Queer Theology

Queer Theology

Rethinking the Western Body

Edited by
Gerard Loughlin

Blackwell
Publishing

BLACKWELL PUBLISHING
350 Main Street, Malden, MA 02148-5020, USA
9600 Garsington Road, Oxford OX4 2DQ, UK
550 Swanston Street, Carlton, Victoria 3053, Australia

First published 2007 by Blackwell Publishing Ltd

2 2008

Library of Congress Cataloging-in-Publication Data

Queer theology : rethinking the western body / edited by Gerard Loughlin.
      p.   cm.
   Includes bibliographical references and index.
   ISBN: 978-0-631-21607-0 (hardcover : alk. paper)
   ISBN: 978-0-631-21608-7 (pbk. : alk. paper)
   1. Sex—Religious aspects—Christianity.   2. Queer theory.   3. Body, Human—Religious aspects—Christianity.   4. Homosexuality—Religious aspects—Christianity.   I. Loughlin, Gerard.

   BT708.Q44 2007
   233'.5—dc22

                                    2006025869

A catalogue record for this title is available from the British Library.

Set in 10.5/12.5 pt Dante
by SNP Best-set Typesetter Ltd, Hong Kong
Printed and bound in Singapore
by C.O.S. Printers Pte Ltd

The publisher's policy is to use permanent paper from mills that operate a sustainable forestry policy, and which has been manufactured from pulp processed using acid-free and elementary chlorine-free practices. Furthermore, the publisher ensures that the text paper and cover board used have met acceptable environmental accreditation standards.

For further information on
Blackwell Publishing, visit our website:
www.blackwellpublishing.com

Front Cover: *Madonna with crying infant*
But God there in the manger cried and moaned;
And these tears were jewels the bride brought to the wedding.
(St John of the Cross)

in memoriam

GARETH MOORE OP
1948–2002

GRACE JANTZEN
1948–2006

Contents

Notes on Contributors

James Alison writes, lectures and teaches in the UK, the USA and Latin America. He is the author, among other books, of *Knowing Jesus* (1998), *Faith Beyond Resentment* (2001), *On Being Liked* (2003) and *Undergoing God* (2006).

Tina Beattie is Reader in Christian Theology at the University of Surrey Roehampton, UK. She is the author of *God's Mother, Eve's Advocate* (1999), *Woman* (2003) and *New Catholic Feminism: Theology and Theory* (2006).

Daniel Boyarin is the Hermann P. and Sophia Taubman Professor of Talmudic Culture at the University of California at Berkeley, USA. Among his many books are *Carnal Israel: Reading Sex in Talmudic Culture* (1993), *Dying for God: Martyrdom and the Making of Christianity and Judaism* (1999) and *Border Lines: The Partition of Judeao-Christianity* (2004).

Virginia Burrus is Professor of Early Christian History at Drew University, Madison, NJ, USA. She is the author of *"Begotten, Not Made": Conceiving Manhood in Late Antiquity* (2000) and *The Sex Lives of Saints: An Erotics of Ancient Hagiography* (2004).

Gavin D'Costa is Professor of Christian Theology at the University of Bristol, UK. He has published several books, including *Sexing the Trinity: Gender, Culture and the Divine* (2000) and *Theology in the Public Square: Church, Academy and Nation* (2005).

Paul Fletcher is Lecturer in Christian Studies at Lancaster University, UK. His recent work considers the relationship between theology and the political and he has published in journals in cultural and political theory as well as theology. He is the author of *Disciplining the Divine* (forthcoming).

Christopher Hinkle is a doctoral student at Harvard Divinity School, where he is studying contemporary theology. He has published articles in several journals, including *Modern Theology*.

Amy Hollywood is the Elizabeth H. Monrad Professor of Christian Studies at Harvard Divinity School, USA. She is the author of *The Soul as Virgin Wife: Mechthild of Magdeburg, Marguerite of Porete, and Meister Eckhart* (1995) and *Sensible Ecstasy: Mysticism, Sexual Difference, and the Demands of History* (2002).

Grace M. Jantzen was Research Professor of Religion, Culture and Gender at the University of Manchester, UK. Among her many publications are *Power, Gender and Christian Mysticism* (1995), *Becoming Divine: Towards a Feminist Philosophy of Religion* (1998) and *Foundations of Violence* (2004).

Mark D. Jordan is the Asa Griggs Candler Professor of Religion at Emory University, USA. Among his many books are *The Invention of Sodomy in Christian Theology* (1997), *The Ethics of Sex* (2002) and *Blessing Same-Sex Unions: The Perils of Queer Romance and the Confusions of Christian Marriage* (2005).

Gerard Loughlin is Professor of Theology and Religion at the University of Durham, UK. He is the author of *Telling God's Story: Bible, Church and Narrative Theology* (1996) and *Alien Sex: The Body and Desire in Cinema and Theology* (2004) and the editor, with Jon Davies, of *Sex These Days* (1997). He is also a co-editor of the journal *Theology & Sexuality*.

David Matzko McCarthy is The Father Forker Professor of Catholic Social Teaching at Mount St Mary's University, Emmitsburg, MD, USA. He is the author of *Sex and Love in the Home: A Theology of the Household* (2001/4) and editor with Therese Lysaught of *Gathered for the Journey: Moral Theology from a Catholic Perspective* (2006).

Rachel Muers is Lecturer in Modern Theology at the University of Exeter, UK. She is the author of *Keeping God's Silence: Towards a Theological Ethics of Communication* (2004) and co-editor with David Ford of the third edition of *The Modern Theologians* (2005) to which she contributed the essay on "Feminism, Gender and Theology."

Catherine Pickstock is Lecturer in Philosophy of Religion at Cambridge University, UK, where she is also a Fellow of Emmanuel College. She is the author of *After Writing: On the Liturgical Consummation of Theology* (1998) and, with John Milbank, *Truth in Aquinas* (2001).

Eugene F. Rogers Jr is Professor of Religious Studies at the University of North Carolina at Greensboro, USA. He is the author of *Sexuality and the Christian Body: Their Way into the Triune God* (1999) and *After the Spirit: A Constructive Pneumatology from Resources Outside the Modern West* (2005). He is also editor of *Theology and Sexuality: Classic and Contemporary Readings* (2002).

Kathy Rudy is Associate Professor in Women's Studies at Duke University, North Carolina, USA, and the author of *Sex and the Church: Gender, Homosexuality, and the Transformation of Christian Ethics* (1997).

Jane Shaw is Dean of Divinity and Fellow of New College, Oxford, UK – the first woman to hold this post in the college's history. She was a founding member of the Movement for the Ordination of Women (MOW), and is the author of *Miracles in Enlightenment England* (2006).

Elizabeth Stuart is Professor of Christian Theology and Director of the Centre for the Study of Sexuality and Religion at the University of Winchester, UK. She is the author of many books, including *Just Good Friends* (1995), *Gay and Lesbian Theologies: Repetitions with Critical Difference* (2003) and *Exploding Mystery: A Queer Science of the Sacraments* (2006). She is also a co-editor of *Theology & Sexuality*.

Graham Ward is Professor of Contextual Theology at the University of Manchester, UK. He is the author of several books, including *Cities of God* (2000), *True Religion* (2003), *Christ and Culture* (2005) and *Cultural Transformation and Religious Practice* (2005).

Linda Woodhead is Professor of Christian Studies at Lancaster University, UK. She is the author of *An Introduction to Christianity* (2004) and *Christianity: A Very Short Introduction* (2004). She has edited many books on contemporary religion, including with Paul Heelas, *Religion in Modern Times* (2000) and *The Spiritual Revolution* (2005).

Preface

This book has been several years in the making, and I must thank all those who have worked on the project over that time. My greatest gratitude is of course to the contributors, to those who have been with the project from the first, and those who joined later, when others had fallen away. To all of them I owe more than it is possible to say.

I must also thank the equally stalwart team at Blackwell, who patiently kept faith with the book. Alex Wright was the commissioning editor, but Rebecca Harkin has seen the book through to completion, and with Rebecca an always cheerful and endlessly helpful team of people, including Linda Auld, Sophie Gibson, Kelvin Matthews, Karen Wilson and most especially Louise Cooper. And I must also thank my long-suffering copy-editor, Elaine Bingham, who worked with me on *Alien Sex*, and who also copy-edits *Theology & Sexuality*, the journal that I co-edit with Elizabeth Stuart and Heather Walton.

I was teaching in the Department of Religious Studies at the University of Newcastle upon Tyne when I began this book, but during the course of its writing, Newcastle University decided to close the Department and transfer its permanent staff south of the Tyne, to the newly named Department of Theology and Religion at Durham University. That move has not been without its stresses, but on the whole it has been a happy one, and I gladly acknowledge the kindness and support that my colleagues at Durham – and in particular John Barclay – have shown to the newcomers from Newcastle. But the closure of the Newcastle Department was less happy for the overall provision of teaching and research in theology and the study of religion in the United Kingdom. The nearby University of Sunderland had already closed its departments of Philosophy and Religious Studies in 2001, and Newcastle its Department of Philosophy in 1989. It is increasingly the case that universities do not know why they are so named.

What little there is of theological substance in my own contributions to this book is the result of others, who over the years have enriched my life with their writings and conversation and friendship. I am happy to say that many of them are contributors to this volume, and they will know who they are. In addition I must also thank – for various kinds of help and support, friendship and insight – Pamela Sue Anderson, Jeremy Carrette, Sarah Coakley, Elaine Graham, Fergus Kerr OP, Janet and Nicholas Lash, Rob MacSwain, Alison and John Milbank, Andrea and Paul Murray, George Newlands, John Sawyer, Paul Julian Smith, Janet Martin Soskice, Will Sweetman, Mark Vernon, Alison Webster and Alex Wright, Jane and Rowan Williams. There will be many I have forgotten, and though unnamed they too will know who they are, and I thank them all. Finally I must remember Andrew Ballantyne, not only for being there, but for being there with such quiet good sense and infinite patience.

Some of the chapters in this book were first published elsewhere, and I am grateful to the authors and their publishers for permission to reproduce them here. Kathy Rudy's chapter on "Subjectivity and Belief" first appeared in *Literature & Theology* (15.3 [2001] 224–40),

Catherine Pickstock's chapter on *"Eros* and Emergence" was first published in *Telos* (127 [2004] 97–118) and James Alison's chapter on "The Gay Thing" was first published in *Sexuality and the U.S. Catholic Church: Crisis and Renewal*, edited by Lisa Cahill, T. Frank Kennedy, and John Garvey (Herder and Herder, 2006). Other chapters have had earlier outings, but appear here in modified, extended versions. Mark Jordan's chapter is a revised version of chapter 5 of *Telling Truths in Church* (reprinted by permission of Beacon Press, 2003), and Gerard Loughlin's chapter first appeared in a shorter version as "The Body" in *The Blackwell Companion to the Bible and Culture*, edited by John F.A. Sawyer (Blackwell, 2006). Daniel Boyarin's chapter is an augmented version of an earlier essay asking "Are There Any Jews in 'The History of Sexuality'?" in the *Journal of the History of Sexuality* (5.3 [1995] 333–55), while Virginia Burrus's chapter manages to both contract and expand on chapter 2 of her study *"Begotten Not Made"* (2000). The excerpt from "The Dark Night" is from *The Collected Works of St. John of the Cross*, translated by Keiran Kavanaugh and Otilio Rodriguez (copyright © 1964, 1979, 1991 by Washington Province of Discalced Carmelites, ICS Publications, 2131 Lincoln Road, NE, Washington, DC 20002-1199; www.icspublications.org).

This book is dedicated to the memory of two people who died too young; two theologians who sought – though in very different ways – to queer how we think about the world and God, about ourselves as bodies in church and society.

Gareth Moore OP (1948–2002) had many interests, including music and philosophy. Like many of his Dominican brothers he was deeply influenced by the work of Ludwig Wittgenstein, and this is evident in his book on *Believing in God* (1988). But the writings for which he will be remembered – and which are nowhere mentioned in the memorial collection of essays published in *New Blackfriars* (July/August 2003) – are about sex and truthfulness. In *The Body in Context* (1992) and *A Question of Truth* (2003), Gareth interrogated the official teaching of the Roman Catholic Church on sex and sexuality, and found it deeply wanting. In the earlier of these two books he did not deny that there might be good arguments in support of the Church's teaching, but merely showed that if so they had yet to be found. But in the second book he suggested that the Church's commitment to truth – which is the truth of Christ – is seriously compromised by the failure to offer cogent arguments in support of its teaching; the failure to admit that there are no such arguments to offer. (It is the failure in honesty that disheartens, and not only in the Catholic Church.)

After Gareth published *The Body in Context*, I urged him to write a book that would display the reformed Catholic teaching on sexuality and human relationships to which I thought his book pointed. It would be a book in which the humanity of certain sexualities were no longer in question, in which the full complexity of human desire, as it gets caught up into the desire of God, is told truthfully and without prejudice. In response he suggested that it was perhaps something I should write. *Queer Theology* may not be what either of us imagined at the time, but I would like to think that it is something like. For it imagines what the church may yet be on the basis of what it has been, and what it has been in the light of what is yet to come and is even now arriving in the lives of queer Christians.

Grace Jantzen (1948–2006) was also a philosopher of religion. But unlike so many of her fellow philosophers she was from the first aware that reason has a fleshy nature – that we think as bodies. In her first book – *God's World, God's Body* (1984) – she identified the divine *logos* with the world's materiality. She sought to uncover and challenge the gender bias in philosophy of religion, a discipline which presumed to view the world (and God) from a genderless perspective, but which everywhere betrays the locatedness of its (mostly male) practitioners. Like Gareth, Grace's interests increasingly turned to questions of culture, gender, and sexuality, which she pursued in both historical and contemporary contexts. She produced two important studies on medieval mystics – *Julian of Norwich* (1987) and *Power, Gender and Christian Mysticism* (1995). But the latter was as much about writing on the mystics as on the mystics themselves. As the title of the book indicates, Grace had come to see that the mystics cannot be studied apart from the cultures and dynamics of power by which they were made: the cultures in which they lived and live again in modern discourse, in the appropriations of theologians and philosophers. And as Grace always insisted, we must constantly ask whose interests are served by such making and remaking.

More recently Grace sought to reinvigorate philosophy of religion by developing – alongside such philosophers as Pamela Sue Anderson – a feminist philosophy of religion that has proved to be the single most important development in the field in recent years. In *Becoming Divine* (1998) Grace began to develop a philosophy of natality that she opposed to what she saw as the West's fascination with death, with a theology and philosophy of mortality that looks to our ending rather than beginning and becoming for the meaning of life. This theme was but in embryo in *Becoming Divine*, for it was to grow into an ambitious project to map the West's morbidity in a multi-volume work on "Death and the Displacement of Beauty." The first volume of this bold undertaking was published in 2004 as *The Foundations of Violence*. In this last book, as in all her work, Grace confronted our complacencies with the possibility of a different imaginary, one that queers the world we take for granted. Like all good evangelists she wanted to open up "new ways of being," and like all wise ones she knew that these new ways arrive in our venturing upon them – like the divine "rule" for which Jesus taught his disciples to pray.

In an essay on the "Contours of a Queer Theology" (Jantzen 2001) Grace argued the need for a "lesbian rule" to measure the "multiple shapes and curves and differences" of such an undertaking (Jantzen 2001: 285). The rule takes its name from the island of Lesbos where it was invented to deal with the "queer shapes" that give the otherwise straight columns of classical architecture "their beauty" (Jantzen 2001: 277). Made from lead it bends to the shape of its object (Aristotle, *Nicomachean Ethics*, V.10), deviating with the deviant, becoming what it measures. With such a rule of beauty Grace imagined building a theology "with curves and flutes and rounded columns set far enough apart so there [is] plenty of room for the wind of the spirit to blow through" (Jantzen 2001: 278). Grace may not have cared for all the rooms that have been constructed in this volume, but I like to think that she would have seen something of the "lesbian rule" with which she sought to build a queer theology.

Gerard Loughlin
Newcastle upon Tyne
The Nativity of the Virgin Mary 2006

The wedding at Cana
Libellus for John the Evangelist (Upper Rhine before 1493)
Öffentliche Bibliothek der Universität Basel (A.vi.38, fol.4r)

Introduction

The End of Sex

Gerard Loughlin

Everyone knows that Jesus went to a wedding at Cana in Galilee (John 2.1–11). But who got married? Strangely, we are not told. The story is not about the happy couple, but about some of their guests – Jesus and his mother and his disciples – and how one of them – Jesus – turned water into wine, the best wine at the feast, and how this was the first of Jesus' signs: a revelation of his glory. But who got married? Who was the bridegroom to whom the steward spoke in his amazement that the best wine had been kept until last, when everyone was drunk (2.10)?

The story of the wedding is not a simple tale, or not only a simple tale, but also a parable, a story that reveals theological truths. It is not a parable that Jesus tells, but one in which he is told, in which he is revealed. Everything in the story has a double meaning, at least a double meaning. It is itself and more than itself. The wedding takes place on the third day (2.1); the third day after Jesus has talked with Nathanael (1.43–51) and told him that he will see visions of glory (1.51), which – in a liturgical setting – is also the third day after Jesus' death, when he rises in glory. The latter "third day" resonates in the former for all Christian readers who encounter this story in the setting of the Eucharist, at the thanksgiving meal in which Jesus' last three days are ritually recalled and inhabited. Moreover, the story itself recalls the Eucharist in which it is told, for Christ turns water into wine just as now – in the liturgical present – he turns wine into blood, when the cup of the new and everlasting covenant (his death) is shared in the eucharistic meal. Thus in the wedding at Cana, Jesus gives a sign of what will come to pass – is coming to pass – and has come to pass, in the church's recollection of the story, which thus turns out to be as much about its narrators as about Jesus: they are the guests at the feast where now wine, not water, is turned into something much more potent than the "best wine" that so amazed the steward. They are the guests at the wedding and the bridegroom is Christ himself.

In the Scriptures, God is the husband of Israel, and, in the gospels, Christ is husband to his church, he is the bridegroom of new Israel. The motif is common to all the gospels. Jesus identifies himself as the bridegroom whose presence dispels mourning and invites feasting rather than fasting (Matthew 9.15; Mark 2.18–20; Luke 5.33–5). And so similarly John the Baptist, who declares that he "who has the bride is the bridegroom. The friend of the bridegroom, who stands and hears him, rejoices greatly at the bridegroom's voice" (John 3.29). John is the friend who rejoices, whose "joy has been fulfilled" (3.29). John is bride to Jesus, and the same is true of all who believe in Jesus. At the end of the story of the wedding at Cana, after Jesus has worked the first of his signs, we are told that "his disciples believed in him" (2.11). They became the brides of Christ, and this is why the story does not tell us who was getting married at Cana, at whose wedding the wine was wondrously replenished. Or rather it does: Christ was marrying his disciples, and all who come to believe on the "third day," who come to share in the new wine of the resurrection. The entire story rests on the ancient idea that God is to Israel as husband to wife, bridegroom to bride, and that now, in Jesus, that relationship is perfected: the bridegroom arrives in person, and all are called to become his bride. But it is, as we cannot help but notice, a queer kind of marriage: the bonding of men in matrimony.

Most churches – at the start of the third Christian millennium – are being asked to acknowledge the marriage of same-sex couples, to acknowledge the union in Christ of men with men, and women with women, as they already witness to the union of men with women and women with men. But most churches are resistant, refusing to see, let alone sanction, the same-sex bonds that are everywhere present in their midst. And yet, as so often, the very thing denied is affirmed and celebrated at the level of the Christian symbolic – in the church's imaginary life, in her stories and songs, parables and prayers. This is one of the queerest things about the Christian Church; that it celebrates in its symbols what it denies to its members.[1] Jesus goes to a wedding at Cana and marries his disciples; John the Baptist marries his friend, the bridegroom Jesus. But this is all imaginary, symbolic. It is not to be taken seriously, or not seriously in this way. So who did get married at Cana?

"Doubtless no one will any longer want to try and guess who the bridegroom was" (Bultmann 1971: 115 n. 3). Some have suggested that it was Simon the Cananaean (Mark 3.18), but others that it was the author of the gospel, traditionally identified as John the son of Zebedee, who left his wife or wife-to-be to follow Jesus, becoming the disciple whom Jesus loved. Indeed, John – in the second-century apocryphal Acts of John – tried three times to get married, and each time Jesus intervened, until John eventually succumbed and gave up the "foul madness" of female flesh and bound himself over to Jesus: "who didst make my joining unto thee perfect and unbroken: who didst give me undoubting faith in thee, who didst order and make clear my inclination toward thee: . . . who didst put into my soul that I should have no possession save thee only: for what is more precious than thee" (James 1924: 269)? Later versions of the story – as in a sermon preached by the Venerable Bede – have John as the bride-groom of Cana, who leaves his bride for Jesus (see Greenhill 1971: 408–9). And in some versions of the story, the woman whom John jilts for Jesus is Mary Magdalene, though Jacobus de Voragine, of all people, dismissed this as a "false and frivolous" tale (Jacobus de Voragine 1993: I, 382). It is not quite clear why Jacobus found the story so preposterous, but he seems to have wanted John betrothed to a respectable virgin, since he assures us on the authority of his contemporary St Albert the Great OP that she, whoever she was, "persevered in virginity," accompanied the Blessed Virgin Mary and "came at last to a holy end."

In one amazing rendition of the story – in a tradition which stretches from at least the eleventh to the fifteenth century, when it became quite popular in Latin and High Middle German texts – John leaves his betrothed on their wedding day, and marries Jesus. It is Jesus and John who get married at Cana. The scene is delightfully pictured in a miniature of the Basel Libellus for John the Evangelist, produced in the Upper Rhine sometime before 1493 (see frontispiece and Hamburger 2002: 159; pl. 25). It shows John with long golden curls and rosy cheeks. Beardless and wearing a wedding chaplet, John is seated at a table beside an equally rosy cheeked but bearded Jesus, and both appear to be taking a great delight in one another, as are their companions – including the Virgin Mary to John's right. John's hands are clasped in prayer as he gazes into Jesus' eyes. They are seated for the wedding banquet, behind a table on which are placed loaves of bread, and in front of which are the six jars of water-turned-to-wine, from which a serving lad is proffering a cup to the happy couple. Above them, at the top of the picture, angels with ruddy cheeks are playing musical instruments, a flying wedding band.

A presentiment of John's marriage to Jesus is also found in an illustrated text of St Anselm of Canterbury's *Prayers and Meditations*. It comes from the monastery of Admont in Styria, and was probably produced in about 1160 for the Abbess Diemuth and her nunnery in Upper Austria (Pächt 1956: 71). Produced some three hundred years before the Basel libellus, the Admont codex illustrates Anselm's prayers to St John with a framed picture of two couples. On the left we see John leaving his betrothed, with both figures standing; while on the right we find John reclining on Jesus' breast, with both of them seated: *"Tu leve conjugis pectus respuisti supra pectus domini Ihesu recumbens"* is inscribed on the frame (see Pächt 1956: pl. 21a). Unlike the later illustration, the Admont Jesus is beardless; as pretty – perhaps prettier – as John's doleful fiancé, abandoned on the left of the picture. Thus its style is an interesting combination of Byzantine and Italian (Pächt 1956: 77), and its picturing of John and Jesus as a couple – separate from the story of the Last Supper (John 13.23) – was a novel development in the twelfth century. As Otto Pächt notes, the "Admont miniature is the earliest example of this iconographic type," and it almost certainly gave rise to what would become the much better known sculpted devotional images (*Andachtsbilder*) of John and Jesus in fourteenth-century Germany (Pächt 1956: 78). As such the image derives from Anselm's prayer to St John – as its illustration – rather than from the Last Supper, and shows the ascendancy of spiritual (*pectus domini*) over carnal (*pectus conjugis*) love: a nuptial mystery.[2] And yet of course, as both twelfth- and fifteenth-century images reveal, the ascetic is imagined in utterly carnal, tender terms. In the Admont miniature, Jesus affectionately caresses John's chin. And who, looking at the Basel scene, can doubt that Jesus is about to kiss John?

The medieval John was exemplary of virginal life, and as such was often paralleled with the Virgin Mary. If she figured virginity for female religious, he provided a model for the male monk, and together they fittingly betokened single-hearted devotion to Christ for those men and women who lived in double monasteries, as at Admont. Mary took precedence, but John was her male double, to the extent that sometimes his conception was viewed as "immaculate," his death an "assumption," and, as we have seen, he could play the *sponsa Christi* as well as the Virgin could – who, as church and second Eve, had become bride to her son in medieval imagination.[3] As bride, John played a feminine role, the wife to Jesus' husband; almost, as it were, the *erōmenos* (beloved) to his *erastēs* (lover), the *malakos* to his *arsenokoitēs*.[4] But in context John was more likely to be thought of as angelic, as enjoying that androgynous life which "subsumes" the "polarities of gender" (Hamburger 2001: 303). In *Les Lounages de Monseigneur Saint Jehan L'Evangelist* (c. 1375–80) John appears alongside the nine orders of angels; and he often appears – as in the Basel libellus – like a young wo/man.[5]

> John's virginal body represents a *conjunctio oppositorum*: not just male and female, but also body and soul, desire and bliss, change and stasis, corruption and transcendence. In John the opposites enshrined in the doctrine of the Incarnation – divinity and corporeality – are conjoined. Like the Virgin, John is utterly free of concupiscence, and like her, he, alone among the saints, is assumed bodily into heaven. (Hamburger 2001: 313)

Jesus, of course, was the original *conjunctio oppositorum*, and as such was also feminized in medieval piety. Though a man, he was yet able to give suck like a nursing woman, feeding

Christian souls with the (eucharistic) blood from his side (Bynum 1982: 110–69; Bynum 1991: 157–65). Indeed, Jesus could give suck to John. In her *Revelations*, Katharina Tucher (d. 1448) longs to drink, like John, from Christ's breast (Hamburger 2001: 310): "John, dear friend, Let me suck there [from Christ's side] the wisdom on which you rested and from which you sucked out all sweetness. O, the noble little bed of holy rest! O, dear God, if I could rest there, that would be everything in the world to me!" (Tucher quoted in Hamburger 2002: 170). This is what John is about to do in the Admont illumination; to suck sweet wisdom on Christ's bed of holy rest. And, in turn, John's body is also able to feed the devout. For when – in the *Golden Legend* – he lies in the grave that he has had dug before the altar of his church, and entreats God to take him to the heavenly feast, the congregation are dazzled by a brilliant light, and, when it fades, John is gone and the grave filled with manna (Jacobus de Voragine 1993: I, 55). His body, like Christ's, has become food.

While the marriage of John and Jesus was considered symbolic of their spiritual union – with John a "virgin" bride – its carnal rendering, not least in such images as that of the Basel libellus, was sufficiently suggestive of physical as well as spiritual intimacy, for the story to be condemned by such as Joannes Molanus (Hamburger 2002: 160). It was not to survive the European Reformations. With the decline of vowed celibacy and the rise of familialism in most Western Christian churches – first in the Protestant and then the Catholic – a story such as that of John and Jesus, with its wonderful sense of fluid genders, became unpalatable. It spoke of a world in which bodily identities were insecure against the movements of desire, and above all the desire of and for God, which flowed through and beyond mundane affections. This desire affected both men and women. In the fifteenth century, John left his wife for Jesus, just as Margery Kempe (c. 1373–c. 1440) sought to leave her husband – or at least her conjugal obligations – for the caresses of her savior (see Kempe 1994; Loughlin 2004a: 17–19). Richard Rolle – in the previous century – spurned women's allures for the fire of Christ's love (see Rolle 1972: Loughlin 2004a: 11–12).[6] The men and women of Admont's double monastery sought a lover whose embraces exceeded the comforts of merely human amours; they sought the pleasures of the *gloriosum pectus*.

Such sacred eroticism is not beyond criticism. It contrasts carnal and spiritual desire, elevating the latter above the former, so that the former is always in danger of denigration, as something to be shunned by those who would truly know God. More worryingly, it genders this contrast as one between man and woman. John leaves Mary for Jesus. And though this upsets any straightforward mapping of gender unto sex, as John becomes wife to Jesus, and Jesus mother to John – feeding him from his breast – this incestuous union (which repeats that between Jesus and Mary, Christ and the church), never – or hardly ever – mobilizes the masculine gender, which remains tied to the male body.[7] But as we have seen this denigration is always paradoxical, because the ascetic ascent is figured in bodily terms of fleshly longing, as the language that is alone most appropriate to heavenly *eros* (see further Turner 1995b). Here we realize that the spiritual can grow out of the carnal, by which it is taught and then teaches in turn; so that spiritual asceticism is not the denial but the transformation of yearning – even in and through that yearning: the attraction of the beautiful.

Gay Marriage

Here we cannot discuss all the complex questions raised by the idea – and now the practice – of civil same-sex marriage or partnership. These issues have been creatively and entertainingly addressed by Mark Jordan (2005). But we may note some of the ironies in the hostility of many Christian pastors, but not only pastors, to same-sex marriage, and wonder why they find such marriage unacceptable. For on the face of it, the advent of legal same-sex marriages would seem to mark the triumph of heterosexual matrimony, as the romantic ideal to which all lovers aspire. Gays and lesbians want to be like everyone else – to get married, settle down, and even (sometimes) have kids. And yet they are told that such marriages will bring about the end of (heterosexual) marriage, family, and even society. It is not entirely clear why or how this would happen, but perhaps it is because such marriages are not "naturally" open to the having of children. Yet when gay and lesbian couples seek to have children – whether through previous relationships, adoption, or genetic donation (means already employed by heterosexuals) – they are told that they should not do so; that their parenting will somehow be more disadvantageous to the children than that of even the least able of heterosexual parents – or the "care homes" that are the best that heterosexuals provide for many of their offspring. Moreover, the threat posed by gays and lesbians to family and society is often proclaimed by men – named "fathers" – who have vowed never to beget children. The pope lives in a household of such men – a veritable palace of "eunuchs" for Christ – that reproduces itself by persuading others not to procreate. Why is this refusal of fecundity – the celibate lifestyle – not also a threat to family and society?

Many of those who oppose same-sex marriage deny that they are homophobic, and insist on human rights for homosexuals; just not the right to get married and have children. They often speak of marriage as a "natural kind" – as natural to heterosexuals. This of course is a fantasy. Marriage is only natural in the sense that it is natural for human beings to invent different forms of social organization, and marriage – variously invented – is one of those forms. And since marriage is social it is only contingently heterosexual. As we have seen, the Christian tradition has always imagined same-sex marriage – at least for men. Men have always been able – if not required – to play the bride to Christ's groom, for "all human beings – both women and men – are called through the Church, to be the 'Bride' of Christ" (John Paul II 1988: n. 25). Why then should same-sex marriage be so troubling for the Christian churches, when it is what Christian men have been doing all along? The answer is contained in the latter clause of the question. It has to do with (men) falling for a male deity, and is in this sense a christological problem (see further my chapter below – chapter 7). But rather than pursue that problem here – for this entire book is in part a preparation for the pursuit – I want to consider the trouble that is the idea of same-sex *marriage*.

Marriage would seem to be a step too far. Many can accept the homosexual "condition" if not the "practice"; many can tolerate the practice in the secular realm – they would not seek its recriminalization; many can even accept the practice in the church, as a kind of "second best," and as long as it is not practiced by priests (Church of England 1991: para. 44–7; 5.13–5.22). (And yes, these tolerations are intolerable!) But they cannot accept homosexual *marriage*. One reason for this might be that marriage poses a different problem from that posed by sex. The latter – same-sex practices – can be understood as private, individual behavior, individual "sin"; a failing that anyone might fall into. But marriage is public rather than private, an "institution," as people like to say. Gay marriage challenges by making a claim to legitimacy on behalf of same-sex couples. It requires the churches to recognize what has been happening in their midst; the signs of grace they have denied. And this is where the advent of civil same-sex marriages (partnerships) is most worrying for the churches. It presents them not only with claims for gay sex, but for the legitimacy of affectionate gay relationships: the avowal, celebration, and undertaking of *love* between women or between men. Many in the churches find love difficult, but they still believe that they are somehow committed to love, to the practices of faithful care and mutual abandonment by which we participate in the very life of the God who is love (1 John 4.16). Must they not then accept the love that people find – by which they are found – even when it is queer love?

Mark Vernon – after Michel Foucault – has presented a version of this argument in terms of friendship. It is not just that same-sex relationships – gay marriages – challenge society to recognize a greater range of human affections than hitherto, but that such relationships deepen what has been previously understood by friendship. They allow "everything that can be troubling in affection, tenderness, friendship, fidelity, camaraderie, and companionship" to escape the channels in which they are normally contained and form "new alliances . . . tying together . . . unforeseen lines of force."

> To imagine a sexual act that doesn't conform to law or nature is not what disturbs people. But that individuals are beginning to love one another – there's the problem. The institution [of society] is caught in a contradiction; affective intensities traverse it which at one and the same time keep it going and shake it up. . . . These relations short-circuit it and introduce love where there's supposed to be only law, rule, or habit. (Foucault 2000: 136–7)

And these "affective intensities" challenge the churches to remember that the family to which they are called by Jesus is not one of biology, but of friendship (John 15.15). Christian identity is not to be constituted by human parents, patrilineal and matrilineal affiliations, but by sharing in Christ's blood, given for all. That friendships between men, and between women, might be erotic, and that erotic relationships between men and women might be friendships, is a challenge for the churches, which have usually separated *eros* and friendship, thinking men and women unequal (see further Loughlin 2004b: 99–101[8]). Changing these fundamentally unchristian ideas will not destroy society, but it will "trace new lines in the 'social fabric'" and in the fabric of the church (Vernon 2006: 222; see further Vernon 2005). It will make the church more herself. But there is another reason why gay marriage unsettles the church; for as we have seen gay marriage is what the church has always been about, while denying it. The advent of civil gay marriages undoes this dissimulation.

Imagining Jesus married to John poses a conundrum for Christian theology. For even if we take their marriage as a metaphor for the spiritual relationship between the soul and Christ, the metaphor is still a sexual one, since it has long been held that there is no marriage where there is no sexual "consummation" (fulfillment).[9] Thus the marital relationship is no less sexual for being spiritualized. Moreover it makes *union* rather than procreation the point of matrimony – neither Jesus nor Paul offer offspring as a reason for marriage. It is the meeting of human and divine that is given in the joining of bodies. Furthermore, it is today less easy – less comfortable – to set the spiritual over against the carnal, since the latter has been taken up into the former: we discover the spirit in the flesh. And is it so obvious that Jesus wedded to John – the church to Christ – is merely metaphorical, for if nothing else, this "metaphor" has to do with bodies and their sacramental relationships, and such relationships are not other than bodily and never merely metaphorical. The consecrated bread and wine are not metaphors for the body and blood of Christ, but really Christ's body and blood, given for us to eat. Pope Benedict XVI does not shy away from this when he acknowledges that the "imagery of marriage between God and Israel" is now realized as *union* with God through sharing in Jesus' body and blood (Benedict XVI 2006: 16–17; para. 13).[10] Certainly the Eucharist is as intimate as sex – taking another body into one's own – and just insofar as it unites men and women with Jesus, it is gay sex as well as straight sex, gay marriage as well as straight marriage.[11]

It is thus not possible for Christians schooled in the gospels and tradition to believe that gay people are ordered to an "intrinsic evil," since all are ordered to God, and those ordered to God through their own sex are ordered as were the two Johns – the beloved and the baptist – who were ordered to Jesus: a lover who does not distinguish between the sex of his brides; who welcomes all alike. Christ is the lover of both St Teresa of Avila *and* St John of the Cross (see further chapter 12 by Christopher Hinkle). And he is a lover whose own sex is less than stable; since as Jesus he is man, but as Christ woman also. It is not possible to place gay people outside Christ's eucharistic embrace, the very space where we learn "the concrete practice of love." For eucharistic communion "includes the reality both of being loved and of loving others in turn." As such, it is where "[f]aith, worship and *ethos* are interwoven as a single reality which takes shape in our encounter with God's *agape*" which is also God's *eros* (Benedict XVI 2006: 17, para. 14; 13, paras. 9–10: "God's *eros* for man is also totally *agape*"). There is only one Christian *ethos* – the diverse life of eucharistic union that includes all in the body of Christ – and it is radically *queer*.

Queer Theology

Theology is a queer thing. It is has always been a queer thing. It is a very strange thing indeed, especially for anyone living in the modern West of the twenty-first century. For theology runs counter to a world given over to material consumption, that understands itself as "accidental," without any meaning other than that which it gives to itself, and so without any fundamental meaning at all. Against this, theology relativizes all earthly projects, insisting that to understand ourselves we must understand our orientation to the unknown from which all things come and to which they return, that which – as Christian theology ventures – is known and received in the life of Jesus. But even when theology was culturally dominant it was strange, for it sought the strange; it sought to know the unknowable in Christ, the mystery it was called to seek through following Jesus. And of course it has always been in danger of losing this strangeness by pretending that it has comprehended the mystery, that it can name that which is beyond all names. Indeed – and despite its own best schooling – it has often succumbed to this danger, which it names "idolatry."

To name theology as queer in this sense is to invoke "queer" as the strange or odd, the thing that doesn't fit in. Theology doesn't fit into the modern world; and if it did fit in too snugly it would be forgetting the strangeness of its undertaking: to think "existence" in relation to the story of a first century rabbi. But "queer" has other meanings, other uses. As well as strange, it is also *insult*; hurled at the one who doesn't fit in. "The insult lets me know that I am not like others, not normal. I am *queer*: strange, bizarre, sick, abnormal" (Eribon 2004: 16). And "queer" is the insult thrown at gay men and lesbian women, the sign of their "social and psychological vulnerability" (Eribon 2004: 15).

> All of the studies done in homosexual populations (of either sex) show that the experience of insult (not to mention of physical violence) is one of the most widely shared elements of their existence – to different degrees, of course, according to which country, and, within any country, according to where they live and in what environment they grow up. But it is a reality experienced by almost everyone. . . . It is not hard to understand why one of the structuring principles of gay and lesbian

subjectivities consists in seeking out means to flee insult and violence, whether it be by way of dissimulation or by way of emigration to more hospitable locations. (Eribon 2004: 18–19)

Given this use of "queer" it is perhaps perverse to describe theology as queer, for theology serves the very churches where such insults are thrown, where those who love their own sex were once named as "sodomites" (to be burned) and are now described as "objectively disordered" (to be reordered). The churches are places where queers are harassed. But language, like life, is never tidy. "Queer" can have more than one use, and the churches are ambivalent places, as much harbingers (hosts) as harassers of gay people (see Jordan 2000). And then there is another, more recent use of "queer" – one that we have already been using and from which this book takes its title.

Queer is also the insult *turned*. No longer a mark of shame it becomes a sign for pride, like "gay." But unlike gay, it names more than erotic interests – a sexual orientation – and it names more than marginal, minority interests. It finds itself curiously central to culture at large, disavowed but necessary for a heterosexual normalcy that defines itself in terms of what it rejects. This is already to speak in terms of the "queer theory" first propounded by Teresa de Lauretis (1991), who argued for queer as the name of an emergent force within the cultural field.

[R]ather than marking the limits of the social space by designating a place at the edge of culture, gay sexuality in its specific female and male cultural (or subcultural) forms acts as an agency of social process whose mode of functioning is both interactive and yet resistant, both participatory and yet distinct, claiming at once equality and difference, demanding political representation while insisting on its material and historical specificity. (Lauretis 1991: iii)

And later queer studies have gone on to find queer interests to have been always already at play in the dominant, supposedly straight culture. As Henry Abelove's queer students say: "[d]on't focus on histories that require the trope of marginalization for their telling. . . . Focus on the musical comedies of the 1950s. What could be queerer? . . . Or go back some years further and focus on the songs of Cole Porter. All these cultural productions were central rather than marginal. By ignoring or neglecting them, we misconceive the past and unwillingly reduce our presence in and claim to the present, they say" (Abelove 2003: 47). Queer studies will take us back to some of the most established authorships in Anglo-American literature, which also turn out to be some of the queerest; to the likes of Henry James (Sedgwick 1990; Moon 1998) and Henry David Thoreau (Abelove 2003: 29–41). "'I am that queer monster the artist, an obstinate finality, an inexhaustible sensibility,' James famously wrote in a late manifesto-letter to Henry Adams (March 21, 1914), and if we give that word 'queer' any less force and range than he does, it is our failure of nerve and imagination, not his" (Moon 1998: 4).

Queer theology aspires to just such "nerve and imagination" in its reading of the past and its address to the present. It is queer because – like all theology – it answers to the queerness of God, who is not other than strange and at odds with our "fallen" world. God's "kingdom" is not ours. When God appeared amongst us he was marginalized and destroyed; and yet he was the one who let his killers *be*. They would have had no power – no life – if it had not been given to them. It is only natural to love one's friends and family; to love one's enemies is perverse.

But queer theology is also queer because it finds – like queer theory – that gay sexuality is not marginal to Christian thought and culture, but oddly central. It finds it to be the disavowed but necessary condition for the Christian symbolic; and not simply as that which is rejected in order to sustain its opposite, but upfront on the surface of that opposite, playing in the movement of stories and images that constitutes the Christian imaginary. The most orthodox turns out to be the queerest of all. Moreover, queer theology – like queer theory – reprises the tradition of the church in order to discover the queer interests that were always already at play in the Spirit's movement, in the lives and devotions of saints and sinners, theologians and ecclesiastics. What could be queerer than the thought of Gregory of Nyssa, St John of the Cross or Hans Urs von Balthasar? (See chapters 9, 12 and 13 below.)

Finally, there is another and more important sense in which queer is more than a name for "gay" or "lesbian" interests. Those latter terms betoken identities built around erotic interests, and liberatory movements that sought to form new social spaces. They turned the pathological homosexual into the political gay. The Lesbian and Gay Christian Movement (LGCM) is still battling on this front within the churches (see further Gill 1998b). But "queer" betokens something other than political and sexual identity, it includes more than just gay or lesbian identified people. As David Halperin puts it, queer is "an identity without an essence. . . . [I]t describes a horizon of possibility whose precise extent and heterogeneous scope cannot in principle be delimited in advance" (Halperin 1995: 62).

Queer seeks to outwit identity. It serves those who find themselves and others to be other than the characters prescribed by an identity. It marks not by defining, but by taking up a distance from what is perceived as the normative. The term is deployed in order to mark, and to make, a difference, a divergence.

> "Queer," then, demarcates not a positivity but a positionality vis-à-vis the normative – a positionality that is not restricted to lesbians and gay men but is in fact available to anyone who is or who feels marginalized because of his or her sexual practices: it could include some married couples without children, for example, or even (who knows?) some married couples *with* children – with, perhaps, *very naughty* children. (Halperin 1995: 62)

Halperin might also have mentioned the sexual practice of celibacy, which was once and is now again a strange deviancy. But queer is used in this book with the kind of inclusiveness that Halperin suggests. And yet at the same time we must acknowledge the dangers of this inclusivity. It can, as Halperin notes, occlude the differences between queers, the tensions of taste and politics that drive them apart, while also admitting those who have not experienced the insult or fear of insult that marks out the deviant. It lets in "the trendy and glamorously unspecified sexual outlaws who . . . [don't have] to do anything icky with their bodies in order to earn" the name of queer (Halperin 1995: 65). And it can turn all too quickly from a positionality into another positivity, another identity. It was for this reason that Teresa de Lauretis, having coined the term "queer theory," abandoned it within a few years. For her it had become a commonplace of the trendy and glamorous, with no power to subvert the dominant codes of heteronormativity. But the term – and its deployment – is less well known in theology, and so it is still possible that this positionality, this distancing or divergence from what is held as normative, will serve to destabilize and undo that normativity: the surety of heteropatriarchal Christianity. But in the case of theology there is something more.

Halperin describes the aim in deploying queer as ultimately to open a "social space for the construction of different identities [from the heteronormative], for the elaboration of various types of relationships, for the development of new cultural forms" (Halperin 1995: 67). But this might be as well said of the church, which is called in and by Christ to open up ways of living that will enable us to live in the "Kingdom of God" when it arrives in its fullness. With the Kingdom arriving already in Christ, but not yet fully with the return of Christ, Christians are called to live – like Christ – as the sign of the Kingdom's arrival. That heteropatriarchy is not such a sign is affirmed by queer theology on the basis of that "identity without an essence" which it sees in the radical practices of Jesus, in the new social spaces that Christ opens up through his self-gift at the altar, and in the "nerve and imagination" with which queer Christians persist in their loving of God and neighbor. Thus queer theology is a call to return to a more fully realized anticipation of the Kingdom, which is not a return to the previous or the same, but to the new and the future, since the church is to be the sign of what is to come. In this way queer is also an undertaking. As with becoming Christian or woman, one is not born but becomes queer; one learns to live as a promise of the future.

There is one other congruity between queer theory and theology that should be noted. As an "identity without an essence," queer might be offered as a name for God. For God's being is indubitable but radically unknowable, and any theology that forgets this is undeniably straight, not queer.[12] One of the first things that Thomas Aquinas tells us about God – about our speaking about God – is that we do not know what God is, only what God is not (*Summa Theologiae* [*ST*] I.3). Instead of a definition we have to make do with God's effects – i.e. everything (*ST* I.1.7 *ad* 1). God in Godself is an identity without an essence, or, as Thomas puts it, God's essence – which is identical with God (*ST* I.3.3) – is God's existence (*ST* I.3.4). This makes God pure actuality (without potentiality). The most that we can say about God is that God *is*, which is not a description but a point of theological grammar. In an analogous way we can say that *queer is*, even if we cannot say in what queer consists other than by pointing to the effects of its deployment.

Queer Lives

Much early feminist theology made its way by appealing to the experience of women; an "experience" that – previously excluded by male hegemony – now spoke with an undeniable power of lives lived (by women) rather than projected or theorized (by men). But with time this category of critique and reproach was weakened by its fragmentation into multiple experiences and by the rise of *discourse* as the productive – constructive – context for any and all experience. Experience is no longer an innocent, prelapsarian value. And yet an appeal to experience remains important for any queer theory or theology, since it is precisely an experience of dissonance between desire and discourse which for many gives rise to the realization that socially entrenched discourses of desire are not truthful but ideological; normalizing the particular as universal. The queer body answers to different discourses. It is for this reason, if no other, that *Queer Theology* begins with two chapters on experienced dissonance between desire and discourse, life and ecclesial community. In a sense they are essays of "coming out."

In a deeply personal, pain-filled essay, **Kathy Rudy** relates how she came out – was turned out – of the Methodist Church where she worshipped, and the Methodist divinity school where she taught, and all because she had come out as who she was and was becoming. All this happened before she published her profoundly humane and lucid study of *Sex and the Church* (1997), a work of queer theology that would grace any school of divinity. Rudy's experience of finding herself estranged through speaking her life is repeated in any number of other lives that bear witness to the loves by which they have been rejected and encountered, changed and made to grow. It is a venerable Christian motif and experience. But Rudy's conversion is a story of falling out of love, and what it is to remember the love that has now passed but still haunts new relationships. This leads Rudy to reflect on the difficulty of understanding belief from inside and outside the believing community; understanding from outside the inside that was once herself, inside herself. Rudy finds guidance in memoirs and subaltern studies, but they fail to adequately measure her own experience of living in or between worlds, of having different worlds within. It is as if Rudy still lives within the faith she has "lost," and out of this she looks for an account of subjectivity that will express her fragmentation, her sense of a self that is moving, becoming.

Rudy draws on the work of Elspeth Probyn and Vivian Gornick in order to offer an account of the self – herself – as one who is haunted by "ghosts," by multiple, often contradictory affiliations and relationships, by hurts and happinesses that together make for what many will recognize as a postmodern self; the condition of *living between*. This will resonate with the experience of many queer Christians, who have both lost and not lost their faith, finding themselves in Christ but rejected by his church. When they find themselves talked at, but never with – made the subjects of confused and incoherent condemnations – many queer Christians give up on the practices of the church; for who wants to remain in an abusive relationship? But where should they go? Rudy seeks a place where such people can live with their ghosts, somewhere like the culture of black African-Americans, who, she believes, have an ability to live between worlds. But she is not sanguine that this is a real possibility for white queers, let alone Christian ones. For the most part, the other contributors to *Queer Theology* are more hopeful than this; hopeful of finding in the church not ghostly affections, but the presage of a future wanting to be born. But queer theology cannot be written except out of something like the experience Rudy describes with such clarity and wisdom, for it grows from the experience of dissonance; from learning that bodies are not as they are said to be – as the church has taught them to be – but that they are something more.

James Alison also knows about dissonance and inhospitality. But in his chapter – which Alison first gave as a lecture by a Catholic to Catholics – he points to what he sees as the recent experience of many if not all Catholics in Western societies, the experience of finding a more or less general acceptance of gay people and their relationships. Alison argues that Catholics as a whole now more or less accept what the wider society accepts, that there are such people, and good luck to them – for finding love and nurturing relationships is difficult for everyone. This is the "gay thing" which has befallen the Catholic Church, that is befalling the church and making its official teaching on "homosexual persons" increasingly incomprehensible, as somehow not quite Catholic. Thus the experience of dissonance which interests Alison is that between the acceptance of gay people in the church and Vatican teaching against them; and it leads him to find a much more serious disjunction between that teaching and the Catholic doctrines of creation and original sin.

Vatican teaching on homosexuality is notoriously incoherent, so much so that it is most plausibly read as an attempt to foil thinking about homosexuality and so silence its discussion in the church (see Jordan 2000). So it is a measure of the clarity and charity of Alison's thought that he is able to offer an irenic reading of that teaching, and of its yet fatal flaws: the abandonment of a properly Catholic view of desire as always perfectible through grace, and the refusal to wait upon the experience of lesbian and gay Catholics – the testimony of grace in their lives. The latter is where ordinary Catholics – following the church's ordinary teaching about grace and sin – will start their thinking about human loving. They will start by following the "still small voice." For queer bodies answer to more traditional, orthodox discourses than those proffered by ecclesial authorities at the beginning of the twenty-first century.

Queer Church

The chapters in the second part of the book remain with the church, and consider how Christian thought queers accepted notions of sexual desire, difference, and fecundity. For as the authors show, Christianity's eschatological orientation changes the way these things are thought. The point is not to queer the tradition, but to let its orientation queer us.

In many ways, **Elizabeth Stuart**'s chapter is programmatic for this book; certainly for the argument of this introduction. For Stuart highlights two ways in which queer theology ends sex: in the sense of overcoming sex as an untruthful, oppressive regime, and in showing the *telos* of sex to be other than reproduction. The first of these has been accomplished by queer theory, but the second is the gift of theology, and it shows how we can evade the melancholy that Judith Butler finds in sexual desire and identity. For Butler, our (sexual) identities are hard won through the repudiation of other possible identities, and these repudiations have to be tirelessly repeated if our identity is not to slip. We must constantly repudiate what we are not in order to maintain who we are.[13] But this means that we are forever in mourning for the selves we have rejected, and this is as true for homosexuals as it is for heterosexuals. Against this, Christian theology offers an identity constituted not through exclusion, but through a radical inclusion.

Queer theory has shown the instability and malleability of sexual identities, as these are variously constructed and reconstructed in different times and places. But this insight is in one sense belated, because Christian theology has always already found the body of Christ to be fungible flesh, a transitioning corporeality; never stable but always changing, becoming other. Christ's body is transfigured, resurrected, ascended, consumed. Born a male, he yet gives birth to the church; dead, he yet returns to life; flesh, he becomes food. As Stuart says, the "the body of Christ is queer."

And it is in becoming part of this queer body that our own bodies – and their identities – are set upon a path of transfiguration, resurrection, and ascension: a baptismal path of eternal transformation. It is also a way of desire, of movement toward an end that is itself always moving, leading us on. Baptism is the gift of wanting "the endlessness of God" (Rowan Williams 2000: 211). This process of endless becoming eludes melancholia because the identity it gives is not constructed through disavowal, but received through grace; it is not achieved but bestowed, and in bestowal we participate in the movement of desire that is always leading us on, to an end that always eludes our grasp. Baptismal identity is not something we make, but is being made in us.

Stuart is aware that the identities by which we are socially built – of race and class, sex and gender – are not such that they can be remade easily. Indeed, such identities and their remaking can be a means of grace to us; as when, in "coming out" – as "gay" or "straight" – we discover the freedom of owning our desires, a sense of homecoming. But finally, all these identities are (to be) washed away in the baptismal waters. They have no ultimacy in Christ. And this is shown in the way that Christians – in the past and still today – are called upon to parody all existing, potentially idolatrous, identities. As Stuart argues, parody – "extended repetition with critical difference" (Linda Hutcheon) – is a way of taking what is given and "playing it out in such a way as to expose the other world breaking through it."

The church was once much better at parody than it is today – infected by modern sobriety. When it more fully parodied heterosexual marriage in vowed celibacy – the polygamous marriage of all celibates, male and female, with Christ – it knew that carnal intimacies were not ultimate, and ultimately served to teach desire for God, to whom all desires are (to be) ultimately ordered. But now even the churches seem to think heterosexual marriage of ultimate significance, to be constantly lauded and safeguarded at all costs (for strangely, it seems that heterosexual marriage, despite its natural ubiquity, is a very fragile achievement, easily destroyed – and civilization along with it – by a few gay marriages).[14]

If baptism is the sacrament by which bodies are liberated for participation in the life of Christ, then it is in the Eucharist that they more fully receive – and learn to receive – that life. Stuart notes how a single-sexed priesthood distorts the sign enacted by the priest: for the priest represents the multi-gendered Christ who does not destroy, but passes beyond gender. When only men are priests, the priesthood fails to signify the "eschatological horizon" to which the church is called by Christ. (This argument is further addressed by Gavin D'Costa in chapter 18.)

Christianity queers sex by making it a means by which we may be sanctified, and so only secondarily a means of reproduction, which itself becomes a means of grace when taken up into the gift of sanctified and sanctifying bodily desire. Heterosexual marriage is sanctified through its likeness to the queer marriage of Christ and church, when even the supreme pontiff becomes a bride yearning for his/her lover. In this sense queer theology becomes an utterly conservative endeavor, recalling the church to Christ's call to transgress the boundaries of men.

But when queer theology recalls the church to its queer origins, gay and lesbian people should not assume that their desires more perfectly figure the divine, for all sexual identities are finally brought to naught in Christ. And in Christ this is figured through the death to which baptism gives birth. As Stuart notes, it is through participation in Christ's death and resurrection – dying to death – that Christian faith refuses melancholy, and in dying to death the Christian in life and death passes beyond all identities constructed through exclusion. As Stuart shows this is nowhere better figured than in the liturgy of the Christian funeral: "All bonds, associations and worldly achievements pale into insignificance beside the status of the deceased as a baptized member of the body of Christ." None of our humanly made divisions and distinctions survive the grave. All that is left is God's creation, made for love – as the Catechism teaches.

Like Stuart, **Graham Ward** also understands Christian life as a way of undoing those identities by which we seek security against others – including Christ. And one of those identities is named "sexual difference": the idea that we are either man *or* woman, and that sexual relationship arises out of *this* irreducible difference. "[S]exual difference is original, nonderived, nondeducible (incapable of representation), because it presents itself as an immediate dimension of fundamental human experience" (Scola 2005: 221). Against this biological fundamentalism – which is of course discursive and historically contingent – Ward argues that sexual relationship does not so much arise out of (hetero)sexual difference, as that bodily difference arises out of relationship, sexuality out of *eros*. Ward sets his arguments about sexual difference against those of Karl Barth and Hans Urs von Balthasar, but like them, he articulates his arguments through a close reading of Scripture; in Ward's case the Johannine stories of the resurrection encounters between Christ and Mary Magdalene, and Christ and Thomas. These paralleled meetings are both powerfully erotic and subversive of any attempt to read them as simply heterosexual or homosexual. Ward moves deftly between the original texts and their highly sexualized reading in later Christian cultures, and not least in the Western tradition of painting; in – say – Caravaggio's seductive chiaroscuros. Ward also moves deftly between phenomenological and ontological modes of discourse in order to find an ordering of human flesh and desire as *diastasis*, one which is more properly theological than the disguised biologism of a Barth or Balthasar.

Queer theology thus has an interest in reminding the church of its remarkable early antipathy to sexual congress, which was, of course, an antipathy to sexual reproduction. The interest is not to advocate a return to such extreme sexual abstinence, but to relativize modern obsessions with heterosexual marriage. In the light of the tradition this obsession is aberrant, and very strange when the concern of celibate men, who have themselves abjured sexual fecundity. But of course, sexual abstinence was mainly honored in the breach, and tradition changes, and today the church recognizes that marital sex is graced, and that children – the fruit of sex – are gifts of grace. So what can queer theology offer to the theology of family and parenting?

David Matzko McCarthy reflects on fecundity, and on what should be the church's understanding of family in the modern world, a concept and practice which are now so resolutely compromised by the interests of consumer capitalism. McCarthy is more wary than some contributors to this book of thinking sex and sexuality "constructed." But this does not mean that he advocates a "nature" which operates independently of our social selves. Rather he wants an account of the self and its desires which attends to their constitution as natural *and* social. Society and nature are not agents which stand over against the self, and which the self must either accept or reject. Rather they are the domains in which the self acts and is acted upon; and McCarthy is concerned to argue that within these interwoven domains, sexual activity is reproductive, both naturally and socially: "sex is social reproduction." Sex not only produces children but reproduces patterns of desire that are as much social as they are natural. And McCarthy fears that the dominant patterns in Western societies follow from viewing the self as the source of natural consumerist desires, which society must satisfy through selling what is wanted. But these desires are themselves produced through society, and their satisfaction is met by an array of social products, which include sex and children. "If sex is socially reproductive, then a grammar of desire, market capitalism and contractual individualism fit together as a dominant network of social reproduction."

It is against this economy of social reproduction that McCarthy sketches his vision of the Christian household, which is not one thing but many, within a confederacy of households. McCarthy argues that sex should be understood within the practices of the home. Sex has an intrinsic worth, but it is not an end in itself, since that worth – as Stuart argues – is the nurturing of our desire for God, and the nurturing of such desire is the *telos* of the Christian household. But sex will not deliver this in and of itself, as in various versions of Christian romanticism. Rather it must be set – practiced – within a larger array of household practices – mundane hospitalities – that constitute the body of Christ at home. "The household, set within the formative practices of the church, is an economy that is directed toward reproducing the social body and shaping the self in imitation of Christ." Sex is thus part of the household's social reproduction, and in many households – and not only heterosexual ones – this will happily result in the production of children, who arrive, not as the satisfaction of needs, but as forms of that divine desire which is ever burgeoning in charitable life.

Queer Origins

Having encountered the lives of queer Christians within and without the contemporary church, we now turn to consider the Western tradition, beginning with two of its "paradigm" texts: Plato and the Bible. For it is through the reading – interpreting – of these textual bodies that later Christians and Jews developed their theological understanding of the body and its desires. Not only these texts, of course. But these two are fundamental for thinking about *eros*, and then *agape*; for thinking about human and divine love – an erotic *agape* or agapeistic *eros*. The Bible is the word of God and so interpretative of all other words; but by that very movement, susceptible to their reverse elucidation. For the Jewish or Christian reader, Plato's truth (platonic and neoplatonic) will be found in the Bible, or, as we might say, in the movement between the texts. Today, nearly all serious thinking of *eros* will return to Plato, and not least to the *Symposium* and Diotima's encomium to *eros*; all Jewish and Christian debates about gender and sex will return to the Bible, to certain "proof" texts, and to what will turn out to be some very queer views about the bodies of men, women, and God.

Catherine Pickstock is well known for her part in "radical orthodoxy" (Milbank, Pickstock and Ward 1999), and more particularly for her reading of Plato against Derrida in *After Writing* (Pickstock 1998). Here she returns to Plato's wily, aporetic thought in the *Meno*, *Ion* and *Symposium*, in order to tease out his connections between knowledge, desire, and inspiration. She begins with Meno's puzzles about knowledge: how do we know that we are ignorant of that of which we are ignorant, and being ignorant, how will we know that we have found knowledge, if and when we find it? Socrates answers with "a mythical presentation of a doctrine of *a priori* understanding"; his story of a prior life and knowledge, now forgotten but waiting to be recalled. Augustine similarly worried about how he could seek the God he did not know unless God was already present to him, and so in some sense known? It is not inappropriate to link these *aporias*, Pickstock argues, because both philosopher and theologian appeal to a preceding knowledge – gained through recollection or illumination – which is at the same time elicited through interlocutors – through teaching or revelation. Moreover, Socrates performs his answer by claiming to have learned it from those who are wise in divine things, from the priests and priestesses recalled by the poets, from those who sought to give a "rational account" of the mysteries they practiced, *mythos* and *logos* combined. Both Socrates and Augustine appeal to a divine tradition. And for both, recollection/illumination is triggered through education.

But Socrates offers not only to show that the ignorant can recall what they have "forgotten," but that in so doing they learn their ignorance and come to desire its undoing. It is this "desiring ignorance," as Pickstock calls it, which both enacts and transmutes the *aporia* of knowledge, since it shows us that we learn through a *desire* for that which we do not know. The learning of his own ignorance – which incites the desire to know – is the one thing that Socrates claims to know with certainty; everything else is at best but true opinion, *orthos doxa*. This is why – Pickstock argues – Plato's philosophy needs mythology in order to show that we can never really know what it is to know and want to know, other than by thinking it a desire that comes from *elsewhere*, and that has to be triggered in us by the learning of our ignorance. And here we are not so far from Augustine's reflections on the God whose unknowability he has to learn.

We learn because we desire, and we learn desire through the attractions of beautiful others – most obviously for Plato the beauty of young men – which then leads us on to the beautiful itself. (But human beauty is not merely instrumental, since all loves are gathered into love.) For some, desire comes to an end when it is fulfilled, when it attains what it seeks. But this is not Plato's view, which imagines a desire into the unknown, in which "the vision of truth replenishes our desire." Desire (to know) emerges in our desiring (learning). We do not regain what we have lost but instead learn to repeat what is yet to come – and is coming ever more intensely in our wanting. The *Symposium* offers various eulogies on the nature of *eros*, and from and against which Socrates takes the view that love is not a goddess, but the *daimon metaxu*, the demonic "between," which binds the cosmos, and which we should follow, as it leads us from human to divine beauty. Socrates has learned of love from the prophetess and magician, Diotima, from whom he has also learned the magic of dialectics. From her Socrates has learned that *eros* is not a lack, but – as Pickstock has it – "a kind of pregnancy which brings to birth." Desire is a becoming or emerging, a wanting which leads us on, which leads itself on, "generating itself." And in generating itself, it comes as the third between lovers. "What any two desire in desiring a union is not merely this union, but always also the fruit of this union in whatever sense, something that is both them and neither of them: a baby, a work of practice or understanding, a new ethos that others may also inhabit." Thus sex is always a kind of birthing: an emergence of desire's fecundity.

In the second part of her chapter, Pickstock seeks to understand emergence after Kierkegaard, as "forwards repetition." She finds it more fundamental than causation, since a cause "emerges" as such in the appearing of its effect. The emergent is aporetic because it "comes from" or "out of" and is yet a new thing; it is both connected and disconnected from what has gone before. Like presence, emergence is something we "live and inhabit," but cannot quite think. But then what we think also escapes our thinking, since thoughts also emerge from we know not where. "In all our activity, ethical and political, as well as artistic, we seem almost to be spectators of emergent processes." And yet we can recognize what emerges as such, and desire its emerging. For Pickstock, the phenomenology of emergence bespeaks an arrival that is neither from space nor time, past or future, but an elsewhere that theology names the *eternal*. In a move that will be familiar to anyone who has read in "radical orthodoxy" more generally, Pickstock suggests that only theology allows us to think the "new." Building on Thomas Aquinas's idea of God as "pure act," she is able to suggest that "God is the eternally emergent action which rescues finite emerging from arbitrariness or predictability, and therefore saves the phenomenology of the emergent." And this then leads to the Trinity.

For Christian theology, *eros* is not daimonic but divine, purely emergent in the mutualities of the divine perichoresis. What we know in time as successively want and fulfillment, anticipation and arrival, is eternally coincident in God; and thus what we know in time as desire and emergence is the divine movement in our lives, which we inhabit but can barely think, and which we know – desire to know – through the incitement of revelation. Moreover, this revelation was born from the unique coincidence of desire and emergence in Mary. She "desired the bridegroom, the *Logos*, and from this desire the *Logos* emerged from the enclosure of her womb." From Mary's desire to see the Father in her son, emerges the new Adam, who will also be her lover, as was Eve to Adam, born from his side. (These queer themes are further explored by Tina Beattie in chapter 20). And as in Mary, so in us, the *Logos* is born in our soul when we also participate in the *eros* that comes to us in the "between" of our desiring, opening for us the elsewhere of its movement and our journeying: the eternal in our loving.

Gerard Loughlin turns to the primary Christian site – after the Eucharist – for revelation's incitement of our desire to know the whence from which it arrives and to which it would return us. The telling of the Bible – Jewish and Christian, but here more particularly Christian – opens a space in which the God who came to Moses and Mary can come again, arriving for those who listen in holy anticipation. God always arrives in the distance between teller and listener, who are sometimes the same person. But Loughlin's chief concern is with the arrival of another, darker undertaking, an imaginary that has troubled Western thought and culture as much as the metaphysics of desire narrated in Pickstock's chapter. This is a concern with the Bible's bodies, with the flesh of its men and women, and of its God.

The Bible is like a body. It is a whole composed of many parts, in the pages of which we find other bodies, identities that even now haunt the Western imagination. Pre-eminently these are the bodies of Adam and Eve, who have been read into all following bodies, as those bodies into them. But they are also the bodies of those ancient men who slept with men *as if they were women* (Leviticus 18.20), and the much later bodies of gay men who have been read back into those earlier practices. And then there is the strange, rarely glimpsed body of God and its sex, which is both seen and unseen; and the queer relationship that is set up between this terrifying body and the men of Israel (and later the church), who are made to play the woman to their oftentimes jealous husband-God. They are to be his glory, clinging to him like the cloth around his loins (Jeremiah 13.11).

It is sometimes said that God's sex is merely metaphorical. But if so, it is far from being a dead metaphor. God's sex still orders human lives. But it does so from behind a veil; from behind the homophobia and misogyny of Western culture and religion. Loughlin's chapter is concerned with the Bible's mythopoeic ordering of these cultural constructions, and the violence against queer people – which is finally against women – that is used to conceal the fact that in relation to God all men are queer. (Something of this will return in Rachel Muers' chapter on Hans Urs von Balthasar – see chapter 13.) There are several dismembered bodies in the Bible, but most especially God's, the parts of which are scattered throughout the pages of Scripture. Loughlin takes a similarly disjointed approach to his subject – discussing bones, mouths, and phalluses – but also finding the ligaments that bind them all back to the Bible's opening myth: the story of a man without a mother, who gives birth to his wife (as later, matrimonial readings would have it). It is this utterly queer body that disturbs all later attempts to find a stable, heterosexual flesh in the Bible.

Queer/ing Tradition

The first two chapters on queering the Western tradition are concerned with two sets of men – "fathers" – who have dominated later Western thought and practice, Jewish and Christian, and that more nebulous – doubtful – Western site, the Judeo-Christian. We may think we have got it straight about these fathers, but as so often, matters turn out to be queerer than at first appears.

Daniel Boyarin starts with a celebrated biblical text – Leviticus 18.22 – and asks what it prohibited and why. The first question is easily answered – male-male anal intercourse – but the second is more difficult and interesting. Boyarin is concerned with the meaning of this text (and others) for rabbinic interpreters in late antiquity, and while it cannot be certain that they reflect the readings of "biblical" people themselves, they may as likely as not do so, and either way no text has meaning except as it is read. So why – according to the rabbis – does Leviticus abhor male-male anal intercourse?

First, it was not because it abhorred homosexuality. The rabbis – as Boyarin argues – knew nothing of homosexuality, and had no concept of "sexual orientation" such as is now taken for granted. What concerned the framers of the levitical law, as understood in later rabbinical reading, was that a man should take the part of a woman and allow himself to be penetrated. As Boyarin shows, it was penetration rather than same-sex affections and other practices that Leviticus condemned. The rabbis classed other same-sex practices as masturbation, and treated them less seriously. Female same-sex practices were also discussed, but not treated as analogous to the activity proscribed in Leviticus. Leviticus is no more concerned with homosexuality than is the story of Sodom (Genesis 19.1–12), or its parallel, the story of the Levite and his concubine (Judges 19). Rather Leviticus is concerned with the violation of categories.

David Halperin and others have shown that in the Greco-Roman world, contemporaneous with the rabbis, male-male anal intercourse was considered reprehensible when the penetrated did not belong to the category of the penetrable, when he was not a woman, slave or boy, but a free man. Such intercourse was a violation of status, of proper social order. Boyarin argues for something similar but also significantly different in regard to Leviticus. A man lying with a man as with a woman violates not status but the proper distinction of kinds. It is condemned along with cross-dressing (and both are condemned in similar formulas) because both are mixings of kind, which is to say, abominations (from *tebhel*, a mixing or confusion). As Boyarin admits, this is at first perplexing, because two men are surely of the same kind. But when one man uses another man as a woman (and "uses" is used advisedly), he uses one kind (male) as if it was another kind (female), and so crosses the border between them. It is strictly analogous to transvestism – condemned as abhorrent in Deuteronomy (22.5) – when clothing is synecdochic and one kind (fe/male attire) is confused with another (fe/male body). As Boyarin puts it, Leviticus condemns male-male anal intercourse because it "is an instance of cross-dressing!" It is not condemned because it is an instance of homosexuality.

Boyarin concludes by noting that Jewish theology is narrative theology. It is the reading of biblical texts, and any Jewish discussion of "homosexuality" has to begin by recognizing that neither the Bible nor the rabbis have anything to say about it. Much the same could be said for Christian theology – or at least Christian narrative theology – and its reading of the Christian Bible, since the New Testament also fails to mention homosexuality, and discusses same-sex activity in terms broadly similar to those addressed by Boyarin (see further Loughlin 2007). It may seem a small point, but one of the achievements of queer theology is to have found the Bible – Jewish and Christian – empty of homosexuality, but full of queer intimacies.

A similar disregard for our modern sexual categories is evidenced by the Christian fathers, and not least in the writings of Gregory of Nyssa (c. 330–c. 395). In a provocative reading of this Greek father, **Virginia Burrus** offers an essay in patristic thought that is both powerful and playful. Burrus finds David Halperin's definition of queerness as an "identity without an essence" useful for thinking about asceticism in Gregory, for so many of his terms – such as "virginity" – turn out to have a less than stable meaning. Even to describe Gregory as a father is querulous, because he may have been one of the "fathers" to have really been a father, or at least really married; or then again, perhaps not. Terms like "marriage" and "virginity" are often used metaphorically by Gregory, but it is not always clear when they are so used, which makes their nonmetaphorical meaning also shifty.

But more importantly for queer theology, Gregory makes desire central to his theology, so that when our desires are rightly ordered they come to participate in the desire of the Trinity, the longing of God for God. This is not desire as want, but as active pursuit of the good. It is desire as donation. Burrus pursues this and other themes through a consideration of "virginity" in Gregory, which for him is a practice for the weak, for those who are not strong enough to order their marital relations in pursuit of God, but fear the waywardness of bodily desires. Moreover, the virginal life seeks a return to the original – and final – sameness of a life without sexual difference, which is the life of the angels in heaven. At the same time this virginal life is marital, since the soul desires the embrace of the bridegroom, and yet this eschatological embrace passes beyond sexual difference, so that as the feminine disappears, homosexuality is established in heaven. But what is masculinity without femininity?

Burrus also pursues Gregory's Moses, who – as exemplary of the mystical man – pursued God on Mount Sinai, in the darkness of the cloud. And here again, words shift in meaning and significance, and Gregory proves to be a fascinating but perilous guide for queer theology. Fascinating in that he so resolutely unsettles any complacency regarding the primacy of the heterosexual. Gender is not a stable category for Gregory, and like Elizabeth Stuart after him, he holds that it is destined to pass away. But that passing is where peril lies, for on one reading it passes to leave a regnant masculinism: a genderless subject who is really a man; a man who has assumed the feminine. But nothing is ever certain when reading Gregory; or in reading Gregory's readers.

In recent years Gregory has become important for a number of prominent theologians, such as Sarah Coakley and John Milbank, and Burrus offers some thoughts on their appropriations of Gregory in relation to queer theory and subjectivity. In relation to Coakley, Burrus raises important questions about the appropriation of queer theory by theology, a supersessionist tendency – not entirely avoided in this introduction – to find theology in advance of a theory that only that theory has made possible. And in relation to Milbank, Burrus finds a certain drawing back from Gregory's "radical orthodoxy," which proves to be a bit too queer. There is a sense of grasping after a masculine essence. Burrus seems to suggest that if we really want to learn from Gregory, we really must learn how to let go.

Until the fourteenth century, theology and what we now refer to as mysticism were one; or at least sufficiently related for prayer to be the setting for intellectual inquiry, for theology to be itself spirituality: seeking to know the mind of God through living in God's Spirit, nourished by God's Word in word and sacrament. Up to the fourteenth century, mystical theology developed an approach to God that was both affective and apophatic, and queer: the "mystical queer." And this is nowhere more evident than in the tradition of the Rhineland mystics, which for many culminates in the writings of Meister Eckhart (c. 1260–1329). But his thought, as **Amy Hollywood** notes, grew out of the "highly experiential mysticism of women monastics, mendicants, and beguines . . . among whom he lived and worked" (Hollywood 2002: 320 n. 1). And it is with three such women – Mechthild of Magdeburg (1207–82), Hadewijch of Anvers (thirteenth century) and Marguerite Porete (d. 1310) – that Hollywood's chapter in *Queer Theology* is concerned.[15] Many – but most notably Caroline Walker Bynum – have shown how these medieval women developed, out of the Song of Songs and other vernacular writings, a highly erotic language for the soul's journey into the divine; for the soul's union with Christ. Such sacred eroticism, however, remains resolutely "heterosexual," until one begins to notice how the medieval feminization of Christ queers the devotions of these female mystics. For Christ's body is not only maternal but erotic, and so a desired female flesh, eliciting "lesbian-like" devotions in those women who long for its embrace; to drink from the slit in Christ's side, the wound in his/her flesh (like Katharina Tucher mentioned above). But here Hollywood finds not only a female same-sex eroticism to match that already available to men (in desiring the male Christ), but also the difficulties in reading any straight/queer, gay/lesbian dichotomy out of and into these medieval, mystical bodies.

It is not only that the mystics did not think in our terms, but that they sought to move beyond their own gender categories, making fluid what was otherwise stable. Their Christ is both male and female; their soul both female and male; and their self seeks dissolution through union with that which is both utterly far and near.[16] This condition of the *between* subverts any attempt to retrieve stable identities, whether of desire or practice. Nevertheless, Hollywood argues that we can look for past experiences in the medieval texts when we take them as the discourses in which their authors sought to think – and so experience – their lives in relation to Christ and church. If we resist the temptation to reduce the erotic to the religious – for which Hollywood chides Bynum – and the corresponding temptation to reduce the religious to the erotic (as in a crude Freudianism), then we can find an erotic-mystical language which challenges both theological and gender categories, of both the thirteenth and twenty-first centuries. In subverting – as in Hadewijch (according to Hollywood) – any simple association of divinity with masculinity and femininity with humanity, the mystics recall Gregory of Nyssa's fluid bodies and pose an ongoing challenge to heterosexual stabilizations of divine and human genders, as in Hans Urs von Balthasar. And this is what Karma Lochrie calls the "mystical queer."

We might hesitate to describe Thomas Aquinas (1225–74) in similar terms, but he also stands in the Christian mystical tradition, being deeply informed by the neoplatonism of Augustine and the Pseudo-Dionysius. Indeed – as **Eugene F. Rogers Jr** shows – Thomas's undertaking of the *via negativa* after Denys, led him closer to queer theory than away from it, because – as already indicated – he sought an identity whose essence cannot be known, but only undertaken. Rogers' own way into this unknowing is to consider the relationship between body and discourse (already broached by Kathy Rudy and James Alison in relation to queer experience) through an examination of Thomas's approach to the "natural law," with which he is often associated, but of which he has remarkably little to say (only one question – I-II.94 – in the *Summa Theologiae*).

For Thomas, the natural law allows us to participate by reason in the eternal law, which is the "prudence" of God. Thus Thomas's natural law has very little to do with the natural laws of modern science. It does not govern the behavior of animals, which have no prudential reasoning, and above all it does not offer a universally available, non-religious guide to the good life. Rather it is known under guidance from Scripture. (Thomas learns that homosexual behavior is unnatural from Paul, not nature – which of course now tells the opposite, see Bagemihl 1999.) In itself, natural law tells us little beyond the injunction to do good and avoid evil (I-II.94.2 *responsio*). Thomas's account of the good life is relentlessly pursued through his account of the virtues and their corresponding vices. But there are two occasions when Thomas does appeal to "nature" for substantive ethical content, and these concern the vices of "lying and lying with a member of the same sex." It is this little noted conjunction of vices to which Rogers attends.

Rogers suggests that homosexuality and lying may have come together for Thomas because of his reading of Romans 1, in which – for Thomas – same-sex practices are presented as God's punishment for Gentile idolatry, and idolatry is a form of injustice; and where there is no justice there is no true understanding of nature. Lying goes against the truth and also against nature, because it goes against the nature of mind, which naturally wants to express itself truthfully. "For since spoken words are naturally signs of things understood, it is unnatural and undue that someone signify by voice that which she does not have in mind" (*ST* II-II.110.3 *responsio*). In this way lying parallels homosexuality, which goes against the truth of the body. As Rogers puts it, "actions of tongue or genitals can both make the whole person a liar." (But note that the vice of the genitals is against our nature as animals, while the vice of the tongue is against our nature as humans – since animals cannot lie.)

Thomas thought that humans should tell the truth of their bodies as well as their minds, and so avoid homosexual behavior, which is a lie of the body, as Thomas believed. But it is the demand that bodies tell their truth that leads Rogers to connect Thomas's apparent "essentialism" with Judith Butler's apparent "anti-essentialism." For when Butler offers something like a definition of the body, she describes it as that which *demands* to come into language, and that – Rogers argues – is remarkably like Thomas's Aristotelian idea that "form gives existence to matter" (*forma dat esse materiae*). By "form" Thomas understands that principle of *change* that is known through the *performance* of the body to which it gives existence. Thus Thomas's essentialism is rather constructivist, for like Butler he holds that "words bring bodies into the street, and bodies in the street call for new words." And that leads Rogers to offer his Thomistic argument for "coming out."

For if bodies demand to be spoken truthfully, then gay bodies should be spoken as such, and not described, say, as "objectively disordered" heterosexual bodies. It is the failure to speak the truth of such bodies that leads to a state of injustice in which it is not possible to know the truth of nature. Thus in a rather surprising way, Eugene Rogers not only finds that Thomas's understanding of natural law has rather little to tell us about the good life, and that what it now has to say about the "vice against nature" (*ST* II-II.154.11) is almost the exact opposite of what it has been taken to say, for that vice turns out to be a virtue now that we know that gay bodies are not lying when they want to lie with bodies of the same sex. Thomas teaches that gay bodies must not lie but tell their truth.

Christopher Hinkle traces the queer erotics of the Christian mystical tradition into the early modern period with a consideration of St John of the Cross (1542–91). John's reworking of the Song of Songs in his poetry and commentaries is an example of how the language of carnal desire provides a language for spiritual ascent. But at the same time Hinkle is also concerned with the dangers in eliding the erotic with the spiritual. For while queer theology is always more celebratory than condemnatory of sexual desire, one cannot ignore the cunning of the latter to disorder spiritual longing. Jacobus de Voragine witnesses to the intimacy of these desires since in the stories he rejects that name Mary Magdalene as the betrothed of John the Beloved, she is said to have turned to "voluptuousness" when John ran off with Jesus, and when she repented of that and "had to forgo the heights of carnal enjoyment", Jesus filled her with the "most intense spiritual delight, which consists in the love of God" (Jacobus de Voragine 1993: I, 382). John also is given "special evidences" of Jesus' affection, because he had to forgo the "aforesaid pleasures" with Mary. It may be that Jacobus objected to these stories because they offer "spiritual delight" as a compensation for "carnal enjoyment," but the link between the two is clear: union with the divine is presented as a more intense form – a transfiguration – of sexual pleasure. And it is thus always possible that the would-be ascetic will mistake the latter for the former, pursuing the flesh rather than God.

To find St John of the Cross teaching the due ordering of sexual to spiritual desire, and not least for gay men, is not to find John a gay saint, even if there are aspects of his life and character that tempt this identification. But such naming would be anachronistic, and our concern has to be with the queerness of his writings, with John's written desire for the embrace of his divine lover, though of course – and most obviously in the original Spanish – he adopts the persona of the feminine soul. Nevertheless, Hinkle does borrow a number of historical queer identities – the effeminate man, the pederastic sodomite, the intimate friend and the sexual invert – in order to analyze John's account of the spiritual ascent. John's biography suggests the "effeminate man," but in his texts Hinkle finds John adopting a pederastic passivity in relation to God, deriving from an "appropriate submission and humility, as well as hope concerning whatever benefits may follow the divine pleasure." And this ancient model of sexual relationships between men answers well to the traditional Christian view of humanity married to God; of a soul that *wants* to submit. The soul does not merely permit penetration, but desires it; the soul *burns* with want of God's love. Hinkle reads this as a shift from "pederasty" to "inversion," and then, as the ascent proceeds, the difference between the lovers seems to disappear, the soul growing ever closer to God, until "the soul appears to be God more than a soul" (John of the Cross 1991: 165). Needless to say, the homoeroticism of John's mystical ascent is "shaped by a picture of God as male."

But while John enables us to affirm the appropriateness of male homosexual desire for articulating, and indeed experiencing, spiritual growth, he also – Hinkle argues – cautions against any easy identification of sexual and spiritual experience, for John, like his great friend Teresa of Avila, feared the misdirection of desire and the experiences to which it gives rise. Sexual experience can distract from the spiritual, while seeming its instantiation, just as spiritual experience can distract from true knowledge of the unknowable God. The danger is that one becomes fixated "on some particular pleasure, image of the divine, or means of religious sensation, and thus loss of God."

But to warn against the delusions of spiritual experiences – as did both John and Teresa – is not to deny their joy and significance, and the same is true for sexual experiences. But both need to be ordered, disciplined, stripped of their distractions and practiced within a prayerful ascesis that teaches discernment and self-dispossession. As Hinkle notes, this stripping of desire is not unlike its deconstruction, when queer theory dissects its social affiliations and constructions. But Hinkle – after John and against much secular queer theory – insists that these constructions belie a more primordial desire, the origin of which is that which gives all to be. One might say – with Thomas Aquinas – that insofar as we desire we desire the good (no matter how mistaken we may be in identifying the good), and the desired good is that by which we desire, for to desire is to participate in the desiring of the Good. And it is for this reason – that our desires are participative in God's desire – that the discernment and ordering of our desires is such a necessary and perilous undertaking, and we need the guidance of the saints, like St John.

The last chapter on queer/ing tradition takes us from the sixteenth to the twentieth century and to the work of Hans Urs von Balthasar (1905–88), whose theology brings the fourth part of the book to an appropriate close. Balthasar's work not only seeks to encompass the entire Western tradition – and not least the *via negativa* of the mystics – but it also stands at the beginning of the twenty-first century as an invitation and warning to the project of thinking a radically queer orthodoxy. Near the end of her chapter, **Rachel Muers** quotes a simple but immensely profound sentence from the final pages of Balthasar's *Herrlichkeit, The Glory of the Lord*:

> The Trinitarian love is the only ultimate form of love – both the love between God and men, and that between human persons. (Balthasar 1982–91: VII, 484)

Balthasar's theology stands as a challenge to think queer love in relation to love of the Trinity; to think our human loves in relation to our love for God and God's love for God, which is also God's love for us, whom God makes for/to love. But Balthasar's work also stands as a warning on how not to queer these relationships, for his own reflections on the Trinity reveal an undoubtedly queer but baleful reading of the trinitarian relationships (on which Gavin D'Costa also comments in his chapter). Balthasar makes sexual difference central to his thinking of God and humanity – with God's "supramasculinity" *and* "suprafemininity" analogous to human femininity and masculinity – and it is this privileging of sexuality which makes his work so important and stimulating for any sexual, let alone queer theology. But what turns out to be most stimulating about Balthasar's work is the way in which it identifies "masculinity" and "femininity" in terms drawn from a certain ecclesial culture, that then cause Balthasar to get into endless tangles as he tries to hang onto his misogynistic sentiments within a symbolic system that has become too labile to serve his regressive interests.

Muers takes us into Balthasar's thinking of sexual difference by way of one of the rare passages in which he directly mentions homosexuality – a brief reference to the men of Sodom, whom he likens to those (in non-Christian religions) who pray in a masculine fashion, seeking to take rather than be taken by God. Such prayer is a kind of "religious homosexuality" (Balthasar 1986a: 188), an attempt to be male with a male God. One might say – going a little further than Muers herself – that on the part of men such prayer is insufficiently *perverse*; it is not queer enough. The men of Sodom should have waited on God's messengers – and so on God – as *women*, in a posture of feminine passivity, waiting to be "taken" (i.e. raped), as Balthasar has it.

As Muers pursues Balthasar's masculinity and femininity, she discovers how he identifies femininity with Mary's mission, which is not so much a mission as the condition of any and all mission, the condition of *waiting*; and how – strangely – Balthasar's masculinity begins to disappear, since in the church all men are to become women in relation to the male God, who, while he contains suprafemininity, is always pre-eminently supramasculine: always first and last Father. (Beattie 2006 identifies the disappearance of masculinity in Balthasar – its near sole identification with the divine – as the cause of his theological angst; and D'Costa's chapter in this volume questions the privileging of the supramasculine over the suprafeminine in God).[17] And yet, despite the dark and vertiginous places into which Balthasar has led Christian thought, Muers finds that at the last, Balthasar – like Elizabeth Stuart – envisions an eschatological state in which it is not our sexual identities, however these are constructed and deconstructed, but our *creatureliness* which determines our joy and freedom.

Queer/ing Modernity

Hans Urs von Balthasar can be placed as easily under the heading of modernity as that of tradition. For while he stands in a line of queer Christian thinkers – of those who thought within the queer symbolics of Christianity – he is also exemplary of modernity's straightening of that tradition: of its heterosexualization. **Jane Shaw**'s chapter on the Reformed and Enlightened Church, on the effects of Reformation and Enlightenment on Christian thinking about the sexes and their relationships, ably shows how new concerns with marriage and sexual difference (and complementarity) broke with earlier tradition and led to a peculiarly modern obsession with heterosexual monogamy.

Both Margery Kempe, in the fourteenth century, and Mary Astell, in the seventeenth century, argued for the right of women to reject marriage and embrace celibacy. But for Astell this set her at odds with the Christian Church as she knew it, the Reformed – though not entirely Protestant – Church of England. Whereas for Kempe it merely set her at odds with her husband; celibacy being an entirely acceptable, indeed laudable, undertaking within the Catholic Church (of England) of her day. In between these two lives came the Protestant Reformation, and, in particular, Martin Luther's championing of marriage over celibacy. As Shaw shows, the impact of the latter was to lead the Protestant traditions – and later the Catholic – away from Paul's preference for celibacy in favor of his allowing marriage for the sake of decency (1 Corinthians 7). As a result, woman's identity – and worth – was increasingly seen in relation to the husband she did or did not have.

A different revolution was to occur in the eighteenth century and then, more fully, in the nineteenth. This revolution was as much social as scientific, but passed itself off as the latter. It was the (scientific) discovery of sexual difference, of an apparently absolute dichotomy between the sexes, such that woman was no longer viewed as an imperfect version of man, but as a body in her own right, though still – of course – weaker than the male. Shaw rehearses this discovery after Thomas Laqueur (1990), who has described it as a transition from a "one-sex" to a "two-sex" model of the human body. This changed understanding of the nature and relationship of the sexes came most fully into its own at the end of the nineteenth and beginning of the twentieth centuries – even as developments in embryology were beginning to show the almost genetic indifference of male to female, and the priority of the latter over the former (the fantasy that women depend upon and are entirely different from men is everywhere in modern culture, including Balthasar).[18]

If nothing else, Shaw's history of the church in the modern period shows that the so-called "traditional" values of heterosexual complementarity and marriage are modern aberrations when viewed against earlier Christian traditions. And these ideas were being developed at the same time as ideas about homosexuality and heterosexuality were also being constructed, and with them an understanding of sexuality as determined solely by the sex of a desired person. As Eve Kosofsky Sedgwick remarks, "[i]t is a rather amazing fact that, of the very many dimensions along which the genital activity of one person can be differentiated from that of another . . . precisely one, the gender of object choice, emerged from the turn of the [nineteenth into the twentieth] century, and has remained, as *the* dimension denoted by the now ubiquitous category of 'sexual orientation'" (Sedgwick 1990: 8). The Christian churches have too easily bought into this modern heterosexualizing of the body and its desires, and so not only opened themselves to acrimonious and seemingly endless debates about who can sleep with whom, but more grievously led them to lose sight of the learning of God that sexual desire can open for us.

As Shaw notes, the church's privileging of heterosexual marriage in modernity, along with the strange idea of complementarity – which imagines an equality-in-difference between the sexes which is actually an inequality, since the difference is "woman as complement to man" – constitutes a history of "female sexuality" as narrated by men. For it is not only that "woman" as symbol has remained mobile in Christian thought – so that men can be womanly in a way that women cannot be manly – but that actual women have been fantasized in differing ways, first as "cooler," weaker versions of men, and then as men's opposites and complements. And these changing identities have been biological and social and thus political. But modern men have paid so much attention to what makes for a woman, that what makes for a man has become increasingly doubtful. This is evident in theologians like Balthasar, but also more generally in Western culture. It has led to a so-called "crisis of masculinity," or series of such, the retorts to which are ever more absurd displays of hypermasculinity – by both straight and gay men, and some women (see chapter 19 by Mark Jordan for more on the problem of securing Jesus' masculinity).

Linda Woodhead also argues that the history of sex and the modern church is ultimately a history of women and their changing desires. Though she sees less of a break between the pre-Reformation and modern church than Shaw – arguing that the church has always promoted some form of family values, even when idealizing celibacy – she nevertheless agrees with Shaw that the Protestant Reformation of the sixteenth century saw the rise of a new concern with the family as the only legitimate place for women. And this was only intensified in the nineteenth century, when the church, increasingly without influence in the political sphere, focused its power on the domestic, becoming in turn an increasingly feminized institution. Woodhead argues that at first this served the church well, aligning it with a newly dominant middle class, which used sexual sobriety to differentiate itself from both aristocratic debauchery and proletarian incontinence. But it did not fit the church well for the "sexual revolution" of the 1960s, and the emancipation of women from the thrall of domesticity. The church's identification with the "angel in the home" could not survive her flight into a new world of personal autonomy and self-realization.

While it remains the case that many of the most vigorous and voluble Christian churches are those which maintain an allegiance to "family values" and "conservative" sexual mores, Christianity has declined throughout most Western societies – including the United States of America – just insofar as women no longer find their lives recognized, valued, and enhanced through its ministries, which are often closed to them. As Woodhead notes, more women than men have always participated in church life, but since the late 1960s, women have been leaving the churches at the same rate as men, which – if nothing else – is proving disastrous for the transmission of faithful practices from one generation to the next. And this despite the feminization of the churches, for this gendering only celebrates "woman" and her supposed qualities at a symbolic level, while occluding real women from the life of the church. As with Balthasar, the church in general forgets women when it fantasizes "woman." But it is not only the church which does this; even (male) queer theorists can forget that human being is not only one.

Michel Foucault would be prominent in any genealogy of "queer theory," for his own practice of genealogy is exemplary for the interrogation of those discourses which serve to establish and maintain an essentialized view of sex and gender, of body and sexuality. But like any great master, Foucault must be subject to his own insights and interrogations, and it is just such a questioning that **Grace M. Jantzen** undertakes with regard to Foucault's own gender blindness – the moments when he lost sight of the fact that human being is not one but at least two. Jantzen acknowledges her own debt to Foucault's work, his disinterring of various medical, legal, and ecclesiastical discourses, of madness and sexuality, of crime and punishment. But she cannot let pass Foucault's (sometime) denial of women's subjectivity, nor his association of their degradation with death, both human and divine. On Jantzen's reading, Foucault queers the (male) subject – unsettles its givenness – at the expense of woman, whose subjectivity goes unrecognized, let alone undone, for she is always already undone by the ministrations of a (masculine) power that looks for death, forgetting birth. For Jantzen, Foucault too easily succumbs to what she sees as the West's fascination with death, a beguilement that runs from Plato to Heidegger, and from which Christianity, despite its discourses on new life, also suffers. For the trope of second birth – being "born again" of the Spirit – only occludes our first birth or natality.

Not everyone will agree that Jantzen has the full measure of the Christian tradition in this regard, but it cannot be denied that Christians have done as much to serve cultures of death as resist them. Reflection on human mortality – on the mortality of all life – need not, and should not, lead us to forget our natality, our coming to be from another. That after all is the Christian doctrine of creation: that we are "born" in every moment of our lives. Thus even as Jantzen finds Foucault too enamored of death, insufficiently queering its gender and dominion, she yet learns from him how to listen to the silences in his own texts as well as those of others, and hear there the voices of the silenced. It is because she is such a faithful disciple that she can so question the master, and find in his work – in his practice of genealogy – "promising ashes" that may be made to glow and burn again with new life. In one way or another all the chapters in this volume query past discourses. They practice Foucauldian genealogy, seeking to disinter forgotten possibilities and unsettle present complacencies.

Anyone who reads the Christian Scriptures and the church "fathers" cannot but be struck by the difference between their views of marriage and that of the Christian churches today. For the latter find marriage and the family to which it gives rise to be the key building blocks – the bulwarks – of society, while the former find them to be at best but passing practices, distractions from Christian discipleship. Needless to say, the practices of marriage and family extolled by the churches are rather modern, bourgeois productions, developments of eighteenth- and nineteenth-century romanticism. They are units of consumption that do indeed sustain modern, consumer capitalism; the very modernity that the churches elsewhere seek to resist. It is this irony that occasions **Paul Fletcher**'s trenchant critique of marriage and his advocacy of divine *eros* over against the micro-fascism of the churches.

In a startling analysis, Fletcher argues that the church's advocacy of sexual moralism against the commodification of sex merely repeats, if in a different mode, the extreme experience (of violence) offered by the fight clubs of David Fincher's 1999 film, *Fight Club*. Whereas the fight clubs of the film offer (men) an escape from the stasis of a life of interminable consumption through the experience of controlled brutality, the church offers an equally deathly discipline – "a modern sarcophagus" – of exclusive and exclusively heterosexual *eros*. It is deathly not only because it denies rather than transforms desire, but the very command to desist from pleasure "engenders the desire to transgress and so constitutes the ground of capitalistic enjoyment." At the very point where the church seeks to challenge contemporary society it merely colludes with its economy, since it has forgotten that God's desire is not capitalistic but utterly unconstrained and plenitudinous.

In Paul, Fletcher finds an entirely different economy – a *noneconomy* – from that of either capitalism or the modern church. Paul's orientation to the future of the resurrected Christ leads him to suspect all civil and religious institutions, including marriage. Paul lives in and for – waits upon – the return of the Messiah, and so refuses anything like the realized eschatology embraced by modernity and the church in modernity. Capitalism – which oscillates between desire's fulfillment (immediate gratification) and its infinite delay – knows nothing of an *eros* that exceeds death, that wants more than life's interminable extension, that looks for genuine joy in the passing moment. It is this desire which the church must want, a *delectatio* that – like pleasure – comes in the moments of present life, as the ground of their gratuity; drawing bodies together, and together to God.

Queer Orthodoxy

In the sixth part of the book we turn to consider some key doctrinal topoi: the doctrines of Trinity, Christ, Mary, and the saints. Here the point is not to queer an ostensibly straight tradition, but to show that the tradition's doctrinal heart is already queer, and that as a named undertaking "queer theology" is itself belated.

Angelo Scola, in a study of the "nuptial mystery" which largely draws on the work of Hans Urs von Balthasar, notes the "great perplexity" caused by those who have gone so far "as to try to 'sex' the Trinity, in an effort to find an argument in favour of homosexuality" (Scola 2005: 394).[19] But such writers (Loughlin 1998b, 1999b; D'Costa 2000) are merely following after Balthasar, who has already sexed the Trinity, and in a very queer way. If there is a problem, it is not that Balthasar has sexed or queered the Trinity, but that he has not done so enough. The Trinity is always queerer than we think. This, at any rate, is the argument put forward by Gavin D'Costa.

Like Rachel Muers, **Gavin D'Costa** applauds Balthasar's insight that the "trinitarian love is the only ultimate form of love – both the love between God and men, and that between human persons" (Balthasar 1982–91: VII, 484). D'Costa argues that all Christian thought should start from and return to the trinitarian mystery, as the source from which all things come and to which they return, as their perfecting and fulfillment. Thus if we are to argue for women priests – as D'Costa does – it will be on the basis of the Trinity rather than human rights; and in this we will be following after – if reversing – Balthasar, who argued from the Trinity to an all-male priesthood. Like Balthasar, D'Costa engages in some very "high" trinitarian theology, but he does so in order to address a very concrete issue: the forgetting of women in the modern church. And like Balthasar he argues on the basis of Balthasar's doctrine of the Trinity, arguing that Balthasar forgets one of the most important insights of his own theology when he argues against women priests: the insight that God is radically queer.

Of course this is not how Balthasar puts the matter. He does not describe the Trinity as "queer." But he does say that the revelation of God in Jesus requires us to use sexuate language of God, though analogically. As we have seen already, Balthasar ascribes supramasculinity and suprafemininity to God, indeed to each of the persons of the Trinity, including the Father. Balthasar understands (supra)masculinity and (supra)femininity in highly patriarchal terms, above all as *activity* and *passivity* respectively. These are also highly Aristotelian terms. But unlike Aristotle, Balthasar affords them equal value: God is both active *and* passive, giving *and* receiving – donation *and* reception. And so God is radically fluid in his/her "gender," and both men and women can represent the divine life. (Indeed, perhaps transgendered people will most perfectly figure this fluidity for us.) This is a queer God indeed.

But then at certain points, which D'Costa discusses in detail, Balthasar goes back on his radical revaluing of Aristotle's values, and ascribes a primordial supramasculinity – née masculinity – to the Father, and so argues for the necessity of not only masculinity but the male sex for representing Christ's representation of the Father. D'Costa argues that this is an entirely arbitrary move within Balthasar's understanding of the Trinity, rendering his doctrine not only incoherent but idolatrous, since it returns us to a pre-Christian, prescriptural privileging of masculinity over femininity, activity over passivity.[20] (One might say that it turns God into a man and men into gods – as Mary Daly always alleged against Christianity.)

D'Costa also questions Balthasar's willingness to ascribe a female biology to God – for both Son and Father are said to have a "womb" – while denying an absolute value to receptivity conceived as "woman." The female body disappears into the manliness of God. Moreover, in transgendering the Son as feminine in relation to the Father – as capable of "fertilization" by the Father (Balthasar 1990b: 78) – D'Costa detects in Balthasar a (male) same-sexing of God, which works against the queer theology Balthasar otherwise espouses: a God whose gender is not one. This is not to disparage same-sex relations, but to argue that all people find their fulfillment in a queer, rather than a "heterosexual" or "homosexual" God. But Balthasar can hardly avoid the idolatry of the latter when he locates suprasexuality in the Trinity, and privileges supramasculinity over suprafemininity. A more fully queer theology will be more analogical and less univocal in its deployment of these terms, and so more open to the indeterminate dynamics of God's desiring. It will think that women can represent God in Christ at the altar because it will not think Son and Father two "male" principles playing at being "man" and "woman" in bed. Indeed, it will think – as a number of authors have taught us to think (most notably Beattie 2006) – that the priesthood fails to fully represent the multi-gendered plenitude of Christ when it is reserved (by men) to men alone.

We may think it queer enough that the Christian God should be three "persons" in one "substance" – as it were a threefold dynamic of desire – but how much queerer that this God should love the world so much that s/he comes to us in the body of Jesus. This, Paul thought, was a stumbling block for the Jew and foolishness to the Greek (1 Corinthians 1.23). It is an absurdity for everyone, including most Christians. If we should think ourselves immune to the comforts of docetism, **Mark D. Jordan** reminds us just how queer it is to think God a body, how reluctant Christians have been to think the body of Jesus beyond a certain point – below the waist.

Jordan meditates on the parts of Jesus' body the tradition has been less than willing to think, and on why this should be so. After all, the Christian tradition, and in particular the Catholic tradition, has not been unwilling to show and meditate upon the body of Jesus, as child and adult – at birth and in death – cradled in his mother's arms, and naked, or nearly naked, in both instances. The body of Christ is strikingly displayed on countless crucifixes, except for the genitals that are nearly always covered with a loincloth. And why is this? Jordan wonders if it might not be as much to cover our eyes as Christ's sex. For it cannot be that God's genitals are shameful but that our gaze is shamed. We look with fallen eyes, mistaking the shame of our looking with what we look upon. For how shameful it is that we so easily view tortured flesh but flinch from its sex.[21]

There is of course no one gaze, everyone sees differently: men from women, straights from gays, and each from all other points of perception in and around these abstractions. As Jordan's meditation proceeds we realize that there are no straight answers to the questions he poses – that Christ's body poses for us; for in thinking about Christ's body we are thinking about our own. But as Jordan reminds us, the incarnation does not condemn but vindicates the body, including its desiring, so that we can learn to see the glory of God in all bodies, beautiful or ugly. Perhaps only the saints will see with this clarity, but it is a vision to which all are called.

Jordan also reminds us that while Christ's sex has been hidden, his gender has not. Indeed, it has been made the means for hiding another sex, that of woman, excluded from the symbolic representation of Christ. Covering up Christ's penis has allowed it to return as *phallus*, as the symbol of Christ's (masculine) power over all things, including death (see Steinberg 1996 and Loughlin's chapter in this volume – chapter 7). And yet how easily this power is deflated. For Christ's masculinity is always being subverted by the femininity it is used to rule and conceal, for he is a *passive* man who turns the other cheek to his enemy. (And do we not already want to describe this as an *active* passivity, to inject some manly vigor into the debased term?) Christ's solicitude for the sinner and his abjection on the cross can seem too wimpish to be followed by other than women and weakling men. In 1999, the Churches Advertising Network – a UK independent advertising agency – produced an Easter poster depicting Christ in the style of Alberto Korda's famous photograph of Che Guevara, with the tag line: "Meek and mild. As if!" It was not without its critics, but it neatly indicates how uncomfortable Christians can be with Christ's masculinity – or lack thereof. For them, Christ's peaceableness (passivity) is too queer, and they have to imagine him as a man of violence. Learning to look upon God's body is difficult for all, as it confronts us with the truth of our own bodies and their looking. It speaks to us of our desires and fears, of fleshly longings and repulsions. In Christ we see ourselves. But as Jordan concludes, there is "no other place to start Christian truth telling than face to face with Jesus."

That God should come to us as flesh means that s/he is also born of a body, made by a woman, and for Christian faith, this woman gives him her flesh so that he can give us his. Christ has no father other than the Father we see in him; his body is entirely his mother's, a womanly body from the first. And how strange that this woman should give birth to God, and not because she is "taken" by a divine or human lover but because she welcomes the Spirit – who is not manly but womanly in the Syriac Christian tradition – when s/he comes upon her. Moreover, this woman, who is the first to receive God in her child, will be to him the church he makes out of and into his own body, the bride to his bridegroom. And thus graced, she will become the mother of all, the queen of heaven. This doctrinal unfolding of Mary's story is rigorously orthodox and utterly queer. And in this story **Tina Beattie** finds healing for a world torn between "identity and otherness, love and abjection, desire and loss."

Like so many other contributors to this volume, Beattie thinks that the modern church has lost sight of the queerness of Christ's story in Scripture and tradition, and in this story the meaning of Mary's life, of her conceiving, motherhood and womanliness. By the end of the nineteenth century Mary had been both torn from her son – having become the encherubed but childless "immaculate conception," who appeared to Bernadette Soubirous in 1858 in confirmation of Pope Pius IX's *Ineffabilis Deus* of 1854 – and placed under the watchful eye of Joseph, the somewhat feeble patriarch of the "holy family" of Nazareth, which was honored with a feast day in 1892 by Pope Pius XIII. Thus by the end of the century Mary had been both domesticated and heterosexualized. She was no longer the woman whose *fiat* brought God into her, and from her into the world; the woman whose relations with God and men were decidedly queer. In order to retrieve this earlier, more orthodox woman, Beattie returns to the Greek Fathers of the ancient church, to such mystics as Ephrem of Syria, who had a sure insight into the strangeness and complexity of Mary's life in God and God's life in her.

Beattie shows how writers like Ephrem and other "fathers" understood the queerness of Mary's virginity, maternity, and womanhood. Her virginity is a sign of the "divine mystery" that takes place in her and as her. But it also shows that the life that grows in and from her is not contained by the "cycle of sex, procreation and death." It is instead the life we know as Jesus – risen and ascended. Christians do not seek immortality through children, but eternity in Christ. But while Jesus is a "new creation," his mothering by Mary shows his humanity, his dependency on others. Like the rest of us he is formed through relationships. Even if, as judge, Christ stands over against us, he first stands with us, as a fellow human being and friend. And the conjunction of virginity with maternity opens the "space of wonder" where we can begin to see the Other in the same; in a body like our own. Finally, in Mary's womanhood we see the new Eve, who is not Eve's replacement, but redemption – our redemption. Mary is Eve's healing, the sign to us – the children of Eve – that Christ's life is fulfilled, will be fulfilled, in all.

In the final parts of her chapter, Beattie relates mariology to psychoanalysis, for in the first she finds hope for what the second seeks, for what it has already half-seen. Julia Kristeva sees psychoanalysis succeeding religion, as articulating the diremption of human life that was expressed – but unknown – in Christianity. And fundamentally this is the tear between the maternal – the semiotic – within which we once lived, and the paternal – the symbolic – in which we come to ourselves as ourselves: but a self that is torn from the mother, and that always has this otherness (*chora*) within. We need to be able to speak the semiotic within the symbolic, a language of motherhood that will heal, though not undo, the trauma of our birth into language. Kristeva thinks that modern society lacks this language of an original maternity, but Beattie argues that it still thrives in the Christian cultures where Mary is known, where life is lived – prayed – in hers, in her birthing of God's body in ours. There the stranger we are to ourselves is taken up into the ever stranger life of God, who comes to us in Mary and Jesus, woman and man, in the mystery of the *incarnation*. And there we will discover that this difference of strangers is not threat but promise: the joy of creature in creator, the ever queerer life of God.

The Mary of Beattie's reflections is the Mary of Christian faith. We have access to no other, and she is the Mary of faith throughout the centuries, whose story has grown in the telling. The faithfulness of the story to the one of whom it is told is tested in and through its telling, through a sense of its fittingness – of its fitting with other stories – which will be known fully in the fullness of time, when the telling of stories runs out into the eternity of their consummation. But how do we think the stories of those other saints who are otherwise located in historical time, of whom biographies as well as hagiographies can be told? This is the question with which **David Matzko McCarthy** opens the closing chapter of *Queer Theology* on the desire of saints.

McCarthy takes for his argument two women who chose virginity rather than matrimony, and he considers how their choice has been narrated in subsequent tellings of their stories. One is Queen Elizabeth I (1503–1603), as told in Shekhar Kapur's film, *Elizabeth* (1998), and the other is St Rose of Lima (1586–1617) as narrated by Sr Mary Alphonsus OSSP (1968). Both women are thus told within hagiographies – life stories which seek to convince their readers of their heroines' virtues. Elizabeth desires love but chooses a single life in order to preserve her freedom and that of her country. In Kapur's telling she is a kind of martyr, who sacrifices her sexuality for the independence of her throne. Elizabeth is contrasted with Mary Tudor (1516–58), who lacks the sexual spontaneity that Elizabeth enjoys but must relinquish. Elizabeth finds herself through sexual desire, even as she learns that she must forgo its fulfillment. She is thus a very modern tragic heroine.

St Rose – a near contemporary of the historical queen – also chooses virginity over marriage, and in order to find a certain freedom, a certain "route to power." But Rose does so in order to be free for her divine lover, Jesus. She does not so much give up her sexuality, as mortify it through strenuous chastisements of the flesh, so that freed from all earthly attachments she is perfectly free for the man – or rather the child – who wants her for his own. Rose's life is dominated by visions of the infant Jesus, reaching out from his mother's arms, to caress Rose with his own. And yet even as she abandons herself for God's embrace, she finds herself abandoned by God, her spiritual life delivering but rare intimacies of its desired consummation. Rose's strange pedophiliac desires render her "nuptial moments with the infant Jesus" unerotic. Hers is a very sexless sexuality.

But it is not that Rose sought to deny the body in favor of a purely spiritual rapture, as that in the mortification of her flesh she sought to find the God whose own body suffered on the cross. It was an attempt to make that body present in her own. "She acts out the burning of God's own anguished passion." McCarthy does not ask us to approve what many will see as a pathology – a dangerous identification with a child phantasm – but he does yet ask us to consider how Rose's passionate attachment to her savior disrupts our expectations of seemly spirituality. Rose's love causes us to wonder. "We see a dangerous, undomesticated love of God." We see – McCarthy seems to suggest – a God whose passion for us burns so brightly that it consumes the bodies it touches. In the saints we see a very queer, extreme desire that fascinates and appalls, moving us to pity and terror.

The medieval saint evoked not so much imitation (*imitatio*) as wonder (*admiratio*). Indeed the saint was not to be imitated but marveled at: *non imitandum sed admirandum*. "When we read what certain saints did . . . we should wonder at rather than imitate their deeds" (James of Vitry quoted in Bynum 2001: 51). To imitate was to stigmatize, to inscribe or incorporate the other into oneself, as Christ in the body of St Francis of Assisi. But to wonder at was to be faced with the inimitable, the nonconsumable, the altogether other; that which one might admire but not become. Elizabeth and Rose, but especially Rose, astonish in just this way. They unsettle our comforts. And to some extent all saints are so queer. But to wonder at these lives is in some way to share in their strangeness, to exceed ourselves – if only for a moment – and so to become wonderful in our wonderment. And this, after all, is the undertaking of queer theology: to make the same different, the familiar strange, the odd wonderful; and to do so not out of perversity but in faithfulness to the different, strange, and wonderful by which we are encountered in the story of Jesus and the body of Christ.

Queer *Mixtio*

For Bernard of Clairvaux, Mary the mother of Jesus was a cause of astonishment, for in herself she was an impossible mixture of virginity and maternity, and so a marvel like the child to whom she gave birth: the supreme *mixtio* of humanity and divinity. With "faith and the human heart" mixed we can only wonder at her and her child.

> For it is marvellous what the human heart can accomplish in yielding to faith, how it can believe God became man and Mary gave birth and remained a virgin. Just as iron and clay cannot be joined so these two cannot be mixed if the glue of the Holy Spirit does not mix them. Who can believe that he was laid in a manger, wept in a cradle, . . . died between thieves, is also God, majestic and immense? . . . And the first mixture [of divinity and humanity] is a poultice to cure infirmities. The two species are mixed in the Virgin's womb as in a mortar, with the Holy Spirit the pestle sweetly mixing them. . . . The first union is the remedy but only in the

second [mixture of virginity and maternity] does the help truly come, for God wills that we gain nothing unless it passes through the hands of Mary. (Bernard of Clairvaux quoted in Bynum 2001: 122–3)

Mary with her crying infant is a perfect figure for queer theology. She is a virgin who yet gives birth; a mother for whom there is no father other than the one she comes to see in her son. And her son, when grown into the Christ of faith and heart, in turn gives birth to her, to the *ecclesia* he feeds with his blood as once he was fed with her milk. And then this son takes her – his mother and child – as his bride and queen, so that we can hardly say who comes from whom, who lives in whom, or how we have come to find our own bodies remade in Christ's: fed with his flesh which is also Mary's.

> When the time had come for him to be born,
> He went forth like the bridegroom from his bridal chamber,
> Embracing his bride, holding her in his arms,
> Whom the gracious Mother laid in a manger
> Among some animals that were there at that time.
> Men sang songs and angels melodies
> Celebrating the marriage of two such as these.
> But God there in the manger cried and moaned;
> And these tears were jewels the bride brought to the wedding.
> The mother gazed in sheer wonder on such an exchange:
> In God, man's weeping, and in man, gladness,
> To the one and the other things usually so strange.
> (St John of the Cross, *Romances*)

Notes

1 For example, in the story of Adam and Eve, Pope Benedict XVI finds authorization for heterosexual monogamy: "Adam is a seeker, who 'abandons his mother and father' in order to find woman; only together do the two represent complete humanity and become 'one flesh'. . . . Corresponding to the image of a monotheistic God, is monogamous marriage" (Benedict XVI 2006: 15; para. 11). Apart from the fact that Adam didn't have a mother and father (and so here we must presume that "Adam" stands for all other men – including the pope? – and the "woman" he seeks for all women), and the fact that the claimed correspondence between monotheism and monogamy is hardly biblical, we may think this a fairly standard ecclesial reading against the grain of Scripture and experience. But turn the page and we find something much queerer. Benedict reminds us that Christ gives himself to be eaten in the Eucharist, and that this is a "previously inconceivable" realization of the "marriage between God and Israel," so that the consumption of Christ's flesh becomes a matrimonial act; a lovers' intimacy. Moreover, in joining with Christ we are united "with all those to whom he gives himself. . . . We become 'one body', completely joined in a single existence" (Benedict XVI 2006: 16–17; paras. 13–14). Thus the marriage practice that corresponds to the one God turns out not to be monogamy after all, but polygamy. This of course better suits Scripture if not the pope's (mis)reading of Genesis. It is as if the pope can think thoughts at the level of the Christian symbolic that he would otherwise find unpalatable.

2 "John, who reclined familiarly on the glorious breast [*gloriosum pectus*] of the Most High; God gave you to his mother as her son in place of himself when he left her at bodily death. To you, blessed one, so loving and so loved of God, this little man who is accused of God appeals with

prayers, so that by the intercession of one so loved he may turn from himself the threat of the wrath of God" (Anselm 1973: 157; First Prayer to Saint John the Evangelist, lines 8–15).

3   For John as *sponsa Christi* see Hamburger 2001: 301. Ephrem of Syria (c. 306–73) – in a hymn on the nativity of Christ (16.10) – was one of the first to describe Mary as Christ's bride (Ephrem of Syria 1989: 150; Gambero 1999: 117–19; see also Tina Beattie's chapter below – chapter 20). Peter Chrysologus (c. 380–c. 450) – who found Mary to be the "enclosed garden" of the Song of Songs (4.12) – married her to Christ as "God's spouse," taking care to note that this union did not impair her marriage with Joseph. For the two marriages, as Luigi Gambero puts it, took place on "different levels," the eternal and the temporal, the spiritual and the material (Gambero 1989: 297). And yet is there not something adulterous or bigamous in the arrangement? For later twelfth-century developments of this trope – when Mary became Christ's seducer and lover – see Balthasar (1988–98: III, 309).

4   This is to map the Pauline terms – *malakos* (1 Corinthians 6.9) and *arsenokoitēs* (1 Timothy 1.10) – onto the earlier "classical" ones and so understand them as respectively referring to the "passive" and "active" parties in pederastic relationships. This is of course disputable – see John Boswell (1980: 106–7; 335–53) – but here I more or less follow Martti Nissinen (1998: 113–18), who allows for this interpretation while pointing up the obscurity of the terms. It is unlikely that we will ever really know what Paul and pseudo-Paul intended.

5   If one likes – and *pace* Dan Brown (2003) – it is not Mary Magdalene as John who appears in Leonardo da Vinci's painting of the Last Supper, but John as the Virgin Mary, as "bride" of Christ. Leonardo's predilection for androgynous figures suits the traditionally feminized John, and Leonardo's John, with his downcast eyes, resembles Leonardo's Virgin of the Rocks (commissioned 1483), and so figures the tradition of the *sponsa Christi*. In a strange way the picture of the Last Supper also reminds us of the *Andachtsbilder*, the devotional images of Christ and St John, in having John lean away from Christ, his body recalling their intimacy even as it presages their rupture, at the moment when Christ reveals his impending sacrifice.

6   It is appropriate to think of English mystics in this regard, because the Admont illustrator may well have been English, or copying an English model. Though the "Admont miniature is Salzburg work, yet the text it illustrates is from the pen of an Italian who was an English archbishop" (Pächt 1956: 79).

7   For just such immobility in Karl Barth and John Paul II see Loughlin (1998a).

8   It should be noted that there might be more reason to describe the friendship between Jonathan and David as homoerotic than I allow in this article. See further Olyan (2006).

9   This is nicely evidenced in the difficulty of explaining how the marriage of Joseph and Mary was complete but not sexual. Thomas Aquinas responded by understanding the perfection of marriage as twofold, as between its form and operation. The form is the "inseparable union of souls . . . a bond of affection that cannot be sundered," while its operation is the begetting and rearing of children. Thus the union of Joseph and Mary was complete in its form, and almost in its carnal operation, since Jesus was reared though not begotten by Joseph and Mary (*Summa Theologiae*, IIIa.29.2 *responsio*). So even Thomas had to admit that their marriage was not fully consummated. Elsewhere, Thomas allows that the lack of carnal intercourse allows a spouse to leave the married state for the religious. "Before marital intercourse there is only a spiritual bond between husband and wife, but afterwards there is a carnal bond between them. Wherefore, just as after marital intercourse marriage is dissolved by carnal death, so by entering religion the bond which exists before the consummation of the marriage is dissolved, because religious life is a kind of spiritual death, whereby a man dies to the world and lives to God" (*Summa Theologiae*, Supplement 61.3 *responsio*).

10 Note how Benedict makes "union" the primary meaning of marriage. And of course it is not possible to do otherwise when the primordial marriage is between Christ and the Church. From this it follows that Christian "procreation" is always spiritual before it is biological, with the latter a figure for the former.

11 And we might as well note that this eucharistic "sex" is "oral sex" and so "contraceptive," and yet no less fecund for that. "[I]n spiritual marriage there are two kinds of birth, and thus two kinds of offspring, though not opposite. For spiritual persons, like holy mothers, may bring souls to birth by preaching, or may give birth to spiritual insights by meditation. . . . The soul is affected in one way when it is made fruitful by the Word, in another when it enjoys the Word: in the one it is considering the needs of its neighbor; in the other it is allured by the sweetness of the Word. A mother is happy in her child; a bride is even happier in her bridegroom's embrace" (Bernard of Clairvaux 1980: 209; 85.13). At the heart of the Christian symbolic we find the very reversal of the Church's modern obsession with heterosexual procreation.

12 God's being is indubitable because the world's being is not: it might not have *been*. Why is there existence rather than nothing?

13 "Gays in the military threaten to undo masculinity only because this masculinity is made of repudiated homosexuality" (J. Butler 1997: 143).

14 See, for example, the ravings of the late Elizabeth Fox-Genovese.

15 Eckhart knew and borrowed from Porete's work (see Turner 1995a: 138).

16 This theme – which identifies the "nothingness" of God and self – is most extreme in Porete and may have led, along with her refusal to desist from publishing *The Mirror of Simple Souls*, to her death by burning in 1310. If so, she was misunderstood; being orthodox rather than heterodox – as Denys Turner (1995a: 139–40) argues.

17 The disappearance of masculinity is perhaps better discussed in French, where masculinité is a feminine noun.

18 The story goes that when present, the SRY gene on the Y chromosome tells the developing embryo to become a male. When this gene is absent the embryo develops into a female by default. But now it would seem that the story has to be somewhat more complex; that the SRY gene helps to fulfill an earlier negotiation within the developing embryo towards a male sex. See further Roughgarden (2004: 196–206).

19 It should be needless to say that queer theology does not oppose God's creation, and so does not seek an argument for or against homosexuality. But queer theology does seek to understand the development and deployment of the term "queer," and the interests its usage serves.

20 Here we may recall the similar retreat from a radically queer theology that Virginia Burrus finds in John Milbank's reading of Gregory of Nyssa.

21 How shameful is it that a President of the United States of America can oppose same-sex marriage but defend the use of torture? How is it that Christian values can be so inverted?

Part I

Queer Lives

Chapter 1

Subjectivity and Belief

Kathy Rudy

Because the mountain grass
Cannot but keep the form
Where the mountain hare has lain.
(William Butler Yeats, *Memory*, 1916)

In the Fall of 1995, I completed the first draft of *Sex and the Church* (Rudy 1997), a book which argued that sexism and homophobia were inextricably intertwined (especially for the Christian right), that the socially constructed distinction between heterosexuality and homosexuality was a poor way to conceptualize Christian ministry, and that progressive Christians should stop encouraging gays and lesbians to take up monogamous relationships and try instead to understand the value of a lifestyle built on community. Although it would be 18 months before the book would be published, I felt happy that Fall to be finished with the first stage, and sent the manuscript to my editor and to several of my colleagues at Duke University.

At that time, I was just starting my second year of a joint appointment at Duke between the Divinity School and Women's Studies. It was a great job for me because my partner also taught at Duke, we owned a house in Durham (North Carolina), had two dogs and a kid in middle school, and having this Duke job meant no more commuting. I had completed my PhD in the Duke Religion Department several years before getting that job, and most of my teachers knew Jan, and knew that we were together; thus, although my sexual orientation was never discussed during the hiring process, I assumed that all parties knew about me and had tacitly consented to these arrangements. I had convinced myself that even though many of my colleagues were blatantly homophobic in their work or in their casual conversation, I was somehow an exception in their minds.

I was wrong. In the beginning of my second year, I was "outed" by several conservative Faculty members, was accused of theological heresy for my current work on homosexuality as well as for earlier publications on abortion, had my credentials questioned by a group of students, and finally was told that although my initial contract would be fulfilled, I would no longer be able to teach courses on gender, sexuality, or feminism without the written approval of the entire Department. To their credit, university administrators realized that this was not a healthy environment for a junior scholar and stepped in immediately to move my position full-time into Women's Studies.

These events produced a number of professional and personal changes for me that bear on my thinking in this chapter. At one level, I feel that my professional career as a scholar of religion ended that Fall. In pursuing tenure in the emerging field of women's studies, I would now need to attend new conferences, make new contacts, publish in different arenas. I would engage different students, different arguments. I would no longer be speaking and writing within the community called "Church."

The more important changes took place on a deeper level where for the first time since college I began to question the value and coherence of my own faith. For many people, disappointments like the one I experienced that semester often function only to bolster belief; God, after all, can provide solace and assurance that can make such hard times easier. However, for me, these months produced the reverse; the entire world of faith and religion seemed tainted, filled with hurt, unwelcoming. This shift came for me not as a result of reasoned deliberation but rather as one of those life events where your emotions seem to reconfigure themselves, where the meaning of many things is altered, almost without your consent. I think of how these events organized my life into "before" and "after" frames. Before, it never bothered me that my partner and our daughter never liked to go to church; I went by myself when I couldn't convince them to come. After, it seems too hard to leave them relaxing on Sunday morning to go off by myself into hostile territory. Before, it didn't bother me that there was not one gay-affirming Methodist church in Durham or Chapel Hill; most of the people in my home church knew and accepted, right? After, such self-deceptions were unconvincing. Before, on the occasions when I really needed a spiritual high, I went to one of the white or black evangelical churches in Durham; even though I had encountered homophobic sermons there, I was able to ignore these proclamations and enjoy the music and the way the Holy Spirit was present. After, rage consumed me so profoundly that I could hardly bear to drive by these places. Before, I felt thrilled with the handful of religion scholars who knew what I was writing and supported my efforts; I worked through my ideas with them. After, the Christian Church seemed filled only with hateful and homophobic hypocrites, and I simply could not will myself into conversation with them. Before, the world felt driven by the love of God. After, the world seemed to go forward based only on sheer force of my own will.

So, before *Sex and the Church* even saw print, my connection with the institution called "Church" was troubled. What I attempt to trace out in this chapter are the ways that this shift has affected my work and my thinking; that is, I am interested not in the impact that *Sex and the Church* has had on readers, but rather the effect the text has had on its own author. Writing several years after these events, I find myself asking a series of questions that potentially shed light not only on matters of faith but also on issues of human subjectivity. How does one cope with a shift in which things that were once "impossible for humans but possible for God" were now just plain impossible? How does one make the transition from a world where "God will provide" and "God knows best" into a world where little is certain except death, taxes, and maybe late capitalism? What happens to the form of belief when the object of faith is questioned, when the controlling institution is revealed to be corrupt? What happens to the meaning that drains out of daily life when you lose your faith? How is that life altered when simple acts that used to function as an intimate connection between the imminent and the transcendent no longer have spiritual value? And, perhaps just as important as any of these questions, in what ways does that life, finally, stay the same?

Over the past several years I have sought answers to these questions in many different forms of scholarship and writing. These investigations have led me to a set of hunches or intuitions about the way that religious belief molds and shapes a human subject, and the various ways that that human subject retains the form or outline of that belief, long after faith has been lost. I would like to review here some of the work that has been most helpful in leading me to these insights; I will conclude by summarizing these ideas in relation to questions of gay and lesbian life in the church.

Fragments and Ghosts

To start with one interesting and perhaps unobvious example, the theories produced by the emerging discourse of subaltern studies can be very helpful, I found, in understanding the experiential shift of being inside and outside of faith communities. Beginning in the middle 1980s, the subaltern studies group attempted to transport the insights of Antonio Gramsci into rural India, not by writing a traditional "history from below" or incorporating disenfranchised Indians into existing paradigms, but rather, as Gyan Prakash articulates it, by repeatedly demonstrating that the process of including the forgotten must always fail. Throughout the last 15 years, these projects have called into question secular universalisms of the dominant culture, and insisted that the inability of the subaltern to represent itself in Western rational terms is an illustration of the limitation of those terms. These scholars argue that the subaltern is intractable and resides outside dominant culture, that peasant mentality remains outside the field of reason. Their goal is not to reinscribe the subaltern into the ruling discourse, but to disable the power of dominance.

In his exceptional work in the field, Dipesh Chakrabarty is keenly aware of the damage done to a culture when religious events are treated by scholars – in this case historians – in non-religious terms. Because the concept of "history" must be made universal in order to fit everywhere, supernatural activity must be overlooked in all historical narratives. People may *think* a God acts, but the historian and the anthropologist must begin with the assumption that God(s) actually do not act. As Chakrabarty claims:

> a secular subject like history faces many problems in handling imaginations in which gods, spirits, or the supernatural have agency in the world. Secular histories are produced usually by ignoring the signs of divine or superhuman presences. In effect, we have two systems of thought, one in which the world is ultimately disenchanted and the other in which humans are not the only meaningful agents. For the purpose of writing history, the first system, the secular, translates the second into itself. (Chakrabarty 1997: 35)

This translation, according to Chakrabarty, uses the seemingly neutral universalism of secular society to express and mediate the world, and thus renders the reality of the subaltern, once again, unspeakable. A metanarrative of non-transcendence is inadvertently applied and people are robbed of the shape of their world. Because "claims about agency on behalf of the religious, the supernatural, the divine, and the ghostly have to be mediated in terms of this universal" we can never accurately portray the lived reality of those inside the religious worldview (Chakrabarty 1997: 39). Our commitments to secular realities and truths diminish and dilute the world of gods and spirits. As Chakrabarty claims, "[t]he moment we think of the world as disenchanted, we set limits to the ways the past can be narrated" (Chakrabarty 1997: 51).

Although this review of subalternity is too brief, I mean only to demonstrate here that the academy has an awareness that religious worldviews differ from dominant secular worldviews. And to my thinking, the tension between the subaltern and dominant history is analogous to the difference between belief and non-belief. For a person of faith, spirits and gods operate in history; for a person who has lost her faith, such assertions seem implausible. In one setting, the world is almost magical, operating under the whims and desires of benevolent or malevolent unseen but palpable forces; in another, the world is rational, operating under the rules and forces of nature, science, objectivity, repeatability. Examining the differences between these two worldviews is a helpful way of capturing what it feels like to lose faith. The world you lived in before, where God operated as a force in your life, seems unrepresentable in the new language. No set of reason-based mechanisms or functions take the place of that potential; fate, desire, power, ambition, and even hope, fall short of adequately portraying the world before. The shape of life inside religious belief is, as subaltern studies theorizes, unrepresentable in secular terms.

A second and unrelated body of literature that has helped me process my own shift in faith has been the genre of memoir. In the last ten years, public intellectuals have become less interested in making abstract arguments that apply universally, and have taken up instead the project of examining, discovering, and revealing who they are and why. Few general-reader books are written today void of the author's presence. Memoirs bring high advances from publishers. Narrating life seems of utmost importance. In an essay examining "The Memoir Boom," Vivian Gornick declares, "[o]ur age is characterized by a need to testify . . . Urgency seems to attach itself to the idea of a tale told directly from life" (Gornick 1996: 3). Or, as Ruth Behar puts it, "autobiography has emerged, for better or worse, as the key form of storytelling in our time, with everyone doing it from Shirley MacLaine to Colin Powell to professors of French and psychiatry" (Behar 1996: 26). And, religion, it seems, has played a part in almost everyone's story, or to be more accurate, confessing rejection or loss of religion often constitutes an essential component of coming of age.

In many of these stories, coherence becomes fixed on the narrating/narrated subject itself; the loss of belief (and/or the assessment of damages incurred as a result of that belief) become the glue that holds the subject together. Where once – in an individual's childhood – the center of one's life was provided by religious discourse, and where once – in a certain historical moment – reason provided a clear foundation for human existence, now neither holds us together. The result is a new, postmodern, self-help-driven subject who coheres around any story she is able to cobble together. Thus, memoir becomes the activity which reconciles us with loss and memory.

While many recent best-selling memoirs deal with loss and religion from interesting perspectives (including Frank McCourt's *Angela's Ashes*, 1996 and Mary Karr's *The Liar's Club*, 1995), two books stand out for me as sophisticated and sagacious models for wrestling with the holes left by intensely religious childhoods. Kim Barnes' *In the Wilderness: Coming of Age in Unknown Country* (1996) is the story of a young girl raised within a Pentecostal community in rural Idaho, and Barbara Wilson's *Blue Windows: A Christian Science Childhood* (1997) is the story of another young girl raised within the pre-modern, faith-healing world of Mary Baker Eddy. What both stories do so well is capture the ways that faith can shape the heart and soul, as well as describe the emptiness that remains when faith fails.

Into the Wilderness begins in the logging camps of rural Idaho, where a young Kim Barnes and her family lead a poor but relatively happy communal existence, where the costs of Christianity live in balance with the benefits. In her early childhood, logging is prosperous enough to keep the extended family afloat, but by the time she is twelve, the industry begins to fail, the extended family departs for city life, and Barnes is left in the woods with only her immediate family and the impending threat of religious fanaticism. Although her mother has been the dominant spiritual force of the family throughout childhood, it is Barnes' father who takes up religion with a vengeance during this time.

> Given his life – the seemingly haphazard set of circumstances and catastrophes that
> had beset his family – the sterile reasoning of an all-knowing God negated the need

to question. What comfort it must have seemed for a man and his family come to the wilderness, escaping whatever demons that had threatened to destroy them. What he believes is that it was the Spirit that spoke to him, that it was my mother's faith and prayers that led him to pick up the Bible she had left on the table and begin reading the words that would change and direct his life. (K. Barnes 1996: 50–1)

The family works hard to accommodate themselves to, and even participate in, the father's conversion. They denounce worldliness, pray constantly, and intensify their awareness of all spiritual matters. Involving themselves deeply in a small non-denominationalist, charismatic country church (one which had a long history of ferocious but problematic leadership), the family falls deeper into the grips of fanaticism, and the teenage girl is forced to repress and hide her emerging sexuality and personality in order to dodge the label of evil. She is sexually abused and simultaneously blamed for that abuse, denied basic human dignity during adolescence, sent away and punished severely. She is able to look back on these years from her perch of adulthood and conclude that although religion had its attractions, she is better off without it.

Barbara Wilson grows up during the same period on the West Coast in a family committed to Christian Science beliefs. *Blue Windows* chronicles the life of a daughter to an observant Christian Science mother, who suffered first from prolonged and disturbing mental illness, and later from breast cancer. In keeping with her religious convictions, Wilson's mother refused all medical treatment, relying instead on practitioners (faith healers). Wilson is intrigued by Christian Science, in part because its teachings dominated her mother's life, in part because Mary Baker Eddy's teaching now seems to serve as a backdrop for many components of New Age religion, in part because she once believed it and remembers its intensity. As she writes:

Christian Science is a religion that still secretly intrigues me, if only because of how completely different its world is than almost anything I'd come across since. I may have only understood it with a child's understanding, but I knew that it was far more than just about going or not going to the doctor. It was a far stranger, far more complex system of beliefs that turned reality on its head, that said that only spirit existed, not matter; that there was only good in the world, not evil. It was a belief system that based its power to heal on keeping the mind fixed firmly on God, who was all-powerful and all-loving. It was choosing to see only beauty and happiness, no matter what. (Wilson 1997: 7)

Wilson knows that, although many of the beliefs of Christian Science now seem ridiculous, she once thought they were true, and that her past has left her with the desire to explore the religion not as a participant, but not as a total apostate either. In describing someone she once met who also grew up as a Christian Scientist, Wilson says "she absolutely loathed the religion, and would pinch together her mouth to show the prissy expression her mother got when she was expounding Mrs Eddy's principles. I never dared talk about Christian Science with her. She had clearly never believed a word of it; she had never been fooled like me, or like my mother" (Wilson 1997: 8). Wilson craves an audience who will appreciate the worth and value of such a religion, while at the same time condemning, with her, the harms incurred by such harshness and rigidity, an audience who will be both understanding and critical. In the end, this desire is met by leaving, by declaring her life as outside the fold, outside the possibility of all belief. "I knew that once I let go of this God, this God of my childhood, I would not be able to believe in another one. And that meant I would cease to believe . . . And one day, when I was worn out and lying on my back on the floor, the simple thought crossed my mind, 'There is no God.' And that was that" (Wilson 1997: 286, 288).

The structure of both these narratives is similar; Barnes and Wilson are fascinated with their religious roots, and are attracted, at some level, to the way their respective religions made them feel as if they belonged, as if they were set apart from the world, as if they were special, as if they were saved. As Barnes recalls:

> I remember the call. I have felt the purging and radiating calm of being born again. I have spoken in tongues, have healed and been healed. I have seen demons cast out and watched a man live forty days without food. I remember these things without doubt, beyond reason . . . Even now, more than two decades later, I can still remember feeling saved, pulled from the brink of hell. (K. Barnes 1996: 256)

However, both writers experience a rupture with intense religiosity – a rupture based on politics, on the improbability of narrative, on problems with sexuality and gender, and on someone else's misuse of power – a rupture which drives them to the higher ground of individualism, to undefined greater power, or to the process of memoir itself. Both once were "found," and now are "lost," and write to us of the relative benefits of the latter. For both, although a lot is lost in the loss of religion – things like security, belonging, salvation, love – the benefits of freedom outweigh the costs.

There is much to be said for the Ur-narrative that celebrates the joys of being released from some of the bizarre strictures that often accompany religion. Although Duke Divinity School is a far cry from backwoods fundamentalism or Christian Science, the idea that educated Christians would be so censorious of my choice of partners that they would want me fired from my job seemed deeply problematic. I read both *In the Wilderness* and *Blue Windows* after the Divinity School incident, and found a great deal of comfort in being divided, disconnected, and detached from such a patently troubled institution. At the time, their stories comforted me, told me that my lack of faith was for the better. Whatever I would become without religion, I would be better off than if I stayed.

In recent rereadings of these memoirs, however, a new problem emerges for me in their attempt to reconcile themselves to their intensely religious childhoods, for Barnes and Wilson (and many others) end up with an all-or-nothing approach to religion. While these authors can at some level appreciate how that background contributed to who they became, there is no way for them to locate even a small part of themselves inside the plausibility structures of the worlds they have rejected. Coping with the intensity requires distance. Religion demands of us an all-or-nothing attitude, we are either in or out. One person can only occupy one truth at any given time. Although people can change, they must change as a unified subject, they must say "I once believed and now I don't." We are required to write our stories either as participants in a faith community (as *Sex and the Church* was written) or as outsiders, to audiences that may remember religion, but are not now comfortable embracing it (*In the Wilderness* and *Blue Windows*).

This same "all-or-nothing" problem of unified subjectivity also haunts subaltern studies, it seems to me. Once the subaltern becomes the least bit imbricated in a system of dominance, that dominance reinscribes the entire life. After all, one cannot be an illiterate peasant part-time, one cannot long for the magical world of spirits once the discourse of Western rationality has been installed.[1] Thus, any given individual must be either inside the system (and engage in practices that signify such membership – such as avoiding dancing or doctoring), or outside and takes on the world as a rational, reasonable being. Doing either half-way or part-time only makes you look foolish from both perspectives.

The problem with this approach is that it does not accurately reflect the way I feel in losing my faith. It was and is a much more jagged process, an uneven development. I find myself longing for things I no longer believe in, believing in things that seem patently absurd. (A friend of mine and fellow dog-lover said to me recently that she doesn't believe in God but she does believe in a God that sends people the perfect dog for them; I realized that this incoherence was exactly how I feel about most issues of belief today.) While, on the one hand, Christianity has wounded me beyond repair, on the other I can't just will myself to stop seeing the world in Christianity's terms. To be fair, these memoirs – especially Wilson's – understand that the loss of faith is a process; indeed her story is itself a sort of exploration of alternative spiritual paths, new ways of retaining the good things about spirituality and creativity.[2] Nevertheless, for marketing purposes she has to declare herself as a unified person who stands in a different place than self-identified Christian Scientists, in much the same way that I have to declare myself here as having "lost my faith." What I need is a theory of subjectivity that would allow me to be two contradictory things at the same time, that would allow me to say "I believe" and "I don't" in a way that does not require coherent explanation. I need a theory that will allow me to be fragmented, not as a temporary stopgap measure until I figure out where I will end up, but a theory that will allow me to understand myself as divided, now and forever. I need a model that does not obligate me to be only one, unified person, that does not rest its idea of subjectivity on Enlightenment individuality, that sees fragmentation as a natural state and not one to be worked through.

While the work of any number of scholars from Michel Foucault to Gloria Anzaldua could be invoked here, one of the most insightful new approaches to human fragmentation, I believe, can be found in the work of cultural studies and queer theorist Elspeth Probyn. Despite the fact that concepts such as fragmented identity, multiple identification, and performativity have become part of the vocabulary of everyday life for many academics, few scholars actually attempt to describe the experiences associated with these ideas. What does it actually feel like to be divided against ourselves, to be aware of the multiple and contradictory discourses running through us and constructing us differently at different moments? In her *Outside Belongings* (1996), Probyn not only describes the ways that multiple belongings work inside us, she also cogently argues that the desires associated with the movement from one identity to another are themselves constitutive of social engagement. Thus, the various fragmentations and incoherencies that exist inside of us produce new ways of being; in standing here and desiring to be there, we imagine new possibilities, become new people. As she puts it:

> desire is productive; it is what oils the social; it produces the pleats and the folds which constitute the social surface we live on. It is through and with desire that we figure relations of proximity to others and other forms of sociality. It is what remakes the social as a dynamic proposition, for if we live within a grid or network of different points, we live through the desire to make them connect differently. (Probyn 1996: 13)

Thus, it is not simply the case that we belong in different and sometimes contradictory places, but rather that these belongings circulate within us and produce desires which constitute who – precisely – we are.

Probyn's work is part of the tradition of scholarship that argues that pleasure cannot and should not be boxed in along the lines of any one single identity, orientation, or membership. According to her, for example, the very desire that produces an interest in sexual pleasure is often stifled and repressed by the unnecessarily narrow boundaries of sexual identity. Probyn recapitulates with ease the jumble of desires that roil around in her – riding horses, loving women, speaking French, traveling, collecting, singing – taken together, her writing conjures the way she (and we) are projected forward by our desires to be and belong right now here (but later there). Thus, throughout her work, Probyn demonstrates how "the inbetweenness of belonging, of belonging not in some deep authentic way but belonging in constant movement" actually functions productively (Probyn 1996: 19). In showing that we need not live our lives within the boundaries of sexual, gender, ethnic, religious, or nationalist categories, she illustrates how the specificities of our identifications and desires spill over the boundaries of any single classification.

The work of Avery Gordon also helps to illustrate that all of the fragmented pieces of a person's subjectivity do not operate on the same plane of awareness. People forget and remember, are unaware of the things that drive their desires, lose sight of the things that matter, are captured by things they can't explain. This crisis in self-awareness is compatible with Probyn's view of fragmentation, but also goes beyond it. As Gordon explains:

> At the core of the postmodern field or scene is a crisis in representation, a fracture in the epistemological regime of modernity, a regime that rested on the reality effect of social change. Such a predicament has led to, among other consequences, an understanding that the practices of writing, analysis, and investigation, whether of social or cultural material, constitute less a scientifically positive project than a cultural practice that organizes particular rituals of storytelling told by situated individuals. (A. Gordon 1997: 10)

Gordon calls these new understandings of social life "hauntings," a concept which attempts to capture the anti-positivist ideas that things are not always what they seem, that buried interpretations often emerge without warning, old stories linger. In her *Ghostly Matters* (1997), Gordon claims that hauntings are an ever-present part of postmodern subjectivity; as she articulates, "haunting is a constituent element of modern social life. It is neither premodern superstition nor individual psychosis; it is a generalizable social phenomenon of great import" (A. Gordon 1997: 7). For her, the presence of ideas, thoughts, motivations, desires, etc., that seem, at one level, absent, marks the emergence of postmodernism. "The ghost or the apparition is one form by which something lost, or barely visible, or seemingly not there to our supposedly well-trained eyes, makes itself known or apparent to us, in its own way, of course" (A. Gordon 1997: 8). Thus, according to Gordon, circulating inside of us with all those fragments of identities and memberships are also ghosts and apparitions of former and forgotten interpretations and lifestyles that, of course, have their own agendas for us as well.

I find Probyn and Gordon helpful in thinking about my predicament in a number of ways. Probyn's description feels like the way I experience things. That is, even when I called myself a Christian, I was never only that; I was also a feminist, a lesbian, a southerner, an animal-lover, a sci-fi fan, etc. All these identities circulated inside of me and informed one another, producing sometimes exciting critiques, and other times almost devastating inconsistencies. What Probyn's version of fragmentation theory enables me to understand is that such internal dissimilarity is all that ever happens with anyone, that productivity depends on movement from one desire to another (and that perhaps some people are better at normalizing paradoxes than others). Gordon's work adds to this an awareness that our physical practices and our bodily responses are not always fully governed by what we think we believe, but by "ghosts" of former and other understandings. For me, then, just because at one level I feel I have left the church, that leaving does not mean that the ghosts of former interpretations have necessarily disappeared. This insight matches my experience well: still today, several years after leaving, when I feel scared about something I (almost involuntarily) pray, when I am anxious I hear a voice that says God will provide, when I face something that seems insurmountable I remember (and I ask myself, is *remembering* the right verb?) that with God, all things are possible. The ghosts embedded in these thoughts and practices continue to circulate in my life, even though I would like them to be gone. Probyn and Gordon both help me explain why religion is not just a part of my past, but also a part of my present. At an almost physical level of flesh and emotions, the church constitutes and constructs a part of who I am, and no amount of rejection or willful apostasy can ever alter that.

So, for purposes of clarity, let me recap. I am drawn to the all-or-nothing narratives of subaltern studies and the memoirs reviewed here, because they seem absolutely true to my experience; they enable me to say to you "I have lost my faith." Sometimes. I am comforted by the stories that tell me that leaving the church will lead me to a more fulfilling, less oppressive life. Sometimes. I enjoy my new life in Women's Studies and the secular academy where being a lesbian is pretty much a non-issue and where I think I understand the rules of the game. Sometimes. I enjoy the feeling of being a whole, secular subject and enjoy projecting that wholeness into my future. Sometimes. Other times, I miss the church terribly. Feel lost without the reconciling wholeness it once offered me. Other times, I notice religious impulses hidden deep inside me, almost as if they were located in my bones. My desire for God sometimes feels beyond my rational control. So what I really need, it occurs to me, is not simply an explanation that says "I am a fragmented subject that is both religious and secular," but rather a three-dimensional theory that will sometimes allow me to be always and only secular, and other times will allow me to see myself as divided, fragmented, and perpetually confused.

Black and White Communities

In an ideal world, this chapter would end here, with a call for a complex subjectivity and a way of seeing myself as both inside and outside the condition of faith. My pragmatic side, however, insists on a conclusion that addresses how we might execute a way of life that refuses the paradox of belief and non-belief, one that embodies fragmented subjectivity. What follows from here does not (and cannot) detail that life in full, because, quite honestly, I haven't yet found such a reality. Rather, this ending stands more as a hypothesis or question, an intuition about the directions I intend to head in with my scholarship and life, to solve the problems that accompany the loss of faith.

At a practical level, one way of formulating this proposal would be to suggest that what I need really isn't a fine-tuned philosophy articulating the operations of unity and fragmentation, but rather a group of people around me who can see me both as a fully secularized subject, and as a fragmented subject for whom religion is part of who I have been and who I am. In other words, perhaps my problems can't be solved with Jameson, Baudrillard, or even Foucault himself; maybe they can only be addressed on the level of practice, in the ways that our cultures circulate inside of us and that people reflect back to us what is and isn't important. Maybe what I need is not abstraction, but a group of people around me saying "yes, we see you are rational and have left all that nonsense behind" one minute, and the next minute lend me a sympathetic ear about the value of faith; a group of people who will not see those positions as inconsistent with each other. Maybe what I need is a group of people who understand that faith, for any individual, comes and goes, that people are complicated and sometimes need to believe and not believe at the same time, and that self-identification isn't finally what matters anyway. Maybe what matters is the struggle, and the people around you helping you through that struggle. Maybe what I need is not a three-dimensional theory, but a community.

What might this community look like? My intuitions tell me that certain kinds of marginalized communities are very practiced at refusing the distinction between belief and non-belief. While trying to avoid both romantic or essentialist implications, it seems important to ask how certain ethnic and racial enclaves inside US boundaries negotiate this paradox, and can maybe serve as a model for the kind of reflection and support I so long for. I want to think – for a moment – about the possibility that the practices associated with African-American communities, for example, might provide a design for coping with the three-dimensional fragmentation I have described here. The way religion and spirituality often operate in black communities, I believe, captures the kind of environment that would enable someone to both believe and not believe at the same time.

It is an indisputable fact that the black church operates as one of the central institutions in most black communities such that most African-Americans share a common perception that whether one believes or not, there is value in the church that cannot be denied. C. Eric Lincoln expresses it this way:

> The Blacks brought their religion with them. After a time they accepted the white man's religion, but they have not always expressed it in the white man's way. It became the black man's purpose – perhaps it was his destiny – to shape, to fashion, to re-create the religion offered him by the Christian slave master, to remold it nearer to his own particular needs. The black religious experience is something more than a black patina on a white happening. It is a unique response to a historical occurrence that can never be replicated for any people in America. (Lincoln 1973: vii–viii)

Or, as Katie Cannon articulates it, "the Black Church expresses the inner ethical life of the people" (Cannon 1988: 1). Even among those who have rejected faith, there is rarely a sense of bitterness, and more often a sense of nostalgia for the good things that have been lost. As a former Duke student Kim McLarin depicts in her first novel *Taming it Down*:

> There were no hymnals in my church. Everybody knew all the words to every song, even the youngest children, and if by some chance you didn't know the words, it was easy enough to catch on, because the chorus was always sung again and again, with such joy and purpose and driving rhythm that only a dead man could resist

joining in. Unhappiness was impossible when the music was swaying the church. So was disbelief. I'd always believed in God, of course, the way I believed that night followed day, but the only time I really felt His presence, the way the elders of the church said they did every day, was when I was singing. After twenty or thirty or forty minutes of singing to glory, I'd sink down in the pew. Moist and happy, knowing that God knew who I was. If church had been just music, I'd have gone every day and gotten saved over and over again. (McLarin 1998: 172)

The church takes up its role in the black community in a way that rarely needs to be hidden or disguised. We almost always expect that a black person will have been part of the church, at least as a child; as a consequence, a religious past in black culture is never a secret that must be either hidden away or painfully revealed. There are no black memoirs (to my knowledge) about the loss of faith, no public confessions of apostasy. Faith comes and goes for African-Americans; not attending church for a period is not usually considered a disaster, the slack can be picked up by friends and family. It seems to me that most African-Americans have an easier time with the kind of fractures and contradictory identifications that seem to obsess me. For them, the ability to almost fluidly move back and forth and in and out is at least in part due to the way others around them perceive such movement as normal. There is no critical divide that must be traversed and explained, because at the very core of what it means to be black rests some association with religion.

Moreover, this fluidity flows both ways, such that African-American writers often express a deep interest in spiritual matters, even when all interest in institutionalized Christianity has been lost. Spirituality and belief have become a part of the culture such that even when association with institutions is gone, avenues for expressions of faith are present. Black writers – especially women such as Toni Morrison, Alice Walker, Tonu Cade Bambara, Paule Marshall, Octavia Butler, and Ntozake Shange – provide the stories that allow us to realize that ghosts and spirits are part of the operation of the world. As Akasha (Gloria) Hull writes:

Black women writers produce literature from historical-cultural specificities of black women's lives in the US, and more particularly, from African-American spiritual traditions, which include revering the dead, acknowledging the reality of ghosts and spirit possession, honouring "superstition" and the unseen world, giving credence to second sight and other supersensory perception, paying homage to African Deities, practicing voodoo and hoodoo, rootworking, and so on. (Hull 1998: 332)

Rather than living in a world that declares and devalues the spirit realm, black writers have addressed the ways that ghosts and spirits work in the lives of their communities, and in much the same way that subaltern studies seeks to represent the faith-world of the non-modern subject. Rather than living in a world where loss of church means loss of faith, African-Americans recreate new and interesting relationships with spirits. They manage to hold on to, it seems to me, that which is essential. Even for those who no longer go to church, there are ways to believe.

I pick up, for example, Ntozake Shange's *Sassafras, Cypress, and Indigo* (1982) and the book takes me into the world of sisters and spirits, where I glimpse the workings of transcendent beings. I set the book down, and imagine making the casserole or casting the spell Shange describes, negotiating with spirits for small things; the line between my life and her book grows thin, just as the line between spirit and materiality fades. I am transported and transformed and see the world differently. I believe what she believes. And for a moment – even though I am not black – it almost doesn't matter precisely what I believe because there is someone out there able to articulate all of this so well.[3]

It is this tradition which seems absent from my white life. Virtually everyone I know is either inside the fold of church membership or outside it, either Christian or secular. The insiders can talk about spirits and saints, the outsiders can only refer to these entities metaphorically. Spirituality is something that exists inside the sanctuary of church or the privacy of homes; it is not something that, for white people, is supposed to be in our blood and bones.

Queer Communities

When I was writing *Sex and the Church*, I might have argued that the queer community could function in a similar fashion to the black community. Now I'm not so sure. Part of the problem is simply that a huge schism seems to exist between secular queers and religious queers. Secular queer books and conferences have rarely (never in my experience) included religious components, and gay and lesbian Christians rarely reach out to include substantial dialogue with non-religious audiences. We could consciously try to bridge this gap from both sides, organizing meetings and discussions which would include believers and non-believers. However, such projects seem to me both insurmountable and unlikely. Queers inside the church expend much of their energy struggling for recognition within their own denominations, queers outside usually experience the church as an irrecoverable site of oppression. Maybe if we just worked harder such bridges could be built, such paradoxes could be embraced.

But maybe it is also true that the thing that divides us (that is, religious and non-religious queers) originates at a deeper level. For example, new scholarship suggests that whiteness – and even the whiteness expressed in the gay and lesbian subcultures – is actually the absence of the kind of cultural particularities that can offer structure to a life filled with paradoxes. Because it includes so many different things, whiteness can never be constituted by only one cultural narrative, but rather can only be signified by lack. As David Roediger articulates it, "[w]hiteness describes not a culture, but precisely the absence of culture. It is the empty and therefore terrifying attempt to build an identity based on what one isn't and on whom one can hold back" (Roediger 1994: 13). The projects of new studies on whiteness simultaneously challenge the emptiness and privilege of white culture.

Black people are often able to embrace the divide between belief and non-belief not because they subscribe to philosophies or principles of fragmentation, but rather because they share a rich heritage of what it means to be black. It doesn't matter if or precisely how a black person believes, their families and communities often reflect back to them a coherence based on common culture, history, and practices. Because whiteness dominates queerness in North America today, I can't help but wonder if some of the emptiness and absence isn't leaking into the communities we are attempting to build. Thus, even though many gay and lesbian communities seem analogous to blacks in terms of marginalization, for historical reasons that have to do with the dominance of whiteness in queer worlds, we (white) gay people have not embraced spirituality with the same necessity as blacks.

In closing, I want to suggest that if we have any hope of addressing the needs and desires of queers who have grown up in church, who have left or been turned away, who have returned and left again, if we have any hope of addressing the lives of our gay sisters and brothers who have experienced fragmentation at the hands of Christianity, we must begin to reject the privilege associated with whiteness by understanding race and sex struggles (as well as gender and class) as deeply interconnected. That is, coalition is important not only for the ultimate liberation of all marginalized peoples, it is also important because in working together, we can learn from each other. As long as we view sexual preference as the sole oppression that unites us, the lessons that other people might share with us are shrouded, the worldviews that might solve our paradoxes remain invisible. We need instead to continue to build coalitions that reject the absence associated with white culture by recovering histories, forming neighborhoods, strengthening visibility of cross-cultural, multi-racial queer/straight communities. Working together in alliance with people in other connected struggles will help us develop new skills and strategies that can help those of us in lesbian, gay, bisexual and transgendered (LGBT) communities highlight the importance of the spirit-world in everyday life. Only when queerness is thoroughly integrated into racial struggles will we become a community of faith strong enough to let people come and go. And only then will those of us who have been deeply wounded really be free to come back.

Notes

1   Thus, despite domestic social problems like poverty, alcohol abuse, incest, etc., it is not clear to me that any Westerner would ever qualify as subaltern.
2   See also Barbara Wilson's novel, *If You Had a Family* (1996), where Wilson covers similar issues from a fictional perspective and is even more adept at portraying the link between spirituality and creativity.
3   This is not to suggest, of course, that black communities are always welcoming of homosexuals. For an insightful study of race and sexuality, see Boykin (1996).

Chapter 2

The Gay Thing

Following the Still Small Voice

James Alison

What I hope to do in this chapter is to further the possibilities for adult discussion in the Catholic Church. One of the things about adult discussion is that it presupposes people who are both capable of being wrong, and yet who take responsibility for what they say. One of the things about Catholic adult discussion is that, in addition to those two dimensions, it should be charitable and generous-spirited towards differing opinions within the discussion. Please forgive me in advance if I fail to live up to these demanding criteria, but I will certainly try to attend to them, and will expect to be held to them.

My first intention is to try and create a sense of "we." I am not by my words seeking to create party spirit, but rather to work out who the "we" is when we say that we are Catholic. For this reason I am deliberately not setting out to talk uniquely about experience, truth, and argument as lived by gay and lesbian Catholics. That rather assumes that there is a certain sort of "we," a gay and lesbian Catholic "we," which has a special sort of experience and that I am some sort of privileged exponent of the experience of this "we." To start in this way would be to start by setting up sides for some sort of confrontation. I would be delivering to you a set of arguments which you could use to wield against other catholics, and this would be, from my perspective, a failure of charity and of catholicity. Instead of this I want to take a step back from experience, truth, and arguments, as lived by gay and lesbian Catholics, and raise instead the more ecumenical question of these matters as lived by Catholics, period. In other words, as something lived by all of those of us who are Catholics independently of our sexual orientation.

Now it is of course impossible to be comprehensive about the experience of Catholics as regards the gay issue, but there are some suggestions which I can make which point to what I would hope we can all consider to be elements of shared life which are ours by virtue of being Catholics who have been alive in the last 20–50 years, give or take a few. The first of these is the emergence among us of the phenomenon which we might now call "the gay thing." Fifty years ago, the word "gay" was only occasionally used with its current meaning, and the idea that there might be public discussion of loving relationships between people of the same sex except in the most shocked or whispered terms would have been incomprehensible. Yet, now, 50 years later, this is increasingly normal at every level of society, and indeed is being legislated for in more and more countries with fewer and fewer objections.

Fifty years ago there were hardly any figures who were publicly known to be gay, and such gay characters as existed in the media tended to be either heavily coded, as in the plays of Tennessee Williams, or depicted as depressive, self-hating and prone to suicide. Now we have a major musician and his same-sex partner walking up the aisle of Westminster Abbey to play for the funeral of Princess Diana, with the BBC commentator's recognition of the partner being beamed throughout the world,[1] while over the last 10 years, programs broadcast all over the planet like "The Real World," "Will and Grace," "Queer as Folk," and more recently "Queer Eye for the Straight Guy," have introduced a different set of images: good, bad, risible, provocative, gentle and so forth, but definitely different, into the public consciousness. And of course this has affected Catholics just as much as anyone else. In fact, as far as we can tell from surveys, practicing Catholic lay people are significantly more likely to be completely relaxed about gay people than their practicing Protestant counterparts – and for some interesting reasons which will emerge below.

Fifty years ago, if someone had suggested that as many as half the men serving in the priesthood were homosexuals, that person would be assumed to be a bigoted anti-Catholic agitator who might be expected to go on in their next breath to claim that nuns regularly ate droves of the small babies who had been illegitimately born in their convents. Yet now someone who claimed that 50 percent of men currently in the priesthood are gay would not be considered mad, or anti-Catholic. Many, myself among them, would hazard that 50 percent seems a conservative estimate, at least in major metropolitan dioceses.

Whatever the figures were 50 years ago, and whatever they are now, one thing is certain: an angry denial that half the priesthood was gay 50 years ago and an angry denial of it now would be greeted by Catholics with entirely different reactions. Fifty years ago, an angry denial would have been expected, now an angry denial would be regarded as a sign that the denier was either ideologically driven or was suffering from some sort of extraplanetary mind warp.

I point this out not because I want to claim that it is a particularly Catholic thing, but rather because there is no evidence at all that being Catholic makes any of us less likely to have been affected by this huge change in social perception, which has worked its way through English speaking society, and, at different speeds and in different ways, through at least those other societies with whose languages and cultures I am familiar.

So here is the first point. In the first place what I call "the gay thing" is something which has just happened, and is just happening, to all of us, whatever our own sexual orientation is. You can be as straight as you like, but being straight is no longer the same as it was when there was no such thing as "gay." Our picture of what it is to be male or female has undergone, and is undergoing, huge changes which affect us not only from without, but from within. We find ourselves relating, whether we want to or not, with each other, and with ourselves, in new ways as a result of something which is far bigger than any of us and which is just happening. But please note that none of this makes any claim about whether this change is good or not, nor does it make any claim about what, if anything we should do about it. It merely notes that it has happened and is happening to all of us, Catholics and non-Catholics alike.

Now our experience as Catholics is not only that we have experienced this change, but we have also experienced our religious authority reacting to this change in particular ways. And this is not a matter of merely noting that religious authority has, from time to time, spoken out on these issues in the years since 1975, and that their pronouncements have reached us. We have all, religious authorities, lay people and clergy, undergone the changes together, and we have lived with each others' reactions to those changes. One of the things which it is worth pointing out, given the passions which this subject raises, is how few and far between have been the public pronouncements of Catholic religious authorities in this area, until very recently, especially if we compare them with the abundance of such pronouncements emerging from Protestant churches. There has been much more reticence to speak about the gay issue than might have been expected. And this for two obvious reasons: it has not been a particularly important matter for the Catholic laity until recently; and the clerical world has been, in this area, a glass house in which it was not wise to throw stones, and discretion seemed the least scandalous option.

This too is part of the Catholic experience: our undergoing the change which has permeated society has been mediated to us not only through television and so on, but also through a discretely, but nevertheless, thoroughly, gay-tinted clerical system. In other words, unlike many Protestant groups, as Catholics we have never really had the option available to us of seriously pretending that we didn't know any gay people, or that there weren't any gay people in our Church. The result is that for us, part of the experience of "the gay thing" as Catholics has been a set of reactions provoked not so much by the official pronouncements of the Church as by the way the clergy live in relation to those official pronouncements: whether they have reacted by being honest, dishonest, frightened for their jobs, open about their partners, leaving, staying, being blackmailed or whatever. This "living with the change" by living with the way in which the clergy are coping with the change is very definitely part of the Catholic experience of this issue. It too is entirely independent of the ideological slant or the moral position taken by Catholics who are reacting to all this: some such Catholics may excoriate the dishonesty, some may lambast a modernist plot to infiltrate seminaries and go on to demand that the gays be weeded out, some may be puzzled that there should be so many, or that so many should stay despite everything. Nevertheless, the comparative discretion with which this matter has been treated by Catholic religious authority over the last 30 or so years, the fact that "the gay thing" has come upon us, usually rather quietly, and is going on all around us, has been an ineluctable part of the Catholic experience in this area, whether we have been aware of it or not.

Now, here I want to say the obvious thing: that our access to the question of truth in this area has not been independent of this experience. Indeed it has only been through this experience that the issue has gradually begun to crystallize into questions of truth. And this is because one of the ways in which "the gay thing" has come upon us has not been merely that outsiders, non-Catholics, start to agitate about this issue; it is not something which is merely felt from outside pressure. Rather, "the gay thing" of its nature, happens within us. And I don't mean merely within the Church considered as a numerical body in which a similar percentage is gay to that found in the rest of society. I mean within the lives of people within the Church. It has become an ineluctable part of how we find ourselves coming to be adult humans at this period, whether or not we are ourselves gay or lesbian, that some of our number find it increasingly important, and at a younger and younger age, to identify themselves as gay or lesbian, aware that this is something they find themselves to be, that the label makes sense to them and is going to be an important dimension of their lives: it is going to be one of the ways they find themselves articulating their relationship with each other, family, friends, employers, and of course, church. And of course, they are aware, as are their contemporaries, that it is a word which is associated with a certain moral courage.

I guess that everyone knows that the kid who comes out at high school, or the student at university is being to some extent brave. I think that this point has much more importance than is usually attached to it. For most gay people, as for an increasing number of their straight contemporaries, "the gay thing" is not in the first instance anything to do with sex. It comes upon us as something to do with how we relate to other people in our peer group – whether we stand up for the effeminate kid who is being bullied by the jocks in the class, or whatever. And this kind of group dynamic through which "the gay thing" comes upon us is extremely important for our moral and spiritual development. It is here that we learn to stand up for the weak, or, in my case, to my shame, how to hide myself, join in the crowd of haters and "pass" for straight until a later time. And the interesting thing is that in this sense "the gay thing" comes upon straight kids as well – they too make moral choices, know what is right and wrong here. More and more adults and kids are reporting that straight kids are increasingly reluctant to go along with gay bullying, whether they see it being done by fellow students or by adults. This is not because they have become hedonistic, oversexualized decadents. It is, on the contrary, because they seem to sense that such behavior is unworthy of them: they are less than straight if they need to beat up on the gay kids.

But part of the Catholic experience has been that alongside the way in which this process of moral and spiritual growth is happening as young people start to react to the way "the gay thing" is irrupting into our midst, has also been the way in which Church authority appears to regard "the gay thing" as exclusively an issue to do with sex. And simultaneously to ignore the experienced moral dimensions that "the gay thing" has in the lives of those who are undergoing it. This leads to a disjunction being lived by us as, on the one hand we learn all about good Catholic values like solidarity, refusal to beat up on the weak, respect for the other. On the other hand, we perceive that in order to handle "the gay thing" themselves, Church authorities, which often enough includes such lay authorities as run Catholic educational enterprises, reduce the whole matter to sex. They are often enough notoriously bad at dealing with any of the lived moral issues which those not dependent on the clerical system for their employment have perceived to be psychologically and spiritually central to dealing with the whole gay thing – being brave, coming out, putting friendship at risk, being socialized transparently, and so on.

And this of course leads to one of the further disjunctions which is part of the Catholic experience of "the gay thing," which is the disjunction between the different sorts of truth-telling which "the gay thing" has brought upon us. On the one hand we have people who can be "out" as gay people, who can say "I am," and who are in all our parishes, neighbourhoods and so forth, and for whom truth-telling involves a certain form of sincerity, and desire to be transparent in their dealings with others, often quite pacifically so, sometimes infuriatingly and provocatively so. And on the other hand we have people who cannot say "I am." At least in public. And for whom truth-telling in this area involves talking about a "they." It involves an attempt to give an objective description of who "they" are who are being talked about, even when a considerable number of people suspect that the person saying "they" would be more honest to say "we." Yet, and this is important, the official characterization of the "homosexual person" in the recent documents of the Vatican Congregations is something which can only be applied to a "they," because even when the person talking is referring to himself, he is accepting the need to treat part of his "I" as a "they," as something that can never be brought into a personal relationship, can never become part of an "I" or a "we," never be addressed as "thou." That's what saying that an inclination "must be considered to be objectively disordered" implies.

This, too, is part of the experience of living as a Catholic as we undergo the "gay thing" – that there is a disjunction between two different sorts of truthfulness, neither of which seems quite adequate: the one because it suggests that sincerity is really all it takes to be honest, and that one can grasp an identity as gay and then "be" that thing, be wholly implicated in it, and the other because it suggests that truthfulness – holding fast to an official definition of what is true – requires dishonesty, makes self-knowledge the enemy of truth, and removes someone from the ordinary demands of charity, and solidarity.

I've tried to deal elsewhere with the subject of honesty in the Church (Alison 2003), but here I would just like briefly to indicate that it seems to me that the challenge for us as church now, and as a church widely perceived to have an honesty deficit, is to understand that honesty is not the same as either sincerity or "holding to objective truth" because both of those involve a certain grasping onto something. Honesty is something undergone as a gift of being brought into truthfulness by being given a self-critical faculty, and it can never be grasped. It is precisely appreciated by others when they see someone undergoing an experience of dealing with something which is making them more truthful. I don't want to major on this here, merely to point out that my choice of approach to this chapter, which may or may not be successful, has been chosen because it seems to me that we are more likely to reach truthfulness if rather than battling each other with incommensurable forms of truth, we start to learn to tell the story of what we have been undergoing together.

As Catholics we have a number of resources to help us work our way through some of these disjunctions, resources which I think we are in fact using already. I'd like to try and highlight how just one of these comes into play. Curiously, I'm going to look at an unlikely resource, which I consider to be absolutely central to finding our way through this particular upheaval, which is the Catholic doctrine of original sin.

Original Sin

One of the principal points of conflict at the time of the Reformation in the sixteenth century was the view of human nature held by either side of the discussion. The Reformed side tended to hold a view of human nature which claimed that after the fall, having been created good we became radically corrupted.[2] We are saved by God imputing to us a counter-factual goodness which is not really ours at all, but which is made available for us to put on, by Jesus' sacrifice on the cross. The important thing about this for us here is what it means about our moral and spiritual life. It means that all our "goodness" is so much fakery, not real goodness, and God's goodness must be given to us through our being ordered to behave in ways which have nothing to do with our natural inclinations. God may order us to go totally against our natural inclinations, because our natural inclinations have been totally corrupted, and there is no proper analogy between what we think of as good, what we desire, and what really is good, what we should desire.

The sort of life story which this underlying theology asks us to tell about ourselves is one involving a radical conversion: how once I was a sinner (and so behaved in certain ways) but now, very suddenly, I am saved, and I have a completely new life story, one with no real organic continuity with my old life story. One where there is a real rupture. Whoever I was is now dead, and now there is a new "I," someone totally new.

Now perhaps you can see how this understanding of original sin and salvation would affect the discussion concerning "the gay thing" which I have just described as having come upon us, if we were strict heirs of the Reformed tradition. It would, in a sense, make life much easier for us by making it much clearer. Because we could say "Well, this business of 'the gay thing' coming upon us is what you would expect in a corrupt and depraved humanity. It is merely another wave of decadence and corruption. Anyone who is given the gift of being saved by Jesus must just obey the biblical commands, however little sense they may make. Given that the Bible, which is God's Word, and not affected by corruption, clearly teaches that homosexuals are a bad thing, and that God created man and woman for each other, it is quite clear that one of the signs of someone being saved is that they are learning to obey God's command which includes not being gay, and they should in fact be undergoing therapy to become straight. The new nature which they are receiving from God is certainly straight, so we can expect them to cease to be gay as part of being converted. Homosexual desire is intrinsically evil. Only divinely given straight desire is intrinsically good."

The reason I say that this would make life easier for us as Catholics is as follows: it would enable us to make a deduction from the teaching of the Church about who we really are, and dismiss any social changes taking place as so much evil. Being Catholic would then be a matter of being on the obedient side of things, not the disobedient, and of course, anyone who agreed that being gay is part of who they really are, rather than the ghastly corrupt former person that they should be leaving behind, isn't really a Catholic, just a hell-bound sinner. Following this model, we couldn't and shouldn't learn anything about ourselves from what is going on around us, from what is just happening to us, because we can't start from there, it is totally untrustworthy. We can only start from something which comes from God covering us over and giving us an entirely different story. A moral command is good because it is a moral command come from God, not because it causes any sort of flourishing of any sort of inclination of our own.

Now, strange though this may be to some, this is not the Catholic faith. The Catholic faith concerning original sin and salvation is slightly and subtly different, and because of that, we have the possibility of quite a different way of dealing with "the gay thing." The Catholic understanding, as set out by the Council of Trent (1545–63), whose ardent fan I am, is that the word "desire" (*epithumia*), which the apostle Paul sometimes uses in such a way as to give the impression that he considered it a purely negative thing, has never been considered by the Church to be a purely negative thing, to be sin in the strict sense of the word. It is in fact an entirely good thing which is, in the case of all of us, very seriously disordered, so that the way we find it in us is as something which comes from sin and inclines us towards sin, but which is nevertheless capable of being gradually transformed and ordered by grace so that we are brought to a flourishing starting from where we are. This means that in the Catholic understanding grace perfects nature, takes something which, while good, is severely damaged, and transforms it starting from where it is, whereas in the "radical corruption" account I gave you, grace cannot transform nature, because nature has become instrinsically corrupt. Grace has to abolish the old nature and start again.[3]

Now, as you can tell, this means that any story of salvation told by Catholics is of rather a different sort from the one I outlined to you earlier. It means that because our nature is not radically corrupt, just accidentally corrupt, and because grace perfects our nature, and because grace meets us starting from where we are, so what salvation looks like is our undergoing a process of divinely initiated transformation, together, in, and as church. It also means that the whole wave of changes in society which "just happen" and which are bigger and more powerful than any of us, are not simply entirely evil and corrupt, but are part of what enables us to be brought into being, which is in itself something good. Furthermore, these waves of change in society may be, amongst other things, ripples out from the way the leaven of the Gospel and the Kingdom is working in the midst of humanity, destroying our belief in the culpability of our victims and so enabling us to come to learn who we really are and how we can learn responsibility for what is. So, such waves of change need to be worked through, understood, discerned, analyzed slowly and carefully, not just written off. It also means that where we are is not an entirely untrustworthy place from which to start, and something of what is true and good can be discerned and learned in the midst of all this mess. And this is something vital: it also means that we can, over time, learn things about who we are as human beings such that what had seemed to be moral commandments turn out to be commandments which are not moral, because they go against our flourishing.[4]

You remember that in the picture of the Reformation understanding which I gave you, it didn't matter at all whether something leads to our flourishing or not. What matters is that it is right because it is commanded by God. In the Catholic understanding it is not the case that something is right because it is commanded by God, rather something is commanded by God because it is good for us: this is what you would expect from a good Creator who wants to make something even better out of his good creation, messy though it may look. But this means that in the Catholic understanding it must be possible for us as humans to learn that something which appeared to have been commanded by God cannot in fact have been commanded by God, because it goes against what any of us can see leads to human flourishing. And this means that we can learn that we are not rebelling against God, but doing his deepest will when we learn that something which seemed to be holy and sacred is neither holy nor sacred, but a way of diminishing people. This of course lays upon us a huge burden of intelligence and responsibility in working out what really is God's will for us.

The funny thing about this Catholic understanding is that it is one of the parts of Catholic teaching that Catholics generally do really "get," at a pretty instinctual level. That we are all in a mess together, none really better than the other, but that we are all rescuable, and must be merciful to each other, is a kind of basic default understanding of Catholic inter-relationship with each other. The notion that the Church is a refuge of sinners, that Our Lady has a soft spot for us in our weakness, and that no one should really be thrown out is kind of written into our souls. And I think that because of this, it is not surprising that one of the typical Catholic ways of dealing with "the gay thing" just having happened among us is to say "Well, of course, it does seem to go against the Church and all that, but, well, if she just is that way, well then, what do you expect, she must just get on and be the very best sort of lesbian, and I hope she finds happiness." I suspect that the ease with which Catholic lay people have got their heads round the idea of at least some sort of marriage for gay couples is related to this.

In contrast to this, the official teaching in this area has come to seem more and more out of line with the default self-understanding which I have been describing, because it seems to be creating an exception to the general rule of original sin, which applies to everybody, equally. It seems to be suggesting that there are some people to whom the Catholic under-standing of original sin should not be applied, and instead, a Protestant understanding should be applied, but only in their case. This disjunction, I should say, is becoming more and more evident as "the gay thing" has come upon us, and come to be seen more and more to have something to do with "who people are" and not so much with "what they do."

In the old days, the discussion was entirely about "acts" – there is an undisputedly ancient Christian tradition of objecting to sexual acts between persons of the same sex. And of course, you can condemn acts without saying anything at all about the being of the person. But over the last 50 years or so, this distinction has become ever less tenable, as people we would now call "gay" have begun to say "I am gay, it's not just that I do certain sexual things which are same-sex acts, but I just find myself being in a way which is best defined as gay, and which is to do with far more of me than sexual acts, furthermore there are other people like me, and we have recognizable traits in common, we can be studied, and we don't appear to be less healthy, more vicious than straight people" and so on.

Well, here is where Church authority had a problem: while the discussion was about acts, the acts could be prohibited, and yet the person could be urged to flourish and find appropriate happiness. But as it became clearer that the acts and a certain sort of person belonged together, were more or less well bound up as part of a package, Church authority was stuck with a dilemma: "Can we maintain the traditional prohibition of certain sorts of acts if they are merely natural functions of the being of the person, capable of being exercised well or badly as that sort of person grows and develops? No, we can't. So we have to make up our minds: either we just concede that the traditional prohibition doesn't apply to those for whom growing and developing in this way is natural, and only applies to those for whom to engage in such things would be to leave their typical usage; or we have to insist that the traditional prohibition does apply, in which case it must be true that gay people aren't really what they say they are, but just have intrinsically disordered desires and must obey the commands of the Church even though these don't seem to help them flourish. But if we do that, we come perilously close to the Reformation position of seeing some part of people as incapable of flourishing, as something which must simply be abolished and covered over by grace, so that they become something different".

This is a difficult dilemma: how could they both maintain the traditional prohibition, one which was at least tenable before it had become clear that "some people just are that way," and yet not simply declare a person to be intrinsically corrupt? You must remember that shortly before they were dealing with this, Paul VI had maintained the traditional prohibition of any sexual act which separated the procreative from the unitive function of sex (*Humanae Vitae*, 1968; Paul VI 1970). So they could scarcely say "Well, such acts as separate the procreative from the unitive are wrong for straight people, but fine for gay people." The phrase they came up with is a pretty good compendium of the difficulty they had in dealing with the dilemma.

As you probably know, the phrase says that "the particular inclination of the homosexual person is not a sin, it is a more or less strong tendency ordered toward an intrinsic moral evil; and thus the inclination itself must be seen as an objective disorder" (Ratzinger 1986: para. 3; in Rogers 2002: 250).

Let's unpack that a little bit. In the first place, those who wrote it show they are good Catholics by indicating that the homosexual inclination is not itself a sin, for no Catholic can understand someone's basic pattern of desire to be intrinsically corrupt. That would be a Reformed position. However, they move on rather fast from this recognition that the homosexual inclination is not itself a sin, and I'd like to slow down a bit. For there is more than one way of recognizing that an inclination is not in itself a sin. There is the way, for instance, that would be true of all heterosexuals. All heterosexual humans find that the package of their growing up and their sexual desire is extremely difficult to humanize and to socialize in an appropriate way. Many heterosexual people find that it takes a long time before they are able to find themselves capable of a monogamous relationship in which each is capable of treating their spouse as an equal, sharing responsibility for procreation if, indeed, they are ever able to get there. But in principle, the notion that their inclination is a good thing, but is always encountered by them in a distorted way, referred to in official teaching as "concupiscence," and that their salvation is, in part, worked out in their creative struggle with their concupiscence, is quite comprehensible.

So, the question arises: is the homosexual inclination, which is not in itself a sin, a subsection of heterosexual concupiscence? Or is it its own sort of concupiscent desire? This is an important distinction. If the homosexual inclination were a subsection of heterosexual concupiscence, then it would be something that couldn't lead to anything good in itself. It would simply be a symptom of the sort of thing that goes wrong in a basically heterosexual human being, like lusting after someone to whom you are not married, or wanting sexual relationships with as many partners (of the opposite sex) as possible. And of course, the life of grace would gradually lead the person whose heterosexual concupiscence takes the form of a homosexual inclination toward recovering an ordered pattern of heterosexual desire, and this would be public and visible in the relationships of the person concerned.

If, on the other hand, the homosexual inclination were its own sort of concupiscent desire, then it would be something which does lead to something good in itself. It would have all the capacity for things to go wrong that exist in the case of heterosexual desire, but, just like heterosexual desire, it would also have the capacity for something to go right. That is, the life of grace would lead the person with the homosexual inclination to become less possessive, more merciful, more generous, more honest, more faithful, but without changing the gender of this person's potential or actual partner(s), and this would be public and visible in the relationships of the person concerned.

Now I would like to point out that both of these are perfectly possible interpretations given the Catholic doctrine of original sin. What the Catholic doctrine of original sin does not allow us to do is simply to refuse on *a priori* grounds the possibility that a long-term, persistent pattern of desire, may, after all, be a sign of how the Creator's love for us wills us to flourish. And therefore we cannot simply refuse the possibility that we can come to learn that what seemed like a subsection of heterosexual concupiscence may just be a different thing. In other words, the Catholic doctrine of original sin does allow the possibility that we come to discover, over time and with difficulty, that, in a regular minority of the population, long-term stable same-sex desire just is, and is the basis from which they flourish, rather than that which has to be "dealt with" in some way before they can begin to flourish.

Given the possibility of this distinction, you can see why I think that the Congregation for the Doctrine of the Faith (CDF) rushed rather fast into their next claim: that the homosexual inclination "is a more or less strong tendency ordered toward an intrinsic moral evil; and thus the inclination itself must be seen as an objective disorder."

The only circumstance in which it would be true that behavior tended to by a homosexual inclination were intrinsically evil is if it were simply true that there is no other intrinsic human pattern of desire than the heterosexual one, tending towards marriage and procreation, and therefore that the homosexual inclination is a subsection of heterosexual concupiscence. And this is what the CDF is implying is in fact the case, as a deduction from its own teaching on marriage and procreation.

In other words, from the Church's teaching on marriage and procreation an attempt is being made to reach a deduction about empirical truth concerning what really is. To flesh this out further: an aspect of revelation, here from the moral sphere, is being asked to bear the weight of defining truth in an anthropological sphere, where whatever is true in this sphere might instead be reached by empirical means. This same intellectual pattern did not work well in the Galileo case, and it did not work well with Genesis' account of Creation in six days. We would be wise to be extremely suspicious of it here.

Now it is, of course, perfectly conceivable that we will eventually discover (rather than presume) that all human beings are intrinsically heterosexual. But this is not a conclusion to which we are obligated either by the Church's teaching on original sin, or by the Church's teaching on marriage. Yet here a deduction from the Church's teaching on marriage is being used to try and foreclose the sort of process of discovery which is allowed for by the Church's doctrine of original sin.

And logically enough, if the homosexual inclination were indeed a subsection of heterosexual concupiscence, leading to nothing in itself, then of course it would be true that it must be considered objectively disordered. Here I would like to point out that I have nothing against the notion of an inclination being objectively disordered *per se*. We would all consider kleptomania to be objectively disordered. But we have come to this conclusion after studying people who are affected by it (rather than those who are just thieves) and seeing what it is that it is a distorted form of, and how those affected can be helped back into a more pacific possession of their own goods and respect for other people's. And this is the point: we can learn what is objectively disordered or not from studying people, their relationships, their habits, their happinesses and so on. Our objectivity is gleaned from within the process of discerning experience, of learning. It is not reached by appealing to an *a priori* deduction from revelation which is supposed to cut short any process of discovery.

And of course, by yoking together, on the one hand, the concession to the Church's teaching concerning original sin and, on the other, an *a priori* deduction about intrinsically evil acts, the CDF does leave us with a *de facto* Reformed teaching regarding the relationship between the homosexual inclination and original sin. What it concedes verbally it removes existentially. Anyone who lives with a homosexual inclination is taught that it is in itself not a sin, but that on the other hand, it can lead to nothing starting from itself, and that if they don't find that the process of grace in their life tends to make them heterosexual, then they must just be paralyzed as sexual beings. Existentially, this is no different from the Reformed position that homosexual desire is intrinsically corrupt and must be just covered over. It is, if you like, a piece of Catholic icing perched precariously atop a Protestant cake.

Well, here is our lived disjunction all right, and it is a disjunction between two forces of Catholic doctrine which hadn't been on a collision course before, but have entered into collision as part of the way that "the gay thing" has come upon us all. For the moment, it looks as though the only way to maintain the traditional Catholic prohibition of same-sex acts is to act as though the homosexual inclination were in fact an intrinsically corrupt desire, even though this is something alien to a Catholic anthropology, because the moment you consider that "being gay" is not an individually defective form of heterosexuality, but is just something that is, then the Catholic understanding of original sin would oblige you to regard grace as transforming that way of being, which is as much in need of transformation as its heterosexual equivalent, and as much in need as its heterosexual equivalent of all the help it can get, starting from where it is. A phrase like marriage is a "remedy for concupiscence" comes to mind. And of course, the Catholic understanding of original sin is such that we can in fact learn, with difficulty and over time that certain ways of being just are, are given, are part of being human, and as such are capable of leading to flourishing and sharing the divine life.

This, too, is part of Catholic experience: at the moment, it does appear from official discourse that everything to do with being gay is somehow an exception to the ordinary teaching of the Church about grace. The moment you apply the Church's ordinary teaching about grace to any aspect of life as a gay or lesbian person, then it is going to lead to all the things which it is in fact leading to, and most ordinary lay Catholics are aware that it is leading to: growth in healthy self-esteem, creative ways of living together, new forms of religious life, enriched sacramental participation, recognition and respect for different forms of flourishing, including appropriate legal guarantees against mistreatment, discrimination and so forth, some sort of marriage laws and eventually publicly recognized religious blessings of such partnerships.

Well, this point of disjunction is where we are at! Now, I think it very unlikely that any Church authority will suddenly wake up and say "Good Lord, we've been missing the whole point of our own doctrine of Original Sin!" My ambition here is more minimalist than that. I merely want to point out, for the day when Church authority finally gets tired of heading up the dead end of trying to make spiritual and political sense out of its own current teaching, that there is a perfectly good Catholic way out of their cul-de-sac which is available for them whenever they want it. They are not condemned, like characters in a Greek tragedy, to carry on being paralyzed by the fatality of their own teaching, just as we are not.

My suggestion for us as Catholics at this point is this: if the Vatican congregations really want us to believe that there is something so wrong with being gay that it in fact constitutes an exception to the ordinary teaching of the Church about grace and original sin, then they must try a great deal harder to make their case. Or alternatively, they must demonstrate, not just to those whose livelihood depends on their publicly agreeing to it, but especially, as an urgent pastoral priority, to ordinary gay and lesbian Catholics, that there is no such thing as being gay; that what we call "being gay" is a mistake, and is simply a severely defective form of heterosexuality. If the Vatican congregations can do that, then they stand a chance of being able to show that the intrinsic heterosexuality of the falsely gay person can flourish, and thus that their own teaching is compatible with the ordinary teaching of the Church about grace. However, if they can't do that – if they can't produce regular and sustained witnesses to heterosexual flourishing emerging without violence from the life stories of people who had assumed they were gay on something like the same scale as there are regular and sustained witnesses to gay and lesbian flourishing emerging without violence from the life stories of people who had been taught that they were heterosexual, then they should reconsider their definition.

However, until they come up with their demonstration, and the burden of teaching effectively is surely on the teachers, who have insisted so loudly on their unique role as teachers, then, faced with the disjunction, any ordinary Catholic should stick with the ordinary teaching of the Church, held uninterruptedly and reaffirmed by a major Church Council, about grace and original sin, and learn to apply it to their lives and the lives of those around them. And this means, starting where we are, and not where someone else tells us we must be considered to be. One of the geniuses of the Catholic doctrine of original sin is that rather than it being a form of general accusation of how wicked we are, it is in fact a recognition of how we are all in the same boat as regards wickedness, and that it is a really terrible thing to do to judge others, because in doing so we become blind to the way we are judging ourselves.[5] Any way of characterizing people which makes them an exception to the general rule, by suggesting that they have a different kind and degree of original sin than others is of course a defection from the Catholic faith, because it is giving permission to judge them, when the whole purpose of the doctrine is to make such permission impossible.

The Still Small Voice

You may have noticed that the subtitle of this chapter is "following the still small voice." And you may also have noticed that I have got to the end of the chapter without making any reference to the title. So I would just like to make explicit that the title is a reference to what I hope to have been hinting at all along. I take it that one of the joys of being Catholic is that we are not a group united by an ideology, nor a group who adhere to a text, nor a group under the command of a leader or set of leaders, but a group being brought into being along with an ordered way of life as we undergo a certain form of listening, listening to a crucified and risen victim as he shows his forgiveness of us and undoes our ways of being together, which tend to be judgmental, violent and so on, so that we can share God's life forever. What keeps us as Catholics, and what is the central element of experience and truth as lived by Catholics in the gay issue, is that we can count absolutely on the crucified and risen Lord, present in our midst especially in the Eucharist, who is gradually teaching us how to reinterpret our world in such a way that we build each other up, and do not fear the truth which will set us free. The presence of the crucified and risen Lord teaching us, together, as Catholics to inhabit words like "Go and learn what this means, I want mercy and not sacrifice" or "the Sabbath is made for humans, not humans for the sabbath," his presence *is* the still small voice that is at work through and in all our debates and disjunctions, and will always be opening us up to being made anew starting from where we are.

Heaven and earth will pass away, but my words will not pass away. (Mark 13.31)

Those words are the living interpretive presence of one who loves us starting exactly where we are, one who reaches us in the midst of all the collapses of what seemed sacred, and the coming upon us of new dimensions of ourselves which seem terrifying until we learn to look at them through the eyes of one who loves us so much that he longs to be us, and longs for us to be free and happy with him, forever.

That we are learning to relax, together, through hearing his words, into being loved, is, surely, the central Catholic experience.

Acknowledgments

This chapter derives from a lecture sponsored by Boston College Allies, and was originally given in Boston College on November 18, 2003, on the day when the Supreme Judicial Court of Massachusetts in the United States of America recognized that gay and lesbian couples are included in the equality and liberty provisions of the constitution of the United States Commonwealth, and are thus free to marry. The present version of my lecture contains significant modifications which are much indebted to the lively discussion following the lecture on that occasion, and in particular to the responses and questions with which Professors Lisa Cahill, Jim Keenan SJ, Stephen Pope and John Baldovin SJ honored me. It has also benefited greatly from a critical reading by Professors John Ranieri and Andrew McKenna. Needless to say, the fact that all these respondents agreed to engage me critically does not imply their agreement with my conclusions.

Notes

1 The marriage (civil-partnering) of Elton John and David Furnish on December 21, 2005 – at the Guildhall, Windsor, UK, where a few weeks earlier Prince Charles and Camilla Parker Bowles had been married – was also widely covered by the British media.

2 I do not know how widespread this is as a genuinely Reformed position. However, this is how Trent depicted the Reformed position. My purpose in adducing it here is to show that, whether

or not the position has ever been held by heirs of the Reformation, it is certainly not one that can coherently be held by Catholics.

3   The Catholic and the Reformed positions are identical in recognizing the completely free and gratuitous initiative of God who saves. The difference between them is an anthropological one concerning who we are who are being saved and what that salvation looks like as a human process over time.

4   See, for instance, Exodus 22.28 and the different reactions to it at Jeremiah 19.5–6 and Ezekiel 20.25–26.

5   See, among other places, but here particularly poignantly, Romans 2.1.

Part II

Queer Church

Chapter 3

Sacramental Flesh

Elizabeth Stuart

Queer theology derives its origins not from the fictitious construction of human sexual "experience" as so much modern sexual theology has done with ultimately disappointing, though sometimes exhilarating results, but from the very life of God incarnate in the body of Christ and particularly in the sacraments, each one of which, every time it is celebrated, makes Christ as truly present as he was in a crib in Bethlehem or on a cross at Calvary. Sarah Coakley sees in Judith Butler's program of gender trouble and in the whole queer project an unconscious "gesturing to an eschatological horizon which will give mortal flesh final significance, a horizon in which the restless, fluid post-modern 'body' can find some sense of completion without losing its mystery, without succumbing again to 'appropriate' or restrictive gender roles" (Coakley 2000: 70). Queer theory itself nudges the theologian towards a different horizon to that which has defined the vision of most contemporary theological discourse on sexuality. It propels the theologian toward the eschatological and the mysterious, to the sacramental heart of the Christian tradition.

In a book she wrote several years after *Gender Trouble* (1990) Judith Butler suggested that in modernity "I" is predicated on the foreclosure of certain forms of desire with the result that the subject is grounded in melancholia and shrouded in an unacknowledged and irresolvable grief for impossible love, for to acknowledge this love would mean the destruction of the self. Both heterosexuality and homosexuality are dependent upon each other for their existence but that dependence is based upon repudiating the desire each identity rests upon. Gender and sexual identity are then a kind of melancholy (J. Butler 1997b: 132–50). For Butler modern Western humanity is mourning and weeping in this vale of tears, unable to escape melancholia without risking annihilation. Butler's work raises two key questions. First, is there any place where it is possible to be truly queer, to perform maleness and femaleness in such a way as to expose their performativity? And, second, can there really be no escape from melancholia? Only the Christian theologian can answer in the affirmative to both these questions and therefore save queer theology from self-destructive despair. For the church is the only community under a mandate to be queer and it is under such a mandate because its eschatological horizon teaches it that gender and sexual identity are not of ultimate concern, thus opening the possibility for love.

The incarnation inaugurates a new creation which is at the same time a recapitulation of a prelapsarian world, a redemption of a world fractured by sin and an anticipation of a final perfection. Graham Ward has drawn attention to the ways in which the church scripted and performed the body of Jesus, the first born of this new creation, as destabilizing the symbolics of gender. Jesus is born male but from purely female matter, he emerges from the womb in a complex web of symbolic relationships with his virgin mother.

The baby boy is husband and bridegroom, spouse and prefigured lover of the mother who gives him birth, whose own body swells to contain the future Church. The bridal chamber is the womb which the bridegroom will impregnate with his seed while also being the womb from which he emerges. The material orders are inseparable from the solid and transcendent orders, the orders of mystery. The material orders are caught up and become significant only within the analogical orders. And so here Jesus' body is brought within a complex network of sexualised symbolic relations that confound incest and the sacred. (Ward 1999: 164–5)

The body of the baby Jesus is stretched, pre-figuring the crucifixion (at his circumcision), resurrection, and the creation of the ecclesial body. The instability of the body is further played out in the displacements of the transfiguration, the Eucharist, the resurrection, and finally the ascension. In the transfiguration, the body of Christ becomes transparent to divinity – our attraction to this figure is taken through the male gendered Jew through the second Adam which he is revealed to be, towards God in whom desire is finally satisfied. In the Eucharist, Jesus' body is transposed, extended into the gender neutral form of bread and, as Ward notes, bodies are revealed as things not only transfigurable but also transposable and, "in being transposable, while always being singular and specific, the body of Christ can cross boundaries, gender boundaries for example. Jesus' body as bread is no longer Christ as simply and biologically male" (Ward 1999: 168). In its crucifixion and death, Jesus' body becomes liminal and soaked in iconicity, it becomes a floating signifier which the medieval church could represent as a maternal body – the side wound representing a womb from which the church springs – and nourishing breast.

The resurrection recapitulates and plays out all previous displacements, revealing the body as essentially mysterious and beyond grasp because the body is finally transposed into the church at the ascension. Jesus becomes the multi-gendered body of the church. As the revealer of true humanity, Jesus reveals this because all bodies are situated within and given significance within his body. They too are "permeable, transcorporeal and transpositional" (Ward 1999: 176). Christian living then becomes a participation in this "permeable, transcorporeal and transpositional body" in an individual and corporate arena. Feminist theologians who have been vexed by the issue of whether a man can save a woman and gay theologians have speculated on the sexuality of Jesus have, according to Ward, simply failed to understand the nature of the body of Christ.

The body of Christ is queer. That body is made available to Christians through the sacraments, the very possibility of which, as Ward notes, is grounded in the queer nature of the body of Christ. Not only is this body available to Christians, they are caught up in it, constituted by it and incorporated into it, sharing in its sacramental flesh. They are in the process of becoming what he is, uniting themselves to him, and it is the sacraments that provide the moments of divine encounter which make this possible.

Rowan Williams (2000: 189) points out that baptism constitutes a ritual change of identity, a setting aside of all other ordinary identities in favor of an identity as a member of the body of Christ. A queer theorist, like Alison Webster, might want to respond by arguing that surely Christian identity is as unstable or slippery as a sexual identity, a mere matter of performance as well (Webster 1998). But Williams argues that it is not. What we receive in baptism is not an identity negotiated in conversation with our communities or culture such as our sexual and gender identities are; it is an identity over which we have no control whatsoever. It is sheer gift. In the sixteenth century Lancelot Andrews pointed out that the presence of the Trinity at baptism reminds us of creation which is a purely gratuitous gift, and baptism constitutes a new creation equally gratuitous (Stevenson 1998: 56–61). It is God's great "yes" to us, based not upon our own merits but upon divine love revealed in Christ. The nature of the elements of our Christian identity may be obscure to us and how we best act out our identity in our various contexts might be a legitimate subject of dispute but the identity itself is not negotiated, it is given.

Baptism, according to Williams, exposes the place outside of it as a place of loss and need (Rowan Williams 2000: 209). In particular, the baptismal rite in the 1662 *Book of Common Prayer* (which is the basis of Williams' reflections) understands baptism as a movement from enslavement to the desires which will destroy us – because they drive us to "objects that fill gaps in our self-construction, so that what we desire is repletion, which is immobilisation, a kind of death" – to a realization that all desire has its proper end in the divine. "[W]e must receive the grace to want the endlessness of God" (Rowan Williams 2000: 211). In other words, baptism unmasks the melancholia at the heart of society, reveals the inadequacy of all other forms of identity and the desire caught up in them and therefore, "the rite requires us *not* to belong to the categories we thought we belonged in, so that a distinctive kind of new belonging can be realised" (Rowan Williams 2000: 209). This new belonging is based upon a solidarity that we have not chosen and is grounded in a radical equality that comes from our all being here through grace alone, a grace which, as Eugene Rogers reminds us, Paul described as an act of God *para phusin* (Romans 11.14). Paul's use of this phrase in Romans 11.14 is shocking considering his previous use of the phrase earlier in this letter to describe, not "homosexual" people, but Gentiles who characteristically engage in same-sex activity, a characteristic that distinguishes them, not from "heterosexuals," but from the Jews. Rogers points out that by Romans 11 Paul is making the outrageous claim that God stands in solidarity with these Gentiles, God like them acts against or – more accurately – in excess of nature. "Just as God saved flesh by taking it on and defeated death by dying, here God saves those who act in excess of nature by an act in excess of nature," an unnatural act that deconstructs the whole notion of the "natural" for evermore, as is evident in the performance of the body of Christ (Rogers 1999a: 65).

Baptist theologian Timothy Bradshaw, reflecting on the use of baptism in some recent gay and lesbian theology, has emphasized the fact that baptism does involve a death – a death to self, sin, and to the ultimacy of certain types of identity (Bradshaw 1999: 458–9). Bradshaw believes that arguments about baptism are dangerous for "radicals" precisely because the New Testament emphasizes the discontinuity of baptism; "participation in this new life is transformed and challenging, life in the tension of the already but not yet" (Bradshaw 1999: 461). It is true that gay and lesbian theology when it has drawn upon the theology of baptism usually fails to appreciate this discontinuity. So Marilyn Bennett Alexander and James Preston in their book, *We Were Baptised Too* (1996), argue that the churches, by marginalizing lesbian and gay people and depriving them of certain sacraments such as ordination, have reneged on the promise made to them at their baptism to support their lives in Christ. It is a clever argument but one that does not appreciate the really radical nature of the Christian understanding of baptism. For the church has always taught that baptism changes people in the depths of their very being, which is why that change is described as a new creation brought about through a death to sin and also, in the Catholic tradition, as the bestowal of a character which configures the baptized to Christ so that their very selves are united to Christ through the church and constituted in and through that union. M.J. Scheeben argues that the character bestowed at baptism is a reflection of the hypostatic union and an extension of the incarnation (Scheeben 1961). What Alexander and Preston have not grappled with is that at baptism the ontology of the baptized is radically changed, they become what might be called ecclesial persons. This personhood is characterized by a new subjectivity which is communal and corporate, for it both shares in and constitutes the body of Christ, the new human. Thus there is a radical difference between the selfhood of baptized and non-baptized which in itself does not determine God's relationship to the non-baptized because God is not bound by her sacraments. The church, though in a constant struggle against the power of sin, nevertheless testifies to and anticipates a humanity in which human beings "coalesce indissolubly into a single existence" with Christ (Ratzinger 1973). This is why the Council of Trent could state:

> For, in those who are born again, there is nothing that God hates; because, there is no condemnation to those who are truly buried together with Christ by baptism into death; who walk not according to the flesh, but, putting off the old man, and putting on the new who is created according to God, are made innocent, immaculate, pure, harmless, and beloved of God, heirs indeed of God, but joint heirs with Christ; so that there is nothing whatever to retard their entrance into heaven. But this holy synod confesses and is sensible, that in the baptized there remains concupiscence, or an incentive (to sin); which, whereas it is left for our exercise, cannot injure those who consent not, but resist manfully by the grace of Jesus Christ; yea, he who shall have striven lawfully shall be crowned. This concupiscence, which the apostle sometimes calls sin, the holy Synod declares that the Catholic Church has never understood it to be called sin, as being truly and properly sin in those born again, but because it is of sin, and inclines to sin (Waterworth 1848: 23–4).

The baptized manifest a new type of creaturehood/humanity, one in which sin has no ultimate hold. It is still perfectly possible to act sinfully, but sin no longer has the power to alienate humanity from God – hence the sacrament of penance.

The baptized belong to another world. To be baptized is to be caught up in a kingdom that does not yet fully exist, that is in the process of becoming; it is to be caught up in the redemption of this world. It is not that the baptized are called to live beyond culture, which is both impossible and undesirable because the Spirit is active in human culture, but that they are called to transform culture by living in it in such a way as to testify to the other world being born within it. All our cultural identities are placed under "eschatological erasure," as Malcolm Edwards has put it (Edwards 1998: 176–7). Heterosexuality and homosexuality and maleness and femaleness are not of ultimate importance, they are not determinative in God's eyes and in so far as any of us have behaved as if they are, we are guilty of the grave sin of idolatry, and if we have further behaved as if they are grounds upon which to exclude people from the glorious liberty of the children of God, we are guilty of profanity and a fundamental denial of our own baptismal identity which rests in being bound together with others not of our choosing by an act of sheer grace.

Culture is humanity's contribution to creation, the means by which we strive to perfect nature. But sin distorts our vision. There is many a slip between the cities we build and the city of God and yet the Spirit is active within our creations, prompting and subverting. Sexual and gender identities have to be subverted because they are constructed in the context of power and are part of a matrix of dominance and exclusion. This has been the great insight of queer theory. Therefore these identities grate against the sign of baptism. This is not to say that on a non-ultimate level these identities may not have some use and been mediations of God's grace, for indeed they have. Categories of sexuality have been used by "lesbian" and "gay" people to subvert the very assumptions that led to their creation in the first place. In giving some people a new and strong sense of self they enabled men and women within the context of philosophical and theological liberalism and liberation to expose and challenge assumptions about same-sex desire. Feminism similarly took the category of "woman," exposed its patriarchal construction and then reinvested it with meaning. These were all movements of grace but in themselves they are not complete and by their inadequacy – exposed in their failure, in their theological forms, to convince the wider church of their claims and, more importantly, in their tendency to become less and less theological in character – we are led back to the theology of baptism which demands something even more radical from Christian theologians, a questioning of the very categories of identity themselves.

Christians are then called to live out their culturally negotiated identities in such a way as to expose their non-ultimacy, to take them up into the processes of redemption, to let their flesh become sacramental. They do this by parodying their culturally negotiated identities. Parody is not a simple sending up. Linda Hutcheon defines parody as "an extended repetition with critical difference" which has "a hermeneutical function with both cultural and even ideological implications" (Hutcheon 1985: 2–7). Parody has long been the habitual Christian *modus operandi*. The Eucharist is an extended repetition with critical difference of the Last Supper, the critical difference being that in the Eucharist the meal element is caught up in a new reality, the reality of the heavenly liturgy opened up to us by the cross and resurrection. The Last Supper itself was probably an extended repetition with critical difference of the Seder meal, the critical difference being the inauguration of a new covenant and the creation of a new community called to live out the outrageous hospitality of God. As David Ford has noted, improvising on a theme, non-identical repetition is intrinsic to the Christian faith, which "is true to itself only by becoming freshly embodied in different contexts . . . Theologically understood, they [such repetitions] are testimony to God's creativity and abundance . . . They show the particularising activity of the Holy Spirit – a flourishing of distinctive and different realisations of the eventfulness of God" (Ford 1999: 144). Modernity's quest for identical repetition – evident in the banality of mass-produced goods or in the dangerous quest of fundamentalism to endlessly reproduce the "original" text or meaning in every age and context – demonstrates a lack of faith in and understanding of the Spirit. Parody is then the Christian way of operating, of taking what is given to us and playing it out in such a way as to expose the other world breaking through it.

Earlier generations of Christians were much better at parodying gender than us. The prominence given to the religious life in a Catholic context right up until the mid twentieth century was crucial to the parodic performance of maleness and femaleness. The vowed celibate testified to two ultimate truths. The first is that heterosexuality, marriage, and family life, are not identical with Christian discipleship. The second is that all desire is ultimately orientated towards God. Our desire for the other is ultimately desire for the Other and will not be satisfied until it reaches its *telos*, its end in God. The decline of and increasing invisibility of the religious life in Western Christianity constitutes a huge crisis for the church in general and for its discourse on sexuality in particular. It is both a product of and has contributed towards the collapse of Christian discipleship into heterosexual marriage. In public discourse on sexuality the Western churches currently give every impression of wanting to produce heterosexual desire rather than desire for God and contemporary society does not need yet another agency producing such desire.

The immensely popular "Seeing Salvation" millennium exhibition at the National Gallery in London contained a number of pictures of Christ exposing his wounds to Thomas or to other disciples. The imagery was most certainly erotic but the erotic gaze was diverted from the genitals, imparting the message that ultimately human desire could only be fulfilled through the wounds of Christ, through God's sheer gift of himself. Vowed celibates in their own persons testify to the *telos* of desire. They further testify to the end of history inaugurated by the birth of the Christ child – the perfect human being – and by his death and resurrection which together dissolve the need for human beings to reproduce, because the perfect child has been born, and in the resurrection which he inaugurated all will be re-membered and remembered, and so the need for heirs is cancelled. The celibate also parodies singleness – living without a partner – but with a critical difference, the critical difference being that in the church no one is actually single, no one is alone, all are bonded together in the body of Christ. One of the causes for the crises we have witnessed among religious and the celibate priesthood in recent years is the fact that the church as a body has left them alone, has forgotten how to nurture and love them, has failed to take responsibility for them. And one of the reasons for this forgetting is the church's idealization of marriage and family life.

The religious life has also traditionally been a place in which cultural constructions of maleness and femaleness have been parodied, at least in part. Celibates became "mothers" and "fathers" in their communities, presiding over groups in which a new type of kinship, no longer based upon blood relationships, united people as "brothers" and "sisters." In my youth it was common for religious women to be known by men's names. The queering was not perfect because it did not usually work the other way round (although there is a tradition in some male religious communities of referring to the male superior as "mother") but it was a queering nonetheless. Growing up surrounded by men wearing clothes that society labeled feminine, whom I had to relate to as "father," and taught by women who were my "sisters" or "mothers," with names such as Augustine and Bernard Joseph, taught me that societal categories were not fixed, that they could be played around with and that the church was a space in which gender shifted.

Thomas Laqueur has demonstrated that until the Enlightenment, Western culture constructed female bodies as imperfect inversions of male bodies. There may have been different genders but there was one sex. This allowed for the possibility of flux and change, a possibility that was closed off in the Enlightenment period, when male and female bodies were sharply differentiated in reaction to the earliest forms of feminism (Laqueur 1990). Mollenkott has drawn attention to the rich tradition of gender bending in Christian hagiography. This tradition was, of course, constructed in the context of patriarchy so the transitions tend to be female to male. Maleness was identified in much early Christian discourse with perfect humanity and femaleness with fallen humanity. Some early church fathers taught that women could become "manly" by exercising virtue and actually become models of manliness for men (Cloke 1995). Even though manifesting many patriarchal assumptions, these traditions nevertheless undermine one of the central props of patriarchy by constructing gender as fluid and therefore as lacking in ultimacy.

In the writings of the early church father and ascetic, Gregory of Nyssa, a number of theologians have identified a queer theologian who predates Butler by hundreds of years. Gregory in his reflections on the resurrection constructs a body which is fluid. Unlike some early theologians, Gregory does not associate change with decay but with movement towards the next life. Reading Genesis 1.27 with Galatians 3.28 Gregory argued that the original human creature was not sexed and it was to this angelic pre-lapsarian state that human beings would return in the resurrection. This state can to some extent be anticipated in the ascetic life and indeed was in the body of Gregory's sister Macrina who is portrayed as performing both male and female roles. Gregory describes her as going "beyond" the nature of a woman which, for Gregory, does not mean that she has reached manly perfection but rather that she is anticipating in her own body redeemed and restored humanity. For Gregory, as the soul ascends to God it moves from an active courting of Christ as "Sophia" (therefore taking a "male" role) to a passivity in which it is the bride embraced by Christ the bridegroom (V.E.F. Harrison 1990). It became common in the Christian tradition and in Christian art to represent the soul as female, in the ultimate nuptial relationship between the soul and God. Gregory then looks to a life beyond gender which can be anticipated in this life.

Foucault perceived a common cause between queer theologians and ancient ascetics. For the pre-modern Christian ascetic lived under constant self-scrutiny, conscious of being a self in production, seeking to desexualize itself (Foucault 1990–92: I). It is becoming increasingly obvious that in the marginalization of the monastic tradition within contemporary Christianity the church has cut itself off from a radical sexual discourse, an ancient form of queer theory which, though it often needs to be read through the lens of feminism to counter its patriarchal assumptions, nevertheless anticipates contemporary queer theory and provides an answer to its pessimistic nihilism.

It is in the Eucharist that the baptized learn about and anticipate the eschatological life, a life in which gender and the sexual identities built upon it are rendered non-ultimate. The Eucharist is, as Cardinal Joseph Ratzinger has noted, a rehearsal of the life to come, a form of play in which we learn about and prepare for a life "which St Augustine describes, by contrast with life in this world, as a fabric woven, no longer of exigency and need, but of the freedom of generosity and gift" (Ratzinger 2000: 14). In the Eucharist Christians gather and face eastwards towards the rising sun, towards the risen and returning Christ. They also face the cosmos, for the Eucharist is a Eucharist of the Church living and departed. In the Eucharist the church stands on the edge of heaven in the company of cherubim and seraphim, angels and archangels and the whole company of heaven, and standing on the edge of heaven gender differences dissolve. All face the same way, orientated to heaven. In the pre-Vatican II Catholic rite the priest too faced east. Bruce Harbert has suggested that one of the consequences of the new liturgy is a loss of a sense of heaven. The liturgy now fails to physically orientate the congregation towards the eschatological horizon that is the space which the Christian inhabits (Harbert 2002). Furthermore one of the most unfortunate results of the introduction of the Eucharist *versus populum* is that it draws attention to the gender of the priest in a manner that the old rite did not. In the old rite the priest stood with his back to the people in imitation of the stance taken by God in relation to Moses (Exodus 33.23), an act which Howard Eilberg-Schwartz (1997) argues was designed to veil the divine sex.

The priest is one who has received the sacrament of ordination which builds upon the sacrament of baptism, bestowing another indelible character which no sin can dislodge or dissipate, and which configures the recipient to Christ's priesthood. As one who functions as an image of Christ to Christ's church it is in fact essential that the priesthood consist of many genders, because the resurrected body of Christ is multi-gendered and therefore beyond gender. But it is also appropriate that in the act of celebrating the Eucharist, as the ones who lead the people into the heavenly liturgy, priests should have their gender concealed by their position and vestments, as a sign of the dissipation of culturally negotiated genders at the eschatological edge. This is why confining the priesthood – or any other liturgical ministry – to one gender grates against the sign of baptism and the eschatological dimension of the Eucharist. Confining any order, ministry or role to one gender or sexual orientation (or to one race or class) solidifies rather than dissolves non-eschatological reality. It signifies the lack of an eschatological horizon. At the consecration of the elements the church learns again and again of the instability, fluidity and transposable nature of the body. In the Eucharist the church reconstitutes itself as the bride of Christ and the body of Christ. Desire is refocused on the divine. The intercourse is between Christ and humanity.

Feminist theology made the abolition of exclusive language – whether used of God or of the church – one of its primary aims, and rightly so, because the use of a monolingual gender language further solidifies gender and helps to create and reinforce structures of exclusion. However, the use of gender specific language can in fact help the process of queering. Culturally constructed forms of identity cannot hold much power over those women who are used to being addressed as "brothers" or men who are forced to under-stand themselves as the brides of Christ.

In his study of the sacraments, Paul Haffner notes that the sacrament of marriage sym-bolizes the union of Christ with his church, which in turn is a reflection of the union at the heart of the Trinity. It "prefigures her [the church's] definitive triumph in heaven", for "when the Marriage of the Lamb has come (Revelation 21.2) the Church will have no further need of sacraments, since her members will see God face to face; the veil will have been removed from the face of the Bride" (Haffner 1999: 219). But the trinitarian and eschatological dimen-sions of the sacrament of marriage are rarely fully worked out in orthodox Catholic theology. Rogers points out that a theology of marriage that has its origins in the Trinity must contend with:

> [t]he ambiguity and fluidity – even gender bending – of its symbolics. God as the Trinity without reference to persons can, in traditional Christian exegesis, both require masculine pronouns and be "our Mother"; God is Father but not male; Jesus is Mother but not female; the Spirit is male, female, or neuter depending on lan-guage, and also denied to have gender. . . . Analogy is more flexible than to require that one occupy a gender to represent it. Unlike, therefore, most uses of divine marriage, the Trinity resists sharp definitions of gender and denies the image of the fertile union of a private two. (Rogers 1999a: 197)

The Trinity is an eternal dance, a perichoresis of grace. The Father eternally sends out the Son and receives him back and the Spirit eternally delights and celebrates this move-ment. Creation, the result of God's good pleasure and eternal nature, generates the very possibility of marriage because it allows for the movement of the dance of grace under the conditions of finitude. There is no procreative principle enshrined in the Trinity, both Augustine and Richard of St Victor explicitly rejected the idea that the Spirit is the child of the Father and the Son. Sex's primary purpose is sanctification, the creation of the children of God. Furthermore,

> the whole pattern of adoption, ingrafting, and resurrection, which goes to the heart of God's extension of the covenant to the Gentiles, transfigures procreation, insist-ing that all human beings (that is, Jew and Gentile) find fulfilment in sanctification, that is, in God. (Rogers 1999: 208)

Therefore the "family resemblance" by which same-sex partnerships may be called marriages is nothing to do with the issue of procreation but their resemblance to the union between Christ and his church and this, indeed, is the only reason why opposite-sex unions may be justifiably called marriages.

The "choice" between the vocations of marriage and monasticism is not a choice between asceticism and non-asceticism but between different types of asceticism. Marriage is a form of asceticism in which denial and restraint is practiced for the purposes of sanctification. Monasticism is also a form of marriage. Both involve the obligation to welcome the stranger. The tradition makes this clear: ascetics are married to God. Both forms of asceticism require time and intensity. Furthermore if, as John Chrysostom claims, in marriage the partners participate in the life of the Trinity because marriage is the form of Christ's relationship to the Father, marriage is part of each Christian's baptismal identity. Rogers argues that incorporating lesbian and gay people into marriage would be to incorporate them into the *kenosis* that Christ demonstrated to the church and to incorporate them into the practice of Christian hospitality which, though it may not manifest itself in terms of procreation, will still welcome the stranger as the great monastic same-sex communities have always done.

The church's refusal to incorporate lesbian and gay and transsexual people into marriage demonstrates a lack of engagement with the eschatological and christological dimension of the sacrament, for if the sacrament is a symbol of Christ's union with the church then that union is a union between one whose body and gender are "permeable, transcorporeal and transpositional" and a multi-gendered body which is in the process of being configured to the body of its spouse so that it too becomes "permeable, transcorporeal and transpositional."

However, as Haffner notes, though marriage has an eschatological dimension, it itself is dissolved in the eschaton when the marriage between the Lamb and his Bride is complete. Marriage – whether heterosexual or homosexual – ends at death. It constantly points beyond itself, preparing the partners for a greater consummation. The church has in the past seen same-sex (particularly male) friendship as anticipating heaven in a manner marriage could not because unlike marriage friendship could survive death. Friendship is to a large extent the answer to melancholia in the Christian tradition. It is ironic that in Western modernity it has been the lot of gay people to keep the tradition of passionate same-sex friendship alive. Gay people have then functioned as uncomfortable reminders of an eschatological horizon that the church has largely lost sight of in modernity.

"Death should be looked on . . . as a 'basic sacrament', mysteriously present in the other sacraments . . . As the supreme, most decisive, clearest and most intimate encounter with Christ . . . death summarises all other encounters" (Boros 1962: 165). The baptized are people who in their own beings carry around with them the death that society fears, the ultimate destruction of sexual and gendered identity which is part of the death into which they are plunged by the waters of baptism. The church makes this clear at the end of the earthly life of the baptized.

The *Order of Christian Funerals*, approved for use in the Roman Catholic dioceses of England, Wales and Scotland, makes clear that the source of hope for the deceased lies in their baptism, that is in their status as persons initiated into the paschal mystery of Christ's death, resurrection, and ascension. Indeed this is their only hope and the funeral rites constantly return to this fact not only in words but also in gestures and symbolism. The positioning of the Easter candle near the coffin recalls the Easter vigil in which the church celebrates the paschal mystery into which Christians are baptized. Holy water sprinkled over the deceased at various points in the funeral rites "remind the assembly of the saving waters of baptism" and "its use calls to mind the deceased's baptism and initiation into the community of faith" (Catholic Church 1991: 10). Incense is used not only to symbolise the community's prayers for the deceased rising to God but "as a sign of honour to the body of the deceased, which through baptism became the temple of the Holy Spirit" (Catholic Church 1991: 10). A pall may be placed on the coffin as a reminder of the baptismal garment of the deceased and also as a symbol of the fact that all are equal in the eyes of God. The clear preference for liturgical color (with due deference to local custom) is white, which "expresses the hope of Easter, the fulfilment of baptism and the wedding garment necessary for the kingdom" (Catholic Church 1991: 11). The Eucharist is the ordinary and principal celebration of the Christian funeral because it is the memorial of the paschal mystery and the place where the faith of the baptized in that paschal mystery is renewed and nourished.

Furthermore, though the family and friends of the deceased are encouraged to play a significant part in the preparation and execution of the funeral rites there is a strong emphasis on the involvement of the whole local Christian community not only in offering a ministry of consolation but in active participation in the rites from the vigil to the committal, an involvement which has practical consequences in, for example, the timing of funerals (Catholic Church 1991: 4). The deceased belongs primarily to the church of which the family is a subgroup. Other elements reinforce the priority of this ecclesial personhood. The general introduction is emphatic that "there is never to be a eulogy" only a homily on the content of Christian hope (Catholic Church 1991: 8). Non-biblical readings are permitted only in prayer services with the family, not in the funeral Eucharist itself. Only Christian symbols such as a Bible or cross may be placed on or near the coffin as a reminder of the faith of the deceased. "Any other symbols, for example, national flags, or flags or insignia of associations, have no place in the funeral liturgy" (Catholic Church 1991: 11). All bonds, associations, and worldly achievements pale into significance beside the status of the deceased as a baptized member of the body of Christ.

So "in the end," as the church commits the whole person – body and soul – to God, the church teaches something so radical about our sexual and gendered identities that it itself seems unable at the present time to digest its own teaching. The church teaches that in the end all other identities other than that conveyed through baptism are relativized (which is not to say that they are dismissed as unimportant as the involvement of friends and family and the opportunity provided for some personal remembrance of the deceased in some rites indicates). There is only one identity stable enough to hope in. At death my church teaches me that all my secular identities are placed under eschatological erasure. They are not matters of ultimate concern. At my death all that has been written on my body will be once again overwritten by my baptism as it was a few weeks after my birth when I was immersed in the waters of death and rebirth and a new character was given to me which nothing can ever destroy. In the end (anticipated every time the Eucharist is celebrated) before the throne of grace everything will dissolve except that identity. Gender, race, sexual orientation, family, nationality, and all other culturally constructed identities will not survive the grave. They will pass away, the "I" that is left, the I am that I am is not, as the popular song would have it, "my own special creation" nor the creation of human communities, the I am that I am is God's own special creation and that is my only grounds for hope.

The church is the only community under a direct mandate to be queer, and it is only within the church that queer theory reaches it *telos*, with the melancholia of gender replaced by the joy born of the death and resurrection of Christ – into which the Christian is incorporated through baptism – and the delight of sacramental growth, whereby the Christian is conformed more and more closely to the body of Christ – which parodies and subverts all culturally constructed identities. Queer flesh is sacramental flesh nudging the queer performer towards the Christian eschatological horizon and sacramental flesh is queer flesh nudging the Christian towards the realization that in Christ maleness and femaleness and gay and straight are categories that dissolve before the throne of grace where only the garment of baptism remains.

Chapter 4

There Is No Sexual Difference

Graham Ward

In Christian theology of the twentieth century Karl Barth and Hans Urs von Balthasar each attempted to situate the creation and vocation of man and woman within their wider systematic concerns (see Barth 1936–75: III/I–IV; Balthasar 1986b: 183–266 and Balthasar 1988–98: II, 365–95). For Barth sexual difference was a repetition on a horizontal and social level of the vertical covenant between God and human beings. Sexual difference rehearses the dialectic of the self and the other; the dialectic itself is constitutive of being human. That is, a human being is such only in relation to other human beings. Man and woman together constitute what it is to be human, making marriage fundamental anthropologically as well as theologically.[1] Marriage is the fulfillment of sexual difference; the fulfillment also of a certain *analogia Christi* insofar as it imitates the old covenantal relationship between Yahweh and Israel and the new covenantal relationship between Christ and the church. For Balthasar, sexual difference is related to the operation of specific offices within the church – the Marian and the Petrine – which, in turn rehearse the difference and hierarchy between Christ and his church. The male and female perform the twofold character of the Christian life, service and obedience. These are the distinct vocations of men and women, in which women are the answer or response to *Mensch*. Each theologian, as has been remarked by several commentators, struggles with but cannot avoid the hierarchy in which the male has priority (see Beattie 1998; Loughlin 1999b; Moss and Gardner 1998; Gardner and Moss 1999; Muers 1999; and Ward 2000: 182–202). Each theologian also cannot avoid a biological essentialism that structures and determines the difference that is subsequently enquired into theologically. The sexual in sexual difference is fundamentally physiological – it is that which can be read off from bodies. Although, these bodily signs have first of all to be recognized as significant, determinative in a major way. And, as historians of medicine and genealogists of corporeality inform us, we have been taught to identify and read certain bodily signs as sexually different only over the last 150 years or so (see Laqueur 1990). Barth and Balthasar's biological essentialism, their beginning with the determining physiological factors of distinct gonads, is itself historically and culturally determined. As such their starting point is relative; relative to other future possibilities and other conceptions of the body's determinative signs in the past.

My enquiry in this chapter issues from wondering what would happen if we started somewhere else – and it is no less relative and no less culturally and historically determined. In fact, it might be said, my starting point can only issue from the debates over the last 20–30 years concerning alterity and difference. For I wish to begin with a series of questions concerning difference as such (and concomitantly, what constitutes affinity as such). We might list such questions as: Why is difference theologically significant? How is difference recognized? What is the effect of the recognition of difference? What is theologically significant about the operations of the recognition of difference?

No doubt Barth and Balthasar would both inform me that they did not begin with the biological body but with Scripture. For both "arrive at" their accounts of sexual difference by way of exegeses of specific scriptural texts: the Genesis story of the creation of Eve, understanding this story as prefiguring the New Testament theology of Christ the Bridegroom and the church as his Bride and, for Balthasar, the scene of the Annunciation and the renaming of Simon as Peter. For both authors, Scripture is used to support a case that had validation elsewhere (in the medical sciences and their respective doctrinal traditions); they cannot escape the hermeneutical circle – of finding in Scripture what they already, to some extent, expect and anticipate. I want to offer two other accounts as scriptural starting points for a theological inquiry into sexual difference. Again neither the choice nor the exegesis that follows escapes the hermeneutical issues raised by Barth and Balthasar. But by beginning with Scripture I place my thinking within a Christian theological tradition working on the basis of what has been revealed and passed on through the church. The particular passages have been chosen to focus our attention upon a wider ecclesial erotics (thus dissolving some of the fixation with physiology by enquiring into the operations of desire) and to open the questions concerning difference, affinity, and its recognition. Both of these accounts occur in John's Gospel and, to some extent, each reflects (albeit non-identically) the concerns of the other. Both are post-resurrection experiences of and encounters with Jesus. This is theologically significant, for I will claim that it is Christ who installs difference; and therefore it is with respect to Christ that all difference has to be understood, when understood theologically.

The first account is Jesus' encounter with Mary in the "Garden" (John 19.41):

> Mary stood at the tomb outside, weeping. As she wept, she peered into the tomb; and she saw two angels in white sitting there, one at the head, and one at the feet, where the body of Jesus had lain. They said to her "Woman, why are you weeping?" She answered, "They have taken my Lord [*Kurion*] away, and I do not know where they have laid him." With these words she turned round [*eis ta opiso*] and saw Jesus standing there, but did not recognise [*edei*] him [*Iesous*]. Jesus said to her, "Woman, why are you weeping? Who is it you are looking for?" Thinking it was the gardener, she said, "If it is you, Sir [*Kurie*], who have removed him, tell me where you have laid him, and I will take him away." Jesus said, "Mary!" She turned to him and said, "Rabboni!" (which is Hebrew for "My Master" [*Didaskale*]). Jesus said, "Touch me no more [*Me mou aptou*], for I have not yet ascended to the Father. But go to my brothers, and tell them that I am ascending to my Father and your Father, my God and your God." Mary of Magdala went to the disciples with the news, "I have seen the Lord! [*Eoraka ton Kurion*]" (John 20.11-18)

The second passage follows this narrative after a space of five verses:

> One of the Twelve, Thomas, that is the "Twin" [*ho legomenos Didumos*], was not with the rest when Jesus came. So the disciples told him, "We have seen the Lord [*Eorakamen ton Kurion*]." He said, "'Unless I see the mark [*tupon*] of the nails on [*in*] his hands, unless I put [*balo*] my finger into the place [*tupon*] where the nails were, and [*balo*] my hand into his side [*pleuran*], I will not believe". A week [*emeras okto*] later his disciples were again in the room, and Thomas was with them. Although the doors were locked, Jesus came and stood among them, saying, "Peace be with

you!" Then he said to Thomas, "Reach [*phere*] your finger here: see my hands. Reach [*phere*] your hand here and put [*bale*] it into my side. Be unbelieving [*ginou apistos*] no longer, but believe." Thomas said, "My Lord [*Kurios*] and my God!" (John 20. 24–8)

In both of these encounters a transaction takes place between self and other that results in a vocalized recognition – "my master" and "my Lord." In both accounts the transaction takes place through emphatic bodily actions and gestures (Mary's turning and embracing; Thomas's reaching beyond the boundaries of his own body to penetrate [*pherao*] and thrust [*balo*] himself into the body of Christ). In both accounts there is an economy of response, a structured dialectic between self and other, in which difference and affinity, distance and proximity is negotiated in a sensuous move from sight to touch. In both accounts there is an eroticism. Mary and Jesus embrace in a garden; the pupil/teacher relation is conflated with the relation between a man and a woman that is suggestively mythologized as a return to the Garden of Eden. And stories of Mary's sexual intimacy with Jesus that have issued from readings of this scriptural text (among others) testifies to the awareness of the eroticism – from the Gnostic Gospels to Martin Scorsese's *Last Temptation of Christ* (USA 1988). Thomas touches the raw flesh of Jesus, placing his hand into the very wound that in John is symbolic of the vaginal opening through which the community of Christ's body is born (John 19.34). The disciples only see, they only behold. A far greater intimacy is granted to Thomas, a more corporeal intimacy than the head of the beloved disciple resting on Jesus' breast (John 13.23). It is again a suggestively mythologized intimacy – thrusting into the side of the second Adam from which the new Eve issues. Caravaggio captures the eroticism of that action – its carnality, its penetration – in his famous painting of the scene, *The Incredulity of St Thomas* (1601–2).

In the first passage, to employ an entirely anachronistic word, the eroticism is heterosexual. In the second passage, to employ a similarly anachronistic word, the eroticism is homosexual. In both there is difference, a difference between self and other that remains even in the epiphany of recognition that overcomes, to some extent, that difference. In both accounts what is sex – being male and female, being male and male – is highly ambivalent. It is ambivalent partly because of the suggestive mythologizing – Mary as Eve, Jesus as Adam; Jesus as a hermaphrodite and Thomas as opening up the womb of Christ. But then sex is always a mythopoetic affair; riding on fantasy (see Zizek 1994).

The difference, the affinity, the eroticism and the sex of those involved in the actions is inseparable from speaking, from words and the translation of words from one language to another. The knowledge that comes through recognition, through the economy of responding to the other and the other responding in return, is a vocalized knowledge. It takes the form of an exchange. Although, with Thomas, the words are spoken to the disciples directly and, one assumes from the story, overheard in some sense by Jesus who then returns them to Thomas when they meet. The cameos of relations with the Christ are themselves written compositions by "John" who, throughout his narrative, is conscious of the creative power of language, and who thinks powerfully about the nature of signs. He is aware of the theological significance of his own written, semiotic act (John 20.31). The text moves across the Aramaic acknowledged as the language being spoken by the disciples and Jesus, translating those conversations into Greek. It is a text concerned throughout with the act of naming: in the first account there is Jesus as Lord and Master and the response elicited by being called "Mary"; in the second there is Thomas called "Didymus" and Jesus is called both Lord and God. Furthermore, the common theme is paralleled in the common structure of these two economies of responding to the resurrected Jesus – the other man whose otherness is manifest in his conquest of death and a certain inability to recognize who he is: coming to know through speaking with and understanding the other, through desiring and engaging with the other, through seeing, naming, and touching the other. In both accounts a topography of bodies is sketched. Mary stands, stoops to peer, turns, turns again at the mention of her name, moves forward to embrace, moves back from the embrace and withdraws to tell the disciples what she has seen. Jesus stands in the midst, confronting Thomas, then offers his body for examination. Thomas moves forward, extends his finger, stretches out his hand, pushes it into the side of Christ, withdraws. This topography of bodies in both passages focuses on Jesus' body, coming to understand, coming to an identification of who he is through engaging with this body. The knowledge then that issues in identification is both carnal and theological.

Let us follow these economies of response a little further to see how this topography of bodies maps onto a relationality in which difference and affinity, distance and proximity, are understood, and ask how difference and affinity, distance and proximity, are not only established but what they signify about Christian relations. First, we can note the play of absence and presence. When Mary stands at the tomb, Jesus is, in one sense, not there because the tomb (and the positioning of the angels accentuates this) is empty. And yet he is there in Mary herself, contained within her, internalized as Lord and Master (or Teacher). In a revealing passage on the body's knowledge, Merleau-Ponty observes:

> When I imagine Peter absent, I am not aware of contemplating an image of Peter numerically distinct from Peter himself. However far away he is, I visualize him in the world, and my power of imagining is nothing but the persistence of my world around me. To say that I imagine Peter is to say that I bring about the pseudo-presence of Peter by putting into operation the "Peter-behaviour-pattern". . . . Peter in imagination is only one of the modalities of my being in the world. (Merleau-Ponty 1962: 210)

In the same way Jesus' presence is part of Mary's presence, and it is the physical absence of that presence that remains within her, displacing both a sense of herself and him, that installs her desire. The question the angels ask her elicits a vocalization of her desire: to have present even if only as a corpse the body of Jesus. Jesus himself not only reiterates the angels' question but he elicits a more precise naming of her desire. Like the night watchmen in the Song of Songs speaking to the Beloved, he asks "Whom do you seek?" Secondly, we can observe the states of knowledge. We begin with incomprehension because the body is missing while the presence of Jesus in her and to her remains strong. We continue with misrecognition for she thought it was the gardener. Turning and turning about (where the body imitates a coming to consciousness of what it itself understands), she turns into a hearing of her own name. The calling calls her not only to herself and into a new knowledge, but to an identification through his voice of herself with him (in him if we can understand the name dwelling in his mouth and mind). The absence that previously filled her disappears, and the two bodies come together (again imitating a state of knowledge) as they embrace.

The negative command, *Me mou aptou*, installs a distance again, but it is not an absence. Although neither is it presence as possession or the unity of the identification of herself in him and with him. In a sense, when he speaks her name he speaks her into existence as part of himself, when he explains to her why she should stop touching him he speaks *to* her and so demonstrates they are not one. His speaking *to* her is a communication *with* her, but also a separation *from* her. (In a sense this is the condition of all theological understanding, that works between a sacramental presence and an inability to grasp fully what faith understands.) Thirdly, we can identify the modes of address as they shift from interrogation to affirmation, to the giving of a command, to the giving of an explanation, to the giving of a commission, to a final acclamation and testimony before witnesses: "I have seen the Lord."

The topography of bodies maps then onto an economy of response that begins with the paralyzing contradiction of absence and presence, issuing dramatically into a consummating knowledge which is then followed by a dialectical relation of affinity (or recognition) and difference, knowledge, and desire. The economy of response is composed of four complex movements – of bodies, of language, of knowledge, and of desire. The movements are not equally distributed between the two figures. The body of Jesus the Christ is more central to the narrative than Mary's body, though it is Mary's body that moves whilst Jesus' body stands still. The language operates upon and within Mary for the most part – she answers or she listens until she makes her statement before the disciples. She does not control the direction of the language. She speaks within a language given to her by invitation (from the angels, from Jesus). The movement of knowledge is time-bound: *eureka*, I have seen. She understands then by remembering. Her moment of identification with Jesus is crossed by ignorance that he is not yet ascended. She makes no answer to the account of going to the Father, of ascending to God. What is known is always being crossed by what is unknown. The language says more than is understood. It operates as an expression of desire as it changes in the moves from loss and longing, to being united, to being separated and given the task of going ahead to speak to others. Desire remains because it cannot fully attain the understanding that faith seeks. Desire remains – confused and lacking an object (fetishizing the corpse), finding and uniting with its object, being displaced on to another object, desire knows difference whilst knowledge has identified again what it knows: "I have seen the Lord." All the various aspects of the economy of response are orientated towards a future state. Mary must go and tell the disciples, Jesus must ascend; the knowledge and the language is not yet perfect. The body receives and responds (it sees, it hears, it touches) more than the mind understands, and what the body knows is not incomprehensible, it merely sketches a knowledge that has yet to be entered into; and the future is carried on the wings of desire. The very secret of the structure of time is contained in that moment of embrace and recognition.

The economy of response in the account of Jesus and Thomas is more truncated, though also more visceral. The theme of absence and presence opens this account too, though it is Thomas's absence to begin with, followed by Jesus' absence when Thomas returns to the upper room and the disciples. There is a different choreography of bodies. But again, Jesus is present in Thomas as his pronouncement to the disciples makes evident. For Thomas rehearses the wounds inflicted on Jesus by the crucifixion. In fact, he returns us, like the victims of trauma return the trusted enquirer, to the scene of the crime: the nails hammered into the hands, the lance puncturing the side. Jesus' death lives in Thomas; lives in his memory, his language and his understanding of who this man is/was. Let us interpret this generously, as Caravaggio did. This is not atheism, nor even agnosticism. This is love that cannot come to terms with loss; this is belief that cannot yet take on the burden of hope. Jesus comes to Thomas as Thomas imagines him, as Thomas has internalized him. There is no mention of Jesus' wounds in Mary's encounter, nor in the encounter with the other disciples that takes place off-stage, so to speak. But something more is needed than seeing these wounds. These wounds have shaped within Thomas an understanding of this crucified man; that understanding must now undergo a transformation. Jesus invites Thomas to plunge into the very depths of the tortured Messiah that he has internalized. The touch is demanded of Thomas; it was Mary's spontaneous response. Thomas must go where no other man or woman has been allowed to go – into the very flesh of the Christ. He must be brought to a new knowledge and identification through the engagement of bodies. His future in Christ is only possible on the basis of the carnal reception of and response to flesh touching flesh. Touch and identification are, as with the early account, inseparable, but a new and more dramatic crossing of bodily boundaries is required. Thomas has to be brought not to announce his desire but to perform it. It is the same desire as Mary's – to be one with Jesus. But in neither case is seeing enough. Mary has to hear first and then embrace. Thomas has to be commanded. Subsequently, he has to submit to that command (which is only voicing what Thomas himself had voiced within himself). Thomas has to be brought to a knowledge; a knowledge Mary seizes in an utter surrender of herself at the call of her name. Caravaggio captures this leading, this manuduction, in his painting; for it is Christ who guides Thomas's finger into the wound. And the wound is opened by that finger as if lifting the lid of an inner eye, or even parting vaginal lips. Thomas is led to an intimate, carnal, and spiritual knowledge; his face is fixed with both a curiosity and an incomprehension.

But let us go just a little further – further than Caravaggio's depiction of Thomas, towards Caravaggio's depiction of and response to embodiment itself. For the painting as a whole – Thomas in his context – suggests the touch is commanded, solicited as an act of love, and initiating a process of healing. Is Jesus' pain in being wounded somehow lessened, healed, by Thomas's touch? Is that touch akin to those visions of mystics who kiss the wounds of Christ not out of some gruesome masochism, but out of a love that wishes to touch the very place of pain with love, and begin its healing? Thomas's hand remains forever touching the torn flesh of Christ; and when does touch become caress? The composition suggests a healing of relation; a distance remains (registered in the look on Thomas's face of absolute incomprehension), but it is a distance known in proximity.

The four aspects of the economy of response that we have examined are different in this second account: what is being performed by and upon the body; the coming to know [*Erkenntnis*][2] and identify; the language which is not of interrogation and explication, but of command; and the operation of desire in which the scene is almost freeze-framed as Thomas reaches into the side of Christ. But the *telos* is the same – the learning of difference and affinity, distance and proximity, through the establishment of a relation that is erotic beyond being simply sexual.[3]

Distance

What do these economies of response with respect to the body of Jesus, the Christ, enable us to understand about theology and sexual difference?

First, I have throughout paralleled the notion of difference with that of distance. This is partly to ensure that difference is always thought relatively, as distance is. There is no pure difference. Difference *qua* difference is an abstraction no one could recognize. Difference is relative, and distance spatializes that relativity and also suggests the possibility of a temporal dynamic. That is, because distance is relative so also actions with respect to that distance will alter it – reducing or expanding proximity. In the same way, difference now understood not as an abstraction but as an aspect of a temporal situation concerned with the relational spatializing of bodies with respect to each other, admits degrees thereof and modifications to those degrees. To associate difference with distance – that I will go on to suggest is a profoundly theological notion that the early Greek Fathers termed "diastema" – prevents any difference, sexual or otherwise, from becoming a stable marker of a living body.

But a question now arises about the adjective "sexual" with respect to difference. Put plainly, how does difference get sexed? From the analysis above I would suggest – and this is the second point in a developing understanding of sexual difference – that difference, to the extent that it concerns the bodies of other responsive beings, is always erotic and therefore sexually charged to a greater or a lesser degree.[4] This is because it is only constituted in relation, and relations between responsive bodies become increasingly eroticized through proximity. The move from seeing to touching in the scriptural accounts we have examined, marks a degree of erotic charge between the bodies as well as a change in what the body knows. The body's knowledge is, I suggest (following Merleau-Ponty), profoundly related to desire. Although I would not want to draw a sharp line between the senses of sight and touch – voyeurism would warn us against doing this – certain forms of seeing can indeed be tactile. There are certain exchanges of glances that can wound or excite, that can caress or puncture the body. A look can make me feel ugly, feel aroused, feel pain. It is somewhere in the engagement between sight and touch that bodies become sexualized, somewhere in the junction between reception and response within the body's own knowing. Such that desire for knowing or being with the other is simultaneously an *attraction* to the other. Is it at such a moment of sexualization, in the arrival of attraction, that bodies take on a sexual difference? What I am arguing here is that in the same way as there is no difference as such, there is no sexual difference as such. Sexual difference is not a given, a fundament, a starting point. It is always an "achievement," in Hegel's understanding of that term – it is produced in and through specific acts of encounter. To take this further, with respect to Christian theology: there is no theology of sexual difference, only the production of sexual difference in a theological relation. And we will have to ask what is a theological relation in a moment.

The difference which arises from any encounter is not sexual with respect to the physiology of the bodies involved. Of course this is not to deny the physiological or the aesthetic (the beauty, which accords with fashion, of this man or that woman). Neither would I want to deny the role that having sexual organs plays in the performance of an explicit sexual encounter or the adrenalin rush that comes with stimulation. Throughout my exegesis and analysis of Scripture, I have emphasized the interplay between what the body receives and responds to and what the mind understands.[5] But the bodies themselves, I suggest, become sexualized by the consciousness of being-in-relation – they are not sexualized before it. In other words, there is no pure physiological state. To return to a point I made with respect to the mythologizing of relations in Jesus' encounter with Mary in the garden, the erotic experience is already mythopoetic, shot through with images, fantasies, and mythemes. Thus when I speak of "consciousness" here I do not simply refer to a mental state as distinct from a physical state. The central argument of this chapter would reject the dualism of mind and body, *psuche* and *soma*. Orientating oneself round a city, anticipating other vehicles and pedestrians whilst driving, reaching for and choosing a shot at tennis in response to a return, are all examples of the body "thinking" and consciously moving with respect to other bodies without necessarily reasoning in these situations. The body is taught to "think" in this way through habituating practices. One can then "know" one is in-relation without the physical proximity of the person. And similarly one can know of being-in-relation without necessarily being mentally attentive to the person one is in relation to. Bodies, I suggest, become sexualized through a consciousness of being-in-relation of various kinds, through attentive rationalizing and responsive readings of body language. In being sexualized bodies negotiate both difference and affinity, distance and proximity – they do not just encounter difference/distance. Attraction, key to the dynamic of desire, operates through economies of both difference and affinity, distance and proximity. It would be as absurd to label the erotic encounter between Mary Magdala and Christ as "heterosexual," as it would be absurd to label the meeting of Thomas and Christ as "homosexual." Both of these labels treat sexuality as a self-subsisting thing, a property that can be attributable to relations, a predicate of persons that encounter awakens. This would be Freud's understanding of the libido as a substructure of selfhood. My analysis would suggest this is an entirely wrong way of understanding sexuality. The erotic nature of a sexual relation is intrinsic to relating itself. The relation itself, in its constitution, participates in an *eros* and a pathos pertaining to all relations between responsive bodies. (And I would be at a loss to say at what point an organic body is unresponsive.) Any understanding of sexual difference has to think through what is relation and embodiment as such.

Let me begin with embodiment, and a distinction as important to St Paul who distinguishes body (*soma*) from flesh (*sarx*) as it is, more recently, to Michel Henry (2000: 7–9) who distinguishes flesh (*chair*) from the corporeal (*le corps*). The distinction is this: there is the material order of things and there is what I will term the ethical order of things. A distinction is not a division. I am not suggesting the world of genetic pools and carbon compounds is divorced from the world of values and significances. In fact, what I understand by the theological term "incarnational" would describe the material order as already inhabited by – only made possible by – the ethical order of things. But the distinction nevertheless remains a useful strategic tool for disrupting the empirical and positivist assumption that what is real and what is true is constituted by the basic elements of carbon and DNA alone. The corporeal (St Paul's *sarx*, Henry's *le corps*) is the material in itself, the pursuit of which for both thinkers is nihilistic and atheistic. The corporeal as such is, on one level, a philosophical abstraction or isolation proceeding from the complex knowledge of the body (St Paul's *soma*, Henry's *le chair*). On another level, the corporeal as such is only possible on the rejection of the theological and ethical orders that give value and significance to the body.

Positivism assumes the opacity of objects; it assumes objects are as they appear. Appearance is the starting place for understanding and thinking about them. Ontology *is* epistemology. It is exactly this assumption that I wish to "queer" with respect to human bodies and how we reflect theologically upon them. To a certain extent phenomenology has already begun to think this disruption of appearance, by asking not about appearance as such but about the how of an appearance, the intentionality of the gaze. Phenomenology asks a prior question about the object of scientific enquiry – how does it give itself to appear as such. Understanding is not the discovery of what is the state of affairs but an "achievement" in and through relating to that which gives itself. Phenomenology distinguishes between an object's appearance and its manner of appearing – for Henry there is "*l'apparence*" and there is "*l'apparaître*." As such, phenomenology is not asking questions about the material composition or contents of the object, it is asking about how it gives itself to be understood. The phenomenological investigation, as Heidegger realized, gives way to an ontological enquiry that is distinct while remaining inseparable from that which makes its appearance. The ontological question is then secondary and dependent; the mystery of what gives itself, the mystery that invests what is with its values and significances, the mystery of donation,[6] remains primary.[7]

Now let us take this one step further with respect to embodiment. For what I am suggesting here is that the meaning and significance of bodies is ultimately ungraspable. Their giveness cannot be accounted for – except mythopoetically or theologically – and they cannot account for themselves (as empiricists would like us to believe). If Jesus the Christ can be understood as the second Adam, then incarnation does not just characterize his body, but, in some sense, all bodies. This incarnational nature is the mark of the mystery of the body's donation, or what Rowan Williams (2002) has called "the body's grace" (being donated). Of course, Christ as the second Adam does not repeat identically the first Adam since Adam was made "in the image of God"; he was not God. And so when I say all bodies are "in some sense" incarnational they are not identical repetitions of Christ's body, but nevertheless participate in that incarnation in their own creaturely way. Embodiment, therefore, is analogically related to incarnation, and it is as such, that Paul's *soma* can refer both to (a) the historical and physical body each possesses, even Christ, and to (b) the transhistorical, spiritual body that is Christ's alone but which is made of several members constituting the church. This rich, analogical understanding of *corpus* is detailed in Henri de Lubac's study of medieval sacramentality, *Corpus Mysticum* (1948). Embodiment maintains its mystery, rendering the particularity of its thereness continually open to a transcorporeal operation. This transcorporeal operation is not beyond the body or *supra*-corporeal. The body's transcorporeality is constituted in and through its relations to other bodies.

This brings us to the second of the two categories that, from my exegesis, will determine a different, theological account of sexual difference: relation. A body is always in transit, always exceeding its significance or transgressing the limits of what appears. The body is constantly in movement and in a movement. It is these complex movements in and upon the body that the economies of response attempt to sketch. Put differently, the body exists fluidly in a number of fluid operations between reception and response, between degrees of desire/repulsion, recognition/misrecognition, and passivity/activity. These operations maintain the body's mystery by causing it always to be in transit. As such a body can only be reduced to a set of identifiable properties of its appearance (such as identifications of sex as "male" or "female") by being isolated from these processes and operations; by being atomized. Embodiment maintains its excess, maintains its transcorporeality in and through its congress with the mysteries of other bodies. It is with respect to other bodies that the operations of reception and response, reading and rereading, acting and withdrawing are not only conducted but constituted. These operations bring into being systems of dependence and interdependence, which any singular body can always resist but from which no singular body can ever finally extract itself. I suggest it is from within these systems, with respect to these operations, that the sexuality of embodiment and its distinctiveness in relation to other sexual embodiments emerges. There is no sexuality or sexual difference as such, just as there is no difference as such, only distances and affinities occurring across networks of relation. Put briefly, and theologically, if the mystery of embodiment and its *eros* is articulated with respect to the body of Christ, then the ambiguities and latitudes of difference and relation are articulated with respect to the operations of a God who is three and who is also one.

In contrast to the determinative biological starting point for discussing sexual difference (filtered through scriptural exegesis) of Karl Barth and Balthasar, I have offered here another place from which to begin – with the "operations" or economies of embodiment and relation. Gregory of Nyssa – writing *On "Not Three Gods"* – provides us with a theological formula for this post-Nicene basis: "every operation which extends from God to the Creation, and is named according to our variable conceptions of it, has its origin from the Father, and proceeds through the Son, and is perfected in the Holy Spirit" (Gregory of Nyssa 1994: 334).

Notes

1   There is an interesting question in Barth's theology of sexual difference concerning "marriage" as a social, contractual institution and "marriage" as a covenantal relation. Barth allows for divorce on the grounds that the relation may not have been and subsequently misunderstood as being covenantal. The "marriage" seems then the relation issuing from the consummation of sexual difference; a relation that is ontologically prior to any ceremonial procedure.

2   This is a Hegelian term, "recognition." In German the prefix *er* establishes the sense of a coming-towards or proximity to. For Hegel identification or recognition is never final; it is a process that remains incomplete. It is a moment in the coming to self-consciousness of any notion or idea. It is a term used extensively in the Lordship and Bondsman discourse of *Phenomenology of Spirit* (1807). Through the dialectic process, '[t]hey *recognize* themselves as mutually *recognizing* one another' (Hegel 1977: 112; #184). The mutually constitutive knowledge that each attains is a work that takes place in the interchange between them; the knowledge in this sense is "achieved," not discovered or revealed.

3   See Henry (2000) for a discussion of the relationship between nihilism and an eroticism that is simply reduced to sexuality. This reduction is found even in Merleau-Ponty, who in his celebrated chapter on sexuality and the body speaks of Eros as Libido.

4   The history of bestiality points to a long-standing awareness of erotic relations between human beings and animals that has, at times, been sexual. Hence I speak about "responsive beings," but I am also aware others have found erotic relations between human beings and other natural forms – trees, water, mountains, and landscapes. In the opening sequences of *The English Patient* (USA 1996), for example, the camera pans erotically over the undulating North African desert as if it were the body of a woman. In Nicholas Roeg's film *Walkabout* (Australia 1970), trees are given a similar erotic charge.

5   Neither is there any need to label the "performance of an explicit sexual encounter" the "consummation" of sex, as if all other forms of erotic relationship were inferior to explicit sexual congress.

6   "There is a difference between calling something a gift, and calling it a donation; it can be a gift even before it is given, but it cannot be called in any way a donation unless it has been given" (Augustine 1991b: 200; V.16).

7   Levinas, following Plato – and evidently the Christian tradition has been indebted to Plato – would concur: the ethical (or the Good) is beyond being and prior to the ontological. This distinction between Good and Being does not imply an absolute difference between ethics and ontology, only a distance (*diastema*) that separates them. One might say that what makes the Good good is that it gives all things, it delivers being or donates.

Chapter 5

Fecundity

Sex and Social Reproduction

David Matzko McCarthy

Sex produces children. This statement might disturb many, inasmuch as it rings of sexual repression and frustrated desire. Surely sex ought not to be constrained by an archaic procreative end? But although out of step with the times, it seems straightforward to begin with simple procreation when introducing a discussion of fecundity. Among the countless things done and intended through sex, sexual activity has an orientation to producing as well, and the end of this orientation is a baby. That is not to say that every sexual act does or must have a procreative outcome. However, procreation is inevitable if a man and woman are not vigilant about avoiding it (or if one of them "suffers" a dysfunction). Most couples who decide to have a child actively do so by discontinuing their resistance to the procreative intentions of their acts. By "intentions of their acts," I mean, not their thinking or their conceptual intentions, but their bodily agency. Our bodies are generative in disposition.

The body intends. A pregnant woman might not intend to be pregnant in the narrowly cognitive sense of intention, and she will not need to make up her mind in order for gestation to proceed. Instead, she is likely to say, "Look at what is happening to me. My breasts are getting heavy, my stomach is poking out, and somebody is moving around in there. Isn't it amazing?" Although she might refer to these events as happening to her, she is not passive by any means. She, in her full bodily sense, knows what to do and intends to do so. This character of our agency has given St Augustine good reason to worry, at least from his understanding of the unity of intellect, will, and body. Augustine makes much out of the fact that our bodies are not entirely under rational control. A man might not think to have an erection but experiences one nevertheless. Modern romanticism simply turns the Augustinian hierarchy on its head. The natural impulses and movement of desire impinge upon us in ways that cannot be, and therefore ought not to be, suppressed. In this case, a man cannot and ought not to ignore his erection. He must respond to his nature. Regardless of what makes rational sense, his sexual responsiveness must be speaking the truth.

Pregnancy is representative of the body's agency, but too often a woman's body has been presented through a dualism that sets rational will over against the body, intellect over against nature, and man as independent thinker and social agent over against woman as bodily creativity and affective unity. Note, for instance, that recent interest in the "theology of the body" is more precisely an interest in the formal differences between male and female bodies. Some distinction between the male and female body is important, but more needs to be said, first, that our embodied activity is social, and second, that bodily agency is not generic in character but specific to you or me. Certainly, the human body *per se* indicates how human beings inhabit the world, but my corporality is lived and acted out in a social world where, it is hoped, I cannot be exchanged with another. The sexual givens of the body are usually used to indicate natural as opposed to social agency. But ironically our bodies are the fundamental medium of our social world (i.e., our only world). My bodily intentions shape and are shaped by the particulars of my everyday life.

This chapter interprets fecundity in terms of the socially situated body and a cultural grammar of desire. It undertakes the difficult task of dealing with sexual generativity in a socioeconomic world that separates the meaning of sex from reproduction and conceives of procreation less as economically productive and more as a form of consumption. The first section of the chapter offers an analysis of sexual desire as it is reproduced within the market economy. Sex, in this setting, is productive of both desire and a naturalism that conceals the expansion of dominant social forms. We live in sexually agonistic times. Masked by the idea of the natural sexual self is an economy of desire that perpetuates the struggle by pushing contentment out of the everyday world. The second section criticizes recent currents in the theology of marriage insofar as a modern turn inward sustains this other-worldly economy of desire. By beginning with my reference to a woman's agency in carrying a child, I hope that a stark contrast has already been established. The sexual/bodily agency of women and men, as it is conceived within the dominant social economy, hinges on our freedom from bodily generation. I am asserting otherwise. My only alternative is to rarefy and spiritualize, to set forward the implausible and empirically false notions that sex "makes love," produces a "relationship," and builds on the true "sexual" self. Sex makes people, not love. Sexual practices mediate the social body, not only through making babies, but also through the course of our bodily-living out in common life.

My concern, in this chapter, is to consider fecundity as social reproduction and sexual agency as it is situated in quotidian endeavors. Ultimately, I will claim that conceptions of marriage and family, as they are carried by practices of the Christian life, do indeed domesticate sex. Sexual practices are a means of being at home; they reproduce the social economy of the household and are satisfied in our belonging.

Sex without Ends

The history of modern sex can be told as a turn inward, toward sexual subjectivity over against social constraints, toward personal fulfillment over against economic alliances and household management, toward love over against procreation. Modern sex, at its best, is an inter-subjective reality. It is an expression of the sexual self, and the self is drawn, through this need for expression, into relationships that are conceived as "sexual." Those who identify a relationship as something social, as a marriage or friendship, are likely to identify a distinct sexual relationship that coexists along with or within their practical or public relationships. This relation between the sexual self and a discrete sexual sphere corresponds, ironically, with the dominance of an impersonal industrial economy and anonymous political relations. While sex has been freed, supposedly, from social and economic constraints, the very idea of a pre-social sexual sphere has come to serve contractual individualism and the market economy. The dominant social economy is reproduced by the inviolability of desire, sexual and otherwise. To be inviolable, desire must be conceived as preceding the social. The sexual self is the natural self that stands outside social relations, and sexual relationships are believed to enliven personal subjectivity in an impersonal social world.

The subjective structure of sex is complemented with a modern conviction that each of us is, inescapably, a desiring subject. Sex and sexual desire point to a truth about us. We are sexual beings. As such, we communicate who we are, sexually, through a variety of interchanges: some overtly sexual, others not, some casual, others profound, some whimsical, others dutiful. Sexual activity need not fulfill any purpose other than the ends determined by the persons who engage in the activity (e.g., physical pleasure, emotional intimacy, love, mutual conquest, or procreation). Sex is defined by the willful making of our subjectivity. If, in ages past, the desired product of sexual activity was children and a display of social position and hierarchy, the desired outcome, in recent times, is both self-determination and a display of the sexual self. If Hebrews, Greeks, and Romans worried about producing progeny and reproducing the social body, modern Americans worry about themselves. In this regard, sexual desire is a product that comes out of the self. Self-referential sexuality is, in a word, romantic.

Because sexual activity is thought to express the self, the end of desire represents a loss of self. Children, pleasure, and power may be goals of sexual activity, but they will not bring sexual satisfaction insofar as "satisfaction" implies an end to motivation and desire. Rather than enjoying the tranquility of their maturity, middle-aged men would rather feel yearnings from within. A sexual drive (or Viagra) restores the self, inasmuch as personal contentment is found through inextinguishable desire. Medieval troubadours, in celebration of the beloved's lure, did not strive for consummation as much as for the abandonment of self in the striving. Consummation marked an end never to be reached, particularly since romantic love was defined outside of the social bonds of household and marriage (Rougemont 1983). Late twentieth-century romantics, in contrast, gain a self through desire. Their true love requires no sacrifice, and now, sexual objects are expected to be both accessible and exhaustible. Romantic love need not endure to be true. Likewise, consummation has been converted, no longer a boundary line but an intermediate point of consumption. If modern adolescents brag about "doing it," mature adults fantasize about "doing it all night long." Good sex will not satisfy as much as spur a lover on for more and more. In other words, sex flounders when it can be sated. Sex must reproduce desire.

This reproduction of desire for the sake of desire is produced within the dominant market economy. Late twentieth-century capitalism is an economy, not of products, but of consumption. It requires ever-expanding markets and innovation for its continuation, and as a result, it must produce desire through the introduction of a product or service. The economy creates markets and reproduces choices and social relations friendly to market rationality (Rifkin 2000). This kind of social reproduction has been used by free trade advocates, as an argument for opening and expanding trade with China. Certainly, China's political system is reprehensible to Americans, but what better way to change their culture of oppression than open our economy to them (McGrory 2000; Mufson 2000; Vita and Eilperin 2000). This familiar argument assumes that the economy carries forms of subjectivity and social relations. Likewise, consumer capitalism pervades a cultural code of sex and sexual desire, and this code impinges on social relations that are ostensibly non-sexual. We all know that sexual cues are used to attract us to one toothpaste rather than another. We all know that non-sexual social exchanges often have a sexual sub-text or operate through a tacit sexual code. It is less recognized or accepted that our sexual desires are structured and constrained by the systems of exchange where they appear (Illouz 1997).

The logic of "reproductive desire" demands that our desires appear to us as only natural (e.g. it is only natural that the Chinese people, as opposed to their oppressive government, would want our market choices). If pre-social, desire can be conceived as a personal reality that impinges upon the world. If not a personal choice, then our sexual impulses must be pre-determined naturally, as sociobiologists will confirm (Dawkins 1976). In either case, desire is conceived as a foundation outside social and economic constraints. As a foundation, it is assumed to produce social relations rather than vice versa. In this regard, market desire justifies its own ends.

By lifting desire out of the "only natural," I do not intend to take what is typically called a constructionist view of sexuality (i.e., that sexual desire and practices are *merely* historical and cultural constructions). Such a theory is the inverse and complement of a modernist reduction to nature. The constructionist tends to view cultures as mechanisms that stand outside and work upon the people that inhabit them; yet, the constructionist argument is often used to justify personal lifestyles and choices, since all "sexualities" are arbitrary anyway. In other words, it is used as a counter-position to those who claim that sex has a normative pre-social basis. Like the naturalist position, the constructionist view is often shaped by an individualist conception of culture and social formation. Culture is considered a collective individual who is self-determined by force of the will (or the majority will) over against a never-to-be-known "nature." In any case, when all desire is defined as arbitrary, the desire of individuals is once again freed from social constraints, just like the modern individual is freed from determination by the social body.

My point is that sex is social reproduction, that sexual practices cohere with and perpetuate forms of social production. With this claim, culture *as such* is not set over against nature *as such*, but neither are they considered a seamless whole. There are a variety of contending and coextensive social forms, and it is plausible to propose that any given culture or era will be a complex of dominant, emergent, residual, and auxiliary social forms, all of which impinge upon, contend for, and form feelings, impulses, rationality, and conceptions of the social or pre-social self (Raymond Williams 1977: 121–8). Some social and sexual practices, perhaps, are reproduced more "naturally" than others, but it is a particularly modern notion that it is important (or possible) to distinguish difference between natural and social, and that the difference can be determined without a conception of human beings as created with an end. Modern "sex without ends" lacks a conception of human fulfillment that interprets and unifies both social and natural life. If sex is socially reproductive, then a grammar of desire, market capitalism and contractual individualism fit together as a dominant network of social reproduction. They represent a dominant set of constraints on conceptions of the sexual and the logic of sexual practices. A challenge to this reproduction of desire is not a turn to the individual or pre-social self, but an alternative social body, which presents contending practices of social reproduction.

Family and Social Reproduction

Marriage and family, inasmuch as they form a social economy, appear to provide an alternative site for social reproduction. If sex in late capitalism is "sex without ends," the meaning of sex is constantly negotiated. Often, sexual encounters are assumed to imply certain ends, by the nature of their context and the signals of a common script. For instance, I can narrow the possible meanings of a sexual interchange if I take an acquaintance home to my bed as a stranger. Sex among friends and companions, on the other hand, will bring a host of ambiguities that will need to be explicitly negotiated. Marriage and family, insofar as they imply binding commitments, seem to present an entirely different (non-negotiable) set of sexual practices. Within the dominant cultural code, they are means to constrict the "natural" reproduction of desire and the free self-determination of the sexual self. From a common theological angle, settling into commitments and setting up a home are conceived as alternatives to the dominant reproduction of desire.

When discussing love and the ideology of reproduction, Niklas Luhmann notes that "the increasing differentiation of the economy on the one hand as the sector of production, and the family on the other . . . led to the family being relieved of having to fulfill any role over and above its immediate concerns" (Luhmann 1986: 145). In other words, family replaces the ancient and medieval household. Affective kinship replaces the household as an economy and as a medium of social duty and political rule (Shorter 1975). In effect, the purpose of family, within the modern economy, is to reproduce itself through emotional ties. Family will continue to convey social and economic benefit, but these forms of distribution are instruments of family's more basic distribution of love (Walzer 1983). Luhmann adds "that, while the stratified order and family systems remained intact, a semantics for love developed to accommodate extra-marital relationships, and was then transferred back into marriage itself" (Luhman 1986: 5–6). Family has become a site for the reproduction of love, but love takes its antecedent or native form from outside family.

The same can be said about sex, particularly as it appears as an expression of love, or as "love-making." Marriage continues to be understood as a basic site for reproducing a sexual relationship, but it is invested with an extra-marital code of desire. Within the dominant reproduction of desire, binding relationships, partnerships, and marriage are understood to be individualist, pre-social contracts, that are, nevertheless, clothed in social dress – like splendid church-weddings, morning coats, and flowing white gowns. Social trappings amount to a matter of style, and the value of sex will be judged in the usual terms – whether or not the sexual relationship generates desire, whether or not the natural sexual self is enlivened. To be justified, binding sexual relationships must mediate an antecedent sexuality that originates and flourishes outside of family. Marriage must reproduce native desire.

These questions of social mediation present the key problematic for recent developments in the theology of conjugal union and sex. The character of family as a mediating institution is consistent with traditional conceptions of the household, whether in the household codes of the New Testament, the role of the Roman citizen-family, or Catholic social teaching of the late nineteenth and early twentieth century. In obviously different ways, household is understood to replicate or to convey the social body or the *polis*. When the household is relieved (in Luhmann's terms) of its political and economic functions, marriage and family begin to be conceived as interpersonal alternatives to basic political institutions and structures of economic exchange (Lasch 1977). Soon marriage becomes the interpersonal foundation of family. By the mid-twentieth century, it is considered a community of two in itself without reference to the social functions of the household or to a larger whole at all. Marriage now mediates the person.

In Dietrich von Hildebrand's groundbreaking book on marriage, conjugal union is assumed to be unique, with no social antecedents (Hildebrand 1984). Spousal love is presented as original, as emerging through the inter-subjectivity of two in order to establish a foundation for a new community. This inter-subjective or personalist interpretation of marriage gives new, romantic meaning to marital companionship. The companions turn their relationship inward. According to Hildebrand, "conjugal love in itself constitutes a completely new kind of love. It involves a unique mutual giving of one's self, which is the outstanding characteristic of this type of love. It is true that in every kind of love one gives oneself in one way or another. But here the giving is literally complete and ultimate. Not only the heart but the entire personality is given up to the other" (Hildebrand 1984: 5). Hildebrand is fond of Martin Buber's language of "I and Thou," but rather than use it to distinguish a personal encounter from the objectifying "I-It," Hildebrand uses the concept as a contrast to "We." If friendship, traditionally defined, is walking "side by side, hand in hand," marriage is gazing "face to face," an I-Thou. If friendship is oriented to common social goods and the good, the marriage partnership is unique because, unlike typical partnerships that are based in common work or an outward vocation, the marital union is self-directed. It is an exclusive inter-subjectivity of two. Conjugal love "tends to . . . a community where two persons constitute a closed union . . . a relationship in which the regard of each one of the two parties is turned exclusively upon the other" (Hildebrand 1984: 5–6).

This inter-subjective account of conjugal love is romantic in its refusal to define partnership in terms of the virtues or character of the beloved. Love is conceived as a formal interchange of subjectivity without reference to whether or not a good partner is needed for a good partnership. Without reference to the selves that are given and received, Hildebrand's personalism romantically appeals to the formal qualities of "total" self-giving. The marriage would have to be so heroic as to carry the weight of a total self, or the self would have to be shallow and one dimensional, so that it could be completely unveiled in a single relationship. Otherwise, total self-giving is merely a hyperbolic way of saying "we do all that we can." In any case, Hildebrand's understanding of nuptial union resonates more with private moments of passion than washing the dishes, dinner with the in-laws, cooperating with neighbors, and managing a home. His account is romantic in its apparent otherness from the everyday world.

Hildebrand's conception of companionship is otherworldly. His view of conjugal love is not invested with erotic passion, but he does sustain a romantic ideal of the transparent private self, where "he is different with me than he is with any one else" or "we get connected only when we have time alone." The unique face-to-face love of Hildebrand's I-Thou has no clear connection to the side-by-side nature of quotidian endeavors. His story of love implies a typical trial of modern romance. Although we have cultivated our I-Thou throughout our courtship, through gazing into each other's eyes under a moonlit sky, we may not be able to sustain the side by side of sharing a household, working for each other's good, and sustaining the goods of common life with friends and neighbors. Great lovers do not necessarily make for good housekeeping. In the dominant mode of desire, it is likely that our focus outward (beyond the face to face) will be experienced as a dissipation of the inter-subjective love we once shared. Love and passion die once partners settle in at home.

Sex, as well, is oriented inwardly. Recent personalists consider inter-subjective union as the primary end of conjugal intercourse. Although Hildebrand considers love and communion to be the meaning of sexual intercourse, he continues to speak of procreation as an intrinsic end of marriage. His account of marriage, it could be argued, is made more consistent when sexual acts are freed from procreation, which is best conceived as an extrinsic end rather than one internal to sexual intercourse. Arguing for the procreative character of sex, as it is understood from the personalist view, depends upon archaic notions of human sexuality and is sustained by retrograde fronts within Roman Catholicism. As the personalist argument goes, we ought to speak of marriage, rather than sex, as procreative and open to procreation. Sexual acts are understood to establish and sustain a sexual relationship as the key expression of nuptial unity. Families raise children, while sex cultivates intimacy and is a basic sign of total self-giving.

When all is said and done, holding to the primacy of nuptial unity is considered, by liberal and conservative proponents alike, to be a counter-cultural position. The dominant cultural code of desire sets good sex apart from marriage. Good sex is judged in a variety of ways, according to standards of passion, emotional investment, personal happiness, novelty, technique, and frequency. Each of these criteria may exist in or outside of marriage. In contrast, personalists argue that sex is intrinsically unifying, and that true sexual relationships integrate physical aspects of sexuality with the "whole person." Their arguments give more credibility to lifelong commitments insofar as the "whole person" and his or her "integration" are matters of a lifetime, but the necessity of sexual-unity-as-marriage is hardly secure.

This theological personalism attempts to outrun (that is, out-subjectify) extra-marital sex on its own terms. If modern sex is an inter-subjective affair, modern personalists try to narrow the sexual context, by giving sexual subjectivity profound meaning and by arguing that marriage is the only context able to sustain it. Heterosexual intercourse is understood, in line with Hildebrand, as a total unity, integrating physical and psychological aspects of the person. Sex, then, becomes a basic sign of our humanity, created in the image of God as male and female. It is conceived as a sacrament of human community *as such*, a unique but still paradigmatic two-in-one flesh. *Eros* is celebrated as a natural (pre-social) drive to communion that transforms an otherwise isolated self. Sex is considered a foundational experience, basic to the true and social self.

Consider an example from a prominent writer (and Catholic-cultural icon) in the United States of America. Andrew Greeley, in cooperation with his sister, Mary Greeley Durkin, provides a good inter-subjective description of falling victim to love. While developing the idea that sex is a sacramental experience, Greeley and Durkin hold that falling in love is a humanizing encounter. "We feel a call to move beyond ourselves. Our beloved becomes the focus of our attention. Our self-complacency is shattered. Our independence is threatened. Yet we make no effort to resist the attraction" (Greeley and Durkin 1984: 115; see also Durkin 1983). Such passion moves us beyond reason, beyond our principles of autonomy, and beyond our need for security. Sexual desire moves two to become one flesh. "We delight in the discovery of this other person and experience a desire to be with her or him for the rest of our lives." With this natural movement, sex and our sexual relationship become sacramental. "Though we might not even be aware of it, when we fall in love we are involved in a deeply religious experience. Falling in love reveals for us the exciting possibilities in human existence. We are like Adam and Eve when they discover each other in the garden and are called to be the image (revelation) of God in Creation" (Greeley and Durkin 1984: 115).

While they focus on *eros*, Greeley and Durkin include personalist elements common to those who conceive of conjugal love in less passionate terms of companionship. Before Greeley and Durkin's lovers meet, they are self-complacent and independent, but love enters as an irresistible force that creates a community of two. Built into this narrative of love is a story of the "normal" or impersonal self. This self, pre-passion, is impersonal inasmuch as he or she is constrained by things as they are, by dominant forces of our impersonal world. Greeley and Durkin assume that self-contentment (complacent satisfaction) must be overturned by passion, by a force that comes from outside of our everyday world. The sexual self is the true social self, enlivened and made transparent in private moments of desire. Likewise, sexual desire must reproduce itself in order to sustain the sexual self. Although desire has the end of "self-giving," the self is a formal category with no identifiable content except its indomitable desire. Greeley and Durkin offer no account of how passion and their binary conception of the social self are, themselves, reproduced within an economy of desire. Love is set against the everyday; yet it creates the true social self from within. The personalist account sustains a dominant economy of desire, and insofar as it does, it reproduces the desire of its own undoing.

Fecundity and the Social Body

I have argued that sex is a means of social reproduction, and in the dominant "economy of desire," the social reproduction of desire must be concealed. Sexual desire appears as natural and a self-validating end-in-itself, so that the economy of desire is justified, it seems, by the needs of the unencumbered self. Sex offers liminal moments of pleasure, but it can never be satisfied as a matter of course, in the everyday world. Everyday we want to want more. This is a basic principle of life in the restless growth economy of late capitalism. Desire is enlivened by dissatisfaction, and sex is known to be gratifying when it reproduces more unsatisfied desire. The needs and mandates of reproductive desire present a critical challenge to any discussion of marriage and family, and particularly theological accounts of sex. As reproduced within the dominant social economy, sexual desire is undomesticated, that is, both natural and wild, pre-social and nomadic. The theology of marriage attempts to relocate sex and sexual desire, giving them a stable home, but the predominant theological personalism begins with a modern naturalism that continues, first, to conceal the social reproduction of desire, and second, to position fulfillment in liminal moments of other-worldly space.

My comments, in the introduction, about procreation and bodily agency offer a contrast to the reigning sexual subjectivity, but they have no necessary implications for conceptions of marriage and family. A starting point in procreative givens imposes no clear conclusions. Highly reproductive polygamy is probably the most logical next step. Theological proposals about marriage and family ought to be grounded in some account of our nature, but they hardly can be defended or secured by appeals to pre-social desire or nature *as such*. The best that can be said (not second to naturalism but better) is that Christian practices of marriage fit with wider practices of the Christian life, and when in good working order, they reproduce social practices that also define the church. Steadfast faithfulness in marriage, for instance, points to a grammar of bodily presence formed through the practices of the body of Christ.

When an argument is made from nature or the "givens" of sexual desire, it should take its route, not from the body to marriage, but through the practices of the social body to claims about human nature, family, and marriage. A natural defense of marriage, it seems to me, would begin with basic practices of the church as they represent and offer possibilities for human flourishing, and then would turn to how certain conceptions of marriage follow naturally from those basic practices. Fortunately for me, this is not my task. I need only indicate, first, how fecundity fits with a particular kind of social reproduction and, second, how procreation presents the social agency of the body.

First, the production of children locates sexual activity in the household. Household, in this regard, is not a synonym for the contemporary family or for filial relationships. While family is often defined by its affection, the household is a social and economic unit. It is constituted by people who share living space and meals, pool resources, and cooperate for mutual benefit. Not all households include children, but children make housekeeping unavoidable. While family is a relation, the household is a place. Householders without children are likely to (and ought to) occupy that same socially reproductive space. Through their commitments to home, they are taken out of the "economy of desire" and taken into a network of households in neighborhood and community. The household, set within the formative practices of the church, is an economy that is directed toward reproducing the social body and shaping the social self in imitation of Christ.

Quite different than the market economy, good housekeeping and household networks generate a subsistence economy that operates through gift-giving (1 Corinthians 11–13): through reciprocal, asymmetrical, and delayed systems of exchange. Children, for instance, return little of what they receive, and the social bond is extended by the disproportion and difference of giving without contractual return. The gift binds (Gouldner 1973: 241–2; Bourdieu 1977: 4–6: Milbank 1995). Equilibrium is achieved, not through immediate exchange or by compensation between individuals, but only over time, through generations perhaps and between households. Household activities encourage routine and entrenchment, but they are also characterized by a regular course of change. The young grow old, and the old grow older. Desire rises, diminishes, rises and diminishes again. In contrast to the static, adolescent character of the "economy of desire," sexual desire within the household is subsumed by the character of the life cycle.

Within the household, sexual desire is domesticated; that is, it follows the lead of common life. Couples will have their days or years of indomitable passion, mixed together with frequent times of minimal or subsistence-level desire. Childbearing and housekeeping show Hildebrand's romantic I-Thou to be an infrequent delight that is hardly a basis for love or community. The desires of the household are less directed to mutual self-absorption than to common, outwardly purposeful work. It is through the outward movement of shared activity where friendship and affection grow. In the "economy of desire," passion is work, and sexual desire is the end of social regeneration. In contrast, passion in the household, for its own sake, is only modestly regenerative. It is simply play, and because play, it is free to be nothing at all, that is, to be spontaneous. In good Pauline tradition, the practices of the household settle desire, and ironically, sexual practices are expected to exceed mutual desiring (1 Corinthians 7). Pauline access takes sex beyond desire and into mutual belonging.

Second, sexual reproduction is a basic activity of social belonging and possessiveness. Possessiveness carries negative connotations of control and domination, but when we refer, positively, to mothers and daughters, husbands and brothers, we use the possessive pronouns "my" and "our." We belong. Childbearing is the concrete "bone of my bone, flesh of my flesh" from which nuptial unity and social "brotherhood" gain their meaning as analogies. Marriage is a derivative social relation. When making reference to fecundity, theological personalism reverses the primacy of procreation and moves toward abstraction, toward making children a symbol of a married couple's prior unity and vocation in community (see, for example, Hanigan 1988: 89–112). Here, fecundity bypasses procreation in favor of more abstract social productivity. As a result, the personalist strategy considers the body a symbol as well. In Hildebrand, Greeley–Durkin, and others, the body symbolizes a psychological/personal relationship, so that a single sexual act (the heterosexual act) is conceived as a sign, trope, and ritual display of "total" human communion and the social body *as such*. The meaning of the body's continuing agency, in this sense, is merely a repetition of the initial unifying act. It is a liminal return to original, psychological unity.

Childbearing, in comparison, sets bodily agency within the protracted setting of the household. In this regard, we can say that gestation and childbirth do not mark a difference between men and women, as much as they reveal the common character of sexual desire in the context of housekeeping and the irregular reciprocity that children require of community. Procreation gets us into something that extends over a lifetime and puts a common venture upon us. In contrast to the abstract unity of personalism, fecundity gives common life an open-ended and fluid character. Sexual practices are unified, not by a single ideal meaning, but by their context in the course of common life. Some nuptial acts might be uninteresting, while others might be exhilarating; some might express a deep sense of unity, while others might simply relieve sexual tension; some acts and relationships are pro-creative, while others are not. Some couples might hardly have sex at all. Sex may have no consistent psychological or personalist symbolism, but it is a binding of the body. A procrea-tive social economy cultivates a bodily desire for belonging, a desire to be "bone of my bone, flesh of my flesh." Sexual practices take on the grammar of shared life (for richer and for poorer), sleeping in the same bed, breaking bread, and carrying on bodily presence in sickness and in health.

Sex, within practices of the church, is analogous to the body-language of adoption. Adoption is not symbolic of childbirth, but the day-to-day bodily presence that makes us who we are. Monogamy and practices of fidelity and lifelong endurance are a way of the body, a cultivation of intimacy and mutual possession through the everyday agency of our embodiment. We bear each other's presence. Through our bodily agency, we belong over time such that our presence cannot be exchanged for another. Through this binding, our bodies are made and made known. In this way, sexual practices are intrinsically fecund.

Part III

Queer Origins

Chapter 6

Eros and Emergence

Catherine Pickstock

Ever since Plato, philosophy has seen that there is a profound link between the question of knowledge and the question of desire. Why is it that we desire at all, when it involves so much labor? And is the question of the motivation of learning a clue to the nature of knowledge as such? This link is particularly apparent in Plato's *Meno*, one of the most important loci for the Platonic doctrine of recollection. Socrates' interlocutor Meno puts to him a problem which has come to be known as the "aporia of learning":

> Why, on what lines will you look, Socrates, for a thing of whose nature you know nothing at all? Pray, what sort of thing, amongst those that you know not, will you treat us to as the object of your search? Or even supposing, at the best, that you hit upon it, how will you know it is the thing you did not know? (Plato 1924: 80d)

This presents a double problematic: how can one seek to find out about that of which one is ignorant? How does one recognize a truth when one finds it, if previously one had been ignorant of this truth? As everyone knows, Socrates' solution to both sides of the *aporia* is to argue that before birth, our souls possessed perfect understanding, and that the process of human learning in time is less a matter of new discovery than of remembering. He dramatically argues for this solution by putting a slave-boy through his geometric paces, and shows that, untaught, he can derive new conclusions from a few given postulates.

Very often this argument has been seen as fallacious. Equally often, it has been regarded as a mythical presentation of a doctrine of *a priori* understanding. It makes sense, it is contended, for Socrates to argue that geometric knowledge is "in" the boy's soul already, in the sense that the mind applies logical principles which in some sense are pre-inscribed within the mind – whether transcendentally, or psychologically, or in terms of the mind's access to some sort of logical universe – rather than being discovered empirically. But the myth of pre-existence is entirely excessive to the truth of this argument: in consequence, the myth represents either Plato's merely half-grasp of the notion of an *a priori*, or else just a colorful and rhetorical presentation of the latter.

These common readings all suppose that the dialogue "resolves" the *aporia* in a straightforward fashion. In effect, this overcomes and explains the moment of desire in the process of learning. Socrates, according to the mythical mode of presentation, desires to know what he does not know, because once in a previous life his soul had been perfectly acquainted with the thing, and therefore had no need of any desire to know it. The more he is able to recall this knowledge, the more his desire to know is outrun and becomes redundant. He is now replete with knowledge, so he no longer desires to know. Demythologized, this means that Socrates recovers through reflection his innate understanding. In this process, desire is once again fulfilled and thereby once again canceled.

But is this really what the dialogue says? In his *Confessions* (I.i), Augustine famously presents a Christian version of the problematic of the *Meno* (of which he was unacquainted in its original version). He asks how he can search for God, call upon him, without God being already present. Augustine presents a double answer in the long course of the text: he can search for God because God has already rendered himself present to his mind in every act of thinking; to be able to think is to be illuminated by the divine light. However, for Augustine, this light has been severely impaired by sin, and must now be mediated to us again through divine grace conveyed by the church. Augustine knows to search for God because he has heard from a teacher of the complete descent of the divine light upon earth in the Incarnation.

Thus one could say that in the *Confessions* the Platonic doctrine of recollection is reworked as the theory of illumination and that this is supplemented in terms of the historical exigency of revelation.

However, a rereading of the *Meno* suggests that the contrast between the Augustinian reworking and the Platonic original can be overdrawn. Meno derives the following from his problematic skeptical conclusions: learning is impossible because either we know something already, or if we do not, we are unaware of our ignorance and so do not seek to remedy it. Socrates claims that he is able to refute this skeptical implication. However, he does not in the first place offer an argument; instead, he says that he has "heard the sayings of men and women who were wise, and knowing in divine things" and that these people were "priests and priestesses" whose teachings are also found in "Pindar and many other of the poets." These sayings concern the doctrine of the immortality and transmigration of souls (Plato 1924: 81b).

Is this dramatic aspect of the dialogue itself part of the merely colorful and rhetorical invocation of myth? Perhaps, but two points may give us pause. First of all, the priests and priestesses are said to have "made it their business to be able to give a rational account of those things in which they were employed" (Plato 1924: 81b). It seems then that their teaching is not to be regarded as a mere *mythos* but is already a *logos*. These learned people had a rationally reflective relation to the rituals and stories of which they were the conveyors. This circumstance may suggest (though does not by itself prove) that Plato did not see any sharp separation between the religious and the philosophical realms of discourse.

In the second place, the artfully literary character of the Platonic dialogues renders it certain that Plato deliberately insinuates a parallel between the problematic "desiring to know" involved in all learning, on the one hand, and Socrates' claiming to possess the solution to this problematic because he has been taught it, on the other. One trivial solution to the *aporia*, but also one aspect of any solution, is that we seek to know about something because we have been informed of it. A child may seek to know what a molecule is because by chance one day she hears the word "molecule" uttered. Or she may know that Africa is a country but no more, and seek in her Atlas to find out where it is and who lives there. It cannot be accidental that Socrates invokes the fact of teaching at this point. Indeed, that he has been taught the solution to the *aporia* of learning itself, in part performatively resolves the *aporia*. However, exactly like Augustine in this respect, he does not simply invoke any old teaching, but rather the teaching of a divinely revealed tradition. And as with Augustine, this sacred pedagogy forms a third term linking the "education" solution to the *aporia* with the "recollection/illumination" solution. And in either case, the reader is left wondering how this third term of linkage works: would not education on its own work as a solution (albeit a relativistic one)? Or else, recollection/illumination on its own? Why does an ontological solution need a historicist supplement? Is there not more a kind of mutual redundancy than a complementarity present here?

Leaving the latter issue in suspense for the moment, one can nevertheless say that Socrates' dramatic narrative suggests that the religious/mythic dimension is for Plato essential to the philosophic dimension. To confirm this suggestion, however, it would be necessary to show that his philosophical understanding of human knowledge in this dialogue does indeed require such a dimension.

But it is possible to demonstrate just this point. It requires taking Socrates at his word, which in this case there is no reason to doubt. Crucial here are the details of the geometric example. It is not the boy's manifestation of new and untaught knowledge which for Socrates alone demonstrates recollection. To the contrary, Socrates brings the boy to the point where he thinks that he should be able to discover certain pieces of geometric knowledge which at the outset he would not have supposed himself able to find out. This circumstance confirms the role of the teacher in the unraveling of the *aporia*, now in a more mundane context. Plato does not, here or elsewhere, like Descartes or Kant suggest that we can scour the recesses of our soul to excavate units of wisdom by remaining in solitary confinement. To the contrary, for Plato recollection is triggered by a human encounter, whether pedagogic or erotic or both. But if this is the case, then one may ask why a mere invocation of the *a priori* should require such a trigger? (Chrétien 2002: 1–40). The operation of the triggers seems much more to sublimate ordinary empirical recollection of lost facts. For example, only the chance meeting again with a person after many years may allow us to recall their face and voice. By contrast, even if we have forgotten our nine times table, we retain the innate resources to reconstruct it in any circumstances. Hence Plato's constant recourse to "triggers" is of a piece with his invocation of the role of teaching in relation to recall and suggests that the mediation of teaching is essential to recollection.

However, there is a further point to be made. Socrates not only causes the boy to recollect; he also stuns the boy, following his gadfly reputation, bringing him to the point where he thinks he should be able to find something out but cannot in fact do so. And this is what Socrates offers as his proof: namely, that he has taught the boy a desiring ignorance that is also an obscure sort of inkling as to knowledge: "from this sense of his ignorance, he will find out the truth in searching for it with me" (Plato 1924: 84c). This example does not dispel the mists of the *aporia* of learning so much as reproduce dramatically the circumstances of this *aporia*. Because the *aporia* persists, one must have recourse to a mythical solution. It is in this way that Plato's philosophical position regarding knowledge is also ineliminably a religious one. The argument for recollection does not proceed as follows: the boy has desire for the unknown because deep in his soul he already knows this thing (although the later Plotinian reading of recollection somewhat anticipates the *a priori*, whereas Proclus, by contrast, appeals to the "mythical/ritual" account). Rather, it proceeds as follows: the boy has desire for the unknown because this desire is an aspect of a memory of something primordial and pre-historical and so strictly speaking inaccessible and not entirely re-memorable at all. On this reading, desire is not the mask of a concealed awareness; rather desire is the only thing that allows any initial cognitive awareness whatsoever.

If memory of a pre-existent knowledge is also at one with a desire to recover this knowledge, and this desire is precipitated when we are stunned into ignorance by a teacher trying to incite our desire, then desire here is akin to an obscure oracular revelation, a harbinger of a mystery into which the slave-boy is initiated by Socrates. Of course, one can object here that, in the end, the boy moves beyond ignorance and arrives at the knowledge he sought, thereby canceling his desire. However, geometric figures and arithmetical numbers, as we are told in the *Republic*, lie beneath the realm of the absolute abiding truth of the Forms (Plato 1936: V, 106e). They are more accessible than the latter, and knowledge of them is repeatedly seen by Plato as merely illustrative of knowledge of the Forms. If one can indeed have full *episteme* of mathematical realities, and so eventually cancel desire – even if one has to pass through an inescapably mysterious moment of inspiration by the muses even in mathematics, wherein one does not yet know that for which one seeks, like Meno's slave-boy – this may not be true of the Forms themselves.

This is suggested in the *Meno*. Socrates here, as elsewhere, proclaims his ignorance: he is himself like the slave-boy as one "stunned" – by the priests and priestesses, by his own reflections, just as he stuns others, in this way resembling the "torpedo fish" (Plato 1924: 80b–d; 84b). However, this condition of ignorance does not reside in a hostile relation with the condition of knowledge of the Forms; to the contrary, Socrates repeatedly indicates that such ignorance is itself just that other knowledge which is the knowledge of recollection and of the Forms. In order to show this other knowledge, he first reduces the boy to a simulacrum of his own ignorance. The Forms are recalled precisely through the operation of a desiring ignorance: the desire for absolute timeless truth, for *episteme*. But, as in the case of mathematics, can one fully recover this truth and leave desire behind? The answer is no. Socrates presents even his "other" knowledge of the Forms as only an "*orthos doxa*," a true opinion falling short of grasped certainty. Only in one paradoxical respect does he claim to exceed *orthos doxa* – namely, in knowing the difference between this and that absolute *episteme* which belongs to the pure beholding of the Forms: "for my part, I speak not thus [he has just said that in true *episteme* one thing follows from another like a chain of magnets] from knowledge; but only from conjecture. But that right opinion and science are two different things, this, as it appears to me, I do not merely imagine or conjecture" (Plato 1924: 98b).

It follows that Socrates' knowledge of the Forms is akin to a kind of religious belief and divine inspiration. This opens the possibility that his overall argument is that outside such belief, skeptical arguments would indeed be valid. On this view, the mythical dimension is essential to Plato's philosophy: it is a necessary way of going on speaking in order to try to illuminate the fact that we think we know and try to know, even though we cannot really ever envisage what makes our knowing and learning possible. To learn and to know are to participate in divine inspiration and this is mediated to us externally as much as internally. This is why the "teaching" and the "recollection" solutions to the *aporia* of learning are complementary rather than mutually redundant.

If this reading is correct, it is perhaps supported by the main argument of the *Meno*. What is primarily at issue here is the nature of virtue. The dialogue moves to show that virtue comes neither by nature nor by nurture: unlike other modes of excellence, there can be no discipline directly concerned with teaching virtue as a practice – as opposed to the philosophical study of "ethics" (Plato 1924: 95c). Yet, if virtue belongs to wisdom, this appears to be contradictory. Socrates rules out the idea that the wisdom involved is any sort of certain *episteme*; rather, it is a matter of approximate *phronesis* deployed in specific situations, and of a securing of justice in a manner for which no exhaustive rules can be found. Virtue then, although it is knowledge of the Good (the highest of the Forms according to the *Republic*), is a matter of *orthos doxa* rather than certainty. Moreover, it is a rather extreme mode of the former, since it cannot be taught. It seems that one cannot here offer even approximative guidelines (and this sounds more extreme than Aristotle). In consequence,

Socrates concludes that virtue "must come by a divine portion or allotment" and there is no real reason to view this conclusion as ironic, given Socrates' association of his own wisdom with divine inspiration (Plato 1924: 99c–d, 99e).

This interpretation also fits with Socrates' claim that "true opinion" can be every bit as good as firm knowledge. This is because, if an opinion is "true," its truth is no less than the same truth known with final certainty. However, one could only in practice make this equation if something like faith or trust made up the difference between opinion and certainty. Only the sense of a divine presence of some kind can elicit such a trust.

The recollection of the Good to produce virtue is clearly central for Plato. Yet this is a matter of something triggered by examples of the beautiful which cannot be taught, at least in any normal fashion. Here, desire for knowledge persists even in the partial holding of knowledge, because this is a matter of the obscure reception of a divine gift. Indeed, were virtue teachable, then it would most likely be definable as something like "good government," which Meno favors, and would concern the pragmatic logic of strength (in the city, in the individual). According to the logic which Meno indicates, virtue might or might not be just: but for Socrates, virtue is always just as it is always prudent. But virtue as always just is a matter of harmonious distribution of goods as much as it is a matter of strength and self-control. This renders the display of the Good as beautiful indispensable for our sense of virtue and tied to a judgment of the harmonious for which there are no rules but is rather a gift of the muses.

Against this reading of the *Meno*, it might be argued that Socrates wishes ironically to contrast those currently good in a hit or miss way by "inspiration," with the figure he invokes at the end of the dialogue who would be "as it were the truth and substance of things, compared with shadows, in respect of virtue" (Plato 1924: 100a). This man, whom one must assume to be somewhat akin to the philosopher-king of the *Republic*, would indeed be "capable of making another man a good politician"; in other words, of teaching virtue, presumably by both example and counsel. However, Socrates never denigrates entirely the existence of a sporadic and unsystematic virtue, and, as we have seen, he indicates that even philosophy cannot entirely escape the realm of mere *doxa*. So how can one resolve this?

The clue may well lie in the invocation of the learned priests and priestesses who reflect on their religious performances. Just as they do not thereby render those performances superfluous, so also the philosopher does not stand any less in need of divine gift as regards virtue: it is more that he has a more reflexive and conscious awareness of the source of virtue as the heaven of the Forms, and intimates somewhat more of the "magnetic" link between the Form of the Good and examples of virtue. Since these examples, as we see in the *Meno*, are highly various and this is part of the reason why virtue cannot be taught, the philosopher's stronger sense of this link perhaps provides the clue as to why he, after all, can teach virtue. It is because he is in this respect, as in all others, a generalist.

One can go a little further than this by invoking the discussions which take place in the *Ion*. The issues here can be seen in parallel with those of the *Meno* because, once more, it is a question of inspiration versus science. Socrates suggests that the rhapsode Ion owes his wisdom to divine inspiration rather than to any sort of *episteme*. It can be suggested that this is not to be taken ironically (or at least entirely ironically) if one bears in mind the implications of Socrates' view of rhapsody for his view of philosophy. Ion does not possess *episteme* for two opposite reasons. First, his knowledge is far too particular (Plato 1925b: 533d–e). He only knows about Homer, and in this respect is like the poets on whom he is parasitic. Poets are confined to lyric, epic, or tragic genres, according to the different inspirations they receive from different muses. Rhapsodes cling to the skirts of inspired poets in the manner of components of a chain of magnets – there is an echo here of the chain of epistemic reasonings in the *Meno*, according to which "deduction" may be closely linked with "inspiration" in Plato's mind – or wild dancing intoxicated corybants. Thus Ion is able by inspiration to speak of Homer, even though, were he really speaking in a learned scientific manner, he could only speak of Homer by comparing him with other poets, and the same skills he applies to Homer should be applicable elsewhere.

Yet, inversely, his knowledge is far too universal. Homer's *Iliad* can be broken down into descriptions of fighting, navigation, charioteering and so forth: experts in all these areas, says Socrates, should be able to speak of these passages with far more sophistication than Ion (Plato 1925b: 536d–542b). The latter protests that he is an expert on "Homer" and not on chariots; Socrates responds that Homer can only be the sum of his parts. If, nevertheless, Ion has a mysterious capacity to speak regarding the "whole" of Homer, then once again this must be a strange divine gift.

Here one is reminded of the question of the nature of ruling or politics in itself in *Republic* I and II. To be more than a power-play, it seems to need a content, yet has none (Ophir 1991). In that dialogue, Plato eventually provides a content, in terms of the contemplation of the Forms and application of this vision via the exercise of *phronesis* to the life of the city. This reveals that the question of a strange knowledge of the whole in excess of that whole's parts is a question that applies most of all to philosophy which claims to know about everything, even though, once again, such knowledge would appear to be both amateur and redundant given a division of academic labor among experts. It is no wonder that Plato invokes the issue of the likely expulsion of the philosopher from the *polis* where he can only ever appear (if he is true to himself) as an imposter, a sophist, a show-off and seducer. These apparent crimes conceal his standing in a heavenly presence which cannot of course appear to view, but which provides him after all with a role and a specific way of talking about the general. Finally, this comes down to the following: it may be that there are only goods, only beings and only truths and only beauties. But the philosopher is one who envisages the Good itself and relentlessly shows that without this, the specific goods are so diverse as not to merit the name good at all, in such a way that virtue nihilistically evaporates, along with truth, being, beauty, and unity.

In a certain sense, then, the figure of the rhapsode is a foil for the figure of the philosopher and provides an allegory for all human understanding. The latter as expert of a particularity has not the benefit of comparison or generally applicable method and therefore his expertise can only be possible as an inexplicable kind of knack; a form of "tacit understanding" as one might now say. But the more it becomes universal, the more it appears to become vacuous, unless it possesses an even stronger degree of divine inspiration; a sense of the analogical derivation of diverse particulars from a common eternal source.

This is perhaps why Plato saw even philosophy, or rather especially philosophy, to be a "musical" art and a "musical" discourse. One can now read the *Meno* as saying that those virtuous without philosophy are still virtuous in a somewhat merely particular way and are therefore inspired by the Muses; while those truly virtuous in a universal way are philosophers or philosopher-kings, and therefore also inspired by the Muses.

Plato can in consequence be read as deconstructing the claims of both particular and general knowledge to be purely human and immanent. Only if it displays always the divinely inspired arts of the muses can it possess any truth and banish the shadow of skepticism. In ancient Athens, it seems, there were no humanists, only materialists in contrast to religious "postmodernists."

Amongst the latter, for Plato, the highest knowledge remained a matter of desiring, because it remained a matter of divine inspiration.

Eros

So far, we have seen that for Plato desire is always involved in human knowing. We have also seen that a desire for knowledge is provoked initially by desire for beauty. Several dialogues show that this is in the first place characteristically the physical beauty of a human other. It is clear that human erotic desire, and of course most often the *eros* of male for male, is crucial for Plato's account of human understanding. But does this mean that he is not interested in the biologically and often culturally unavoidable link between desire and giving birth present in human heterosexuality?

The answer to this question may lie in the *Symposium*. If Plato clarifies the nature of knowledge by showing its link to desire, he seeks to clarify the nature of desire by showing its link to birth, or to the phenomenon of "emergence." But this second clarification redounds dramatically upon the first. It might seem that the ideal goal of recollection is to leave behind the "triggers" as so many temporarily necessary instruments, and gradually to abandon desire in the intensified serenity of contemplation. Even if the exigency of the triggers suggests that the theory of recollection requires a certain positive validation of time, the latter is still to be left behind, and the trope of this dismissal is the idea of a pre-historic eternal past for which one forsakes both the present and the future. This is how Kierkegaard read, respectfully, the Socratic theory, contrasting retrospective recollection with forwards repetition, where the latter, in looking to the future eschaton, establishes an ideal consistency not through melancholic recovery of the lost, but rather through sustained commitments through time forming a kind of liturgical patterning (Kierkegaard 1985).

However, as Jean-Louis Chrétien (2002) and others have argued, something akin to Kierkegaardian repetition is already envisaged by Plato. This is particularly shown in the *Symposium*. If it were the case that desire were only a kind of melancholic lack, then desire would be asymptotically banished the more recollection was engaged. The model for this manner of relating desire to knowledge is a certain conception of inter-human love. For this conception, one desires the other and then this desire is satisfied by her presence, and the fullness of this presence. Desire in this way is consummated, satisfied and vanishes. But is desire only desire to know or desire to "meet" (in every sense)? Is desire only desire for knowledge or desire for social and physical intercourse with the other? Is it only, as in either of these cases, desire for a withheld but nonetheless given distance? But in that case, what about desire to do something or make something or bring something about? Sometimes, one is not certain quite what one is desirous to bring to fruition; in fact (echoing the *Meno*'s problematic in another mode), this is perhaps always the case, because if one knew entirely the lineaments of the thing one desired to bring about, it would already be actualized and the desire would be superfluous.

One can complicate this question. Is desire to bring something about not also involved in the desire to know and the desire to meet the other? Do our souls merely look at knowledge, or do they also repeat it in bringing it forth? And is the meeting of the other only a mutual gaze or does something "happen" between the two? Is the meeting also an upshot? If the answer in both cases is yes, then desire is not in time asymptotically left behind; instead, if the more we know the Forms of truth, the more we give rise to the emergence of truth in the temporal future, then as long as we are alive in time, the vision of truth replenishes our desire. Likewise, the encounter with the other is needed not merely as the occasion for a recalling, but more radically as the seed of a new vision of the eternal which can only be nourished in just this soil.

This perspective would mean that the eternal is invoked not merely as a past that we can never fully recover but as always radically present to us in a way that we are not entirely aware of (though forgotten, it is also radically "unforgettable," as Chrétien puts it), but also as a future which we can never fully anticipate (a hope for the "unhoped for," as Chrétien says).

But in the *Symposium*, Plato offers just such a perspective which is complementary to his teaching on recollection. Desire does not just recall the absolute past; it also gives rise to, causes to emerge, the unreachable future. In this dialogue, he names *eros* the daimonic *metaxu*, the "between" (which he only otherwise alludes to in the *Philebus*), thereby revealing another dimension of his religious vision (Plato 1925a: 202a–e).

The *Symposium* shows that because we must reach forwards as well as backwards, we do not tend to cancel *eros* in favor of the primordial, but rather, at least in time, remain within the *metaxu*, in the midst of desire to which we must return if we wish to know and to encounter the truth.

How does Plato indicate this doctrine? First of all, through Socrates, he refuses the idea that love is a goddess and insists instead that it is a *daimon*. Perhaps one should take this religious assertion quite literally; perhaps it is an intrinsic aspect of Plato's philosophical treatment of love. This is in part confirmed by the association he sets up between a pre-philosophical, merely eulogistic treatment of love, and the view that love is a goddess. If love is a goddess, then she is ineffable and given and must be contemplated and praised.

Five different eulogies are given: by Phaedrus, Pausanius, Eryximachus, Aristophanes, and Agathon. In the first, love is seen as the unbegotten oldest goddess who motivates lovers to form the ideal city of devoted affines. In the second, love is seen as both the lustful earthly Aphrodite and the refined heavenly Aphrodite; the latter should be followed and this permits, as in Athens, persuasion of the beloved, in contrast to Western civic forcing of the beloved and oriental tyrannic denial of free wooing. In the third, a medical account by the physician Eryximachus, love is seen somewhat pre-socratically as a binding physical force. In the fourth, love is seen as a consequence of the primordial splitting of either male or else female or yet again hermaphroditic individuals, to produce respectively true males and females who are homoerotic, and heterosexuals whose attachment to their own sex is ambivalent. In the fifth (the exact opposite of the first view), love is seen as the youngest divinity, who gives rise to peace and harmony after an earlier reign of blind necessity which produced an agonistic cosmos.

Just as in the case of the rhapsode and the non-philosophic men of virtue, Socrates does not explicitly deny the truth of these eulogies. Indeed, it is arguable that he himself offers a synthesis of their respective emphases. For Socrates, following the same order: (1) love is unbegotten since it is the daimonic *metaxu* and love exists in multiple affinities (see Desmond 1995); (2) we should indeed follow a higher *eros* (though he is a *daimon* and not a goddess) and the civilized Athenian codes of courtship; (3) *eros* is also a cosmic binding force; (4) homoeroticism is higher than heteroeroticism; (5) love is not really eldest since it mediates the divinities and in this sense is "younger" than them.

Socrates' account of love is not a eulogy, but an exercise in dialectics. However, unlike the eulogists, who seem to lay claim to direct musical inspiration, Socrates provides mediated cultic credentials for his claims. Once more, he invokes a meeting with a teacher: this time, the prophetess Diotima, whom he says taught him the art of dialectics, although she is also presented without qualm as a magician who held the plague away from Athens for ten years by propitiatory sacrifice. (Perhaps we must hermeneutically assume that "doing dialectics" and "performing magic" were for Plato in some kind of natural alignment, unless there is evidence to the contrary.) At the same time as teaching Socrates dialectics, Diotima also taught him that love is a *daimon* and that it is productive. One must assume, then, that there is an intimate connection between three things: Diotima's unusual (for Plato) femaleness; dialectics; and the "female" view of desire as substantive rather than as a lack: a kind of pregnancy which brings to birth. This may well imply that knowledge is something produced through desire as well as something longed-for and recollected through ardor.

Instead of eulogy, Socrates offers a dialectic of love which remains nonetheless to some extent a eulogy and a "mythos" of love, for Socrates offers his own personification of *eros* and a narrative account of its origin. There is, however, an important match between the dialectical argumentative form of Socrates' discourse and the substance of what his discourse is about, namely love. First of all, the idea that love is a *daimon* that mediates between the higher and the lower corresponds with the idea of a dialectical and contemplative ascent. Marcel Detienne has shown how the Pythagorean/Platonic tradition inherited an ancient form of religiosity which concerned the "voyaging" of the soul to transworldly regions rather than the official Greek civic cults (Detienne 1963). Secondly, whereas the eulogists present love in "spatial" terms as a given state of affairs, Socrates stresses that desire is a movement and a striving, and points out that for this reason it is involved in all human practical and theoretical activities and not just in the field of "romance" as we might now designate it. Thus, if the *Meno* deals with knowledge and virtue in terms of desire, the *Symposium* refers desire to knowledge and to virtue.

In Socrates' myth of *eros*, love was born at the same time as the goddess Aphrodite and this ensures the occult bond between love and beauty. However, love itself is not a goddess but a *daimon* who hovers "between" beauty and ugliness, good and bad, gods and mortals. As belonging to the realm of the *metaxu*, love also belongs properly to *orthos doxa* and not to heavenly *episteme*. It is to do with the lure towards the Forms. However, it is also linked with bringing to birth a life that expresses the truth of the Forms. It is important that love is not primordial and ungenerated, as for Phaedrus in the first eulogy. Love itself is brought to birth, love itself emerges and is therefore not just a "given," nor something drawn towards another given. Rather, it is itself an emerging event. As something born, it does nevertheless emerge from lack and need, and indeed Socrates points up this deficient, possibly tragic and "ugly" dimension of love in opposition to his interlocutors. He indicates a certain alliance of love with time and becoming. However, for Socrates this alliance has also another positive and creative dimension. If love is the child of its mother, "lack" (here the associations are with the womb and also with the fertile ignorance taught by Diotima, into which Socrates has been "initiated") is also the child of its father "resource." In accordance with aspects of Greek biology, the positive aspects of giving birth are associated by Plato with the male part, just as later in the dialogue he speaks of the consummation of male heterosexual love as itself a giving birth and realization of a "pregnancy." The same thing applies analogically to male homoerotic love (the Greeks arguably did not have the concept of this as "sexual," even though it could be physical), where in a higher spiritual sense, something is conceived and delivered. As also the child of resource, desire is not simply lacking the other, but rather is lacking what it can itself bring into being through its own powers (one could compare the emphases of Deleuze and Guattari at this juncture).

Eros is therefore dynamic. It responds to the other but also generates itself. It constantly "dies and rises." It is not simply provoked by the presence of the beautiful, as if this were something love merely pursued; rather, to love is to "bring forth upon the beautiful, both in body and in the soul" (Plato 1925a: 206e). So although love is instigated by the beautiful, it also further emerges in conjunction with the beautiful, repeating in time the birth of the *daimon eros*. To love the beautiful is always already to copulate with the beautiful and to engender a child. Diotima famously speaks of an erotic ascent: one must begin with desire of a beautiful body; ascend to love of all physical beauty; then to the spiritual beauty of souls and institutions and finally to the eternal beauty of truth (Plato 1925a: 210a–e). This can sound as if finite beauties are mere occasions and instruments to be left behind. However, this would be to read the *Symposium* only in terms of the "backwards recollection" of the *Meno*. To the contrary, in this dialogue, worldly beauty does not just remind us of the spiritual; it causes us to become conjoined with it and engender both new physical realities in time and new psychic realities which also emerge into being for us through the course of time, since for Plato our soul (unlike for Plotinus later) lies for now within time. One can suggest that the "occasions" for bringing to birth remain necessary (since we do not arrive at a full *episteme* of the Forms) and must constantly be returned to. This reading would align the *Symposium* with the *Phaedrus* where it is said that erotic alliances on earth remain even in heaven. Since, one can infer, *eros* even as a heavenly reality is generated on a transcendent occasion, all earthly occasions and births are finally gathered up into this transcendental event.

In the *Symposium*, Plato does not see the satisfaction of desire as merely the possession of the object of desire. Rather, he sees it also as the "end" of a "travail," the delivery of an expression of self that was always bursting to come forth but could only do so by way of the other "on the body of the beautiful" (Plato 1925a: 206c). This event is an expression of knowledge and of wisdom. Because it can only emerge by way of the other, it is also the emergence of a third thing that could only arise by way of a relational conjunction. This moves beyond the finality of the circuit of reciprocity. What any two desire in desiring a union is not merely this union, but always also the fruit of this union in whatever sense, something that is both them and neither of them: a baby, a work of practice or understanding, a new ethos that others may also inhabit. In this way, for Plato, desire welds together inseparably both erotic gift-exchange, and the "agapeic" offering of a new gift to "anyone" that does not return to the givers in any ordinary fashion.

Emergence

From Plato we have learned that desire is not merely a matter of being drawn by the attractive, the beautiful and of a lack which must be fulfilled. It is equally a matter of travail, of expectant and obscure pregnancy, of frustration in something one is trying to say, make, or do. If desire is about "sex," it is equally about "birth." But both aspects are always present: "to have sex" is "to bring to birth." To "bring to birth" is to enter into a new erotic union with the world in some fashion.

But if the dimension of lack has been often explored, we understand less about the phenomenon of emergence. Likewise, applying desire to knowledge, we know more about "backwards recollection" than "forwards repetition." How are we to understand emergence?

The first thing to see here is that emergence is more fundamental than causality. In physical and cultural reality, there are genuinely new occurrences which cannot be deciphered merely in the terms of that from which they proceed. Indeed, one might say that unless causality is only a banal and mysterious repetition, causality itself involves emergence, because when something is a cause, it has mutated and emanated beyond itself. If something is acting as a cause, it has developed in some way. This is only predictable if one includes the development or the tendency to develop in the definition of the causing agent itself. One has to factor in the incalculable. As soon as one recognizes that there are such radical new events in reality, and that the ordinary is also newness, then one has to allow that emergence is a more fundamental phenomenon than causality.

It might seem, therefore, as if the notion of emergence marks a postmodern consciousness, and the end of an ultimately theological view which explains the world in terms of preceding causes and intentions. One can interpret the Enlightenment perspective as a secularized version of this outlook in which both teleology and eschatology seem to be linked with the notion of an all-governing intention or plan. This remains the case even where the intention or plan is immanentized and depersonalized.

Presently, I will somewhat question this assumption. But let it for the moment stand. One can in any case venture that the notion of emergence can be seen as postmodern insofar as it destabilizes reality and opens up aporias. This can be seen in relation to space, time, and the processes of subjectivity.

First of all, in terms of space. The very word "emergence" is instructive here. It was first used in relation to the distillation of something from a liquid. It is linked therefore to chemistry, which, since the days of alchemy, has been the mysterious sphere of physical properties not reducible to physical operations, at least in the sense of mechanical operations. It often seems to be concerned with merely describable phenomenal properties – color, viscosity, smell, corrosive effects, and so forth. It is in fact the sphere of emergent properties. The latter are curiously elemental, and yet also already secondary. The word also suggests things coming out of the sea, yet it does not denote the coming-to-the-surface of concealed sea-creatures. Rather, it suggests things that are only defined when they do come to the surface.

This is an arrival in a radical sense. It does not betoken the invocation of another reality apart from the sphere of emergence, as would be the case when one adds one brick to another brick, and a wall starts to take shape. Rather, something new arises in an unexpected way merely from given resources. Nothing is really added, because this would suggest something coming from outside; yet neither is this predictable from within because the new thing needs the space into which it emerges, the externalizing action, in order to define itself.

One would in consequence be tempted to speak of a mutation, but even this is not quite right, because it would suggest something unfolding from within, perhaps like a butterfly from a chrysalis. Yet this cannot apply, because the emergent thing is definitely a new reality in its own right, with no traceable continuity of a developmental or mechanical sort with what went before.

Here is the problem of something new in space that is not from pre-given space, nor from super-added space. There seems to be no space anywhere for the emergent event, perhaps because it is what provides space in the first place. The problem is compounded by the fact that an emergent thing must be in some way connected with what went before, otherwise it would not be recognizable at all. Something wholly discontinuous could not be described or deciphered in any available categories whatsoever. So, we would simply not know about it. This raises the problem of the link between objective emergence and subjective recognition of emerging things. Nevertheless, the sense of continuity involved here will of necessity be very incomplete, and we will go on having to debate its nature (because it cannot be reduced).

This kind of connection between an antecedent and a consequent more or less defines the relation of passage from past to present, and so we cannot think through the problems of spatial emergence without invoking, in the second place, temporal emergence.

Here, we can only see a present event if we connect it in some way with what has gone before, and yet the present event was neither hidden in the past, nor is it added to the past, as it were, from another past; rather, the present emerges from the past and the future. But just as we saw that there is no space for emergence, so equally there is no time for emergence. The present moment, as soon as it occurs, takes on the aspect of something that was already there and somehow we had failed to notice – and this accounts for our odd sense of inevitability about things, and maybe for a sense of the uncanny or *déjà vu*. For just the same reason, the present moment has already transgressed on the sphere of the future, as if it were added to the past from the future. One can see this as the aporetic impossibility of presence.

But, more radically, one can also see this as the unthinkable primacy of presence, which is what gives rise to time in the first place. We may not be able to think presence and emergence, and yet we can live them and inhabit them, and thereby we somehow prove their reality beyond the inverted rationalisms of deconstruction.

This is of relevance, in the third place, to the question of subjectivity. First of all, the subjective "I" is also something only emergent. Its specificity and ability to reflect is an intense example of something that arises from the past and yet in an unpredictable fashion. Secondly, the subject is tangled up in the problems of space and time as just delineated. It emerges within space and time problematically, and its peculiarity is that it can reflect upon its emergence, as Judith Butler (2003) has indicated. As she also argues, the subject cannot perfectly carry out this reflection because emergence is an inexplicable phenomenon, and therefore the constitution of the subject is always more primary than its reflective reconstitution, even though the latter is always going on from the subject's birth, like a kind of emergence from emergence (perhaps rather like a return to the sea).

This inability to catch up with itself does not just apply to the past, which tends to be the compass of psychoanalysis. It also applies to present and future intentions. One often finds oneself saying "it has occurred to me that . . . "; this phrase exposes the way in which we are not in command of our ideas; they come to us almost as if from without, and Plato, as we have seen, for this reason thought of knowledge and all "arts" as derived from divine inspiration. We can exercise a kind of secondary censorship or editorial role, but that is all.

It is very extraordinary that most thought hitherto, forgetting Plato, does not seem to take much account of this state of affairs. What seems to be the case is that responsible thinking involves a kind of state of mystical responsive receptiveness, rather than technical control. Martin Seel is right to suggest that all of human activity is in the situation of creative art where we do not quite know what it is that we are bringing about (Seel 2003). In all our activity, ethical and political, as well as artistic, we seem almost to be spectators of emergent processes.

Yet just because emergence is not something pre-given, this is not quite true: in subtle ways that we cannot scrutinize, we elicit emergence, and we are able to refuse or accept an emergent thing in the name of a norm that seems to be itself only emergent. The fact that to recognize a new emergent object we must develop a new emergent capacity to recognize what emerges, suggests that there is a kinship between the deepest dimension of reality that is radical innovation and thought itself. As Plato indicated, knowledge is bound up with an obscure desire, both for what has always been there, and for an emerging which anticipates an eternal future.

Without this Platonic "postmodernism," then, it would seem that the priority of emergence opens up a chaotic or nihilistic prospect. It might seem to do so, if nothing is commanded in advance, and nothing occurs according to a graspable teleology. One might read the situation in terms of the rule of a random flux that throws up everything beyond the reach of choice or reason. However, this is not really what happens, according to the phenomenology of emergence in human culture. Rather, it seems to disclose an order beyond disorder which we cannot fully grasp.

We have already seen this in various ways: to be emergent, the radically new thing not only reveals its own new logic, but reorders the past in terms of this new logic, so that we can make some – but never perfect – sense of the reality of the thing's emergence. This is perhaps most intensely true in the sphere of the creative arts, where we are confronted with radically new things which nonetheless make sense to us, and to some extent cohere with what we already knew about. This does not mean that we are awakened to a logic we should already have known about, because the new way of looking at things is inseparable from the new beautiful object which we apprehend.

Is one to say, then, that this new meaning is simply a willed meaning, or else a kind of impersonal arbitrariness of which we are the passive recipient? The latter option would in effect negate the experience of art, or indeed the experience of a new social awareness. What we are confronted with here is the sense that something objective, as Alain Badiou acknowledges, has arrived, not from the past, in which it was hidden, nor from a concealed immanent eternity which was always available. We need these historical events to emerge if we are to see just this or that. As Badiou (2001) says, this is exactly like an event of grace.

Can this be a secular grace? It is hard to see how, because the secular alternatives of the permanently given, on the one hand, or the arbitrary, on the other, seem to be exhaustive. If the new compels us and redefines what went before, then, irreducibly, we have the sense of an arrival which cannot be from space, the past, or the future. To have this experience, and not to disbelieve it in a moment of rationalist deconstruction, is already to have entered in some fashion upon the field of theology. The arrival can only be the reflection in time of the eternal. In this way, only the eternal saves the new.

It is true that traditional theology did not fully recognize the paradigm of thought as occurrence, yet, at the same time, pre-modern theology did not have our modern reductive notion of causality. For example, neoplatonic emanation sees causation as development of that which is causal; what is more, the pre-Newtonian God was not seen as a God with a plan plus a series of whimsical interventions. Instead, for Thomas Aquinas, for example, God's thinking is only contained in the emergence of the *Logos* or the Son from the Father, which is like a kind of infinite comprehension within God of his external creative action. This does not proceed according to a plan, but it is itself the plan. God is only self-constrained by the beauty of what He tries to produce externally and internally. There is therefore a case for saying that for Thomas and much pre-modern theology, God is not before the emergent but is himself the eternally emergent act (but not in a Hegelian pre-determined sense, since he does not depend on his emergence); rather, God is the eternally emergent action which rescues finite emerging from arbitrariness or predictability, and therefore saves the phenomenology of the emergent (Kerr 2002: 181–207).

Trinity

If emergence resides in God himself for Thomas, it is because God is triune. In Plato we remain in the "between" of desire because we remain in *orthos doxa* and never attain to *episteme*. We remain in the realm of the daimonic sphere between gods and mortals. Our orientation to the eternal is both to a primordial past by recollection, and to a never-arriving future (since arrivals are in time) through emergence. The "between" of *eros* is for Plato also of heavenly birth or emergence; nevertheless, it is born to reside in a realm between the heavenly and the earthly.

In the Trinitarian conception, however, the daimonic is entirely the divine and not in any sense an ontological *lapsus*. God is lover, *eros*, and *agape*; the mutuality of Father and Son and the emergent unilateral gift of the Spirit. But the latter expresses the mutuality of Father and Son, and the mutuality only arises as the further emergence of the Spirit. Moreover, the mutuality is itself the birth of the Son from the Father in anticipation of and communion with the Spirit which will arise from the bond of Father with Son. Desire as aspiration and desire as emergence are complexly interwoven. The "between" of daimonic *eros*, in seeking the unforgettable past and the unhoped-for future, seeks itself alone, the eternal *metaxu*. It is also the case that Plato's later dialogues, particularly the *Sophist*, themselves envisage an eternal interplay, or eternal betweenness that is a bond of harmonious love.

In the generation of the Son from the Father and the spiration of the Spirit, aspiration and emergence, need and resource, entirely coincide. For us as human beings, they do not, but rather ceaselessly oscillate in successive phases. This oscillation participates in the eternal daimonic coincidence of the two.

However, human fallenness amounts to the obscuring of this participation, a descent into the skeptical abyss of merely futile emerging. The alluring beauty on which to bring about has been hidden from us. How else could it be shown to us again except through renewed divine daimonic descents; indeed, most dramatically and appropriately through the historical image of the descent of God in the Incarnation. Here we are shown in time the eternal birth of Aphrodite as the beauty that incites desire, just as the Greeks presented the goddess as born from the waves of a human sea.

But how are we shown the coming about of this supreme event? Is it simply that God first appeared in beauty as human and elicited our desire which was first of all exhibited as lack? No, it was rather shown that God became Incarnate through the desire of a woman to give rise to the god-like in humanity, through a desire for emergence. In the case of Mary, uniquely, the divine coincidence of desire as bond and as emergence is shown in humanity. Mary desired the bridegroom, the *Logos*, and from this desire the *Logos* emerged from the enclosure of her womb. So she desired the Father of her baby as the baby and the baby as its Father, since this Father was indeed eternally a Son. Mary's human sexual desire was not canceled but rather optimally exhibited in the Virgin Birth from which her divine lover emerged.

Yet this unique demonstration of divine power in time also echoes the male pregnancy (one thinks again of the *Symposium*) of Adam which gave rise to his lover Eve. As Hildegard of Bingen put it:

> O how great
> in its powers
> is the side of man
> from which God produced the form of woman
> which He made the mirror of all His beauty
> and the embrace of all His creation.
> (Hildegard 2003: 4a, II, 24–9).[1]

Mary's action in the Incarnation is a recreation of the human race which undoes the lapse of Eve ("Sprouting, you flowered/in a change different/than Adam would have been producing/the whole human race" – Hildegard 2003: 1b, II, 4–7), and establishes here the female (one can logically say) as the new Adam as well as the new Eve, since she has performed again the Adamic act of single-sex birth: the emerging of a baby that is also an adult mutual communion. But Adam himself emerged from a single parentage in so far as he was created by God. Because she begins the new creation as a new Adam, Mary is herself the beginning of a new creation, and was so seen by many thinkers in the Middle Ages. Though she had two human parents, she is, according to Hildegard, in a special sense a direct new creation of God himself:

> O flower, you did not spring from dew,
> nor from the drops of rain,
> nor did the air fly over you
> but divine brightness
> brought you forth on the noblest branch.
> (Hildegard 2003: 2b, II, 12–16)

Mary, restoring Adam, shows the desire of God (in creating) for the Creation through her emergence. But since humanity is in the image of God as love, both mutual and giving, she had also to repeat the act of Adam in giving birth to his lover Eve, by giving birth to her lover Christ.

According to a long mystical tradition beginning with Origen, we are not united with God only by the rising up of our souls to the heavenly realm, but also by giving birth to the *logos* in our soul, in a repetition of the action of Mary (see C. Hart 1980). As for Plato, desire for the divine is an emergence of the new as well as a longing for the distant. Again as for Plato, knowledge, the *logos* itself, is possible through this emergence as well as through this longing. As desiring and knowing, we remain in the daimonic between. But since Origen, we are also said, in giving birth to the daimonic, also to give birth again to the divine and to repeat in ourselves an eternal birth that remains in the eternal even as it descends into time. For now the eternal is also the between, and now the between in us which emerges is also the eternal.

> Now is born full-grown this Child
> Who was chosen by humility,
> And is full-grown in sublime Love
> And carried to term nine months.
> And each month has four weeks
> And each calls for preparation and adornment
> Before the great high day,
> So that Love can be born perfect.
> (Hadewijch 1980: 350, "Allegory of Love's Growth")

Acknowledgments

I am profoundly grateful to the convener Professor Hans Ulrich Gumbrecht and all the participants of the Stanford Colloquium on Emergence which took place at the Stanford Humanities Center (August 2002), for their discussions of the phenomenon of emergence. This chapter is in manifold ways indebted to those discussions, and especially to discussions with Sepp Gumbrecht and Robert Harrison.

Note

1   I am grateful to Dr Stephen D'Evelyn for making available to me his translation of, and commentary on, this "Sequence for Mary." See further his brilliant doctoral dissertation, D'Evelyn (2003).

Chapter 7

Omphalos

Gerard Loughlin

The Bible is like a body. It is a whole composed of many parts, in the pages of which we find other bodies, identities which even now haunt the Western imagination: like so many dead bodies in a library. The biblical body is not singular, but many: malleable and multiform. St Paul imagined that the Christians to whom he wrote in Corinth constituted a body, whose head was Christ (1 Corinthians 12.12–31). Making Christ head changes the body of the Bible, both in form and in meaning. When the Bible no longer ends with the second Book of Chronicles, as in the Hebrew Bible, but with the Book of Revelation, at the end of the Christian New Testament, and when the Bible no longer witnesses to the Messiah who is to come but to the Messiah who, having arrived and departed, is to come again, then we are dealing with very different books. We are dealing with different textual bodies, and different orderings of the bodies inside them – the bodies who live in the texts as characters and encounter them as readers, the believers who are bound over and into their bindings. And while both Jewish and Christian Bibles open with apparently the same book – Bereshith/Genesis – they are in fact different texts, for when Christ is head all other bodies are ordered to his flesh; they become figures of his physique. And this even includes the Bible's first human bodies, those of Adam and Eve, who, it turns out, were already too late; imperfect copies of a perfect humanity that would succeed them.

In the Bible, God's Torah is written on stone (Exodus 24.12) and flesh, in the hearts of the people (Jeremiah 31.33; 2 Corinthians 3.2–3), and in the Gospels it arrives in a body, in the life of Jesus (Luke 4.16–21). The Bible writes our flesh, its meanings and possibilities. But writing is nothing if it is not read, and the distinction between writing and reading opens a space for movement, for a field of energy. This, indeed, is the field of religion, in which believers are bound (*religare*) over to the reading, again and again (*relegere*), of the texts by which they are both bound and set free. The divine Hermes lives in this space, as its *energeia*, as the movement of bodies who read themselves differently. How we understand ourselves determines our reading of the texts by which we are written.

As already suggested, to think about the bodies in the Bible is to think about the Bible itself, and its hold on our imaginations. This chapter will mention only a few of the Bible's bodies, and offer the merest sketch of their effects on later Western tradition(s). Many of the most significant bodies go unmentioned, or if mentioned, undiscussed, and of those discussed only some of their modalities are explored. As Averil Cameron notes, all "the central elements in orthodox Christianity – the Incarnation, the Resurrection, the Trinity, the Virgin Birth, and the Eucharist – focus on the body as symbolic of higher truth" (1991: 68). Indeed, for all these elements, the body is not just a symbol of their truth, but the site where it is realized. But this chapter can only touch on a few of these elements. In particular, this chapter does not attend to those biblical bodies whose lives are largely lived outside the texts. In one sense this is true of all biblical bodies, which live not just in the Scriptures, but in their interpretation. But this is more true of some than of others. It is more true of the New Testament's women, especially the Virgin Mary and Mary of Magdala. Moreover, in leaving these bodies out of account, we curtail the lives of those bodies we do discuss, for all biblical bodies are interrelated. Just as one cannot understand Christ without Adam (1 Corinthians 15.20–8; 45–9) – and so Adam without Christ – so one cannot understand Eve without Mary, since in Christian tradition Mary is Eve's repetition, her second life, as Christ is Adam's (Gambero 1999: 51–8). Nor can one understand Christ without Eve-Mary – from whom Christ takes his flesh, and to which he returns the church (John 19.26–7), which is also his own body as well as his bride (Ephesians 5.25–32), the body-bride that will become Eve-Mary herself (Gambero 1999: 117–18, 198–9, 296–7; see further Beattie 2002). Christian symbolics are utterly incestuous and conceptually vertiginous.

Biblical bodies are never discreet and self-enclosed. There are places in the Bible where attempts are made to police borders, as in Leviticus, which arguably is one of the Bible's most anxious books, being concerned with the ritual purity of ancient Israel's priestly class. The holy is pure and its priests have to be perfect, with undefiled bodies, free of those flows that unsettle the boundaries between one thing and another: between male and female, inside and outside, us and them. Polity and purity were intimately related because the security of the social body was maintained through the due order of the priestly body, as it served the Lord who in turn protected Israel from her enemies. "The Israelites were always in their history a hard-pressed minority. . . . The threatened boundaries of their body politics would be well mirrored in their care for the integrity, unity and purity of the physical body" (M. Douglas 2002: 153). Thus the priestly concern with purity became an obsession with the body's porosity, with the ejaculations and seepages of its fluids, which could cross the borders of skin and country. Human flesh is always traversing and transgressing boundaries; its fluids seeping out, its skin touching other skins, its limbs entangling aliens – human and divine. It leaves one land and enters another, traveling from one book to the next, and, above all, it slips beyond the scrolls on which it was first written, beyond the pages of its inception, to live in the imaginations of those traditions we call religions, and, beyond them, in the cultures they once wrote and still write.

If nothing else, this chapter is intended to show that the Bible as body inhabits the bodies that come after it and live within it. Present bodies – in the West but in other cultures also – become biblical bodies, and biblical bodies become present lives. And sometimes this is for good, and sometimes for ill. The Bible can irradiate flesh with God's glory and condemn it to hell's fires. It was Eric Auerbach who imagined the Bible as a voracious, all-consuming text. "Far from seeking, like Homer, merely to make us forget our own reality for a few hours, it seeks to overcome our reality: we are to fit our own life into its world, feel ourselves to be elements in its structure of universal history" (Auerbach 1953: 13). But the Bible does not do this by itself. It has to be fed by those communities – Jewish and Christian – upon which, in a sense, it feeds.

As bodies changed over the centuries, formed and reformed by changing cultures, different biblical texts were written (read) upon them, or old texts in new ways. Thus, when homosexual bodies were discovered in the nineteenth century, and, in their wake, heterosexual ones also – in 1869 and 1887 respectively (Foucault 1990–2: I; Halperin 1990: 15–40) – the Bible had to be newly read, its writing of flesh descried anew. Before there were homosexuals there had been sodomites – whose predilection, *sodomia*, was first coined by Peter Damien in the eleventh century (Jordan 1997) – and, before the sodomites, in the ancient Greco-Roman world, there had been *molles* and *tribades*, soft men and hard women. The soft men were passive when they should have been active, enjoying penetration rather than penetrating; while the women were the reverse, assuming an inappropriate, dominant role in sexual relationships (Brooten 1996: 143–73). But though these sexual "characters" bear some relationship to the modern "homosexual," it is a very distant one, for the determining criterion was not whether you desired your *own sex*, but whether you desired to be the *other sex*, and the other sex was never just a biological form, but always also a social role. It was reprehensible for a man to (want to) be penetrated, but not for him to penetrate a boy, since a boy's standing – until he became a man – was akin to that of a woman, and woman was made for penetration. This ancient way of thinking – which always understood sexual congress to be asymmetric, between a dominant and a submissive, with one *using* the other, and their relationship coded as that between man and woman (Halperin 1990: 29–38) – is even further removed from modern conceptions of gay and lesbian people, who understand themselves as wanting to be their own sex, while also desiring members of it. Gay men are thus very different from those men in Leviticus who sleep with other men *as if with women*, as also from the *malakoi* and *arsenokoitai* in Paul (1 Corinthians 6.9–11; 1 Timothy 1.9–10), whose sexual practices – whatever they were – may have resembled modern ones, but which would have had very different meanings, and so have been different acts.

Past biblical bodies are continually being written into present gay and lesbian ones, while at the same time the latter are being read back into the Bible. Thus homosexuals appear in the Bible, but only in modern, twentieth-century Bibles, as when the New English Bible finds "homosexual perversion" in Corinth, or the New Revised Standard Version discovers "sodomites" in the same place (1 Corinthians 6.9). These are careless, ideological translations, passing off modern personages as ancient, biblical bodies, which thus seem to appear in the present, or rather, not so much the ancient bodies themselves – which have been replaced with modern ones – as the ancient, Levitical, and Pauline antipathies to those past bodies.

The chief focus of this chapter, however, is the body of God and its sex. It is often asserted – in both Jewish and Christian traditions – that God has no sex, and that concern with God's gender, as raised in feminist thought and theology, is beside the point. And indeed one can use the distinction between sex and gender, as between biological and social categories, to argue that God has no sex but is gendered, and gendered predominately, though not exclusively, as male in both Jewish and Christian traditions. But while the distinction between sex and gender, biology and culture, serves a purpose, it rests on the fallacy that biology escapes its mediation, and is not itself a social category: the myth that science is not a cultural product. But biology is cultural, and our ideas of sex are gendered, and God's gender affects his sex, and this becomes all too evident when divinity is used to underwrite certain human orderings, and most notably those that exclude women from certain kinds of power. It is then that we discover that women are not fully human because not really divine – in the way that men are. We discover that gender neutrality is a ruse of male partiality. This is the legacy of the biblical tradition with which Western culture – both religious and secular – is now engaged, and it would seem that only the Bible's hesitations and indeterminacies will allow it and its culture(s) to think God beyond gender, and so free the bodies that live within it for a more fluid life (Loughlin 1998a).

Bones

Philip Gosse (1810–88), a member of the Plymouth Brethren and a marine zoologist, famously argued, in his book *Omphalos* (1857), that though Adam did not need a navel – having been born of the earth rather than a woman – he nevertheless had one (Philip Gosse 2003). Adam gave every appearance of being a normal body, even though he had never been born, had never been a baby, nor grown and gone through puberty to become the father of the human race.[1] In just the same way, the trees in the garden of Eden gave every appearance of having grown from seed, rather than having been recently planted, fully limbed and leafed; just as the earth's sedimented rocks, with their fossilized bones, give every appearance of vast millennial age, when in fact only a few thousand years old. In this way Gosse sought to reconcile the body of the biblical text with the dead bodies in the body of the earth. "This 'Omphalos' of his," as Gosse's son, Edmund, observed, "was to bring all the turmoil of scientific speculation to a close, fling geology into the arms of Scripture, and make the lion eat grass with the lamb. . . . But, alas! atheists and Christians alike looked at it, and laughed, and threw it away" (Edmund Gosse 1949: 77).

But if Gosse had been less of a zoologist and more of a theologian, he might have argued that Adam had a navel because, being made in the image (*tselem*) and likeness (*demuth*) of God, he was made in the *image of the image* of God – the deity embodied in Christ – who not only had a navel, being the son of his mother, but was also the Omphalos of the world.[2] By this circularity – Christ made in the image of Adam (and Eve) made in the image of Christ – one can overcome the biblical conundrum of how bodies can image that which has no body. Adam and Eve are belated. Chronologically, they precede Christ, but ontologically, they come after him, as types of his prototype, repetitions of the one true "image of the invisible God, the firstborn of all creation" (1 Colossians 1.15), the embodied deity. But of course this would not have answered Gosse's real problem, which was the existence of relics seemingly older than the earth which contained them; a problem that he could only have answered by learning to read the Bible better than he did.

The Bible – in all traditions – begins with the making of bodies. Out of primal chaos God forms the bodies of the heavens and the earth and on the earth the bodies of plants and animals, and in the sea the "great sea monsters," and in the air the birds of "every kind" (Genesis 1.21–3). And then God makes humankind (*adam*) in God's own image, after God's own likeness: humankind in two kinds, "male and female he created them" (Genesis 1.26–7). God makes by speaking; God's words form matter, their meaning bodied forth. God makes like from like, humankind from the dust of the ground, *adam* from *adamah* (a masculine from a feminine noun), and then breathes life into the earthlings (Genesis 2.7).

The bodies of Adam and Eve are the most protean in the Bible, since they will become figures for all other bodies, the templates for all future generations, giving dignity and decrepitude to all following flesh. The only other biblical body that is more significant is Christ's, and, as we have already seen, his body will encompass theirs. The order of Adam and Eve will become the order of men to women, and all later orderings of the sexes will be judged by how far they adhere to or depart from that of the primal couple. Eve made from Adam's bone has suggested her secondariness – woman's dependency – down the ages, even to the day when "natural selection" replaced God as the maker of humankind.

> The greater size, strength, courage, pugnacity, and energy of man, in comparison with woman, were acquired during primeval times, and have subsequently been augmented, chiefly through the contests of rival males for the possession of the females. The greater intellectual vigour and power of invention in man is probably due to natural selection, combined with the inherited effects of habit, for the most

part able men will have succeeded best in defending and providing for themselves and for their wives and offspring. (Darwin 2004: 674)

Even when the Bible had been reduced to myth, its culture was being written onto the bodies of its now doubtful readers. Previously, people had thought the difference between the sexes to be one of degree rather than of kind, the woman being but a "cooler" version of the "hotter" man. This ancient, "one-sex" biology – in which male and female were but permutations of a single sex, polar moments of an altogether fungible flesh – lasted throughout the middles ages and into the early modern period (Laqueur 1990). Eve's flesh was not different in kind from Adam's, and their difference from one another was not onto-logical but spectral. A woman could become a man; and a man might fear to become a woman, to become effeminate, losing that balance of humors which women could only hope to enjoy through the guidance of their husbands (P. Brown 1988: 5–32).

But with the arrival of modernity and the emergence of new interests, pressing for the entry of women into male domains, a new biology was needed to establish and maintain the difference between the sexes, so that women could become something altogether dif-ferent from men, from a newly discrete male body and its privileges. By the end of the nineteenth century, the eminent Scottish physician Patrick Geddes (1854–1932) found that male and female bodies were composed of fundamentally different cells, and for theolo-gians the same became true for Adam and Eve, so that the removal of Adam's rib was understood to have constituted a new creation, a different species altogether (Balthasar 1988-98: II, 365–6; John Paul II 1981: 155–6).

Adam and Eve were expelled from Eden for eating forbidden fruit, and this story tells us more about the ordering of the sexes, since they were expelled with a differential curse which marks their "fall" as a fall into patriarchal order. The woman will bring forth chil-dren in pain, and yet still desire to have more of them with her husband, who will rule over her; while he will toil to wrest food from the earth, out of the dust from which he was made and to which he will return (Genesis 3.16–19). Modern readers have recognized that this subordination of the woman to the man is a disorder, consequent upon their learning the difference between good and evil (Genesis 3.22). But Augustine, who did not doubt that women were more bodily than men, and men more rational than women, did not find here a story about how women are properly or improperly subordinate to men, but about how learning good habits is painful and requires subordinating the flesh to reason, as if to its "husband" (Augustine 2002: 91). For Augustine, the "carnal" meaning of the story makes little sense – something about women turning to their husbands after giving birth, when everyone knows that husbands are rarely present at the "delivery" – and so it must be read "spiritually," allegorically, and the curses as commands rather than punishments.

When Genesis first narrates the making of humankind the text becomes uncertain as to whether this is the making of one thing – humankind – or two things – man and woman – and this equivocation extends to, or flows from, a similar trembling over the singularity of the divine, which is signified with a plural name, 'elohim (Genesis 1.26–30). This uncer-tainty will resonate in later hesitations over human identity, whether it is one or two, man or woman-and-man. For many men – for Tertullian (*On the Apparel of Women*, I.i–ii) and Palladius in the third century – it seemed that women must first become men if they were to be saved; that in being saved they will become the "self-same sex as men," for man alone was made in the image of God (Tertullian 1994: 14–15). In learning virtue (*virtus*), woman becomes man (*vir*); she becomes – as Palladius had it – a "female man of God" (Cloke 1995:

214; see also Miles 1992: 53–77). And if this language seems merely rhetorical – the use of strong metaphor for an androcentric ideal of virility – we have Augustine's testimony in the *City of God* (XXII.17) that many imagined a change of body, "because God made only man of earth, and the woman from the man." It is thus reassuring to learn that "the sex of a woman is not a vice, but nature," and that God, "who instituted two sexes will restore them both" in the resurrection. And this much is taught by Christ when he denied that there would be marrying or giving in marriage in the resurrected life, and so implied the presence of both men *and* women in heaven (Matthew 22.29; Augustine 1998: 1144–6).

Later commentators find in Genesis a story of bodily complementarity: Eve is the difference that complements Adam's singularity, his aloneness. But in fact, while Eve is numerically distinct, she is ontologically the same as Adam – "bone of my bones and flesh of my flesh" (Genesis 2.23) – and so not his complement but his companion, the same-but-different who will breach his solitariness. But this companionability is almost immediately undone by the insinuation of the serpent that leads to the fall into hierarchy. Henceforth – from Aristotle to *When Harry Met Sally* (USA 1989) – friendship between men and women will seem impossible. The attempt to establish the equality necessary for true friendship will become a paradisal project: the attempt to live ahead of – in preparation for – the arrival of a promised restoration, the coming of a Messianic equilibrium.

Mouths

In the Bible God's body is not so much seen as heard, for God speaks, and speaking is the voicing of a body: the exhalation of semantics. God's body is everywhere because God is always speaking, from the first to the last page. God speaks in the speaking of others – "The Lord your God says . . . ." But God must first speak (to) them, draw close and breathe upon them, before they can speak after him. We may of course imagine God speaking with a *disembodied* voice, as when a speaker is out of sight, in another room, another space. But by its nature, the dis*embodied* voice bespeaks a bodily origin, even if it is now only the body of the text, which breathes when it is read, given voice in the singing of the cantor in the synagogue, the reader in the church.

God, being mouthless, must speak through the mouths of others. But in the Christian Bible, God gains a mouth in the person of Jesus, who speaks not just in God's stead, but as God. He is God speaking. But no sooner spoken, than he too, like all speaking, passes away, like breath on the wind. But in finding Christ the Omphalos of the world, Christianity finds the world spoken into being by Christ (John 1.3), so that the *Logos* – God's utterance – speaks the world, and is its breathing, and all mouths can be – because in some sense they already are – the mouth of God.

But mouths, like the body itself, are manifold; multiple organs. Mouths are not just for speaking, but also for eating; as well as for blowing and sucking, and, indeed, kissing. And these uses are not absent from the Bible and its reading. Indeed, the Bible itself is like a mouth, for it speaks the Word of God and is to be spoken; and it is to be eaten, like food; and kissed like lips. Both Jews and Christians kiss their Scriptures, in church and synagogue and in private devotion; an intimate sign of their love for God's word.

There are many kisses in the Bible – from those of David and Jonathan, who "kissed each other, and wept with each other" (1 Samuel 20.41) to Judas, who betrays his "friend" with a kiss (Matthew 26.49–50); from Naomi, Orpah, and Ruth, who kissed and "wept aloud" together (Ruth 1.9), to the "holy kiss" with which the early Christians were enjoined to greet one another (Romans 16.16; 1 Corinthians 16.20; 2 Corinthians 13.12; 1 Thessalonians 5.26; 1 Peter 5.14) – but perhaps the most significant kiss, because the most potent for later readers, is the kiss importuned at the beginning of the Song of Songs: "Let him kiss me with the kisses of his mouth" (1.2)! More than any other verse in the Song of Songs, more than any other biblical kiss, this entreated intimacy would become an enduring symbol for the soul's union with God in the Christian mystical tradition, which is to say, the theological tradition, at least until the fourteenth century, when theology began to be torn from spirituality. This tradition, being infatuated with the incarnation, with the conjunction of divine and human in Christ, was deeply paradoxical, using the body and its amours to explore the soul's embrace in the arms of a bodiless God.

For Bernard of Clairvaux (1090–1153), in his *Sermons on the Song of Songs*, the entreated kiss evokes multiple intimacies: between the bride and her bridegroom, the (monkish) soul and Christ, the church and her Savior, and between Christ and the Father. This kiss is first the kiss of incarnation, when the Word's mouth was pressed to the mouth of Jesus. "A fertile kiss therefore, a marvel of stupendous self-abasement that is not a mere pressing of mouth upon mouth; it is the uniting of God with man" (2.3; Bernard 1971: 10). And having kissed Jesus on the lips, the Word in Jesus kisses the ascending soul, who, however, must start her ascent with first kissing Christ's feet. "Prostrate yourself on the ground, take hold of his feet, soothe them with kisses, sprinkle them with your tears and so wash not them but yourself. Thus you will become one of the 'flock of shorn ewes as they come up from the washing' [Song of Songs 4.2]" (3.2; Bernard 1971: 17). Then, when you have received forgiveness for your sins, you may aspire to kiss the hands of Christ – as he raises you up – and then, at last, to receive the kiss of his mouth (3.5–6; Bernard 1971: 19–20). For Bernard, the soul ascends to Christ by moving up his body, covering it with kisses; a ladder of arousal that rises to a returned kiss on the mouth, "at the summit of love's intimacy" (4.1; Bernard 1971: 21). It is because the bride asks for a kiss on the mouth, rather than just a kiss, that Bernard inserts the other kisses (of feet and hands) before the first kiss of the Song. And it is because the bride asks to receive *the kisses* of his mouth, rather than to be kissed on her mouth or by his mouth, that Bernard is led to find the kiss at the heart of God. Bernard distinguishes between mouth and kiss because the lips that kiss and are kissed become for him the lips of the Father and the Son, with the Spirit the kiss itself that flows between the lips of the divine lovers. The soul participates in the erotic life of the Trinity – between the divine lips – when she receives the kiss which is the Spirit, and which Christ gave to the church when he breathed upon the disciples (John 20.22). "That favour, given to the newly-chosen Church, was indeed a kiss."

> Hence the bride is satisfied to receive the kiss of the bridegroom, though she be not kissed with his mouth. For her it is no mean or contemptible thing to be kissed by the kiss, because it is nothing less than the gift of the Holy Spirit. If, as is properly understood, the Father is he who kisses, the Son he who is kissed, then it cannot be wrong to see in the kiss the Holy Spirit, for he is the imperturbable peace of the Father and the Son, their unshakeable bond, their undivided love, their indivisible unity. (8.2; Bernard 1971: 46)

Augustine, in his book on *The Trinity*, famously likened the divine triunity to the relationship of lovers. Carnal love is the "coupling or trying to couple" of two things, namely the "lover and what is being loved." And if we raise this image to a spiritual plane, to love of the spirit in the friend, rather than of the friend's body, we will arrive at a more fitting triad for modeling the divine relationships: "the lover, what is being loved, and love" (8.5.14; Augustine 1991b: 255). In a sense, Bernard returns this image to the carnal, even as he finds in it the soul's perfecting: as she kisses the lovers' kiss that moistens their pressed lips. It is perhaps only in the twentieth century that we will find a revered theologian offering a theology as sexualized as Bernard's.

Hans Urs von Balthasar (1905–88), who died shortly before he was to become a Roman Cardinal, was steeped in the Christian tradition of "sacred eroticism" (Rambuss 1998), and, like Augustine and Bernard before him, found the triune God to be the "lover, responding beloved, and union of the fruit of both" (Balthasar 1990b: 32). The Spirit as fruit of the union between Father and Son is an obviously sexual metaphor. Picking up on the Song of Song's "well of living water" (4.15), in which Gregory of Nyssa (c. 330–c. 395) had seen the bridegroom's mouth, gushing with the words of eternal life (quoted in Balthasar 1995a: 157–8), Balthasar does not hesitate to imagine the divine life as an ejaculatory flow; "a flowing wellspring with no holding-trough beneath it, an act of procreation with no seminal vesicle, with no organism at all to perform the act." It is just a "pure act of self-pouring-forth" (Balthasar 1990b: 30). The same biblical image informs Balthasar's (masturbatory) vision of the bridegroom's return to life on the first Easter morning; but now the fountain's mouth is a wound, from which the seminal flow gushes forth.

> Is it the beginning? It is small and undefined as a drop. Perhaps it is water. But it does not flow. It is not water. It is thicker, more opaque, more viscous than water. It is also not blood, for blood is red, blood is alive, blood has a loud human speech. This is neither water nor blood. It is older than both, a chaotic drop. Slowly, slowly, unbelievably slowly the drop begins to quicken. . . . But look there: it is indeed moving, a weak, viscous flow. It's still much too early to speak of a wellspring. It trickles, lost in the chaos, directionless, without gravity. But more copiously now. A wellspring in the chaos. It leaps out of pure-nothingness, it leaps out of itself. . . . The spring leaps up even more plenteously. To be sure, it flows out of a wound and is like the blossom and fruit of a wound; like a tree it sprouts from this wound. . . . Deep-dug Fountain of Life! Wave upon wave gushes out of you inexhaustible, ever-flowing, billows of water and blood baptizing the heathen hearts, comforting the yearning souls, rushing over the deserts of guilt, enriching over abundantly, over-flowing every heart that receives it, far surpassing every desire (Balthasar 1979: 151–3; see further Crammer 2004 and Loughlin 2004a: 146–61).[3]

The mouth is not only for kissing, it is also for eating, and as such is associated with bodies in the Bible and with the Bible as food. "My soul is satisfied as with a rich feast, and my mouth praises you with joyful lips when I think of you on my bed, and meditate on you in the watches of the night" (Psalm 63.5–7). In the Book of Revelation (10.8–10), John is given the word of God to eat, on a little scroll. "So I took the little scroll from the hand of the angel and ate it; it was sweet as honey in my mouth, but when I had eaten it, my stomach was made bitter" (10.10). It is a word of judgment, just like the scroll-food given to Ezekiel for his eating and prophesying, a word of "lamentation and mourning and woe," but as sweet as honey in his mouth (Ezekiel 2.8–3.3). As both the Word of God, Bible and Christ are one, scroll-flesh and scroll-food, since Christ is the word-body given for eating.

Then he took a loaf of bread, and when he had given thanks, he broke it and gave it to them, saying, "This is my body, which is given for you. Do this in remembrance of me." And he did the same with the cup after supper, saying, "This cup that is poured out for you is the new covenant in my blood." (Luke 22.19–20)

In one fourteenth-century illustration of the meal that the angel gives John to eat, the Eucharistic aspect of the scroll-book is suggested by the postures of the messenger and the visionary, who have become celebrant and communicant. The angel supports John's arm as he raises the book to his mouth, as if it were a chalice (see Loughlin 1999a: frontispiece). It is above all in the Christian Eucharist – performed, interpreted and contested throughout the centuries and across the world – that we see the Bible's most audacious body realized in the bread-become-flesh and community-become-Christ; in Christ become food and embrace.

Phallus

When pushed, most people will admit that God has no body, but they will still think that he does, and how could they not when they think *him* a "he." For popular piety the learning of the theologians is neither here nor there, let alone the teaching of the church's mystical tradition that if we are to understand God we must begin to abandon the images by which we strive to comprehend God. We must learn to let them fall away, like the rope that helps to hoist a glider aloft, and which the glider must release in order for it to spiral upwards on nothing but rising air. Unless the rope is released the glider will never rise, but fall back to the ground. In order to know the God of the Bible we have to let the Bible go. When Augustine and his mother Monica looked out on the garden in Ostia, and, through their conversation, ascended together to the divine wisdom, they did so by moving beyond – if only for a moment – the words and bodily images by which they climbed, and with which Augustine afterwards recalled their ascent in his *Confessions* (9.10.24).

> Step by step we climbed beyond all corporeal objects and the heaven itself, where sun, moon, and stars shed light on the earth. We ascended even further by internal reflection and dialogue and wonder at your works, and we entered into our own minds. We moved up beyond them so as to attain to the region of inexhaustible abundance where you feed Israel eternally with truth for food. There life is the wisdom by which all creatures come into being, both things which were and which will be. . . . And while we talked and panted after it, we touched it in some small degree by a moment of total concentration of the heart. (Augustine 1991a: 171)

The description that has done most to establish God as a body, as an old man with a white-beard – an image of patriarchy with an almost pathological hold on the popular imagination – is that of the Ancient of Days in the Book of Daniel. "His clothing was white as snow, and the hair of his head like pure wool" (Daniel 7.9). William Blake's 1794 picture of the Ancient of Days engraved this image on the modern mind. It shows a strong, naked deity, half-squatting on his haunches and leaning forward to set the bounds of the firmament with his compasses, while his white hair and beard (which is not directly mentioned in Daniel) streams in the winds of creation. This is Daniel's Ancient turned into the Creator God of John Milton's *Paradise Lost* (1667 / 1674), who comes forth, "golden compasses" in hand, "to circumscribe/This universe, and all created things" (VII.224–6). Milton, as Blake saw, had turned the Creator into a demiurge, who comes forth from heaven in order to calm and order the "vast immeasurable abyss/Outrageous as a sea" that washes up against the shores of heaven (VII.210–2). For Blake, Milton had succumbed to the newly forming scientism of the seventeenth century, that reduced the world to the material and measurable, and which Blake associated with John Locke and Isaac Newton. As named in Blake's *Milton* (1804–8), the God of these deists had become "Satan": "Newton's Pantocrator weaving the woof of Locke" (I.iv.11; see further Raine 1968: II, 53–83). The path that would lead from the unseen God of the Bible to the demiurge of modern deism was taken as soon as people began to imagine the Bible's God as an old man in the sky.

The Bible is very reticent about seeing God. But instead of refusing us sight of God's body, it shows it variously, first one way, then another, so that in this way – a *via positiva* brimming over with images – the Bible becomes a *via negativa*, obscuring (and so revealing God's hiddenness) by showing us too much; too many fragmentary images. In Deuteronomy (4.12–24), the Israelites are reminded that they cannot picture God because God has no form to be seen. Moses, in the Book of Exodus (33.20–3), wanted to know God (*da'ath 'elohim*; Exodus 33.13) – like the men of Sodom, who wanted to know Lot's visitors (Genesis 19) – a subtle, or not so subtle, intimation that to know God is to sleep with him. But Moses is told that he cannot see God's face and live, so that when God makes his "goodness" to pass before Moses, he covers Moses with his hand, so that Moses sees only God's departing back (see also Judges 13.22). And yet Moses has already seen God and lived, because only a few verses before he was in the tent of meeting, speaking to God, "face to face, as one speaks to a friend" (Exodus 33.11; see also Numbers 12) – up close and personal – and a few chapters further back, Moses, and Aaron and Nadab and Abihu, and seventy elders, sat down and ate a covenant meal in God's presence, and they all saw God and lived (Exodus 24.9–11).

But what did they see? Perhaps they saw only a part of God? "Under his feet there was something like a pavement of sapphire stone, like the very heaven for clearness. . . . [T]hey beheld God, and they ate and drank" (24.10). Perhaps they saw only God's feet? Perhaps God can be seen only in parts? As in other visions and sightings of the deity (Amos 9.1; Job 42.5; 1 Kings 22.19; Isaiah 6.1–2; Ezekiel 1.26–8), divinity is oddly indistinct or dismembered in the strange stories of Moses in the cleft of the rock and eating with the elders and God; a pointer, it might be thought, to the metaphorical nature of God's body.

For Thomas Aquinas in the thirteenth century, in his *Summa Theologiae*, God is not even a being, let alone a body, and so the Bible's bodily metaphors for God – including references to God's eyes, arm and hand (Psalms 33.16; Job 40.4; Psalms 117.16) – have to be taken as symbols of God's power (1a.3.1 *ad* 1; 1a.1.9). "Parts of the body are ascribed to God in the scriptures by a metaphor drawn from their functions. Eyes, for example, see, and so, we call God's power of sight his eye, though it is not a sense-power, but intellect. And so with other parts of the body" (1a.3.1 *ad* 3; Thomas Aquinas 1964: 23). God is no more a man, or like a man, than he is a lion or a bear or a rock (Hosea 13.8; Deuteronomy 32.4).

But there is something uncanny about these stories, as also about the story of Jacob wrestling throughout the night with the man he meets by the Jabbok (Genesis 32.22–32), and whom he takes to be God (32.30); the man/God who gives him the new name of Israel (32.28). Howard Eilberg-Schwartz has argued that the reason why Moses is only allowed to see God's back, and why those with whom God eats only see his feet, is because to see more, or to be told more of what they saw, would be to see, or to be told about, God's front, and so God's sex: the divine phallus. God's member is often intimated, but never seen, and this despite the fact that God's relationship to Israel is like that of a cloth that clings to his loins (Jeremiah 13.11). Ezekiel, who does not hesitate to tell us about the Egyptians "whose members were like those of donkeys, and whose emission was like that of stallions" (Ezekiel 23.20), is teasingly coy when it comes to his vision of God, his sighting of the "something that seemed like a human form." He tells us what every part of this body looked like, except for its loins.

> Upward from what appeared like the loins I saw something like gleaming amber, something that looked like fire enclosed all around; and downward from what looked like the loins I saw something that looked like fire, and there was splendour all around. Like the bow in a cloud on a rainy day, such was the appearance of the splendour all around. This was the appearance of the likeness of the glory of the Lord. (Ezekiel 1.27–8)

The Bible, and later rabbinical commentaries, hesitate over God's sex – Ezekiel looks upwards and downwards from God's loins, but not at them – and this is because to see God's genitals is to remember that the divinity who commands his creatures to reproduce (Genesis 1.28) does not himself do so. God has no consort, and so no use for the genitals that he yet gives to his human likenesses. It was in order to solve this conundrum – Eilberg-Schwartz argues – that ancient Israel imagined herself as God's consort. The patriarchs of Israel are wife to God's husband, who has entered into a marriage contract with them – as the prophets Hosea, Jeremiah, and Ezekiel testify – and who ravishes them. God has watched over Israel from infancy, when no one else would have her. And when she is old enough, he "takes" her for his own.

> [O]n the day you were born your navel cord was not cut, nor were you washed with water to cleanse you, nor rubbed with salt, nor wrapped in cloths. No eye pitied you, to do any of these things for you out of compassion for you; but you were thrown out in the open field, for you were abhorred on the day you were born. I passed by you, and saw you flailing about in your blood. As you lay in your blood, I said to you, "Live! and grow up like a plant of the field." You grew up and became tall and arrived at full womanhood; your breasts were formed, and your hair had grown; yet you were naked and bare. I passed by you again and looked on you; you were at the age for love. I spread the edge of my cloak over you, and covered your nakedness: I pledged myself to you and entered into a covenant with you, says the Lord God, and you became mine. Then I bathed you with water and washed off the blood from you, and anointed you with oil. (Ezekiel 16.4–9)

God washes away the blood of Israel's "deflowering"; and male circumcision becomes the mark, in her flesh, of God's possession; the mark, on each man, of his deflowering. Prudish commentators overlook the euphemism of the spread cloak (see Ruth 3.3–9), and like to describe God's "bedding" of the girl Israel as a marriage. It is, but it is more nearly a rape than a willing seduction; Israel becomes more nearly a "kept woman" than a wife, dressed in fine clothes and adorned with jewelry – bracelets on her arms, a chain on her neck, a ring in her nose, earrings in her ears, and a crown on her head (16.10–13). She herself becomes a piece of jewelry: the girl on the arm of her "sugar daddy," reflecting his power back to him. "Your fame spread among the nations on account of your beauty, for it was perfect because of my splendour that I had bestowed on you, says the Lord God" (16.14). But this girl is Israel – the *men* of Israel; and this solution to the problem of finding a use for God's sex now has the result of queering Israel's men – as we might say, but they could not. The men of Israel must either acknowledge that they are like men who sleep with men as if with a woman (Leviticus 18.20), or imagine that they are women. It is then this dilemma that is partly overcome – hidden – by hiding God's phallus; by averting one's gaze.

As Eilberg-Schwartz notes, the same kind of discomfort afflicts Christian men who are enjoined to think of Christ as their bridegroom (Ephesians 5.25–30; Eilberg-Schwartz 1994: 237). If only at a symbolic level, all Christian men are queer, as when St Bernard and his monks yearn for the kiss of Christ. This truth can be occluded in several ways. The early church's enthusiasm for celibacy (see Clark 1999) – enjoined on those who would be perfect, if not on all – enabled the use of erotic language and imagery, its spiritualization being underwritten by the celibate's spiritualization of his or her own body through chastisement of its fleshly desires. And when celibacy lost its attraction, and marriage – especially in Protestant Christianity – became more desirable, the homoeroticism involved in men loving a "male" God was secreted away by an increased discernment and destruction of all sodomitical bodies. This is why twenty-first century debates about (male) homosexuality and same-sex marriage are so unsettling for the Christian churches.

Christian men also learned to avert their gaze, while peeking at the same time. In the Western tradition of Christian art, Christ's infant genitalia were constantly exposed in order – so Leo Steinberg argues – to establish his full humanity, as against any lingering docetism. The Christ child is really male, really human. But the tradition also sought to show, while concealing, the genitalia of the adult Christ. Certain pictures of Christ crucified, entombed, or as the "man of sorrows," display his erect member through the elaborate folds of the cloth by which it is covered. Like Ezekiel's God, nothing and everything is to be seen. In the absence of explanatory texts, Steinberg suggests that this sixteenth-century motif – especially favored by Maerten van Heemskerck (1498–1574) – was intended to show Christ's perfect humanity; for Christ, unlike fallen man,[4] could excite himself by will alone, even in death. "[T]he necessarily voluntary erection in the Ghent *Man of Sorrows* [Heemskerck 1532] triumphs over both death and sin. It is the painter's way of writing Paradise Regained on the body of Christ" (Steinberg 1996: 324–5; compare Balthasar 1979: 151–3). Steinberg describes these images and their possible meanings with relish, as also the anxieties they occasion in modern historians, who would rather look the other way.[5] But even Steinberg draws back from noting the obviously (homo)erotic interest – to speak anachronistically – that these pictures must have had for at least some of their viewers, and, more importantly, the manner in which they figure the unspoken – unspeakable – fears and longings of a religion that understands union with God as a bridal mystery, a nuptial intimacy. The queerness of Christian culture is shown in its pictures of the aroused (resurrected) Christ.

Once men can marry men – can lie with a man *as with a man* – the relationship between men and the "male" Christian God is fully revealed as queer. (This is why Balthasar is such an unsettling theologian, for he can even locate "sodomy" within the Trinity when he imagines the Father "fertilizing" the Son; Balthasar 1990b: 78.) Once gay relationships are allowed, the pretence that a man can really only lie with a woman, and a woman can really only lie with a man, are revealed as pretences. But these pretences are but modes of an even deeper pretence: that women depend on men, as Israel depends on God in Ezekiel's tender but terrifying vision. This, finally, is the deep pretence at the beginning of the Bible, in the

story of woman made from man. It is the great mystifying reversal at the heart of all biblical cultures and their secular successors: the myth of a man without an omphalos. Which
is to say, the myth that man is not dependent on woman, does not really need her; the fear
that man is no more than woman – her offspring rather than she his; the fear that what he
does to woman is – will be/has been – done to him by the God to whom man is woman.[6]

Christianity, of course, rewrites this myth by finding Adam but an image of the true man
– Christ – who is indeed born of a woman. But then Christianity makes the woman dependent on a "male" deity, to whom she is of course "actively receptive." It reinscribes the myth
differently. It is only when Christianity acknowledges that incarnation is not one but two,
and not two but many – in the co-redeemers of Mary and her son, and in those incorporated in him and so in her (see D'Costa 2000: 32–9, 196–203) – that God can be released
from the constraints of the heterosexual regime (the differential valorization of sexed
bodies), and men and women from sexual hierarchy. And this is what is at stake in acknowledging that men can lie with men as men, and women with women as women.

Notes

1   Though it may be noted that Irenaeus of Lyons (c. 130–c. 200) unusually – if not uniquely –
    thought that Adam and Eve were created as children and had to grow to adulthood before they
    could procreate. See Irenaeus (1996: 455; *Against Heresies*, 3.22.4).
2   Though some have thought that Christ was born by a kind of miraculous Caesarean section,
    which left Mary perfectly intact.
3   I am grateful to Tina Beattie for bringing this text to my attention. For her own discussion of the
    passage see Beattie (2006: 170–3). Balthasar's ejaculatory image of the resurrection is not entirely
    without precedence. It can be related to a Germanic tradition in "low" culture and "high" art
    which associated resurrection with penile erection. See Steinberg (1996: 315–17).
4   Infamously, Augustine saw humanity's fallen state figured in the unruliness of the male member,
    which seems to have a life of its own. In paradise, Adam's sex was completely ruled by his will,
    and he copulated – if he did copulate – without lust; sex without concupiscence. See Augustine
    (1998: 623–7; *The City of God*, XIV.23–4).
5   For example see Bynum (1991: 79–117) and the response in Steinberg (1996: 364–89).
6   This is a version of an argument borrowed from Tina Beattie's reading of Balthasar's fearful
    theology (Beattie 2006). Balthasarian man lives under erasure once he comes to see "all created
    Being as essentially feminine when compared to the Creator God" (Balthasar 1986a: 214).
    Balthasar's strange, contradictory and often simply daft theology arises from trying to evade this
    disappearance.

Part IV

Queer/ing Tradition

Chapter 8

Against Rabbinic Sexuality

Textual Reasoning and the Jewish Theology of Sex

Daniel Boyarin

In this chapter I do not so much want to indicate content for a Jewish theology of sex, as point to the peculiar ways that a peculiar people undertake the theological enterprise itself. Not given to forms of philosophical discourse that other Jews (including Christians) mobilize in their doing of theological work (and which might possibly, at least, be the only form of discourse that merits the name "theology"), the Rabbis, famously or notoriously, work out values and religious ideas through two very different discursive means, hermeneutical elaboration of norms, as expressed in the Torah (the five books of Moses), and the expansion of biblical narrative (midrash). These two processes, which bear some relationship to modern "narrative theology," have been dubbed by a school of thinkers following Peter Ochs, as "textual reasoning," a mode of rationality that is always/already second-order, and, indeed, does not recognize the very opposition between first-order and second-order reasonings. Hence, the present contribution to a theological elaboration of sexuality (or rather its privation) within rabbinic textuality.

Penetrating Leviticus

"Do not lie with a man a *woman's lyings* [*miškəbei 'iššā*]; that is *tô ʿēbā*" (Leviticus 18.22).[1] This verse is usually taken in both scholarly and popular parlance to prohibit "homosexuality" *tout court*. What I would like to show is that the rabbinic culture of late antiquity did not understand this verse in terms of sexuality at all, although it did, of course, in terms of sex.[2] I begin with the assumption that there is no more reason *a priori* to assume that ancient Jewish culture – biblical or talmudic – does have a system of sexuality than to assume the opposite. Given Michel Foucault's work and the work of historians who have shown how "sexuality" develops at a particular moment in history (Halperin 1990; Davidson 2002), it becomes at least equally plausible – indeed much more so – to begin by assuming that the Jewish culture of the biblical and talmudic periods was not organized around a system of sexual orientations defined by object choice (or in any other way for that matter). I know of no evidence that would support the claim for a system of sexual orientations (there is no talmudic equivalent even for the *cinaedus*).[3] Any positive evidence, therefore, that militates against the assumption of the production of a category of sexuality in the rabbinic discourse becomes highly significant.

There is a further methodological point that must be made.[4] The base of data on which I describe late antique Jewish culture is highly skewed in that it includes the expression of one, very limited social group within the culture, a learned, hegemonic, male rabbinic elite (and even within that I am almost exclusively concentrating on its Babylonian variety). In fact, I know almost nothing, aside from what I can read between the lines or against the grain of the Talmud, of what the rest of the (Jewish) world was doing or thinking. This is particularly significant, because from the much more variegated remains of Greek culture we learn of a heterogeneous cultural situation, wherein certain types of texts – medical texts, for example – have an entirely different ideology of sex than do the high cultural literary artifacts of, for example, Hesiod. This is even more the case in the later Greek and Hellenistic worlds than in the archaic period. There might very well have been an analogous cultural situation in late antique Jewish culture. Precisely what I am investigating then are particular discursive practices, not whole cultures – whatever that might even mean – and claiming that these discursive practices are fully comprehensible without assuming a cultural sub-system of sexuality.[5] Since this discursive practice – rabbinic halakhic discourse – is the normative base for Jewish religious practice, it is at least plausible to argue that it is this which must be the basis for a rabbinic Jewish theology of sex. I wish to argue that such a theology must base itself on a radical rejection of the discourse of sexuality, in order to be faithful precisely to the tradition that any "orthodox" Judaism must claim for itself.

My first argument in demonstrating the lack of a binary opposition of hetero/homosexuality in talmudic textual practice will be a text that shows that the Talmud did not read such a category into the biblical prohibitions on male intercourse, understanding that only anal intercourse and no other male–male sexual practices were interdicted in the Torah. In the Babylonian Talmud *Niddah* 13b, we find the following colloquy:

> Our Rabbis have taught: Converts and those who sport with children, delay the Messiah. I understand "converts", for Rabbi Helbo has said that converts are as difficult for Israel as *sappaḥat* [a skin disease]! But what is this about those who sport with children? If I will say it refers to male intercourse [*miškāb zākor*, a technical term referring to male–male anal penetration], they are subject to stoning! Rather, [shall we say] it refers to intercrural [between the thighs, (Heb.) *děrěk 'ēbārim*, (Gk.) *diamêrizein*] intercourse? But that is like the children of the flood [i.e., masturbation – Rashi]. Rather it refers to those who marry minor girls who are not of childbearing age, for Rabbi Yossi has said that the son of David will not come until all of the souls in the "body" are finished [i.e. until all of the souls that were created at the Beginning of the universe have been born into bodies, the Messiah will not arrive].

The Talmud quotes an earlier text (tannaitic, that is Palestinian and prior to the third century of the Christian era) that condemns converts to Judaism and pedophiles in what seems to be rather extreme language. The Talmud (Babylonian and post third century) asks what is meant by sporting with children. From the answer that the Talmud suggests to its question, it is quite clear that the Talmud sharply distinguishes male–male anal intercourse from other same-sex practices, arguing that only the former is comprehended by the biblical prohibition on male intercourse. This point already establishes the claim that this culture, insofar as we can know it, does not know of a general category of the homosexual (as a typology of human beings) or even of homosexuality (as a bounded set of same-sex practices).

It is important, however, to understand the intricate cultural coding of this passage. Rabbinic discourse frequently uses exaggerated language to inculcate prohibitions and inhibitions which are not forbidden in the Torah. There is, accordingly, an inner-cultural recognition that such prohibitions, precisely because they are expressed in extreme language, are not as "serious" as those that are forbidden in the Book. It is as if there is a tacit cultural understanding that the more extreme the rhetoric, the less authoritative the prohibition. Thus, just as in the case of masturbation, where there is no biblical text indicating that it is forbidden, and it is therefore designated hyperbolically as being like "the children of the flood," so also for "sporting with children," the text finds highly hyperbolic language with which to express itself.[6] "Preventing the Messiah" has about the same status of hyperbole as being one "of the children of the flood," and neither of them are taken as seriously as those prohibitions for which the Torah explicitly marks out an interdiction and a punishment.

Thus, since male anal intercourse is forbidden explicitly by the Torah and a punishment marked out for it, there is no need to utilize obviously hyperbolic language like that of delaying the coming of the Messiah. Far from strengthening the case, it only would weaken it. As the canonical commentary of Rashi has it: "*Only* delaying the Messiah? But it is forbidden by the Torah and punishable by stoning!" [emphasis added]. Therefore, claims the Talmud, this cannot be what is meant by "sporting with children" in the commented upon text. The Talmud then suggests that what is being spoken of here is the practice of intercrural intercourse between men and boys, according to some authorities the standard sexual practice of Greek pederasty (Dover 1989: 98, 106). This, however, is *merely* a type of masturbation, for which another axiological category exists. Masturbators are not Messiah-delayers but Children of the Flood.[7] All that is left, therefore, for our category of delaying the Messiah is intergender pedophilia, forbidden because it is anti-natalist.

The tannaitic text itself will bear, however, some further analysis. The term I have translated "sport with" means variously "to play" and "to laugh," but frequently is used as an explicit term for sexual interaction, as it undoubtedly is meant here. The term for "children" here is a gender-indeterminate word that refers to anyone from infancy to puberty. The first question to be asked of the original statement is: What is the association between converts and those who sport with children? I would suggest that at least a plausible answer is that Greco-Roman converts are taken to be those who sport with children or even tempt other Jews into such sport. If that be granted, it would seem clear that it is pederasty that is being spoken of. The third interpretation that the Talmud offers, then, for the earlier text, namely that intergender pedophilia is referred to, seems highly implausible. On the other hand, the Talmud's refusal to understand here anal intercourse as being the intention of the original text seems well founded, for it would be, as I have indicated above, highly unusual to use hyperbolic language such as that of Messiah-prevention to refer to that for which an explicit biblical reference could be cited. It seems, therefore, that some other pederastic sexual practice is connoted by "sporting with children," and intercrural intercourse seems as good a candidate as any. In other words, my hypothesis is that the second suggestion that the Talmud makes in order to interpret the original source seems the most likely one, namely that "those who sport with children" refers to pederasts who practice forms of sexual behavior that do not include anal intercourse. If this reading is accepted, it would follow that both levels of the talmudic discourse, that is the original Palestinian tannaitic statement and its later Babylonian talmudic interpretations, understood the Torah's interdiction to be limited only to the practice of male anal intercourse, of use of the male *as* a female. If this interpretation is deemed finally implausible, then the tannaitic evidence falls by the wayside. Whether or not my reading of the tannaitic text be accepted, in any case, it is clear that this is how the Babylonian Talmud understood the Torah, as we see, I repeat, from the explicit distinction made between anal intercourse, forbidden by the Torah, and intercrural intercourse which the Torah has permitted. At the very least, then, we have here positive evidence that late antique Babylonian Jewish culture did not operate with a category of the "homosexual" corresponding to "ours." As the Talmud understood it, male–male sexual practices other than anal intercourse are not prohibited by the Torah and only fall under the category of masturbation which is the same, whether solo or in concert.[8] This provides, then, strong evidence within the Talmud for the absence of a category of homosexuals or even of homosexual practices isomorphic with that of modern Euroamerican culture.

Further evidence for the absence of a category of the "homosexual" in talmudic culture may be found in (the admittedly very rare) discussions of female same-sex genital practices, for instance Babylonian Talmud *Yevamoth* 76a:

> Rav Huna said: "Women who rub each other may not marry priests", but even Rabbi Eliezer who said that "an unmarried man who has intercourse with an unmarried woman without intending to marry her makes her a *zōnā*[9] [and thus unfit to marry a high priest]", his words only apply to a man [who lies with a woman] but as for a woman [who lies with a woman], it is mere lasciviousness.

Also Babylonian Talmud *Shabbat* 65a-b:

> Shmuel's father did not allow his daughters to lie with each other. . . . Shall we say that this supports the view of Rav Huna, for Rav Huna said: "Women who rub each other may not marry priests"? No, he forbad it in order that they should not learn [the feel] of another body [and they would then lust to lie with men (Rashi)].

The only reason, according to this text, that unmarried women should not excite each other sexually is because it might lead to immorality – that is, sex with men![10] Female same-sex practices just do not belong to the same category as male anal intercourse any more than other forms of male same-sex stimulation. We see from here, moreover, that the notion that the Talmud, like Queen Victoria, just didn't believe in the possibility of female homo-eroticism, is not a true assumption. It was understood that women could pleasure each other, but this did not form a single category with male intercourse. Male anal intercourse is *sui generis*, and its genus is clearly not, then, in any way identical to "our" category of homosexuality.

This provides us then with further evidence that not only is there no category, no "species of human being," of the homosexual, there is, in fact, no category formed by same-sex *acts per se* either. Neither people nor acts are taxonomized merely by the gender of the object of genital activity. Male-male anal intercourse belongs to a category known as "male inter-course," while other same-sex genital acts – male and female – are subsumed under the category of masturbation, apparently without the presence of another male actor intro-ducing any other diacritic factor into the equation.[11]

A thousand years (and in the case of the Babylonian Talmud, several thousand kilome-ters) separate between the Torah-sources and their talmudic interpreters. While it is impossible, therefore, to use the Talmud as direct evidence for biblical culture, it neverthe-less provides highly significant indirect evidence, since it is counter-intuitive to assume that in the biblical period, the category of homosexuality existed and later disappeared in the same *Kulturgebiet*. Still, such an assumption, while implausible, is not impossible. In any case, however, at the very least the talmudic testimony suggests that the "homosexuality" inter-pretation of the biblical material is not ineluctable and that other options should be considered.[12] If it is not same-sex eroticism *per se* that worries Leviticus, what cultural force is it that could have produced the powerful interdiction on male anal intercourse? Cross-cultural comparison points us in a promising direction here. David Halperin contends that for the Romans (the contemporaries roughly speaking of the Rabbis), as for the earlier Greeks, the relevant distinction between sexual practices was not between same-sex and other-sex desire but between status positions.[13] Adult free males penetrated. Some preferred boys and some women, and many liked both. There was something pathological and depraved, however, in the spectacle of an adult male allowing his body to be used as if it were the body of a person of penetrable status, whether the man did so for pleasure or for profit (Halperin 1990: 22–4, 88–112; Winkler 1989: 45–70; and Richlin 1993). "It is sex-role reversal, or *gender-deviance,* that is problematized here" (Halperin 1990: 23). In other words, the fulfillment of the pleasure of the penetrating male involved either an appropriate ascription of lower status to the passive partner or an inappropriate degradation to that status. I would like to suggest that in the biblical culture also – at least as received by the Talmud – "sexuality" rather than being the controlling figure of other subsidiary discourses is rather subsumed under larger cultural structures. If in the Greco-Roman formation sexual patternings were subordinated to larger structures having to do with power and status, in biblical culture also I will claim sexual taboos were subsidiary to another cultural structure. Here, I suggest, also penetration of a male constituted a consignment of him to the class of females, but rather than a degradation of status, this constituted a sort of a mixing of kinds, a generally taboo occurrence in Hebrew culture. Just as in Greece, then, the prohibited forms of sexual practice were parts of entire cultural systems. Their violating the body of the free, adult male sexually constituted one offence within a category of many against such a body. As Halperin has demonstrated, other such offences included even placing a hand on his body without his consent. "It was an act of *hybris,* or 'outrage', which signified the violation of a status distinction, the attempted reduction of a person to a status below the one he actually occupied ('using free men as slaves', Demosthenes loosely but vividly defined it)" (Halperin 1990: 96; see also Dover 1989 and D. Cohen 1991).

I would like to suggest the following hypothesis: In biblical culture as well the sexual taboo enters into an entire system of forbidden practices, but one of a completely different nature – not of *hybris,* but of *hybrids.* In that system, one may not hybridize or even plant two species together, mate a horse to a donkey, weave linen and wool into linsey-woolsey, etc. God-given categories must be kept separate. Anthropologist Mary Douglas already made this point with regard to sexual prohibitions in general in ancient Israel:[14]

> Other precepts extend holiness to species and categories. Hybrids and other confusions are abominated. "And you shall not lie with any beast and defile yourself with it, neither shall any woman give herself to a beast to lie with it; it is perversion" (Leviticus 18). The word "perversion" is a significant mistranslation of the rare Hebrew word *tebhel, which has as its meaning mixing or confusion* (Douglas 2002: 66; emphasis added).

I suggest that the interdiction on male–male anal intercourse enters, in the biblical cultural system, into the sub-system of such violations of the symbolic realm. In its immediate literary context, the verse just cited that prohibits male anal intercourse follows immediately on the verse that prohibits "bestiality" within which the word "confusion" [of kinds] is emphasized, hinting that there may be a connection between the two prohibitions on this level as well. A much stronger argument for this point is derived from the parallelism in language and form to the taboo on cross-dressing. This prohibition is phrased in the following fashion: "The woman shall not wear that which pertains unto a man, neither shall a man put on a *woman's garment* [*śimlat 'iššā*], for all that do so are *tô ʿēba* unto the Lord thy God" (Deuteronomy 22.5). The latter appears as: "Do not lie with a man a *woman's lyings* [*miškəbei'iššā*]; that is *tô ʿēba*" (Leviticus 18.22).[15] Both the usage of the term "*tô ʿēba*" and the semantic/syntactic parallelism of "a woman's garment || a woman's lyings" are common to the two prohibitions, suggesting a cultural relation between them. (The seeming lack of parallelism in that the first verse is gender symmetrical while the second only mentions men forms a key argument for my thesis below.)

Thus when one man "uses" another man as a female, he causes a transgression of the borders between male and female, much as by planting two species together he causes a transgression of the borders of species. Now at first glance this explanation seems somewhat paradoxical, because the other cases of levitically prohibited category crossing involve the keeping apart of things that are different. Thus, one does not mix wool with linen in a garment. One might have thought, therefore, that if anything, homoerotic relations would be more consistent with the idea of keeping the different separate. This paradox is, however, only apparent. What we must think of, in order to understand the levitical system, is the "metaphysics" underlying it. These prohibitions belong to the Priestly Torah that emphasizes over and over in its account of the Creation in Genesis 1 that God has created from the beginning the separate kinds of creatures.[16] Male and female are among the kinds that were created at the very beginning (Genesis 1.27). Now if we understand that it is the kinds that have to be kept separate, that is, the categories or types, because confusing their borders (*tebhel*) is an abomination – as opposed to a mere necessity to keep physically separate the tokens of the categories – then we can understand the specifics of the Torah's interdiction of male anal intercourse. The Torah's language is very explicit; it is the "use" of a male as a female that is "*tô ʿēba*," the crossing of a body from one God-given category to another, analogous to the wearing of clothes that belong to the other sex, by nature as it were. Moving a male body across the border into "female" metaphysical space transgresses the categories in the same way as putting on a female garment, for both parties, since both participate (presumably willingly) in the transgressive act.

Now it is clear why only male anal intercourse and not other homoerotic practices are forbidden by the Torah. The issue is gender (as the verse of the Bible explicitly suggests) and not "homosexuality," and gender is conceived around penetration and being penetrated. The lack of a prohibition on female homoerotic behavior, a fact about which "there has been considerable speculation" according to the latest interpretations of biblical law, now receives a fresh explanation (Levine 1989: 123). Up until now, this omission has generally been explained as the sign of a general lack of interest in what women do when it does not lead to possible illicit pregnancy and thus confusion in the realm of the Name-of-the-Father.[17] However, as we have seen from the above-quoted verse from Deuteronomy, it is simply not the case that female behavior is not controlled by this system, nor that the Torah is uninterested in what women do. For cross-dressing, the male and female are equally controlled. The same point holds for intercourse with animals as in the verse quoted above. We see, therefore, that female sexual behavior is every bit as much of interest to the Torah as male sexual behavior, even in situations where illicit pregnancy could not possibly result. Were there a category of the homosexual whose activities are condemned *per se*, there is no reason that only the males would be included in it, nor any reason that only one male–male genital practice would be forbidden. It follows, then, that there was no such category in either biblical or talmudic culture and that some other explanation than a horror of "homosexuality" must be advanced for the taboo on male anal intercourse. The explanation for this taboo generally accepted among biblical scholars is that "homosexuality," being allegedly a regular practice of the Canaanites, or even part of their cult, the Bible abjected it as part of its project of differential production of Israelite culture. There is very little (or no) evidence that I know of to support such a view; indeed, virtually none that the Canaanites were especially given to homosexual practices. I submit that it is a reasonable hypothesis to subordinate the sexual practice under the category of gender-crossing, and conclude that only male anal intercourse was considered as a kind of cross-dressing owing to the penetration of one body by another. The Rabbis (in contrast apparently to the Romans)[18] did not imagine female–female sexual contact as involving any form of penetration that they recognized as such.[19]

The very word for female, *nəqēbā* in both biblical and talmudic Hebrew, as well as talmudic Aramaic, means "orifice-bearer," as if male bodies did not possess orifices. A talmudic text emphasizes to what extent gender was constituted by penetration and being penetrated within this cultural system. The Talmud is trying to determine what sorts of jealousy on the part of a husband will invoke the ceremony of the Waters of Curse – that is, the biblical ritual whereby a wife suspected of adultery drinks water in which a passage from a Torah scroll has been dissolved. If she is "guilty" God causes certain bodily diseases, and if "innocent," God leaves her alone (and promises her progeny):[20]

We have learned, "sexual intercourse" – excluding something else.

The verse says that the husband suspects his wife of having had sexual intercourse with another man, and the midrashic passage quoted indicates that this is to exclude a situation in which he suspects her of "something else":

What is "something else"? Rav Sheshet said: "It excludes anal intercourse [literally not according to her manner]."

For Rav Sheshet, anal intercourse does not constitute intercourse at all and therefore it is not adultery, so if a husband suspects his wife of this, she does not undergo the "test" for adulteresses, but Rava dissents:

Rava said to him: "But with reference to anal intercourse, it is written 'a woman's lyings'!" Rather Rava said: "It excludes a case where he suspected her of intercrural intercourse."[21]

Rava argues from the verse that treats of male anal intercourse. His argument is that since that practice is defined, as we have seen, as "a woman's lyings," it follows that anal intercourse with women is indeed defined as intercourse. Crucial in the context of the present inquiry is Rava's proof that male-female anal intercourse counts as full intercourse for the purpose of definitions of adultery from the fact that male-male anal intercourse is defined by the Torah as "a woman's lyings (i.e. as intercourse in the fashion of lying with women)." From the verse prohibiting this behavior between men, we learn that it *is* appropriate when practiced between a man and a woman. The exact talmudic term for male-female anal intercourse is "penetration not according to her way," which we might be tempted to gloss as penetration that is not natural to her, but this is precisely the interpretation which the Talmud denies us by assuming that such intercourse *is* natural to women, indeed can be defined by the Torah as "a woman's lyings." (Compare Herodotus i.61.1f., cited in Dover 1989: 100.) Moreover, in a further passage (Babylonian Talmud *Sanhedrin* 54a), the Talmud argues explicitly that with reference to women there are two kinds of intercourse, that is, vaginal and anal, because the verse that deals with male-male anal intercourse indicts it as "a woman's lying*s* [plural *miškəbei*]," thus two kinds of lying with women exist. "According to her way" means, then, simply something like in the more common or usual fashion and a discourse of natural/unnatural is not being mobilized here. It follows, then, that the manner of lying with women is penetration *simpliciter* and no distinction of anal/vaginal is intended by the Torah but only a distinction between penetrative and non-penetrative sex.[22] Men penetrate; women are penetrated, so for a man to be penetrated constitutes a "mixing of kinds" analogous to cross-dressing.

A contemporary temptation would be to reverse the relation that I have suggested and propose that the reason that cross-dressing is forbidden is because it leads to, simulates, or somehow is associated with "homosexuality." Indeed, some have gone so far as to suggest that the entire system of forbidden "mixtures" – and especially, of course, the taboo on cross-dressing – is to support the prohibition on so-called homosexuality. As Terry Castle has remarked, "The implication . . . that sodomy follows from transvestism – became a standard notion in the eighteenth century" (Castle 1986: 46, 47; cited in Garber 1992: 381). I am, as it were, turning this notion upside-down – leaving it for the eighteenth century and ours – and interpreting that male anal intercourse is for the biblical culture not the result of cross-dressing, nor is transvestism an index of deviant sexual practice, but rather anal intercourse with a man is an instance of cross-dressing![23]

Note, then, both the similarity and the enormous difference between this explanation of the biblical culture and the interpretations of Greek culture of the Foucauldian school. In both, that separate realm that we identify as sexuality is subsumed under larger cultural structures and discourses.[24] In the latter, since the issues involved are social status and power, there is no shame in (or taboo against) an appropriately higher status male penetrating a lower status male.[25] In the biblical culture, on the other hand, where the issue does not seem to have been status so much as an insistence on the absolute inviolability of gender dimorphism – since such violation would constitute a mixing of categories – *any* penetration of a male by another male constitutes a transgression of this boundary for both parties. In either case, we now understand why other male-male sexual practices are not mentioned in the Torah at all and need to be subsumed by the Talmud under the rubric of masturbation. We also understand why female-female sexual practices are not spoken of by the Torah and treated very lightly indeed by the Talmud. It is because they are not perceived as simulacra of male-female intercourse. They do not confuse the dimorphism of the genders, because they are not conceptualized in this culture around penetration.[26]

Were the Men of Sodom Sodomites?

It is important at this point for me to discuss the story of the Destruction of Sodom, since this text has often been interpreted as encoding a condemnation of – and therefore production (or presupposition) of – a category of homosexuality (Cantarella 1992: 195).

The story is as follows (Genesis 19.1–12). God, having become aware of the evil of the people of Sodom has determined to destroy the city and sent angels in the form of men to announce this to Lot, so that he and his family can be saved. In the evening the people of Sodom come to the door of the house and demand access to the strangers, desiring to "know them." Lot offers instead his two virgin daughters. The people are very angry: "This one has come to dwell among us, and he is judging us. Now we will do more evil to you than to them" (Genesis 19.9). At this point a miracle is produced, the people are struck blind, and Lot and his family escape.

Both writers who want to insist that the Bible condemns homosexuality and writers who wish to argue against this proposition have operated with the assumption that if this is a story about homosexuality then it provides strong support for the idea that the Bible operates with a category of homosexuality that it violently condemns. Typical is Eva Cantarella, who, in arguing against Robin Scroggs' claim that the Leviticus verses are totally isolated in biblical literature and probably late (Scroggs 1983: 73), writes, "The proof of how forced this interpretation is comes from the celebrated story of the people of Sodom" (Cantarella 1992: 195). Rightly dismissing interpretations which deny the sexual nature of the Sodomites' intentions, she concludes, "It seems very difficult to deny that the biblical account should be taken to mean that homosexuality is an execrable type of behaviour" (1992: 197). Difficult or no, this is precisely what I intend to do.

I begin by stating that there is no possibility, so it seems to me, of denying that the intention of the Sodomites was to rape the strangers. Commentators who attempt to interpret "know" here in a non-sexual sense are ignoring the simple and clear fact that Lot "offers" his daughters as sexual substitutes for the strangers. Does he do so because he condemns their "homosexuality" and is trying to convert them to "heterosexuality"? Some interpreters would have us believe this proposition, but the story makes absolutely clear why he is protecting the men: "Only to these men do nothing, seeing that they have come under the protection of my roof." The offer of his daughters in exchange is simply because, as his "property," he has the right to do so, while he is obligated to protect guests from all harm. Far from a rebuke, Lot is simply offering them an alternative to protect his honor, and one that he expects, moreover, that they will accept. (One could, of course, query why he offers his daughters and not himself, and two answers could be given. Either he expects the daughters to be more attractive to the men than he himself would be or that women are generally dispensable in his culture. This question will be further addressed below.) The rejection of his proffer is not portrayed in terms of a homosexual preference on the part of the Sodomites but as a furious response to Lot's judgmental stance toward them. This is, after all, the stated reason for their anger: "This one has come to dwell among us, and he is judging us!" Any "hermeneutics of suspicion" here that suggests some other reason for the fury runs the serious risk of anachronism, of simply filling in a gap where there is none and doing so, moreover, with our own cultural expectations. Their expressed intention, moreover, to do worse to him than they intended to do to the strangers is not at all erotic in its implications. There is, accordingly, no warrant whatever for Eva Cantarella's conclusion that "The Sodomites do not want Lot's daughters: they want the foreign visitors. This is their sin" (1992: 195). Had they taken Lot's daughters, they would have been equally sinful – a proposition that will be further verified from a parallel text immediately below.

The point has been made that in the myriad references to the Sodomites in later biblical writing, not once is their alleged "homosexuality" even mentioned. Scroggs has collected eleven such allusions (Scroggs 1983: 74). Where they make mention at all of the nature of the Sodomite sin, it is always violence that is at issue, not sexual immorality. Typical is Isaiah 1.10–17, where the "officers of Sodom" are addressed and their sin is described as "their hands being full of blood" (v. 16), and their atonement is to do justice with the orphan and the widow (v. 17). He argues from this that these writers either did not know of or did not accept the "homosexual dimension of the story of Sodom." On the other hand, there is a parallel story – almost surely modeled on the Sodom narrative – in which the sexual aspect is clearly presupposed – I shall presently be returning to this text – and therefore, Scroggs writes, "Contrary to later references, the homosexual dimension of the story of Sodom is accepted" (Scroggs 1983: 75). It seems to me that Scroggs has missed the point, although he is tending in the right direction. There is no reason to assume that the prophetic writers did not know of the homosexual rape aspect of the Sodom story, but it was considered by them a synecdoche for the violence of the Sodomites, *not an issue of sexual immorality*.

The same point ought to be made about rabbinic interpretations of this story. As Scroggs correctly points out, there is nothing in the rabbinic readings of the Sodom story that indicates that their particular sinful nature was "homosexuality." The emphasis is always on their violence and murderousness (Scroggs 1983: 80). Scroggs, however, draws the wrong conclusion from this premise. Thus he writes, "The Palestinian Targum's clear statement of the sin as sexual does not, perhaps surprisingly, seem to have informed rabbinic midrash of this time" (Scroggs 1983: 81). Scroggs has been misled by the modern category of sexuality to assume that the Rabbis would certainly have marked off sexual inclination as a separate and unequal determiner of human moral status. There is no reason whatever to assume that the Rabbis, assiduous readers of the Bible with no reason to apologize for the Sodomites, denied the sexual nature of their intention towards the "men." They almost certainly did understand it this way, as did everyone else in the ancient world. It was not understood by them, however, as it was not understood by the inner-biblical interpretive tradition, as being the essence of the Sodomite sinfulness or the point of the story. Indeed, judging from this Jewish interpretive tradition, the homosexual aspect of their violence was hardly worth remarking; it did not add to the heinousness of their brutality. For the interpretive tradition that locates the sin of Sodom in their "unnatural" sexuality, we look neither to the inner-biblical allusions nor to rabbinic midrash, but to first-century Hellenistic (Greek-speaking) Jewish texts, whether Palestinian or otherwise. Not surprisingly, here as elsewhere, the New Testament is closest to these other Hellenistic Jewish traditions.[27] The crucial element that enters, it seems, with Hellenistic culture is the notion of nature and the possibility of an act being *contra naturam,* as opposed to being merely forbidden. This is a peculiarly Greek idea, whether or not Greeks applied it in the same way – obviously they did not – as Hellenized Jews were to (Koester 1968). For the ancient Near East, and ancient Israel among them, acts were taboo or permitted, abhorred, or praiseworthy, but never consonant with or against nature itself. Consequently the notion that a type of desire was "unnatural" and the people who possessed it were somehow monstrous had to wait for the grafting of Greek thinking onto biblical culture that took place among Hellenistic Jews.[28] This story in the Bible and in the (Hebrew/Aramaic-speaking) Rabbis is no more a condemnation of homoerotic desire than a story about a heterosexual rape would be a condemnation of heteroerotic desire, and the parallel text from Judges, to which I turn now, makes this clear.

In the story in Judges 19 the account is similar to the Sodom story. This is also a story of inhospitality and violence toward strangers. The inhospitality of the men of Gibeah is focused on right at the beginning of the story. The Levite, his concubine, and servant are wandering in the town at nightfall, and contrary to the customs of Israel, not one of these Israelites takes them into their home for the night (v. 15). An elderly foreigner, not one of the natives of the place – like Lot – finally takes them in and exhibits the appropriate friendliness and generosity toward strangers (v. 21). The wicked inhabitants of the place surround the house and make exactly the same demand that was made of Lot, that he bring out the stranger to be raped. Once more, the host pleads with them, "because this man has come into my house" (v. 23), and offers his virgin daughter and the concubine as "substitutes." The man pushes his concubine out, and she is gang-raped and abused all night, until in the morning she is found dead with her hand on the doorstop, having died desperately trying to get in. This is an absolutely horrifying story of violence toward women, and while the men of Gibeah are punished terribly for their murder of the woman (v. 4), the Levite who threw her to the dogs to save his skin is let off scot-free by the text.[29] A story of primitive male privilege of the most repulsive sort, this is not in any way, however, a discourse about homosexuality. Indeed, here, the acceptance of a "heterosexual" substitute shows that the people of Gibeah are not being anathematized as "homosexuals." Their punishment is explicitly owing to their violence toward the woman and not to their supposed homoeroticism. In both of these stories we find, then, a representation, perhaps with some historical basis, of a tradition of aggression toward strangers, acted out as "homosexual" rape (and murder – the Levite expected that he was to be killed as well [v. 5]).[30] These accounts have nothing whatever to do with either legal or discursive practices related to same-sex *desire*.

We should indeed be appalled by both of these narratives, but not for an alleged condemnation of homosexuality which they do not inscribe, but rather for the callous indifference to the fate of women that they do. The final conclusion is that there is no evidence in the Hebrew Bible for a category of homosexuals or homosexuality at all, and whatever explanation be adopted for the prohibition of male anal intercourse, there is as little reason to believe that it extended to other forms of homoerotic practice.[31] The hypothesis offered here, namely that male anal intercourse was understood as a category violation, a kind of cross-dressing, while not provable, certainly seems to me to be a plausible one.

Epilogue: Philology as Theology

If there is anything distinctive about the Jewish way of doing theology, it is that there is no distinction between systematic and biblical theology, no distinction between dogmatic and narrative theology. Jews traditionally have done theology through reading narratives and producing narratives on narratives. There can be, I assert as a dogmatic claim, no Jewish theology without philology, no Jewish theology without close reading and textual reasoning. If the philology is not adequate, if the point of the talmudic text is being missed, there is no grounding for a Jewish theological claim. If the philology holds up here, then a Jewish theology of sexuality will have to operate without sexuality, without homo and hetero.

Neither the Bible, nor as I hope to have shown here, the Talmud, knows of such a typology – of that entity called by us "sexuality," whose "chief conceptual function," according to Halperin, "is to distinguish, once and for all, sexual identity from matters of gender – to decouple, as it were, *kinds* of sexual predilection from *degrees* of masculinity and femininity." And as Halperin further observes: "That is what makes sexuality alien to the spirit of ancient Mediterranean cultures" (Halperin 1990: 100, 25). This is as true for the biblical/talmudic Jewish culture of the ancient Mediterranean, as it is for the Greek. Both biblical and talmudic texts confirm rather than refute Foucault's general hypothesis of the "history of sexuality." Neither of them divide off sexual practices from the general categories of forbidden and permitted. Precisely because there is no separate realm of sexuality with all its definitional fraughtness for self-identification and that of others, there is also no separate realm of the sexually forbidden. Of course, I do not mean that forbidden genital practices do not form distinct corpora within either biblical or talmudic law codes. Where a man put his penis was categorized as a separate area of experience than what he put in his stomach, for instance. What I mean is that it does not have a separate ontological, axiological, or even moral status. As opposed to our culture where violating the rules against homoeroticism provokes an entirely different set of reactions from the violation of other moral taboos – *including* sexual ones such as adultery – there is no evidence in biblical/talmudic culture that suggests that that was the case there. Tabooed practices may have been ranked according to severity, but they did not at any time constitute different "species" of human beings. Violating the Sabbath, for instance, produced precisely the same category of transgression (punishable by death) as did male intercourse.

The element common to both classical culture (with all of its variations) and biblical culture (with all of its variations), is that the taboos and tolerances of the culture vis-à-vis same-sex genital practice were tied precisely to structures of maleness and femaleness, to gender and not to a putative sexuality. The absence of "sexuality" does not obviously preclude violence against those who engaged in male anal intercourse, although it should be emphasized that there is not the slightest bit of evidence to suggest that such violence was actually practiced in talmudic times.[32] It does, however, seem to permit a much greater scope for other forms of male intimacy, eroticized and otherwise. "Who is a friend?" a midrash asks, "he that one eats with, drinks with, reads with, studies with, sleeps with, and reveals to him all of his secrets – the secrets of Torah and the secrets of the way of the world" (Shechter 1967). "Sleeps with" does *not* have the metaphorical value that it has in English or German, but the text is certainly reaching for a very intense and passionate level of male-male physical intimacy here. The "way of the world" is a somewhat ambiguous metaphorical term that can refer to several areas of worldly life, including business, but especially sex.[33] Male intimacy, it seems, for the talmudic culture includes the physical contact of being in bed together, while sharing verbally the most intimate of experiences, a pattern not unknown in other cultures. The image of two men in bed together talking of their sexual experiences with women is reminiscent of ethnographic descriptions of Barasana (Columbian) tribesmen, lying in hammocks, fondling each other and talking about sex with women (D. Greenberg 1988: 71). Another way of saying this would be to claim that precisely because biblical and talmudic cultures did not have, according to my reading, a category of the homosexual, they therefore allowed for much greater normative possibilities for the homoerotic. The break in categorical continuity between anal intercourse, which did threaten gendered male identity in that culture as in ours, and other same-sex intimate practices, which did not, allowed for such practices to be engaged in, more or less normatively, without calling up the specter of a threatened masculinity.[34] Eve Kosofsky Sedgwick has perhaps best captured the oddness of our present system:

> It is a rather amazing fact that, of the very many dimensions along which the genital activity of one person can be differentiated from that of another (dimensions that include preference for certain acts, certain zones or sensations, certain physical types, a certain frequency, certain symbolic investments, certain relations of age or power, a certain species, a certain number of participants, etc. etc. etc.), precisely one, the gender of object choice, emerged from the turn of the century, and has remained, as *the* dimension denoted by the now ubiquitous category of "sexual orientation." (Sedgwick 1990: 8)

It is only after the production of a category of sexuality *per se*, of a sexual identity determined by object choice, that any form of physical intimacy between men, and indeed almost any form of intimacy at all, becomes so problematic for our culture. In this sense the ancient cultures of the Mediterranean are more like each other – for all their differences – than any of them are like our own.

Although the theological work remains largely yet to be done, it seems to me that this recognition built on close textual work with the biblical and especially talmudic texts which are definitive for rabbinic Jewish thought has to be the basis for any modern Jewish theological reflection on sexuality. Wherever we begin, we cannot found theological reflection on the assumption that the Bible or the Rabbis have anything to say about "homosexuality."[35]

Acknowledgments

The philological analysis in this chapter has already been published as Boyarin (1995a); the theological reflections are new.

Notes

1   The word *tô 'ēbā*, usually translated "abomination" or "detestable," means something like "transgression of borders." It is used biblically for many types of ritual transgressions that are not sexual. In any case, there is no warrant whatever for the accepted renderings which are obviously loaded with later cultural meanings and would quite beg the current question.

2   I hasten to add this, because I am not claiming that some forbidden cultic practice is being referred to.

3   See Richlin (1993). Although the Talmud does abjure the use of perfumes for men "in places where male intercourse is common," because this would lead people to suspect them of such behavior. Generally, as in this instance, when the Talmud speaks of a predilection for anal intercourse, it attributes such tastes to geographical or ethnic groups – not to individual proclivities.

4   Initially brought to my attention by Marion Bodian when I presented an early version of this chapter at the University of Michigan.

5   By using the term "culture," then, I mean to be asserting that the textual practices that I analyze are not mere language but are a significant cultural practice, however widespread their acceptance or not.

6   The Onan story in the Bible itself has, of course, nothing to do with masturbation at all. Onan's "sin" was coitus interruptus for the purpose of preventing the mandated conception of a child by his brother's widow. "Onanism" for masturbation is thus, as Amy Richlin points out to me just as much a misnomer as "sodomy" for homosexual intercourse is (for the latter see below).

7   Because the flood was caused by those who "destroyed their way upon the ground," taken by the rabbinic commentaries to refer to spilling of the seed.

8   To be sure, the text does not mention other types of homoerotic practice so it is impossible to determine even normative, let alone actual and popular, dispositions towards them.

9   The term refers to a category of women forbidden to priests because of past sexual practices. I am leaving it untranslated here, because it is precisely its definition that is at stake here.

10   I will argue below that this does not reflect a general lack of interest in what women do as long as they don't do it with men. The prohibition on female cross-dressing is every bit as severe as that on male cross-dressing, just to take one highly salient example. Further, there is little reason to assume that the point here is that they will turn to men because sex with women is an inadequate substitute as modern male chauvinists would have it, but simply that once acquainted with the joys of sexual stimulation, they might very well seek it with men also, and *that* is forbidden.

11 It nevertheless remains the case that having intercourse with a non-fertile girl or woman or having anal, intercrural, or oral intercourse with a woman does *not* constitute masturbation, while having oral or intercrural intercourse with a man does.

12 Olyan (1994) has also argued on inner-biblical philological grounds alone that "male intercourse" comprises solely anal penetration.

13 For studies critical of Halperin's position (and of the Foucauldian stance generally), see Thornton (1991) and Richlin (1991). I continue to find the evidence for the thesis compelling in spite of some difficulties and occasional seeming counter-evidence.

14 It has been brought to my attention that Thomas Thurston (1990) has already suggested the possible pertinence of Mary Douglas's work to our question.

15 I have somewhat tortured English syntax to reproduce the parallelism which is obvious in the Hebrew. To be sure, Deuteronomy and the "Holiness" Code of this portion of Leviticus are generally considered different documents according to modern biblical criticism. However, Deuteronomy also interdicts "mixtures of kinds." Whatever its subcultures, biblical culture certainly showed degrees of coherence as well.

16 This connection was realized by the Rabbis. In the Palestinian Talmud, Tractate *Kil'aim* [Forbidden Mixtures] 27a, Rabbi Shim'on ben Lakish remarks: Everywhere that it says "according to its kind," the laws of forbidden mixtures apply. The phrase, "according to its kind" appears no less than five times in the verse immediately preceding the verse that describes the creation of humankind in separate sexes, called also in Hebrew "kinds." Technically, biblical critics assign the laws of forbidden mixtures to a source known as the Holiness Code (H), produced, as was the Priestly Code (P) according to them in temple circles. According to the latest scholarly opinion, H is a secondary elaboration of P, and the "authors" of H were the redactors of P in its current form (Knohl [1992] 1994, whose conclusions have been accepted by Milgrom 1992). Even, however, according to older critical views according to which H is older than P, there has never been a doubt as to their common provenance in priestly circles such as those that produced Genesis 1 as well and no reason to assume, therefore, major cultural differences between them.

17 Compare the opposite but structurally similar explanation that Foucault gives for the differential treatment of male-male sex and female-female sex in Artemidorus, where only the latter is considered as "contrary to nature" (Foucault 1990–2: III, 24–5).

18 See Hallett (1989). Some of Hallett's evidence is, however, questionable, especially her interpretation of Phaedrus's Fable in which he accounts for "tribadic females and effeminate males" by recounting that Prometheus got drunk when making human beings and attached some male genitals to female people and some female genitals to male people by mistake. Hallett interprets this to mean that lesbians are women with male genitalia (1989: 210), a contradiction of biological reality that she understandably finds quite unsettling. To me it seems quite patent that the purport of the fable is that tribades are the men who got female genitals by mistake, and the *molles* are the women with male genitals attached to them. This actually provides beautiful evidence for Halperin's definition of sexuality as that modern cultural entity whose chief conceptual function "is to distinguish, once and for all, sexual identity from matters of gender – to decouple, as it were, *kinds* of sexual predilection from *degrees* of masculinity and femininity" (Halperin 1990: 100). For Phaedrus it was impossible to imagine a woman loving women, so a lesbian must "really" be a man in a woman's body "by mistake," and this was, in one version or another, the most common way in Euroamerica of accounting for same-sex eroticism until the early twentieth century. Even a Krafft-Ebing, towards the end of the nineteenth century still conceived of lesbians as men with female bodies, i.e. as male souls in bodies with female genitalia (Mosse 1985: 106). For "us," the situation is precisely reversed. Monique Wittig's (1992) intervention notwithstanding, lesbians *are* in our contemporary culture clearly women, thus explaining Hallet's misreading – if I am correct. The best (in fact, for me, the only cogent) evidence that Hallett cites for her claim that tribadism was understood as involving penetration is the text by

Martial that describes a tribad who penetrates boys (anally) as well as women (1989: 215–16). In any case, the very etymology of the Greek loan word *tribas* suggests that at least at one time female same-sex eroticism was understood to involve only rubbing and not penetration, just as in the Talmud.

19 This can be demonstrated philologically. The term that is used, and which I have translated as "rubbing" is used in another sexual context as well: "Our Rabbis have taught: One who is rubbing with her son and he enters her, Bet Shammai says that he has rendered her unfit to marry a priest, and Bet Hillel says that she is fit to marry a priest" (Babylonian Talmud, *Sanhedrin* 69b). From this context we learn clearly two things: "Rubbing" involves contact of external genital with external genital, and it does not include penetration, for the rubbing here is contrasted with the entering. We also learn, by the way, of a fascinating sexual practice that, as long as it did not include penetration, was apparently hardly even disapproved of to judge from the tone of this passage.

20 Surprisingly little work has been done on this important site for understanding both biblical and talmudic gender politics. I hope to do much more with this. Certainly by the time of the Talmud – if not actually *much* earlier – the practice itself had fallen into complete desuetude.

21 Interestingly enough, according to Dover, representations of male–female intercrural intercourse are unknown from the vase paintings (1989: 99).

22 I owe this last formulation to David Halperin.

23 Note that this is entirely different from the (false) association between cross-dressing (transvestism) and homosexuality in contemporary folk culture, on which see Garber (1992: 130). I avoid the term "sodomy" as anachronistic for the biblical culture, although not, of course, for the culture of the eighteenth century.

24 Indeed, it is highly symptomatic that in the talmudic analogue of Artemidorus, sexual dreams are taken as symbolic of other activities, just as in the Greek text; while, of course, in "our" formation the opposite is the case.

25 There was, paradoxically enough, some shame attached to the status of the *erômenos* if he grants his favors to the *erastês*. See Dover (1989: 42 and especially 81–4). See also his simple comparison between this situation and the discourse of heterosexual "seduction" in twentieth-century English society (1989: 88–9). Although it has been said before, it is worth once more remarking Dover's exemplary quiet good sense and taste.

26 There is even a slight bit of evidence but very inconclusive that might indicate that solo masturbation with a dildo was more blamable for women than mutual non-penetrative rubbing (Babylonian Talmud *Avodah Zara* 44a), where a certain female ruler is disparaged for having had made for herself an imitation penis which she used every day. Since this is, however, in a non-legal discursive context, it is impossible to determine what the normative status of such activity would have been. Were this evidence more conclusive, it would provide strong confirmation for my interpretation.

27 Cantarella (1992: 200–1). In the New Testament, as in first century Jewish literature and not in the Bible nor the Rabbis, the Sodomites' sin is identified as homosexual (contrast Jude 1.7, where the sin of Sodom is identified as sexual immorality and perversion to Ezekiel 16.49–50, where it is referred to as arrogance and lack of concern for the poor and the needy). See Boyarin (1995b) for other examples in which the New Testament's discourse of sex is closest to that of such texts as the *Testaments of the Twelve Patriarchs* and different from that of the Rabbis.

28 The Rabbis themselves, as I have argued at length in Boyarin (1993) and elsewhere, resisted and rejected Hellenistic philosophy, although they were heavily influenced in other ways by Hellenistic culture.

29 As Phyllis Trible has remarked, "These two stories show that the rules of hospitality in Israel protect only males. Though Lot entertained men alone, the old man also has a female guest, and no hospitality safeguards her. She is chosen as the victim for male lust. Further, in neither of these stories does the male host offer himself in place of his guests" (Trible 1984: 75). Trible's

further suggestion, however, that the woman was not dead, and the husband's dismemberment of her to call for revenge was a sacrifice of a living victim is totally unsupportable. Her claim (pressed at least as a question) that, "the cowardly betrayer [is] also the murderer" and that "no mourning becomes the man" (1984: 80) seems to me just plain wrong. She is certainly already dead; this is what the Bible tells us when it says that she did not answer him, and the dismemberment is pursued in a sort of extravagance of mourning and desire for revenge for the violence done to her – to be sure engendered by his cowardice and callous domination of her. He was willing for her to be sexually abused; the violence done to her that causes her death appalls even him.

30 Dover (1989: 105). A more modern analogue can be found in John Boorman's *Deliverance* (USA 1972), where a group of "hillbillies" attack and rape one of a party of middle-class canoers who have "invaded" their territory. For anal rape described as formalized or official aggression, see also Mekilta derabbi Ishmael Amaleq 1, where a foreign conqueror punishes the king of Israel by "standing before him ruffians who had never known woman in their lives and they tortured him with anal intercourse." (Incidentally this does not mean that they were "homosexuals" but that they were virgins and very randy.) See also Richlin (1992: *passim*).

31 Contra Cantarella (1992: 198) who is still speaking of "homosexuality" as a transhistorical category, ten years after Foucault's work (which she cites but neither accepts nor contests). My point is not, of course, that Foucault has become some sort of received doctrine that must be acknowledged but that he has opened questions that must be addressed whenever we speak of "sexuality." Whether or not he is explicitly brought in, we simply cannot *assume* a category of homosexuality for any and every cultural formation and text; it must be argued for.

32 In the Mishna, *Makkot* ch. 1, the point is explicitly made that the death penalties of the Bible are no longer operative, except possibly for murder.

33 As indicated by the following text among others: "When his wife died, Rabbi Tarfon said to her sister during the mourning period: Marry me and raise your sister's children. And even though he married her, he did not behave with her according to the way of the world until after thirty days" (*Kohellet Rabba* 9; see also *Bereshit Rabba* 22). Now, although the sexual meaning is not the most frequent one for this collocation it is certainly a readily available one. Thus while it is a meaningless claim (because unfalsifiable) that this is what the author of this text "intended," it is hard to escape concluding that the sexual association would have been present for any recipient of this text.

34 Of course, I do not know and cannot speculate precisely what expressions of intimacy the actual talmudic rabbis permitted themselves. Precisely one point of this study is, however, to suggest that the borders of erotic experience were not nearly as sharply defined then as now.

35 For important resources towards a Jewish theology of sexuality see Steven Greenberg (2003) and Simcha Dubowski's very important documentary film, *Trembling Before G-d* (2001).

Chapter 9

Queer Father

Gregory of Nyssa and the Subversion of Identity

Virginia Burrus

What might it mean to perform a "queer" reading of Gregory of Nyssa? (And what would be the point?) Oddly enough, it might mean to read Gregory for his *asceticism*. For asceticism and queerness are, arguably, heavily overlapped terms: both designate practices that center on *resistance* to normative discourses of sex and sexuality. Thus, David Halperin's paradoxical definition of queerness as an "identity without an essence" might also be applied to asceticism. Like queerness, asceticism can be said to demarcate "not a positivity but a positionality vis-à-vis the normative – a positionality that is not restricted to" monks and nuns, even as queerness is not restricted to "lesbians and gay men" (Halperin 1995: 62).[1]

Both Gregory's reputation as a married man and his appropriation of Platonic concepts of desire complicate the interpretation of his asceticism. Gregory, then, is a *queer ascetic* not only because asceticism and queerness may sometimes amount to much the same thing, but also (or all the more so) because his asceticism fails to conform to expectations. First, his anti-marital doctrine of "virginity" stubbornly resists literalization as a specifiable "lifestyle," thereby leaving the referent of "marriage" equally in question – like "an identity without an essence." Second, his concept of sexual sublimation evades a strict dualism of flesh and spirit at the same time that it unmoors active and passive erotic positionalities from stable hierarchies. Christian "love" (*agape*), according to Gregory, is the result not of the repression or control of desire but rather desire's disciplined *intensification*; a mere man is able not only to receive God's penetrating Word and Spirit but also to desire the divine bridegroom *actively*; and even a Father and his Son are to be conceived (however improbably) as equals in transgenerational love. Gregory's erotic theory, intricately woven into his soteriological scheme, is also implicated in his relational doctrine of God: indeed, it is in the context of the masculinist formulation of Trinitarian theology that the homoeroticism of his revisionary Platonism most clearly surfaces.[2]

At first glance, the *least* "queer" (the most painfully conventional) aspect of Gregory's theory of sexuality would seem to be his conviction that *the only proper object of desire is God* – who turns out, however, to be *no proper object at all*. Indeed, Gregory stresses that divinity – being both infinite and incomprehensible – absolutely eludes objectification. Thus the sublimity of desire lies in its (theoretically) limitless extension, in the repetitions by which it is prolonged and through which not only the object but also the subject are held in (eternal) suspense. It is, however, at this point of seeming greatest difference – the radical transcendentalizing of *eros* – that Gregory's ascetic theory of desire also proves queerly resonant with the positions of some radically "pro-sex" gay and lesbian theorists, as I shall discuss briefly in closing.

Meanwhile, I have left another question in suspense: what is the point of a queer reading of Gregory? The point, for me, is surely not to defend patristic orthodoxy by arguing that it is more politically or intellectually "correct" than formerly thought (or for that matter, that is "naughtier").[3] The point is, in the words of Judith Butler, to perform "a repetition in language that forces change," by taking up an interpellative of theological hate speech – "hey, *queer!*" – and reproducing it as the site of an insurrectionary "counterspeech" lodged within the texts of the Church Fathers themselves (Butler 1997a: 163, 15). My motivations in reading Gregory as queerly as I can are thus primarily therapeutic, in relation to theology itself. To be sure, the "healing" of theological "sin" does not occur all at once or once for all; and yet by the same token the ongoing effectiveness of injurious address should not be taken for granted. The forceful momentum of repetition – intrinsic to a theological orthodoxy's constitution as a self-perpetuating "tradition" – ensures, for better and for worse, that no word is final. Or, as Gregory himself might put it: this present attempt to queer the Father's *logos* is just a drop in the rhetorical bucket.[4]

Gregory's Virginity

In the treatise *On Virginity*, the earliest of his surviving writings,[5] Gregory skillfully demonstrates his humility by representing himself as lacking what he nonetheless dares to praise – namely virginity. He expresses regret that his own knowledge of virginity's beauty is like water placed out of reach of a thirsty man – "vain and useless." "Happy they who have still the power of choosing the better way, and have not debarred themselves from it by engagements of the secular (τῷ κοινῷ . . . βίῳ) as we have, whom a gulf now divides from glorious virginity" (*On Virginity* 3; Gregory of Nyssa 1994: 345a).[6] In a state of lack, Gregory is also in a state of yearning for what he does not have (*for what no one really has?*) – no less a good than the incorruptible divinity of the spiritual realm, as he has defined the virginal condition (*On Virginity* 1–2; Gregory of Nyssa 1994: 343b–345a). Gregory does not possess virginity, but he hints that he is in pursuit of it in so far as he is capable of recognizing the poverty of the "common life" and thus of longing for something better (*On Virginity* 3; Gregory of Nyssa 1994: 345a–348b).[7]

The "common life" is metonymically represented by marriage in Gregory's text. His uncompromising denunciation of family life proceeds by cataloguing the daily course of intimacy between spouses, parents, and children, and the repeated woundings of grief that necessarily accompany any finite love. As Michel Barnes (1996) has shown, Gregory's description of marriage draws heavily upon Stoic tradition, while placing new emphasis on the paradoxical conjunction of joy and sadness that is woven into the fabric of mortal existence. "They are human all the time, things weak and perishing; they have to look upon the tombs of their progenitors; and so pain is inseparably bound up with their existence, if they have the least power of reflection." Page after page, Gregory sustains the spectacle of familiar suffering in an excessive and yet still seemingly insufficient attempt to answer his own challenge: "How shall we really bring to view the evils common to life?" Setting out to write of life as a tragedy, as he puts it, he raises his voice in the hyperbolic language of lament, taking the role attributed to the servants who, "like conquering foes, dismantle the bridal chamber" of the young wife who has died in childbirth: "they deck it for the funeral, but it is death's room now; they make useless wailings and beatings of the hands."

Gregory introduces Elijah and John the Baptist as positive biblical models of the single-mindedness of the virginal soul who has avoided the vicissitudes of the familial. "It is my belief that they would not have reached to this loftiness of spirit, if marriage had softened them," he remarks (*On Virginity* 6; Gregory of Nyssa 1994: 351b). The theme of single-mindedness is further developed through the image of a stream's flow; while refer-ring explicitly to the gush of a mind's creative potency, it also enfolds within its meaning the rush of generative fluids that produce a man's bodily "issues." "We often see water con-tained in a pipe bursting upwards through this constraining force, which will not let it leak; and this, in spite of its natural gravitation," remarks Gregory. "In the same way, the mind of man, enclosed in the compact channel of an habitual continence, and by not having any side issues, will be raised by virtue of its natural powers of motion to an exalted love" (*On Virginity* 7; Gregory of Nyssa 1994: 352a). If this comparison suggests that spiritual trans-cendence must be achieved by closing down all other erotic channels, above all the physi-cally sexual, Gregory nevertheless makes it clear that he has no intention of deprecating "marriage as an institution." Nor, as it turns out, does he intend to present marriage as merely an honorable alternative to virginity for those too weak to abstain from the conve-niences and satisfactions of family life. On the contrary, he now audaciously proposes that it is a literalized virginity that is the refuge of the less muscular Christian: "He who is of so weak a character that he cannot make a manful stand against nature's impulse had better keep himself very far away from temptations, rather than descend into a combat which is above his strength." Another biblical type is placed alongside Elijah and John, as Isaac is introduced as the privileged model for the man who is able both to put "heavenly things" first and to "use the advantages of marriage with sobriety and moderation" in order to fulfill his duty (λειτοργια) to the civic community.[8] The biblical father had intercourse with his wife up to the point that she gave birth, as Gregory tells it; his dimness of sight in old age is taken as a sign that he subsequently shut down "the channels of the senses" and gave himself wholly to the contemplation of the invisible. Here Gregory turns to the example of the experienced farmer who is able temporarily to divert a portion of water for irrigation and then skillfully redirect it back into the stream, thereby meeting multiple needs without significantly weakening the water's flow (*On Virginity* 8; Gregory of Nyssa 1994: 353a). How are we to read this illustration in light of the previously offered example of "water contained in a pipe bursting upward" (*On Virginity* 7; Gregory of Nyssa 1994: 352a)? The water bursting from a single pipe may seem excessive in comparison with the measured flow of the second farmer's diversified irrigation system (this somewhat idiosyncratic position is argued quite forcefully by Mark Hart 1992: 4). Equally plausible, however, is that the second farmer's compromise with the fleshly demands of marriage may be seen to distort and even parody the singular heroics of true virginity. Resolution is deferred.

Having thus left his definitions of virginity and marriage suspended in ambiguity, Gregory draws on the Platonic myth of ascent and the biblical creation narratives to refine his erotic theory further. In a lengthy passage that is among the most overtly Platonizing in his works, drawing particularly heavily on the *Symposium*,[9] Gregory notes that, for the "climbing soul," material beauties "will be but the ladder by which he climbs to the prospect of that Intellectual Beauty," or "the hand to lead us to the love of the supernal Beauty." "But how can any one fly up into the heavens, who has not the wings of heaven?" he queries, adding that "there is but one vehicle on which man's soul can mount into the heavens, namely, the self-made likeness in himself to the descending Dove" (*On Virginity* 11; Gregory of Nyssa 1994: 355a–357a). Rising heavenward on the wings of the one-and-only bearer of desire, the soul achieves "union" with "the incorruptible Deity" in a match based on sameness. A recep-tive lover, "she places herself like a mirror beneath the purity of God and moulds her own beauty at the touch and sight of the Archetype of all beauty." "The real Virginity – the real zeal for chastity – ends in no other goal than this, namely, the power thereby of seeing God," Gregory concludes (*On Virginity* 11; Gregory of Nyssa 1994: 357a).

Sliding from Plato's vision of the end to the Genesis account of the beginning, Gregory notes that the human being originally possessed that untarnished image of the Divine Mind prerequisite for the act of love as the mimetic consummation of likeness. Disruptive "passion" came later, bending free will to the fabrication of evil. Sin thus entered with the force and "fatal quickness" of a bad habit, darkening the soul's mirror with the rust of corruption, smearing the reflective purity of the original creature with a coat of filth, by which it acquired a "resemblance to something else." "Now the putting off of a strange accretion is equivalent to the return to that which is familiar and natural," explains Gregory. The Platonic ascent is thereby scripted as a return to created nature. Like the woman of Luke's Gospel who searches her home for a lost coin, the "widowed soul" need only turn within to recover her lost self, which is also to say to find the divine lover in whose image she is molded. Gregory exhorts the reader to "become that which the First Man was at the moment when he first breathed," stripping off the "dead skins" of sin and death. Innocent of sexual relations with his "helpmeet," the First Man "found in the Lord alone all that was sweet" in those blessed times before marriage was instituted as "the last stage of our separation from the life that was led in Paradise." Marriage's institutionalized heteroeroticism – a concession to the taint of difference that was introduced into love's economy – remains a barrier between humanity and Paradise. Marriage, then, is also "the first thing to be left" on the path back to future bliss. Virginity's salvation is for those who know how to love in a spirit of sameness, its goal the consummating absorption of all sexes in the one (*On Virginity* 12; Gregory of Nyssa 1994: 357a–359a).[10]

Of course, virginity's version of same-sex love cannot possibly have anything to do with fleshly procreation: "life and immortality instead of children are produced by this latter intercourse." By refusing to perpetuate life's cycles, the virginal body becomes a barrier against mortality; the "virgin mother" conceives only "deathless children" by the Spirit. Having now (with a little help from Paul) wed Plato's concept of philosophic motherhood as a property of men to a biblical notion of a fecund virginity originally Adam's and recovered in Mary, Gregory once again bemoans the "agonies of grief" brought in with marriage, while acknowledging its attractions. Marriage, he here suggests, is like a sword. It's hilt "is smooth and handy, and polished and glittering outside; it seems to grow to the outline (τύπος) of the hand"; "it offers for the grasp of the senses a smooth surface of delights." Gregory will, however, allow our thoughts to linger only so long on the smooth surface and sensual pleasures associated with that swellingly swordlike member that molds itself so delightfully to the contours of the grasping hand. A sword is, after all, more than a friendly hilt: "the other part is steel and the instrument of death, formidable to look at, more formidable still to come across"; it becomes, for man, "the worker of mourning and of loss." The instrument of pleasure is thus the organ of birth and therefore tainted with the violence of death, the cause – on this reading – of all pain accompanying the loss of children, parents, spouses. For one who would avoid the sword wounds of grief, God is the gentlest bridegroom, and the virginal soul who becomes his spouse, conceiving with the divine spirit, "brings forth wisdom and righteousness, and sanctification and redemption too," children who will never die. To live thus virginally is to anticipate the angelic nature that will belong to humanity once again in Paradise. "In fact, the life of virginity seems to be an actual representation (εἰκών τις) of the blessedness in the world to come," as Gregory remarks (*On Virginity* 13: Gregory of Nyssa 1994: 360b).

By this point Gregory has made it abundantly clear that virginity is not a matter of mere abstention from sexual relations: as a psychic condition, it is certainly much more; remembering Isaac (and also Plato),[11] we might ponder again whether it is not also somewhat less. Gregory's particular poetic art resists the sharp distinction between literal and figurative language, which is part of what makes his treatise *On Virginity* so difficult to interpret tidily.[12] "Virginity" as the sign of the fecundity of desire always means more than it did before; no reader can get to the bottom of it; and yet it does not simply mean something *else*, as if the trick of reading lay straightforwardly in the cracking of a code.

Gregory's biblical exemplars, like his aqueous metaphors, complicate the relation between sign and sense, literal and figurative virginity, physical and sublimated desire. Gregory takes Miriam to be "a type of Mary the mother of God," whereas her thoroughly dry "timbrel" (τύμπανον) "may mean to imply virginity." Having been separated from all sources of moisture, as Gregory describes it, the membrane stretched over the vessel of the virginal womb of this first Mary has become as resonant as a drum. "Thus, Miriam's timbrel being a dead thing, and virginity being a deadening of the bodily passions, it is perhaps not very far removed from the bounds of probability that Miriam was a virgin," he concludes. Adding that "we can but guess and surmise, we cannot clearly prove that this was so," he proceeds to discuss the strengths and weaknesses of various arguments from silence that this woman identified as her brother's sister might have been no man's wife. By now, however, Gregory seems a bit deflated by his own act of Marian desiccation, with its withering threat of infertility. Proceeding quickly to cite the examples of Isaiah and Paul, whose self-descriptions privilege a juicier but still spiritualized fecundity, he returns finally to Mary the Godbearer, in whose female body virginity and motherhood coincide despite seeming contradiction. Paul's teaching that each human being is in some sense "doubled," consisting in both an inner and an outer man, leads Gregory to the notion of a doubled marital status, in which the ruling of fidelity dictates that one "self's" virginity must correspond to the "self's" marriage. "Maybe," he concludes coyly, "if one was to assert boldly that the body's virginity was the co-operator and the agent of the inward marriage, this assertion would not be much beside the probable fact." Thus, for Gregory, the virginal mother becomes not so much a paradoxical conjunction of opposites as an icon of consistency, easily harmonized with a version of the Platonic myth of ascent in which the soul's desire for union with the beautiful moves it ever upward, as virginity gives birth continually to a higher fecundity in the progressive displacements of erotic sublimation (*On Virginity* 19; Gregory of Nyssa 1994: 364b–365b).[13]

Virginity is, then, the bottomless womb of the self-transcending infinitude of Gregory's desire. Isaac models the measured progress of the soul's upward climb, in which each stage prepares the way for the next, youth's passionate rush giving way to a sedate marriage in manhood's full maturity (resulting in a single act of birth), marriage itself giving way to a more divine love and more lasting progeny. Isaac himself is superseded, in Gregory's text, not by Christ but by Mary. What Isaac pursues sequentially, with a fragmented grace, she accomplishes with thrilling integrity, at once virgin and parent, at one in flesh and spirit, salvation's end looping back to creation's beginning. Sometimes inclined to gush, sensitive to the pleasurable touch of a sword's hilt, Gregory reaches for the timbrel's saving aridity: dry now, he leads the dance of the virgins, all the more man in that he is more woman. Icon of "a teleology of reabsorption of fluid in a solidified form," Gregory's text models the congealing of an idealized masculine subjectivity that transcends the "mechanics" of fluids, in Irigaray's phrasing (Irigaray 1985b: 110). And yet, startlingly, *On Virginity* does not repress the sticky "reality" of the male body's ebb and flow but rather projects the desire for the reassuring constancy of solid matter onto female form.

Was Gregory married? Have we not here a married Father? Well, Gregory does – near the end – try to make an honest man of himself. Establishing an elaborate comparison between bodily and spiritual marriages, which correspond to Paul's "inner" and "outer" men, he represents the inward or spiritual self as a man who courts a bride who is Wisdom herself, in the guise of the good wife of Solomon's Proverbs. Gregory is seemingly not, however, altogether happy to remain with this "straight" version of the divine union. It is clear, he notes hastily, that the marital metaphor applies to male and female subjects alike; he cites the assurance of Galatians 3.28 that in Christ "there is not male and female," adding the explanatory gloss that "Christ is all things and in all." If Christ can be all things to all people, any gendering of the object of desire will also do: the beloved is equally divine whether figured as the queenly Sophia or the incorruptible Bridegroom, concludes Gregory (*On Virginity* 20; Gregory of Nyssa 1994: 365a–366b). Indeed, most of the time Gregory's "inner man" seems happy to play the woman in relation to the "Good Husband" for whom he bears deathless children, protects his chastity (*On Virginity* 15; Gregory of Nyssa 1994: 361a–b), and even keeps house (*On Virginity* 18; Gregory of Nyssa 1994: 363a–364b).

Was Gregory married? Was he a virgin? What counts as marriage, what counts as virginity? If this text insists on putting marriage in question without offering virginity as an easy answer, then it seems to me that one of its perhaps unintended but not accidental jokes is to have been taken almost universally as conclusive evidence that *Gregory was married*. Regarding Gregory's protest that his engagement in the "common life" now separates him irrevocably "from glorious virginity" (*On Virginity* 3; Gregory of Nyssa 1994: 345a), Michel Aubineau notes, "One cannot reasonably discount such a categorical disclosure" (Aubineau 1966: 66). We have seen, however, that the disclosive *logos* of this treatise consistently eludes the particular clarities of the categorical. Isaac did, after all, beget in a single act not one but two sons: perhaps Gregory is not the married Father but the trickster Jacob who rides in on the heel of his brother. Wrapped in a deceptively hairy skin, underneath he is actually beardless and smooth – like the hilt of a sword – like a sister or a virginal mother – like Mary. Maybe he was, maybe he wasn't: a "marriage" that stretches desire across the gulf of sexual difference is truly beside the point, from Gregory's perspective. Mobilizing androgyny's fluidity on behalf of a different love, Gregory's vertically oriented "philosophic *logos*" does not flow in channels of gendered plurality but begets a singular – and singularly graceful – masculine subjectivity that derives its position of transcendent dominance "from its power to eradicate the difference between the sexes" (Irigaray 1985b: 74).

God's Bottom

Readers of Gregory's *Life of Moses* find their view of the biographical subject screened not only by the original biblical text of which Moses is both subject and (presumed) author but also by the added layers of Gregory's narrative simplifications and theoretical expansion. Inscribed, reduced, sublimated – in the end, Moses is made as fine and light "as the thread of a spider web," enveloped in a tunic the color of air (*Life of Moses* 2.191; Gregory of Nyssa 1978: 103).[14] One begins to suspect that it is not only Moses' request to see God but also Gregory's request to see this man that "has been both granted and denied" (Ferguson 1976: 310): following in the footsteps of Moses, he finds himself suddenly staring straight into the cleft of the unrepresentable. The scholarly tendency to categorize this subtle text as the fruit of old age and a contemplative – even "mystical" – lifestyle is not hard to understand.[15] On the one hand, there *is* something consummative about the work; on the other hand, unfurling seamlessly, it moves beyond even consummation's finality. For the author of the *Life of Moses*, there are multiple climaxes on the never-ending ascent of the ever-receding peak, where satisfaction always opens out into the desire for something even better. Slipping into the hole in the rock is not a regress to the smug stasis of the maternal womb but rather a conversion of the womb's abysmal potentiality into the expansive site of a man's absolute transformability:[16] pursuing Moses, Gregory surges forward toward perfection, his only goal to make the chase last forever.

The work opens to the accompaniment of the pounding hooves of racehorses. Acquiescing to a friend's request that he offer some advice on the "perfect life," Gregory represents himself playfully as one of the spectators who shout encouragement "even though the horses are eager to run." Introducing a treatise that will argue for the importance of *theoria*, or visual contemplation, as well as mimesis, or the imitation of divine perfection, he here gently mocks those who rivet their gaze on the charioteers and mime their gestures, "leaning forward and flailing the air with their outstretched hands instead of with a whip," as if they might help speed the teams along. The joke is perhaps on his own initially misplaced Platonic identification with the charioteer of the soul rather than the horse of passion.[17] Moreover, agreeing merely to exhort a younger man who is already "lightfootedly leaping and straining constantly for the 'prize of the heavenly calling,'" he may appear to be taking himself out of the race (*Life of Moses* 1.1; Gregory of Nyssa 1978: 29). In reality he is setting the pace, a "father" who models obedience for the son (*Life of Moses* 1.2; Gregory of Nyssa 1978: 29). Galloping smoothly by now, he warns his disciple that this course has no end: "The one limit of virtue is the absence of a limit. How then would one arrive at the sought-for boundary when he can find no boundary?" (*Life of Moses* 1.8; Gregory of Nyssa 1978: 31). The joy is in the running itself. Gregory's concern in this *Life* is "not with logical connection but with progress, not with chronology but with sequence," as Everett Ferguson notes (1976: 314); the main thing is that the text, like the quest for virtue, must be prolonged. Or, to borrow Ronald Heine's words, "each [event] represents another upward step, and in this sense all are of equal importance in showing that Moses never stopped on the course of virtue" (Heine 1975: 102).

Moses' birth is the birth not of a male but rather of the principle of maleness, marked by "austerity and intensity of virtue" and shaped by ongoing resistance to the "tyrant" who favors "the female form of life" (*Life of Moses* 2.2; Gregory of Nyssa 1978: 55). As mutable creatures, human beings are constantly giving birth to themselves, remarks Gregory, and gender is a matter of choice: "we are in some manner our own parents, giving birth to ourselves by our own free choice in accordance with whatever we wish to be, whether male or female, molding ourselves to the teaching of virtue or vice" (*Life of Moses* 2.3; Gregory of Nyssa 1978: 55–6). Free will assists in the begetting and delivery of virtuous male selves, protected by the ark of education from "the stream made turbulent by the successive waves of passion" in which the less well-endowed children drown (*Life of Moses* 2.5–7; Gregory of Nyssa 1978: 56). Fruitful Christianity is the "natural" mother to whom the male child must return for milky nurturance, while a secular education, "which is always in labor but never gives birth," may serve as an adequate, if temporary, foster mother (*Life of Moses* 2.10–12; Gregory of Nyssa 1978: 57).

To the one who has given birth to himself as male, the truth which is God comes, illumining his soul with its flame. If Christ is the flaming truth, the Virgin is the thorny bush that is miraculously not consumed by the fire. (As elsewhere, Gregory's Mariology engulfs his incarnational Christology.) In order to get close enough to see the light shining through the womblike container within the bush, the man Moses removes the coverings of skins – materiality itself – from the feet of his soul. Stripped naked, he finally perceives the difference between being and non-being, between the "transcendent essence and cause of the universe" and the created order that exists only by participation in true being (*Life of Moses* 2.19–26; Gregory of Nyssa 1978: 59–61).

One of the first miracles to occur following this theophany, continues Gregory, is "the rod's changing into a snake" (*Life of Moses* 2.26; Gregory of Nyssa 1978: 61). However, Gregory assures his readers that "the change from a rod (βακτηρία) into a snake should not trouble the lovers of Christ" (*Life of Moses* 2.31; Gregory of Nyssa 1978: 61). "For our sakes [the Lord] became a serpent that he might devour and consume the Egyptian serpents produced by the sorcerers"; "this done, the serpent changed into a rod" (*Life of Moses* 2.33–4; Gregory of Nyssa 1978: 62). Seeming to associate philosophy with the serpent of sorcery, he adds that circumcision is necessary to "cut off everything that is hurtful and impure" as is the case with "philosophy's generative faculty (γονή)" (*Life of Moses* 2.38–9; Gregory of Nyssa 1978: 63). Its fleshly excesses sheered away, the snake is once again refashioned as a sleek rod. Although admitting that "we have probably already sufficiently interpreted the rod (ῥάβδος)" (*Life of Moses* 2.63; Gregory of Nyssa 1978: 68), Gregory cannot resist elaborating his account of the marvels of "that invincible rod of virtue which consumes the rods of magic" (*Life of Moses* 2.64; Gregory of Nyssa 1978: 68). Vanquishing the serpentine forces of a hyper-masculinity, the rod also purifies the man of the swampy mire of a "frog-like life" (*Life of Moses* 2.77; Gregory of Nyssa 1978: 72). However, when struck against the dry rock that is Christ, the rod "dissolves hardness into the softness of water," so that the rock "flows into those who receive him" (*Life of Moses* 136; Gregory of Nyssa 1978: 87).

Heine's insistence that all of the events "are of equal importance" in this ongoing narrative disrupts a scholarly obsession with its theophanic moments, which have, following the influential work of Jean Daniélou (1954), been invoked to support a reductive and anachronistic reading of Gregory's *Life* as descriptive of a tidy, three-stage "mystical" ascent.[18] Heine urges us to attend, instead, to the continuous flow of the text – to listen (as it were) for the relentless pounding of the hooves of horses that never stop in the race for perfection. Heine's interpretation is compelling, yet it might be admitted that Gregory himself does suggest that the three theophanies are privileged purveyors of the message of eternal progress,[19] even if they are not ends – or indeed quite climaxes – in themselves. Discussing what Moses saw on Sinai, Gregory explicitly relates this vision to his hero's earlier glimpse into the virginal bush: "What is now recounted seems somehow to be contradictory to the first theophany, for then the Divine was beheld in light but now he is seen in darkness" (*Life of Moses* 2.162; Gregory of Nyssa 1978: 94–5). Having passed through a period of spiritual adolescence – all that preoccupation with the contests of rods! – Moses reaches a higher level of erotic knowledge. True sight now turns out to be partly a matter of blind touch, as the mind pushes ever deeper into the "luminous darkness," yearning to understand that which exceeds understanding (*Life of Moses* 2.163; Gregory of Nyssa 1978: 95). Within this account of penetration, the movement of Moses' ascent keeps repeating itself: it is "as though he were passing from one peak to another." Ascending beyond the base of the mountain, he hears the trumpetlike cry of a God who is at this point apparently beyond words; next, "he slips into the inner sanctuary" where divinity is to be found; finally he reaches "the tabernacle not made with hands" (*Life of Moses* 2.167; Gregory of Nyssa 1978:

96) – a "limit" that itself quickly expands into the capaciousness of the all-encompassing (*Life of Moses* 2.177; Gregory of Nyssa 1978: 99). If the clarity of light has been converted to the mystery of a womblike darkness, the ascent of the peak has been transformed into a dive into the bottomless deep. In the process, Moses himself has also been entered and changed: "It was not marriage which produced for him his 'God-receiving' flesh, but he became the stonecutter of his own flesh, which was carved by the divine finger, for 'the Holy Spirit came upon the virgin and the power of the Most High overshadowed her'"(*Life of Moses* 2.216; Gregory of Nyssa 1978: 110–1). God's own finger having written on his body, impregnating him with its word, Moses is still a virgin after Sinai.

But there is (always) more. Seemingly not satisfied with the limits of his own historical retelling, Gregory thickens his interpretation with a supplemental theophany not mentioned in the initial recounting of events. Pulled out of sequence from an earlier chapter in the biblical text, the episode is refashioned into a divine encore whose structural excessiveness merely underlines the point that even expansion into the all-encompassing "tabernacle" is not the end of knowing God. "He still thirsts for that with which he constantly filled himself to capacity, and he asks to attain as if he had never partaken" (*Life of Moses* 2.230; Gregory of Nyssa 1978: 114). If Moses has now asked to see God "face to face, as a man speaks with his friend" (*Life of Moses* 2.219; Gregory of Nyssa 1978: 111), God both satisfied his desire and leaves him in an eternal state of frustrated excitement. What he wants exceeds his human capacity, he is told. "Still," reports Gregory, "God says there is 'a place with himself' where there is a 'rock with a hole in it' into which he commands Moses to enter." Entering, Moses cannot see, for God has placed his hand over the mouth of the hole, but Moses hears God call out to him. Coming out of the hole, he sees "the back of the One who called him" (*Life of Moses* 2.220; Gregory of Nyssa 1978: 112). The reader, it would seem, is, like Moses, invited both to see and not to see what is being described in such charged passages. "These sentences raise mystery to sublimity, so that my understanding rests in a state of quiet apprehension of something beyond my powers to decipher. I am confused, I do not understand . . . unless – I do. But if I do, I perform a rapid, even instantaneous gesture of cancellation," writes Geoffrey Harpham.[20] Gregory, for his part, admonishes the reader to perform just such a "cancellation," explaining, "If these things are looked at literally, their concept of [God] will be inappropriate" (*Life of Moses* 2.221; Gregory of Nyssa 1978: 112). Continuing nonetheless to peek behind the veil of his own reluctance, Harpham observes: "the conjunction between the mysteries of faith and the groaning, heaving processes of homosexual fornication is so grotesque, impossible, ridiculous that it could not be admitted." Indeed, it is as Gregory has predicted: "If therefore one should think of the back of God in a literal fashion, he will necessarily be carried to such an absurd conclusion" (*Life of Moses* 2.222; Gregory of Nyssa 1978: 112). "Thus the homoerotic serves as an explanatory model in the material world of desire for faith," theorizes Harpham, "one that illuminates without defiling because it is so altogether defiled that its function is never actually admitted" (Harpham 1995: 366).[21] Gregory seems to offer elusive agreement: "All of this would more fittingly be contemplated in its spiritual sense" (*Life of Moses* 2.223; Gregory of Nyssa 1978: 113).

Perhaps because his confidence in theory's sublimating power is so strong, Gregory does not attempt to cancel the impulse of desire itself but only to *reorient* it – indeed, there is no other horse for the race! If bodies have a "downward thrust," he admits readily that the soul is not so different but simply "moves in the opposite direction." "Once it is released from its earthly attachment, it becomes light and swift for its movement upward, soaring from below up to the heights" (*Life of Moses* 2.224; Gregory of Nyssa 1978: 113). It does not just soar, it expands: "Activity directed toward virtue causes its capacity to grow through exertion; this kind of activity alone does not slacken its intensity by the effort, but increases it" (*Life of Moses* 2.226; Gregory of Nyssa 1978: 113). No longer bound to a fleshly cycle of filling and emptying (*Life of Moses* 2.61; Gregory of Nyssa 1978: 68), the soul's longing for God's swells ever larger. Engorged with an endlessly expansive desire, it can only rise – paradoxically, "by means of the standing." "I mean by this," clarifies Gregory, "that the firmer and more immovable one remains in the Good, the more he progresses in the course of virtue" (*Life of Moses* 2.243; Gregory of Nyssa 1978: 117). The place of stasis is the rock, repeats Gregory, and the hole in the rock where God directs him to take his stand turns out to be the heavenly tabernacle (*Life of Moses* 2.245; Gregory of Nyssa 1978: 118). It is also the place where the race is run (*Life of Moses* 2.246; Gregory of Nyssa 1978: 118). And so goes the progression of conversions: through the virginal bush into the all-encompassing taber- nacle of darkness, thence via the naturalized topography of the cave to the masculinized backside of the Supernatural himself (see Harpham 1995: 363–4). Face-to-face is not after all the best position for love: "for good does not look good in the face, but follows it" and Moses is "the man who has learned to follow behind God" (*Life of Moses* 2.253–5; Gregory of Nyssa 1978: 119–20).

And still (as Heine points out) the story is not finished, however much we may be tempted to rest with the satisfying finality of a seemingly climactic moment. "Let us proceed," Gregory urges briskly (*Life of Moses* 2.264; Gregory of Nyssa 1978: 122). The last episode before Gregory's tumbling recapitulation of the route of continuous perfectibility (*Life of Moses* 2.305–18; Gregory of Nyssa 1978: 133–6) centers on the figure of Phineas. Here, at the beginning of the *Life*, Gregory underlines both the gendered structure of erotic sublimation and the violence inherent in the renunciations demanded. Captured by lust for foreign women, the Israelites "were themselves wounded by feminine darts of pleasure," as Gregory tells it in his most sternly moralizing voice; "as soon as the women appeared to them, showing off comeliness instead of weapons, they forgot their manly strength and dis- sipated their vigor in pleasure" (*Life of Moses* 2.298; Gregory of Nyssa 1978: 131). It was Phineas who re-established the order of virility. Piercing a mixed and mingling couple with a single thrust of his spear, "he did the work of a priest by purging the sin with blood" (*Life of Moses* 2.300; Gregory of Nyssa 1978: 131). Thus did Phineas defeat Pleasure herself, "who makes men beasts." Gregory amplified his own disgust at manhood's disgrace through this contamination with the female and the foreign: "they did not hide their excess but adorned themselves with the dishonour of passion and beautified themselves with the stain of shame as they wallowed, like pigs [or frogs!], in the slimy mire of uncleanness, openly for every- one to see" (*Life of Moses* 2.302; Gregory of Nyssa 1978: 132).

"After all these things," Gregory continues (*Life of Moses* 2.313; Gregory of Nyssa 1978: 134), Moses – forgoing the finality of arrival in the promised land – did not so much stop in his race toward perfection as pass beyond our sight. His is a "living death, which is not followed by the grave, or fills the tomb, or brings dimness to the eyes and aging to the person" (*Life of Moses* 2.314; Gregory of Nyssa 1978: 135). Imitating him, his followers will prolong the tale of true perfection, which emplots the unfolding desire of ageless, bright- eyed men "To be known by God and to become his friend" (*Life of Moses* 2.320; Gregory of Nyssa 1978: 137).

Reading this as a "late" work, it is tempting to conclude that Gregory has at last grown into his manhood – indeed, how he has grown! If dry Miriam was the star of *On Virginity*, in this text she makes only a brief appearance as a degraded symbol of "female" envy (*Life of*

Moses 1.62, 2.260; Gregory of Nyssa 1978: 47, 121), while Moses controls the ground of dryness (*Life of Moses* 1.31, 2.311; Gregory of Nyssa 1978: 38, 134). No longer content with the desire either to "have" or to "be" the woman, Gregory, standing tall with Moses on the rock of Christ, seems to have achieved the pinnacle of an active virility in and through his imitative desire for God. Perfectly self-disciplined, the horse of his hypermasculine passion no longer even requires a driver.

And, yet, to reach my conclusion, in relation to this work in particular, would perhaps be a mistake. Master of style, and never at rest, this fluid author is always giving birth to himself anew. In another work generally assigned to Gregory's last years (May 1971: 64), "he" is the bride of the Song of Songs, "constantly making progress and never stopping at any stage of perfection." The bride's lover is compared to an "apple tree" whose shadowy house she enters. Wounded by the lover's dart, "then she herself becomes the arrow in the hands of the archer, who with right hand draws the arrow near and with left directs its head toward the heavenly goal." Called to leave the shadow, the bride rests "in the cleft of the rock." Finally coming to bed, thinking to achieve "that more perfect participation" in her union with the divine Spouse, she finds herself, "just as Moses" did, suddenly enveloped in the inner space of a secret, sacred darkness. In the encounter with her ambiguously feminized divine partner who is all fruit and shadow and cleft, the bride transforms the potential emptiness of mutual receptivity into a swollen plenitude of *eros* that knows no end: "far from attaining perfection, she has not even begun to approach it" on her wedding night (*Homily 6 on the Song of Songs* 888C–893C; Gregory of Nyssa 1961: 201).[22] "Are we unsatisfied?" she might (he might), with Irigaray, query rhetorically. "Yes, if that means we are never finished. If our pleasure consists in moving, being moved, endlessly" (Irigaray 1985b: 210).

Love's Wound

Some might perhaps think that these are the words of one in pain, not those of one in joy, especially when she says: "They struck me: they wounded me: they took away my veil." But if you consider the meaning of the words carefully, you will see they are the expressions of one who glories most in what she enjoys. . . . The soul that looks up towards God, and conceives that good desire for His eternal beauty, constantly experiences an ever new yearning for that which lies ahead, and her desire is never given its full satisfaction. . . . In this way she is, in a certain sense, wounded and beaten because of the frustration of what she desires. . . . But the veil of her grief is removed when she learns that the true satisfaction of her desire consists in constantly going on with her quest and never ceasing in her ascent, seeing that every fulfilment of her desire continually generates a further desire for the Transcendent. (*Homily 12 on the Song of Songs* 1029A–1037C; Gregory of Nyssa 1961: 263–71)

The soul is now a distillation of sense such that one conceives its life . . . as an orgasmic experience in which wanting only comes with fulfilment and fulfilment does not cancel wanting. In other words, an entirely active and in no sense passive or lacking desire; but just for that reason, all the more erotic. (Milbank 1998: 106)

Of course one can never really say what she wants to say – that is why we keep writing. That is also why we keep having sex. Roxanne . . . never has that one great orgasm that would put desire for all other orgasms to rest. But she keeps on trying,

even though she knows it is impossible, indeed because she knows it's impossible.
. . . Masochists are particularly adept at turning delayed gratification into pleasure,
and even when "consummation" occurs, the dynamic is not to arrive at an end-
point but to reproduce the conditions that guarantee the necessity for endless
returns. (L. Hart 1998)

Fantasizing a human nature healed of the perversity of sexual difference, Gregory of
Nyssa reconstructs the lost paradise of sex before marriage. He posits a *non-reproductive* sexuality that is crucially *not quite Platonic*. By destabilizing the ontological hierarchy inscribed
by active and passive sexual roles, Gregory also queers the mimetic economy of pederasty,
in which a beloved "son" is erotically reproduced as the perfect image of a mature, paternal-
ized lover. Feminized as a soul "wounded by the arrow of love," Gregory is an ardent
Divinity's receptive beloved, playing the "Bottom" almost (but not quite) as a Platonist would
expect – *because playing it too well*.[23] His rhetoric not only names but furthermore exuberantly
performs a masochistic deferral of satisfaction that effectively exceeds the limits of temporality itself, unfurling into eternity's bliss of boundless love.[24] Gregory can also, however,
survey the suspenseful scene of desire from the perspective of the "top." As he rides the horse
of his passion for Christ right up to the abysmal edge of knowledge's consummation (where
he glimpses the *divine bottom!*), he appears to be the active lover in pursuit of the infinitely
desired Son, or (to underline the paradox) the Son in pursuit of the Father. Following behind
is thus, as Gregory performs it, a complex positionality, oscillating between discipleship and
domination. Seemingly, a man can have it both ways, where divine plenitude is matched by
the limitlessness of human desire. But perhaps the two "ways" are not really so different. In
a context in which the ostensibly active top is said to "surrender" and the passive bottom to
"control" the act, even the extreme power- and role-differentiations ritualized within contemporary sadomasochism produce, as Lynda Hart puts it, "a 'queer' act, based on a
relationship that privileges the sharing of similarities" (1998: 68).[25]

For Gregory, "there can be no grasp of essences, since the essence of the world is a mirroring of divine incomprehensibility," notes John Milbank; instead, there is "infinite
bestowing and bestowing back again" (Milbank 1998: 101). Milbank's insightful reading
allows us to place Gregory's erotic theory – in which "it is possible . . . to be in the same
instance both receptive and donating" (Milbank 1998: 95) – in the context of neoplatonism's
break with the irreducibly hierarchical logic of the mediated ontology of Middle Platonism
– in which it was possible to be both receptive and donating but precisely *not* in the same
instance. Under an earlier model of subjectivity as *self-mastery*, cosmological and political
hierarchies were internalized and mimetically reproduced as mind acting on passive/pas-
sionate matter. In later antiquity, however, the subject's speculative interiority is understood
as the product of an unmediated reflection of externalized being – an image, but not a reproduction. Thus desire does not any longer lodge with the "passions" that must be controlled
but is identified with the act of reflection, "the infinite bestowing and bestowing back again."
Desire, reason, and will are essentially one. "There is still hierarchy, of course, of source over
mirror, but formally speaking there is no limit to the receptiveness of the mirror, and nor
does the hierarchy require to be repeated within the space of the mirror; government is
now by the external, transcendent other, and is no longer in principle a matter of self-
government of the cosmos over itself which is microcosmically reflected in the individual
soul composed of heterogeneous and hierarchically ordered aspects." Gregory, on Milbank's
reading, takes neoplatonic theories of subjectivity to their logical extremes, rejecting the

notion of "any receptacle other to what is received, and which is thereby passionate over against the rays of actuality," so that "the mirror is truly nothing but the apparent surface of light itself in its rebound" (Milbank 1998: 108). "Gregory discovers the body and society as a site of pure activity," Milbank concludes, protesting that "there is little that could be construed as a cult of weakness in Gregory," in marked contrast to "a certain sickly version of Christian Hegelianism, exalting pathos and dialectical negativity, which has persisted from the nineteenth century into the late twentieth" (Milbank 1998: 109).

This closing polemic gives me pause. Has Milbank uncovered in this Father something that he finds a bit *too queer*? I wonder.[26] The thematized paradox of "active receptivity" troubles his text and must be resolved rhetorically into "pure activity" (thereby banishing the specter of passivity): "weakness" is actively repudiated, lest it spread like a sickness. Hegel, seemingly brought in as a whipping boy, serves rather to whip the weakness out of Gregory. The philosopher's master/slave dialectic is, after all, notoriously in danger of discovering itself muscle-bound: to the extent that the figure of the slave is thoroughly negated (sublated) as object – via incorporation into the identity of the sovereign subject – he becomes, problematically, "unworthy" to perform his necessary duty of "recognizing" the lord.[27] I would argue that if Gregory may be seen both to anticipate and to finesse the dilemma that haunts modern theories of subjectivity – as Milbank persuasively argues that he does – it is in large part because, like the masochist (and Hegel?), he is acutely aware of the limits of mastery and the weakness of identity, attuned to "how the subject is formed in submission" (Butler 1997a: 2) and to how the erotic submission may performatively "shatter" the shackles of subjectivity itself.[28] Beaten, wounded, stripped – there is no limit to what can be suffered in love, the Cappadocian suggests. Gregory of Nyssa is a queer Father not because he is purified of passion but rather because he is purely passionate, nothing more (or less) than the abysmal creature of divine desire.

Acknowledgments

Thanks are due to Marion Grau, Catherine Keller, and Stephen Moore for helpful conversation and criticism. This chapter is dedicated to the memory of Lynda Hart.

Notes

1 Note that Halperin also emphasizes that there are distinct dangers attending "the lack of specifically homosexual content built into the meaning of 'queer'" (Halperin 1995: 64); in this instance, for example, reading asceticism as "queer" risks eliding the particular political oppression of gays and lesbians.

2 I discuss the erotic economy at work in Gregory's Trinitarian doctrine more fully in Burrus (2000: 97–112). Note that, although my reading of Gregory's trinitarianism is in many respects sympathetic, I by no means view its masculinism as merely benign, to put it simply. I am thus wary, for example, of Graham Ward's suggestion that a two-natured Christology centered on the ascension (i.e. on the aporetic, lost, or withdrawn Christ) effectively "displaces" the male body of Jesus and thereby "continually refigures a masculine symbolics until the particularities of one sex give way to the particularities of bodies which are male and female" – a theological "fact" that (in Ward's view) renders the theological concerns of feminists naive and irrelevant, evidence of an unredeemed "essentialism" and failure "to understand the nature of bodies and sex in Christ" (Ward 1999: 163, 177). I agree with Ward that the maleness of the historical Jesus may not present an insurmountable theoretical obstacle for feminist theology: the problem lies rather with the

"displaced" body of masculinity itself, i.e. with the transcendentalized masculinism of trinitarian theology.

3 I hope it will be clear that an apologetics that has blossomed into full-blown Christian triumphalism interests me even less. Thus, I find extremely disturbing the supersessionist positioning of Gregory of Nyssa vis-à-vis Judith Butler in Sarah Coakley (2000). If Butler's works can help us understand Gregory's, that is because Gregory already knows everything Butler knows, and then some, Coakley suggests. By the same token, what Butler is seen to lack – namely, an asceticized Christian eschatology – Gregory already possesses. That this is supersessionism in the classical sense, despite the chronological inversion, is evidenced by Coakley's careful marking of Butler as Jewish. Butler's treatment of "power" (in contrast to Gregory's) "suggests comparison with the 'Yahweh' of her Jewish heritage who still lurks at the corners of her discussion," notes Coakley; also "lurking" at the most optimistic edges of Butler's purportedly generally pessimistic thought is "the myth of the cross and the resurrection," she adds (Coakley 2000: 66). "Odd, is it not (or not so odd?), that we needed the anguished insights of a secularized Jewish lesbian feminist to remind us of this deep strand of longing and wisdom" in Gregory's eschatology, Coakley concludes with a flourish (Coakley 2000: 71). Interestingly, Butler, as far as I am aware, does not in her published work locate herself as either "Jewish" or "lesbian"; this is not perhaps surprising, given that Butler's most well-known book bears a subtitle that announces its resistance to "identity" (as cited by this chapter's subtitle): *Gender Trouble: Feminism and the Subversion of Identity* (J. Butler 1990).

4 Compare *On Virginity* 1: "A man who takes this theme for ambitious praise has the appearance of supposing that one drop of his own perspiration will make an appreciable increase in the boundless ocean . . ." (Gregory of Nyssa 1994: 344a).

5 Establishing a chronology of Gregory's life and works is likely to remain a vexed task. *On Virginity* is, however, the only one of his texts that can be dated with some certainty to the period before Basil's death, and was thus probably written between 370 (when Basil was consecrated bishop) and 378 (when he died); see G. May (1971: 55). Michel Aubineau (1966: 31) is among those who have read Gregory's probable address of Basil as "our bishop and father" as implying that Gregory himself is not yet a bishop, thereby dating the work before 372, by which point Gregory had been appointed to the episcopacy of Nyssa. But as has been suggested by Jean Gribomont (1967: 25), Gregory could have referred to Basil in these terms when already a bishop himself.

6 English translations of *On Virginity* follow Gregory (1994: 343–71). J.P. Cavarnos's critical edition of the Greek is in Gregory (1952: 215–343).

7 Compare Mark D. Hart's provocative and carefully argued suggestion that we should "doubt the sincerity of Gregory's . . . lament in chapter 3 that his own marriage holds him back from a more noble way of life" (Hart 1992: 2; see also Hart 1990: 477). I interpret the passage as both more "sincere" than Hart takes it to be and more rhetorically arch than most other commentators assume.

8 Mark Hart (1990) gives a fine account of Gregory's "ideal of marriage as public service," especially in relation to his use of the term λειτουργία in this passage.

9 Gregory's Platonism, however "overt" in its reference to themes derived ultimately from texts like the *Republic*, the *Symposium*, the *Phaedo*, and the *Phaedrus*, avoids literal or explicit citation, so that it gives the impression of reflecting a rather indistinct, highly mediated, and widespread cultural *koine*. Thus Aubineau (1966) comments that a perusal of the Platonic texts is useful for the contemporary reader not because Gregory cites them verbatim but because "they restore a mentality, diffuse in time and space, in which Gregory shared, following so many others, and which impregnated every student who haunted the universities in the fourth century of the era" (Aubineau 1966: 99). In *On Virginity* (11), however, the references to the *Symposium* are unmistakable, as Aubineau himself documents. In a much-cited study, Harold Fredrik Cherniss (1971) argues that Gregory is deeply familiar with the Platonic corpus itself, as well as with the

biblical Platonism of Philo and Origen and the pagan neoplatonic school of thought represented by Plotinus and his followers.

10 In *On the Making of Man*, Gregory is more explicit on the point that sexual difference is a secondary accretion to humanity's original creation "in the image" of God, in whom there is no male and female. A sexed bodily nature was added to a prior sexless rational nature as an advance compromise with the need of a fallen humanity to reproduce itself in the face of mortality (*On the Making of Man* 16; Gregory of Nyssa 1994: 404a–406b). Resurrection will return humanity to its roots, with the elimination of marriage as the site of both sexual difference and procreation (*On the Making of Man* 17; Gregory of Nyssa 1994: 406b–407b). See V.E.F. Harrison (1990).

11 Underlying the ambiguities of Gregory's conception of virginal desire are the ambiguities of "Platonic love" as represented in some of the very dialogues of Plato of which Gregory makes heaviest use. At issue is the structure of sublimation in both linking and opposing carnal and spiritual desires, as well as an implicit question of how the homoerotic functions in ancient philosophic discourse from Plato to Gregory. In reference to the *Symposium*, A.W. Price (1989: 226) notes that Plato "clearly believes that there is a natural connection between pederasty and pregnancy in soul" where the goal of love is defined as a mental or sublimated procreation "in beauty," structuring an erotic "succession" mimetically between like but unequal minds; "if pederastic desire is particularly susceptible to sublimation, then it is natural those particularly capable of sublimation should incline towards pederasty."

12 It may also be related to what Christopher Stead (1976: 113) refers to (with considerable philosophic dismay) as a "really extraordinary flexibility and imprecision of terminology" resulting from a tendency to slide all too easily (from Stead's perspective) between the concrete and the abstract. Verna Harrison (1992: 97–9) takes a far more sanguine view of the matter, at the same time offering a broad but concise discussion of the relation between philosophic "concepts" and poetic "images" in Gregory's work.

13 See V.E.F. Harrison (1996) for a thoughtful account of Gregory's Mariology in the broader context of the significance of motherhood as a privileged image for spiritual generation in his thought. Plato, Philo, and Origen are discussed as the bearers of a tradition that constructs a feminized masculinity through the development of an image of spiritual childbearing in Harrison 1995.

14 English translations of the *Life of Moses* follow Gregory of Nyssa (1978). There are two critical editions of the Greek: Gregory of Nyssa (1964) and Gregory of Nyssa (1955).

15 The dating of the treatise and the question of its "mysticism" turn out to be closely related; see Heine (1975: 1–26).

16 "The womb must be denied, or converted, before one can honourably return to it. . . . The womb is converted by being naturalized. But it is naturalized by being masculinized, which is to say, unnaturalized. The natural form of the cave is made available for human purposes by being routed through the masculine, a two-stage conversion that renders the cave an object of desire, an object to desire instead of the womb: One lives in a cave instead of with a woman. This is, to the ascetic, a natural desire that takes natural form, the form of the cave. . . . But life in a cave also represents a renunciation of natural desire, a will to desire the nonnatural, the unnatural, to have an unnatural desire, the very type of which is anal intercourse. The cave – or anus – is the natural and human site of gender conversion or transformation" (Harpham 1995: 363–4).

17 In the *Dialogue on the Soul and the Resurrection*, Gregory engages and revises Plato's theory of the soul and the passions, displacing a model in which reason (as the "charioteer") controls desire and anger (the "horses") with a model in which a purified desire (*agape*) overwhelms or encompasses reason; see my discussion of this text in Burrus (2000: 112–22).

18 Heine (1975) follows Ekkehard Mühlenberg (1966) in challenging a narrowly "mystical" reading of Gregory's *Life of Moses* as well as his *Commentary on the Song of Songs*. Like Mühlenberg, he sees a close connection between the more "philosophically" framed theological and

epistemological issues debated in *Against Eunomius* and the "spiritual" concept of eternal progress thematized in these less overtly polemical works; he argues furthermore that Gregory is at least as concerned to engage and counter Origenism's concept of spiritual "satiety" as Eunomius's concept of divine knowability. Closer attention to the philosophical context of the *Life of Moses* is offered by the recent work of Thomas Böhm (1996).

19 See, for example, the careful discussion in Böhm (1996). Regarding the broader question of Gregory's "mysticism" – with which the interpretation of the *Life's* "theophanic" passages is deeply entangled – Verna Harrison (1992: 61–3) observes with characteristic good sense that it is possible to reject a simplistic three-stage model of mysticism, accept the importance of polemical contexts, and still find in a work like the *Life of Moses* a central concern with describing "a path to participation in divine life" figured in terms of the soul's pursuit of an unmediated union with God.

20 Although I have borrowed Harpham's voice for my reading of Gregory's *Life of Moses*, Harpham (it should be noted) is himself actually interpreting a Renaissance painting of Jerome's *Life of Paul*.

21 At the risk of stating the obvious, I would add that the (male) homoerotic also "illuminates without defiling" because it has eliminated the female.

22 This English translation follows Gregory (1961: 197–203). Note that Franz Dünzl (1993: 380–8) emphasizes the intertextual complexity and fluidity of Gregory's erotic imagery in his *Commentary on the Song of Songs*, which by no means confines itself to the metaphors explicitly suggested by the biblical text.

23 In contemporary sadomasochistic parlance (and elsewhere), "bottom" and "top" designate passive and active sexual roles, performed in such a way as to both intensify and denaturalize such distinctions.

24 On masochism and deferral see Lynda Hart (1998: 79) and Deleuze (1989: 33–5).

25 Hart is here (if only provisionally) invoking Deleuze's claim that sadism and masochism represent not identical or even complementary erotic practices (as is commonly argued) but are "entirely dissimilar" phenomena; thus, the masochist's torturer is not a sadist but "a pure element of masochism" (Deleuze 1989: 13, 42). Hart implicitly assumes that the particular erotic practice that interests her (lesbian s/m) is "masochistic" in Deleuze's terms, and that she can refer to s/m partners as "two masochists." In the end, however, she does not find Deleuze's claim that sadism always turns on a father figure and masochism on a mother figure nearly queer enough (L. Hart 1998: 164–5).

26 Note that Sarah Coakley likewise appears alarmed at what she has unveiled in her own reading of this Father. Having undertaken to interpret Gregory through the theoretical lens of the "secularized Jewish lesbian feminist" Judith Butler, she too finds it necessary to deliver a stern admonishment in closing: "it is not, note, the goal of Gregory's vision to enjoy various forms of previously-banned sexual pleasure; or to escape or sneer at a supposedly 'repressive' pornography law" (Coakley 2000: 70–1).

27 See, for example, the comments of Lynda Hart (1998: 164); this critique of Hegel's theory of subjectivity (largely a product of Hegel's French reception) has, however, itself been critically interrogated by Judith Butler (1987).

28 The ways in which (masochistic) sexuality exceeds and indeed undermines the formation of the ego are explored in Bersani (1986) and Bersani (1988).

Chapter 10

Queering the Beguines

Mechthild of Magdeburg, Hadewijch of Anvers, Marguerite Porete

Amy Hollywood

You can reduce religion to sex only if you don't especially believe in either one.
(Michael Warner 1996)

In the face of what the social historian Judith Bennett refers to as "the virtual absence of actual women from the sources of medieval lesbianisms," a number of literary and cultural scholars have recently turned to texts by and/or about women to uncover homoerotic possibilities within the metaphoric structures of their writings or in the practices ascribed to women or female characters within literary and religious documents (Bennett 2000: 7).[1] Karma Lochrie, for example, looks to a number of medieval devotional texts and images in which Christ's bloody side wound becomes a locus of desire.[2] According to Lochrie, not only is Christ's body feminized through its association with women's (and particularly the Virgin Mary's) nurturing breasts, as Caroline Walker Bynum famously argues, but religious representations also "genitalize" Christ's wound, associating it both imagistically and linguistically with the vulva.[3] When women mystics write about eagerly kissing the sacred wound, then, their relationship with Christ is queered, for the body they desire and with which they identify is both male and female.[4] For Lochrie, "neither the acts/identity distinction nor the focus on same-sex desire is adequate or desirable as a framework for queering medieval mysticism" (Lochrie 1997: 195). Rather, Lochrie argues, the complex interplay of gender and sexuality in medieval texts and images effectively queers simple identifications of sex, gender, and/or sexuality.

Bennett describes the work of Lochrie and other cultural and literary critics with care and enthusiasm, yet worries that while "as literary criticism, these readings reach plausible conclusions . . . as guides to social history, they are considerably less convincing" (Bennett 2000: 8).

> It's great fun, for example, to read Lochrie's impressive exploration of the artistic, literary, and linguistic ties between Christ's wound and female genitalia, and to speculate, therefore, that the kissing of images of Christ's wound by medieval nuns somehow parallels lesbian oral sex. Yet Lochrie very wisely does not claim that any medieval nun who contemplated Christ's wound ever, in fact, was thinking about last night's tumble in bed with a sister nun. (Bennett 2000: 8–9)

Bennett's worries about "actual people" and "plausible behaviors" (Bennett 2000: 8) lead her to argue that queer readings like Lochrie's are "intriguing-but-not-fully-historicized" (Bennett 2000: 9). Bennett's argument depends, however, on assuming that the history of lesbianisms is and/or should be centrally concerned with same-sex acts or identities derived from the pursuit of such acts, precisely the categories of analysis questioned by Lochrie (and, she would argue, by at least some medieval texts and images).

Bennett herself introduces the notion of "lesbian-like" in order to broaden lesbian history beyond its focus on "certifiable same-sex genital contact." Where she differs from Lochrie is in her focus on "broadly sociological" affinities between contemporary lesbians and women in the past – "affinities related to social conduct, marital status, living arrangements, and other behaviors that might be traced in the archives of past societies" (Bennett 2000: 14–15; see also Bennett and Froide 1999). The pursuit of these affinities is certainly important historical work, both for women's history and for what Bennett calls the history of lesbianisms. Yet Bennett's argument is problematic if she means to suggest that these sociological categories give access to "real women" in a way that attention to the religious imagery and desires found in texts written and/or used by medieval women do not. Some medieval religious women did use intensely erotic language and imagery to talk about their relationship to the divine. No matter how implausible it might seem to us to understand Christ's side wound as a bloody slit that feminizes and eroticizes his corporeality, this is in fact what some medieval women (and men) did.[5]

Lochrie and Bennett are surely right to resist an easy movement from the relationship between the woman believer and Christ to sexual relationships between women (or between men and women).[6] Yet why shouldn't the complex interplay between sex, gender, and sexuality in representations of relationships to the divine have as much significance for contemporary lesbian and/or queer history as the marital status of late medieval women – especially when the fluidity and excess of categories within discussions of divine desire may work to undermine the seemingly unquestioned supremacy of heteronormativity within medieval Christian culture (a heteronormativity itself also often seen within devotional language and imagery)?[7] Sociological questions might seem more "real" to us in the early twenty-first century, but for many Christians in the later Middle Ages, one's relationship to Christ and the language and images through which one attempted to achieve and convey something of that relationship had equal, if not greater, reality. So while Bennett and Lochrie no doubt pursue different kinds of historical question, I think it is important to recognize both as *historically* valid and of significance for contemporary discussions about sexuality and gender.

At stake here is not just the question of what constitutes reality, but also how we are to understand the relationship between the often highly erotic and sexual imagery used by late medieval religious writers to describe the soul's relationship to Christ and human sexuality. Caroline Walker Bynum's magisterial work on late medieval religiosity has set the tone here, for she argues against what she sees as a modern tendency to equate the bodily too quickly with the sexual. In an attempt to refute the widespread reduction of late medieval religiosity – particularly that of women – to sex, Bynum is in danger of denying even the metaphorically sexualized nature of many women's – and men's – religious writings. Her explicit aim, both in *Holy Feast and Holy Fast* (1987) and the essays collected in *Fragmentation and Redemption* (1991), is to expand the meanings that we ascribe to corporeality in late medieval texts and practices. Yet as Lochrie and Richard Rambuss convincingly show, Bynum "herself can be quick to delimit the erotic – and especially the homoerotic – potentialities of her own devotional polysemy of the medieval body" (Rambuss 1998: 48).[8] When Catherine of Siena writes of "putting on the nuptial garment," Bynum explains, "the phrase means suffering" and so is "extremely unerotic." She goes on to argue that in:

Catherine's repeated descriptions of climbing Christ's body from foot to side to mouth, the body is either a female body that nurses or a piece of flesh that one puts on oneself or sinks into. . . . Catherine understood union with Christ not as an erotic fusing with a male figure but as a taking in and taking on – a becoming – of Christ's flesh itself. (Bynum 1987: 178)[9]

Bynum makes many contentious (and, not surprisingly, vehemently anti-Freudian) assumptions about sexuality and erotic desire – most crucially, that erotic desire can be clearly distinguished from suffering, the maternal, and identification – yet as Rambuss suggests, perhaps the most salient point of Bynum's interpretation is her refusal to see same-sex desire as potentially sexual. If Christ's body is feminized (and so becomes a point of identification for women), Bynum assumes it cannot also be the locus of female sexual desire (or even of a desire for the divine *analogous* to sexual desire). Her insistence on the feminization of Christ serves two functions, then, both providing a locus for female identification with the divine and protecting the divine-human relationship from even metaphorical sexualization.

What I want to show here is that some late medieval women did use explicitly erotic language to discuss their relationship with Christ and they did so, often, in ways that challenge the prescriptive heterosexuality of the culture in which they lived. This challenge occurs not only through the feminization of Christ's body discussed by Lochrie, but also through an intense, hyperbolic, and often ultimately self-subverting deployment of apparently heterosexual imagery. This excess often involves a displacement of Christ as the center of the religious life and emphasis on a feminized figure of divine Love. Among the beguines – semi-religious women who flourished in thirteenth-century Northern Europe and are most well known for their so-called "bridal mysticism" (and hence, it would seem, for a resolutely heterosexual, non-queer sexual imaginary) – we find accounts of insane love and endless desire in which gender becomes so radically fluid that it is not clear *what* kind of sexuality – within the heterosexual/homosexual dichotomy most readily available to modern readers – is being metaphorically deployed to evoke the relationship between humans and the divine.[10] Rather, as Richard Rambuss argues with regard to early modern male-authored religious poetry, the absence in these texts "of a polarizing system of sexual types tends to open these works in the direction of a greater plasticity of erotic possibilities, possibilities not entirely containable by our own (often only suppositiously coherent) sexual dichotomies" (Rambuss 1998: 58). This very inability to contain medieval divine eroticism within modern categories points to its potential queerness.[11]

Religious desire and sexual desire are not the same, as Bennett usefully reminds us, but if "religion makes available a language of ecstasy, a horizon of significance within which transgressions against the normal order of the world and the boundaries of the self *can be seen as good things*," as Michael Warner argues (1996: 43), religious writers often use the language of eroticism to express that ecstasy, excess, and transgression. Perhaps this is because erotic language is able, in ways that devotional language both exploits and intensifies, to engender affective states that push the believer beyond the limitations of his or her own body and desires (see Rambuss 1998: 11–71; Bataille 1962 and Hollywood 2002: 36–119). At the same time, the intensity of divine desire forces sexual language into new, unheard of configurations. Hence the emergence in the later Middle Ages of what Lochrie aptly calls the "mystical queer." These religious representations do not reflect, nor even legitimate, particular configurations of human sexual relations – they often indeed seem to involve a movement beyond sexed and gendered bodies, even that of Christ, as the locus of pleasure and desire – but they do de-naturalize and de-stabilize normative conceptions of human sexuality in potentially radical ways.

Mystical Queer

The centrality of the Song of Songs to medieval Christian devotional literature, images, and practices sets the stage for an intensely erotic and, at least on the surface, heterosexualized understanding of the relationship between the soul and God. Origen (c. 185–254), the first Christian commentator on the Song of Songs whose work survives, reads the series of erotic poems as an allegory both for the relationship between Christ and the church and for that between Christ and the individual believer.[12] The latter reading provides a central source for twelfth-century mystical exegetes like Bernard of Clairvaux (1090–1153), William of St Thierry (c. 1080–1148), and Rupert of Deutz (1077–1120), who increasingly emphasize the intensely erotic nature of the relationship between the lover and the beloved, the bridegroom and the bride, or Christ and the soul (see McGinn 1994: 158–224, 225–74 and 328–33; and Krahmer 2000). When undertaken by male authors, these allegorical readings often involve a kind of linguistic transvestism, whereby the male devoté becomes the female soul joined in loving union with the male figure of Christ.[13] When undertaken by women, on the other hand, apparently normalized sexual roles often prevail.

So, for example, in Mechthild of Magdeburg's (c. 1260–1282/94) *Flowing Light of the Godhead*, an understanding of the soul as the bride of Christ is joined with traditions derived from courtly literature.[14] In Book I, Mechthild describes the soul as a lady, who dresses herself in the virtues so as to be prepared to welcome the prince. After much waiting, in which the soul watches other holy people dance, "the young man comes and says to her: 'Young lady, my chosen ones have shown off their dancing to you. Just as artfully should you now follow their lead.'" The soul replies:

> I cannot dance, Lord, unless you lead me.
> If you want me to leap with abandon,
> You must intone the song.
> Then I shall leap into love,
> From love into knowledge,
> From knowledge into enjoyment,
> And from enjoyment beyond all human sensations.
> There I want to remain, yet want also to circle higher still.
> (Mechthild 1998: 44, 59)

Their dance is recorded in song: the young man sings: "Through me into you / And through you from me," while the soul responds, like the alternatively joyful and despondent bride of the Song of Songs, "Willingly with you / Woefully from you."

Mechthild makes explicit her preference for erotic over maternal metaphors in her conception of the relationship between the soul and Christ. Weary of the dance, the soul says to the senses that they should leave her so that she might refresh herself. The senses, wanting to stay with the soul, offer a series of refreshments in which they too might take part: "the blood of martyrs," "the counsel of confessors," the bliss of the angels, and finally, the milk of the Virgin enjoyed by the Christ child. To this, the soul replies, "That is child's

love, that one suckle and rock a baby. I am a full-grown bride. I want to go to my Lover"
(1998: 61). Although there the senses will "go completely blind," the soul asserts that her
true identity is found in the nature of God.

> A fish in water does not drown.
> A bird in the air does not plummet.
> Gold in fire does not perish.
> Rather, it gets its purity and its radiant color there.
> God has created all creatures to live according to their nature.
> How, then, am I to resist my nature?
> I must go from all things to God,
> Who is my Father by nature,
> My Brother by his humanity,
> My Bridegroom by love,
> And I his bride from all eternity.
> (Mechthild 1998: 61)

Just as Mechthild will insist that she is both God's child by grace and by nature (1998:
VI, §31), so here she claims to be daughter, sister, and bride of Christ, multiplying metaphors
(all derived from the Song of Songs) without undermining the eroticism of the dance of
love in which the dialogue appears.

Moreover, identification does not preclude, but rather seems to follow from the intensity of desire. After asserting the commonality of her nature with that of the divine, the
bride of all delights goes to the fairest of lovers in the secret chamber of the invisible
Godhead. There she finds the bed and the abode of love prepared by God in a manner
beyond what is human. Our Lord speaks:

> "Stay, Lady soul."
> "What do you bid me, Lord?"
> "Take off your clothes."
> "Lord, what will happen to me then?"
> "Lady soul, you are so utterly ennatured in me
> That not the slightest thing can be between you and me." . . .
> Then a blessed stillness
> That both desire comes over them.
> He surrenders himself to her,
> And she surrenders herself to him.
> What happens to her then – she knows –
> And that is fine with me.
> But this cannot last long.
> When two lovers meet secretly,
> They must often part from one another inseparably.
> (Mechthild 1998: 62)

As long as the soul remains within the body, the lovers can only meet fleetingly. The
intensity of her desire and fusion with the divine both demands the use of erotic language
and subverts it, for the body cannot sustain the experience of the divine embrace. (Although

as I will show below, Mechthild insists that the body will ultimately be reunited with the soul and share in its final glory.) The suffering to which God's presence and absence gives rise is then itself taken up as crucial to the path of desire for and identification with Christ.[15]

The interplay of suffering and desire is also crucial to the poetry and prose of Hadewijch (fl. 1250) in ways that ultimately disrupt the heteronormativity of the relationship between the soul and the divine prevalent in Mechthild's work.[16] In a poem on the seven names of Love, Hadewijch makes the spectacular claim that Love, Hadewijch's favored name for the divine, is Hell.

> Hell is the seventh name
> Of this Love wherein I suffer.
> For there is nothing Love does not engulf and damn,
> And no one who falls into her
> And whom she seizes comes out again,
> Because no grace exists there.
> As Hell turns everything to ruin,
> In Love nothing else is acquired
> But disquiet and torture without pity;
> Forever to be in unrest,
> Forever assault and new persecution;
> To be wholly devoured and engulfed
> In her unfathomable essence,
> To founder unceasingly in heat and cold,
> In the deep, insurmountable darkness of Love.
> (Hadewijch 1980: 356)

For Hadewijch, the constant "comings and goings" of Love are a source of continual suffering, for the soul is caught between the ecstasy of the divine presence, Love's unrelenting demands for fidelity, and the constant threat of God's absence. Suffering does not preclude erotic desire, but is central to it. As Karma Lochrie argues, "aggression, violence, masochism, and dark despair are as fundamental to the visions of some women mystics as the tropes of marriage and . . . languorous desire." For Lochrie, this kind of excessive, violent desire is "queer in its effects – exceeding and hyperbolizing its own conventionality and fracturing the discourses of mystical love and sex" (Lochrie 1997: 184).

Hadewijch, like Mechthild, argues that this suffering love itself becomes a part of the soul's identification with Christ. As she writes in a letter to fellow beguines, "we all indeed wish to be God with God, but God knows there are few of us who want to live as human beings with his Humanity, or want to carry his cross with him, or want to hang on the cross with him and pay humanity's debt to the full" (Hadewijch 1980: 61). Yet this demand that the soul identify with Christ in his suffering humanity does not preclude a desire for the divine best expressed through the language of eroticism. Again like Mechthild, Hadewijch, particularly in her visions, makes use of imagery derived from the Song of Songs as the basis for her understanding of the union between the soul and Christ. One day while at matins, she writes:

> My heart and my veins and all my limbs trembled and quivered with eager desire
> and, as often occurred with me, such madness and fear beset my mind that it seemed

to me I did not content my Beloved, and that my Beloved did not fulfill my desire, so that dying I must go mad, and going mad I must die. (Hadewijch 1980: 280).

This leads Hadewijch to desire that her humanity "should to the fullest extent be one in fruition" with that of Christ, so that she might then "grow up in order to be God with God" (Hadewijch 1980: 280).

The vision that follows is the fulfillment of that desire. Looking at the altar, she first sees Christ in the form of a child of three years, holding the eucharistic bread in his right hand and the chalice in his left. The child then becomes a man and administers the sacrament to Hadewijch.

> After that he came himself to me, took me entirely in his arms, and pressed me to him; and all my members felt his in full felicity, in accordance with the desire of my heart and my humanity. So that I was outwardly satisfied and transported. Also then, for a short while, I had the strength to bear this; but soon, after a short time, I lost that manly beauty outwardly in the sight of his form. I saw him completely come to naught and so fade and all at once dissolve that I could no longer recognize or perceive him outside me, and I could no longer distinguish him within me. Then it was to me as if we were one without difference. . . . After that I remained in a passing away in my Beloved, so that I wholly melted away in him and nothing any longer remained to me of myself. (Hadewijch 1980: 281–2)

Full union with Christ, expressed here through intensely erotic language, leads to a fusion and identification with profound theological implications. Although heterosexual in its imagistic operation, moreover, the melting away of the soul into the divine radically undermines any stable distinction between male and female and, more importantly for Hadewijch, between human and divine. The incarnation, in which God becomes human, becomes the basis for humanity's full identification with the divine.

Yet Hadewijch's work undermines associations of masculinity with the divine and femininity with the human, for it includes a series of poems in which the divine is represented as Love (*minne*, which is feminine), the unattainable female object of desire, and the soul as a knight-errant in quest of his Lady.[17] Love cannot be clearly identified either with Christ, the Holy Spirit, God the Father, or the Trinity; Hadewijch continually shifts and overlaps various divine referents. These poems again stress the cruelty of Love and the anguish to which her demand for desirous fidelity reduces the knight.

> Sometimes kind, sometimes hateful,
> Sometimes far, sometimes to hand.
> To him who endures this with loyalty of love
> That is jubilation;
> How love kills
> And embraces
> In a single action.
> (Hadewijch quoted in Murk-Jansen 1996: 58)

Those who are "Knight-errants in Love" live in an endless oscillation between darkness and light, the divine presence and her absence.[18] The knightly soul is suspended between activity, "laying siege" to Love in desire and fidelity – ("the brave," one poem advises, "should strike before Love does")[19] – and recognition that his "best success" lies in the suffering he undergoes when "shot by Love's arrow" (Hadewijch 1980: 162). Even as Hadewijch stresses the gap between the (feminine) divine and the (masculine) soul, then, she both undermines rigid gender distinctions and lays the groundwork for the eventual union of the soul and the divine through the soul's "mad love" and suffering desire – a union that occurs through Christ but is often poetically imagined without reference to his human body.[20]

In the dialogues that make up Marguerite Porete's (d. 1310) *The Mirror of Simple Souls*, Porete similarly employs the feminine figure of Love as the most prominent representation of the divine. She goes even further than Hadewijch, moreover, in suggesting that while Christ and Christ's body play a crucial role in the path of the soul to union with Love, ultimately the role of the body and of Christ will be surpassed. Instead, the female soul engages in a loving dialogue both with Lady Love and with the feminine Trinity, giving the text an intensely homoerotic valence absent in Mechthild's heterosexual account of the love between the soul and Christ and Hadewijch's transvestism, in which the soul becomes male in order to pursue Lady Love. Love and the soul provide a representation of those souls who have become so free of all created things, including will and desire, that they are indistinguishable from the divine. I have argued elsewhere that Porete's pursuit of annihilation is a result of her desire to escape the intense suffering engendered by endless desire and "mad love." Absolute union with the divine occurs through the sacrifice of desire by desire. Yet the resulting loss of distinction between the soul and the divine also radically subverts, even erases, gender distinctions, a move both dependent on and subversive of the text's homoeroticism. (Porete uses the femininity of the soul and Love to elicit pronominal ambiguities in which the gap between them is erased.[21]) Porete's work, with its distrust of spiritual delights, ecstasies, and visions, stands in a critical relationship to that of her beguine predecessors. This is evident in her relationship to the imagery of erotic love. For Porete, like Hadewijch, Love is the primary name of the divine and she at times make use of language and imagery derived from the Song of Songs, yet always in ways that undermine the initial gendered dichotomy between the lover and the beloved. This subversion seems dependent, as it is in Hadewijch, on a displacement of Christ's body.

The process can be seen most starkly in a crucial scene toward the end of the *Mirror* in which a now masculine God challenges the soul concerning the strength of her fidelity. As Nicholas Watson argues, the series of hypothetical scenes recounted by the soul "are eccentric versions of the love-tests found in the tale of patient Griselda." Just as Griselda is honored for patiently submitting to the various tests of her fidelity posed by her distrustful husband, so the soul imagines a series of tests posed by God. She asks herself,

> as if He Himself were asking me, how I would fare if I knew that he could be better pleased that I should love another better than Him. At this my sense failed me, and I knew not how to answer, nor what to will, nor what to deny; but I responded that I would ponder it.
>
> And then He asked me how I would fare if it could be that He could love another better than me. And at this my sense failed me, and I know not what to answer, or will, or deny.
>
> Yet again, He asked me what I would do and how I would fare if it could be that He would will that someone other love me better than He. And again my sense

failed, and I knew not what to respond, no more than before, but still I said that I would ponder it. (Porete 1993: ch. 131, 213–14)

Using the imaginative meditative practices recommended within contemporary devotional treatises as a means of participating in and identifying with Christ's passion, Porete here enacts a Trial of Love reminiscent of those within secular courtly literature.

The trial leads to the death of the will and of the desire (that same desire more often elicited and exploited through such meditative practices). In acquiescing to demands that go against her desire to love and be loved by God alone, she "martyrs" both her will and her love, thereby annihilating all creatureliness and, paradoxically, attaining a union without distinction with the divine. In Watson's evocative words, Porete "out-griselded Griselda," taking the test of submission to such extremes that subservience becomes the means by which the soul forces God to merge with her (Watson 1996: 3). Porete takes the cultural stereotype of the patient bride who will submit to anything in fidelity to her bridegroom and converts it into an account of how the soul's fall into nothingness is itself the apprehension of her full share in the divine being.[22] Like Mechthild, who insists that the soul is God's child by nature, thereby challenging late medieval versions of the doctrine of grace, Porete stresses throughout the *Mirror* the ways in which the soul, by emphasizing and embracing her sinfulness, abjection, and humility, can become one with God.[23] Most crucially, as Watson argues, Porete shows the soul achieving "mystical annihilation of her own volition, *by telling herself stories*" (Watson 1996: 6). This particular story both depends on and subverts the hierarchically ordered gender expectations of late medieval culture.

Porete's use of erotic and gendered language is, like that of her fellow beguines Mechthild and, particularly, Hadewijch, remarkably complex.[24] As the example offered here suggests, however, unlike Mechthild and Hadewijch – or perhaps better, more starkly than they – Porete posits the goal of the soul as the eradication of any distinction between herself and the divine. Porete evokes this union without distinction through the unsaying or apophasis of gender and the displacement of Christ's body as the center of religious devotion. With the overcoming of gender comes also the annihilation of desire and radical detachment from the body.[25] Porete never mentions the orthodox doctrine of the resurrection of the body, for example. With the annihilation of gender, will, and desire, also comes an end to the painful and ecstatic eroticism that runs throughout the texts of Mechthild and Hadewijch.

Porete's utopic subversion of gender difference (grounded, needless to say, in her desire to overcome the gap between the soul and the divine), leaves no room for the vagaries of desire expressed in the closing dialogue of Mechthild's *Flowing Light*. There we hear the words of a body and soul who refuse, finally, to renounce their ambivalent and multivalent desires.

This is how the tormented body speaks to the lonely soul: "When shall you soar with the feathers of your yearning to the blissful heights of Jesus, your eternal Love? Thank him there for me, lady, that, feeble and unworthy though I am, he nevertheless wanted to be mine when he came into this land of exile and took our humanity on himself; and ask him to keep me innocent in his favor until I attain a holy end, when you, dearest soul, turn away from me."

The soul: "Ah, dearest prison in which I have been bound, I thank you especially for being obedient to me. Though I was often unhappy because of you, you nevertheless came to my aid. On the last day all your troubles will be taken from you.

Then we shall no longer complain.
Then everything that God has done with us
Will suit us just fine,
If you will only stand fast
And keep hold of sweet hope.
(Mechthild 1998: 335–6)

This promise depends on the body's self-denial, for "the less the body preserves itself, the fairer its works shine before God and before people of good will" (Mechthild 1998: 336). It is precisely the intense suffering of this desire and the self-denial to which it leads that give rise to Porete's attempt to save the soul and body through the martyrdom of the will.

Porete's utopic vision involves an effacement of differences – between God and soul, uncreated and created (including the body, will, and desire), and male and female – that, paradoxically, both queers heteronormative desire and sacrifices the bodies and desires from which, in their multiplicity, contemporary queer theory and practice emerge. There is clearly no straight road from medieval mystical writings to contemporary practices and politics. In the writings of the beguines, desire is both a resource, an opportunity, and a problem – a problem to which Mechthild, Hadewijch, and Marguerite respond in very different ways. The divergence between them shows that although we can't simply identify these women's accounts of religious experience with human sexual practices, what they write about their relationship to the divine originates in and remains tied to their experiences of themselves as embodied and desirous human beings. And even the most apparently heteronormative texts queer sexuality in that the object of this desire is not another human being, but (a) divine (Godman). The ecstasies of religion and those of sexuality are metaphorically linked at least in part because of their shared bodiliness, intensity, and tendency toward excess, an excess that, in the case of Marguerite Porete, leads to the subversion of the very grounds from which it emerges.[26]

Notes

1   See also the essays collected in Sautman and Sheingorn (2001), and for groundbreaking theoretical and historical work on the early modern period see Traub (2002). For materials directed toward specifically religious texts see J. Cohen (2003: 154–87); Wiethaus (2003); Dinshaw (1999: 143–82); Lochrie (1997); Holsinger (1993); Campbell (1992); and Lavezzo (1996).

2   Lochrie does not provide a full history of the image. An early, intensely erotic and eucharistic example can be found in Aelred of Rievaulx's "Rule of Life for a Recluse," a general guide to the religious life written, perhaps not surprisingly, for women. In meditating on Christ's body, Aelred encourages the reader: "Hasten, linger not, eat the honeycomb with your honey, drink your wine with your milk. The blood is changed into wine to gladden you, the water into milk to nourish you. From the rock streams have flowed for you, wounds have been made in his limbs, holes in the wall of his body, in which, like a dove, you may hide while you kiss them one by one. Your lips, stained with his blood, will become like a scarlet ribbon and your word sweet" (Aelred of Rievaulx 1971: 90–1; cited in Bestul 1996: 39). As Bestul points out, the passage brings together language from the Psalms and the Song of Songs. Although this kind of highly erotic devotion to Christ's wounds becomes characteristic of late medieval meditational practice, the example from Aelred shows that it has roots in mid-twelfth-century texts and practices. For further examples from fourteenth-century and fifteenth-century devotional texts, see Bestul (1996: 56–7, 59 and 62); D. Gray (1963); F. Lewis (1996) and Areford (1998). See also Camille (1994: 77).

3   Both Bynum and Lochrie cite Raymond of Capua's *Life* of Catherine of Siena (1327–80): "With that, he tenderly placed his right hand on her neck and drew her towards the wound on his side. 'Drink, daughter, from my side,' he said, 'and by that draught your soul shall become enraptured with such delight that your very body, which for my sake you have denied, shall be inundated with its overflowing goodness.' Drawn close in this way to the outlet of the Fountain of Life, she fastened her lips upon that sacred wound, and still more eagerly the mouth of her soul, and there she slaked her thirst" (Bynum 1987: 172 and Lochrie 1997: 188). Bynum, in reading the side wound as a breast and Christ's blood as milk, explicitly rejects a sexualized reading, whereas Lochrie insists that the maternal does not exclude the sexual. In the Middle Ages, it was believed that breast milk was created from surplus menses not released in childbirth. The association of the blood with Christ's side wound, then, ties it both to the vagina *and* breast milk, thereby enabling the threefold association of wound, vulva, and breast. On these associations, see Wood (1981: 710–27). For the highly suggestive and erotic visual images, see Lochrie (1997) and F. Lewis (1996). On the linguistic association of the Latin for wound and vulva, see Lochrie (1997: 189, 198 n. 26) and Riehle (1981: 46). One wonders about the relationship between these vulvic wound images and the blood-drenched Christ discussed by Hamburger (1997: pl. 1). For a warning against the dangers of assuming all penetrable sites are feminine see Rambuss (1998: 19–32).

4   This queering can also be seen in a text that Lochrie mentions but does not cite, Angela of Foligno's (c. 1248–1309) *Book*, particularly the *Memorial*, dictated by Angela to a Friar. In two places she discusses the wound in Christ's side: "In the fourteenth step, while I was standing in prayer, Christ on the cross appeared . . . to me . . . He then called me to place my mouth to the wound on his side. It seemed to me that I saw and drank the blood, which was freshly flowing from his side. His intention was to make me understand that by this blood he would cleanse me." And later, she writes that "At times it seems to my soul that it enters into Christ's side, and this is a source of great joy and delight" (Angela of Foligno 1993: 128 and 176; and see also 246). These two passages are compressed in a highly erotic and homosexuated or queered reading by Luce Irigaray: "Could it be true that not every wound need remain secret, that not every laceration was shameful? Could a sore be *holy*? Ecstasy is there in that glorious slit where she curls up as if in her nest, where she rests as if she had found her home – and He is also in her. She bathes in a blood that flows over her, hot and purifying" (Irigaray 1985a: 200). For more on Irigaray and mysticism see Hollywood (2002: 187–210) and Hollywood (2004a). For other examples of "possibly queer female desire for Christ's wounds," see Lochrie (1997: 199 n. 34).

5   I realize that this is not quite where Bennett places the implausibility – for her it is the purported jump between religious representations and actual sexual practices between women that are implausible. But I think that behind her sense that religious representation tells us little about "actual people" lies the irreality of medieval religious beliefs for many modern readers.

6   Judith C. Brown's descriptions of the trial records concerning Sister Benedetta Carlini (1590–1661) suggest that one *might* in fact lead to the other. In this case, Benedetta Carlini's visions, in which she speaks as Christ and as a male angel, serve as the pretext for her sexual relationship with another nun assigned to care for her. As Brown explains, Benedetta's "male identity consequently allowed her to have sexual and emotional relations that she could not conceive between women." In addition, the requests she made as the angel Spenditello did not differ substantially from erotic mystical language. See J.C. Brown (1986: 127).

7   On the potential problems with using modern notions of normativity to understand medieval materials see Hollywood (2001: 173–9).

8   Rambuss points to similar problems with Leo Steinberg's theological readings of Christ's penis as it appears in Renaissance art. See Steinberg (1996). For a related argument about the body of Christ in the York cycle see Epp (2001).

9   For many, this would be an apt description of intense sexual desire.

10   The beguines – as women who did not marry, living singly or in groups, often supported themselves through manual labor, and sometimes refused or attempted to escape from the

strict jurisdiction of male ecclesial or monastic hierarchies – are also "lesbian-like" in the terms discussed by Bennett. Their modes of religious imagery, however, as I will argue in what follows, were queer in varying degrees.

11 At least from the standpoint of the contemporary reader. Whether these idealized conceptions of divine-human relations would have been similarly "queer" for medieval readers is not yet clear to me. See again Hollywood (2001).

12 For a useful introduction to Origen and his interpretation of the Song of Songs, see McGinn (1992: 108–30). On the "queering" of the Song of Songs in the Christian tradition see Moore (2000). The "individual believer" is a potentially gender neutral category, yet in many male-authored texts on the Song of Songs the presumption of *reversal* in calling oneself a bride depends on the marking of that believer as male.

13 For the intensity of such gender crossings (and re-crossings) in seventeenth-century English devotional poetry, and the ways in which they destabilize sex, gender, and sexual categories, see Rambuss (1998). The texts of a number of medieval male authors might usefully be subjected to a similar analysis, most particularly perhaps, Rupert of Deutz, Bernard of Clairvaux, Richard of St Victor, and Heinrich Suso.

14 For an overview of Mechthild's life and work see Hollywood (2004b); Hollywood (1995: 1–86); and McGinn (1998: 222–44).

15 This leads in the later books of *The Flowing Light* to Mechthild's claim that the "well-ordered" soul becomes the "housewife" of God. See Mechthild (1998: VII, 3, 277) and Hollywood (1995: 78–86).

16 For a general overview see McGinn (1998: 199–222). On the homoeroticism of Hadewijch's poems and letters see Matter (1989). On the "queering" effect of the intensity of her desire see Lochrie (1997: 184). For a more "normalizing" reading of Hadewijch's language, in relationship to late medieval theology, see Murk-Jansen (1996: 52–68).

17 For Hadewijch's debts to secular courtly love lyric, see Murk-Jansen (1992: 117–28), Murk-Jansen (1996: 54–55) and the literature cited there. According to Bynum, medieval religious men used gender reversal (the soul as the bride of Christ) to stress their humility in the face of the divinity. Murk-Jansen carries this argument to Hadewijch's poems, arguing that since "within the conventions of the courtly love lyric it is the lady who has all the power" and "the man who is represented as of lower status," Hadewijch too uses gender reversal as a form of renunciation. This is certainly right, at least in part. But as I will argue here, Hadewijch's knight is not simply passive in face of the unattainable Love, but actively seeks her, through pain, passion, and desire. In this he combines activity and passivity (as does the bride in the Song of Songs, who goes into the streets looking for her beloved).

18 On the one hand, Hadewijch stresses that this is the case as long as the soul is in the body or on earth, holding forth the promise of the continual union and coming to fruition of the soul and the divine after death. Yet at other times, the doubleness and cruelty of desire and its passionate, painful, ecstasy seem, literally, endless.

19 Murk-Jansen (1996: 58). This is reminiscent of *The Rothschild Canticle's* representation of Song of Song 4.9 – "You have wounded my heart, my sister, my spouse" – in which the bride holds the lance with which Christ's side is wounded on the verso side, and Christ on a stylized cross displays his side wound on the recto. (Rothschild Canticles, New Haven, Beinecke Rare Book and Manuscript Library, MS 404, fols 18v–19r.)

20 According to Murk-Jansen (1996: 66), "the fluid movement between masculine and feminine imagery emphasizes the basic similarity of male and female before God," leaving any account of Hadewijch's own understanding of "womanhood" "necessarily speculative." Yet doesn't the fluidity of human gender before God tell us *something* about how Hadewijch experienced gender, at least on the level of her relationship to the divine (itself central to her life)?

21 See Sells (1994: 180–217); and Hollywood (1995: 87–119, 180–93).

22 For the "fall into nothingness" and the dialectic of All and Nothing in Porete see Marguerite Porete (1993: ch. 118, 192–3).

23   The term grace rarely appears in the *Mirror*, and then to refer to the very lowest stages of the soul, which are clearly subordinated to the life of the spirit and that of the annihilated soul. See, for example, Porete (1993: ch. 60, 137–8).

24   Porete deploys gendered language in a number of different ways throughout the *Mirror*. Her dialectical subversions of the gap between the soul and Love (or the Trinity), for example, often depend for their linguistic operation on the fact that these terms are feminine and so take feminine pronouns. The resultant pronominal ambiguity elides the gap between the soul and the divine. There may also be echoes in Porete of the uniting of male and female characteristics in Christ's body through the bloody side wound. In general, Porete focuses attention on Christ in the third and fourth realms. Yet she calls the divine in the higher realms the "Farnear," thereby evoking both courtly and biblical allusions to the Beloved. This male beloved, moreover, in the sixth stage (the highest the soul can achieve in this life), opens an "aperture" to the soul in which she sees her own eternal glory (Porete 1993: ch. 61, 138). For more on this and other uses of gendered language in the *Mirror*, see Hollywood (1995: 100–1, 108–9) and Sells (1994: 180–217).

25   Although Porete retains the orthodox position that full union between the soul and the divine can only occur after death, she clearly holds that the soul, while on earth, can annihilate its will and desire. In doing so, the soul overcomes the need for corporeal aids to salvation and is able to "give to nature what it wills." But it is able to do so only because the body is fully subservient to the virtues and so will ask nothing contrary to God's will. See Hollywood (1995: 109–12).

26   For a related argument about the self-subverting nature of sexual desire see Bersani (1988: 197–222).

Chapter 11

Bodies Demand Language

Thomas Aquinas

Eugene F. Rogers Jr

In what follows I elaborate on the claim, common to Thomas Aquinas and Judith Butler, that a body is that which demands language. First, I undermine the claim that natural law functions in Aquinas primarily to give content to morality, particularly in the case of what he calls, in the *Summa Theologiae* and the *Commentary on Romans,* "the vice against nature," and I heighten the surprisingness of the claims with a comparison to Butler. Second, I take up a possible objection to the claim that natural law chiefly functions otherwise than to give content, since in two cases it does seem to do so, namely in Aquinas's explications of lying and lying with a member of the same sex. The account becomes an exhortation to come out, to obey the "natural" demand of the body for language.

Natural Law Meets Judith Butler

"Natural law" in ethics sounds like the very heart of an essentialist program. And the greatest exponent of natural law is supposed to be Thomas Aquinas. Not only Catholic, but even Protestant, Jewish, and non-theistic accounts of natural law cite and claim him.[1] Yet a queer natural law it is. It is a natural law of which we can know with certainty only the proposition: do good, avoid evil. It is a natural law in which animals do not properly participate.[2] It is a natural law that no human being fulfills, and one whose presence humans infer in the absence of its effects, in the breach. It is a natural law that occupies only a very small part of the corpus of its supposed chief defender. It is a natural law entirely overshadowed by a theory of the virtues, to the extent that its existence depends upon the virtue of prudence (God's), and knowledge of it depends on the virtue of justice (ours). It is a natural law explicitly subject to social construction. It is a natural law that parallels not physics but narrative. It is a natural law founded not upon experiment but upon interpretation of text.

The present chapter appears in a volume called *Queer Theology.* Perhaps the most prominent theorist of queerness is Judith Butler. To put Judith Butler into conversation with Aquinas seems a doomed encounter between abstract stereotypes. He's a realist; she's not. But I use "seems" in the way that Thomas does: what "seems" to be the case is always the objection that Thomas disputes.

I write too because I instantiate that encounter in a bipolar reaction to Butler.

Hearing her positions reported, I tend to get annoyed. I don't know what essentialists she has in mind; when I think of Aquinas, the "essentialist" best known to me, the critique seems to sail right past the author. I worry that despite her intention her analysis constructs bodies to the extent that they float away. An Aristotelian standpoint leaves me far enough away to become tone-deaf, so that when I hear about Butler it sounds to me like Kant. In both cases one starts with the things themselves, whether phenomena or hermaphrodites. In both cases one ends with things constructed, whether in the mind or in a community of language users: just more noumena? Kant rendered communal? I find myself clinging to the Aristotelian supposition that either the world and the mind are made for each other, or intelligibility demands that we treat them that way. I find myself impatient with the dualisms of realism and constructivism that I encounter in cocktail references to Butler; Plato versus Aristotle, late medieval nominalists versus high medieval realists; German idealists versus Viennese positivists: haven't we been through all this before, so many times before?

Reading Judith Butler, however, I have a different reaction. I find my objections anticipated and qualified away. I find much to appreciate in her interest in performance, in her observation that matter is what demands more language. For Aristotle and Aquinas, too, matter demands form, is unintelligible without it. I wonder if the essences to which Butler objects are the very ones to which Aristotle objected: Platonic ones, imagined (truly or falsely) as static, unearthly, away in the sky.[3] Aristotelian forms are no longer confining shapes or lacks of shape; they are internal principles of *change,* including changes of shape. And the changes are motivated by *desire.*[4]

Consider Judith Butler's anti-essentialist definition of a body:

> [W]hat persists here is *a demand in and for language,* a "that which" which prompts and occasions . . . calls to be explained, described, diagnosed, altered . . . fed, exercised, mobilized, put to sleep, a site of enactments and passions . . . the constitutive demand that mobilizes psychic action. (Butler 1993: 67)

See how Aquinas sums it up, like this:

> Forma dat esse materiae.[5]

Or at greater length:

> Materia enim est id in quo intelligitur forma et privatio.[6]

In irenic moods, Aquinas held that since the truth is one, all things true participated in the First Truth. There was no truth without its source in the Father, its demonstration in the Son, its becoming known in the Spirit. If that sounds too *philosophia perennis,* I should refer instead to a rapprochement between the philosophical forebears of Aquinas and Butler, namely between Aristotle and Freud. Deep in the background lies Jonathan Lear's *Love and Its Place in Nature* (1990), an account of how much better sense Freud makes if you try to unpack his actual clinical practice not with the reigning natural-science paradigm of which Freud himself was covetous, but with a little Wittgenstein and a lot of Aristotle. Discovering id, ego, and superego becomes a form working itself out (or per-formance). Without pursuing a critique of Butler, therefore, or making much of necessary distinctions, I shall first deconstruct the received Aquinas on natural law to show its dynamic and performative Aristotelian roots, roots less uncongenial to scholars formed by Butler than one might suppose. I then reconstruct a Thomistic case for coming out, by considering apparent parallels between Thomas's account of the vice against nature and the unnaturalness of lying. For Thomas as for Butler, bodies demand language.[7]

The Construction of Natural Law in the *Summa* and the *Commentary on Romans*

In the *Secunda Pars* of the *Summa Theologiae* (*ST*), Thomas devotes only a few pages (six, in a standard Latin edition) to natural law. He devotes many more (157) to other forms of law: The Old Law, the New Law, Ceremonial Law, Human Law, and vastly more to the virtues, their background and context (around 1200). Law generally is the deliverance of the prudence of a ruler. Eternal law is God's prudence (*ST* I–II.91.1), and concerns singulars (including people and events – *ST* I–II.93.5–6); natural law is an abbreviation of eternal law (*ST* I–II.91.2, 94.2, 94.3), God's taking human beings into participation in the divine prudence by allowing them to understand certain generalizations from the particulars, at least: do good and avoid evil (*ST* I–II.94.2). Note that in this way natural law is defined in terms of the virtues (God's prudence). Furthermore, as other scholars have argued, human beings require prudence to understand the natural law, and, as I have argued elsewhere, justice and gratitude to carry it out (Rogers 1998; Rogers 1999a: 87–139 and Rogers 1999b). But the great surprise to non-Thomists about Thomas on natural law is textual: he says so little about it, and he does so little with it. While in theory the wrongness of an action might be stated both in the language of law,[8] and in the language of virtue, in practice Thomas almost always chooses to state it in the language of virtue. Natural law answers not the modern, essentialist yearning for something commanding transcultural, universal agreement. On the contrary, Thomas explicitly claims that something as obviously wrong as stealing admits of cultural determination, so that natural law signally *fails* to command agreement (*ST* I–II.94.4). Rather, natural law answers the Stoic objection that the life of virtue may not lead to happiness if fate can defeat it (see Bowlin 1999). Natural law claims that fate is under the control of God's providence, and that if human beings participate in God's prudence, then the vagaries of fate will be such as *can* lead them to greater virtue and *need not* defeat the blessedness of the virtuous.[9] In particular, it is prudent, and a parameter around the vagaries of fate attempting to defeat happiness, if we attend to the natural goods of food, shelter, sex, living in society, and seeking to understand (*ST* I.94.2 *post med*). This attention does not so much give content to the virtues, as put a fence around fate. Not that natural law *cannot* supply content. Aquinas would never make a form-and-content distinction go all the way down. Rather, to read natural law rather than the virtues as the ordinary, surface site of appeal for content is bizarrely to misread the *Summa*, to take the half of a percent for the 99.5.

There are at least two places, however, where Aquinas seems to favor an appeal to natural law over an appeal to the virtues: lying and homosexuality. Can these two cases restore a natural law that dictates content to morality? Marriage-like homosexual relationships may lead adherents of virtue and law approaches to rival conclusions. Natural law theorists may call them unnatural, a parody; virtue theorists may applaud the sites of love and justice. Only oblique approaches may generate more light than heat. I address the tension between natural-law and virtue-theory ethics among Thomas scholars in complementary ways: (1) by turning to his biblical commentaries, and (2) by relating his discussion of homosexuality to his discussion of lying. The biblical commentaries reveal premises that modern ethicists on both sides of the debate no longer share with Thomas, and the analysis of lying applies differently to modern and medieval conceptions of homosexual activity, however evaluated.

In Aquinas's *Commentary on Romans,* chapter 1, the results look surprising. Aquinas *mentions* homosexual acts in the commentary for the most obvious reason, but one that often goes unstated: because Paul does, and Aquinas is attempting to follow Paul's reasoning. Aquinas bases his *account* of apparent homosexual acts in the Romans commentary (unlike elsewhere?) penultimately on natural law but ultimately on the virtues of justice and gratitude. Homosexuality is God's punishment for Gentile injustice and idolatry.[10] Indeed, idolatry is a "holding truth captive in injustice."[11] Liberation theologians can now appeal to Thomas Aquinas to claim that human beings cannot reach correct intellectual conclusions under unjust conditions. Rather, injustice leads human beings to mistake the truth about what is natural.[12] That claim will not *settle* any debates about natural law, but it may complicate and enrich them. For it makes social justice crucial and allows disputants to differ on what justice entails.

That is so not least because no one will now hold *Aquinas's* view of how social justice relates to homosexuality. In the *Commentary on Romans*, homosexuality does not originate as an independent sin, but as a punishment for *previous* sins of social injustice, a punishment causing the unjust society to die out – in this case, idolatrous Gentile societies. According to Aquinas (who seems to have learned this from the rabbis), God began and increased the practice of homosexuality among Gentiles just as they began and increased the practice of idolatry. The beauty ("convenientia") of it is, that idolatry kills itself off.[13]

In the very biblical passages, therefore, that Aquinas elsewhere adduces as the *warrants* for arguments about natural law and the virtues, natural law turns out to be no *independent* source of knowledge. Natural law is here (unlike elsewhere?) epistemologically *subordinate* to the virtues, because Aquinas reads Romans 1 to make homosexuality follow from injustice. Following Paul, Aquinas tells a story in which ignorance of natural law succeeds a lack of justice. Here, natural law shows itself to be at bottom a mode of biblical exegesis and critique, rather than a discipline of secular provenance and goals. In the presence of injustice, it becomes a self-consuming artifact, a non-functional, feckless knowledge, a knowledge *manqué*. Aquinas's account may therefore show more flexibility than many give it credit for, and prove susceptible of different uses by those with ideas different from his about what justice and gratitude entail. Proponents of religious blessing or civil recognition of same-sex unions can argue, for example, that those are conditions of social justice without which the truth about homosexuality simply cannot be known. Textual resistance to such a revisionist usage of Aquinas's reasoning arises less from his view of nature than his view of Scripture. But that is another argument (see Rogers 1999a: 127–39).

Theses on Aquinas and Butler

The account lends support to a non-standard but textually compelling series of observations about Aquinas's use of natural law that distinguish it sharply from many modern uses.

In the Romans commentary, human beings cannot expect to reach correct conclusions about natural law under conditions of injustice – so that Aquinas's account unexpectedly allows different uses by those differing on what justice and gratitude entail. Although there is no budging Aquinas from his conclusion about the illicitness of homosexual acts, in his Romans commentary the account depends upon two premises that modern readers, whether they agree with his conclusions or not, are unlikely to share: homosexual activity, before it is a sin, is a punishment for prior social injustice; and as such it should occur among Gentile idolaters, but not among Jews – or Christians.

Thus natural-law thinking in Aquinas is much less "essentialist" than its modern successors, for a number of reasons: recognizing the natural moral law depends upon habits of virtue, that is, in postmodern parlance, upon a performance. Indeed, insofar as human beings know natural law, they not only perform, but participate in a performance of God's: natural law is the this-worldly performance of God's prudence, God's prudence in act. As we participate in God's prudence, natural law is no *independent, totalizing* source of knowledge, but part of a changing mix. The natures in question are defined not Platonically as essences off in some ideal space, but Aristotelianly as *internal* principles of *change*. They differ from modern essences then in two further crucial ways. They are internal, not external. They express what is our ownmost; they do not constrain but empower us. And they are principles of *change*, not static but dynamic through and through. Thus we know them not by introspection, not directly, but indirectly, by observing ourselves (*ST* I.87). That is, we know them from our *performance*. They are, in other words, surmises or extrapolations or inferences or generalizations from performance. "What one must characterize theologically as a piece of the doctrine of God or of creation appears philosophically as transcendental reflection" (Pesch 1988: 294–5). In the order of knowing, performance comes first. Properly understood, therefore, Aristotelian natures cannot oppress in the way that Platonic essences can. To be sure, anything fallen can oppress. But not everything can oppress in the same way.

For those and similar reasons, Aquinas's realism is not a Platonic essentialism, but learns enough from Aristotle to escape much of Butler's critique. I assert the theologian's license to sum up in theses.

1   Form is dynamic, not static.
2   Nature is "an inner principle of change," that is, an abbreviation of performance (Lear 1988:15-25).
3   The human being knows herself only by observing her own activity (*ST* I.87), or performance.
4   Knowing takes place over time, in language, and in community (by reference to justice,[14] to the *maiores in fide* (*ST* II–II.5.3 ad 2, II–II.5.4), *per ecclesia, per longum tempum, et cum admixtione multorum errorum* (*ST* I.1.1)).
5   All language rests on analogy, or "appropriate equivocations" (Preller 1967: 243), so that it cannot foreclose further demands for language.
6   God is unimpeded activity, or boundary-crossing performance.
7   Nature is defined by form, matter, and privation,[15] or construction, that which calls for more language, and the constitutive other.
8   Form ("construction") defines both matter and language. It applies "indifferently to minds and things" (Irwin 1988: 7).
9   First principles are never of the Cartesian, foundational sort. They always appear in the context of an explanation. For that reason Thomas does not only admit, but says explicitly that they are "positioned," that is, they occupy a *positio*.[16]
10 Matter requires more language, and language materializes bodies – both through form, which is the working out of a dynamic (*dynamis*, power) indifferently in words and things.
11 The attention to habit is attention to the persistence or iterability of a performance.
12 Iterability turns the spatial into the temporal.
13 The truth of bodies is that bodies matter, that is, they signify, and in so doing they demand and call forth language; the truth of language is that language matters; it calls forth and materializes bodies. Or, in Aristotelian terms, metaphysics considers that which is as *intelligibilia*, that is, for humans, as linguistically constructed. But that which

is does not come before intelligibility; rather, intelligibility and that which is both arise, equiprimordially, from form, or construction. So words bring bodies into the street, and bodies in the street call for new words. Aquinas and Butler agree that sexuality is all tied up with language, and language is all tied up with sexuality.

That brings us to the second part of this account, one in which language and sexuality come together. Is it the case that animals do not lie, and do not lie with members of the same sex, for a similar reason?

Lying and Lying Together, or How Do Bodies Tell the Truth?

A second oblique approach to Aquinas on natural law turns to his account of lying. In the *Summa,* Aquinas almost always bases his account of a vice, in Aristotelian fashion, on its corresponding virtue. At least twice he departs from that procedure. Both times he appeals to the law of nature rather than the virtues. The odd cases have never become important to a comprehensive account. Both anomalies resonate most powerfully *not* with the natural theory of Aristotle, but with the natural theory of Paul's Epistle to the Romans. As far as I know, no one has previously noted this anomaly in print.[17] The cases are the vice against nature and lying. The vice against nature is said to depart from the "natural" use of sex by animals to propagate the species.[18] In like manner, lying seems to depart from a natural use of expression by animals. At least in passing, Aquinas regards animals as unable to express something different with their bodies from what is in their minds. When humans do so, is it therefore unnatural? Does Aquinas's analysis of homosexuality go the same way? Does he regard sex as communicative on the model with language, so that sexual sins miscommunicate as falsehoods do? If so, what difference would the recent concept of sexual orientation make?

In the *Summa Theologiae,* Aquinas classes lying as a "vice opposed to the truth." It is also one of those *contra* vices: it is enunciating something contrary to what the mind adheres to as true.[19] As the vice against truth counters the nature of the mind, so the vice against nature counters the truth of the body. Indeed, lying is unnatural: "For since spoken words are naturally signs of things understood, it is unnatural and undue that someone signify by voice that which she does not have in mind."[20]

When Aquinas comes to explicate this contrariety further, however, an ambiguity opens up. The contrariety becomes inordinance, a matter of degree rather than direction. "Lying has the sense of sin not only from the evil that it inflicts on the neighbour, but also from its own inordinance."[21] Aquinas says this just where the harm to the neighbour is hardest to see, that is, when someone tells a lie to save a life. Reasoning from a sin's inordinance echoes loudly in the treatment of the vice against nature. Aquinas treats the vice against nature as a vice of *luxuria,* or inordinance *par excellence.* In that discussion he shows a strict understanding of the Greek, *para phusin,* that underlies the Vulgate's *contra naturam.* The Greek speaks of something precisely *beyond,* rather than contrary to nature, a sin of excess – just as Aquinas's classification. Lying too exceeds something: an excess of words, it exceeds one's true state of mind. What is the problem with that excess, and how does lifesaving count as excessive? That question goes unanswered. The section on the vice against nature raises a similar one. In both cases Aquinas's decision seems to elevate the rightness of the act itself over the practice of virtue, indeed the virtue of charity. Here deontology rules. Yet in the very next article, charity decides whether the lying is mortal or not. The tension is palpable. Aquinas stresses that lying to save a life is not mortal (to the liar!): how small a step to say, not a sin at all? Or a sin only because one finds oneself (why?) trapped in a situation with no innocent solution? Aquinas will not say these things.

Under the sin of hypocrisy Aquinas explains further. The objective wrong of lying departs from this principle: "The exterior work naturally signifies the intention."[22] It is in the nature of truth that "signs concord with things signified."[23]

Lies of the genitals resemble lies of the tongue because both are better described as acts of the whole person; actions of tongue or genitals can both make the whole person a liar. This commonality seems most present when Aquinas indicates that animals do not or cannot lie. Speech is a manifestation or enunciation of something by a rational act conferring a sign upon something signified.[24] "Whence even brute animals manifest something, although they do not intend the manifestation, but by natural instinct they do something upon which manifestation follows."[25] That seems to imply that animals do not lie. But the remark is subtler than may at first appear. Aquinas does not say that animals do not lie because they form no intentions to mislead, or because animals naturally tell the truth. Rather, animals can neither lie nor avoid lying, because animals do not form intentions at all. The mention of animals is by the way, and not what one might expect. The truth-telling animal plays no role in the argument; the instinctually manifesting animal comes as an extra. The nature in the background here is not the nature that human beings share with animals, but the nature that distinguishes them from animals. Because humans form intentions, because they confer signs intentionally on things signified, they retain a moral responsibility that animals lack. That does not look like modern natural-law argument at all, but it looks a lot like Aquinas.

At last the vice against nature does differ from the vice against truth. The vice against nature counters – or sometimes exceeds – the nature of the human being as animal. The vice against truth counters – or sometimes exceeds – the nature of the human being as human.

And there is another problem. Thomas defines the natural moral law as human participation in God's eternal law by *reason*, and (non-human) animals, by the definition of "human," do *not* use reason. God governs their natures by instinct, not by participation in the *reasonableness* of his rulerly prudence. Aquinas famously defines natural law as the human, rational participation in God's eternal law.[26] It is much less often noted that, since other animals are not rational, "The natural law is given to *human beings,* not to the other animals: the most important transformation since Antiquity" (Pesch 1988: 294).[27] That is because Aquinas develops "the teaching about the natural law, like that about the eternal law, on *theological* grounds," so that "the *philosophical* result of Thomas's teaching claims that *there is no natural law,* in any case not in the sense in which it is usually taken account of, namely as a catalogue of prescribed and obligatory directions of content that bind each human lawgiver" – where "lawgiver" means not legislator, but rational agent (Pesch 1988: 294; italics in original). The eternal law of God is not "natural" to irrational animals, because they do not govern themselves by a providence or prudence analogous to God's, or as participant law-givers.[28] Rather, as sometimes noted, the human mind knows with certainty only the first principle of natural law, that good is to be done, evil avoided (*ST* I–II.94.2c). Indeed, German and American scholars now argue independently that Thomas's account of natural law serves rather to give the conditions for the possibility of the success of virtue (Pesch 1988: 294–5): God's prudence so bounds contingency that misfortune cannot finally defeat the happiness of the virtuous (Bowlin 1999 *passim*).

In that context the appeal to animal nature can at most serve to abbreviate an appeal to the reasonableness of the law to humans and the possible exercise of human virtue. Otherwise, the mention of animal activity can count as a remark only quoted in theology from biology. Biology, like metaphysics, stands outside theology's formal rationale, a discipline from which sacred doctrine may not mount its own, proper arguments. Arguments from biology, as from metaphysics, count merely as "extraneous and probable" in sacred doctrine (*ST* I.1.8). Sacred doctrine treats them as foreign matter. Should it take them in, it includes them *ad hoc,* or as "extraneous," and without vouching for their truth, or as "probable." What authority they may possess, sacred doctrine does not recognize, except by courtesy. Nothing in sacred doctrine can depend upon arguments extraneous and probable.

For Aquinas to be true to his lights he has to (not discard or ignore) *bracket or transmute* certain appeals to experimental science – a claim that will sound queer to both conservatives and liberals. On the conservative side, one would expect that natural law marked the *continuity* between human beings and animals, and that therefore one could argue from animal behavior to human behavior. It may indeed mark continuity, but we cannot know that *in sacred doctrine* by arguing from animal behavior. That move marks the argument as one in biology. The argument from biology might indeed be part of the warrant for modern natural-law theorists who must elide Thomas's commitment to the Scriptures because they are trying to use natural-law theory – as he did not – to generate agreement where disagreement is widespread. Where disagreement is widespread, they dare not appeal to Scripture for fear it would expose a sectarian enterprise. In the modern period, the whole *point* of the appeal to natural law is to provide an apparently universal, extrascriptural basis for a morality traditionally based upon Scripture. But Thomas Aquinas will have none of it. Thomas has the confidence of one who can assume that all readers will accept the authority of Scripture, and who also knows that the best available natural science is subject to change, and that furthermore the hierarchy harbors deep and sometimes theologically justified suspicion of the best available natural science, as represented by Aristotle.

On the liberal side, one would expect that the way for critics to gain leverage against traditional natural-law theory would be to point to the incidence of homosexual activity among animals (Bagemihl 1999), or undermine the essentiality of the sexes by pointing to the incidence of various hermaphroditisms among human beings (Butler 1999). Detractors might find it ironic that modern natural-law theory opens a space to counter rather than learn from natural science. Yet these too are biological arguments extraneous to sacred doctrine. At most experimental science could *raise questions* for an account of natural law; since the truth is one, incidence of homosexuality among animals could be cause only for checking one's exegesis. Exegesis correct, sacred doctrine may exercise the theological privilege of judgment over against biology (as some are raising objections against reductionist versions of Darwinism) at least in sacred doctrine's own discipline. In his bracketing of natural science Aquinas again resembles Butler. Both demand that scientific disciplines reveal their political commitments – where "political" means what sort of community they serve.

When Aquinas remarks that animals do not lie, has he temporarily abandoned a commitment to properly theological argument, to argument based on Scripture? If so, we could simply throw out the comment that animals do not lie.

On the other hand, Aquinas may have a scriptural warrant that goes without saying. If so, he adduces extraneous argument to illustrative effect, while his actual premises lie elsewhere. A prohibition against lying appears in the Ten Commandments, and a prohibition of the vice against nature arises from a reading of Romans 1.

One strain of thinking about the relation of natural to biblical law in Aquinas, prominent in German-language discussion since the mid-1960s (beginning with Kluxen 1964: 218–41), but less known in the Anglo-American context, makes much of Aquinas's extreme under-determination of the natural law, and his specification of it by the Ten Commandments. Thus, in Question 100, Thomas announces that God gave the Ten Commandments to specify the principle of natural law: do good and avoid evil. Since the Ten Commandments contain an explicit prohibition of lying, and, in many medieval interpretations, a prohibition of homosexual intercourse under the prohibition of adultery, and since Thomas uses them to specify the natural law, one might expect to find in his commentary on the Ten Commandments[29] the following result: since animals neither lie, nor lie unnaturally with one another, these breaches of the law of nature are specified in the Ten Commandments. But Thomas does not so argue. Rather, the commentary on the Ten Commandments makes no use of natural law argument. It concatenates biblical passages, sometimes organized as first, second, and third reasons. Indeed, on second thought, that is what we should have expected instead. The Ten Commandments do not need to be explained by natural-law reasoning. Rather, natural-law reasoning needs to be specified by the Ten Commandments – just as Thomas announced in Question 100. Thomas is only being consistent.

And yet, that result makes the switch from virtue-reasoning to law-reasoning even stranger when it comes. If the purpose of natural law is to give the conditions under which virtuous action is possible – as German and American authors have independently argued (Pesch 1988 and Bowlin 1999) – then why does Aquinas *ever* use it to give content?

But Aquinas reasons more complexly, because his account of nature depends not simply on what animals do, or what a sexual orientation might be. It depends – I surmise – on his understanding of Paul, who brings the two atypical cases, lying and homosexuality, together in Romans 1.24: "Therefore God gave them up in the lusts of their hearts to impurity . . . because they exchanged the truth about God for a lie." That is a surmise, because, although it seems to explain the pair, the Romans Commentary offers no evidence beyond the words of Paul. For Aquinas the "natural virtue" of truth-telling seems to have applied to bodies as well as speech, and told against homosexuality. Many modern thinkers would conclude instead that gay people ought to come out.

Homosexuality, one infers, is for Thomas in some respects a lie of the body. We might today adopt the similar reasoning to an opposite conclusion: heterosexual activity by gay and lesbian people is exposed when their bodies give them the lie, and coming out is the bringing into community, the semiotic offering, of the body's truth telling.

The communicative acts of coming out certainly entail self-definition, but these acts of signification come through surrender to an interpretive community. Coming out is opening one's life to be told by others. This exposure is the source of dread and panic in coming out. It is also the outcome of a desire to be known, a desire for wholeness and a promise of unity of oneself and the world. Coming out articulates the sign-giving character of human, bodily life.

For the church, a similar statement of identity and desire is at stake when the members of the body come out with their sexual commitments. Marriage and the celibate life write the body into the story of redemption. Both are communicative, sexual acts. They are means by which the story of redemption is written through human lives, as signs of God's recon-ciliation, a reconciliation of the body. Coming out is a wager, opening the body to a language of redemption, opening a way for the body's agency not only in the movement of desire but in the donation of one's agency as an interpretive sign.

Any argument for or against same-sex unions in the church needs to attend to the desire of gay and lesbian Christians to make their desires known and to offer their bodies as signs of God's self-giving (McCarthy 1998: 101–2).

For the most part same-sex rather than cross-sex marriages would better befit the desire of gay and lesbian Christians to make their desires known and offer their bodies as signs of God's self-giving.

John Paul II puts this desire in a particularly graphic way: "God, according to the words of Holy Scripture, penetrates the creature, who is completely 'naked' before Him: 'And before him no creature is hidden, but all are open (*panta gymna* [naked]) and laid bare to the eyes of him with whom we have to do' (Hebrews 4:13)." Even more surprisingly, this "penetration" cannot be as male-centered as it sounds. John Paul immediately blocks that supposition, noting that "This characteristic belongs in particular to Divine Wisdom," gendered feminine. He cites the gender-bending Wisdom 7.24, where "Wisdom . . . because of her pureness pervades and penetrates all things." (If penetrating women go too far, the Greek supports the more feminine translation "Wisdom . . . envelopes – χωρεῖ – all things.") The human being is bound for communion with God because God sees human beings and calls them good, that is, desirable. God grants the human being "a body that expresses the person" because God destines the human creature for not merely spiritual but *nuptial* community, a marriage between human beings or between the human being and God (John Paul II 1981: 98 n. 1, 109).

Coming out responds to the body's demand for language, and not for individualistic reasons, either. For language is a gift and a demand of a community. Marriage, too (along with monasticism), responds to the body's demand for language, in a way especially suited to receiving and returning a communal gift. As "iron with iron together, so a man is sharpened in the presence of his friend."[30]

Notes

1 Westberg (1994); Novak (1998); Stout (1992). For accounts congenial with that offered here, see especially Nelson (1992); Hall (1994) and above all Bowlin (1999).

2 Although all things are subject in some way to God's providence (*ST* I–II.91.2c.), irrational creatures cannot participate in the rationality of God's providence, or its specifically legal character, so that in animals God's providence "cannot be called law except by similitude" (*ST* I–II.91.2 *ad* 2). Oddly for us moderns, natural physical law as constructed by modern science – say Newton's law of motion – also cannot properly be called law by Aquinas's lights. It too lacks the prudence of a ruler.

3 For hints in this direction, see Butler (1993: 31–44), with accompanying notes.

4 For a particularly dynamic, change-oriented account of Aristotle, see Lear (1988: 15–25).

5 Form gives existence to matter. Aquinas, *De principiis naturae*, 2.

6 For matter is that in which form and privation (or construction and passion) are understood. *De principiis naturae*, 2.

7 Cf. Aquinas, *De principiis naturae*, 2.

8 This may grant too much to natural law, since "not all virtuous acts are prescribed by the natural law," I–II.94.3 *in fin*.

9 Cf. *ST* I.92.1: whether an effect of law is to make human beings good.

10 "Idolatriae poenam," *In Rom.* 1:28, #151; cf. also v. 24, #139; v. 28, #153. I cite by verse and paragraph number from the Marietti edition of *Super Epistolas Sancti Pauli Lectura* (Thomas Aquinas 1953).

11 *In Rom.* 1:18, ##111–12.

12 "Nam vera Dei cognitio quantum est de se inducit homines ad bonum, sed ligatur, quasi captivitate detenta, per iniustiae affectum," *In Rom.* 1:18, #112.

13 "Est autem notandum quod satis rationabiliter Apostolus vitia contra naturam, quae sunt gravissima inter peccata carnalia, ponit idolatriae poenam, quia simul cum idolatria incepisse videntur, scilicet temporae Abrahae, quando creditur idolatria incoepisse. Unde et tunc primo leguntur in Sodomitis punita fuisse, ut Gen. XIX. Simul etiam idolatria crescente, huiusmodi vitia creverunt." *In Rom.* 1:27, #151.

14 *In Rom.* 1:18, #109; *ST* I–II.57–8, as interpreted in Rogers (1996).

15 *De principiis naturae,* 2.

16 *In post. anal.,* bk. 1, *lect.* 4, no. 7; Chenu (1957: 71–3 n. 1).

17 I owe my attention to it to Jeffrey Stout, who learned it from Victor Preller.

18 "Natura hominis potest dici vel illa quae est propria homini: et secundum hoc, omnia peccata, inquantum sunt contra rationem, sunt etiam contra naturam, ut patet per Damascenum, in II libro. Vel illa quae est communis homini et aliis animalibus: et secundum hoc, quaedam specialia peccata *dicuntur* esse contra naturam, sicut contra commixtionem maris et feminae quae est naturalis omnibus animalibus, est concubitus masculorum, quod specialiter dicitur vitium contra naturam" (I–II.94.2 *ad* 2). But note that this is said in answer to an objection. The question asks whether all acts of virtue are in accord with natural law, and the objection points out that only some vices are called vices specifically "against nature." In reply, Thomas is licensing, or supplying the rationale for, a prior linguistic usage that does not particularly fit with his way of putting things, but has biblical and traditional support. In the corpus of the article, Thomas catalogues the view in two lines, but does not reason from it: "Secundo inest homini inclinatio ad aliqua magis specialia, secundum naturam in qua communicat cum ceteris animalibus. Et secundum hoc, dicuntur ea esse de lege naturali 'quae natura omnia animalia docuit,' ut est coniunctio maris et feminae, et educatio liberorum, et similia" (I–II.94.2 *post med*). In the Romans commentary, note the absence of a homosexual orientation. Same-sex sexual activity is something into which "human beings," and not just homosexually oriented people, may be expected to fall as soon as God removes the grace that prevents them; strictly speaking, same-sex sexuality is as (un)natural as falling: "Sed [Deus] indirecte tradit homines in peccatum, in quantum iuste subtrahit gratiam per quam homines continebantur ne peccarent" (*In Rom.* 1.24, #139). "Alio modo dicitur esse aliquid contra naturam hominis ratione generis, quod est animal. Manifesturm est autem quod, secundum naturae intentionem, commixtio sexuum in animalibus ordinatur ad actum generationis, unde omnis commixtionis modus, ex quo generatio sequi non potest, est contra naturam hominis inquantum est animal. Et secundum hoc dicitur in Glossa 'naturalis usus est ut vir et mulier in uno concubito ceant, contra naturam vero ut masculus masculum polluat et mulier mulierem.' Et eadem ratio est de omni actu coitus ex quo generatio sequi non potest" (*In Rom.* 1.26, #149).

19 "Mendacium nominatur ex eo quod contra mentem dicitur" (II–II.110.1).

20 "Cum enim voces sint signa naturaliter intellectuum, innaturale est et indebitum quod aliquis voce significet id quod non habet in mente" (II–II.110.3).

21 "Mendacium non solum habet rationem peccati ex damno quod infert proximo, sed ex sua inordinatione" (II–II.110.3 *ad* 4).

22 "Opus exterius naturaliter significat intentionem" (II–II.111.2 *ad* 1).

23 "Veritas dicitur secundum quod signa concordant signatis" (II–II.111.3 *ad* 2).

24 "Quae quidem manifestatio, sive enuntiatio, est rationis actus conferentis signum ad signatum" (II–II.110.1).

25 "Unde etsi bruta animalia aliquid manifestent, non tamen manifestationem indendunt, sed naturali instinctu aliquid agunt ad quod manifestatio sequitur" (II–II.110.1).

26 "Lex naturalis nihil aliud est quam participatio legis aeternae in rationali creatura" (I–2.91.2c *in fin*).

27 "In creatura autem irrationali non participatur rationaliter: inde non potest dici lex nisi per similitudinem" (I–II.91.2 *ad* 3 *in fin*).

28 "Inter cetera autem rationalis creatura excellentiori quodam modo divinae providentiae subiacet, inquantum et ipsa fit providentiae particeps, sibi ipsi et aliis providens" (I–II.91c *in med*).

29 *Collationes in decem precepta,* collected in various editions with the *Opuscula*. Critical edition in Torrell (1985a: 5–40, 227–63); ET in Torrell (1985b).

30 Proverbs 27.17, quoted by Aquinas to close *De perfectione spiritualis vitae* (ch. 30). I follow the Hebrew rather than the Vulgate.

Chapter 12

Love's Urgent Longings

St John of the Cross

Christopher Hinkle

One dark night,
Fired with love's urgent longings
– ah, the sheer grace! –
I went out unseen,
My house being now all stilled.
(*The Dark Night*, stanza 1)[1]

Poet, mystic, and theologian, St John of the Cross (1542–91) has inspired numerous Christians with his passionate accounts of human desire for God and of the mystical consummation, both devastating and delightful, toward which this desire draws us. This sometimes controversial Spanish Carmelite describes a contemplative path along which all passions, capacities, and faculties are stilled and then transformed as the soul enters into more intimate relationship with God. What sustains us through this transformation, according to St John, is a desire for God strong enough to face trials of sensory and spiritual deprivation. This urgent longing leads John into erotic raptures as he describes the search for his divine Lover and then to a point where words fail altogether as he receives the touch of divine union. In this chapter I seek to unfold somewhat the complex relationship between spirituality and sexuality in St John's writings, focusing on desire for God as central to his understanding of spiritual progress and to the spiritual guidance he offers. I also seek to present John as a resource for queer theology or more accurately for those queer Christians and near-Christians who,[2] faced with the destabilization of sexual and theological certainties, mourn the absence of God who seems increasingly inaccessible, while also celebrating new freedoms and an openness to new sexual and spiritual possibilities.

I have written elsewhere on the value of John of the Cross's experience-based epistemology for conceptualizing and defending pro-gay religious convictions.[3] In this chapter I address an audience less confident in and concerning God's presence. Queer sexual desire has been claimed by many as a critical point of access to God, an important clue as to what God may be, and John of the Cross both confirms and gives theological context for this experience. But theological accounts of sex should not ignore that sex also, where it is self-involved, shame-driven, or lacking in charity, can be a rejection of God, a point too often obscured for both straight and gay Christians by the church's single-minded focus on the gender of sexual partners. Drawing on John of the Cross, I advocate here a theological perspective in which sexual desire is known as both means to God and obstacle, a perspective which, with John, celebrates the connection between erotic desire and desire for God without equating them, and affirms the authority of God over sexual desire without denigrating sex or advocating legalistic prescriptions concerning its necessary shape, style, or frequency. John of the Cross offers valuable spiritual direction towards the living of such a queer theology, drawing on his own passionate desires, experiences of abandonment and despair, and new certainty concerning God's continuing presence and promise.

I base my discussion upon what is probably the best known of St John's poems, "The Dark Night" (stanzas of which introduce each section of this chapter), and upon the pair of treatises organized by John as commentaries on this poem, *The Ascent of Mount Carmel* (A) and *The Dark Night* (DN). My chapter is structured as a three-part commentary on John's desire for God, an attempt both to introduce the reader to St John's mystical practice and to show his relevance for contemporary reflection. The first section emphasizes the close relationship of desire for God and sexual desire in St John, addressing the queer shape of John's desire for God. I find here an invitation for queer individuals (gay men in particular) to experience their own sexual desire as congruent with and tending towards desire for God. The second section then addresses sex as a potential obstacle to God, following St John's account of the risk of confusing sexual desire and its pleasures with desire for God and his insistence that they be separated so as to allow further intimacy with God. Finally the third section addresses briefly the challenge of reconciling a queer theology of the sort John describes with the secularizing agenda implicit within much contemporary queer theoretical writing.

The Shape of Desire

> O guiding night!
> O night more lovely than the dawn!
> O night that has united
> The Lover with his[4] beloved,
> Transforming the beloved in her Lover.
> (*The Dark Night*, stanza 5)

The popularity of St John's poetry testifies to the power then as now of communicating religious truths in the language of erotic love. Throughout his prose writings as well John seeks to evoke the more demanding desire for God by employing imagery which stimulates and attracts.[5] This linking of sexual desire and desire for God is not for John a mere technique. Rather John insists that this is the intended significance of sexual desire. In directing us towards desire for God and in readying us for that supreme intimacy, sexual desire achieves its true purpose.

There is of course, prior to John, a long Christian tradition of sexual allegory rooted particularly in the Song of Songs, the text requested by John upon his deathbed. Though one might argue that this entire tradition reveals certain homoerotic excesses, the more predictable consequence of interpreting John within this tradition is to render him innocuous, emphasizing the purely spiritual quality of John's desire for God while simultaneously concluding from John's conventional gendering of the soul as female that he in fact supports heterosexual marriage as uniquely sacramental. I will pursue a reading which instead emphasizes the erotic intensity of John's desire for God and draws attention to the gendered play of passivity, activity, penetration, and consummation used by John to evoke its fluid character. That John finds in such a euphoric eroticism the most adequate means for communicating his love for God invites contemporary queer Christians, particularly those for whom ecclesial homophobia and queer anti-Christian backlash have undermined confidence in God's presence, to explore the resonances of their own sexual and spiritual desires.

In fact, I propose that John of the Cross's account of divine love draws on and perhaps even contributes to the rather different erotic tradition which has helped to shape these desires.

Historian David Halperin identifies four historical classifications of men and male desire which, though still potentially discontinuous, seem frequently to converge in the modern world to form what we recognize as male homosexuality (Halperin 2002: 106–37). These are: (1) Effeminacy, in which the male prefers activities associated with women, such as art or love rather than those expected of men such as war, athletics, or ascetic practices. (2) Active sodomy (or pederasty), in which a normal male sexually penetrates subordinate males and in which the erotic aspect is assumed to be unidirectional and correlated with differences (in age, station, etc.) between those engaged. (3) Male friendship or love emphasizing mutuality in which the more egalitarian nature of the relationship serves to immunize it from erotic interpretation. (4) Sexual inversion or passivity, in which the male not only allows penetration by another man, but desires and takes pleasure in it, this deviancy being the most flagrant among other potential gender failings. Although St John of the Cross would, according to Halperin, have no conception of homosexuality as such, he would be exposed to these frameworks for interpreting gender and sexual performance.

Halperin's categories problematize even the question of whether St John was himself gay. There is no determinate historical evidence for claiming that St John either did or did not himself experience and/or act upon desires such as Halperin describes. Certainly John's poetry seems homoerotic to a contemporary gay gaze, but then we may have a heightened sensitivity to gender deviance. Still, drawing on Halperin's categorization we may claim John, at the least, as in many ways effeminate. Quite small, gentle, fond of gardens and drawing, St John challenged gender expectations. As a young man he nursed syphilis patients, embraced a vocation as a Carmelite marked by celibacy and contemplation, formed a powerful friendship with Teresa of Avila, and became well known for religious poetry with a controversial eroticism and for spiritual direction critical of "manly" asceticism. More passionate than politically savvy in his desire for reform, John was imprisoned as rebellious and contumacious, made a daring nocturnal escape (which figures in the imagery for "The Dark Night") and faced exile during his final, debilitating illness. In short, it is appropriate that John should feel familiar to contemporary gay men, and we are not surprised that he is led to describe communion with God in terms of both excess and hiddenness, attracting us through that hint of heresy which seems inevitably to accompany both mystical and sexual experience.

In the most memorable of his poems, "The Dark Night," St John transforms his own painful experience of isolation into the quivering anticipation of a secret embrace, moved by desire for a divine lover whose masculine beauty calls out, disturbing his sleep, inviting his caress and promising an unparalleled fulfillment. John here takes on the role of the female soul, a standard trope within Christian mystical writing but one which seems particularly significant within John's treatment of desire. In English, the effect is more straightforwardly homoerotic as the gender of John's narrator remains provocatively ambiguous except for the fifth stanza (which introduces this section). In Spanish, however, the female gender is established immediately though suggestively with a string of adjectives and participles: *inflamada* (fired or inflamed), *sin notada* (unseen or concealed), *segura* (secure), and *disfrazada* (disguised). It is by desire and in secrecy that St John takes on this female role, striking a very different tone than that found in his other poetry; noticeably absent is the bride/bridegroom language standard in the longer poems and rather than shepherds, girls of Judea, and animals, here only the wind witnesses the lovers' rendezvous.

Critical here is John's association of gender transformation with desire for God, a pattern further developed in his two treatises describing progress along the spiritual path. We find in the treatises not a constant gender performance, but rather a desire-driven transformation toward an increasing receptivity and passivity before God. The soul is "tempered and prepared for the sublime reception, experience, and savor of the divine" (DN 2.16.4; John of the Cross 1991: 432). John describes this transformation in terms first of active purgations (or purification), practices of self-denial and self-control which increase the soul's spiritual stamina. But as the soul progresses it is the more demanding passive purgations, those more private transformations initiated by God upon a stilled and attentive lover, which dominate. At this point, "God teaches the soul secretly and instructs it in the perfection of love" (DN 2.5.1; John of the Cross 1991: 401).

John's rhetoric of penetration and subordination resonates, I suggest, with Halperin's description of a pederastic[6] model, one in which desire depends upon and draws attention to differences in power and status, and in which obedience is exchanged for other rewards. God's preparation and eventual possession of the soul confirm the vast difference between God and humanity. The soul's passivity derives from appropriate submission and humility, as well as hope concerning whatever benefits may follow the divine pleasure. Though easily caricatured, the pederastic model of sexual desire seems a reasonably appropriate extension of the traditional Christian account of the relationship between an omnipotent God and a humanity which, though loved, is expected also to submit. The spiritual path John describes is one directed finally according to God's desire, and one in which the good is often distinguished from the pleasant. This shaping of desire proves too limiting and one-sided for understanding St John's relationship to God, however. John's submissiveness, though key to the spiritual transformation he hopes to encourage, is motivated more by the soul's own desire than by duty. From the beginning, John asserts, "the soul is touched with urgent longings of love: of esteeming love, sometimes; at other times, also of burning love" (DN 2.13.5; John of the Cross 1991: 425).

To fully understand the import of this shift from esteeming love to burning love, we must recognize the transformation as involving fear, uncertainty, and an awareness of deviance from what has been normal. The soul's inflamed desire for God increases the sense of submission and transformation and, therefore, when contrasted with a self-possessed masculine desire, increases stigma as well, carrying intimations of unnatural pleasures. In Halperin's terms, the shift is from a sodomitic act of submission to sexual inversion in which the previously masculine soul now not only allows divine penetration but sensually and spiritually longs for it and for the transformed identity it implies. Indeed the soul here turns away from natural enjoyments, all the satisfactions which come from creatures and from human agency, swept up in a desire that cannot be accounted for within the limits of its previous understanding. John describes a pleasure which is unfamiliar, symptomatic of a more widespread and radical reordering of our senses and faculties. Although John assumes some level of desire for God to be universal, this further capacity for both desire and pleasure emerges only as one progresses along the contemplative path. Thus increased passivity before God first brings the fear, pain, and emptiness which characterize the dark night, but then makes possible a new and heightened passion. "[T]he spiritual suffering is intimate and penetrating because the love to be possessed by the soul will also be intimate and refined" (DN 2.9.9; John of the Cross 1991: 415). Furthermore this transformation is accompanied by what John calls a "spiritual hiding," a leaving behind of former categories of experience and of the comfort of public acceptance and confirmation of one's experience. "[L]ove alone, which at this period burns by soliciting the heart for the Beloved, is what guides and moves her, and makes her soar to God in an unknown way along the road of solitude" (DN 2.25.4; John of the Cross 1991: 457).

According to Halperin's categorization, the shift from pederasty to inversion represents an intensification of the difference between the sexual participants, as the gender identity of the invert is called into question and "his" deviancy makes "him" a social outcast. St John's rhetoric of a soul, now known as female, stripped before a masculine God seems in part to follow such a pattern and so to reinforce God's superiority. But John also reverses this interpretation, proclaiming a radical sameness between the soul and God in which differences seem to disappear. Following Aristotle, he insists that it is similarity not difference which characterizes the desire between the soul and God. "The lover becomes like the one he loves; for the greater their likeness the greater their delight."[7] In the higher stages of spiritual progress, the soul thus increasingly takes on the appearance of divinity, approaching a divine consummation which is also a kind of identification of God and human. "When God grants this supernatural favor to the soul, so great a union is caused that all things of both God and the soul become one in participant transformation, and the soul appears to be God more than a soul" (A 2.5.7; John of the Cross 1991: 165). Nor does our maturation and growing similarity to God signal a shift in God's or our inflamed desire towards a more heroic, fraternal love in the mold of Halperin's remaining category, but instead further intensifies it, making possible in turn an even closer similarity and intimacy.[8]

While Halperin's categories are helpful for marking the complexity and fluid character of St John's desire, John seems in the end to transcend them. Likewise, though his desire for God echoes with homoerotic overtones, and though the flexibility he brings to sexual categories resonates intriguingly with contemporary queer interests, he seems to draw us beyond these as well. For those socialized to experience queer desire as unpredictable, uncontrollable, and estranged from Christian categories, it is difficult to conceive of homosexual desire as having some broader theological purpose. For John of the Cross, however, desire for God, the transformed sense of identity which accompanies it, and the (homo)erotic passions which contribute to it are all inconceivable without the basic awareness that they come from God and are directed towards a more perfect intimacy with God. His mingling of the sexual and spiritual thus invites us to broaden our own experiences of desire and to become aware of an urgent longing for God which seems both to emerge from these desires and in turn to give them shape and direction. May it be true for us as for John that, "in the measure that the fire increases, the soul becomes aware of being attracted by the love of God and enkindled in it, without knowing how or where this attraction and love originates" (DN 1.11.1; John of the Cross 1991: 383).

As my exploration into the shape of John's desire for God suggests, I find this invitation particularly appropriate for gay men and interpret John's own desire for God as shaped by a picture of God as male. I should note that John's language for God is *not* exclusively masculine. At several points he describes God as a loving mother nursing the soul with good milk, though always with reference to souls in early stages of spiritual progress. As the soul advances and its capacity for a fuller and more erotic intimacy increases, John comes to describe God in more masculine terms. The "sensory breasts" through which the appetites of the immature soul were nourished dry up (DN 1.13.13; John of the Cross 1991: 392). Now rather than milk, "His majesty frequently gives [the soul] joy by paying it visits of spiritual delight" (DN 2.19.4; John of the Cross 1991: 443). Although God's virility seems vital for St John's own religious experiences, we find here a recognition that God's gender too is fluid, or rather that our perception of it stems from individual needs to which God is responsive. Insofar as spiritual progress according to John requires a heightened passivity and openness to penetration, those social codes which label these traits as deviant for men do seem to encourage an experienced affinity between male homosexuality and mystical communion.[9] There is no necessary link implied, however, between desire for God and homosexual desire or desire for men; the emphasis is rather on a willingness to have all of one's desires taken up into desire for God and to be transformed by this blessed intimacy.

The Risk of Desire

When the breeze blew from the turret,
Parting his hair,
He wounded my neck
With his gentle hand, [10]
Suspending all my senses.
(*The Dark Night*, stanza 7)

Given that institutional Christianity represents for many queer individuals the most visible source of oppression, asserting the potential godliness of gay sex from within a Christian framework fulfills a crucial theological and pastoral role. On the other hand, from the far left wing of Christianity and within a more spiritually ambiguous queer popular culture, the association of sex and transcendence has (in the interest of pro-gay apologetics) been made so strongly and so frequently as to become clichéd. We have been told too often that sex is sacred for the force of the claim any longer to influence either our sexual or religious lives. In addition to obscuring the more damaging aspects of sex, this repetition thus risks undermining the effectiveness of the association and, worse even, trivializing the sacred completely. We consider in this section St John's focus on distinguishing divine desire (desire for God) from sexual desire, a necessary condition both for responding to those aspects of sex which are stumbling blocks rather than signposts on the spiritual path and for strengthening and honing the soul's desire for God. As should become clear, John's intent here is not to denigrate or dismiss sexual desire, but, on the contrary, in bringing it to a more discerning alignment with divine desire, to allow the close association between the two to function more effectively.

According to St John, the close resemblance between sexual desire and desire for God encourages us to attribute unwarranted significance to the sensual aspects or accompaniments of religious experiences, a failing evidenced, I believe, in much queer writing. A frequent argument within queer theology (and within other sex-affirming theologies) is that sex provides a unique intimacy, an openness to another which is also an openness to God. Robert Goss, for example, a former Jesuit, self-described erotic contemplative and queer freedom fighter, and the author of several books on queer theology, makes this claim with sometimes shocking vividness, connecting experiences of God (or Jesus) with moments of sexual pleasure.

There was a sense of oneness with each other and a deep sense of Christ's presence in a dynamic energy flow embracing our bodies. There was a letting-go and a surrender to rapture that transported us into a meditative realm of consciousness where boundaries dissolved and where the body of Christ was experienced in intimate touch, taste, smell, play, and so on. (Goss 2002: 22)

From these experiences follows a queer theology accenting the overlap between sexuality and spirituality alongside a harsh critique of institutional religion which has denied these gifts thus alienating us from our bodies and from God. Goss borrows considerably from the mystical tradition in order to evoke the spiritual qualities of these pleasures. "Orgasmic bliss has many of the subtle qualities of intense, sublime, nonconceptual contemplation of Christ," he claims, and also "when one's body and mind are joined meditatively together in love-making, the sexual/spiritual potential moves beyond the ordinary orgasmic threshold of both partners into a new dimension of reality" (Goss 2002: 15, 22). For many gay men in particular, Goss asserts, sex is intrinsic to experience of God, an essential component of any spiritual path (Goss 2002: 78).

My purpose is not to question the genuineness of these experiences, but rather, following St John, to address them as real and therefore perilous. Although John (speaking primarily to the presumably celibate) focuses more on the body's frequent erotic response during times of prayer, communion, meditation, and so on, than on sex itself, the conjoining of experiences of God with sexual pleasure is for him no great stretch. The risk of such association relates instead to St John's surprising ambivalence concerning religious experiences in general and to the various distractions and failings towards which all of those pursuing a spiritual practice are susceptible. Put briefly, one will become overly attached to these experiences, gradually allowing the pursuit of them to replace the desire for God, a desire which is not "an understanding by the soul, not the taste, feeling, or imagining of God or of any other object, but purity and love, the stripping off and proper renunciation of all such experiences for God alone" (A 2.5.8; John of the Cross 1991: 165).

The circumstances of queer religious experience – alienation from institutional authority, the political and theological apologetic value of such experience, its obvious erotic appeal – suggests that the temptation John describes will be particularly strong. This lure of "spiritual savor" according to John encourages a pursuit of pleasure that ignores purity of intention, virtuous moderation, and the discipline of obedience. "Their only yearning and satisfaction is to do what they feel inclined to do . . . They are under the impression that they do not serve God when they are not allowed to do what they want" (DN 1.6.2-3; John of the Cross 1991: 371–2). The tendency in queer theological writing towards self-indulgence would seem to validate John's concerns.

I should say here that I do not find Robert Goss unusually susceptible to this temptation among queer writers. On the contrary, his training and commitment to Christian liturgy seem in his writings to resist allowing God to be subsumed within sexual pleasure. My concern is for the general direction of queer theology, committed to sexual liberation and based in sexual/religious experience, and for the religious (and sexual) lives of those Christians (queer or otherwise) for whom such experience constitutes an important access point to God.[11] The eventual consequence of this confusion of desires is fixation on some particular pleasure, image of the divine, or means of religious sensation, and thus loss of God.[12] One begins to equate God and one's preferred source of pleasure – an offense to God which then leads to pride in the possession of God – to a gluttonous pursuit of more and more intense experiences, and to the habit of measuring God according to human purposes. Excessive attention to sensual pleasure, particularly when linked to religious experience thus, for John, leads towards a perverse reversal in which spirituality becomes a means for sexual advancement rather than vice versa.[13] Taken to its extreme, this tendency makes of queer theology a technology for better sex, an erotic spiritual dimension to supplement the strictly secular pursuit of pleasure. This secularized erotic appetite is never satisfied and leads the soul further and further from God as "those who do not hesitate to order divine and supernatural things to temporal things as to gods" make their souls incapable of spiritual progress (A 3.19.9; John of the Cross 1991: 300).

The error here is not the queer claim that certain experiences of God have homoerotic content (or that certain homoerotic experiences have sacred content) but the privileging of the erotic as the sole, primary, or simply most appealing means for such experience and the concomitant tendency to equate unity with God with the satisfaction of one's own desire.[14] It is in short not true, according to St John, that gay men *require* sex to experience transcendence (though such experiences may indeed occur); furthermore the belief that sex *is* necessary represents a barrier to further intimacy with God. As a spiritual director, St John makes suggestions as to what is required to accomplish the separation between desire for God and desire for these more immediate and sensual experiences. Taken out of context, this can seem a fairly dismal view of sex: warnings against lust, a forceful dichotomy between sensual and spiritual desire, and the suggestion at times that all sexual desire must be eliminated in preparing the soul for God. My hope, however, is for a queer theology which will, instead of dismissing St John, attend to what John seeks here to accomplish.

Let's return again to the question of religious experience. St John's criticism is not of religious experience itself but of a particular emphasis on showy, discrete, unpredictable, and distracting experiences. The experience of union with God he describes by contrast is inseparable from an extended and demanding religious practice, a gradual intensification of desire and awareness of God.[15] Similarly, John calls for a uniting of sensual and spiritual desires which requires self-discipline, a gradual transformation of one's understanding of sexual experience, and the purifying intervention of God. Erotic desire (and practice) can and should serve God, but this requires significant internal renovation, a stripping away perhaps even of those elements which at first seemed most conducive to relationship with the transcendent.

As a spiritual director, John of the Cross would often insist that one of his charges give up, at least for a while, a favorite cross, some specific prayer practice, or a distracting pleasure. In part this self-denial helps strengthen and prepare the soul for greater trials ahead, but more basically it works to distinguish desire for God from those habits (and particularly sensual pleasures) with which it has become too closely associated. Just as for John, "a more intense enkindling of another, better love . . . is necessary for the vanquishing of the appetites and the denial of [sensory] pleasure" (A 1.14.2; John of the Cross 1991: 151), so the discipline of self-denial makes us more attentive to that love of God for which we, our bodies and our desires are created. Such self-denial should be a transitional process not an enduring state. The goal of disciplining sensual desire and of distinguishing it is eventually to bring it more fully into alignment with desire for God such that we, upon "feeling the delight of certain tastes and delicate touches, immediately at the first movement direct [our] thought and the affection of [our] will to God . . . that he be more known and loved through them" (A 3.24.5; John of the Cross 1991: 310–1). Likewise, St John encourages us to apply discernment to our attractions, distinguishing lusts which create remorse from that affection where "love of God grows when it grows" or "the love of God is remembered as often as the affection is remembered" (DN 1.4.7; John of the Cross 1991: 369). Yet even here we sense the risk of mistaking our own pleasure for God's. In the end, it must be God who prepares us for the fullness of divine love, guiding us through a dark night in which, according to John, all our former gratifications disappear and all of our understanding is undone.[16]

St John of the Cross seems here to resist principles of sexual ethics or any permanent rules for sexual behavior (including celibacy). Despite his frequent use of bridegroom imagery for Jesus, it is difficult to forge from his emphasis on ongoing transformation, openness, and continual discernment a firm argument for marriage, gay or otherwise.[17] Those practices which seem the most good may themselves be occasions for forgetting God. What the close interaction of sexual desire and desire for God demands of us is a constant vigilance that sex does not become a substitute for God or an alternative source of authority. We seek here to develop a sexual practice which is also an experience of God, not in the immediate sense described by Robert Goss at the beginning of this section (though again St John assumes such experiences may occur), but as part of a gradual spiritual ascent in which sexual desire contributes to desire for God, both at its peak when it lends its intensity to our love for God and when God completely withdraws it from us so as to turn us to God alone.

The Source of Desire

> I abandoned and forgot myself,
> Laying my face on my Beloved;
> All things ceased; I went out from myself,
> Leaving my cares
> Forgotten among the lilies.
> (*The Dark Night*, stanza 8)

Theology must address the multifaceted relationship of sexual desire to desire for God in order to speak to those who, having felt the full force of the challenge queerness presents to traditional Christian doctrine, still sense (or are at least open to the possibility) that sexual practice can lead us towards God. The fluidity, gender crossing, and affinity with male homosexuality which shapes John's desire for God contributes, I have suggested, to a contemporary harnessing of homoerotic desire towards theological and spiritual ends. Although there is a risk here of confusing sexual desire with desire for God, St John directs us towards practices of discipline and discernment which, in correctly aligning the two, prepare us for their fulfillment in intimacy with God.

What are the prospects for contemporary queer theology to take up these concerns of St John of the Cross? Though I suggested in the introduction that "queer theology" might include any theology directed towards queer people, I cannot ignore the theological significance of the scholarship loosely joined under the term "queer theory" whose influence within the academy and within queer popular culture appears to be increasing. Based on the complex interactions between feminist theory and theology and between Marxism and liberation theology, one may expect that as queer theology further develops it will both draw on and seek to challenge queer theory. As of yet, however, queer theological writings seem with a few exceptions unaware or uncritical of queer theory's antipathy towards the most basic Christian commitments. I described above the way in which St John's fluid experience of a desire transcending social categories resembles a queer theoretical picture of sex as too diverse and unstable to fit within neat categories of sexual orientation. This resemblance must not be taken to imply an acceptance of the secularizing conclusions which accompany these queer theoretical claims, though I do hope based on such overlap that a queer theology opposed to such conclusions is possible.

Perhaps the best way to present the contrast between St John's Christian theology and the assumptions of queer theory is to ask about the source of desire. This question of where desire (or more specifically homosexual desire) comes from is one generally avoided within queer theory, both in order to move away from essentialist conceptions of sexual orientation and because inquiries into the source of desire seem inevitably to be linked to some vision of eliminating whatever form of desire is deemed problematic. Still one finds in queer theoretical writings a fairly uniform account, explaining sexual desire and also desire for God in terms of social forces.

> We must struggle to discern in what we currently regard as our most precious, unique, original, and spontaneous impulses the traces of a previously rehearsed and socially encoded script. . . . We must train ourselves to recognize conventions of feeling as well as conventions of behavior and to interpret the intricate texture of personal life as an artifact, as the determinate outcome, of a complex and arbitrary constellation of cultural processes. (Halperin 1990: 40)

St John's theological task is not utterly opposed to such a deconstructive habit at least as a starting point. The stripping John describes stems in large part from his recognition that much of our desire is tied to these "natural" sources, and that even that which seems supernatural to us in fact can be explained this way. But central to John's entire project is the conviction that there is a desire for God which comes unmediated from God, which is not simply the magnification or refinement of other natural desires. Unless this is the case then it is impossible to transcend the sensual attachments which are stumbling blocks on the spiritual path and John's non-discursive contemplation is nonsense and self-delusion. John thus seeks in the end to direct us towards a very different awareness of desires than does Halperin, one in which beyond all the cultural artifacts and processes there is a source of desire (and thus a purpose for desire) which cannot be encompassed in these terms, which is timeless, and in which both sexual desire and divine desire attain their true form. In this "intimate nakedness" before God, "God does not communicate himself through the senses as he did before, by means of the discursive analysis and synthesis of ideas, but begins to communicate himself through pure spirit by an act of simple contemplation in which there is no discursive succession of thought" (DN 1.9.8; John of the Cross 1991: 380).

The opposition between Christian theology and queer theory on this point is not incidental or superficial. Robert Goss writes that most queer theorists "find Christianity irrelevant at best and too often violent and oppressive" (Goss 2002: 247). I would say more strongly that queer theory emerges as a discipline in part as a strategy for resisting Christian authority over sexual matters, for challenging distinctions between approved and forbidden sexual activity, and for replacing doctrine and tradition with new sexual experts qualified to explain (and incite) our sexualities in secular, liberating ways. At its best, however, queer theory, following Foucault, is well able to recognize in this its own will to power and so to recognize that whatever sexual liberation it describes represents the promotion of new controls and categories for distinguishing good (now healthy, amoral, and polymorphous) from bad (restricted, overburdened with religious significance) sex. Queer theory has the tools (and perhaps, if we trust John's theological optimism, even the desire) to rise above a self-promoting dismissal of Christian claims and even in some cases to be transformed by them. In directing all of his urgent longings towards God, John of the Cross does not pretend to describe a theology in which sex is autonomous and unburdened, but he does describe sexual desire and divine desire, both gifts of God, as means towards an intimacy with God in which all expert knowledge is relativized. Thus St John continues to act as a spiritual guide for contemporary queer Christians whose own divine desires lead towards a queer theology which comprehends queer theory but is directed towards God.

Notes

1 Except as otherwise noted, citations from St John of the Cross are taken from John of the Cross (1991).

2 While cognizant of the shortcomings of the term, and the risk of false inclusiveness, I will use "queer people" as a shorthand intended to include gay, lesbian, bisexual, transgendered people as well as other gender/sex nonconformists. "Queer" accents both instability and transgression, aspects of sexual desire I seek to apply to desire for God.

3 See Hinkle (2001) for a discussion of John's relevance for pro-gay Christian apologetics.

4 The God John desires is unmistakably gendered, though not, I will claim, in a rigid or exclusive sense. In discussing John I will therefore follow his preference of male language for God.

5 In fact Daniel Dombrowski argues that it was the eroticism of John's writing that scandalized persecutors and delayed publication of his works. See Dombrowski (1992: 97).

6 It is difficult, particularly within the present political context, to consider a pederastic sexual model as other than disgusting and damaging. Thus an association of such a model with God threatens to be either highly offensive or to contribute to a dismissal of Christianity. The model I borrow from Halperin should in principle carry no connotation of violence, psychological damage, deception, or coercion, and refers broadly to differences in status, authority, and accomplishment in addition to age.

7 In the context of *The Dark Night*, St John's treatment of sameness refers to the progressive divinization of the human soul to becoming a fitting partner for God. This quote taken from "Romances," a poem concerning the Trinity, actually refers to God's taking on flesh in the incarnation. See John of the Cross (1991: 66).

8 Though John's discussion of growing similarity to God suggests a transcending of gender as of all human categories, rhetorically it also functions as a challenge to longstanding defenses of heterosexual privilege based on gender complementarity.

9 Sensitive to the homoerotic character of John of the Cross's desire for God, Jeffrey Kripal has convincingly argued that Christian mysticism in general, based on intense love of a male God, is awkward for heterosexual men, a claim which, if true, no doubt applies to lesbians as well. See Kripal (2001: ch. 1).

10 Here I follow Daniel Dombrowski in preferring an alternative translation to Kavanaugh's "It [the breeze] wounded my neck with its gentle hand" (Dombrowski 1992: 10).

11 In Hinkle (2001) I argue that any pro-gay theology and perhaps any Christian theology compelling in a religious pluralistic culture must rely significantly on religious experience.

12 "Those who not only pay heed to these imaginative apprehensions but think God resembles some of them, and that one can journey to union with God through them, are already in great error and will gradually lose the light of faith" (A 3.12.3; John of the Cross 1991: 284–5).

13 John discusses this excessive attention to the sensual as the "vice of effeminacy," a suggestive appeal to Halperin's categorization above (A 3.25.6; John of the Cross 1991: 312). The error here is not the passivity of desire or its possible homosexual content but the immoderate valuation of sensual pleasure within the religious life.

14 Consider, for example, this statement from John McNeill (1995), quoted by Goss: "To discern spirits is to listen to our own hearts. Our God dwells within us, and the only way to become one with God is to become one with our authentic self. If any action we undertake brings with it a deepening of peace, joy, and fulfillment, then we can be sure what we are doing is right for us" (Goss 2002: 82).

15 Denys Turner describes John as sharing the modern interest in religious experience but as rejecting absolutely modern "experientialism" (see Turner 1995a: 226).

16 St John's emphasis, I argue, is finally on the transformation rather than denial of pleasure. There is a practical danger in the present ecclesial context of this being interpreted as a transformation from homosexuality to heterosexuality, a point I have addressed more fully in Hinkle (2001). Let me reiterate that St John, as I demonstrated above, resists rather than reinforces heteronormativity.

17 He writes, for example, that "it would be vanity for a husband and wife to rejoice in their marriage when they are uncertain whether God is being better served by it" (A 3.18.6; John of the Cross 1991: 297).

Chapter 13

A Queer Theology

Hans Urs von Balthasar

Rachel Muers

What can the work of Hans Urs von Balthasar contribute to a "queer theology," a critical and constructive rereading of established categories of sex and gender from a Christian theological perspective? The importance of sexual difference, and of gendered roles and subjects, in Balthasar's theological scheme is undeniable. Discussions of Balthasar's treatment of sexual difference have focused variously on his Mariology (Leahy 1996; Beattie 1998), his views on the position of women in the church (Strukelj 1993), his understanding of prayer (Gawronski 1995), and through all these on his trinitarian theology (Moss and Gardner 1998). His valorization of sexual difference, and in particular the significance he accords to femininity, has been used to justify a conservative response to the challenges of feminist theology and of the movement for women's ordination (Leahy 1996; Strukelj 1993; Schindler 1993). On the other hand, the very fact that sexual difference is of such importance in his "theo-drama" has led those with an interest in queer theology to seek to appropriate his work for a rethinking of sex and gender in Christian theology (Bullimore 1999; Loughlin 1999b).

After a brief overview of the opportunities and questions raised by Balthasar's theology of sexual difference in general, and in particular by the use of sexual difference as both theological analogate and ground of theological analogy, this chapter will focus on the relation of sexual difference to Balthasar's concept of personal mission. "Femininity" is for Balthasar a characteristic of the creature before God that enables the acceptance and fulfillment of a personal mission. The undifferentiated "feminine principle" to which the development of this idea gives rise can be traced in its consequences for Mariology and (indirectly) for Balthasar's attitude to politics. Significantly for queer theology, Balthasar's use of "femininity" makes erotic relations between women simply inconceivable. The familiar pattern – gay men are seen and feared, lesbian women are invisible/impossible – is apparent in Balthasar's few explicit discussions of homosexuality, but more importantly is reinforced by the function of sexual difference within his theological scheme. Despite all this, we can see in Balthasar's theology of personal mission, particularly within the perspective of his eschatology, scope for the development of a theological anthropology that would be more conducive to the aims of a "queer theology."

Balthasar and Sexual Difference: Introductory Notes

Why is sexual difference important for Balthasar? *Diastasis* – difference in relation – is of central importance for the structure of his theology. Theologically, the *diastasis* between God and creation, within which the freedom of the creature becomes possible, is grounded in the *diastasis* of the persons of the Trinity. Anthropologically, the human person exists as inescapably ordered towards union with what is other than her, a union that brings about not self-contained completeness but continuing "fruitfulness." In the *Theo-Drama*, the central work of his threefold theological project, Balthasar introduces sexual difference initially as one of the central polarities that determine human existence, and which are observable (in his view) "prior" to the determination of anthropology by Christology (Balthasar 1988–98: II, 365–82). To be human is, for Balthasar, to be sexually differentiated. Sexual difference indicates both our incompleteness and our possibility of self-transcendence.

Following on from this, sexual difference becomes for Balthasar one of the key terms whereby an analogical understanding of the relationship between God and creation can be developed. The biblical imagery of Israel as bride of YHWH and church as bride of Christ is brought forward and developed in the light, both of a phenomenological analysis of sexual difference and *eros* and of the whole history of creation and redemption. A complex passage in the final volume of *The Glory of the Lord* uses the exegesis of Ephesians 5 to develop a vision of creaturely *eros* "sacramentalized" and drawn beyond the "closed circle" of human sexuality by its completion in the *agape*-love of Christ for the church, which in turn has its source in the "selfless self-love" of the persons of the Trinity (Balthasar 1982–91: VII, 480–4). Thus, in a further development of the theme of *diastasis*, sexual difference finds its ultimate ground and analogue in the life of the Trinity itself (see further Moss and Gardner 1998). Balthasar's discussions of the life of the immanent Trinity refer to "supra-masculinity" and "supra-femininity," in all three persons with reference to different "moments" in the self-differentiation of God (Balthasar 1968: 313).

Those seeking to develop a "queer theology" may well see in Balthasar's accounts of the importance of sexual difference a way beyond biological essentialism or the false androgyny of liberalism. If sexual difference is to be given such immense theological significance, existing ideas of what it means to be a sexed being, male or female, must surely become vulnerable to critique from their "higher analogues." Balthasar states at the end of the exegesis just cited, "The trinitarian love is the only ultimate form of all love – both the love between God and men, and that between human persons" (1982–91: VII, 484). The claim is that this theology of love breaks the "closed circle" (the supposed biological "givenness"? the apparent completeness of the male-female pair?) of human sexuality while not separating *eros* altogether from *agape* – which would seem to make it the ideal starting point for a queer theology. Everything will depend, however, on the development of the various analogies implied in Balthasar's use of sexual difference – and, as we shall see, it is here that the problems for "queer theology" begin to arise.

The tensions surrounding Balthasar's use of analogy with regard to sexual difference have been noted by several commentators in recent years. Two basic and interconnected problems present themselves (see Loughlin 1999b; Moss and Gardner 1998). The first is the extent to which the use of sexual difference to "describe" both the existence of human persons in relation to each other, and the relation of these persons to God, makes sexual difference both an analogue and the *tertium quid* whereby analogy becomes possible. Sexual difference – or, to be more precise, the "feminine principle" – is, as a recent article explains, in some respects the basis for the very possibility of the *analogia entis*. The consent of Mary to the bearing of the incarnate Word, which is the fulfillment of her feminine "mission," is the precondition for the entry of the personified *analogia entis*, Christ, into the world.

The second is Balthasar's tendency, implicitly or explicitly, to treat the analogies based on sexual difference as reversible, so that the "ordering" of the sexes on earth that provided an analogy for innertrinitarian relations or the ordering of Christ and the church is in turn valorized or reinforced on the basis of its heavenly analogates. Clearly this acts against any critical interrogation of our assumptions concerning sexual difference. Predetermined understandings of "masculinity" and "femininity" are mapped onto the immanent Trinity, and back onto earth, without being affected by the *maior dissimilitudo* supposedly present in every instance of analogy between the divine and the human. The designation of inner-trinitarian "masculinity" and "femininity" as *supra*-masculine or feminine does not always prevent this reversal of analogies.

Both of these problems, and their consequences for the theological understanding of sexual difference, can be illustrated from one of the few passages in which Balthasar mentions same-sex love.

Queer Prayer?

In *New Elucidations*, Balthasar sets quasi-magical prayer "techniques," such as he believes to dominate most non-Christian practices of prayer, over against the Marian model of creaturely femininity in the worship of God. He describes prayer techniques as "a kind of religious homosexuality, in which the creature would relate himself to God in a masculine fashion . . . whose perverse encroachment on God himself . . . is depicted in the story of Sodom and its destruction. With God there can be no union of the same sex but only a feminine dependence on God . . . no taking but only a being taken" (Balthasar 1986a: 188).

Leaving aside the dubious characterization of non-Christian religions here and elsewhere in Balthasar's work (for a somewhat over-appreciative discussion of which see Gawronski 1995), we should reflect on the implications of this passage. Why is there a reference to Sodom here, rather than (as would seem more obvious in the context of what is actually being discussed) to the actions of the priests of Baal, the request of Simon Magus or the Pharisees' "demand for a sign"? The actions of the men of Sodom clearly are a "perverse encroachment on God" in the form of God's messengers to whom Lot has shown hospitality. But why should these men and their fate be the key image for a quasi-magical prayer technique?

It would seem that at this point Balthasar is attempting to make the analogy of sexual difference face in two directions at once. On the one hand, *assuming* that gay sex can unproblematically be characterized as "perverse encroachment," he uses the image of the men of Sodom to attack "unfeminine" prayer. On the other hand, he seeks to *reinforce* the rejection of gay sex by assimilating it to what he has already demonstrated to be an unacceptable approach to prayer. "With God there can be no union of the same sex" is a Janus-faced phrase; if it is to be applied only in terms of the analogy with prayer, it cannot straightforwardly be transferred to the sphere of sexual ethics. Especially if it has already been stated that both women and men can and should be "feminine," in the sense implied by the "Marian principle," it is clearly illegitimate to transfer a claim about the Creator-creature relationship, unargued, to a claim about human sexual behavior.[1]

Part of the problem lies in the unquestioned assumption that God must invariably be "masculine" vis-à-vis humanity. While Balthasar is quite happy, in the discussion of inner-trinitarian relations, to allow "supra-femininity" as well as "supra-masculinity" in the Persons of the Trinity – even in God the Father, who "receives" fatherhood from the Son – the act by which God enters into relation with creatures can only be understood in terms of God's "masculinity." Balthasar is careful, in his discussions of analogy, to stress the *maior dissimilitudo* that conditions every analogical predication, of God, of the characteristics of creatures. In considering sexual difference, however, this *maior dissimilitudo* can easily be lost. If we want to pursue the sexual analogy with regard to prayer, "perverse encroachment" (and the attempt to control God or take from God) sounds most like *rape*; at which point the demand that God's masculinity be preserved at all costs begins to sound distinctly sinister. Why is the action of the men of Sodom so much better an example of "perverse encroachment" than that of the men of Gibeah (Judges 19)? Is the point at issue, in fact, not the ontological difference but (heterosexual) male sexual power? At the very least, the two have become so entangled through the rapidly shifting analogies that it will be difficult to detach them without some explicit statement of the immense *difference* between divine "supra-masculinity" and human masculinity.

It should also be noted that Balthasar's condemnation of "union of the same sex" is a condemnation of *male* homosexuality; the masculinity of God makes this inevitable. It is no coincidence, as we shall see, that the possibility of a female "union of the same sex" does not enter consideration.

The next section will examine Balthasar's concept of personal mission, as an aspect of his anthropology that, on the one hand, appears to hold out possibilities for a "queer theology" and, on the other hand, through the use of gendered categories makes such a theology more problematic.

Mission and Personhood

In this section, I shall focus on Balthasar's use of gender terms and of sexual difference with reference to one of the key concepts in his anthropology – personal *mission*. The idea that each person is given a unique "mission" by virtue of her incorporation into Christ lies behind many of Balthasar's most distinctive concerns – the importance of contemplative prayer, his interest in the saints as living "apologies" for Christianity, his rethinking of the tradition of the beatific vision and the communion of saints. It is one of the central anthropological presuppositions of the project of "theo-drama," and links that project to many of his more narrowly focused works (on what follows see V.S. Harrison 1999a and 1999b).

For Balthasar the "mission" is in each case the specific way in which the person can become conformed to Christ. The discovery and acceptance of one's mission, of which we shall say more below, is an ongoing lived process of conversion in obedience. In temporal existence it involves the continuing "death" of the self-centered and sinful personality concomitant with growth into new life. Mission is not extrinsic to personal existence, as its goal or end-point; rather, it is the center out of which Christian life is lived. It is, however, an "ex-centric" center, given in Christ and hence not commensurable with any purely immanent project of "self-realization." A life lived in accordance with mission is a *holy* life, and holiness is best defined as the fulfillment of mission (see Balthasar 1988–98: III, 263–82).

At several points Balthasar explains the ontology of personal mission in terms of the *creation* of all things in Christ (Balthasar 1988–98: II, 200–3; Balthasar 1961: 21). Patristic and medieval thought, as Balthasar traces it, modified the Platonic doctrine of the divine Ideas, through reflection on the mediation of Christ, to develop an understanding of the parallel and God-given "ascent" of the creature towards fulfillment of its eternal Idea and the "descent" of the Idea that perfects and completes the creature. Earthly life in Christ is a continual receiving of one's mission and a continual being-drawn towards it. The parallel movements culminate, for Balthasar, in the participation of temporal creatures in the eternal divine life, which is both promise and reality in the resurrected body of Christ. The reality of (something analogous to) "novelty" and "surprise" in God's eternity through the mutual love and self-gift of the trinitarian persons is the reality in which the eternal life of creatures participates (Balthasar 1988–98: V, 385–94; O'Hanlon 1990).

Why should a "queer theology" be interested in Balthasar's theology of personal mission? Mission defines and redefines what we are – as whole persons, body and soul – in Christ, and establishes in each case the possibility of a holy life. At the same time, it forces, or should force, a critical reassessment of whatever we take our "natural" or "given" forms of spiritual and bodily self-fulfillment to be. Personal mission, as Balthasar describes it, is in two important senses undecidable: since it is in each case unique, its contours cannot be determined in the abstract; and because of its relation to God's infinitely fruitful eternity it can never be regarded as "complete." We might see in the concept of mission a way of understanding same-sex relationships and the disruption of traditional gender roles as possible manifestations of Christian holiness. The fact that this is clearly not possible in Balthasar's own work, and the indications that it perhaps *should* be possible, provide the basis for what follows. The problem lies, I shall suggest, with Balthasar's use of "femininity" as the basis of the possibility of personal mission, as demonstrated most clearly in his Mariology.

Femininity and Mission

Any discussion of sexual difference in Balthasar's work must quickly move to a discussion of his concept of femininity. This is partly because, following the logic of Genesis 2, he regards the creation of woman and the emergence of sexual difference as the same moment. Linked with this is the fact that femininity, within Balthasar's work, emerges as a clearly defined set of characteristics and ways of relating. In a familiar pattern, the existence and nature of woman (or "the feminine principle") requires explanation, while the existence and nature of man does not. The very fact that it is possible to set out the characteristics of femininity in Balthasar – characteristics that apply equally in his discussions of creaturely relations, of the relation of creature to Creator, and with appropriate reservations to inner-trinitarian relations – raises questions about the relation of sexual difference to analogy in his theology.

What is the feminine for Balthasar? His most comprehensive discussion is found in his prolegomena to Mariology (Balthasar 1988–98: III, 283–300). Here, woman is described as a double principle, a dyad, in contrast to the masculine monad. Woman's duality lies in the dual answer she gives to man – as bride and counterpart, and as bearer of the child that both results from and transcends their union. The principle of femininity is first and foremost the principle of receptivity and response. It is the principle of the Other in relationship – difference that does not oppose or exclude, that is ordered towards encounter, and that renders that encounter fruitful.

The question then arises: What is the relation of this principle of femininity to particular women and men? It is clear from Balthasar's early work that the "feminine" principle within the church is not restricted to women or to the laity. The attitude of active and fruitful reception is fundamental both to the community as a whole and to each individual. "Indifference," of which Mary as the perfection of femininity vis-à-vis God becomes the ultimate exemplar (Balthasar 1961: 24; for an extended discussion of "indifference" in Balthasar see Gawronski 1995: 113), is in fact the condition of Christian *personhood* as such. The mission that each person is granted by God in Christ, and that defines her role in the theo-drama, is received by each insofar as she becomes receptive to it. To be perfectly conformed to one's mission, and thus perfectly conformed to Christ, requires a perfection of indifference.

The unquestioned masculinity of God in God's relation to the created order, placed alongside the characterization of "femininity" described above, has the effect of rendering same-sex relations among *women* invisible in this passage and elsewhere. The pattern is familiar; male same-sex relations are a very visible threat, female same-sex relations are by definition unthinkable. If femininity is essentially receptive, responsive, an "answer," there is no way of thinking the relation of "feminine" beings one to another, save by the relativization of their femininity. Thus, relationships within the church are structured by the introduction of the office that represents the "masculine" principle; the femininity of the church, meanwhile, is unified in a single person, Mary, who makes her single response to the word of God.[2]

Mary: Perfection of a Mission?

For Balthasar, only Mary, by virtue of her freedom from original sin, has achieved the perfection of indifference, and thus only she can be said to conform perfectly with her mission (Balthasar 1992: 21). The femininity of the church, as its openness to God and its perfect response to the prevenient action of God, is most often described in terms of the "Marian principle." Mary is associated particularly closely with the contemplative tradition (Balthasar 1961: 72), with the (lived, bodily) *experience* of the indwelling of Christ that makes persons holy (Balthasar 1982–91: I, 421–5), and with the obedience of faith.

In all of this, Mary is not merely the exemplar of creaturely "femininity" vis-à-vis God; she is also both its condition and its archetype. She is its condition, because apart from her consent to bear Christ there is no christological "space" – the space opened up in the incarnation – wherein human persons can respond to God and be drawn into the divine life. She is its archetype, in that as "Mary-Church" she perfectly represents and draws together the several and partial responses of individuals within the church. She is, furthermore, the culmination of the apparent paradoxes of mission. What is most inwardly one's own – Mary's immaculate conception orders her whole life towards this mission – is most clearly the gift of another, the immaculate conception occurs through the merits of Christ; the church is born at the Cross.[3] The point of greatest freedom – Mary's free consent – is the point of greatest obedience: "Behold the handmaid of the Lord." The mission is accepted in solitude, but it has both universal and specific social implications. To live one's mission is both to *be what one is* – "nuptiality" – and to *become something new* – "fruitfulness." In one of his longest discussions of Mariology, Balthasar discusses these and other paradoxes of Mary's dramatic "role" in the history of salvation.

It is here that we begin to see the difficulties arising from the links between femininity and mission, discussed above. Mary, as the perfect and archetypal believer, is the perfect fulfiller of her mission. She is able to be this *because* she is the perfection and archetype of the femininity of creation in relation to God. Her immaculate conception leaves her free to respond to God without the "death" of the old self. She possesses preeminently the qualities of the holy person in whom Christ takes form. However, when we ask *what* mission Mary receives through her indifference and obedience, the answer seems to be – simply to be feminine. This impression is reinforced (as David Moss and Lucy Gardner note) by the arrangement of the relevant section of the *Theo-Drama*, wherein "woman" and "the feminine principle" as such is discussed before Mary herself appears. Mary as a *character* in the theo-drama disappears under the mass of principles she is supposed to represent. Her mission is not *a* mission but the prerequisite for, or summary of, all missions.

But where does this leave Christology? We are told repeatedly, after all, that Christ's is the one mission; the unique missions of Christians are incorporated into the single movement of Christ that restores a redeemed and perfected creation to the Father (on the relationship between Christ's mission and the other missions see Balthasar 1988–98: III, 202–29). In relation to the Father, Christ can sometimes be described as "supra-feminine" in his obedience and receptivity – the attributes that make his "mission" possible. At the same time, the *maleness* of Christ in the Incarnation is for Balthasar "necessary" because the act of God vis-à-vis creation is masculine.[4] Mary becomes the point at which the "supra-femininity" in the innertrinitarian relations, which is the basis of Christ's mission and thus of all human missions, appears in the created order.

Women Together

It may seem curious to claim that Balthasar's scheme has no room for differentiation between, and therefore for relationships among, feminine persons. After all, his understanding of mission and holiness is decisively shaped by particular women – by his study of the Carmelites Thérèse of Lisieux and Elizabeth of Dijon, and by his collaboration with Adrienne von Speyr. The Carmelites are explicitly said to have different, if complementary, missions to the Church; Elizabeth learns from and develops Thérèse's work, both Thérèse and Elizabeth learn from their Carmelite sisters. Why choose women as examples of the plurality of divine missions if femininity as such is undifferentiated, "indifferent"?

The answer becomes clear if we refer back to the discussion of personal mission, above. The indifference of the contemplative is – in every case but that of Mary – not the mission itself but the basis of it. In Balthasar's descriptions of Thérèse and Elizabeth, both are termed "womanly" for the *same reason* – their unquestioning obedience to the God who forms them in their distinctive roles and offices (Balthasar 1992: 67, 488). This basic obedience leads to two very different missions "in the Spirit." The missions are inseparable from the historical, social, and bodily specificity of the women who receive them. A man could not have "been" Thérèse of Lisieux. But nor could a married woman; Thérèse's mission is defined not by "femininity" but by Thérèse as she lives out her transformed life in Christ. Moreover, the missions of both Thérèse and Elizabeth seem to involve taking on functions that have elsewhere been described as "masculine." They are teachers of the church whose missions are specifically *theological*. They inform, inspire, shape, "impregnate" their communities and the wider church. In this they do not point to a disembodied androgyny; but they certainly indicate the *maior dissimilitudo* between the ontological difference and creaturely sexual difference, with the infinite priority of the one over the other. Balthasar's decision not to consider at such length the "mission" of any *man* after the apostles (despite his great interest in the individual theological *styles* of particular thinkers) perhaps indicates a difficulty in recognizing the implications of his own location of "femininity" within the ontological difference.[5]

Even this consideration of the missions of Thérèse and Elizabeth, however, leaves the question of the invisibility of erotic relations between women, and the fear of erotic relations between men, unanswered. If we accept the analogy of femininity and creaturely receptivity, even with the complications introduced above, are we not still relying on an assumed "naturalness" of heterosexual relations initiated by the male?

Balthasar has been criticized for his lack of attention to politics, and to the social character of all human, and specifically Christian, life (see Dalzell 1999). His primary focus is, as may already have become clear, most often on the individual person in her relation to God, which secondarily and derivatively becomes an existence with and for others. Clearly, existence "in Christ" must be social existence, mission is given "for the church" and is only comprehensible from within the church, and the call of each person is socially mediated. Nonetheless, it does seem that the focus on the virtue of *indifference*, and on the primacy of finding oneself "alone with the Alone" encourages us, as Dalzell puts it, to regard the theodrama as taking place within the individual soul. The discontinuity between the old and the new covenant, for Balthasar, lies to a considerable extent in the rejection of *collective* relationship between God and a people. The calling of Israel is replaced by individual calling – Mary, the apostles, Mary Magdalene.

Balthasar's interest in the "femininity" of the creature has obvious links to this relative neglect of the social. It is clear that the focus on *bridal* imagery, especially after the Hebrew image of Israel as the bride of YHWH is transferred to Mary as archetype, reinforces the prioritization of the interpersonal over the social. Even "maternal" imagery, oddly enough, is not permitted to broaden the interpersonal perspective towards social relations. As we saw, woman is defined in her relation to man as a "dyad" – bride and mother; so we see her *either* as "mother of a (male) child" *or* as "wife of a man"; the threefoldness of man-woman-child is rarely allowed to appear.[6]

Dalzell notes this with regard to Balthasar's trinitarian theology, suggesting that the personhood of the Spirit (for whose generation the analogy of the birth of a child to a man and a woman is occasionally used) is insufficiently developed, and that this leads in turn to an insufficiently social understanding of human personhood. Queer theology may give more consideration to the second "face" of the Janus-analogy discussed above. If the emphasis on creaturely femininity, understood in terms of the "dyad," makes it hard to understand the social aspects of human existence, this is seen symbolically in the invisibility of women's same-sex relationships. "Women" (all creatures in Christ) can only relate to one another through their relations to a "man" (Christ).

Woman at the Cross

One of the most powerful passages of the *Theo-Drama* is Balthasar's description of Mary's participation in the kenotic "silencing" of the incarnate Word of God. Her silent obedience that makes possible the conception and birth of the infant Christ is mirrored by her solidarity, standing at the foot of the Cross, with the silence of his death – a silence from which the speech of Pentecost is in turn born. Balthasar returns again and again to the Johannine account of the Passion, with Mary and the beloved disciple present to signify the birth of the church from the death of Christ. Mary, especially, is said to *participate* in the passion: "Jesus died suffocated under the weight of the world's sin, and his Mother shared in this event" (Balthasar 1988–98: III, 337).

Mary is, then, a term of continuity in the immense discontinuity of the Cross; the term that enables the response of creation to God to be recognized beyond the "suffocation under the weight of the world's sin." Balthasar, as is well known, grounds the *diastasis* of God and creation in the infinite "distance" between Father and Son that opens up in the abandonment of Son by Father on the Cross. The possibility of Mary's obedience, as the free obedience of the creation to its Creator, is, then, given in the crucifixion and descent into hell. But by her presence at the Cross the outcome of the abandonment of God by God is already proclaimed. Just as, in the "death of the self" involved in the acceptance of mission, the *potentia obedientialis* – itself, it must always be recalled, in each case a gift of God – survives to receive the transforming grace of God, so in the theo-drama the archetype of feminine obedience "survives" the cross and its discontinuity.[7]

What are the consequences of this for Balthasar's understanding of sexual difference? If Mary can be seen to "survive" the death of Christ intact, the ordering of male and female, masculine and feminine, also "survives." The analogies it grounds remain free from the critique implied by the infinite *diastasis* of Father and Son completed in the crucifixion. This is, it would seem, why Balthasar can make his gendered analogies face both ways, secured by Mary's uninterrupted mediation as the pivot between innerworldly and innertrinitarian relations.

Is the attribution of this degree of continuity to Mary justified? We have already noted Mary's *lack* of theological "personhood" as Balthasar understands the latter; she accepts and fulfills her mission perfectly, but her mission simply *is* perfect acceptance. She is assimilated to the feminine principle, and hence defined, not as a particular "answer" to the divine call, but as the essence of "answering." A similar abstractness prevails even in the powerful "recapitulation" of her participation in the sufferings of Christ. Because of the beloved disciple, she is still "mother," and because of her presence at the Cross for the first time truly "bride"; hence she is still feminine, hence, it would seem, nothing in her has changed.

The term of continuity can be more precisely specified; not Mary but Mary's *womb*. Throughout this passage of the *Theo-Drama* there is an interplay of the images of voice and silence, sterility and fruitfulness. Mary's "barrenness" after her son's death is linked with the apparent futility of the suffering of Christ on the Cross; but the message of the Johannine account is that "God . . . can take the 'nothingness' of unfruitful virginity . . . and make of it the fruitful motherhood of the Virgin, with a fruitfulness that extends to the whole world" (Balthasar 1988–98: IV, 361). What "survives" is the *potentia obedientialis*, the "space" for divine action, the womb that (it has always appeared) defines "femininity" and thus makes sexual difference possible. The maternal body must, Balthasar explicitly states, be included within the "antecedent *idea, offer* and *mission* of the Lamb" (Balthasar 1988–98: IV, 360); but at the same time it appears to transcend this mission, to stand alongside it rather than within it. At the same time, Balthasar's account recognizes that Mary's "motherhood," and all the relationships that shaped her particular existence as *a* woman (not as "woman") have been shattered by this death. She has been sent away and handed over to another (Balthasar 1988–98: IV, 360).

Conclusion: Women at the Cross and in the Resurrection

Balthasar's portrayal of femininity as "indifferent" – from which arises, it has been suggested, his inability to establish Mary as a theo-dramatic character – perhaps makes it easy for him to ignore the other presences at the crucifixion. Even in the Fourth Gospel, two *other* Marys appear beside Jesus' mother; in the synoptics, groups of women watch "from a distance." It is these women, both in the synoptics and in the Fourth Gospel, whose actions and encounters mark the beginning of the proclamation of the resurrection.

Mary Magdalene's encounter with the risen Christ is one of Balthasar's favorite examples (the other being Simon/Peter) of the reconfiguration of personal identity through the resurrection. Her calling by name leads to her proclamation of the resurrection – a circumstance to which Balthasar occasionally refers, without consideration of its implications for the "femininity" of this other Mary (Balthasar 1961: 22).

The women who discover the empty tomb, on the other hand, are scarcely mentioned. Their actions, as far as Balthasar's theological scheme goes, are highly ambiguous. Their contemplation is only a contemplation of meaninglessness. Their response in the face of death and silence is not passive waiting, or even "active receptivity," but the observation of the commandments of the old covenant and a commitment – socially undertaken and (potentially) politically oriented – to a work of mourning that would itself almost certainly fail ("Who will roll away the stone for us?"). What they "receive" is unexpected, and their reception of it is undetermined in outcome. They are not subsequently assigned apostolic roles and do not form part of the continuing structure of the church.

Balthasar discusses their presence in Luke's Gospel, where they are assimilated to "the 'daughter of Sion' who has become flesh in woman"; Luke, we read, shows us "Jesus as a man, who from the outset takes up his fellow human beings with their feminine, handmaid's *fiat* into his own work." It is far from clear, however, that the actions of these women from Good Friday to Easter Sunday can so easily be summarized as a "handmaid's *fiat*" (Balthasar: 1982–91: VII, 354).[8]

I suggest that the ability to see these women, their relation to each other and to the dead and risen Christ is *in nuce* what would be required for Balthasar's "theo-drama" to overcome the reification of sexual difference.[9] Seeing these women would entail considering their performance of historically and culturally "female" actions – the anointing of the dead, specific female tasks in the keeping of Sabbath – and the way in which the ordinary significance of these actions is transcended. Seeing them as wom*en* would reinforce this by attending to the plurality of ways in which female embodiment is lived out. Their story is structured by absence and discontinuity, the breakdown of relationship and analogy, and its conclusion intensifies that discontinuity rather than healing it. That conclusion also marks, however, the beginning of a *mission*, the direction of which is specified but the final form of which remains unknown.

I referred earlier to Balthasar's distinctive understanding of the "beatific vision," as the participation of redeemed creation in the eternal movement-in-rest of God. It is essential to his understanding of mission, as having its source in the divine Idea through which all things are created in Christ, that the distinctive missions of creatures persist in eternity. Thérèse of Lisieux's desire to spend her eternity, not in rest but in the love of God and creatures, is for Balthasar a desire most appropriate to the nature of God revealed in Christ (Balthasar 1992: 201; Balthasar 1988–98: V, 394, 413). *Freedom* as the continual enactment of the "always more" of one's eternal existence in God is more truly present in eternal than in temporal life. Furthermore, this participation in the divine life is inseparably linked to knowledge and enjoyment of one another in the communion of saints – "everyone is utterly open and available to each other, but this openness is not like the total perspicuity of states or situations; instead we have free persons freely available to each other on the basis of the unfathomable distinctness of each" (Balthasar 1988–98: V, 485–6).

This latter statement, taken out of its context, could serve as a summary of Balthasar's earlier description of the significance of sexual difference. That description, as we saw, was subsequently in effect undermined by the need to define "femininity" for christological purposes. Here, however, in the vision of the redeemed state, we have a return to non-reified sexual difference – placed, significantly, *after* the discussion of the completion of the "nuptial" relationship of God and creation, so that no further tangling of analogies is possible. Perhaps those who seek to develop Balthasar's work can allow this vision of the communion of saints to cast its light back onto all the difficulties discussed earlier – so that the God-given missions of persons in Christ are seen as leading them, not towards the reaffirmation of gender roles as we know them, but towards the "always more" of life in God.

Notes

1   It is interesting to compare this passage with the exegesis of Ephesians 5, mentioned above. Balthasar notes that Paul begins (5.23–7) by "projecting his thought . . . from the creaturely, sexual sphere (which is the subject of his exhortation) to the soteriological sphere," and "goes on to look back from the latter order to the former" (Ephesians 5.28–31; Balthasar 1982–91: VII, 484). So Paul's nuptial analogy also faces two ways – but in Ephesians, as Balthasar makes clear, the priority of the soteriological sphere over the "creaturely, sexual" sphere, and the consequent relativization of the latter, is made apparent. Even as the imagery of sexual difference is "projected" into the soteriological sphere, its inadequacy to that sphere is indicated.

2   There are several different "masculine" forms or principles within the church – their archetypes being the leading apostles – but "femininity" at the formal level remains essentially undifferentiated. There is only one "Marian principle," and the missions of the other women of the New Testament whom Balthasar mentions most often, Mary of Bethany and Mary Magdalene, are assimilated to it (Balthasar 1988–98: III, 279–82).

3   I am grateful to Alice Wood for discussions of this topic in connection with her BA dissertation "Creation and Redemption in the Doctrine of the Immaculate Conception" (Cambridge Divinity Faculty, 2000).

4   Christ's maleness is, in turn, the basis for male and female roles within the church (the male priest represents Christ, even while being himself "feminine" towards God); again, the analogies point in both directions. See Balthasar (1986a: 187–98) on the question of women priests.

5   This chapter's discussion of the *singleness* of the "feminine principle" invites a complementary discussion – which space does not permit – of the *empty formality* of the "masculine principle" in Balthasar's thought. *Men* as such (as opposed to priests, apostles, particular thinkers) have no specified characteristics or roles that arise from their "being male"; a fact that itself has major ethical and ecclesiological implications – consider the current rise of movements such as the Promise Keepers with the express intention of rediscovering the *role of men* within the churches. Concepts such as "initiating," "creating," "forming," associated with the masculine principle, are insufficient in themselves, since they require completion by the specification of objects to be initiated, created, or formed. (I am grateful to Jon Cooley for drawing my attention to this question.)

6   Balthasar even claims that a woman's nurturing and raising, as well as the bearing, of her child constitutes a "response to man" (Balthasar 1991: 158). Not, let it be noted, a response to the child!

7   Ben Quash has observed, in his reading of *Mysterium Paschale* (Balthasar's fullest treatment of the "descent into Hell" as the point of the greatest separation of Father and Son), the oddity of Balthasar's concentration on the *consciousness* of Christ in this event; Christ *experiences* hell and lostness. Quash asks, in effect, whether a Christ who "sees" Hell is really dead – in other words, whether Balthasar has really done justice to the discontinuity of death. In connection with this, he notes the presence of Mary as a "term of continuity." See Quash (1999: 246).

8   They also appear in Balthasar (1982–91: VII, 197), where they "represent and hint at something that becomes full reality in Mary the mother: accompaniment into the absolute forsakenness" (see also Balthasar 1988–98: IV, 396).

9   Much has been made in feminist theology, particularly in the work of Elisabeth Schüssler Fiorenza, of the contrast between the "empty tomb tradition" and the "resurrection appearances tradition" (Fiorenza 1995: 119). I do not wish to express an opinion here on the historical-critical question, or to imply that the "empty tomb tradition" *must* be the focus for feminist theological consideration of the resurrection. I would argue, however, that Balthasar's implicitly "progressive" model of New Testament theologies allows him to ignore the real tensions between the different gospel accounts – as his attempt to turn the women disciples in the Synoptics into a "foreshadowing" of Mary in the Fourth Gospel shows.

Part V

Queer/ing Modernity

Chapter 14

Reformed and Enlightened Church

Jane Shaw

It is often presumed within church circles that "the tradition" speaks with a univocal and ahis-torical voice. Much gets promoted in Christian sexual ethics, not least in opposition to women (of all sexual orientations) and homosexuality (in both sexes), under the flag of an unchanging "traditional" view (sometimes called "traditionalist") – and this is always posited in opposition to the "liberal" and innovative ideas (sometimes called "revisionist") of those who wish to affirm the full humanity and sexual orientation of women and men, gay and straight. By contrast, one of the remits of this volume is to demonstrate the ways in which those often called "liberal" or "revisionist" are in fact rooted within the Christian tradition, understanding the ways in which the tradition has *necessarily* changed, and will always have this dynamic aspect to it, mediated as it is by culture and language. This chapter therefore looks at two moments when the Christian tradition has dramatically shifted in its under-standing of sex and gender, at the Protestant Reformation and in the Enlightenment. For practical reasons of focusing the topic, this chapter is primarily one of intellectual history and looks very little at "practice." The first part of the chapter looks at several key theological texts that illustrate the changes in thought and direction about marriage during the Protestant Reformation. The second part of the chapter looks at a number of significant changes in ideas about sex, gender, and sexual identity in the Enlightenment period, and then looks at their impact in several texts and debates up to the present day. One purpose of this second part is to introduce a body of historical research rarely discussed in the debates in the church today, but, it is contended, vital to understanding them; for in under-standing the broader culture's shifts with regard to understanding sex and gender, we see that views today promoted as "traditionalist" (especially in the debates about homosexuality) are in fact comparatively modern. In both sections of the chapter, policy and practice are touched on where possible; but in the space allowed here, this aspect is covered only briefly to illustrate certain points. In the course of looking at these two moments of paradigm shift, and the reasons for them, the chapter also attempts to look especially at female sexuality within the Christian tradition, given that we generally have so little evidence about it – except from men. Let me begin, then, with two texts by two very different women.

In 1393, Margery, the daughter of the mayor of Bishop's Lynn (later King's Lynn), married a Lynn burgess named John Kempe. After she had given birth to their first child, she became ill and suffered a great spiritual crisis. The resolution of that crisis occurred when she had a vision of the bliss of heaven, after which she pleaded with her husband that they might lead "continent" lives, for she wished to be a dedicated holy virgin within their marriage.

> And after this time she never had any desire to have sexual intercourse with her husband, for paying the debt of matrimony was more abominable to her that she

would rather, she thought, have eaten and drunk the ooze and muck in the gutter than consent to intercourse, except out of obedience. And so she said to her husband. "I may not deny you my body, but all the love and affection of my heart is withdrawn from all earthly creatures and is set on God alone." (Kempe 1994: 46)

In proposing to lead such a holy life *within* marriage, she was perhaps unusual, but in wishing to follow the path of celibacy, as the higher good, she was simply following the teaching of the church for the preceding thousand years. In wishing to be a holy virgin – though not necessarily a nun – she was following the great examples of the patristic era, woman such as Macrina, sister of Gregory of Nyssa, and the holy virgins who surrounded male theologians such as Augustine. Her husband did not yet relent: "he would have his way with her, and she obeyed with much weeping and sorrowing because she could not live in chastity" (Kempe 1994: 46). He eventually relented but only after 20 years of marriage and the birth of 14 children; his giving way occurred in a dramatic episode, which took place on the side of a road as they were walking from York one hot midsummer evening. After 8 weeks of no sexual activity between them, despite their sleeping in the same bed, her husband once again tried to assert his conjugal rights: Margery pleaded with him and, desperate, said her prayers in the middle of a field. Guided by Christ, who spoke to her, she once again asked her husband not to enter her bed; he agreed, on the condition that she paid his debts (she came from a wealthier family than he did) and he released her saying, "may your body be as freely available to God as it has been to me" (Kempe 1994: 60). Freed to live as a dedicated holy virgin, she went on pilgrimage to Compostela, Rome and other places, and exercised the gift of holy tears (which irritated her fellow pilgrims no end!). The story of Margery Kempe indicates the ways in which virginity was defined not only as a physical state but also as a moral and spiritual state, "that quality of spirit belonging to those whose primary relationship is with God" (Atkinson 1983: 133).[1] She dictated her story – which is why we know about her – to a scribe (she could neither read nor write) and the text, having been lost for several centuries, was rediscovered in 1934; it is the earliest surviving autobiographical text in English.

In 1694, some 300 years later, a high Tory Anglican called Mary Astell wrote *A Serious Proposal to the Ladies* in which she suggested that single women should have a monastery or a "religious retirement" (as she phrased it, "to avoid giving offence to the scrupulous and injudicious by names which though innocent in themselves, have been abus'd by Superstitious Practices") where they could develop their spiritual life and increase their intellectual learning. This was to have a "double aspect, being not only a Retreat from the World, for those who desire that advantage; but likewise an institution and precious discipline, to fit us to do the greatest good in it" (Astell 1694: 60–1). At the heart of Astell's proposal were: a belief that women too have souls and the faculty of reasoning, and should develop them; a desire to cultivate piety in the high Anglican manner, observing the feasts and fasts of the church in community; and a strong advocacy of female friendship. The proposal was directed at the educated, the "middling and upper sorts" who had some financial means and the possibility of choice in their lives. It was directed against the frivolities of the world, in particular the silliness that Astell identified as existing amongst women because of their lack of education and because of their desire to get along in the marriage market. Astell's was a proposal:

whose only design is to improve your charms and heighten your value, by suffering you no longer to be cheap and contemptible. Its aim is to fix that beauty, to make it lasting and permanent, which Nature with all the helps of the Arts, cannot secure: And to place it out of reach of Sickness and Old Age, by transferring it from a corruptible Body to an immortal Mind (Astell 1694: 3).

Its main aim was religious, about that Astell was quite clear, and it was to be a "retreat" – "such a Paradise as your mother Eve forfeited" (Astell 1694: 67) – but she hoped it would have an effect on the world. It should be "a seminary to stock the Kingdom with pious and prudent ladies: whose good example it is to be hop'd will so influence the rest of the sex, that women may no longer pass for those little useless and impertinent Animals, which the ill conduct of too many, has caus'd them to be mistaken for" (Astell 1694: 73–4).

Astell called for those who supported her to provide the money for such an enterprise, and pious ladies came forward to do so. Indeed, *A Serious Proposal* "caught everyone's attention from the start" and inspired both women and men. John Evelyn wrote that he wished that at least some of these foundations for women and men had been spared in the Reformation, and called Astell's writing "sublime." John Dunton the publisher wrote of "the divine Astell" and Daniel Defoe used her idea for a section on "An Academy for Women" in his *Essay upon Projects* (1697). By 1701, five editions of *A Serious Proposal* had already been published (Perry 1986: 105).

Both of these texts, *The Book of Margery Kempe* and *A Serious Proposal*, represent the struggle by women to control their own sexuality within the paradigms of the Christian tradition; the similarity of their aims is particularly striking because in the period between the writing of their two texts a seismic shift occurred in the Christian tradition's thinking about marriage and sexuality. Celibacy was no longer thought to be the higher good; marriage came to be at least on a par with it and, for many of the Protestant reformers, far superior to it. So for Kempe, before the Reformation, the struggle was with a father who wanted her to marry well, and a husband who wished to enjoy his conjugal rights, but there was no doubt that holy virginity was, in the medieval Christian scheme of things, a higher good than marriage. Convents were still thriving; women could still choose to be nuns and holy virgins. Indeed, her struggle against the worldly aims of marriage stood in a long tradition of women attempting to resist marriage in order to lead a more holy life; as early as the fourth century, Ambrose had written his treatise on virginity in part to encourage elite young women to defy their parents' match-making and to take the more holy path. By contrast, Astell, an unmarried and educated woman, in proposing such a "monastery" in the late seventeenth century, in a religious landscape where the monasteries and nunneries had been dissolved at the Reformation, highlighted the uncertain place of women in society if they now *remained* unmarried. Demographics also played a part here. There were more women than men in late seventeenth-century England: it was estimated in 1694 that (as a result of wars especially, but also perhaps because of plague to which men were said to be more susceptible) there were 77 men for every 100 women in London. Not all women could therefore marry: what were the rest to do? Astell provided one answer, but despite the warm reception that Astell's *Serious Proposal* received, and the readiness of pious women to give it support, the idea was squashed by leading churchmen who thought it too "papist" and therefore dangerous. (There were no Protestant convents in England until the mid-nineteenth century when the Anglo-Catholics revived monastic life in the Church of England.)

Astell was, crucially, pointing to the narrowing of choices for women in a society where marriage was now seen as the only option, indeed the only vocation, for women. In particular the virtues of friendship had been lost. "For Friendship is a vertue which comprehends all the rest, none being fit for this, who is not adorn'd with every other Vertue. Probably one considerable cause of the degeneracy of the present Age, is the little true Friendship that is to be found in it; or perhaps you will say that is the effect of our corruption." Astell also seemed to suggest that the emphasis on marriage, coupled with her age's selfish tenor, had weakened the bonds of friendship:

> "The love of many is not only waxen cold, but quite bemus'd and perish'd." Friendship could be the main source of instruction in following the great commandment to love one's neighbour. "For Friendship is nothing else but Charity contracted . . . and therefore tis without any doubt, the best Instructor to teach us our duty to our Neighbour." (Astell 1694: 135–6)

Theologians of the Middle Ages – many of them monks, such as Anselm, who lived in community with others – emphasized the godly nature of friendship. Astell suggests that the emphasis on marriage as the primary "estate" led both to a loss of the bonds of friendship and a narrowing of choices for women. These points we must bear in mind as we turn back to look at that paradigm shift of the Reformation – which led to marriage being given a new importance – and the work of the male theologian, Martin Luther.

Reformed Church

In 1522 Luther declared "How I dread preaching on the estate of marriage!" (Luther 2003: 100) And yet he preached on it many times. Indeed, he wrote and preached about marriage, sex, sexuality, and women throughout the 1520s, 30s and 40s, until he died; he wrote so much that sometimes his ideas are contradictory, and scholars have debated them at some length.[2] Nevertheless, a clear message in favor of marriage and against monastic life, and against celibacy in most cases, is apparent in his writings. Perhaps the most significant of Luther's writings to consider here is his Commentary on 1 Corinthians 7 written in 1523. 1 Corinthians 7 was, above all other biblical texts, key to the prevailing argument, established in the patristic era, that said the celibate life was preeminent. Or, as Luther put it, "this very chapter, more than all the other writings of the entire Bible, has been twisted back and forth to condemn the married state and at the same time to give a strong appearance of sanctity to the dangerous and peculiar state of celibacy" (Luther 1973: 3). The question was, as much as anything, how to interpret vv. 7–9 where Paul writes,

> I wish that all were as I myself am. But each has a particular gift from God, one having one kind and another a different kind. To the unmarried and widows I say that it is well for them to remain unmarried as I am. But if they are not practising self-control, they should marry. For it is better to marry than to be aflame with passion (NRSV).

Did Paul mean that the higher good, the ideal to which all should aspire, is celibacy? Is marriage therefore a second best, something to which one resorts if one cannot control one's lust? Or did he really mean that different people have different gifts – of celibacy and marriage – and that these are equally valid? By the fourth century the majority of learned and leading Christians were quite clear what the answer was: celibacy was the higher good – "I wish that all were as I myself am" was the key verse – and marriage was second best; as we have seen in the example of Margery Kempe, this remained the Church's attitude for over a thousand years. Augustine, for example, who articulated positively the goods of marriage, only wrote about those goods within the larger understanding that "it is good to marry, since it is a good to beget children . . . but it is better not to marry, since it is better for human society itself not to have need of marriage." Others, such as Jerome, wrote far more intemperately against the married life and zealously in favor of the ascetic and celibate life (Augustine 1955: 22).[3]

The Protestant reformers, in attacking the monastic and celibate life and writing in favor of marriage, were embarking upon a paradigm shift of major proportions, and they knew they had to address this key Pauline text: 1 Corinthians 7. In 1522 Melanchthon had written a commentary on it, in which he had accused Jerome of superstitiously extolling celibacy, but Luther felt this commentary was too brief to give proper exegetical proof of the reformers' position. He therefore embarked upon a commentary himself; he completed it in August 1523 and dedicated it to Hans Loser, marshal to the Elector of Saxony, as a wedding song, a Christian "epithalamium" – Loser married the next year, and Luther officiated at the ceremony.[4]

Luther's key message in his commentary was that celibacy is a gift for only a few and should not be demanded of anyone; therefore marriage is an equal calling with celibacy and it is the state to which the vast majority will find themselves called. How then did he deal with the tricky passages in which Paul seemed to be saying that celibacy was the higher good? Of the phrase which had been so important to the patristic writers – "I wish that all were as I am" – he wrote simply,

> True, Paul wishes that everyone might have the great gift of chastity so that he would be relieved of the labour and cares of marriage and might be concerned only with God and His Word, as he himself was. And who wouldn't wish this for everyone, especially since Christian love desires all good things, both temporal and eternal for everyone?

Luther agreed with the statement in a wistful sort of way – if only that might be the case – and then went straight on to the part of the verse which supported his argument: "But, he [Paul] says, "each has his own special gift from God, one of one kind, and one of another." Here he confesses that his wish cannot be fulfilled and it is not God's will to grant everyone this great gift. "Note this phrase well, for there is much in it, and it praises marriage no less than celibacy." In short, Luther makes chastity the preserve of Paul and the very few and then seeks to interpret this text as making "marriage just as much a gift of God . . . as chastity is" (Luther 1973: 16).

His focus was, therefore, on v. 9: "But if they are not practising self-control, they should marry. For it is better to marry than to be aflame with passion." Luther interpreted this bluntly. "This is as much as to say: Necessity orders that you marry. Much as chastity is praised, and no matter how noble a gift it is, nevertheless necessity prevails so that few can attain it, for they cannot control themselves." Luther's argument was entirely pragmatic. He listed all the reasons why people get married and then declared, "But St Paul gives this one reason, and I know of none fundamentally stronger and better, namely need. Need commands it." He interpreted the second half of the verse – "For it is better to marry than to be aflame with passion" – with equal bluntness:

I have no doubt that everyone who wants to live chastely, though unmarried and without special grace for it, will understand these words and what they convey. For St Paul is not speaking of secret matters, but of the common known feeling of all those who live chastely outside of marriage but do not have the grace to accomplish it.

He goes on to say that "aflame with passion" is:

the heat of the flesh, which rages without ceasing, and daily attraction to woman or to man; we find this wherever there is not desire nor love for chastity. People without this heat are just as far and few between as those who have God's grace for chastity. . . . Truly it can be said: for every chaste person there should be more than a hundred thousand married people.

Luther's interpretation of this phrase was so radical that he even interpreted Paul as saying "better an unhappy marriage than unhappy chastity. Better a sour and difficult marriage than a sour and difficult chastity. Why? The latter is a sure loss, the former can be of use" (Luther 1973: 27–30).

In this commentary, Luther wrote as the former monk who had "not desire nor love for chastity" and was delighted by his own marriage in that same year to a former nun, Katherine von Bora. What is striking about Luther's approach is that it was entirely needs-based, and he interpreted Paul in that way. He did write more theologically nuanced defenses of marriage and therefore more positively in favor of marriage in other texts – it was not just a remedy for that "heat of the flesh which rages without ceasing." For example, his defense of marriage connected, importantly, to his doctrine of the priesthood of all believers, a doctrine which formed the basis of his attack on the Roman Catholic idea that the clergy were the standard bearers of morals – being celibate. But his negative experience of being a monk, and his personal struggle with all that was required by that way of life, was never far from the surface in his polemic. Luther's needs-based approach meant that he found it difficult to have any empathy with those who experienced things differently. In particular, he thought that all women should marry, and some of his most abrasive language was reserved for nuns. Take this passage from the Commentary on 1 Corinthians 7, for example:

It is clear how grievously in error are those who glorify nuns, claiming that their state is more glorious and better in the sight of God than matrimony. They contrive fictitious crowns for them and all kinds of virtues and honours, and thus they produce vainglorious, un Christian and even ungodly people who rely more on their station and work than in faith in Christ and on God's grace, despising marriage as something much inferior – even before God – to their own status and calling themselves "brides of Christ." They are rather brides of the devil, because they do not use chastity as it should be used, namely, not to pretend to be better in the eyes of God, but to make people here on earth freer and more capable to give attention to God's word than to marriage (Luther 1973: 16–17).

Luther's defense of marriage had two major consequences: first, monastic houses and convents were shut down, and secondly, marriage was elevated in importance in evangelical theology and practice. While Luther, and indeed his wife Katherine, had found monastic life highly unsatisfactory, this was not the response of all monks and nuns, especially nuns, who understood that their distinctive way of life, in a society where few women had choices, was being destroyed. Women in convents were often the first to challenge the Protestant Reformation. For example, at St Clara Convent in Nuremberg, the nuns were all from wealthy and influential families. When the City Council ordered all cloisters to close, the convent refused. Neither persuasion nor intimidation worked: Protestant sermons were preached four times a week; nuns were refused confessors and Roman Catholic communion; the nuns' servants had difficulty buying food in the town; the nuns were harassed and threatened and finally the Court confiscated the convent's land. None of these measures worked; finally the Council left the convent alone though forbade it from taking in any novices. The last nun there died in 1590 (see Wesiner 1988).

The major Protestant reformers continued to write in favor of marriage and put their beliefs into practice. As one historian has put it, "by 1525, marriage had become one of the litmus tests of commitment to reform" (Carlson 1994: 4). In England, where religious reform was gradual, the question of marriage was equally a litmus test. Once the break with Rome had occurred in the 1530s, tracts in favor of clerical marriage circulated but Henry VIII was strongly opposed to it and in 1539, with the issuing of the rather conservative Six Articles, clerical celibacy was rigorously enforced. With the accession of Edward VI and a more clearly Protestant regime in place, the Six Articles were repealed and in 1549 there was an act permitting clerical marriage. As with Luther, the argument was needs-based rather than theologically nuanced. The statute noted that it was better for ministers in the Church of God to live "chaste, sole and separate from the company of women and the bond of marriage" because then they would be less troubled with the charge of a household and could attend to the administration of the gospel better. However, "such uncleanness of living, and other great inconveniences . . . have followed of compelled chastity" that it was thought better, after consultation with the Scripture, that the commonwealth suffer ministers "to live in holy marriage, than feignedly abuse with worse enormity outward chastity or single life" (*Statutes of the Realm* iv; excerpted in Sheils 1989: 94–5). In 1552, there was a second Act reaffirming the legality of clerical marriage and establishing that children born of such marriages were legitimate. This emphasizes the enormous cultural sea change that was being promoted. Initially – indeed for some time – resistance or, at the very least, suspicion abounded. People sometimes refused to receive communion from married clergymen. For so long, marriage had been seen as distinctly second-class from a Christian point of view, that people now had difficulty discerning the difference between the wife now living in the pastor's house and the "mistress" the old priest used to keep. Dislike of clerical marriage lingered for some time. Mary of course repealed all the legislation allowing clerical marriage in 1553. When Elizabeth became queen in 1559, she was as ambiguous about clerical marriage as she was about just about anything else: it became clear that she did not like it – she especially did not like her bishops marrying – but she did not forbid it. Article 32 of the 39 Articles of Religion of 1563 stated: "Bishops, priests and deacons are not commanded by God's law, either to vow the estate of single life, or to abstain from marriage: therefore it is lawful also for them, as for all other Christian men, to marry at their own discretion, as they shall judge the same to serve better to godliness" (*Book of Common Prayer*). This was finally accepted by the queen in a Bill for subscription to the Articles in 1571 and it became law.

Eric Carlson has argued that the Protestant Reformation brought dramatic changes in the status and legal regulation of marriage on the continent but not in England. Helen

Parish, more recently, has provided a lively revision of Carlson's and most other work on the subject, insisting that the English debate about clerical marriage was as vigorous as that on the continent (see Carlson 1994 and Parish 2000). In addition, she asserts that many of those engaged in the debates for clerical marriage *were* married – contrary to Carlson's assessment. The impact of the 1549 legislation is indicated by the number of clergy deprived of their livings in Mary's reign because they were married – up to a third of London clergy, for example (remembering, however, that London was a rather hotly Protestant area compared to other parts of the country) – though Parish believes that the move towards acceptance of clerical marriage proceeded rather slowly in Elizabeth's reign. Parish notes that a theological stumbling block was in attitudes to the priest's role in the Mass: the celibacy of the priesthood was inextricably linked with the Mass. Simply put, Christ would not be made present on the altar at Mass by words of an unchaste priest. Priests who took wives were therefore seen as administering the sacraments improperly – polluting them in the eyes of a concerned laity – and this was the primary reason why clerical wives received so much abuse and were labeled concubines in the early years. This all, of course, related to raging debates about what happened in the Eucharist: was Christ present or not? If, as the married Zwingli argued, the Lord's Supper was merely a memorial, then this problem was in any case removed. Furthermore as the role of the priest – at the altar and elsewhere – was re-thought, the issue of "purity" became less important. This is illustrated by Article 26 of the 39 Articles of 1563, which concerned "the unworthiness of the ministers, which hinders not the effect of the Sacrament."

The Protestant reformers therefore had to make marriage (especially for themselves, for many of them were ministers) not only the "norm" but even respectable. In England this resulted in a flood of polemical literature. Marriage and family were idealized in a whole series of household manuals and conduct books, written by ministers not least to justify clerical marriage (for a good discussion of these conduct books see A. Fletcher 1994). What all of this amounted to was an enormous shift in cultural and theological expectations and beliefs: marriage went from being second best to the idealized norm as Protestantism spread and made its impact. This occurred surprisingly quickly given the persistence of the former paradigm within the church – namely that celibacy was the higher good. Simply put, the Christian tradition's understanding of marriage in much of Europe and Britain changed dramatically. Scripture was reinterpreted to justify the changes – in particular, Luther's understanding of 1 Corinthians 7 marked a 180-degree turn from prevailing readings of that text – and pragmatic reasons for marriage were unashamedly given: it was seen as a necessity, a place for the expression of natural if lustful desires.

Enlightenment and Church

When we turn to the Enlightenment period, and to our second paradigm shift, interestingly but perhaps not surprisingly we find ourselves turning not so much to the theologians and the churches but rather to the scientists and society, for it was science and society which led the way, and the church followed. Of course, Luther and company assumed without question the prevailing scientific ideas about sex and gender of their own day. In the early modern period, relying still on the ancient sources of Aristotle and Galen, scientists understood woman as an imperfect version of man; that is, there was "one sex" hierarchically arranged. It was thought that men and women had the same genitals (testes and penis), but women's were imperfectly formed and therefore remained inside. This fitted well with

Aristotle's notion, which was also prevalent, that female bodies were formed because of deficient heat in the reproductive process (i.e. they did not quite make it to being men). Women were governed by cold and wet humors, men by hot and dry humors, with the result that all people were on a scale of male to female, according to the quantity and quality of humors they had. It was the heat in men that drove their genitals outside. These ideas about women and men were widespread, even in popular culture, as evidenced by folk tales from this era of women who jumped over fences, with the result that their genitals dropped and they became male. The sixteenth-century surgeon Ambroise Paré told the story of Marie who became Germain, a shepherd, at the age of 15 when she/he jumped over a ditch with too much vigor. The French essayist Montaigne repeated the story and reported that the girls sang a song reminding themselves not to stretch their legs too far in case they became male (Laqueur 1987: 13). The historian Thomas Laqueur has named this the "one-sex model" (Laqueur 1990). An interesting feature of this understanding of gender was the belief that both women and men had to emit seed – both had to have orgasms – in order for conception to take place. Women were therefore seen as just as sexually active as men: Luther's insistence that women were fully sexual beings was quite in step with the scientific understanding of women and men in his day.

This idea was challenged in the Enlightenment. Laqueur has traced the history of the very significant shift from this "one-sex" model to the "two-sex" model and has thus charted the transformation in ideas about sex and gender that occurred in the eighteenth and early nineteenth century. In the latter part of the eighteenth century, scientists sought "sexual difference," thus creating a "two-sex" model. According to Laqueur, this intellectual shift was not a result of scientific discoveries; rather "the eighteenth century created the context in which the articulation of radical differences between the sexes became culturally imperative." Thus "a biology of incommensurability became the means by which such differences could be authoritatively represented" (Laqueur 1987: 35). Scientists sought sexual difference in women's anatomy and physiology. The womb became more important; people began to think that conception could take place without the woman experiencing orgasm, and, as Londa Schiebinger has demonstrated, distinctively different female and male skeletons began to be drawn for the first time (Schiebinger 1987). Both Laqueur and Schiebinger argue that the drive towards sexual difference occurred in a political context where the old hierarchies of society were being questioned, the new language of natural rights was beginning to circulate, and a radical rupture in the hierarchical social and political order occurred in revolutionary France. The question was: who had rights? No one seriously wanted to give women rights, so the question became: how then to deny them rights? The answer was sought in the "facts" of biology: if women were essentially *different* from men then that might lead to all kinds of political and cultural conclusions – and it did. As Schiebinger points out, for example, skull size became extremely important – there was a lot of measuring of skulls and pelvises and other body parts in all of this – because it was thought it could provide an "objective" measure of intelligence: women's skulls were smaller, therefore (it was deduced) women were less capable of natural reason. This meant "the study of anatomical sex differences played a part in underwriting the increasing polarization of gender roles in the Enlightenment" (Schiebinger 1987: 67).

In particular, the notion of the complementarity of the sexes came to prevail – that is, the idea that women and men have distinctly different qualities (and that these are rooted in biology) and this suits them for different (but "complementary") roles in life. Men were seen as hardy and robust with an aggressive sexual appetite, while women were portrayed as frail, rather prone to weakness and sexually passive. This was a dramatic shift from under-standings of female sexuality in the pre-modern era. This emphasis on sexual difference and the notion that women and men were suited for different "roles" in life necessarily set up the terms in which feminists – from Mary Wollstonecraft onwards – argued for women's rights. They either had to argue that women were the same as men, and therefore deserved equal treatment; or that women were essentially different from men but on those grounds "womanly" qualities should be brought to the public spheres of education, politics, and reli-gion. Hence the French feminist, Luce Irigaray, writing in the late twentieth century, has suggested that sexual difference is our modern obsession, the philosophical question that we must work out (Irigaray 1993).

What was the impact of all this on theology and the church? It was everywhere appar-ent that the church readily took on these new scientific and societal ideas. Women came to be especially identified as guardians of morals and religion. This fitted very well with the new economic structures of society, in which work became separated from the home, and the middle classes (as well as the working classes) emerged. For as society was transformed by the industrial revolution, so separate spheres for work and home were developed and the home came to be seen as the special domain of women (at least middle-class women). Leonore Davidoff and Catherine Hall, in their study of middle class families from 1780 to 1850, put it like this:

> The advances in English society which made possible this retreat of women, away from the dangers of "the world" into the home which they could construct as a moral haven, was thus a mark of progress. The idea of a privatized home, sepa-rated from the world, had a powerful moral force and, if women, with their special aptitude for faith, could be contained within that home, then a space would be created for true family religion. Women were more open to religious influence than men because of their greater separation from the temptations of the world and their "natural" characteristics of gentleness and passivity (Davidoff and Hall 1987: 115).

This new ideology of sexual difference was particularly apparent in the evangelical revival of the late eighteenth and early nineteenth centuries where new ideas about the differences between men and women were given a theological grounding by preachers – and blended with old ideas about the subordination of women. Women were seen as *spiritually* equal but, in practical terms, *socially* subordinate. The Pauline texts about headship (1 Corinthians 11.3; Colossians 3.18) still exercised a powerful influence. The result was that sexual com-plementarity did not mean "different and equal," as so often claimed, but rather (combined with Pauline ideas of female submission) it came to mean "different and entirely unequal."

A popular Christian writer on this topic in the nineteenth century was John Angell James, one of the most well-known Congregationalist ministers of his day and a leading figure in the evangelical revival. His *Female Piety* (1853) articulated in theological terms many of these late-Enlightenment ideas about women's proper sphere, once they had filtered down to a more popular level, and argued strongly against women "sullying" themselves in the world of public work. He wrote, "Christianity has provided a place for woman for which she is fitted [the home], and in which she shines; but take her out of that place, and her lustre pales and sheds a feeble and sickly ray." He continued:

The Bible gives her her place of majesty and dignity in the domestic circle: that is the heart of her husband and the heart of her family. . . . A woman who fills well the sphere assigned to her, as a wife, a mother, and a mistress; who trains up good citizens for the state, and good fathers and mothers of other families which are to spring from her own; and so from generation to generation in all but endless succession, need not complain that her sphere of action and her power of influence are too limited for female ambition to aspire to. (James quoted in Dale 1983: 129)

As James's work illustrates, Pauline notions of female submission were made to fit with gender complementarity (just as they had with older notions of gender hierarchy).

Woman scarcely needs to be taught, that in the domestic economy she is second, and not first, that "the man is the head of the woman." This is a law of nature written on the heart, and coincides exactly with the law of God written on the page of revelation. It is first of all an instinct, and then confirmed by reason. (1983: 130)

Woman "instinctively" knew all of this; it was in her nature: "She generally knows her place, and feels it her happiness as well as her duty to keep it. It is not necessity but even choice that produces a willing subjection. She is contented it should be so, for God has implanted the disposition in her nature" (1983: 131).

These ideas about sexual difference did not of course go uncontested: in the nineteenth century, there were vigorous debates about the balance between possible gender equality and male headship within marriage, not least when English marriage law was reformed in the middle of the century (giving wives greater rights to property, for example), and later in the century when women argued for their admission into higher education and the professions, and for universal suffrage (see further Witte 2004). Nevertheless, these ideas have continued to have an impact in modern theology: in the early twentieth century, Karl Barth's writings about women and men illustrate how embedded in the Christian tradition these relatively recent ideas have become. Barth insists on *both* the distinctively different and complementary "essences" (and therefore roles) of women and men *and* the observance of the Pauline texts on male headship. He writes that the distinctive natures of women and men is "the command of God" which tells them "what here and now is their male or female nature, and what they have to guard faithfully as such" (Barth 1936–75: III/IV, 153). For Barth, these distinctive natures lead to sex-differentiated functions, and any temptation to disregard these must be resisted: "the sexes might wish to exchange their special vocations, what is required of the one or the other as such. This must not happen" (Barth 1936–75: III/IV, 154). This notion of sexual difference is regarded by Barth as absolutely rigid: the distinction between masculine and non-masculine or feminine and non-feminine is not, he insists, illusory. He writes:

This distinction insists upon being observed. It must not be blurred on either side. The command of God will always point man to his position and woman to hers. In every situation, in face of every task and in every conversation, their functions and possibilities, when they are obedient to the command, will be distinctive and diverse, and will never be interchangeable. (Barth 1936–75: III/IV, 158)

Barth's insistence upon the distinctively different "natures" of men and women enables him to hold together the seemingly incompatible notions of *both* the mutuality *and* the hierarchy of the sexes. Distinctively gendered natures and consequent roles lead, for Barth, straight to the superordination of the man and the subordination of the woman; the subordination of woman to man indicates the submission of the church as a whole to Christ. The "difference" of the sexes is therefore understood in a christological context in which all Christians must submit to Christ, and women express that submission in their relationship to the "headship" of man. In short, Barth goes straight from his reading of Genesis 2 to the Pauline texts on headship, writing always with the presuppositions of his own day about the "nature" and "roles" of men and women. He ignores not only the first-century context of the household codes to which Paul is alluding, but also the context of Genesis 2, that text which he cites in support of his understanding of the "difference" of the sexes. He writes, "woman is of the man and the man by the woman. Both are told us by Gen. 2. Woman is taken out of man, but man is man only by the woman taken out of him. Yet only an inattentive enthusiasm could deduce from this that man and woman are absolutely alike" (Barth 1936–75: III/II, 309). The irony here is that Barth has his history wrong – or just plain absent – precisely because it was only with the advent of modernity that scientists began to think that women and men were *not*, in their "nature," absolutely alike. It is Barth's "inattentive enthusiasm" for his own views about women and men – deeply influenced by the societal norms of his day – that leads him to read them *into* the Scriptures. Any attempt to re-appropriate Barth for modern (even feminist) purposes necessarily keeps these views about women and men intact. The systematic theologian, Paul Fiddes, makes such an attempt and ends up reiterating the notion of sexual difference: "We have continually to discover what *particular functions of men and women might be*, as these emerge in reciprocal relations" (Fiddes 1990: 153; emphasis added).

Barth's understanding of gender relations points to a prevailing problem within a particular strand in contemporary theology and ethics. Ideas about sexual difference and complementarity that our ancestors would have barely recognized 300 years ago, let alone 3,000 years ago, are regularly mapped back onto the Hebrew Scriptures, especially the creation stories in Genesis 2. This exists in a group of texts today, all aimed at promoting a conservative line about homosexuality in the Anglican Communion in the present climate (in the midst of fierce debates about the subject), in which Genesis 2 is taken as the blueprint for sexual difference and therefore for heterosexuality. The position outlined in these texts is described by its proponents as "traditionalist" and is pitched over and against views which are often more attentive to the nuances and history of the Christian Scriptures and tradition but which are misleadingly called "revisionist." "The narrative in Genesis 2 portrays the creation of male and female as of central significance to humanity" argue the anonymous authors of the recent pamphlet *True Union in the Body?* This narrative "is fundamental to a Christian understanding of marriage" (Anonymous: 22). At the heart of it is a "bi-polar relational nature of humanity" (Anonymous: 11) – in short, sexual difference. But what is that narrative? In a talk given at Sarum College in Salisbury in 2004, Andrew Goddard sketched out the six "acts" of that narrative (borrowed from the New Testament scholar, N.T. Wright). It is in Act One, "Creation," that "the goodness and significance of the distinction in humanity between male and female and the goodness of marriage as a gift of God in creation" are established (Goddard 2005: 48). Genesis 2 is the "shadow" text here (if not directly quoted by Goddard). Goddard therefore argues – echoing directly the language of *True Union in the Body?* – "the traditionalist paradigm is structured around the created bipolarity of humanity as *male and female*" (Goddard 2005: 44). In this scheme, "the traditionalist paradigm holds that marriage between a man and a woman is the divinely intended pattern in creation for human sexual relationships and so for human flourishing" (Goddard 2005: 48). All of this is posited as if there were a seamless line from the world of Genesis to the early twenty-first century; no account of marriage and household relations in ancient Israel is given; no account of prevailing understandings of women and men in ancient Israel is provided; modern notions of marriage and sexual difference are mapped back onto a text from a completely different culture, without explanation. The "revisionists" are then criticized for failing "to take seriously the bodily difference of male and female and the meaning of this material differentiation in God's creative purpose for human sexuality." This misses the point that the "revisionist" position takes material bodies very seriously, recognizing that we cannot make any sense of material bodies without understanding the context in which they operate and in which they are assigned meanings as "male" and "female" – be that ancient Israel, nineteenth-century Britain or twenty-first century America. It turns out, then, that the so-called revisionists take the tradition far more seriously than the so-called traditionalists.

It is the contention of this chapter that powerful ideas from the Reformation and Enlightenment periods, which were startlingly new in their day, namely that marriage is the "norm" in the Christian tradition and that gender relations are determined by an understanding of sexual difference, still powerfully affect our thinking today and are frequently presented as "traditional" with little or no regard for their history. This has repercussions for another historical narrative: that of homosexuality in the West. It is not within the remit of this chapter to rehearse the history of (or, indeed, the complex historiography about) modern homosexuality. But it is important to indicate the significance of the emergence of sexual difference for the creation of "homosexuality" as an identity. For these two concepts are, in fact, two sides of the same coin: only with the advent of sexual difference could heterosexuality emerge as an identity; and only with heterosexuality could homosexuality emerge as an identity. "Sameness" and "difference" must necessarily rely upon one another for their meanings.

There is, then, a parallel – and related – narrative to that told by Thomas Laqueur and other historians about sexual difference and gender complementarity in the modern period, and it is an account of the emergence of sexual identity. This narrative suggests that in the Enlightenment period, sex went from something one did to something one was, from a verb to a noun. In short, heterosexual and homosexual identities were created. Not all historians agree with this story – in particular, the medievalist John Boswell argued strongly for the existence of homosexual identity in the pre-modern period – but it is generally accepted that this shift occurred. This is not to say that sexual activity between two people of the same sex did not take place before the modern period! But all sexual activity – whether between men and women, men and men or women and women – was regarded as just that: *activity*. And, of course, some activities became illegal: in the 1530s, as the Protestant reformation was getting going, sodomy was made a civil crime in England in 1533, and became a criminal offence in 1562. It had long been a capital offence. From the sixteenth century, sodomy was defined as a felony without benefit of clergy – the most serious sort of capital crime. Sodomy, like the activity of prostitution, with which it was often linked and which was also clamped down on in this period, was considered threatening to marriage. Despite this, the number of sodomy cases in the sixteenth and seventeenth centuries remained quite small: in order to prove sodomy, several elements had to be in place – both penetration and ejaculation, and two witnesses (not the participants!) who could attest to both of those activities occurring. Crucially, the activity was not at that time connected with any particular sub-culture. As Diarmaid MacCulloch has put it:

> There was no descriptive term at all in the prescriptive literature for the notion of a homosexual identity; sodomy was a matter of corrupted individuals making choices to carry out certain acts. All people could fall, and the consequences were dire, not just for the individual but for all society. . . . Therefore sodomy was linked to any group which could be represented as threatening the structure of society" (MacCulloch 2003: 622–3).[5]

Most historians suggest that it was only in the late seventeenth century at the earliest, and into the eighteenth century, that "sub-cultures" of "homosexual" men began to gather, first in Amsterdam and London. Male homosexual sub-cultures in London gathered in "molly houses" and in various open-air venues, especially Moorfields and St James's Park. That such an identity could begin to emerge had everything to do with shifting ideas about gender in society. As older Galenic ideas about man and woman being "one sex" on a hierarchical continuum declined, so "male" and "female" developed as distinctively different identities, and there was a new notion of sexual or gender difference (what Laqueur calls the two-sex model). The notion of gender complementarity – the idea that male and female are somehow *naturally* made for each other – likewise developed, and those who did not fit into that scheme began to emerge with a different identity: the effeminate man and the mannish woman, whose sexual desire lay with those of the same sex.

The development of male homosexuality as an identity in the modern West is well charted; in recent years historians have also argued that women formed homosexual sub-cultures in the same way that men did, piecing together the threads of a history of eighteenth-century and early nineteenth-century lesbian identity. There are numerous cases of women living together, running businesses together, sometimes with one of them cross-dressing as a man – as in the case of Charlotte Charke (the daughter of theater man, Colley Cibber) who wrote her scandalous memoirs in 1755 (Donoghue 1993 and Charke 1755). One of the most revealing historical finds has been the diary of one Anne Lister, a gentlewoman from Yorkshire, born in 1791. Her extremely frank diary entries (written in code) suggest the existence of a lesbian sub-culture in the early nineteenth century which was regarded as normal, and was therefore accepted and very much a part of the gentry culture in which she lived (Whitbread 1988; see also Liddington 1993).

When the medical profession started to label, medicalize and pathologize homosexuality in the nineteenth century then a clear homosexual identity emerged. Of course, what followed this medicalization was persecution of the identity as much as of the activity, and pastors and theologians have participated in that as much as any other institutional group.

Conclusion

Anyone who has in the last few months or years picked up a church document about sexuality or marriage will immediately recognize the immense impact of the two major paradigms discussed in this chapter: the ideas about marriage, which were promoted in the Protestant Reformation, and Enlightenment ideas, under which we still labor today, about women, men, sexual difference, and sexual identity. The church too often takes as "given" a particular model of marriage, a particular understanding of women and men, and a particular notion of sexual identity, without historicizing any one of them. And yet, our modern understandings of all of these things have come about as a result of radical shifts in thought and the culture. In the Reformation, a radical new interpretation of Scripture, as well as an appeal to raw need, brought about a new appreciation and promotion of marriage; this shift marked a radical rupture with the patristic and medieval eras' understanding that celibacy was the greater good. In the Enlightenment, new scientific and cultural ideas about women and men and sexual identity were assumed into theological systems of thinking without question; women were seen as "naturally" more religious, and suited for only limited roles in the private sphere. All of these could be understood within – indeed, mapped back onto – a particular corpus of biblical texts (Genesis; certain Pauline letters).

At the heart of the fierce debates about homosexuality in the churches today lie two key factors: Scripture and science. Can Christians re-interpret Scripture to be more tolerant of homosexuality? Why not? The church has done it before with marriage. And can Christians take into account scientific findings about homosexuality that suggest that it is natural, even genetic, and not something out of which someone can be talked or forced. Why not? The church has accepted science at face value before, when scientists made the bold and daring suggestion that woman and man were different from each other.

Notes

1   Atkinson goes on to argue that this moral definition of virginity prevailed in the later Middle Ages "because of the experience and reputations of the late medieval saints."
2   For a helpful introduction to this scholarly debate, see the Introduction to Karant-Nunn and Wesiner-Hanks (2003).
3   Both Augustine and Jerome were writing against Jovinian who – alone in this period – considered the married state equal to virginity. Both Pope Siricius and Ambrose had condemned this "heresy" and Jerome had written *Adveruss Jovinianum* exalting virginity. Augustine felt that he needed to refute Jovinian's position whilst retaining the dignity of marriage.
4   There was a Roman Catholic response, but not until 1527 when Conrad Kollin, prior of the Dominican monastery at Cologne, published his *Refutation of the Lutheran Wedding Song*. But Luther does not seem to have taken any notice of it.
5   But see, for a different perspective, Jordan (1997) and Jordan (2002: 76–106).

Chapter 15

Sex and Secularization

Linda Woodhead

The Christian process . . . demands the sacrifice of the hitherto most valued function, the dearest possession, the strongest instinct. (Jung 1938: 25)

Sex is the single most controversial topic in the churches today. In both northern and southern hemispheres disagreement between and within the churches tends to come to sharpest focus over the issue of homosexuality. But a penumbra of anxiety extends over many related issues, including the breakdown of marriage and the family; the changing roles and expectations of women; the permissibility of contraception, abortion, new reproductive technologies; and – in the African context – polygamy. This situation is unprecedented. Whilst sexuality has always been a particular concern of the churches, it is only in the modern period that it has assumed such central and universal prominence in a Christian agenda.

The first part of this chapter offers some suggestions about how this situation has come about in the modern West. Three factors are isolated as particularly significant: the privatization and "domestication" of Christianity in the modern world, reaction against modern "permissiveness" in the quest for a distinctive Christian identity in a time of rapid change, and historical Christian concern with sexual regulation. The underlying argument is that the contemporary churches' anxiety over the control of sexuality in the modern world has a great deal to do with their struggle to retain social power in a situation where such power is under increasing threat. The central part of the chapter goes on to consider ways in which Christianity has redoubled its efforts to control sexuality in modern times, looking in particular at its defense of heterosexuality, and its impact upon female bodies. Finally, the chapter suggests that the modern churches' heightened concern with sexual regulation may have served as a significant factor in their recent decline. Here the argument is that the widespread cultural turn to "subjective life" which has taken place since the 1960s has involved widespread rejection of attempts by external authorities to impose order on the more authentic claims of inner, subjective life – including, paradigmatically, sexual life. In this context, the churches' stance on sexuality may have served to retain the loyalties of men and women wary of the subjective turn, whilst alienating the larger numbers who find the promptings of inner life more trustworthy than the imperatives of external obligation. In the West at least, "sexualization" may be an important factor in secularization.

Why Sex Became so Important to the Modern Churches

Privatization and domestication of Christianity

To read medieval compilations of canon law, or the writings of Aquinas, or papal documents relating to the investiture struggle, is to be reminded just how wide-ranging the

Western church's sphere of interest and influence once was. What differentiated the medieval church from the early church and the modern church was its lively ideal of Christendom – of what Ernst Troeltsch refers to as "an internally uniform Christian civilization" (Troeltsch 1931: 201). Where the early church had tended to see itself as "ecclesia," a religious body of perfect holiness called out of the world and differentiated from it, the medieval church sought to extend its control not only over culture but the whole sociopolitical realm as well. Today the Christendom ideal has no living force, for the conditions of modernity rendered its realization impossible – even in the United States of America. Indeed, it is possible to characterize modernity *as* the revolutionary overturning of the Christendom ideal, a revolution which has seen social, political, and economic power gradually wrested from the church in a series of both bloody and bloodless revolutions.

From a situation in which it exercised extensive control over government, the economy, law, education, health, and welfare, Christianity in the modern West has been reduced to one in which its sphere of influence grows ever smaller. Yet the churches have not surrendered power without a struggle, and this struggle has not been wholly ineffectual. Nostalgic remnants of political power remain, most obviously in the few remaining state churches in Europe. In Europe some denominations also retain influence in the educational sphere, chiefly by maintaining church schools. In Europe and America denominational and ecumenical boards of social responsibility continue to issue reports on issues as diverse as nuclear deterrence and global capitalism, albeit in diminishing volume. Yet the only realm besides the purely religious one in which Christianity can still claim something like a monopoly of power is that of private life and family life.[1]

As the modern churches' other spheres of influence diminished, their efforts to control the domestic sphere intensified. On this topic, uniquely, the churches in the modern world could not only speak, but could expect to be heard and even obeyed. To be able to exercise power over individuals' private and domestic lives has been a major compensation for institutions which have seen their power in other spheres decline so significantly. For one thing, the family is the context in which the next generation is both born and formed, and it continues to have a major educational role even in modern times. For another, control over intimate life is a very real form of control, for it involves control of the deepest of bodily and emotional pleasures and desires – control of *eros*, no less. As the family grew in significance as "a haven in a heartless world," so this power became the more significant (Lasch 1977). To be able to control the sphere in which men and women invested the greater part of their hopes and energies, not to mention their finances, is to have power indeed. It is to control the sphere most important in the construction of men's and (particularly) women's identity. By insinuating itself into the bedroom, churches were in effect disallowing the one thing many moderns sought in the domestic realm, namely privacy and freedom from control. What more intense form of control could there be than such public control over "private" life?

The power that the modern church exercised through its colonization of the domestic sphere impacted more forcefully on women than on men. The creation of the modern family, and the division of men and women into two "sexes" with different characteristics, went hand in hand with the increasingly rigid demarcation of public and private spheres which was a defining feature of industrialization.[2] This development was associated with the growth of jobs in industry and the professions which took men away from the home, and with an increasing affluence which made it possible for women (particularly of the new middle classes) to stay at home and occupy themselves with "genteel," non-paid tasks.[3]

Some have gone so far as to argue that the "free" labor of women in the domestic sphere, together with that of mostly female domestic servants who were supported at subsistence-level, was a necessary condition of the rise of industrial capitalism (see, for example, McClintock 1995).

As Christianity lost power in the "public" world and consolidated it within the increasingly important "private" realm, so it inevitably "domesticized" and "feminized."[4] Instead of being located in the public world of male power, the church was gradually relocated in the realm of women and domesticity. For women, increasingly excluded from the public realm, the gain was considerable. From the nineteenth century onwards the Christian churches increasingly affirmed and dignified women in their domestic roles and conferred upon them the highest of symbolic statuses – that of God's most blessed and chosen servants. What is more, it offered an escape from the otherwise suffocating constraints of the domestic sphere by providing alternative but complementary social spaces that would not otherwise have been available to them.[5] The worshipping church itself was the most important and obvious of these spaces, but a rapidly growing number of nineteenth-century societies and associations and movements opened up still more opportunities for women. They included temperance movements, home-visiting educational and uplift programs, charitable initiatives, and missionary societies. Many allowed women to escape the home (albeit temporarily), to take on a measure of administrative and organizational responsibility, and to at least sniff the air of public power (see, for example, Ginzberg 1990). These gains were particularly important for middle-class women, and often reinforced an emerging class hierarchy. Working-class women could gain from feminization as well, not least through the domestication of their menfolk.

The gains which domestication and feminization brought the church were significant. Most importantly, they counteracted the congregational decline which might otherwise have accompanied such processes as social differentiation. Indeed Callum Brown goes so far as to argue that the creation of a "salvation economy" centered on women is the single most important factor in explaining the massive impact of Christianity within Western societies from the 1800 through to the 1960s (C. Brown 2001). Quite simply, women sustained the church: the commitment of the most active was unstinting, and their labor was free. Yet feminization also resulted in a loss of status for the churches and for the clergymen who still retained organizational power within them, and there was also the ever-present danger that men would become alienated from the churches – a worry which clergymen addressed periodically through attempts to make Christianity more "muscular" (whether by way of movements like the boy scouts, church-sponsored to football teams, or by the self-conscious selection of "manly" bishops).[6] Whilst men did continue to attend church, there is some evidence that it was increasingly women-folk who dictated their church-going practice (C. Brown 2001: 192).

Reactionary identity and the creation of a counter-culture

As Western Christianity became structurally identified with women, families, and the home in industrial societies, so sex inevitably became a focus of concern. The church's concern was not merely with sex-acts, but with sexual conduct more generally, and so with the whole structuring of relations between the sexes. Marriage, the family, and the heterosexual economy were viewed as part of the natural and/or God-given order of things. Sex must be understood and embodied within this context. It was seen to be "ordered" rather than disorderly when it took place within the married relationship and was oriented to procreation and the building up of family life, rather than to pleasure. In the vast majority of churches, sexuality was also said – or quietly assumed – to be ordered when the male took the active and the female the more passive role, both in desire and its consummation.

So influential were these ideas in shaping the ideals of modern Western society that for much of the nineteenth and twentieth centuries they were not regarded as reactionary or counter-cultural. Far from it. American Protestantism, for example, tended to think of itself and its sexual ethic as at the vanguard of modern progress and civilization. Yet shifts in social and sexual mores allied to broader socio-economic changes and medical/technological developments – most notably the invention of ever more reliable forms of contraception – gradually meant that merely by standing still the churches came to seem increasingly out of step with the spirit of the age. As a result the churches' teachings on sexuality had come to stand out as a more distinctive defining feature of their identities by the latter part of the twentieth century than had previously been the case. Far from making them more hesitant about speaking out on issues of sexuality, the evidence seems to suggest that this development has had the opposite effect. Many churches have actively embraced the fact that their identities have become bound up with what is now perceived as a reactionary sexual stance, and to have "reacted" more as a result. Here is an area, many seem to have felt, where Christian witness to "the world" can and should be heard. Thus it is surely no coincidence that Christian campaigning on sexual issues dates from the 1920s and intensifies after the 1960s, for these dates reflect the points at which shifts in Western opinion on these issues began and intensified. Sexual conservativism did not merely mark Christians off from the "secular" world, however, it also marked them off from one another. As mainline Protestant denominations gradually accommodated such practices as contraception and even abortion in the course of the twentieth century, so Roman Catholicism and more conservative forms of Protestantism increasingly identified themselves over and against such "liberalism" by their robust defense of a "traditional" sexual ethic.[7]

The recent history of Roman Catholic teaching on contraception offers a powerful illustration of these points. Until the end of the nineteenth century, there was little that was distinctive about Catholic opposition to contraception. If we take North America as our context, we find discussion of the alleged evils of contraception abroad in society long before the Catholic Church had attained an important public voice (indeed, one of the arguments against contraception was that it would lead to the overwhelming of white Protestant America by immigrant Catholic families). Yet the situation changed dramatically in the twentieth century. Movements in favor of birth control began in America in the 1910s and had gained wide support by the inter-war period; by the 1960s "family planning" was so uncontentious that its promotion had become an official part of American foreign policy. Whilst the American Catholic hierarchy had long opposed birth control, it was not until after the 1910s that it made a more public issue of it, becoming *the* central organized opponent of the pro-birth control movement (see Burns 1999). This opposition redoubled in the face of a liberalization of the Protestant stance on the issue, and it is telling that opposition gained papal support from Pius XI's *Casti Connubii*, which is itself thought to have been written in reaction to the 1929 Lambeth Conference's approval of contraception within the context of marriages oriented to procreation. Even more significant, given the increasingly wide acceptance of birth-control and the pill after the 1960s, was Pope Paul VI's reaffirmation of the ban on contraception in *Humanae Vitae* in 1968. Though the document was greeted with shock by many caught up in the modernizing spirit of the Second Vatican Council, Pope John Paul II reaffirmed the teaching of *Humanae Vitae*, signaling out contraception and abortion as major symptoms of the "culture of death" with which he believed the church to be surrounded.[8] He also prohibited the discussion of women's ordination, condemned homosexual acts as "intrinsically disordered," and upheld a "traditional" Christian view of the family within which women should assume their God-given role as wives and mothers. One might go so far as to say that in defending the identity of the Catholic Church against liberalism of both Protestant and secular varieties, Pope John Paul II took his defining stand upon the issue of sexuality. The identification between the two is now so close that a change in Catholic sexual policy would threaten the very identity of the church.

A heritage of sexual concern

Modern Christian churches' focus upon sexuality in the defense and consolidation of threatened power and identity cannot, however, be viewed as merely opportunistic, for concern with the control of sexuality has been central to the internal logic of Christianity from early times. Thus modernity has served as a context which has had the effect of activating this part of the Christian legacy with renewed force. This is not to deny the newness of many aspects of this development (see below), nor to underplay the importance of individual choices, nor even to suggest that the churches could not have taken a very different direction had their leaders chosen to do so. It is merely to recognize that the churches' claim to be reasserting "traditional" teachings has significant historical foundation.

Without wishing to rehearse that history here it is interesting to note that in some ways the churches' position in the modern world represents a return to Christianity's earliest mode of social existence. For the first three centuries of its life the "early church" (in actual fact a number of different competing forms of Christian community) had little or no political, economic, or military power. In Michael Mann's characterization, the only power it possessed was "ideological" (Mann 1986). It could not buy, force, or command allegiance, but grew by winning hearts and minds. It was not imposed from above, but grew from below, and it operated not at the level of primary but of intermediate associations, most notably the family. Just as the family had supplied the chief metaphor in Jesus' teaching (God as "Abba," human beings as his children, these children the brothers and sisters of one another, and all bound by the bonds of intimate love), so the early churches were formed on the model of families bound by spiritual bonds. In some cases this was subversive of the biological family, since the ecclesia offered an alternative "higher" (ascetic) family under the authority of a Father God, but the emerging "orthodox" and "catholic" tradition – articulated in the writings of men like Augustine – sought to head off this possibility by affirming the mutually reinforcing value of both the church *and* the domestic unit. Good Christians were also good wives, mothers, fathers, daughters etc., to such an extent that church and family could each supply the hierarchically ordered model of the other. In this way Christianity served not only to legitimate the patriarchal family, but to strengthen its institutional importance, and to gradually root out alternative forms of patterned intimate relationship.

Thus a great deal of the early success of Christianity may be accounted for by its ability to (a) give intense ethico-religious meaning, order and significance to the domestic sphere (b), to appeal thereby to *all* those – including women – who inhabited it, and (c) to use the family as a chief means for the production and reproduction of Christians and Christianity. This is not to underestimate the significance of the ascetic ideal in early Christianity, but to point out that the "winning" form of Christianity was that which accommodated and defended the family, and allowed householders as well as ascetics to entertain the hope of ultimate salvation. Such "catholic," "orthodox" Christianity managed to establish a delicate balance between the ascetic and familial ideals, by endorsing the family yet identifying the "highest" form of human existence with "spiritual" fatherhood and "spiritual" sonship. The figures of God "the Father," Christ "the Son" and Mary "the virgin mother" had the potential both to legitimate patriarchal family relationships on earth, and to subvert them in favor of a higher, sexless, ideal. As we will see below, the general effect of the Reformation was to exalt the ideal of patriarchal family life, and to give more dignity to the domestic role of women. This tendency was intensified by the pressures of industrialization, discussed above, which saw the "one sex" model which had prevailed in Christianity until that time (where true humanity/divinity is male, and the female state a falling away from this higher identity), to the "two sex" model in which men and women were viewed as two separate and distinct "sexes" with their own unique value – though with the male still dominant. In these ways Christian concern with sex managed to keep step with the unfolding history of sex and gender in the West, and to play a key role in the regulation of sex and gender relations right through to the modern period.

Controlling the Female Christian Body

As well as asking why Christian energies have focused so much on the control of sexuality in modern times, it is interesting to consider in more detail how such control has been exercised. This topic can be interestingly pursued in relation to male and female sexuality, heterosexuality, and homosexuality. Here I will concentrate only on Christianity and female heterosexuality, since I will argue in the final part of this chapter that where sexuality is concerned this is the area of greatest importance for understanding the fate of the churches in modern times.

If we go back to the beginnings of Christianity we find a situation in which it was the male rather than the female head of household who had primary responsibility for maintaining the "family ethic" of Christianity. In establishing orderly, loving and respectful relations within the family the *paterfamilias* would realize in miniature nothing less than the relations in the "household of God" (1 Timothy 2.15). Epistles like the latter show how quickly the potentially subversive teaching of Jesus and even Paul – with its tendency to downplay the importance of the natural family compared with the spiritual family of the children of God – was diverted into more conventional patriarchal forms. For the author of 1 Timothy, a male God who commands obedient servants was to be the model for a church order in which a male bishop commands the faithful and a domestic unit in which the *paterfamilias* commands wife, children, and servants. Whilst the pastoral teachings of 1 Timothy were regularly cited by churchmen down the centuries, they were given fresh force by the Protestant Reformation. Like 1 Timothy, the Reformers envisaged a Christianity that was founded on a patriarchal, family-based system (see Roper 1989 and Weisner-Hanks 2000). Despite its defense of the family, the Catholic Church's alliance with monasticism and its elevation of celibacy – not to mention its veneration of the Virgin Mary – was said to have diverted it from Timothy's vision of a church ruled over by proven *patersfamilias*. As much a social and sexual revolution as a religious one, the Reformation revived this "original" ideal by teaching that each family unit should become a church in its own right, responsible for propagating the faith, disciplining its members and ensuring the proper subordination of women, children, and servants. Against a background of changing socio-economic and political relations, the Reformers helped ensure a gradual migration of power from the hands of social and ecclesiastical elites to male heads of increasingly self-sufficient families. The luxurious and indulgent lifestyle of a pope or aristocrat was contrasted with the ordered, disciplined and respectable life of the householder. As a portable social unit of moral and economic culture the sacralized family unit proved both effective and exportable, capable not only of colonizing the "New World" but of helping re-shape the social landscape of the old. Catholicism was not exempt. Motivated in part by concern to avoid Protestant charges of sexual laxity and immorality and in part by its own dynamics of reform including a new piety centered on sacramental penance and the confessional, Roman Catholicism also developed an ethic in which "the holy family" became more important than ever before (see, for example, Delumeau 1983).

Social and economic changes associated with industrialization built on these foundations to initiate a new phase in the development of the family and sex. Though stripped of many of its earlier socioeconomic functions, allegiance to the ideal of "respectable" family life became a marker of the identity and superiority of the emerging middle class. It proved not only an inspiration and ideological support for this emerging class, but a means by which it could bolster its precarious existence by differentiating itself not only from a dissolute aristocracy on the one hand but an "unrespectable" working class on the other. As mentioned above, this development also initiated a new era in relations between the sexes. From now on men would exercise their leadership and vocations chiefly in the "public" world of work, whilst women would have responsibility for the gentler virtues within the private realm – including spiritual matters. Although women's domestic labor was not defined as "work" it had economic significance – not only was it vital to the emerging capitalist system, but because the family was rapidly becoming a major unit not only of production but of consumption (see A. Douglas 1977). "The process overall," comments Anthony Fletcher, "altered the whole notion of what a woman is. We can characterize it in terms of the internalization of social roles as inherent personality traits" (A. Fletcher 1998: 189). People began to talk about belonging to the female "sex" for the first time, and such belonging came "to colour existence to the point of suffusion" (Riley 1988: 18).

In this restructuring of femininity and the relations between the sexes the churches played a central, indispensable role. Earlier models of women as powerful prophets or independent nuns and abbesses gave way to more confined and passive models of Christian womanhood. Femininity was wholly identified with the role of Christian wife and mother and the work of selfless care. It was as if the Reformation *paterfamilias* had delegated his spiritual duties to his wife. It was now up to her to maintain the respectability of her family, and it was on her powers of self-control and discipline that its status depended. Sexual self-control was central here, and became the symbol of the control – Godly and male – under which all female action must take place. 1 Timothy says that:

> Women should adorn themselves modestly and sensibly in seemly apparel . . . Let a woman learn in silence with all submissiveness. I permit no woman to teach or have authority over men; she is to keep silent . . . Yet woman will be saved through bearing children, if she continues in faith and love and holiness, with modesty. (1.9–15)

The slippage in this passage between sexual, domestic, and religious duties is explained by its guiding concern with the control of women's bodies in every sphere of action. A similar dynamic characterizes nineteenth-century Christian teachings concerning women and their bodies. For a woman to "lose control" sexually would be for her to endanger every aspect of her femininity and, indeed, her salvation. Worse, she would be endangering her whole family. Nineteenth-century middle-class and respectable working-class women could lose their respectability and drag down the standing of their families in a way that men could not. A drunken or whoring husband was far from the Christian ideal, of course, but such things were condonable in men in a way they were not in women. Under this system of moral control women were "angels" whereas men were "beasts," with the fall of the former being far more shocking than the fall of the latter.

Thus even though women might have been delegated some of the religious powers that had once been reserved for the *paterfamilias*, she must not forget the importance of male headship and control. Hers was the passive role whilst the man's was the active. The *Free Church Magazine,* discussing "Female Methods of Usefulness" in 1844 cautioned women against:

> zeal and activity . . . lest they sacrifice those meek and lowly tempers which are so calculated to adorn and promote the cause they love and advocate. Female influence should shed its rays on every circle, but these ought to be felt, rather in their softening effects, than seen by their brilliancy. There are certain duties which sometimes call women out of their quiet domestic circles . . . such duties will, we humbly think, be best performed by those who enter this enlarged field, not from any desire of a more public sphere, but because, in obedience to the precepts of their divine Lord, the hungry are to be fed, the sick comforted, the prisoners visited. (Quoted in C. Brown 2001: 68)

It was to display of the "gentle" virtues that women were called. In the USA Catharine Beecher and her father campaigned tirelessly for the training of women in the habits of "order, neatness, punctuality" as well as "patient attention, calm judgement, steady efficiency, and habitual self-control" (Isenberg 1998: 80). If sexuality was the strongest of human drives, and sexual pleasure the most intense of human passions (as so many Christians since Augustine had believed), then control of women must involve the control of female sexuality – that control would now be the stronger for being internalized as self-control.

The ideal of self-controlled, passion-free, angelic Christian womanhood was diffused into Western culture through a range of media and forms of representation. In the visual arts, for example, nineteenth-century depictions of female piety fell into two main categories: the idealized wife and mother – demure, loving, and self-giving – and the pure and innocent nun – usually depicted with lowered eyes. As Jane Kristof notes, both are chiefly notable for the sexlessness of the women they depict (Kristof 2001). Even more influential was fiction, that most widely devoured of nineteenth-century arts – by women in particular. Short stories and full-length novels endlessly replayed a narrative of a thoughtless, careless, or dissolute man who is eventually "saved" by a woman.[9] Though the stories had a romantic flavor – for the heroine/savior is nearly always in love with a man and normally becomes his wife – it is the heroism of the woman and her ability to redeem that is emphasized. Such novels no doubt proved inspiring and empowering for women, rather than merely gratifying or exciting. It was only in the twentieth century that they transmuted into "Mills and Boon" type narratives where romance rather than religious redemption became the climax, with the novel ending rather than beginning with the central characters becoming engaged.

Christianity also consolidated control over women's bodies and sexuality by means of more negative modes of reinforcement. In the medieval and early modern periods there were public means of external control. Both legal and illegal measures were sometimes used to control women's sexuality. They were backed by the use of force, which could be lethal. In the modern period, negative reinforcement was more likely to be internalized, and enforced by way of – for example – the emotional sanctions of shame and guilt. Proscribed sexual activities and stirrings were delimited and policed not only by way of explicit teachings but, just as importantly, by silence. The fact that there was less and less discursive space for female desire, female pleasure, female orgasm and female sexual organs meant that for many women and men these things ceased to exist. Given this negation, any internal stirring of active sexuality would likely be experienced – if experienced at all – as a source of shame and abnormality. Like menstruation, women's sexuality would be represented and received as a "curse" to be controlled, hidden away and, best of all, destroyed. Men were to take the lead in sexual activity, but even they must do so not for pleasure, but for one or more of the higher "goods" which marriage was ordained to serve.

It is testimony to the power of both the negative and positive modes of Christian sexual control over women's bodies that their influence persisted so long, even after the decline of the art and fiction that helped sustain it. As will be mentioned below, it is still alive and well in more conservative wings of the Christian churches. Even more remarkable has been its continuing influence within Western culture more generally, in Europe and especially the USA, right up to the 1970s. I can personally testify to the way in which it shaped my own upbringing in a largely secular English household in the 1970s, and how decisive it was in shaping the ethos of the girl's Catholic school I attended, and where I was trained in the gentle arts of sewing, domestic science, and good manners and exhorted to safeguard my "modesty" in order to protect my "reputation" and make a good marriage. Less anecdotal evidence comes from a source which is in some ways the more revealing because of its blindness to religion, namely Beverley Skeggs' study of working-class women in the north of England. Based on research undertaken mainly in the 1980s, and subtitled *Becoming Respectable*, this study finds that the lives of its subjects (born in the 1950s and 1960s) are still dominated by the negative imperative of avoiding the loss of respectability. What is more, "respectability" still seems to carry the same Christian freight that it did over a hundred years ago: ordered domesticity, hierarchical gender relations, female self-control and sexual continence, the labor of care (Skeggs 1997). All of the women involved in the study view marriage and motherhood as the chief goal of their lives, and those who undertake any form of further education undertake courses in "caring." When it comes to sex, they are wary. Despite the sexual liberation their generation is meant to be heir to, they know that for a women to initiate sex, or show too much interest in sex, or make their sexual desire too explicit is to risk being labeled "tart," "whore," "slapper," and – worse – to risk losing the prospects of a good marriage. For similar reasons, these women are extremely quick to dissociate themselves from "feminism," fearing for their reputations should they be labeled in this way. As 1 Timothy envisaged, it is in childbearing, silence, and submission that they seek salvation, albeit in this world rather than the next.

Despite the long reach of its cultural influence, however, the era since the 1960s has been characterized in many Western societies by a gradual diminution in the influence of this ideal of "Christian" femininity, particularly amongst the educated middle classes. Symbolized by controversial yet popular television shows like "Sex in the City" or "Desperate Housewives," women are increasingly represented as beings capable of sexual desire and of taking sexual initiatives for the sake of their own subjective satisfaction. Thus the "long 1960s" seem to represent something of a hinge in social and cultural history – not only in sexual but in religious terms as well. In the remaining part of this chapter I will suggest that this is more than a coincidence, and that women's rejection of an ideal of passive and sexless womanhood, together with a rejection of the church's "interference" in sexual matters on the part of both sexes, has a direct relation to the sudden and massive decline of the churches, particularly in Europe, since the 1960s.

"Don't Tell Me What To Do with My Body": Sexual Control and Church Decline

A weakness of classical theories of secularization which appeal to "constants" of modernization like rationalization in order to explain religious decline is their inability to account for the accelerated decline of churchgoing in many parts of the West since the 1960s. In Britain, for example, churchgoing roughly halved in the century between 1860 and 1960, then halved again in just three decades (see Bruce 2002). Even in the USA there is growing evidence that the 1960s initiated a new, intensive, phase of de-Christianization.[10] In *The Spiritual Revolution: Why Religion Is Giving Way to Spirituality*, Paul Heelas and I invoke what Charles Taylor refers to as "the massive subjective turn of modern culture" to help explain the post-sixties collapse (Taylor 1991: 26; quoted in Heelas and Woodhead 2005: 2). We argue that a complex and interwoven set of social changes supported a cultural shift which saw traditional values of duty and deference give way to new values of authenticity and expressivism. Rather than relying on external authority as a guide for identity and action, an increasing number of men and women in affluent democracies have come to rely on inner convictions, emotions, and intuitions as the authentic source of wisdom in the living of life. Such a shift favors forms of religion and spirituality which promise to put people in touch with their inner wisdom, but undermines forms of religion – including much church Christianity – which posit a higher authority that overrules the promptings of subjective life.

The idea that a widespread "turn to the self" has been a major factor in secularization can be refined and developed in various ways. As well as paying closer attention to the ways in which a turn to the self may play out differently in men's and women's lives, it is interesting to look in more detail at what the turn to the self rejects as repressive authority, and what it elevates as authoritative in its place. So far as I can see these tasks must go hand in hand, and when they do so they are likely to lead to the same destination – sex.

It is no accident that the cultural revolution of the "sixties" is commonly known as the "sexual revolution," for issues of sex and gender lay at its heart – and thus at the heart of the subjective turn. Following the dislocations of the Second World War, and in the shadow of the threat of nuclear war, the 1950s witnessed a nostalgic return to "traditional values."[11] At its heart was a reassertion of a "two sex" and "separate spheres" ideology undergirded by a harsh sexual division of labor. Political power working through the mechanisms of the burgeoning welfare state was deployed to defend men's right to earn a "family wage," whilst the dignity of womanhood was tied to the dutiful discharge of domestic labors within the home. Numerous cultural agencies legitimated this clamping down on some of the freedoms for women won earlier in the century, from the fashion industry which offered women the "New Look" to the churches which helped sacralize family and home – and were rewarded with a brief upturn in attendance and commitment. Integral to these developments was a new spirit of puritanism in which sexual fulfillment was given new importance but subjected to strict regulation and containment, with women's sexual activity being particularly harshly monitored and controlled. Beneath a new ideal of companionate marriage old ideas of men as sexually active and women as sexless angels who must never take the sexual initiative remained influential. The only appropriate sphere for sexual activity, particularly for women, was that of marriage, and the only appropriate end the reproduction of the family.[12] Both men and women came under enormous pressure to marry, particularly if they were known to be having sex with one another. Women who had a child out of wedlock suffered enormous social disgrace and material hardship, with welfare provisions for single mothers tending to become even more punitive in the postwar period, and some single mothers – in the UK at least – even being placed in asylums for the mentally ill or disabled.[13]

This harsh ethic of sexual containment with its sexual double standard became a key symbol of all that was wrong with the "square," "straight-laced," "up-tight" and "repressive" culture that increasing numbers of young people in the West rejected from the 1960s onwards. The baby boomers continued to pursue the quest for intimacy which had inspired their parents, but rejected the restrictions which had surrounded it. As Elaine Tyler May puts it, they:

> Abandoned the old containers: the traditional family, home-centered consumerism, marriage-centered sex, and cold-war centered politics. The youth culture, as well as the booming economy, encouraged them to be risk takers in ways that their security-oriented parents found unthinkable. (May 1990: 198)

Getting in touch with one's authentic self and freeing one's emotional life from the chains and restrictions that "the establishment" would place upon it necessarily involved expressing one's sexuality in a free and "authentic" manner. Not only in personal but also in public life it was in the realm of sexuality that the "counter-culture" made some its earliest, most publicized and most far-reaching gains. Thus the late 1960s witnessed the most striking changes in the legal framework of sexuality for almost a hundred years. Between 1967 and 1970 there was significant new legislation on abortion, homosexuality, stage censorship and divorce (Weeks 2000: 147).[14] There were also significant changes in individual behavior, with disapproval of premarital sex in the USA dropping from 68 percent in 1969 to 48 percent by 1973, the number of unmarried couples living together tripling in the 1970s, the median age of first marriage rising, the number of single person households rising, the divorce rate rising, and the number of illegitimate births beginning to soar (May 1990: 198–9; and tables on xii–xvi).

Most of these changes directly contradicted church teaching, both Catholic and Protestant. The contradiction became more evident as many churches, including the Roman Catholic, began to reiterate and even intensify their defense of a "traditional" sexual ethic in the later twentieth century. As Western societies became increasingly "subjectivized" in their approach to sexuality, so Christianity retained or even intensified its attempts to regulate sex, and in doing so alienated the large numbers of baby boomers who identified with the causes of the sexual revolution. In this rebellion, issues of sex and gender would often be hard to distinguish, particularly for women, given that their identity as women had become so closely associated with their "sex" – or rather with their sexlessness and lack of sexual desire. Thus the "subjective turn" for a woman would be likely to involve attributing more value to her own appetites and emotions, and treating them as more authoritative in the living of her life than the voice of external, often patriarchal, authorities. Given the power of the sexual appetite, not least in social contexts in which it was being rendered increasingly visible, the quest for "authentic selfhood" would therefore also involve a "sexual liberation" in which a woman admits to and acts upon her own sexual desires, rather than allowing these desires to be shaped or suppressed by the roles to which she is expected to conform. For both men and women it would also involve a new freedom of choice about when, how and with whom sex is performed (depending on what "feels right"), and a lessening of the pressures to confine sex to the boundaries of heterosexual marriage. For men this involved a loosening of identification with the role of paternal care and responsibility, whilst for women identification with the role of mother was loosened by the separation of sex from reproduction, but retained by the "stalled revolution," which saw men cut loose from parenting responsibilities and the work of care to a far greater extent than women.[15]

In arguing that the sexual revolution played an important role in secularization I am not, therefore, wishing to separate sexual activity from the wider issues of gender, power, and identity that surround it. Nor am I wishing to suggest that people left the churches simply because of an intellectual disagreement with church teachings on sex. Such disagreement could certainly be important, but it would often be tied up with a felt dissonance between a person's identity, dress, and self-presentation and what was acceptable in church circles, between the "atmospheric" of a woman's group in church and the sort of circles in which one felt comfortable, between the values and behaviors of one's parents' generation and one's own, and so on. Though there is much more research to be done in this area – and in establishing the causes of secularization more generally – a few indicative pieces of evidence to support my suggestion may help illustrate the argument and suggest avenues for further exploration.

I begin with an extract from an interview I conducted in 2002 with a middle-aged woman born into a working-class family in a mill town in the north-west of England. In the following extract she explains how and why she ceased to be a regular church attender in the 1970s.

> We took the kids to Church Parade on a Sunday . . . it seemed so empty, so hypocritical really . . . I couldn't believe values like respectability and family life . . . There was one occasion at church, we were putting banns up [my husband-to-be and I] and they all knew we weren't married [we were living together] and when they were read out there were these ladies behind me and they said "that's about time", something like that, and I thought "you bitches, supposed to call yourself Christians", and some said "you won't be wearing white then" and I said this to the vicar and he said "it just shows you're pure in mind", and I thought "you hypocrite, I don't think me mind's that pure". But I wanted to wear white just to show them. I just wanted to do my own thing, I wasn't having anyone telling me what to do.

Later in the same interview she describes a later experience of visiting St Peter's in Rome, looking at the fig leaves on the statues of male nudes, and being struck by the thought that Christianity has always been about repression and "covering up" sex and sexuality. Though she does not say this in so many words, there is a clear implication that for her a journey of self-discovery and self-empowerment, and the construction of selfhood upon a new more subjective basis, has been tied up with a dawning sense of the legitimacy of her own sexuality which has involved a dissociation from the identity of "moral womanhood" which she associates with church circles.

Similar issues appear in a study of the attitudes of elderly Catholic churchgoing women to changes in Catholicism post Vatican II. This research, carried out by Mary Beatham, interviewed women in their seventies and eighties, that is to say members of the pre-boomer generation (Beatham 2003). Although these women are still churchgoers, and still shaped and formed by the identification of womanhood with the work of care for family, husband, and church community, they are deeply aware of the changes which have shaped their daughters' lives in different ways to their own, and of the significance of changing sexual attitudes and behaviors in this shift. "In my generation," says one,

> you fulfilled your duty as a good Catholic girl, dutifully committing yourself to your family, as your mother did, sublimating your own desires for the needs of the greater good, of everybody else, and you just got on with it.
>
> You saw it as a privilege, like you'd been given an "exalted" role in your own home [laughter]. Not that young girls, even my own daughter, would see it like that today! She'd laugh at the idea. They would say we were all being duped. Maybe we were. (Beatham 2003: 25)

Nearly all the women in this study speak of the profound impact of *Humanae Vitae* and the ban on contraception on their lives, their comments often hinting at the way in which it was received as "of a piece" with other church teachings which restricted women's lives. For some it led to a long period of disaffection with the church: "I stopped going for quite a long time," says one, "I thought do I really want to belong to this Church?"; "I stopped going to church on Sunday for quite a while," says another, "I wasn't sure if I'd simmer or not . . . it was all so upsetting." And another woman comments, "the men were not encouraged to deal [with these issues] by the church . . . it was considered to be a 'woman's problem' which was most unfair." The women are in little doubt that it is this complex of sex and gender issues – and restrictions – which have led their daughters' generation to distance themselves from church. "It's easier with hindsight to see what happened," says one:

> Today women do what they believe is best for themselves and their families, as they should . . . as I did . . . but they don't have all this guilt and conscience stuff . . . I envy them that . . . although it doesn't affect me in the same way . . . I'm too old now! (Beatham 2003: 40)

Remaining with Catholicism, but turning to the realm of cultural studies, a powerful illustration of the subversion of Christian symbols of female passivity burst onto the scene in the 1980s in the shape of the pop star Madonna. As her stage name suggests, Louise Veronica Ciccone's immensely successful career was founded upon her skillful deployment of Roman Catholic imagery and symbolism against itself in the cause of female sexual liberation. Madonna's subversion consisted in her taking Christian symbols and using them to claim rather than renounce an explicit female sexual identity. "Like a Virgin" invoked the sexual excitement of a convent girl's first sexual encounter, "Papa Don't Preach" asserted a young woman's right to decide the course of her own life, and the cross was used in several of her videos as a phallic symbol. Thus Madonna established her massive success on the reversal of Catholic symbols of female submission – prior to embracing the virtues of motherhood and domesticity, alongside superstardom, in more recent times (see Sexton 1993).

This exclusive focus on women's disaffiliation from Christianity, and the role of disaffection from church-endorsed sex and gender roles – is not intended to deny the importance of similar factors bearing on men. Modern men are every bit as likely as women to agree with Pierre Trudeau that the church has no more place than the state in the bedrooms of the nation. Ideals of masculinity tend to place heavy emphasis on the importance of male agency, not least in sexual encounter – and the idea that this might be restricted by "higher" authority is likely to be correspondingly less palatable to them than to women. So far as we can tell, men ignored or rejected church teachings on issues like contraception and pre-marital sex earlier and more readily than women – which may, of course, be one reason for men's lower levels of church attendance and general commitment right through the modern period.[16] As suggested above, men's growing alienation from paternal masculinities may be a linked reason which helps explain their more rapid disaffiliation after the 1960s. It is still the case that women outnumber men on almost every index of involvement in most con-temporary forms of church Christianity by a ratio of about three to two, which means that although women have defected in larger numbers from Christianity (and hence had a greater impact on church decline than men), they have nevertheless defected at the same rate (see Walter and Davie 1998). In this context it is interesting to note that the most recent evidence from Peter Brierley's Scottish church attendance survey shows women beginning to defect at a higher rate than men – a trend which, if sustained, would have disastrous results for the churches (Brierley 2003: 2.91).

My argument that the churches' implicit and explicit messages about the regulation of sex have played a significant role in secularization can be supported, finally, by compar-ing two recent attitudinal surveys. In response to the question "do you think it is proper for the leaders of religion to speak out on . . ." the 2001 Scottish Social Attitudes Survey finds that whilst a majority of people are quite happy for church leaders to speak out on a range of political and public issues, they are unhappy when it comes to their commenting on sexual and private matters. Eighty percent think it "generally right" to speak out on world poverty, compared with 37 percent who think it "generally right" to comment on "sexual behavior" (Scottish Social Attitudes Survey 2001 analyzed in Bruce and Glendenning 2001). Compare this with Christians from an Anglican evangelical congregation, responding to the question "which issues do you think the church should speak out on," where we find that respondents feel that private issues are at least as important as public ones, with 90 percent saying the church should speak out on "extra-marital affairs" compared with 60 percent on "government policy" (Guest 2002). The conclusion must be that at a time when Christians and their churches have been putting increasing energy into the regulation of sexuality, the general population has become increasingly hostile to attempts to "interfere" with what they view as their personal subjective lives.

Today we see the results of this disjunction in a contemporary religio-cultural landscape in the West in which a diminishing number of people attend church, those that do are increas-ingly conservative in relation to "family values," and a yawning gulf opens up between these two cultures. The most successful churches in both Europe and the USA currently tend to be those which are most socially and morally conservative (see Kelley 1977 and, for more recent confirmation in relation to the UK, Brierley 2000). In the USA such churches fare even better than in Europe, not least because they are able to maintain a distinctive sub-culture centered on the family, churches, and Christian educational establishments, and TV channels.[17] The success of conservative churches would seem to suggest that Christianity still has an impor-tant role to play in defending "traditional family values" and differentiated sex and gender roles for men and women, with few serious competitors to contend with. Such Christianity caters for those who dissociate themselves from the "lax" and "permissive" values of the subjective turn – a minority in Europe, but a sizeable constituency in the USA and in the growing churches in the southern hemisphere. Sensing its ascendance, such family-based Christianity is currently launching aggressive attacks upon more liberal forms of Christianity, taking as the site of battle the latter's "laxer" attitudes to sex role differentiation and sexual regulation. Thus the future of Christianity – in terms of its internal profile, its overall numbers, and its geographical spread – is likely to be determined in large part by issues of sex and gender.

Notes

1 Even in the sphere of sacred power, Christianity's monopoly is under threat. See Heelas and Woodhead (2005).
2 On the rise of a "two sex" model of human identity see Laqueur (1990).
3 On the shifting structural location and changing meanings of the family and domesticity see Davidoff and Hall (1987) and Mintz and Kellogg (1988).
4 The classic statement of this thesis is in Ann Douglas (1977).
5 For much fuller discussion of these key points, and the evidence on which they rest, see Woodhead (2001: 332–56) and Woodhead (2004).
6 See, for example, Vance (1985) and Gill (1998a).
7 For recent evidence of how an issue in sexuality can become a rallying point for conservatives against liberals, see Stephen Bates' (2004) account and interpretation of the evangelical campaign against homosexual activity in the Anglican Church.
8 In *Veritatis Splendor* (1993) John Paul II insisted upon the reality of exceptionless moral norms or "intrinsically evil acts," but confined his discussion of them to sexual acts.
9 See Callum Brown's survey of this literature and its themes in Brown (2001: 58–87).
10 See the work of the American sociologists of religion Penny Marler, Kirk Hadaway and Mark Chaves, summarized in Heelas and Woodhead (2005: 55–60).
11 The classic study of this conservative domestic turn in the US context is E.T. May (1990).
12 In the USA Alfred Kinsey's documentation of widespread pre-marital inter-course, homosexual experiences, masturbation and extra-marital sex gave rise to new efforts to ensure sexual containment within marriage (E.T. May 1990: 88–90 and D'Emilio 1983).
13 On welfare provision in the USA see L. Gordon (1994). I have not found a systematic study of the incarceration of unmarried mothers in mental asylums, but for an indicative case study see Griffiths (1998). Szasz (1975) presents evidence of single mothers incarcerated decades before still being found in asylums in the 1970s.
14 On the debate about what the sexual revolution really amounted to see McLaren (1999: 166–92).
15 The idea of a stalled gender revolution, visible in the continuing unequal division of labor between men and women is taken from Hochschild (1989).
16 For a discussion of the sex differentiation of secularization see Woodhead (2005).
17 On the sexual and moral "backlash" spearheaded by conservative evangelical churches in the USA and embodied not only in New Christian Right movements of the 1980s and 1990s but more recently in men's movements like "Promisekeepers" see Ruether (2001: 156–80), Diamond (1989), and Novosad (1999).

Chapter 16

"Promising Ashes"

A Queer Language of Life

Grace M. Jantzen

"Aren't you sure of what you're saying? Are you going to change yet again, shift
your position according to the questions that are put to you, and say that the objections are not really directed at the place from which you are speaking? Are you
going to declare yet again that you have never been what you have been reproached
with being?" . . . "Do not ask who I am and do not ask me to remain the same:
leave it to our bureaucrats and our police to see that our papers are in order. At
least spare us their morality when we write." (Foucault 1972: 17)

These frequently quoted words could be taken as a manifesto of queer theory. All through
his writings Foucault undermined the idea of fixed identity, whether his own identity as an
author, or any conception of an identity or essence of rationality, health, delinquency, or
sexuality. He showed that things were always more complicated, considerably queerer than
could be captured by any talk of essence. Moreover, he showed that the shape-shifting that
these putative universals have gone through were not simple changes, but that they were
always also interconnected with issues of power and authority, with what counts as truth
and who gets to do the counting. Foucault summarized his method as "a systematic scep-
ticism with respect to all anthropological universals," such as madness, crime, or sexuality.

> Yet the refusal [of such universals] entails more than the simple observation that
> their content varies with time and circumstances; it entails wondering about the
> conditions that make it possible, according to the rules of truth-telling, to recog-
> nize a subject as mentally ill or to cause subjects to recognize the most essential
> part of themselves in the modality of their sexual desire (Florence 1994: 317).

Foucault demonstrated the investment of authority of those who would keep our "identity papers in order." If we have learned anything from Foucault, we have learned first to
look for the genealogy – and therewith the queering – of any putative essence; and second,
to look for the ways in which such queering is resisted by those who want to be able to tell
one true story, whether about rationality, sex, or even God, and make their story compulsory
for all.

Although Foucault thus demonstrates queer strategy, however, he is not consistent in
carrying it through. For example, it is a commonplace of feminist discussion of Foucault
that he writes from an untroubled male perspective and rarely takes into consideration how
differently things might appear if he were to queer gender rather than take unexamined
masculinity as normative (see McNay 1992 and Hekman 1996). I do not mean only that a
woman would write differently, though probably she would. I also mean that the issues
Foucault presents, especially around sexuality and religion, would be contoured differently

if instead of writing as though masculinity were universal or normative he had problematized gender in the way that he problematizes sexuality, say, or madness, or illness. In the first section of this chapter I shall take Jeremy Carrette's collection of Foucault's writings on religion and culture and indicate some of the places where taking gender seriously would give insights beyond what Foucault himself achieved, insights that are crucial for the development of a queer theology (Carrette 1999).

But this, while important, is not new. What I want to go on to suggest is that, just as Foucault is constantly bumping up against gender and yet maintains a blindness about it, so also he keeps bumping up against another category which, like gender, he almost acknowledges but never actually deals with. That category is death. Time after time death crops up in his writings, like an undercurrent with which he is fascinated; and sometimes Foucault seems to recognize that at this point some major work needs to be done. But it is only towards the end of his life, in *The History of Sexuality*, that he begins a project of queering death, destabilizing its conceptual hegemony. I shall discuss this in the second and third sections of this chapter.[1]

Now, what I suggest is that these two lacunae are of a piece; and moreover that they are related to religion in the Western symbolic. Gender and death are linked together in Foucault's thinking, not, I suppose, at any conscious or focused level but as part of the baggage of the Western philosophical and religious tradition. While Foucault challenges many of the assumptions of that tradition and explores many of its silences, he hardly does so in the case of gender, and only begins to in the case of death, but rather for the most part reinscribes their stereotypical identities in his own writings. However, I think that some of the queering strategies that he develops, especially subverting identities by working through a genealogy of what had been taken as a universal and thereby troubling it, would go a long way toward queering his own assumptions on gender and death. Therefore I shall show that although his own stance is from a queer feminist perspective unacceptable, Foucauldian tactics can be fruitfully brought to bear on things which Foucault himself left untroubled.[2]

Gender

To begin with the gratingly obvious, there are in Foucault's writings on religion, as indeed in all his writings, the tell-tale slips and turns of phrase that make it obvious that only a man could have written them, and a man who had not problematized gender or thought much about the power at work in the assumption of masculinity as normative. He writes, for example, of humanism as the "little whore of all thought" (Carrette 1999: 99). He writes of the development of the subject in relation to the government of households, wives, and children: obviously "subject" here is male (Carrette 1999: 154). Could there be a woman subject? How would she develop? Foucault assumes (as has much of Western theology) the connection of the demonic and witchcraft with women, whom "we [who?] were to subject to exclusion" (Carrette 1999: 55). When he contrasts Japanese with Western society he says: "Western man . . . always thought that the essential thing in his life was sexuality. . . . In the West, men, people, individualize themselves" largely in terms of sexuality (Carrette 1999: 129). But who are these "people" who creep into his text as though he is at some level aware of a problem? Does he mean that "men" are the ones who count as normative "people"? Or is he gesturing towards the existence of some people who are not men? But if so, what evidence does Foucault have that such people – presumably women and possibly children

– individualize themselves in terms of their sexuality? Surely until recently only a few privileged women have had any choice about it; and even when we do have choices, perhaps their importance falls otherwise? Foucault may be right, but he has not discussed it, so it is unwarranted on his part just to subsume women, to say nothing of children, as some of these "people." Foucault's assumptions around gender identity, especially masculinity, urgently need queering if they are not to reinscribe male hegemony.

This last example begins to indicate that the problem is deeper than one which a little attention to inclusive language would put right. We can see a bit more of what is at stake when we notice what Foucault says in "A Preface to Transgression" in his discussion (after Bataille) of mysticism. His point is that it was sexuality which gave Christian practice and aspiration a "felicity of expression." He says:

> The proof is its whole tradition of mysticism and spirituality which was incapable of dividing the continuous forms of desire, of rapture, of penetration, of ecstasy, of that outpouring which leaves us [*us?!*] spent: all of these experiences seemed to lead, without interruption or limit, right to the heart of a divine love of which they were both the outpouring and the source returning upon itself (Carrette 1999: 57).

Here is a tangled web of ideas, all of them resting on unproblematized masculinity. First, in this sentence Foucault assimilates the "whole tradition" of Christian mysticism and spirituality to male sexual experience. It is not clear exactly which mystics he had in mind; he does not name any. But brief acquaintance with medieval Christian mysticism makes clear that only a relatively small subsection used the language of sexuality or thought in terms of "erotic" mysticism. Writers ranging from the Pseudo-Dionysius to Julian of Norwich, from Eckhart to the anonymous author of *The Cloud of Unknowing*, use erotic imagery sparingly or not at all, and by no amount of Procrustean stretching could be made to fit Foucault's description (see Jantzen 1995).

Second, the subsection of mystical writers who did use erotic imagery were disproportionately women, including Hadewijch of Anvers, Mechthild of Magdeburg, and Catherine of Siena; and their vocabulary is, predictably, quite different from Foucault's words of "penetration," "ecstasy," and an "outpouring that leaves us spent." They are at least as concerned with tenderness, security, and fidelity as with ecstasy; and they construe love in terms of the unity of the *will* with the divine, and thus in terms of obedience, more than with passion. The one mystic who might spring to mind as fitting Foucault's picture is Teresa of Avila, who does indeed write of the rapture of mystical betrothal and marriage. But even in her case, Foucault's description is much more accurate to the Teresa of Bernini's famous sculpture, in which the angelic messenger is about to pierce her ecstatic body, than it is to the Teresa of her own writings in which the account of this experience occupies only a small proportion of a book devoted to exploring the soul's "interior castle" – a different set of metaphors altogether (Teresa 1946).

The point is that Foucault, by failing to problematize male sexuality, thereby also spreads false generalizations over the tradition of Christian spirituality and with it something so central to Christian thought as what it might mean to experience the love of God. Foucault then proceeds to use his generalizations, as Bataille had done, to reflect on transgression, another central theological theme. So by pulling at the thread of his gender-biased starting point, the whole web begins to unravel. To be fair, I have been quoting from an early essay, written in 1963. In his later work Foucault developed the strategy of genealogy, which when applied to Christian mysticism yields illuminating results.[3] But Foucault himself never made that application, though his late work on Christianity is much more nuanced.

I am, however, not confident that he is any less gender biased in his later writing. In his 1980 essay on "The Beginning of the Hermeneutics of the Self," Foucault describes his concern with "the genealogy of the modern subject" (Carrette 1999: 159) and the various techniques or technologies of the self which must be studied to develop such a genealogy: it is the same theme which occupies the last two volumes of his *History of Sexuality*. He then contrasts the technique of self-examination among pagans and Christians respectively, showing changes in what counted as being a subject. But in his queering of the subject, his refusal of any essential or universal subject, Foucault considers only texts of male subject formation. Does Foucault think women became subjects in the same way – with the con-fession and self-examination and vigilance against fornication that preoccupied the men? Surely not. Does he think there are no sources from which women could be studied? As good an archivist as Foucault would surely know better. Does he think that a genealogy of women subjects is unimportant? What reinscription of patriarchal power is tacitly at work here? Although Foucault is highly effective in queering male subjectivity and sexuality, his very method of doing so assumes and perpetuates masculinist hegemony, and does so in direct appropriation of the history of Christendom. I shall return to this after consideration of my second theme, namely death.

Death

Once one becomes alert to it, it is astonishing how frequently death appears in Foucault's writings, sometimes in its literal meaning, and often as a metaphor or rhetorical trope. Foucault is in this at one with the Western cultural and religious tradition, which, as I have argued elsewhere, is founded and built upon a gesture of death (see Jantzen 1998: 156–70). Indeed, perhaps it is because the Western symbolic is so saturated with death that we are inured to it and at first may hardly notice its prominence in Foucault's writings. But it is there: from the death of God to the death of the subject, from *Death and the Labyrinth* (1963) to death and sacrifice, death and revolt, death and the simulacrum, the mortification of the flesh and the dissection of corpses. Scarcely any of Foucault's writings does not involve an invocation of death, at the very least as a telling metaphor.

Before I proceed to discuss Foucault's treatment of this theme, however, I wish to make clear what I am *not* discussing. I wish to distance myself from the emphasis in James Miller's "psychological life" of Foucault on Foucault's fascination with "limit experiences," whether of sex, mysticism, or death (Miller 1994). Indeed in Miller's book these three seem to be linked in Foucault's psychological make-up, and to lead inexorably to his death from AIDS. Miller's sensationalizing and even pathologizing of Foucault has been thoroughly discredited by both David Halperin (1995) and Jeremy Carrette (2000). In any case, my purpose is not an investi-gation of Foucault's psyche but rather a consideration of the trope of death in his writings, particularly in relation to religion and gender.

Although I believe that there is an unacknowledged link between gender and death in Foucault's writings, I want first to point out a significant difference in his treatment of the two. Foucault, as I have said, never queers gender, or problematizes it at any depth; whereas he does explicitly acknowledge the importance of analyzing death. He writes, for example, of "the relations between experiences like madness, death, crime, sexuality, and several technologies of power" (Carrette 1999: 136, 144): apart from death, this is precisely the list of the genealogies which he developed. There is more than a hint here that although death appears to be a physical and biological fact, it actually has a genealogy too, just as do madness, crime, and sexuality; and that exploring that genealogy would illuminate our situation as we enter postmodernity. In the three volumes of *The History of Sexuality*, Foucault explicitly links changing attitudes to death and immortality with shifts in the genealogy of sex (Foucault 1990–2: I, 135–59; II, 133–9; III, 105–11). I shall return to this. The point here is that Foucault is rather less blind to the significance of death and to its ripeness for queering than he is to gender. However, he never gets around to giving that analysis or genealogy of death; and so, as in the case of gender, a gap is left open which his own strategies can be summoned to help fill.

The significant death, proclaimed by Nietzsche as the defining moment of modernity, is the death of God. This death is related to human subjectivity, sexuality, and transgression. Foucault also links the death of God with the end of philosophy, at least of the kind typified by Hegel; and when he is being careful he points out that the death of God has different meanings for Hegel, Feuerbach, and Nietzsche (Carrette 1999: 85). Of these, it is Nietzsche whose ideas most influence Foucault, especially in connecting the death of God with sexuality, in response to de Sade and Bataille (Carrette 1999: 57). Indeed, in "A Preface to Transgression" Foucault considers how sexuality – in particular sexual transgression, queer sex – reveals what the death of God means.

> What, indeed, is the meaning of the death of God, if not a strange solidarity between the stunning realization of his non-existence and the act that kills him? But what does it mean to kill God if he does not exist, to kill God *who has never existed*? . . . The death of God does not restore us to a limited and positivistic world, but to a world exposed by the experience of its limits, made and unmade by that excess which transgresses it. (Carrette 1999: 59)

Now, if there is one thing we have learned from Foucault's own strategies ever since his *Madness and Civilization* it is to listen to the silences, to be alert to what is not said. As I have already indicated, one of those silences in his own writing is about women; and here again, when he talks of death gender is not scrutinized. Yet obviously it is the *Father* who dies, the *sons* who kill him (who has never existed). It is the *male* subject whose death Foucault elsewhere links with the death of God. And it is *male* sexuality whose excesses and transgressivity exposes all this death, the *male* who is now free, "beyond life and death," to develop an aesthetics of the self (see Bernauer and Mahon 1994: 155).

Where, then, are the women? When we listen carefully, the silence about them is not complete: they are there, but noticing their location changes the rhetorical scene quite dramatically. They are there, first of all, in the scenes of sexual transgression depicted by Bataille (and de Sade) and cited by Foucault; but for the most part they are there as objects for this male sexuality, sometimes for violence and abuse. They are *not* there, however, as subjects. The subject whose death Foucault announces is male. Yet since this death, like the death of God, is evidenced by sexual transgression which involves this abuse – and in the writings of de Sade even the murder – of women, the actual death of women becomes the basis for the rhetorical death of the male subject and the aesthetic actualization of the male self. If Foucault ever wanted a study in silence, projection, and the inscription of power, it is all here in his own writing.

But the female is also present in this scene in another way, for it transpires that it is not just God the Father who is killed but that "God is a whore" (Carrette 1999: 59; citing Bataille). So if God the whore has been killed, and killed through male eroticism, and if it is this which makes for the possibility of a new aesthetics of the male self, surely it is necessary to ask what fantasies are at work here? How will they be enacted on the bodies of actual women? In Western society, where every woman knows herself the potential and too often the actual target of male sexual violence, it will not do to pass these phrases off as only rhetorical. It is necessary first to take seriously how they reinscribe rather than challenge cultural misogyny, and second to queer them so that they can do so no more.

Queering Gender, Queering Death

There is, however, also another silence, even deeper than the silence about women; and that is silence about birth. I am not referring here to motherhood, but to what I have characterized elsewhere as natality: natality as a philosophical category parallel to mortality (see Jantzen 1998). Death, mortality, has been taken as a central category of thought throughout the Western tradition. Plato, at its inception, characterizes a philosopher as someone who makes dying his profession: death will release the soul from the body and will thereby enable the soul to encounter truth in a way that was impossible as long as it was shackled in the body's prisonhouse. At the other end of the tradition we find Heidegger's *Dasein* running ahead toward death: it is death that gives him his authenticity, not in some future-life encounter with truth as in Plato, but in the realization that with death before him, living for "the they" can have no place. The theme of death is also of the first importance for Western Christendom, based as it is on a dying god, the mortification of the flesh, and the hope of a world to come, after the death of the body. Even when Christendom does speak of birth, it is of a new birth, not of man or woman or of the flesh, but of God; a birth, that is, which is ready for death precisely because it has already overcome natality.

With Foucault we find again the instinctive reaching for the category of death that has been so prominent a theme in the Western tradition, death which, as we have seen, is linked in his thought with the objectification of women. The death of the (male) subject is, once again, the means of the liberation of the self, "beyond life and death." But here I suggest that we need to take a leaf from Derrida's book, who showed the importance of investigating, for any theme, whether or not there is something which it simultaneously requires and represses, something both essential and silenced. In Foucault (as in much of the rest of the Western tradition) I suggest that natality operates in just this way. If the male subject dies, when and from whom was he born? If he is capable of mortality, and if that death gives him his liberty to develop an aesthetics of the self, what does – or did – his natality bespeak? What is the origin of the male subject, and by what exclusions did he make modernity his own? And what about God, this Father, this whore, whom the sons kill even though he has never existed? When was he/she born, and from whom?

In Foucault's later writings, especially in the volumes of *The History of Sexuality* and related essays, he does begin to turn slightly in the direction of some of these questions, wanting to investigate the genealogy of the modern subject. Yet as he goes back to antiquity to explore some of the steps in this genealogy, we find again, different though these studies are from his earlier ones, the same entanglements of gender and death. In *The Use of Pleasure*, Foucault considers the relation of sexuality and reproduction to death and immortality in late antiquity, pointing out Plato's view in the *Laws* that (hetero)sexual intercourse and the generation of children was a means of cheating death (Foucault 1990–2: II, 133–9). Then in the development of Christian monasticism Foucault emphasizes the technologies of mortification – literally putting to death – of the flesh, which, he says, is the aim of such Christian practices as examination and obedience. "Mortification is not death, of course, but it is a renunciation of this world and of oneself: a kind of everyday death. A death which is supposed to provide life in another world" (Carrette 1999: 143). Now, what *Foucault* is interested in is how these practices of mortification came to construct a different kind of subject than was found in Greek polity; but what *I* am asking for is a recognition of the ways in which gender and mortality are again entangled while women and natality are made invisible.

Or nearly so: women, to be sure, are again lurking in the margins. In his late essay, "The Hermeneutics of the Self," where Foucault continues his exploration of penance, martyrdom, and mortification, Foucault consistently uses masculine pronouns to refer to the penitent Christian. Yet the one example he gives is that of a woman, Fabiola, who had married a second husband before the first had died, and was obliged to do penance for it (Carrette 1999: 171–2). Again, in "The Battle for Chastity" which continues the theme of the formation of the self in early Christianity, women are portrayed as the source of temptation. Or, more accurately, for the monks struggling for purity it is their memories and fantasies of women, even of their own mothers and sisters, which constitute temptation to fornication; and these memories and fantasies can be eradicated only by severe mortification (Carrette 1999: 189–90). To be sure, these ideas are Foucault's presentation of the thoughts of writers of late antiquity: Jerome, Cassian, Tertullian; they are not meant to represent his own views. Yet he uses them to develop a genealogy of the subject, not remarking that it is the *male* subject only who could be thus constituted – Fabiola notwithstanding – and only by the objectification of women and by the association of women with death.

But the problem is even deeper than that. As Foucault presents it – and I think that at least in broad terms he is right – subjectivity in Western Christendom has indeed been constituted by the effort to escape from the flesh. The salvation of the soul requires the mortification of the flesh. But Foucault does not ask why this should be so, or what it betokens. When we do ask that question, it is clear that we are back with the strong conceptual links between women, the body, and sexuality, while maleness is linked with reason, the soul, and God. To be born of woman is to be conceived in sin and born with a sinful body unto death. Salvation (for men) depends upon being born again of the spirit, mastering and mortifying the flesh, dying to the sinful body and all that is linked with it. It is true that in Christendom from its inception women also could be saved (though Foucault does not comment on it) but only by becoming "honorary men," raised above their gender (see Jantzen 1995: 26–58).

Now, Foucault is exhuming the genealogy of the subject, not praising it; and there is no need to think that he especially liked the ways in which gender played itself out in the Western tradition. Indeed in his writings on the death of the subject we might have looked for the repudiation or queering of these ideas of gender and death which have been so strongly formative of Western religion and Western attitudes to sexuality. And we do find hints towards such queering. As I have already said, Foucault finds in transgression and excess the liberation from the dead hand of the God in whose name so much mortification and guilt had been purveyed. But as I have also said, that excess, as presented, is often at the expense of women, sometimes violent, never seriously considering women as subjects. Thus from first to last Foucault does not challenge the marginalization or abuse of women, does not queer gender or death, and by his silence reinscribes the hegemony of their stereotypes.

"Promising Ashes"

Yet although there is much in Foucault's writings that is unacceptable from a queer feminist perspective, I also find in them resources and strategies that can take us forward. It is after all Foucault who has, perhaps more than anyone else, fostered the tactic of listening to that which has been silenced and thus retrieving the marginalized past. It is Foucault whose example of painstaking archival research has shown just how illuminating the development of a genealogy can be, just how unsettling to our "certitudes and dogmatism" it can be to expose "the history of various forms of rationality" (Carrette 1999: 151). Discovering such a history unsettles the notion that the categories of our conceptual symbolic are fixed essences. It shows them, rather, as social constructions, built up of many layers of sedimentation, but not inevitable or rooted in "nature." By such a strategy of liberating ourselves from fixed ideas, by queering the categories of our thought, it is possible to move to new and more creative ways of looking at our selfhood, finding queer openings.

Feminist writers have been using Foucauldian strategies in this way to queer gender. Judith Butler, for example, in *Gender Trouble*, which has become a manifesto for queer theory, shows how both sex and gender are inscribed on the body by endlessly repeated ascriptions and performances. They are not natural or biological essences. The hegemony of normative heterosexuality, which presents itself as "natural" or as a fixed essence, is thus exposed as a regulatory fiction. Thus gender can be troubled, and the oppressive heterosexual matrix revealed to be the technology of power that it is. Though Butler in many particulars takes issue with Foucault, not least with the implicit misogyny in his representations of women, her highly significant and influential work in queering gender is unthinkable without him.

I suggest that an even more radical destabilization of hegemonic categories can be brought about by queering death. Foucault, as I have said, hints at the need for a genealogy of death. Such a genealogy would show that while death, like sex, is at one level a physical reality, it is no more simply "natural" or part of a biological essence than sex is. Rather, it is multiply inscribed, its meanings and implications sedimented into our subjectivities. The first premise of many a logic lesson, "All men are mortal," is taken to be a platitude; but it is a platitude which preoccupies Western culture and saturates our symbolic structure. However, once we note that the category of death, and indeed what it means to be mortal, has a genealogy, this insight queers death and reveals the heavy regulatory hand that preoccupation with salvation, mortification, other worlds and immortality has laid upon us, especially through Western Christendom. This genealogy remains to be written; but it is not difficult to discern some of its contours, from Plato's prisonhouse of the soul and the Christendom of late antiquity to the medieval emphasis on the mortification of the flesh and the preoccupation with heaven, hell, and the pains of purgatory, to the modern versions of death and other worlds ranging from colonial conquest and space exploration to cyberspace.

Most particularly, such a genealogy allows for new openings, openings which I have called natality. It is after all not in virtue of our mortality but of our natality that we are capable of new beginnings. Foucault in his efforts towards and aesthetics of the self after the death of God and the subject makes much of liberty, transgression, excess; but as we have seen, he locates it with de Sade in sexual practices which involve the degradation of women. With the queering of mortality and the opening of a category of natality as a locus of freedom and new possibility, I suggest that an aesthetic of the self need not be located in oppression. To be a natal is to be one who has come into new life, one who has openings for growth and flourishing. The flourishing of natals depends on care for one another, and on justice in the distribution of material and social goods. As I have argued elsewhere, it is different in its emphasis than is a symbolic of salvation (Jantzen 1998: 171–203). Rather than looking to immortality or to a life after death it looks to the conditions of life on this earth. Rather than depending on a heroic savior coming to the rescue, it emerges as gradual growth, as a plant grows and flourishes from within, drawing on its environment for its resources. Thus the flourishing of natals is not solitary, as death is, but is part of a web of life. An aesthetics of the self that looks for new possibilities of freedom and beauty and mutuality is better signified, I suggest, in a symbolic of natality opened out by a queering of gender and death, than in Foucault's fixation on mortification, mortality, and masculinity. As with the growth of a plant, there can be no fixed certainties, nor is there any uniform pattern or hegemonic ideal; but the conditions of flourishing can be ascertained.

The development of such a queer aesthetics of the self is opened by Foucault's strategies of displacing hegemonies by genealogies, even if he did not always carry them through himself. As he said, it is "a simple choice, but a difficult work. It is always necessary to watch out for something, a little beneath history, that breaks with it, that agitates it; it is necessary to look, a little behind politics, for that which ought to limit it, unconditionally" (Carrette 1999: 134). And perhaps it is also necessary to look a little beyond Foucault, at genealogies that queer gender and death, in order to sweep up these "promising ashes" (Carrette 1999: 60) and breathe into them a queer language of life.

Notes

1   I am indebted in this to Bernauer and Mahon (1994), though I differ from them in some respects.
2   It will be obvious to anyone who knows her work that my vocabulary and to some extent my strategy is indebted to Judith Butler (1999).
3   I am heavily dependent upon Foucault's strategy in Jantzen (1995), which would not be thinkable without it.

Chapter 17

Antimarriage

Paul Fletcher

As if the laws of nature to which love submits were not more tyrannical and more odious than the laws of society! (Berl 1929: 404; cited in Benjamin 1999: 493)

In his *Commentary on the Epistle to the Romans*, Origen attempts, following Paul's bidding in Romans 5.14, to describe the relationship between Adam's sin and the transgressions of his descendants. Central to the description that Origen offers is the question of how Adam's sin came to be borne by all his progeny when many of his children's transgressions are very different in type and character from that primary offense. Origen's explanation is that even while Adam enjoyed the Garden of Eden all his descendants subsisted in his loins.

> And all men who were with him, or rather in him, were expelled from paradise when he was himself driven out from there; and through him the death which had come to him from the transgression consequently passed through to them as well, who were dwelling in his loins; and therefore the Apostle rightly says, "For as in Adam all die, so also in Christ all will be made alive [I Corinthians 15.22]." (Origen 2001: 311)

Sin is disseminated from the loins of Adam and it is only through the refusal of the promptings of the loins that Origen believes the soul can advance to spiritual purity. Sex in Origen's view distributes sin and so it was crucial that the second Adam was conceived without the medium of human seed. There is no hesitation in Origen's portrayal of Adam's bequest to link sex with heredity and reproduction, a fact confirmed by his assertion that sexual relations within marriage are for procreation rather than pleasure. Sex, in this account, has a *natural* role that is to be radically distinguished from its erotic lure.

At the beginning of the twenty-first century, it is obvious that the nature of sex, and especially the partition between nature and *eros*, is not only modified but fundamentally transformed. Sex is not what it used to be! The availability of relatively cheap and effective contraception has been followed by the technical and technological unhinging of sex from an economy of fecundity and reproduction, a process that is intensified with the prospect of techniques of genetic cloning and practices of pleasure (such as teledildonics – see C. Gray 2001: 152) that are a part of the discourse of the present as well as the future. Sex has been unhinged from its reproductive, procreative role and now serves a very different economy of desire. Sex has been socially appropriated for the body and its pleasures and has been removed from the public realm of marriage, state, and church. Sex is no longer about the future – children, security, continuity – but about "experience."

Mark Ravenhill's play, *Shopping and Fucking* (1996), makes this unsettlingly clear. In the context of late-capitalism, *eros* is a figure of consumption (shopping) and the body is a commodity (for exchange at a price). The only route to authentic "experience," echoing Georges

Bataille, is to take that same body to the limit of value, to move beyond a restricted economy of discontinuity and immanent exchange and to transcend the fiscal body in a sacrificial body in which pleasure and destruction, *eros* and *thanatos*, are indistinguishable. But the promise of the limit is never fulfilled and a return to restricted economies of utility and value is always inevitable; life at the edge is only able to realize an experience that is, as it were, Bataille-lite.

The play concerns the (sexual, retail, and narcotic) consumption of three twenty-some-things – Mark, Robbie, and Lulu – and details their precarious involvement with a rent boy, Gary, and a businessman, Brian. While the cast spend an inordinate amount of time consuming a variety of bodies, the nihilism of measurement, utility, and value are constantly disclosed: "If we do anything, it's got to mean nothing"; "Civilisation is money and money is civilisation"; "Are there any feelings left?"

Unsurprisingly, Ravenhill's play attracted a tremendous amount of critical attention and discussion (not least for its title). The right-wing press went into paroxysms of righteous distress when the play opened in 1996 and the (then) UK Minister for Education highlighted the play as an example of moral degeneration. Amid realizations that the "new realism" represented by this play disclosed something rather profound – "What makes this play so dangerous to closed minds is its unnerving knack of opening our eyes to the horrors of our daily lives" (*Sunday Express*) – was the usual condemnation of explicit sexual performativity – "It wallows in the conditions it describes" (*Sunday Telegraph*). Missing from the critical notices, however, was an analysis of the kind of subjects we – who daily participate in a new rendition of the script – have become in consumptive, and I use the word advisedly, capitalist cultures.[1] The play discloses something more profound than a worldview in which we clamor after the momentary *jouissance* available in a tub of Häagen-Dazs, impressed on my Nike™ sneakers or savored in an anonymous blowjob. We are confronted with the sublation and sublimation of identity in a context where the disarticulation of habitus, authority, and tradition leave only an overburdened reflexivity and a quest for the affect. This modification of identity reaches its apotheosis with the triumph of fantasy over the "real."[2] Hence, pornographic material in which the subject looks into the camera and meets the gaze of the voyeur stimulates in a manner that is dependent on the "realism" of a performance that, *in truth*, only exhibits that the act of stimulation is nothing but simulation (Agamben 2000: 94). Or, to put it in less precious terms, sex has become a marker of the loss of experience: sex has become a thing like every marketed thing, something to want when you do not possess it and not to want when you do. This thoroughgoing commodification of love, pleasure, and eroticism cul-minates in the erosion of the significance of the body:

> Never has the human body – above all the female body – been so massively manipulated as today and, so to speak, imagined from top to bottom by the techniques of advertising and commodity production: The opacity of sexual differences has been belied by the transsexual body; the incommunicable foreignness of the singular *physis* has been abolished by its mediatization as spectacle; the mortality of the organic body has been put in question by its traffic with the body without organs of commodities; the intimacy of erotic life has been refuted by pornography (Agamben 1993: 49–50).

And so the church must respond to the "thinning out" of the body politic, the disappearance of the body as the *imago dei* and the compartmentalization of the ecclesiastical body in matters sexual (and much besides). The thrust of this chapter, however, is that the church responds as a micro-fascist organization in order to cure its pain and does so by refusing *eros* and embracing a vapid and lifeless moralism. The church performs the role of a modern sarcophagus that harbors the ideology of moral values and seems to do little more than reflect the so-called ethical positions – particularly with regard to sex – of the moralistic media commentators who despise pluralism and espouse a myopic view of desire, relationality, and fecundity. Nevertheless, it is not simply the church that has failed. In Georges Bataille's *Theory of Religion*, *eros* and *thanatos* converge, as it were, in the quest for a lost intimacy with, and immediacy of, a lost animality (Bataille 1962: 90). The individual disconnection of subjects and the division of the sacred and the profane that is characteristic of advanced human societies is overcome in the convulsions of sacrificial violence and orgasm.

> The act of violence that deprives the creature of its limited particularity and bestows on it the limitless, infinite nature of sacred things is with its profound logic an intentional one. It is intentional like the act of the man who lays bare, desires and wants to penetrate his victim. The lover strips the beloved of her identity no less than the bloodstained priest his human or animal victim. With her modesty she loses the firm barrier that once separated her from others and made her impenetrable. (Bataille 1962: 90)

Bataille's text attempts to uncover an originary economy of unity and continuity that is only attained through violence and the overcoming or, more accurately, the dissolution of subjectivity. This alternative economy attempts to harness and utilize heterogeneous energies, what Bataille calls nonproductive expenditure (*dépense*), in a quest of freedom from utility and commodification (Bataille 1985: 116–20). Sacrifice reintegrates *eros* and nature through *thanatos*.

Unfortunately, this sacrificial vision has itself been inhabited by the logic of consumption as Ravenhill's play reveals. Bodies, clothes, and commodities of all kinds are pretty useless but utility is not the point. Branding, image, and the ubiquity of the product are more urgently sought than profit itself. Hence, the salvific perversion of a sacrificial economy has become the norm. But we know all this! More shocking is the fact that the dominance of an ideology of moral values that dictates ecclesiastical responses to the signs of the times is equally a normalization of perversion. The fantasy of the church, which opposes – though underpins – the fantasy of consumption, is for a disciplinary logic predicated on the moral law. Whereas in consumer societies anxiety is engendered by too much freedom, the sexual ethics of the Christian churches create a body that is rigidly codified in a manner that is a perversion of its scriptural and doctrinal traditions. What is often neglected by theologians is the fact that the declaration of the freedom to enjoy that is the major characteristic and claim of late-capital feeds off the injunction to desist that is so typical of Christian sexual ethics. The law engenders the desire to transgress and so constitutes the ground of capitalistic enjoyment. Capitalism is strangely parasitic upon the moralism of a divinely authorized body in order to perpetuate the illusion that its vacant promises are really "cutting-edge" and beyond the norm. Concomitantly, Christian practice has become strangely parasitic upon capital. Yet again, it is popular visual culture that renders this "double bind" most transparent.

Going Underground

In David Fincher's highly successful adaptation of Chuck Palahniuk's cult novel, *Fight Club* (1992) the viewer is presented with an unwittingly prescient parable for the church of the twenty-first century. The film interrogates the transmutations of desire in the context of late-capital, and the manner in which this culture of desiring consumption is also a culture of death. Released in 1999, *Fight Club* begins with the narrator, possibly named Jack, sitting in a chair with a gun in his mouth in a building that is about to explode. He begins to recall the events that have brought him to this point: that of facing his own destruction as well as that of the many buildings that surround his high-rise vista. "Two minutes to go and I'm wondering how I got here." This beginning that is the end allows "Jack" to take us to a point in his life many months before.

He lives in an unnamed American city, has a decently paid job as an accident investigator for an insurance firm and a fashionable apartment that is a simulacrum of an IKEA catalogue. "I had become a slave to the IKEA nesting instinct. If I saw something like the clever Njurunda coffee tables in the shape of a lime green Yin and an orange Yang . . . I had to have it." And this thirst for lifestyle-simulation mirrors the thirst for sexual stimulation: "We used to read pornography. Now it was the Horchow Collection." "Jack's" life is meaningless, empty and superficial and the somnambulistic status of this life is borne corporeally. "Jack" cannot sleep. He goes to see his doctor and requests sleeping pills but the unsympathetic physician suggests that he attend a testicular-cancer support group to find out "what real pain is." So Jack has his first taste of group therapy, the emotion, the sharing, and the tactility. In becoming a cuddle-junkie, and finding a whole array of supportive contexts – the sickle-cell anemia support group, the "Free and Clear" group, the prostate cancer group, and so on – "Jack" finds freedom in the performance of the loss of hope that is central to each of these meetings. Jack is cured: "Babies don't sleep this well." Cured, that is, until he is confronted with another "tourist" or faker, Marla Singer, whose presence at these sessions brings "Jack's" own deceit into focus. Although they attend meetings for different reasons (Marla says they are "cheaper than a movie and there's free coffee"), they agree, at "Jack's" insistence, to split the various groups between them. Nevertheless, "Jack" has returned to the life of the insomniac because "she" has ruined everything.

Redemption comes twice for "Jack." On a plane, he meets Tyler Durden, a man who is even more cynical than "Jack," who makes a living from selling soap to high-class cosmetic retailers. This chance meeting changes "Jack's" life and sets in motion the transformation of his emotional and material circumstances. When his apartment is destroyed after a (seemingly) accidental explosion, "Jack" moves in with Tyler in the latter's dilapidated house on the margins of an industrial wasteland. This arrangement is, however, conditional. Tyler offers hospitality on the basis that "Jack" hits him. Outside a bar, the two men beat each other up for amusement. Feeding off the pleasure of this violent encounter they start "Fight Club," a secret society that meets in the underground of the city and exists to provide men with the authenticity and reality of experience: they beat each other to pulp. This is no gentlemen's club and the fighting relies on a completely different rationale than the Queensberry rules. But there are rules:

> The first rule of fight club is – you don't talk about fight club. The second rule of fight club is – you don't talk about fight club. The third rule in fight club is – when

someone says "stop" or goes limp, the fight is over. The fourth rule is – only two guys to a fight. Fifth rule – one fight at a time. Sixth rule – no shirts or shoes. Seventh rule – fights go on as long as they have to. And the eighth rule of fight club is – if this is your first night, you *have* to fight.

Everything is going well for "Jack"; he is sleeping, does not care about work, material possessions, or status. Then Marla returns to the fray. She calls "Jack" after taking an overdose. Although "Jack" refuses to go to her rescue, Tyler saves her life by embarking on a sexual relationship with her and thus keeping her awake all night. "Jack" is disgusted and, whenever he sees Marla in the house, treats her with disdain. Although he despises Tyler's relationship with Marla, "Jack" is still beholden to Tyler and his amazing ability to undermine consumer culture and the conventions of capital. Tyler reveals that his soap is made from human fat stolen from liposuction clinics. "From the asses and thighs of rich women, paydirt." But the soap-making process also reveals an ingredient that Tyler will put to work – glycerine.

In the meantime, fight clubs have sprung up all over the country. Out of them Tyler starts "Project Mayhem," a revolutionary organization that thrives on petty vandalistic acts that eventually mutate into terrorist attacks against major corporations and big business. During one mission, a member of Project Mayhem, Bob, is shot and killed by the police. "Jack" is horrified. Bob was the first person that he met at his testicular-cancer support group and his death deeply affects "Jack" who now wants to stop Project Mayhem's activities. Tyler Durden, though, has disappeared.

In order to find him, "Jack" criss-crosses the country following Tyler's footsteps from the airline ticket stubs he had left behind. As he does so, he comes across numerous fight clubs, the members of which believe *he* is Tyler Durden. Realizing that they are right, a fact confirmed by Marla, "Jack" attempts to foil Tyler's plans to blow up a number of skyscrapers (the homes of various credit card companies) but is thwarted by Tyler. In the climax to the film, "Jack" momentarily masters his schizophrenia and shoots himself in the head, only wounding his own body but "killing" his alter ego. "Jack," and Marla, who has been returned to him by the members of Project Mayhem, hold hands as the spectacle begins and the explosions bring down the buildings around them.

Fight Club offers an engaging and thoughtful analysis of the manner in which capital, and the empty and somnambulistic subjectivities it engenders, might be rejected and resisted. In the face of the loss of experience an underground world of embodied, corporate *pathos* is performed and celebrated. This martial dramaturgy is at once both a lament for, and a critique of, the atomization and superficiality of those other corporate existences that define the lives of subjects in so-called advanced Western societies: branding, consumption, and image. But fight clubs are nothing more than a subterranean enactment of the perversion of the new moralism of late capital that takes as its slogan "you are what you consume" and which refuses the establishment or repetition of any acquired habits. The danger with this underground rejoinder lies in the possibility of the normalization of perversion when Fight Club becomes a project. In the filmic text this is exactly what happens as the micro-fascist "Project Mayhem" emerges from the quest for the real, the true, and the certain.[3] Micro-fascist in its logic, "Project Mayhem" does little more than replay, in a different key, the antinomian and anomic character of late capital. This project of resistance rejects any law or tradition (bar those that are constructed within) and instead measures its value and efficacy on the basis of Romantic tropes such as brotherhood, exclusivity with regard to experience, and the purity of identity.

For the Christian churches today, it is both right and proper to offer a critical interrogation of the logic of late capital and to provide and promote an alternative economy of goods, practices, and desires. Nevertheless, the constant temptation for the church is to respond to the transformation of identities, practices, and values in a manner that is analogous to *Fight Club*. The church is in a crisis of its own making. It responds to the proliferation of experiences and promises with its own fantastic promise of an exclusive experience. Take the Alpha course, a full length commercial for a product that will fill your Jesus-shaped hole, a true experience of the fullness of self that sure beats MacDonald's promise to fill your burger-shaped hole (and without the calories). Christianity-lite sees the Scriptures as a way to out-do the Ikea experience and if pornography deludes us with the fantasy of the eternal erection then Christianity offers something even better – eternal resurrection. Ironically, the performagraphic logic of the church seems to change when we turn to sex. Here the church responds to the proliferation of discourses surrounding sex with all the puritanical zeal of an underground sect that seeks to promote the truth. Yet, for the most part, Christian commentators are doing little more than occupying and enjoying the very space that was bequeathed to the church with the rise of modernity. When it comes to sex, Christians (especially evangelicals) expound a sophisticated moral code that is ostensibly biblical in tone and content. Yet, as any reading of the biblical data on sex and sexuality will demonstrate, the creation of a legalistic framework that curtails the flights of *eros* is both a refusal of the multidimensional character of scriptural narrative and a blindness to the crucial influence of a peculiarly modern conflation of religion and morality. As a consequence, Christian reflection on sex tends towards a normalization of a modern perversion of Christianity, one that is micro-fascistic in its emphasis on marriage as the exclusive locale for the practice of erotic performance.

The Conjugal Catacomb

As with *Fight Club*, the Christian churches have moved into the underground as a response to the transformation of eroticism. The catacombs that have been erected – those subterranean tombs – serve only one purpose. It is there that *eros* is made safe through an unholy marriage with the thanatological criteria of the ideology of morality. The proclamation of a new creation becomes little more than a pious platitude and the eschatological ethic of love is definitively eschewed in the assertion of a legalism that is, at the same time, a renunciation of the messianic intention of the church. In the latter's wake we see a Christianity that is domesticated and which refuses to confront the difficulty of the (moral) law and its significance for Christian sexual practices.

Only the persisting dominance of this revocation of the messianic imperative makes us misread the significance of one of the most sustained reflections on marriage in the New Testament. In 1 Corinthians 7, Paul outlines an understanding of marriage from the perspective of one who, according to Peter Brown, "lived his life poised between revelation and resurrection" (P. Brown 1988: 46). Paul describes how the Christian is to live in the between-time, the "time that remains," and how the appropriate *habitus* might be constituted in a messianic time that is, strictly speaking, neither *chronos* nor *kairos*. The overcoming of the law, Paul suggests, demands a radically different rehearsal of what has, and is to, come: "I mean, brethren, the appointed time (*kairos*) has grown very short; from now on, let those who have wives live as though they had none, and those who mourn as though they were not mourning, and those who rejoice as though they were not rejoicing, and those who buy as though they had no goods, and those who deal with the world as though they had no dealings with it. For the form of this world is passing away" (1 Corinthians 7.29–31). This Pauline text consistently repeats a specific motif of the negation of a given historical nature of things in order to set up the possibility of living in the time that remains, a motif that signifies the arrival of a very different temporality to historical time. That motif, repeated five times in this short text, is *hōs mē*, "as if not." It signifies a radical reconstitution of the nature of life, because its *telos* in the wake of the risen Christ is the new creation, and daringly questions the state and status of the order of things, whether economic or affective but especially sexual.

It is this questioning of the *status quo* – whether of the law or of the conventions of the Greco-Roman household – that is forsaken in the modern incarceration of erotic practices. Paul does not compartmentalize eroticism but establishes it within a wider economy of desire, whether for power, status or mammon. Consequently, later on in the same chapter of his epistle, he suggests that "the married man is anxious about worldly affairs, how to please his wife, and he is divided" (1 Corinthians 7.33–4). This bold assertion leads Kurt Niederwimmer to propose that the Pauline uneasiness with conjugal relations, based on a disavowal of their immanent ends, results in an identification of the married person as "half-Christian" (Niederwimmer 1975: 114; cited in Brown 1988: 56). This is not an *ethos* that the moralistic Christian churches of late modernity would want to embrace. Yet the central thematic that is interrogated in Paul's discussion of the problematic status of marriage is that of the end of desire. Desire here is not restricted to any specific characteristics of sexual desire but is a wider erotic category that includes idolatry and immorality more generally and which Paul calls *porneia* (see 1 Corinthians 6.13; 7.2). Consequently, if marriage has any role in the Pauline scheme of (messianic) things, it is little more than a mechanism that guards against the desire for worldly things, a desire that must be discharged from sexual relations within marriage as well as without (Martin 1997: 202). For the churches today, Paul's view of marriage is neglected, even elided, because it threatens the basis of the modern morality that is so resolutely embraced and propounded.[4]

The Economy of Matrimony

The renunciation of the eschatological imperative in Christian thought and practice is consummated in the modern period.[5] It is nevertheless necessary to realize that this transformation of the character of Christianity did not arise through a straightforward rejection of eschatology. Rather, the doctrinal and conceptual territory of eschatology was "reoccupied," to use Hans Blumenberg's term, by the promises of human rationality, techno-scientific progress and the socio-political possibilities that coincided with the extraordinary pretensions of an enlightened "Man" who believed in the perfectibility of the world through the principles of reason:

> Such is therefore the work of the good principle – unnoticed to human eye yet constantly advancing – in erecting a power and a kingdom for itself within the human race, in the form of a community according to the laws of virtue that proclaims the victory over evil and, under its dominion, assures the world of an eternal peace. (Kant 1996a: 153)

Kant's claim, quite remarkable in tone and uncompromising in its expectancy, comes in the seventh, and concluding, section of the third part of his *Religion* book which is entitled

"The Gradual Transition of Ecclesiastic Faith Toward the Exclusive Sovereignty of Pure Religious Faith in the Coming Kingdom." Pure religious faith is not simply concerned with an inner morality but with the juridical framework within which, and through which, peaceable living is engendered and the kingdom might be realized. The disruption of the law that is the sign of the immanent kingdom in Paul's messianic proclamation is wholly dismissed in this concrete establishment of a juridical virtue and an immanent kingdom of goods. Indeed, as Alain Badiou puts it, what is original in the Pauline *non*economy of grace is that it opposes "law insofar as it is what comes *without being due*" (Badiou 1997: 81). Kant, in contrast, requires a measurable duty that economizes on the need for grace. It is impossible to overemphasize the degree to which the Kantian vision of the kingdom is antithetical to a Pauline anticipation that requires not duty but grace of an immeasurable kind.

Unsurprisingly, the legalistic realization of eschatology undertaken by Kant is most fully clarified in his reflections on sexual economy. The law that Paul renders problematic is a central element of the true and rational taxonomy of the human as good. Consequently, "if a man and a woman want to enjoy each other's sexual attributes they must necessarily marry, and this is necessary in accordance with pure reason's laws of right" (Kant 1996b: 62). Only in the context of right, contract and a juridical morality can "Man" be saved from the destruction of his selfhood:

> For the natural use that one sex makes of the other's sexual organs is *enjoyment*, for which one gives itself up to the other. In this act a human being makes himself into a thing, which conflicts with the right of humanity in his own person. There is only one condition under which this is possible: that while one person is acquired by the other *as if it were a thing*, the one who is acquired acquires the other in turn; for in this way each reclaims itself and restores its personality. But acquiring a human being is at the same time acquiring the whole person, since a person is an absolute unity. Hence it is not only admissible for the sexes to surrender and to accept each other for enjoyment under the condition of marriage, but it is possible for them to do so *only* under this condition. (Kant 1996b: 62)[6]

The ideology of morality in practice demands a reciprocal possession that itself requires the sovereignty of the self and the rejection of various modes of desire. Desire that rules the body – be it desire for intimacy, the divine, or erotic enjoyment – can only *rightfully* occur once it is mastered by the law and occurs within the parameters of the contractual, juridical agreement that we call marriage.[7] Once again, Kant accounts for subjectivity and meaning in a manner that is both totalizing and evaluative. While Paul revokes the mastery of desire because of a radical shift in the order of things that is realized in the resurrected Christ, Kant is intent on divinizing order *qua* order in moral terms. It is this ideology that dominates the social and theological teaching of contemporary Christianity, an ideology that achieves its force in the refusal of the Messiah and that provides the very condition of desirability of the enjoyment it rejects.

More seriously, however, the moral evaluation of sexual desire neglects the kind of subjects that we have become, a failing that it shares with the type of sacrificial economy that capital itself has acquired. Late-modern subjects inhabit the limbo that is situated between the moral and the sacrificial, between the absolutely secured subject and the wholly annihilated self. Capital and the church provide the (necessarily) incongruous backdrops for this vapid drama in a perverse symbiosis that engenders debt and guilt in equal measure. There is no longer a specifically human *eros*, yearning for love, politics and ultimately God that drives and fuels existence towards its *telos*. In its wake comes a sentient desire that is fundamentally quiescent and static in character.

In effect, the status of our desiring, and its consequences, was revealed by Alexandre Kojève in a short lecture on Hegel in December 1937. This lecture shocked the champion of the redemptive character of sacrifice, Georges Bataille, because in it Kojève claims that the sacrificial ends in a "'beautiful death' but death just the same: total, definitive failure" (Kojève 1988: 89). And Kantian morality is rejected because it fails in a different manner: it is "utter inactivity . . . hence a Nothingness" (Kojève 1988: 87). In both these cases Kojève is repudiating economies. In the case of Kant, the economy of right and value measures everything against the *status quo*. In the economy of violent transgression in Bataille, everything is measured in relation to its negation. Neither perspective will suffice in the face of a contemporary context that Kojève outlined in detail during the 1930s.

Post-historical Sex

Between 1933 and 1939 Kojève lectured on Hegel at the Ecole Pratique des Hautes Etudes in Paris (Kojève 1947).[8] Kojève placed the dialectic of Master and Slave at the center of, and as the key to understanding, what he considered to be the most significant of the *"écrits hégéliens,"* the *Phenomenology of Spirit*. It is the fight for recognition that is essential to becoming a self – an "I" (Kojève 1980: 7). Kojève, like Hegel (1977: 109–10), posited a distinction between the desire to fulfill instinctual needs or "appetites" and a higher Desire. This higher Desire *is* human desire and must win out over the purely animal desire. Human Desire, however, is not, as is animal desire, simply instinctual:

> Desire is human only if the one desires, not the body, but the Desire of the other; if he wants "to possess" or "to assimilate" the Desire taken as Desire – that is to say, if he wants to be "desired" or "loved", or, rather, "recognised" in his human value, in his reality as a human individual. (Kojève 1980: 6)

This "recognition" is not simply a matter of some supplementary status that sorts the masters from the slaves – it is an essential characteristic of human identity. As Kojève declares, "the human being is *formed* only in terms of a Desire directed towards another Desire, that is – finally – in terms of a desire for recognition" (Kojève 1980: 7; my italics). Thus Kojève, in positing the fight for recognition as pivotal, proposes a reading of the *Phenomenology* in which we are presented with an "account of universal history in which bloody strife – and not 'reason' – is responsible for the progress towards the happy conclusion" (Descombes 1980: 13). The conclusion being, of course, Absolute Knowledge and the End of History. Kojève bequeathed to his readers *"a terrorist conception of history"* (Descombes 1980: 14). For Desire to be Desire, then, *thanatos* must be its precondition in an economy of becoming that is sacrificial and where death only has meaning to the extent that its meaninglessness is wagered.

While commentators and critics have repeatedly emphasized this violent element of Kojève's legacy, there is an often-ignored factor that is central to the realization of the consummation of desire: happiness *is* the ultimate goal of history, conflict, and Man. This point is of the utmost importance not least because the once-certain distinction between human and animal disappears on reaching happiness – the End of History – and desire is once again transformed.

The *Selbst* – that is, Man properly so-called or the free Individual, *is* Time; and Time is History, and *only* History. . . . And Man is essentially *Negativity*, for Time is *Becoming* – that is, the *annihilation* of Being or Space. Therefore Man is a Nothingness that nihilates and that preserves itself in (spatial) Being only by *negating* being, this Negation being Action. Now, if Man is Negativity – that is, Time – he is not eternal. He is born and he dies as Man. He is *"das Negative seiner selbst,"* Hegel says. And we know what that means: Man overcomes himself as Action (or *Selbst*) by ceasing to *oppose* himself to the World, after creating in it the universal and homogeneous State; or to put it otherwise, on the cognitive level: Man overcomes himself as *Error* (or "Subject" *opposed* to the Object) after creating the Truth of "Science." (Kojève 1980: 159–60)

The ends of Man can be discerned with the coming of the "universal and homogeneous state" and the closure of ideology. At this point, when Man is no longer, "life is purely biological" (Kojève 1947: 387). Man is once again pure animality and, in a footnote to the first edition of his *Introduction* in 1947, Kojève confirms and affirms this *telos* of the human: Man becomes an animal who is "in *harmony* with Nature or given Being" (Kojève 1980: 158 n. 6). Although this "annihilation of Man" brings about the end of philosophy and wisdom, there is sufficient consolation in this "state" of being animal: "art, love, play, etc., etc." (Kojève 1980: 159 n. 6). Nevertheless, Kojève's vision is fundamentally horrific: human life has become what we might call "lifestyle as biopolitics," where biopolitics is the constitution of life as little more than "birth, death, production, illness, and so on" (Foucault 2003: 243). Mere survival of the flesh is the logic of the biopolitical era in which traditional sovereign power – to make die and let live – has been superseded by biopower – to make live and let die (Foucault 2003: 241).

In the second edition of his *Introduction à la lecture de Hegel* (1959), Kojève returned to this biopolitical footnote with a change of mind. The animality of the post-historical human that is so persuasively delineated in the first edition is abandoned in the midst of a complete reappraisal of a culture after History.

If Man becomes an animal again, his acts, his loves, and his play must also become purely "natural" again. Hence it would have to be admitted that after the end of History, men would construct their edifices and works of art as birds build their nests and spiders spin their webs, would perform musical concerts after the fashion of frogs and cicadas, would play like young animals, and would indulge in love like adult beasts. But one cannot then say that all this "makes Man *happy*." One would have to say that post-historical animals of the species *Homo sapiens* (which would live amidst abundance and complete security) will be *content* as a result of their artistic, erotic, and playful behaviour, inasmuch as, by definition, they will be contented with it. But there is more. "The *definitive annihilation* of Man *properly so-called*" also means the definitive disappearance of human Discourse (*Logos*) in the strict sense. Animals of the species *Homo sapiens* would react by conditioned reflexes to vocal signals or sign "language," and thus their so-called "discourses" would be like what is supposed to be the "language" of bees. What would disappear, then, is not only Philosophy or the search for discursive Wisdom, but also that Wisdom itself. For in these post-historical animals, there would no longer be any "[discursive] understanding of the World and of self." (Kojève 1980: 159–60 n. 6)

In the wake of pure animality comes pure formalism and the refusal of reflexivity – Japanese aristocratic snobbery is the exemplar of post-History. But Kojève is being disingenuous here. Animal desire, as the merely sentient condition of human desire, is characterized by Kojève as lacking the essential reflexivity or ability to disquiet Man (Kojève 1980: 3–4). This, in turn, remains the very status of post-historical humanity even in its revision as formalism (Kojève 1947: 387). Notwithstanding his reservations, Kojève cannot escape the biopolitical implications of his analysis – political action is no longer possible or commendable and desire is always aligned to the mores of the "universal state" in which the human is a refugee (Kojève 1947: 387). The universal state is now realized as global liberal governance and the latter is enforced, for the most part, by multinational corporations and transnational agencies.

The consequences, for a Christian eroticism, of the ascendancy of constructs of being that are inert in the *civitas terrana* are manifold. In the post-historical, biopolitical context of the end of the Human, desire is essentially a timeless and goal-less satedness that gives birth to the dreamy, technological practices of the inhabitants of late-capitalist societies. The *nature* of the human, as with all existence, has been transformed into a set of material possibilities and potentialities that are managed through an economy of sentient desiring and the capture of that which is imminent to the species. There is no point or end and, as Kojève reminded Bataille, a beautiful death is definitive failure. Is it surprising that the church also expends the bulk of its energy on managing bodies and establishing moral parameters that define what it is to be Christian in the wake of the Messiah? The church is managing its own beautiful death. In contrast, the church might retrieve the fecundity of its reflections upon, and practices of, desire. In doing so, it is not only a question of rethinking Divine desire but of being theologically political by desiring Divine desire. The starting point for such reflections and practices, however, must be a rejection of the ideology of moral values and the violence of sacrificial origins, of the laws that divide the Christian. Only then is a truly radical Christian eroticism possible.

Dying for It!

In many ways, the means to answer the biopolitics of the present and its management of life is to consider the significance of another death that is truly beautiful and desired above all else. Through the biopolitical lens of Western culture death is little more than one physiological stage on life's way, a point at which the body might be incised so that its clues to the mysteries of vitality and pathology may be acquired. Put starkly, death is no longer a watershed but a tractable, if distinct, aspect of material existence. The aim of techno-science is to postpone the point at which that aspect of material existence impinges upon subjects, with a view to the indefinite postponement of definitive failure, the nuisance of dying.[9] In the Fathers moves a very different intuition and experience of death that is wholly desirable in that the purpose of life *is* to die. The time of death is intrinsically linked to the death of Christ and the resurrection of the body. Thus, in the words of Gregory of Nazianzus, the Christian's objective is to make "this life down below – as Plato says – a training for death" (Letter 31 in Gregory of Nazianzus 1961: 39). This insight, like the eschatological imperative, has been expunged from Christianity like those saucy passages of Shakespeare that were censored in children's editions of the great bard's works. Yet its importance can be measured in the vitriol it meets from one of the principal intellectual adversaries of early Christianity.

Do not try to tell us that those who can see are blind and that those who can run are crippled since it is you who are blind of spirit and crippled of soul, teaching a doctrine that relates only to the body and living in the hope of raising a dead thing to life! (Celsus 1987: 112)

The resurrection of the body is at odds with the management of life. Its potency arises from the training for death that is a way of life – body-loving as Celsus sarcastically but accurately terms it – lived in a fundamentally distinctive temporality. In the same way as Paul outlined a Christian comportment in the midst of kairological time, so the resurrection inaugurates a temporal performativity that responds to the irrepeatable that has been but which cannot be possessed (even in the biopolitical vision of the management of life).

This vision of a death transfigured leads us to a Christian eroticism that is adequate to the challenges of the present and the demands of that which is remembered – the Passion of the Christ. Thomas's reflection on the status of pleasure as "delightful desire" (*delectatio*), a desire that has no specific end or anchor and is outside measurable duration offers a clue to the status and temporality of such an erotic practice (*Summa Theologiae* 1a2ae31.2). Pleasure, in Thomas's account, is more akin to an experience that is kairological than anything that is possible in either historical or post-historical time. Pleasure is immune to economies of value or price because it is *given* as an experience and therefore is invaluable. Pleasure, as an apprehension of transcendence, is radically mundane. Pleasure is outside morality. True pleasure does not pursue, at any cost, the empty illusion of a righteous economy of sexual desire. Rather, this experience exceeds time and matter in the messianic interval of pleasure that impresses itself upon history and bodies in those encounters that are irrepeatable gifts. Attending to such time demands a truly qualitative revolution of our understanding of *eros* that draws bodies together in communion – an experience of the "time that remains" which actively embraces the promise of the One who returns.

Notes

1 Indeed, in Gustave Flaubert's *Madame Bovary* – one of the first thoroughgoing analyses of the thanatological logic of *eros* in the context of modern capitalism – desire to consume rules Emma Bovary's life. Her consumption is sexual, retail, and religious and the novel (tragically) ends with her consumption of poison.
2 For a more comprehensive treatment of this triumph of fantasy over experience see P. Fletcher (2003: 157–69).
3 For a thorough analysis of the micro-fascism in *Fight Club* see Diken and Laustsen (2002: 349–67).
4 It ought to be noted that Paul's uncompromising position on marriage forms the antinomian basis for its radical rejection in the Marcionite church. See Blackman (1948: 13).
5 This consummation is epitomized by the war of words that commenced with the publication in 1966 of Hans Blumenberg's *The Legitimacy of the Modern Age* (1983). One of Blumenberg's primary targets in this work (for there were many opponents found wanting at the bar of historical reason) was Karl Löwith's *Meaning in History: The Theological Implications of the Philosophy of History* (1949). Despite the fundamental differences in their respective theses, Blumenberg and Löwith share a common presupposition concerning the status of history and its meaning and significance: the irreconcilable difference between modernity and eschatology, that is to say, a Christian conception of time. In both of these reflections the Christian conception of time oriented towards the eschatological end was obsolete and fundamentally inconsistent with the modern experience of time.

6   See also Kant's contention (1996b: 127) that outside marriage carnal enjoyment is cannibalistic in principle (even if not always in its effect).

7   The emphasis on the centrality of marriage for social, religious, and moral ends also neglects the transformations that have occurred to the imaginary and social practices of the wedding in Western cultures. See Freeman (2002).

8   An abridged version is available as Kojève (1980). Translations from the French edition are my own.

9   See Condorcet's consideration of the problem of immortality as a mathematical challenge that will result in worldly immortality (Condorcet 1966: 282–3).

Part VI

Queer Orthodoxy

Chapter 18

Queer Trinity

Gavin D'Costa

The doctrine of the Trinity shapes the life and practice of the church, even though, of course, such a doctrine is the product of the very church whose life it shapes. Hence, we should not be surprised to find within the doctrine much that tells us about the shapers of this dazzling truth, and about their societies. But we will also glean a sense of the truth that compelled and drove Christians into formulating such a doctrine. How much depends on getting the Trinity right? Most Christian churches would say "everything," as it is a matter of truth, the whole truth, and nothing but the truth. Otherwise, idolatry might live at the heart of Christian worship. Since all practice depends on the shape of God, the life of the church would be severely dysfunctional if its God were not the true God. In queering the Trinity I will focus on one single practice – the admission of only men to the ministerial priesthood – within the largest Christian denomination, the Roman Catholic Church, as it is defended in the theology of one of the Church's most influential modern theologians, Hans Urs von Balthasar (1905–88).[1] I will suggest that this practice of exclusive male ordination is as heretical as the doctrine of God that sustains it. I am not going to argue the case for the ordination of women to the priesthood based on any secular notion of equal rights for women, because that argument is irrelevant; for it is on trinitarian, biblical, and historical-practice grounds that the exclusion is defended.[2] And to those who might say, "but what has the Trinity to do with women priests?" the answer is simple: "everything" – as we shall see. Julia Kristeva, the French feminist psychoanalytical philosopher, recognizes the subtle and complex interrelationships between the Trinity and every aspect of religious practice. Formulating the matter in Lacanian terms she writes: "The Trinity itself, that crown jewel of theological speculation, evokes, beyond its specific content and by virtue of the very logic of its articulation, the intricate intertwining of the three aspects of psychic life: the symbolic, the imaginary, and the real" (Kristeva 1987b: 43). One might equate Kristeva's "real" with the immanent God who is unknowable and unrepresentable, the symbolic with the economic revelation of God and the consequent structure of the church in history, and the imaginary with the ecclesial unconscious.

The forging of Christian doctrine requires *human* language to speak of the *divine*. On the one hand there is the constant danger that we might project onto the divine attributes of our human society and its structures. Feuerbach, Freud, and Marx saw this in profound and different ways, but failed to think this through beyond the idea of projection. On the other hand, and in reaction to such critiques, there are some negative theologians so wary that our language about God is saturated with anthropocentricism that they argue it is best to say nothing at all about the divine; the apophatic is privileged. In response to this dilemma there is a curious form of revelatory positivism where it is claimed that we must simply trust that the divine words are found untarnished in the Bible and accept these words as "God's Word/s." The whole question of mediation is bypassed. However, this positivist view has an interesting element within it: the incarnation of God in *human flesh* in the person of Jesus *does* mean that human beings have the ability to reflect on the divine, but only analogically. In one of its forms, this incarnational path was developed as the way of *analogy*. There are other trajectories, but this is the one I shall be examining.

Thomas Aquinas puts the matter of analogy succinctly: "concerning God we cannot grasp what he is, but only what he is not, and how other beings stand in relation to him" (*Summa Contra Gentiles* 1.30; cited in Catholic Church 1994: 18). This laid the foundation for the teaching of the *maior dissimilitudo*, whereby it is held that any *similarity* between God and creation is known only within the *infinitely greater difference* between the two: "between creator and creature no similitude can be expressed without implying an even greater dissimilitude" (Fourth Lateran Council, Denzinger and Schönmetzer 1965: 806; cited in Catholic Church 1994: 18). This safeguarded against anthropocentricism, but allowed that language might have a carefully qualified, regulative function to play in response to the divine mystery. Failure to recognize the analogical quality of language about God was a sure recipe for heresy: to predicate of God that which belongs to creation, to forget the greater difference. This view of analogy leads me to queer theory.

In introducing queer theory, the sociologist Steven Seidman writes: "[s]exuality is perhaps the last human dimension that many of us refuse to grant is socially created, historically variable, and therefore deeply political. However, this is changing" (Seidman 1996: 2). Seidman contends that this denaturalizing of sex has been generated by disciplines such as psychoanalysis, feminism, post-structuralism and sociology, which have allowed us to see the socially constructed nature of reality, and thereby question it. Seidman never once mentions theology, and this is true of many queer theorists, although *methodologically* I believe that certain types of theology might properly be called queer; that is, they are capable of overturning idols, showing how human constructions so easily masquerade as "God-given reality" or – in its secular trope – as "natural." Such queer theologies are concerned to unmask allegedly revelatory or natural idolatry not so that personal capitalism may flourish (that you can do what you like if you have the power and resources to do it) but to herald in a new order, the "kingdom of God" or, more simply, a church where women priests can properly represent Christ and Mary. Of course theologians are not able to make this critique from any foundationalist standpoint, replicating the problem that queer theory aims to unmask, but from within a complex tradition which they must both criticize and learn from. Hence this chapter is planted in the heart of Roman Catholic theology, in my own ecclesial communion.

Clearly, this type of queer theology is different from *secular* queer theory in a number of ways. First, it is particularly concerned with the question of God language, and not purely in a deconstructive manner, but in the belief that in the forging and practice of God-language lies our salvation (see Nussbaum 1999; and for a careful theological analysis Coakley 2002: 153–67). Second, its accountability is primarily to ecclesial communities, acknowledging the different contours that these have, and not to the academy or specific ideological theories or particular political groupings. This would require considerable unpacking, but my point is that in varied senses theology is an ecclesial practice while queer theorizing is not.[3] Third, the aims of certain queer theorists have been overtly ideological: to "liberate" gay men or lesbian women or bisexuals or transgendered persons. My concern is different: to make space for God within our (eucharistic) language, so that we might listen, see, smell, touch, taste, and worship. While this worship may actually lead to the liberation of gay men and lesbian women it is not undertaken for this reason *per se*, for it is not

possible to know what "liberation" might be apart from the language of the Christian tradition, even if it is within this same tradition that gays and lesbians have been – and still are
– shamefully persecuted.

Queering Hans Urs von Balthasar's Trinity

The theology of Hans Urs von Balthasar has been immensely influential within the Roman
Catholic Church (see Henrici 1991). Balthasar was deeply admired by Pope John Paul II,
and by Pope Benedict XVI, when he was Joseph Cardinal Ratzinger, Prefect of the
Congregation for the Doctrine of the Faith. Balthasar was a key figure in the founding of
the journal *Communio*, a "conservative" response to the more "liberal" journal *Concilium*.[4]
Paul McPartlan (1997: 51) notes Balthasar's profound influence on the shaping of
twentieth-century papal teaching, to the extent of being cited in John Paul II's *Mulieris
Dignitatem* (John Paul II 1988: 101, para. 27).

I want to look at Balthasar's depiction of the Trinity for three reasons. First, it is his
Trinity, his "crown jewel" (Kristeva), which organizes all creation, right down to the small-
est detail, whereby the "symbolic, the imaginary, and the real" are intertwined in complex
and awesome patterns, presenting one of the richest and most nuanced discussions of the
Trinity, in both its immanent (as it is in itself) and economic (as it is revealed in history)
forms. We learn much from this dazzling construction, both in terms of the church's *actual*
and *potential* symbolic life, and of its unconscious imaginary.

Secondly, it is from the Trinity that Balthasar outdoes the Vatican in instantiating an ontological mandate against women priests.[5] I want to call this move into question, as a single
instance of Balthasar's more widespread failure to be queer/analogical enough in the sym-
bolizing/staging of trinitarian life. But I do not want to argue that Balthasar's theology is
redundant because of this. On the contrary, I want to suggest that his trinitarian symbolizing, however inadequate, actually opens up many important avenues whereby "gender" is
recast in a number of ways. It is possible to see how the divine life is capable of being represented in multi-gender terms, even if in Balthasar these terms are rather thinly developed. It
is possible to see how the divine life is capable of being represented in gay, lesbian and heterosexual self-giving, faithful and fruitful love, even if Balthasar's Trinity enacts a *form* of
exclusive misogynist homosexual erotics that is predicated upon the exclusion of the
feminine/woman.

And thirdly – and most germane to my argument – it is possible to see why women are ontologically able to represent Christ and therefore be ordained to the ministerial priesthood, just
as men are able to ontologically represent Mary (and be characterized as the feminine Marian
"church"). I should make it clear that I see Balthasar's particular homoeroticism as the unconscious driving force that excludes women (except for the mother, Mary) from the symbolic
order. This is not an argument against homosexuality *per se,* just as an argument against men
raping women and "queer bashing" is not an argument against heterosexuality *per se* (even if
both of the latter violent actions may be connected with misogyny). Balthasar's argument
against women priests happens because his sense of analogy fails him at crucial trinitarian
moments. This failure is particularly acute as Balthasar is profoundly sensitive to the danger of
anthropocentrism in God-language.[6] In this sense his is a queer theology, even if it fails to be
queer enough.

Balthasar's Trinity is depicted most clearly in his five volume *Theo-Drama* (1988–98),
although I shall be drawing from other works as well.[7] It is only in the final two volumes

of the *Theo-Drama* that Balthasar elaborates on the immanent life of God that both mirrors the economic revelation, and, more fundamentally, shapes it. It is this inner life that draws us into the mystery of salvation.

The Immanent Trinity: Only Incestuous Homoerotics?

How is one to stage the inner life of God? To attain this near impossible task Balthasar employs gender terms, deriving from but transforming Aristotle. And in case we forget that analogy operates within an always greater difference, Balthasar uses the prefix *über* – translated variously as "over," "above," "supra" or "super" – to signify that when supramasculine (*übermännlich*) and suprafeminine (*überweiblich*) are used of God, they are not to be literally or directly related to the "masculine" and "feminine" in the human realm – whatever these terms might mean (see further Gardner and Moss 1999: 98 n. 59). However, the use of these gendered terms does denote something specific about the inner life of God, otherwise there would be no use in employing them. What do they say about the divine life?

Balthasar's Trinity is an ecstatic eternal circle of overflowing love, reciprocally given, received, and shared between the three persons. However, the persons are distinguished by "processions," and in these processions we find the gendered analogical language by which the distinctiveness of each person is secured. We need to recall that in much of the Scholastic tradition, following Aristotle, the "feminine" is related to "matter" and thus understood as "potency." Potency, as possibility, is imperfection. The "masculine" is related to "form" and is thus understood as "act." Act represents perfection in that it is realized. This results in two further implications. First, it leads to a sense in which the feminine is imperfect – like potency – until it is related to act, the masculine. The receptivity of the feminine / matter to its shaping and determination by masculine / form in Aristotle's biology and metaphysics was central to certain misogynistic strands in the vision of the relation between created men and women found in Augustine and Aquinas (on the Aristotelian background see Børresen 1981 and Allen 1985). Man was master, the clear thinker, the active principle and the need of man for women was an asymmetrical completion; the asymmetry deriving from biology. Aquinas puts it thus: "We are told that woman was made to be a help to man. But she was not fitted to help man except in generation, because another man would have proved a more effective help in anything else" (*Summa Theologiae*, 1.98.2 *sed contra*).

Balthasar daringly transforms this gendered metaphysics in two very important ways. He queers Aristotle's and Aquinas's biology and also their metaphysics. First, Balthasar realizes that in the act of love within the Godhead, there is not simply "pure act," as Thomas envisages it. For Thomas anything other than "pure act" would impute imperfection to the Godhead. However, Balthasar, given the drama of the cross, sees that feminine receptivity, previously alien to the (Greek) Godhead, is constitutive in the very life of God.

> Where absolute love is concerned, receiving and letting be are just as essential as giving. In fact, without this receptive letting be and all it involves – gratitude for the gift of oneself and a turning in love toward the Giver – the giving itself is impossible. (Balthasar 1988–98: V, 86; corrected)

This metaphysical claim surpasses both Aristotle and Aquinas in the sense that what was previously viewed as an imperfection (feminine / matter / receptivity) is now, in the light of the incarnation, seen as perfection. There is no divine love without giving, receiving, and letting be. And this development allows Balthasar to move away from defining gender in terms of a defective biology embedded within a natural theology (as in Augustine and Aquinas). Instead, gender is now *constructed within the biblical narrative*. While I will criticize Balthasar's particular reading of the biblical material, the important point is that gender is generated within Christian discourse and not located at a primary, prelinguistic level, on which Christian language is subsequently pasted. In this sense, Balthasar's theology is queer.

When we turn to Balthasar's depiction of the inner life of God, we find that the so-called "reactionary conservative" daringly employs both male and female terms analogically within the divine life, surpassing much (though not all) of the tradition before him. It is this breakthrough that makes Balthasar's theology so important in gender politics. The processions which distinguish each person of the Trinity are given thus:

> In trinitarian terms, of course, the Father, who begets him who is without origin, appears initially as (super-)masculine; the Son, in consenting, appears initially as (super-) feminine, but in the act (together with the Father) of breathing forth the Spirit, he is (super-)masculine. As for the Spirit, he is (super-)feminine. There is even something (super-)feminine about the Father too, since . . . in the action of begetting and breathing forth he allows himself to be determined by the Persons who thus proceed from him; however, *this does not affect his primacy in the order of the Trinity*. (Balthasar 1988–98: V, 91; emphasis added)

This is a key passage and I shall refer to it often. In this radical restaging of the Trinity we see that all three divine persons are dual-gendered, each being both supramasculine and suprafeminine. The feminist critique of the male God/Trinity, so forcefully made by Mary Daly (1973), apparently evaporates in Balthasar's hands. The Son is envisaged as first suprafeminine in his receptivity to the active supramasculine gift of the Father's self. And this suprafemininity is the context from out of which the Son responds, supramasculinely, to the gift of the Father. We should recall that since these "moves" within the Godhead are eternal, one cannot give any chronological priority to the various processions, even if they nevertheless require sequential telling, for how else are we to tell stories except in time?[8] (See Rowan Williams 1999: 177.) So, not only is the Son bisexual in ontological terms, but so also is that most worrying of potential patriarchs, the Father. The Father is not purely supramasculine, for in *always* receiving from and being defined by the Son and Spirit he too has an eternally suprafeminine dimension.

At this point it is worth noting the immense fertility of Balthasar's Trinity in being able to represent three forms of erotic and ecstatic relationship, even if thinly (given the underdetermined senses of "giving," "receiving," and "letting be"). Balthasar's Trinity symbolizes divine love in terms of interpenetrating and reciprocal relationships between supramasculine and suprafeminine, suprafeminine and suprafeminine, and supramasculine and supramasculine (analogically: heterosexual, lesbian, and gay relationships); but *only in so much* as these relationships are self-giving for the wider community, as endless outpourings and sharings. And this should remind us that the Genesis account of heterosexual relationships is *just one* account of how human sociality analogically reflects God's love as covenant fidelity, and it does so along with other ways of incarnating loving practice, ecclesially and bodily: through celibacy, virginity, and permanent gay and lesbian unions. David Matzko McCarthy has included the latter relationships within the two goods of marriage: permanent loving union and procreativity.

McCarthy makes a strong case for permanent lesbian and gay relationships as "anomalies" within the Catholic theology of marriage, for that theology is not an exclusive sanctification of heterosexual love, for "[m]ale–female complementarity does not produce the goods of marriage but is produced by it" (McCarthy 1997: 384). He thereby criticizes the prioritizing of Genesis 1.27, using Vatican II to argue that "[c]reation as male and female is used as the paradigmatic example, but the example does not exclude other ways of imagining humanity's social nature" (McCarthy 1997: 382; see also McCarthy 1998 and Rogers 1999a). In this respect, the medievalist Marilyn McCord Adams rightly extols and at the same time questions the same-gender models of trinitarian love within the trinitarian symbolics of Richard of St Victor and Aelred of Rievaulx. She questions them on the grounds of their exclusion of women–women relations (going back to Cicero's exaltation of male–male friendship as the highest and most noble coupling). She extols them in so much as "Richard's picture of the trinitarian love affair combines with Aelred's account of Christian friendship to suggest how homosexual love can serve – as much as heterosexual couplings – as an icon of godly love, a sacramental participation in Love Divine" (Adams 2002: 336). This avenue is clearly in need of further research.

A further avenue opened by Balthasar's trinitarian symbolics is the rich suggestion that the name "Father" analogically includes both male and female, for the Father is both supra-masculine and suprafeminine, and likewise the Son. This would mean that traditional patriarchy is challenged at its metaphysical roots, finally going "beyond God the Father" (as Mary Daly urged us to do). And more significantly for my present argument, the Son can be represented analogically by both male and female, for he too is both suprafeminine and supramasculine. But we shall see that Balthasar excludes this possibility for the ministerial priesthood precisely because he does not take his own trinitarian symbolics with full seriousness.

While acknowledging that the Father is suprafeminine, Balthasar still asserts – in an almost unintelligible manner – that this is so without it affecting the Father's "primacy in the order of the Trinity" (Balthasar 1988–98: V, 91). How can this be? Despite everything – utter reciprocity and utter self-giving in eternal ecstasy – the primacy of the supramasculine originless Begetter is suddenly prioritized and kept intact. The Father's primacy will not be touched by real ontological reciprocity. Male giving, male activity, male definition, suddenly resurfaces as more primary, more ontological. Balthasar fails to entirely rethink Aristotle by still identifying masculinity with activity and femininity with passivity, and he does so because of a distorted biblical reading whereby Jesus is made "active" and Mary "passive." Balthasar's insistence that the Father's primacy remains untouched by his suprafemininity has the effect of returning us to an untransformed Aristotelian metaphysics, where pure act / male / form is finally more real, more primary, than the relations that actually co-constitute the Father. This regression, which is now a repression, will surface again to mark all of creation. For in Balthasar, the shape of God's Trinity determines the shape and ordering of creation. It is as if Balthasar freezes a frame from an unfinished movie and this frozen frame – the primacy of the supramasculine originless Begetter – is made the dominant frame within which the entire movie is to be viewed and interpreted.

This repression surfaces at other moments in the immanent Trinity, which is perhaps a sign of what is to follow at the economic level. I note two disturbances. First, the female images that Balthasar employs to speak of the Father (as a womb, for example), while radical and important, are at the same time potentially regressive. When speaking of God's "father-hood" – a term that "bursts all analogies" – one way in which Balthasar bursts the analogy is to say that "such 'fatherhood' can *only* mean the giving away of everything the Father is, including his entire Godhead . . . it is a giving-away that, in the Father's act of generation – which lasts from all eternity – leaves the latter's womb 'empty'" (Balthasar 1988–98: III, 518; emphasis added). But note that suddenly the Father's suprafeminine passivity or receptivity has disappeared: active giving-away is the only mark of the first person. Later, Balthasar speaks of Christians who acquire ecclesial traits by virtue of "being born with Christ from the Father's womb" (Balthasar 1988–98: III, 527). The symbolic construction is radical in employing biological imagery from women's bodies to speak of the Godhead, and specifically the first person. Men do not have wombs, so speaking of the womb of God means that women can symbolize the deity. As I noted earlier, it would seem that Balthasar sides with radical feminists who have long argued that patriarchy's God crumbles once women are able to represent/image the divine. However, it is only in an unintended sense that this is so for Balthasar, for his use of female images appropriates woman, removes the womb from *her* body, so as to express the creative power of the supramasculine originless Begetter, the Father who cannot be called Mother.[9] Women are represented as the unimaginable formless Real of both Lacan and Aristotle, requiring phallic (Lacan) or male (Aristotle) definition to gain symbolic (Lacan) or bodily (Aristotle) presence.

Luce Irigaray, the French psychoanalyst feminist philosopher, points out how the womb is often constructed as a passive receptacle within patriarchy, whereby the woman has no claims on its workings, becoming the container for the product made in the father's name, "possessed as a means of (re)production" (Irigaray 1985a: 16). Elsewhere, Irigaray has written what might be a commentary on Balthasar's specific ontological taxonomy:

> The problem is that, by denying the mother her generative power and by wanting to be the sole creator, the Father, according to our culture, superimposes upon the archaic world of the flesh a universe of language and symbols which cannot take root in it except as in the form of that which makes a hole in the bellies of women and in the site of their identity. (Irigaray in Whitford 1991: 41)

It is important not to push Balthasar's texts too far. As we have noted, he is well aware of the problems of language and he constantly calls for a reversal of images and metaphors. But patriarchal primacy stops him from going all the way. Does his inability to allow for the ontological implications of full reciprocity – which would have obliterated the primacy that he wants to retain for the supramasculine originless Begetter – mean that his immanent Trinity ends with a *male biological cross-dresser*: a Father with a womb? It would seem so. If Balthasar allowed his doctrine of analogy to come into operation, and thus fully reciprocal trinitarian relations, his Trinity would indeed open up to a *remarkable* generation of gender representations – as I have already intimated and elsewhere developed (D'Costa 2000). In this sense there is much to commend Balthasar's Trinity.

Another example reveals the unconscious homoerotics within Balthasar's Trinity – the workings of what Irigaray calls "homosexuate language," whereby the feminine/woman is excluded from the symbolic order.[10] I am not wanting to call into question homosexual covenanting relations – or heterosexual couplings – except insofar as they *exclude* other forms of covenant relationship. Balthasar writes that the suprafeminine Son, in first receiving the gift of the Father, "allowed himself to be led and 'fertilized' by the Father" (Balthasar 1990b: 78). This homoerotic incest leads to the spiration of the third person, the Spirit; and this prioritizing of "male" giving or self-giving is, as we would expect, also replicated at the level of the economic Trinity, to which we now turn.

The Economic Trinity: The (Single) Gendered Drama Continues

Balthasar's trinitarian drama – at the economic level – makes two key assumptions. Following the Johannine testimony, Balthasar argues that the Father is known only through the Son. This is the witness of most of the New Testament. Furthermore, for Balthasar, the Son as *male* is key in properly *representing* the supramasculine originless begetting Father. A woman could not represent *this* aspect of the Father. This is why, so to speak, God became incarnate in a man. Balthasar never tells us how the suprafeminine aspect of the Father is represented and one suspects he is unable to, for that aspect of the first person is strangely silenced in the symbolic order. Second, the drama unfolds *only* because of a woman, Mary. Her role is central to redemption. In fact, without her, redemption is not possible at all. This high place for Mary is one of the most exciting aspects of Balthasar's theology, even if traditionally Mary's role in the Roman Catholic tradition is not without misogynistic elements.[11] However, let us look at the way in which Balthasar unfolds this complex economic drama.

Balthasar begins with the story of creation and pre-Christian cosmological accounts of the polarities and tensions between three foci that generate the construction of self and society. These are the tensions between conceptions of spirit and matter, man and woman, the individual and society. Balthasar, with immense learning, shows how these three foci are never properly harmonized in Greek thought, and it is only in the biblical account of Adam and Eve that these three *begin* to be resolved into a coherent *telos*. However, it is only in Christ that the Genesis account is properly understood and completed, for in Christ all three poles are taken up, reconciled, and transformed into a new creation. This new creation – in which spirit and matter, male and female, individual and society begin to be resolved into a divine harmony, analogically reflecting God's life – is the church. Balthasar's supramasculine/feminine within the Godhead comes into play in a remarkable fashion. I will plot one trajectory only within this unfolding drama – the one which leads to the exclusion of women from the ministerial priesthood.

Adam, the first man, and Eve, the first woman, are recapitulated within the second Adam (Christ) and the second Eve (Mary). Balthasar takes up important themes from the fathers that have too often been neglected in modern theologies. He traces many illuminating parallels: from Adam's side comes his bride Eve and out of Christ's side comes his bride, the church; from Eve's disobedience sin enters the world (and Balthasar will have no truck with blaming Eve alone), and out of Mary's obedience salvation enters the world; from Eve's motherhood springs the entire human race, and from Mary's motherhood springs the new creation in a double sense: as Christ the man, and as Mary, the true church. Incest themes are profoundly embedded within Christianity – as Christ is groom to his bride, who is his mother, who is the church. But amidst Balthasar's immensely subtle and fertile exposition, reflecting his breakthrough on the level of the immanent Trinity, we find the return of the Father's regressive primacy. And not surprisingly, this primacy is related to the "priority of the man."

> The reciprocal fruitfulness of man and woman is surpassed by the *ultimate priority* of the "Second Adam", who, in suprasexual fruitfulness, brings a "companion", the Church, into being. Now the "deep sleep" of death on the Cross, the "taking of

the rib" in the wound that opens the heart of Jesus, no longer take place in unconsciousness and passivity, as in the case of the First Adam, but in the consciously affirmed love-death of the Agape, from which the Eucharist's fruitfulness also springs. *The relative priority of the man over the woman here becomes absolute, insofar as the Church is a creation of Christ himself, drawn from his own substance.* (Balthasar 1988–98: II, 413; emphasis added)

Balthasar plumbs profound themes in this passage. However, in relation to our question, one should note that Christ is the "origin" of the church (which is "drawn from his own substance"), as analogously, the Father is the "origin" of Christ (who is drawn from the Father's own substance). This over-masculinizing of the Father and now of Christ (and therefore of Adam) means that the church is primarily feminine receptivity, embodied in Mary, the "first" of all creatures. Admittedly she is analogous to the way that the Son is suprafeminine in his begottenness from the Father, the first before all creation. But note here the same slippage as appeared in the immanent Trinity, and how the mirroring of that "frozen frame" in which the Father's supramasculine primacy was asserted, now re-emerges in the Son and has to *assert* itself in the economic order. Hence, a "reciprocal fruitfulness" is surpassed by the Son's "suprasexual fruitfulness" – causing a rather disturbing relapse into the Aristotelian heritage which earlier seemed to have been so richly transformed. Hence, the inevitable result: "the relative priority of the man over the woman becomes absolute." Once more, woman becomes the place for man's fulfillment: he complements her material formlessness, bringing *her* to birth by his form, by *his* sexual act, even if it is suprasexual. Mary's (woman's) *co-redemptive* status is suddenly relegated, as it has been in much modern Christianity. It is ironic that Balthasar is one of the main forces behind reinstating this Marian doctrine into productive ecclesiology. This absolutizing of male priority is a regress, forgetting the doctrine of analogy so relentlessly employed by Balthasar. This idolizing of a complementary but subordinate sexual symbolics (superior male to receptive and dependent female) at the economic level (where Christ must be groom to his bridal church, just as Adam was to Eve) is linked to the misogynist homoerotics in Balthasar's immanent Trinity, where woman is excluded or subordinated and cannot be represented. Balthasar's trinitarian logic should properly allow that women can symbolically represent Christ just as men can, and likewise, the church can be properly female in a Marian sense and also male in a Christic sense, precisely because Mary also properly represents Christ (in his suprafemininity). Balthasar seems to have forgotten that Christ is himself represented as female and as mother in certain medieval traditions (see Bynum 1982 and Ward 1999).

Admittedly, Balthasar's statement on the "absolute priority" of the male is almost immediately followed by an attempt to draw back, even though such a drawing back undermines the very point Balthasar is wanting to drive home about the centrality of Christ. "All the same, the first account of creation is over-fulfilled here, for in the mind of God the incarnate Word has never existed without his Church (Ephesians 1.4–6)" (Balthasar 1988–98: II, 413). But this qualification fails to work because of the explicit way in which the "relative" priority of the man over the woman *must* become "absolute," for without it the church cannot happen, and the ontological argument for all male priesthood collapses.

One further example of how Balthasar absolutizes the male, amidst so much rich reciprocity, will suffice to indicate the relentless fall from analogy that operates throughout Balthasar's trinitarian taxonomy. Balthasar envisages the Eucharist as the outpouring of seed from the loins of Jesus. He writes:

[T]he Son of God who has become man and flesh, knowing his Father's work from inside and perfecting it in the total self-giving of himself, not only of his spiritual but precisely also of his physical powers, giving not only to one individual but to all. What else is his Eucharist but, at a higher level, an endless act of fruitful out-pouring of his whole flesh, such as a man can achieve only for a moment with a limited organ of his body? (Balthasar 1998: 226)

In many respects this is a rich image and well worth developing, for the Eucharist is generative of new community, and a community which calls itself the body of Christ. But given the earlier problems we have noted this "out-pouring" becomes a troubling image of love and self-giving for it excludes any female imagery, and once more identifies "love" as purely male sexual "self-giving." All mutual reciprocity is surpassed, for this suprasexual fruitfulness is a "giving" without receiving. It excludes the symbolic dimensions of any female imagery other than the imagined passivity of woman, the church, on her knees, awaiting a Eucharist which is nourishment from the male's body, and, tellingly, a Eucharist presided over by men who are the first to drink from the loins of the male Jesus. And it is here that the trinitarian cascade reaches the bottom of a long chain: the exclusive male ministerial priesthood.

Ministerial Priesthood: Men Only "Representatives"?

Balthasar's argument follows the gendered Trinity right into the genitalia of human beings, although, as Schindler notes, "the primitive source of 'gender' at least in the theology of Balthasar is 'ontological' before it is physiological, even if it is through physiology that we first discover gender differences" (Schindler 1996: 259). Balthasar's objection to women priests is clear: "However the One who comes forth from the Father is designated, as a human being he *must be a man if his mission is to represent the Origin*, the Father, in the world" (Balthasar 1988–98: III, 284; emphasis added). Now this logic should be void given Balthasar's use of analogy, for as Schindler, his close and faithful interpreter, writes: "The 'transcendent' meaning of (supra) 'gender' in God . . . cannot be remotely approximated among human beings" (Schindler 1996: 258). But given the earlier slippage in the immanent order of the Trinity, prioritizing the male, it now inevitably resurfaces in a stark assertion: only a male body can represent Christ, because only the male Christ can represent the Father, who, in his mission of originless begetting, is supramasculine. And once more, the Father's eternal suprafemininity disappears, as do women from the symbolic altar on earth, and with them the possibility of a different herstory. The movie is frozen, against its divinely intended motion.

Now it is important to understand why some – like Balthasar – do not see the exclusion of women as a problem. For them, this exclusion *derives from the very nature of God's inner reality* and therefore must be good. For Balthasar, his theology safeguards "equality" between the sexes, because this equality is not based on equal rights but on sexual difference. Hence, he points out that the priestly mission of representation is strictly connected with "roles," and not with power over others, and ecclesial office is just one role of service among the many required to make up the body of Christ's church. For Balthasar, women do not have the "right" to be priests, just as men do not have the "right" to bear children. And after all, this male role is dependent on the female: on the Marian *fiat*. The priest must be baptized into the Marian church before he can undertake the priestly role – and it is exercised within the feminine body. Balthasar writes: "What Peter will receive as 'infallibility' for his office of governing will be a partial share in the total flawlessness of the feminine, Marian Church" (Balthasar 1995a: 167).

Thus for Balthasar, the doctrine of the Trinity rules out women priests, for otherwise God's self-revelation would be perverted. Throughout this chapter I have labored to suggest that the opposite is in fact the case and that Balthasar's Trinity is *not queer enough*: it is not as relentlessly analogical as it set out to be. It fails to transform Aristotle's categories thoroughly enough; it fails to think gender in terms of its complex biblical construction. But Balthasar's theology is still immensely fruitful, and it is because of this that I have looked at his Trinity in such detail. We have nowhere else but the existing tradition from which to work. If Balthasar had followed his concern with the *maior dissimilitudo,* then his account of the trinitarian love – which so radically includes receptivity, letting be and activity (in contrast to so much of the metaphysical tradition) – would be capable of symbolizing homosexual as well as heterosexual love.[12] And if Balthasar had questioned the Aristotelian identification of the male with activity/generation, and not written this into the Godhead, we might have been shown how the Trinity is capable of leading us to envisage a society without patriarchy, without the driving of holes into the bellies of women, and without their eradication from the symbolic order. Instead we might have had a divine symbolic which allowed for a richer hermeneutics of the Bible and for women to be included within the ministerial priesthood. And had Balthasar traced the female morphology in the Bible with more trinitarian openness, Mary's active "yes" to God might be seen to stand *equally and differently* alongside her passivity and receptivity, and she to stand *equally and differently* alongside her Son, as the world's *co-redeemer*. Balthasar has already helped us to see that the many ways of being holy within the church enlarge and enrich the body of Christ, who in the Bible is not only bride, but also inorganic rock, organic and bountiful vine, male and female, not primarily feminine or secondarily masculine. The Bible generates a much more varied and far richer cultural constructivism, even while it bears the marks of patriarchy. To queer Balthasar's already queer Trinity is to begin to glimpse what human "liberation" looks like in the love of God, even if we now see only through a mirror darkly (1 Corinthians 13.12).

Acknowledgments

I am indebted to Gerard Loughlin for helpful comments on a first draft of this chapter and for his daring piece, Loughlin (1999b); revised in Loughlin (2004a: 143–71). Thanks also to Wendy Allen, Jonathan Baxter, Richard Johnson, and Marcus Pound for discussion of this chapter.

Notes

1 For the Church's official teaching on the exclusion of women see *Inter Insigniores – Declaration on the Admission of Women to the Ministerial Priesthood* (Sacred Congregation for the Doctrine of the Faith 1976) and John Paul II's *Ordinatio Sacerdotalis* (1994), and the respective Roman commentaries on them (1977 and 1995). These texts are available in English at www. womenpriests.org.

2 *Inter Insigniores* does not employ trinitarian arguments *per se*, but it does employ gendered ones, such as Balthasar also uses, and which he runs back to the Trinity. One of the best discussions of *Inter Insigniores* is Wijngaards (2001).

3   This is not to deny the gay and lesbian movements within the church and their employment of queer theory. My point stands in so much as queer theory is not *determinative* of theology.

4   For an insightful and complex discussion of Balthasar as "conservative" and Karl Rahner as "liberal" – as symbolized by the two journals, *Communio* and *Concilium* – see Rowan Williams (1986: 11–34).

5   *Inter Insigniores*, unlike Balthasar, fails to explain why Christ was male. Its (faulty) arguments about "natural signs" and priestly "representation" make far better (even if still faulty) sense in the light of Balthasar's Trinity.

6   The theme of the unknowability of God and the *maior dissimilitudo* ends each volume of the *Theo-Drama*, like a chorus at the end of each act of an opera.

7   For the best expositions of Balthasar on Trinity and gender see Schindler (1996) and Pesarchick (2000). The latter hardly takes seriously any criticisms of Balthasar, whereas Schindler is far more sensitive and rigorously illustrates the range of issues opened up by Balthasar's gendering. For an excellent and nuanced appreciation of Balthasar on gender and divinity see Gardner and Moss (1999). See also Saward (1990).

8   See Rowan Williams (1999: 177).

9   At least not in the sections of the *Theo-Drama* under discussion (see also Balthasar 1988–98: II, 262), but elsewhere Balthasar does allow God to be called Mother, but not as a proper name, which must remain Father. See Balthasar (1990b: 30).

10 I define and deploy Irigaray's notion of homosexuate language to engage with trinitarian representations in D'Costa (2000).

11 Marina Warner (1990) tracks these problems. Beattie (1998) nicely takes to task Balthasar's Marian symbolic and his mapping of the "feminine"; and for a startling recovery of Mary from patriarchy see Beattie (1999). I also try to recover Mary from patriarchy in D'Costa (2000).

12 In this sense I agree with Williams' comment that Balthasar cannot be easily written off as simply offering a "rhetoric of sexual differentiation apparently in thrall to unexamined patriarchy" (Rowan Williams 1999: 177). Balthasar's trinitarian theology opens too many *other* doors, intentionally or otherwise, and Williams rightly concludes: "However hard we insist upon the simultaneity of the divine subsistents, we can say nothing of this simultaneity that is not abstract and formal unless we take the necessary (not to say canonical) risk of *evoking* simultaneity by telling a cluster of 'stories' that configure in different and reciprocal ways the relations of the trinitarian persons" (p. 177). See further Riches and Quash (1997: 146–67).

Chapter 19

God's Body

Mark D. Jordan

For many contemporary speakers, telling the truth about Jesus means finding the "real" or "historical" Jesus underneath the stories and theologies constructed around him. The truth about Jesus, they affirm, is the truth about what he really said and did as over against what various Christian communities made of him. So telling the truth about Jesus' body would mean reminding listeners that he was a Jewish peasant who did manual labor rather than an Anglo-Saxon movie star surrounded by a constant halo tweaked by a diffusion filter. The best way to represent the "historical" truth about Jesus' body would be to reconstruct a composite or typical portrait of a Nazarene who was born around the beginning of the Common Era. Just that kind of portrait was constructed for a recent television series, and the composite image circulated widely in the press.[1]

Much can be said for and against truths about Jesus of this sort. On the one hand, they challenge easy suppositions about how we got from Jesus to the churches. Jesus was not a blond screen idol, and he did not go about preaching treatises on the union of divine and human natures in himself. On the other hand, the present search for the historical Jesus supposes both that the experience of an incarnate God must be like any other experience and that texts recording that experience must be like any other texts. It also supposes, at least in some of its versions, that no god could become human in the way theological traditions have supposed. These are curious suppositions and commitments, but my concern at the moment is not to engage them. I want to ask another sort of question – a question based on a hypothesis. The hypothesis is this: whoever Jesus was "in reality," the most important fact about him is that he was a good and perhaps the best way for God to become human. The question follows: If Jesus' body was God's body, how do we begin to tell truths about it?

A devotee of the current pursuit of the historical Jesus might object immediately that my question simply repeats the deviation of the Christian tradition. By hypothesizing that Jesus of Nazareth was God incarnate, I am superimposing the "high Christology" of the Gospel of John onto the much different facts about Jesus that we can discover in hypothesized proto-Gospels or reconstructed oral traditions. My reply is to repeat more fully what I said above: My aim here is not to pit assumption against assumption or method against method. I am asking a question on the basis of a hypothesis. If you want, you can think of it as a thought-experiment. At the very least, the thought-experiment will clarify difficulties of speech in contemporary churches – because in fact the churches find it awkward to talk fully about the implications of the high Christology, that is, of the affirmation of incarnation. Truth telling is not the same as reconstructing facts according to the reigning "common sense." Certainly telling the truth about Jesus requires at least talking about the disconcerting consequences of the traditional affirmations that God took flesh.[2]

The most familiar Christian creeds or confessions, for all of their polemical contingency and philosophical complication, profess the religion of an incarnate God. Their words are repeated in so many Christian liturgies that it seems silly to refer to them. Hear in your memory's ear at least some phrases from an English "Nicene Creed": "Who for us men, and for our salvation, came down from heaven; and was incarnate by the Holy Ghost of the Virgin Mary, and was made man." Or, in a less aggressively masculinist translation: "Who for us human beings, and for our salvation, descended from heaven, and was put into flesh by the holy spirit from the virgin, Mary, and became human." "Incarnate," "put into flesh." Some Christians kneel or bow their heads at the words. Most know them by rote. Christianity as the religion of God in human flesh – it is almost too trite to say and yet still too disconcerting to think.[3]

Roman Catholicism in particular prides itself on being a strongly incarnational practice of Christianity. The sacramental theater of Catholic liturgy culminates when God becomes flesh in bread and wine. We Catholics profess to believe that it is the actual body of Jesus, back among us. Indeed, we preserve unconsumed pieces in tabernacles. Images of the Catholic Jesus are its lesser manifestations. The image-body hovers over our churches in graphic crucifixes, in prints of the Sacred Heart, in scourged statues of the Man of Sorrows. Then the body of Jesus raised from the dead: "Do not touch me," he says to Mary Magdalene, "for I have not yet ascended to the Father" (John 20.17). That single sentence has inspired or provoked dozens of master paintings. The body of Jesus is mirrored in the bodies of his saints, whose relics are venerated and whose martyrdoms or miracles take contours in church art. The events around Jesus' body are also re-performed more straightforwardly. When I was a boy in central Mexico, a young man was chosen to take on the role of Christ during Holy Week. His body became the image of Christ's body. It rode into the dusty recreation of Jerusalem, there to celebrate the meal, to be arrested and scourged, to be tried and condemned. On the afternoon of Good Friday, the young man's body was tied up on a cross.

Alongside these rites and artifacts, Roman Catholics have also cultivated certain ways of meditating on the incarnate God. The meditations picture the body of Jesus at many moments and under different aspects. We have from famous theologians sustained reflections on Jesus as an infant or at the age of twelve, Jesus in desert retreat or preaching on the mount. Ignatius of Loyola asks us to imagine Jesus as a noble commander so that we will respond by joining up.[4] Most famously, theologians and spiritual masters write of Jesus in the days of his Passion: the body of Jesus going down to death. The "Stations of the Cross" is only one of hundreds of texts that picture Jesus' body in order to produce compunction through compassion.

Doctrines, liturgies, icons, and meditations about Christ's body teach many things about it, but hardly everything. There are ambiguities and absences. Indeed, the absences are marked by ambiguities. Consider the ambiguities around the "simple fact" that Jesus' body was male. God incarnate as a human being has to fall somewhere within the range of human sex-differentiation, and that range is often reduced by our societies to a dichotomy: male *or* female. So we know about Jesus' body that it must have had some sex and we accept it as historical fact that the sex was (unambiguously!) male. We also know that it has been very important for most Christian churches that his body was male. Jesus' maleness has been used to justify a number of theological conclusions, as it is still used by some churches to exclude women from ministry. For these churches, it is not trivial that Jesus was marked as male from his birth.

Christian traditions consider it important that Jesus was a male, both because he needed some sex/gender and because he had the sex/gender that claims particular privileges and powers. Christian traditions haven't often considered it important to reflect on what made

Jesus male – that is, on the fact that the incarnate God had genitals of a certain configuration. Indeed, and as you may have felt in reading that last sentence, the genitals of Jesus are typically and normatively excluded from speech. To talk about them is indecent or provocative or blasphemous. To meditate on them would be obscene. We are urged to meditate on Jesus' acts and sufferings. We are asked to gaze on imaginary portraits of him and picture for ourselves his height and weight, the color of his skin or the length of his hair. But if our meditation should drift downward towards his pelvis, we are immediately rebuked and then condemned as perverted or pornographic.

Reflect on the vehemence of those rebukes and condemnations. Reflect on it and then push back against it. Our meditations on Jesus are incomplete without his sex. Telling the truth about him, we ought to try to tell it whole. But there is more: a vehement refusal to think Jesus' sex while insisting on his masculinity suggests that we have yet to tell an anxious truth *about ourselves* in relation to Jesus' body. We are not able even to speak about some parts of it. Why is that?

There follows a meditation on the body of the incarnate God. It meditates on the part of that body that is both necessary and unspeakable, that is fetishized and hidden. So it becomes a meditation on our needs in relation to that body. The aim of the meditation is to make us more capable of telling a truth that we cannot. We need the truth, and we are afraid of it.

Meditations on Christ take many forms, but they often permit themselves graphic and impassioned speech. I have given myself that permission here. Please do not confuse it with the presumption of propositional language that imagines itself capturing God.

Jesus' Corpses

Much Christian theology claims to be about a divine incarnation. It is also, and perhaps more emphatically, a speech for managing that incarnation by controlling its awkward implications. Some particularly awkward consequences can only be managed by passing over members of the body of God in prudish silence. Looked at in this way, the history of Christian theology can be seen as a long flight from the full consequences of its central profession. The big business of theology has been to construct alternate bodies for Jesus the Christ – tidier bodies, bodies better conformed to institutional needs. I think of these artificial bodies as Jesus' corpses, and I consider large parts of official Christology their mortuary.

Take as an emblem for the management of this awkward incarnation a typical Catholic crucifix. On it, a man wearing a loincloth is nailed to a cross. The representation is "realistic": the muscles on the body are sharply defined, nails poke through the strained skin, and the head lolls to one side in agony or exhaustion. If the crucifix before us is an older one from southern European or Latin American churches, the "realism" will be greater still. Vividly red blood runs over creamy skin – runs down from a minutely crafted crown of thorns, from nail punctures, from a bruised and swollen cut just below the ridge of ribs. The face itself is filled by agony, with beseeching eyes and a moaning or screaming mouth. The depiction is strikingly and perhaps appallingly realistic. Or is it? On one antique Mexican crucifix that hung in my mother's home, a corpus of this kind bore only a flimsy bit of parchment as its loincloth. When the paper fell away after one too many moves, it was revealed that there was nothing underneath. The corpus on the crucifix was shockingly detailed, except in the lower abdomen, which was as smooth and abstract as an old-fashioned manikin.

Imagine for a moment a more completely incarnate practice of carving crucifixes. The carver would take special care to carve equally realistic genitals on each corpus, whether or not a miniature loincloth would soon hide the work. The genitals would be considered – as they were in some periods of Christian painting – a powerful sign of the fullness of incarnation.[5] The penis would be circumcised in conformity with scriptural evidence and as a sign of Jesus' obedience to Jewish law. But it would be neither exaggerated nor minimized, fetishized neither as a commodity to be chased nor as a disgrace to be repudiated. We might even imagine a tradition of special prayers or meditations for attending to this extraordinary consequence of an eternal God's love for us perishable creatures, who must reproduce to survive as bodies. The genitals would be carved reverently as a profound teaching inscribed on the surface of the body of God-with-us.

To my knowledge, we Catholics have not had such a tradition for carving crucifixes. On the contrary, we have expected, when we have not required, that genitals be left off a crucifix's corpus, no matter how "realistic."[6] We have also traditionally insisted that Jesus not be shown naked in paintings of the crucifixion. At various times, nakedness on the cross has been explicitly refused even though it was conceded to be more historically accurate.[7] Jesus most probably was naked on the cross, but we cannot show him that way. You can catch here not only a curious disregard for history, but a refusal to accept divine providence. God did not prevent what Catholic art wants to prohibit. God let Jesus hang naked on the cross; our crucifixes cannot. Indeed, and with few exceptions, Catholic art has refused to allow any hint of a penis underneath Jesus' loincloth. The loincloth must cover a vacuum.[8]

Nothing underneath the loincloth – take that as an emblem for our thought about Jesus' body. The loincloth is not so much a rag as a magic cloth that makes things disappear. Why do we need the magic? That is a complicated question, to which I will give several answers. The first of them begins this way: Ask yourself what you have been feeling while reading through the last half dozen paragraphs. Is it recognition and insight? Calm and reasoned rejection? Or have you perhaps been feeling some distaste, embarrassment, disgust, repulsion? Have you been feeling that His genitals shouldn't be talked about – much less imagined as seen? If so, you may understand that we need that loincloth to keep ourselves from being ashamed. The cloth covers part of Jesus, which means that it helps us not to look at ourselves. His loincloth is made to cover our eyes.

Here is the beginning of a second answer: Imagine, again, the tradition for carving detailed genitals onto each and every crucifix. Who is doing the carving? If it is a woman, she might be presumed (in a male-centered theology at least) to be sexually aroused by such detailed attention to images of a penis – unless, of course, she is presumed not to know anything about them. If the carver is a man, he is supposed to be entirely disinterested in the genitals – except that the soul of every believer is Christ's spouse, is as a bride to Jesus considered as spiritual bridegroom. It might even be in some rare cases, in the overheated workshop of an undisciplined monastery, that a pious male carver would begin to find the carving of those members oddly – no, we cannot begin to think that. It is not enough to cover them up. We have to prevent their being carved in the first place. Think of the scandal to (and from) the carvers.

On many traditional readings, sexual shame began in Eden after the fall into sin. "Then the eyes of both were naked: and they sewed fig leaves together and made loincloths for themselves" (Genesis 3.7). Adam and Eve made loincloths because they had sinned. Why do we make loincloths for our images of Jesus, in statues or in paintings? Because *we* sin. We have to cover him up because of what we have become in our fearful denials. Certainly it is not God who is ashamed of human genitals – or God who pulls back from the shame meant to be inflicted on Jesus by crucifying him naked. We are the ones ashamed both of human bodies as created and of what we do to human bodies when we want to humiliate them. We are afraid of how we might respond to a naked savior. We are afraid of what we do to each other when we use nakedness as an insult.[9]

There are many connected questions to be posed about Western iconography of Jesus on the cross. For example, is it surprising or predictable that an officially homophobic doctrine would take as its central image an *almost* naked man being tortured? Do we understand that "choice" as the eruption of the repressed or the cultivation of erotic indifference towards male beauty – as a continual revenge on the threat of male attraction? Again, if the most important male body is standardly represented *almost* naked under torture, suffering apparently the threat or the effects of castration, how does that alter a culture's general conventions for picturing violence, desire, and masculinity? These are important questions, but I set them aside to say again the most basic thing. For the most traditional Christian theology, it would be a sign of full redemption to represent Jesus naked on the cross.[10] His nakedness would be a sign of a redeemed – that is, a humanly mature – community of believers. But we are afraid to look at the body of God as it was. So our typical "Jesus" – as corpus, statue, painting – only adds to the series of Jesus' corpses. The corpses are mutilated. We cannot let Jesus' body be whole, either in death or in life.

Jesus' Sex and Jesus' Gender

Christian traditions have wanted to hide on Jesus' body the organs of male sex at the same time that they have wanted to insist upon his male gender. A full consideration of this division might look to the difference between male organ and male power, between what theorists distinguish as the penis and the phallus. The penis is an organ while the phallus is a totem. I propose for the moment only the beginning of a simpler analysis. Consider how the distinction between sex and gender in Jesus allows his masculinity to be pliable for official purposes.

Two cautions before beginning this consideration. First, the distinction between sex and gender can only be provisional. The distinction has been used to separate (physically determined) sex from (culturally constructed) gender. Sex means roughly the kind of body you are born with. Gender is the way you were taught to handle that sexed body within a certain social regime. Between "sex" and "gender" there appears "sexuality," which sometimes seems physiologically based and cross-cultural, at other times culturally specific and always under construction. But the trichotomy, the triplet of terms, cannot be stable. It is never clear, for example, what should be included in "gender." Analyzed carefully, "sex" is no less troublesome, since external genital anatomy is only one biological marker of sex and since societies disagree when interpreting the marker. So in distinguishing Jesus' (hidden) sex from Jesus' (institutionalized) gender, we can only expect a rough and ready distinction between what cannot be cleanly separated.

The second caution: In talking about Jesus' gender, it is safest not to get entangled in questions about his "sexual orientation." It is very useful to undo the heterosexist presumption that Jesus was of course heterosexual – that he would obviously have been married to a woman if he had entered into an erotic relation at all. As incarnate God, Jesus violated any number of social expectations. Perhaps he would have violated this one too. Of course, the deceptions in applying terms for sexual orientation across history are numerous even when there is an abundance of evidence. There is little or no evidence about Jesus' sexual desires in the canonical Gospels.[11] So while it is helpful to rethink the Gospel narratives without the assumption that Jesus was "heterosexual," it is very wise not to attempt to prove that he was "homosexual." In any case, the point here is precisely not to inaugurate a quest for the historical Jesus' sexuality. The point is to notice the consequences of how Christian traditions have distinguished Jesus' sex from Jesus' gender.

Recall again the contrast between silence on sex and stridency on gender. When canonical theologians have considered Jesus' sex, they have refused to allow it what might be considered ordinary sexual operations. Reasoning from hypotheses about genitals in Eden before the fall, and from rules about the right use of sex, they have suggested, for example, that Jesus never had an erection. Erections in Eden would have been voluntary: Adam would have chosen to have one only for purposes of procreation with Eve. Since Jesus never willed to copulate with anyone, he would not have willed an erection.[12] Again, the disorder of human sexual desire is considered both a cause and an effect of original sin. When I feel the rush of desire for another man, I am only showing that I am objectively disordered in consequence of the sin that long ago disrupted human life. When a heterosexual woman feels lust for a man whom she never intends to marry and without any notion of procreative possibilities, she too is showing disorder. Jesus was not disordered by sin. So Jesus didn't suffer such desires. In sum, for many traditional Christian theologies Jesus had genitals (which need to be hidden), but he did not have anything like what we think of as ordinary sexual reactions. He was like us in all things but sin – and the traditions stigmatize most of our experienced sexuality as sin.

So far, the enforced silence on Jesus' sex. The strident affirmations of Jesus' gender are much more familiar to us. We Catholics hear, for example, that women cannot be ordained to priesthood because they cannot represent or symbolize Jesus. We are told, again, that church leadership is more appropriate to men than to women: not only was Jesus himself a man, but he chose only men as his disciples. So Jesus' masculine gender has enormous significance for church life. Indeed, recent Vatican arguments against the ordination of women suppose that the maleness of priesthood is a divine given that cannot be changed by the church even if it wanted too.[13]

Of course, Jesus' masculinity is somewhat curious. First, most Christian churches have conceived it as a strictly celibate masculinity, since they take it as obvious that Jesus never engaged in sexual activity. Second, though perhaps less obviously, Jesus' masculinity is a sort of eunuch masculinity. If we are to believe that he never "had sex," we are also not to think about his having male organs for sex. Finally, the masculinity of male Christian leaders has often itself strained social expectations of masculinity. In the Catholic Church, the normatively celibate priesthood has not infrequently been treated as a sort of third sex or intersex. It has been assigned gender roles that mix or confuse ordinary gender expectations. There are, I suspect, similar shifts of gender expectations even in the normatively married Protestant clergy. So while Jesus' masculinity is held up as the standard for the masculinity of Christian ministry, it is also complicated in ways that make it seem problematically masculine.

If believing Christians hesitate to accuse Jesus of being effeminate, they have not hesitated to level the accusation against particular representations of him. Bruce Barton, once popular as author of *The Man Nobody Knows* (to be read with emphasis on "man"), was pushed to portray Jesus as an athletic business leader because he was so put off by representations of Jesus as a wimp.[14] If the prevailing images of Jesus were not to be abandoned altogether, they had to be monitored quite closely. Consider Warner Sallman's best-selling portraits of Christ.[15] Sallman himself undertook them precisely in order in present the figure of a masculine Christ, a "real" man's Christ. Alas, Sallman himself was accused of presenting a soft, strange, effeminate Christ, with glistening locks and flimsy robes. So the pictures of Jesus have to be toughened up, butched up. Jesus' portraits have to keep proving their masculinity.

What threatens the masculinity of Jesus' representations? I have mentioned above some reasons why Jesus' official masculinity is problematic from the start, but we should add here another reason that we can notice particularly in portraits. Religious images are objects of devotion. Jesus' masculinity must be troubled because both men and women have passionate and psychologically intimate relations to him. His portraits are meant to attract and direct devotion. They are portraits of someone loved ardently by members of both sexes.

Jesus is our Lord, but also our friend. We go to him with our cares and our concerns. We suppose that he knows all of our shameful secrets, including our hidden sexual desires and acts. He even sees us performing them. So Jesus knows things about my body and what I do with it that an erotic partner of many years may not know, that the sum of my lovers may not have seen. Jesus knows me inside out. He loves me and I love him. He wants to help me in my daily struggle to live rightly, including with regard to sexual desires and acts. How does his gaze on my body affect my gaze on his? How does the intimacy of our relationship trouble my relation to him as someone who has a sexed body? Must I hide his sex in part because I can't figure out how to think of his sex in relation to our intimacy, my devotion? For heterosexual men, Jesus must be a buddy and cannot be only a buddy (since Jesus sees private things a buddy isn't supposed to see). For non-heterosexual men, Jesus can all too easily be more than a buddy – with the dangers that implies. What is it for a "straight" woman to have a superbly attractive man solicit her deepest love even as he knows her intimate history? And if lesbians might seem to escape the paradoxes of reacting with desire to Jesus' physical body, they might seem to be especially subjected to his (male) gaze. Every human body is watched by Jesus everywhere it goes, in everything it does. Is it any wonder that we are so worried about how Jesus appears – and must not appear?[16]

Other reactions to portraits of Jesus are not only possible, but certainly more frequent in conscious experience. I may look at a crucifix and think that it is bad art, a bit of factory kitsch. Or I may look at it and recall how different Jesus may have looked "in fact." Or, again, the sight of a crucifix may lead me to meditate on the many ways in which Jesus appears to me – in the consecrated bread and wine, in the faces of the needy, in the luminous transfigurations of human love. Jesus' physical body may be noted more as absent or as multiplied than as singular and specific. Still, if I am led by a piece of religious art to place myself at the foot of the cross, to walk with Jesus on the road to Emmaus, to follow his commands in a fishing boat on Galilee, I must also meditate on my reaction to his body, which must be sexed as human bodies are.

Why need that confrontation be erotic, someone might ask? Isn't any effort to eroticize Jesus' body a sign more of cultural decadence than of serious thinking about faith? After all, isn't it a hyper-sexualized culture that forces us to consider every body in terms of its sex and to worry that every relation is repressed sexuality? There is a real point to these questions, and I will come back to it in a moment. I would only note now that anxieties over Jesus' sex or gender predate contemporary America. They predate the preoccupations of "muscular Christianity" and the YMCA. We have noticed already old quandaries about the representation of Jesus crucified. We could also have noted that Christians have always been attracted by an ideal of life beyond sex, and have considered such a life an imitation of their Lord's life. Jesus' sex has always been unsettling, both cause and effect of how unsettling any sex has been for Christianity. We deduce our sexual morality from Jesus' rejected sex; Jesus must have rejected sex because of our sexual morality. So we need not be afraid to stand by the insight that troubles about the sexed body of the Messiah are deeply inscribed in Christian living. They are not merely cultural byproducts of the last decades – or centuries. We should not be afraid to continue with our meditations.

Truth about the Body of God

What is it to tell the truth about a human body? Is it the truth of a medical chart or an autopsy report? The body is described with its age and weight, medical conditions, signs of traumatic injury or inward decay. The body is reported science. Or is the truth of a body more like a fashion spread in a glossy magazine? The body has been bathed and prepared with namable products for its skin and hair, new perfumes and make-up colors. It has been regimented or surgically altered to the prevailing type. It will be further tailored with the photo software. The body is a billboard.

For Christians, the truth about Jesus' body would be neither of these – and not just because there was neither plastic surgery nor modern autopsy. The believer's truth about Jesus is always a truth told in love. How do you tell loving truths about a body? We sometimes pretend as if the most loving truth is a truth that lies about bodies by making them more attractive than they are – or than any body could be. Parents dote over their infant children, as those freshly in love gush about the unique and complete beauty of their new amours. We discount descriptions given by new parents and new lovers. To us, the infant looks pretty much like any other, and the new girlfriend or boyfriend has a funny nose and unconvincing hair. Love lies about bodies, we conclude. Or should we rather say: love discovers another way to talk about truths in bodies?

Some older Christian writers held, from reading Isaiah 53.2–3, that Jesus was in fact ugly.[17] Most Christian writers on the Passion have stressed that Jesus was made ugly on the cross. Some representations of the crucifixion seem to vie in representing his deformity – the twisting of the emaciated limbs, the gouges and tears in the flayed skin, or the inhuman agony of the jaundiced and blood-shot eyes. Often this sort of meditation has been linked to claims that Jesus' suffering was absolutely unique in its intensity, that he has suffered the woes of all humanity combined, and so on. I find it more helpful to think of Jesus on the cross as right in the middle of human suffering. Not everyone is executed in public for political or religious crimes, but then crucifixion is an easy way to go in comparison with many other forms of political and religious torture. So I conclude not that Jesus' body on the cross was the most deformed body of suffering, but that it looked worse than some and better than others. Whatever suffering his body showed when it was taken down, other bodies have shown far worse. Indeed, if Jesus had been executed in a more gruesome fashion (say, by being flayed and burned), would traditional iconography have been able to accomplish the transformation of an execution into a generic symbol? The availability of the cross as an image is an indication of his relatively moderate suffering – though also of our culturally induced insensibility to the suffering of that particular body.

What makes the ugliness of Jesus' crucified body important is not that it was the greatest physical ugliness, but that we are asked to see through it to the unspeakable beauty of

God. The crucifixion inverts our ordinary bodily aesthetic by claiming that the radiant source of all beauty was disclosed to us in a scourged, crucified, dead body. Bonaventure says it succinctly: if you want to understand the presence of goodness in this world of bodies, there is no other way than by walking the streets of Jerusalem on the way to Golgotha (Bonaventure 1993: 39).[18] Julian of Norwich describes it more graphically – too graphically for some readers. The head of Jesus, bleeding from its crown of thorns, is held over her while she suffers her own passion, and she looks up at it as most beautiful.[19]

Beautiful because desired, because loved? Both and neither. Paradoxical assertions about Jesus' beauty on the cross invite us to learn that bodies can be beautiful in ways we hadn't expected – or were perhaps afraid to think. A body can be beautiful even after rites of humiliation or pain not because those rites produce beauty, but because its beauty escapes those rites. How much more, then, might a loved body remain somehow beautiful no matter what. The height of sentimentality? Or an insight into the beauty that lies in human bodies being what they are? If the notion of the beauty of Jesus even when crucified is too much at present, or too suspiciously morbid, might we at least learn from it that a desired body can be complete, and so endowed with capacities for the erotic, even when it appears as ugly?

Some Christian theologians have claimed that *eros* couldn't fit with *agape* because *eros* was particular in two senses: it was directed at a specific object and it was choosy in its attractions.[20] This is a polemical notion of *eros*. We are used to having our erotic tastes put into tiny packages for a number of opposed and collusive reasons: to keep them confined, to keep them out of sight, to make them amenable to marketing. How are you going to sell beauty as a commodity unless you can make *eros* a form of commodity fetishism? But couldn't we take *eros* out of those packages to think about how it might not be confined to particular notions of beauty or particular acts and objects? And shouldn't we do so if we regard Jesus' body as a teaching about embodiment in every one of its moments? He shows us a body in which desire is not only for the predictably beautiful and in which *eros* can outlast even well-calibrated humiliations.

In each moment, Jesus' body is a complete human body. Meditate on how to represent that. We need as an emblem for Jesus' body neither the unsexed corpus of a crucifix nor its necessary opposite – a body with gigantic genitals. We don't want to replace the mutilated corpse on the crucifix with a Christian version of one of the ancient satyr statues, in which the body is dwarfed by an engorged phallus. Indeed, our representations of Jesus' body should show us most vividly how a body can be erotic without being only or obsessively erotic. We should learn from it how a body has sex without being just sex. We learn this, not coincidentally, from a divine body that is unafraid to be naked even when it is supposedly humiliated. Here Jesus trumps Nietzsche's Dionysus. Jesus is so divinely erotic that he need not be ashamed of either his "beauty" or his "ugliness." He is thus the god to teach us why our sexual shame really was a product of sin.

We should learn from the unashamed Jesus that our erotic reactions to him, whether we call him beautiful or ugly, are far from being a cause of shame. They are indispensable in our love of God. I am not thinking here again of the familiar and yet mysterious dependence of "mystical" language on the erotic.[21] Nor am I thinking of recent attempts to rediscover the sexuality latent in our theology of God.[22] No doubt our encounters with the divine must actualize our deepest capacities for joy and for intimacy, along with the highly charged sexual languages we have made to describe them. No doubt, too, our Scriptures record how many ways our deepest psychological formations have projected themselves onto representations of God. We have in the incarnation not only a concession to our bodily life, but a vindication of it.

After all, and on the most traditional teaching, our bodies are not something we Christians expect to abandon with a relieved or desperate "Good riddance!" We get our bodies back again and stay with them for eternity. We get them back as the best human bodies there are, which means, as bodies with genitals. Unless you regard human genitals as a sort of cancerous affliction, a disease, a deformity, that came upon us after sin, then you cannot regard them as something that will be missing from our bodies after resurrection – any more than you can hold that Jesus' resurrected body was a eunuch's body. Here again, take the organs as emblem of deeper powers. The erotic powers with which we were created were given not only for this world, hence not only for reproduction. They were given as instruments and enactments of intimate union. That union culminates in union with God.

This might seem a rather pious conclusion to a scandalous meditation. Love of God is also not a cause for shame. Nor is the love of Jesus, as completely embodied. But then I want to insist that we come to the piety only after what seems a scandalous meditation on Jesus as erotic. Indeed, I want to argue more generally that we come to tell loving truths about Jesus only after we have forced ourselves to tell truths about our loves. At the decisive moment of this meditation, Jesus doesn't want you to enlist for his side because you are infatuated with his nobility. He wants you to look at your body with newly loving eyes because you have seen him as humanly beautiful even without nobility.

At the end of our meditation, we can reverse the familiar pronouncement that Christian *agape* defeats, excludes, or totally redoes "pagan" *eros*. The meditation teaches that there is no way into a full language of *agape* except through the language of *eros*. Meditating on our multiple shames before a sexed savior may help us a little out of shame, into salvation, which is wholeness. Meditating on Jesus' beauty even when crucified may help us a little towards a less fetishistic notion of beauty and its *eros*. Certainly meditating on how we speak of our desire for Jesus will show us something about how to talk of his desires for us. Truth telling about *eros* comes before – and remains with – truth telling about *agape*. No other place to start Christian truth telling than face to face with Jesus.

Notes

1 The series "Son of God" premiered on BBC One on April 1, 2001. The image was released to the press on March 27 of that year.
2 There are also silences about the body of Jesus in the current quest for its historical truth. John Dominic Crossan's marvelous chapter title, "In the Beginning Is the Body," covers a text chiefly about healing miracles and patronage. Certainly it doesn't begin with *Jesus'* body (see Crossan 1995: 75–101). Geza Vermes, in his much longer *The Changing Faces of Jesus* (2000), not only avoids the physical face, but deals with other aspects of Jesus' bodily life either by dismissing them as fabulous or by treating them as lived scriptural citations. Jesus' circumcision is another "amusing snippet of a semilegendary nature" (p. 229) and his celibacy refers to interpretations of what is required for prophetic life, as exemplified by Philo on Moses (p. 273). History too can hide the body – or ignore it because of uncertain evidence.
3 We are beginning to get some provocative theological writing on Jesus' body as a sexed body, though much of it is discounted as "feminist" or "queer" theology (see, for example, Goss 1992: 69–72 and 81–5; and Heyward 1999: 123–7).

4 Ignatius of Loyola, *Spiritual Exercises*, Second Week, perhaps especially paragraphs [92]–[98] and [143]–[146] (as in Ignatius 1963: 218–20 and 226–7).

5 See Steinberg (1996). Steinberg is himself nervous that his topic will seem scandalous (see pp. 24, 36, 41).

6 A related example is the famous metal loincloth added by later hands to Michelangelo's statue of the risen Christ in the Roman church of S. Maria sopra Minerva. The loincloth has disappeared and reappeared during subsequent ecclesiastical regimes – a sort of thermometer for official sensitivities.

7 See the examples in Trexler (1993: 113–15); and Perez (1992: 211–14 and 219).

8 I keep speaking of Catholic art because I have lived in it. I suspect that the same is true for other Christian traditions only with significant qualifications. The eastern churches are constrained both by their iconoclastic prohibitions on statuary and by different iconographic emphases. Protestant traditions have long regarded Catholic art – and perhaps especially Catholic representations of Jesus' body – as idolatrous or morbid.

9 There is an old spiritual precept, "Follow the naked Christ naked." It has many allegorical and liturgical applications (e.g., in baptismal rites), but it has also been applied more literally in ascetical and penitential practices. For the desert monks, both demons and great saints arrive in the nude.

10 In this way too, Christians might reply to one of Nietzsche's most pointed criticisms, namely, that any true god would appear as naked because unashamed. "But such a god [as Dionysus] has nothing to do with all this venerable lumber and pomp. 'Keep that,' he would say, 'for yourself and your like and for anyone else who needs it! I – have no reason to cover my nakedness.'" (see Nietzsche 1973: [No. 295] 201).

11 There are tantalizing bits of evidence outside the canonical Gospels, especially in "Gnostic" gospels or other texts that emphasize secret initiation by Christ. But it is perhaps more interesting to recall that speculation about Jesus' "orientation" did not begin with Stonewall. It runs in English literature back beyond the first appearances of the word "homosexuality."

12 Compare Thomas Aquinas, *Summa Theologiae* part 3 question 15 article 2: "And in this way, the flesh of Christ, by the desire of the sensitive appetite, naturally had appetite for food and drink and sleep, and other things for which there can be appetite according to right reason." The roundabout phrasing shows the problem about attributing anything like our sexual desires to Christ. Christ would have had sexual "appetite" only according to right reason, that is, for the sake of procreation in a monogamous and permanent union of a man and a woman. If he had copulated in such a union, he would have indeed experienced sexual pleasure (compare *Summa* part 1 question 98 article 2 reply to objection 3, on hypothetical sexual pleasure in Eden). Since Jesus was not married, it would have been irrational for him to suffer sexual desires. Thomas is not at all hesitant to affirm that Jesus had genitals. He argues elsewhere in the *Summa* that it was appropriate for the Lord to be circumcised partly in order to show "the truth of his human flesh" (*Summa* 3.37.1).

13 John Paul II, *Ordinatio sacerdotalis* [Apostolic Letter on Reserving Priestly Ordination to Men Alone, May 22, 1994], together with Congregation for the Doctrine of the Faith, *Responsum ad dubium* [Concerning the Teaching Contained in *Ordinatio sacerdotalis*, October 28, 1995], and the accompanying, clarifying letter from then Cardinal Joseph Ratzinger (later Benedict XVI) on the same date.

14 Barton's impulses are recounted and analyzed in Moore (2001: 105–7).

15 Worry over the effeminacy of Christ in Protestant portraiture has yielded much to recent study. See, for example, McDannell (1995: 180); Morgan (1998: 111–23); and Moore (2001: 107–17).

16 Robert Neville shows how our (erotic) views on Jesus viewing us can be taken up into the larger language of friendship (see Neville 2001: 199–223, especially 214–17).

17 The tradition is introduced in Moore (2001: 96–9).

18   Not coincidentally, the remark follows a quotation from the Pseudo-Dionysius.

19   Julian of Norwich (1978): 128 ("everything around the cross was ugly to me"), 129 (blood), 136–7 (blood), 141 ("his freshness, his ruddiness, his vitality and his beauty" which, with death, now changes), and so on.

20   See famously Nygren (1957), as summarized, for example, in a chart (p. 210). Elsewhere in the book Nygren simply says that *eros* is the "principal adversary" of Christianity (p. 53). Nygren must be wrong not least because his teaching would deny the incarnation.

21   For help with how to begin examining our supposed familiarity with this language, see Kripal (2001: 15–23).

22   Rediscoveries sometimes happen at surprising sites, say, in Hans Urs von Balthasar (see Loughlin 1999b).

Chapter 20

Queen of Heaven

Tina Beattie

Our Lord, no one knows
how to address Your mother. [If] one calls her "virgin,"
her child stands up, and "married" –
no one knew her [sexually]. But if Your mother is
incomprehensible, who is capable of [comprehending] you?
(Ephrem the Syrian 1989: 131)

"She" is indefinitely other in herself. This is doubtless why she is said to be whimsical, incomprehensible, agitated, capricious . . . not to mention her language, in which "she" sets off in all directions leaving "him" unable to discern the coherence of any meaning. Hers are contradictory words, somewhat mad from the standpoint of reason, inaudible for whoever listens to them with ready-made grids, with a fully elaborated code in hand.
(Irigaray 1985b: 28–9)

Now the apostles were in the place Chritir with Mary. And Bartholomew came to Peter and Andrew and John, and said to them: Let us ask Mary, her who is highly favoured, how she conceived the incomprehensible or how she carried him who cannot be carried or how she bore so much greatness. . . . But Mary answered: Do not ask me concerning this mystery. If I begin to tell you, fire will come out of my mouth and consume the whole earth.
(Gospel of Bartholomew 2.1–15; Hennecke 1963: 492)

There is a riddle which describes a man looking at a photograph and saying, "Brothers and sisters have I none, but that man's father is my father's son." Whose photograph is he looking at? The logical answer is that he is looking at a photograph of his son. The difference between that riddle and family relationships between Mary and the Trinity is that the latter remain resistant to logic no matter how hard one tries to work them out. The fourth-century hymns and meditations of Ephrem the Syrian are a rich resource for these devotional riddles. Ephrem imagines Mary saying to Christ:

> Shall I call You Son?
> Shall I call You Brother? Shall I call You Bridegroom?
> Shall I call You Lord, O [You] Who brought forth his mother
> [in] another birth out of the water?
> "For I am [Your] sister from the house of David,
> who is a second father. Again, I am mother

because of Your conception, and bride am I
because of your chastity. Handmaid and daughter
of blood and water [am I] whom you redeemed and baptised."
(Hymn 16.9–10; Ephrem the Syrian 1989: 150)

In this chapter, I argue that such paradoxical language has the power to lead the believer away from the demands of rationality into the poetics of devotion and prayer, through the expression of forbidden desire. Psychoanalysis provides a resource by which theology might bridge the gulf between the relatively sober language of Marian doctrine and the often unrestrained excess of Marian devotion, reintegrating the two in a holistic encounter between Christian belief and praxis. However, this entails rediscovering a sense of wonder concerning Mary's role within the mystery of the incarnation, a mystery which celebrates the patristic insight that "He is the good Word of the good Father, and it is he who has established the order of all things, reconciling opposites and from them forming a single harmony" (Athanasius 1974: 398–9). It is this reconciliation of opposites and harmonious reintegration of difference which constitutes the incomprehensibility of the incarnation from the perspective of human reason.

"The Radically Redeemed"

As the Mother of God, model of the church and "the radically Redeemed" (Rahner 1965: 218), Mary is a sign of contradiction to the finite mind. Being both mother and creature of the new creation, she reveals to us what we will finally be in a Kingdom and Queendom where love overwhelms the law, life triumphs over death, and the human comes into the fullness of his or her divinization in Christ. This redeeming process is decisively inaugurated with Mary's *fiat*, which brings God into intimate communion with creation and thus overcomes the primal experience of alienation which Christianity interprets as the fall and psychoanalysis associated with the Oedipus complex (Beattie 2002: 45–50, 115–22). However, this process will only be fulfilled with the consummation of human and divine love in the heavenly wedding feast at the end of time. The believer is therefore called to inhabit a paradoxical space expressed in the language of memory and anticipation, yearning and fulfillment, mourning and celebration, constituting a *theopoetics* in which the conceptually impossible world which comes into being in the incarnation is kept alive in the liturgical life of the church, until Christ comes again in glory.

But governed as we are by the laws and concepts of a world still fallen as well as redeemed, we experience Mary as "queer," as an unsettling presence with the potential to disrupt the order of our theological and social systems. As the above quotation from the Gospel of Bartholomew suggests, she is a mystery with the power of a consuming fire to those who seek to question her. This apocryphal Gospel tells that Mary asked the apostles to surround her and hold her "so that, when I begin to speak, my limbs are not loosed" (Gospel of Bartholomew 2.14; Hennecke 1963: 493). As Mary was speaking, "fire came from her mouth, and the world was on the point of being burned up. Then came Jesus quickly and said to Mary: Say no more, or today my whole creation will come to an end. And the apostles were seized with fear lest God should be angry with them" (Gospel of Bartholomew 2.22; Hennecke 1963: 494).

I quote from this third-century Coptic text because its vivid imagery suggests the fascination but also the threat which Mary represents even today for those who seek to comprehend the mystery she symbolizes in Christ. It is a mystery which, were it to be revealed, would have the power to loosen the limbs of the body and burn up the known and familiar world. Perhaps that is why Protestant and Catholic theologians have gone to such extremes to control Mary's place in the story of salvation, in a way which limits her transgressiveness and inhibits her mystical potency. This theological struggle to inscribe her within the laws of rationality finds expression in Protestantism's banishment of maternal feminine symbolism and its commitment to an unambiguously patriarchal Father God. It finds different expression in Roman Catholic theology through a process of systematization which George Shea describes as follows in his study of the history of Mariology:

> Here, as in other areas, the onward march of theology acquired but slowly momentum, direction, discipline, and co-ordination . . . For those who would participate in this endeavour to consolidate and to extend the precious conquests of the centuries, almost indispensable is some familiarity with the history of Mariology. It is not otherwise than with a new commander on a field of battle; to cement his grip on the terrain already won, to plan and effect additional gains, he must first orient himself, striving to understand the position and disposition of his forces by diligent study of the campaign's history. (Shea 1954: 283–4)

This is the kind of knowledge through which, according to Irigaray, "he" seeks to know "her," "with ready-made grids, with a fully elaborated code in hand." Shea's militaristic imagery suggests that Mariology is particularly vulnerable to Michel Foucault's claim that the "history which bears and determines us has the form of a war rather than that of a language: relations of power, not relations of meaning" (Foucault 1984: 56). For women who have played no part in the history of Mariology but who find themselves bodily inscribed within its war-like discourse, the task of liberating theological symbols is complex and multidimensional. It requires going beyond the systematized domain of Mariology itself, in order to construct an alternative theological narrative which draws on different aspects of the Marian tradition. Patristic theology, with its fluid and manifold forms of expression, and Marian devotional writings, provide a language which approximates to the kind of plurivocity that Irigaray associates with a feminine subjectivity which is truly other, and not merely the other of the (masculine) same (see Irigaray 1993: 97–129).

However, although this quest for an alternative symbolics of subjectivity is of particular significance for feminism, it has relevance for all who recognize that the call to follow Christ is a call to a new way of being, in which the alienated subject of the secularized social order becomes a person made in the image and likeness of the tripersonal God, characterized by "loving, forgiving, relational and redeeming indwelling" (D'Costa 2000: xiv). This is what it means to be "radically redeemed." Hans Urs von Balthasar's insight that the Christian character is fundamentally Marian is flawed by his stereotypical representation of sexual difference, but it is nevertheless an invitation to reconsider Mary's significance as the model of Christian personhood for women and men alike (see Balthasar 1988–98: 283–360; Roten 1991). Mary makes Christ present to us when we follow her into a space of radical otherness in relation to the present order, so that we experience the queering of human values which constitutes the foretaste of our redemption. It is, therefore, when the systematic theologian surrenders "his" drive towards rationalization that he might encounter the fecundity of faith in the language of desire constituted as prayer, poetry, art, music, and carnival, but also as a "scrambling of the landmarks" (Lamy 2000) of the kinship systems which structure the patriarchal social order and inscribe its laws on the psyche. With these suggestions in mind, I turn now to consider the theological significance of Mary for the doctrine of the incarnation.

Virgin Mother, New Eve

The riches – some might say the excesses – of the Marian tradition have their origins in three theological insights of the early church: Mary is Virgin, Mary is Mother of God or Godbearer (*Theotokos*), and Mary is the New Eve. In patristic theology, none of these titles is an optional extra – all of them are central to the doctrine of the incarnation and the meaning of salvation.

From the fourth century, Mary's virginity has been increasingly interpreted as a sign of sexual purity, with the implication that there is a fundamental incompatibility between sex and God. However, for the early church, the doctrine of the virgin birth attested first and foremost to the divine origins and nature of Christ, so that it represented the vertical, God-human dimension of the incarnation (see Campenhausen 1964). To quote Ambrose of Milan (c. 339–397) in his Exposition of Luke (2.15), "[a] virgin giving birth is the sign of a divine mystery, not a human one" (Ambrose in Gambero 1999: 192). Mary's virginity is therefore primarily a theological symbol, or, according to Manuel Miguens, a theologoumenon. Miguens argues that this does not mean that its significance is purely symbolic, since "God's real interest in Christ's birth, and coming in general, is by far more aptly and efficaciously signified by a genuine and factual intervention than through a narrative which has to fabricate an imaginary event where, after all, the message remains highly conceptual and dialectical" (Miguens 1975: 162).

But while the doctrine of the virgin birth was primarily theological in the early church, Mary's virginity also had anthropological significance since it symbolized the transformation of the human in Christ. The redeemed person has escaped the cycle of sex, procreation, and death, and therefore the virginal body is a potent symbol of resurrection and eternal life. Gregory of Nyssa (c. 330–c.395) writes in his treatise *On Virginity* (ch. 13) that when death came to Mary, he "dashed his forces against the fruit of her virginity as against a rock, that he was shattered to pieces upon her, so in every soul which passes through this life in the flesh under the protection of virginity, the strength of death is in a manner broken and annulled" (Gregory of Nyssa 1994: 359–60).

Mary's virginity therefore represents the supernatural intervention of God into the human story, and the consequent transformation of the finite human into a divinized and immortal being. This idea is beautifully expressed in the Orthodox concept of *theosis*: "The human vocation is to fulfil one's humanity by becoming God through grace" (Clément 1997: 76).

The patristic understanding of the virgin birth poses a challenge to modern interpretations, both liberal and conservative. Liberals tend to interpret the conception of Christ as typical of mythological couplings in which a human mother is impregnated by a divine father and gives birth to a hero or a god (see Hamington 1995: 58; Lüdemann 1998; Baring and Cashford 1993: 563). But the first Christians formulated the doctrine of the virgin birth as an explicit refutation of pagan ideas of divine sexual procreation.[1] René Girard is more faithful to the early Christian vision than many theologians, when he interprets the virgin birth as a refusal of sexual violence and an affirmation of the essentially peaceful nature of the incarnation. Girard claims that "[t]he birth of the gods is always a kind of rape" (Girard 1987: 220), and he contrasts this with the fact that "all the themes and terms associated with the virgin birth convey to us a perfect submission to the non-violent will of the God of the Gospels" (Girard 1987: 221).

Conservatives share with liberals the tendency to endow the virgin birth with sexual connotations, thereby losing sight of its primary theological significance. Balthasar posits a "suprasexual (and not sexless) relationship between the incarnate Word and his Church" (Balthasar 1988–98: II, 412). In his elaborate metaphysics of sexual difference, this relationship is personified in the relationship between Christ and Mary, and there is an implicit suggestion that the conception of Christ is a transcendent act of divine copulation between an essentially masculine God and an essentially feminine creature.[2] But to suggest this is to deny the theological insight that Mary falls pregnant by the power of God acting through the Holy Spirit in an entirely non-sexual way, which introduces something new and unheard of into the human story. Justin Martyr (died c. 165), refuting comparisons between the virgin birth and the sexual procreation of the gods in his "First Apology" (ch. 33), writes of the Spirit which "when it came upon the virgin and overshadowed her, caused her to conceive, not by intercourse, but by power" (Justin Martyr 1996: 174).

The tendency to interpret the conception of Christ exclusively in metaphors of heterosexual intercourse is undermined even further when one considers that for the early church, particularly the Syriac Church, the Holy Spirit by which Mary conceived was sometimes understood as feminine. Consider, for example, Ode 19 of the second-century Odes of Solomon, which uses startling gender metaphors to describe Christ's conception and birth:

> The Holy Spirit opened her womb,
> and mixed the milk of the two breasts of the Father. . . .
> The womb of the Virgin caught it,
> and She received conception and gave birth. . . .
> And she did not need a midwife
> Because He [God] delivered her.
> Like a man she gave birth by will.
> (Quoted in Harvey 1993: 125–6).

Such "queering" of the conception of Christ renders it inherently unstable so that it defies any fixed positioning within the bounds of human reason and gender constructs. As theological symbols become more literal in gendered and philosophical terms, they lose this capacity to unsettle intellectual theories about the relationship between God and humanity in Christ.

If the virgin birth represents discontinuity and transformation in the story of creation, the motherhood of Mary represents continuity and integration, so that it affirms the fullest possible identification of Christ with the human condition from the beginning. Mary's motherhood is the horizontal dimension of the incarnation, incorporating Christ into the historical, social, and material realities of life in all its contingency and finitude. To quote Athanasius (295–373), in his Letter to Epictetus (7), "[t]he nature which came forth from Mary was human, according to the divine Scriptures, and the body of the Lord was real; real, I say, since he existed like we do. Moreover, Mary is our sister; for all of us surely have our origins in Adam" (Athanasius 1998: 573; in Buby 1996: III, 106).

In the earliest Christian defenses of the incarnation, Mary's motherhood represents the supreme challenge to those who argue that the divine cannot identify itself with the inherent corruption of the flesh. The fact that God was born of a mother affirms that the flesh is good and created by God. Tertullian (c. 155–c. 225), in his characteristically polemical style, gives a graphic account of the gestation and birth of Christ which is, as far as I know, unique among Christian writings on the incarnation. His treatise *On the Flesh of Christ* culminates with a challenge to his opponent, Marcion: "You detest a human being at his birth; then after what fashion do you love anybody? . . . Well, then, loving man [Christ] loved his nativity also, and his flesh as well" (Tertullian 1870: 164). Augustine (354–430) uses a similar argument against his opponents with less vivid imagery. He acknowledges that Christ could have been born without a woman, but says, "Suppose I am not able to show why he should choose to be born of a woman; you must still show me what he ought to avoid in a woman" (Augustine 1991c: 21). He continues by imagining Christ saying:

> To show that it's not any creature of God that is bad, but that it's crooked pleasures that distort them, in the beginning when I made man, I made them male and female. . . . Here I am, born of a man, born of a woman. So I don't reject any creature I have made, but I reject and condemn sins, which I didn't make. (Augustine 1991c: 22)

The motherhood of Mary, therefore, is symbolically significant for two related reasons: first, it affirms the full humanity of Christ, and secondly, it affirms the inherent goodness of the material world and human flesh – including female flesh – as created by God. Gradually, particularly since the Counter Reformation, these insights have been lost to Catholic Mariology. Instead of a fully human mother who incarnates the fully human God, Mary has become a transcendent feminized principle identified with a transcendent and disembodied Christ (see Boss 2000: 26–72; Beattie 2000: 150–9). From the seventeenth century, depictions of Mary in art tend to show her without the child in her arms, an image of idealized femininity divorced from the reality of the flesh. Related to this, the emphasis on Mary's virginal purity has lost its early significance as a symbol of the redeemed flesh free from the corruption of death, and has come instead to signify a body uniquely set apart and preserved from the taint of the flesh itself, especially the sexual female flesh symbolized by Eve. Such shifts in the theological imagination distort the very heart of the Christian faith, for they deny the significance of Mary for the incarnation as a symbol of reconciling peace between the Word and the flesh, the body and God, creation and the Creator.

But the wonder of this reconciling peace lies not in Mary's virginity nor in her motherhood, but in the juxtaposition of the two. It is here that opposites meet and the ruptured world of the fall is restored to a state of integrity and wholeness beyond our human capacity to comprehend. In the words of Irenaeus (c. 130–c. 208) – in *Against Heresies* (3.19.3) – "The Lord has given us a sign 'as deep as Sheol and as high as heaven', such as we should not have dared to hope for. How could we have expected to see a virgin with child, and to see in this child a 'God with us' (Isaiah 7.11, 14)" (Irenaeus in Clément 1997: 36). In an era of genetic engineering and *in vitro* fertilization, it is perhaps impossible for us to appreciate the significance of the term "virgin mother," but for the pre-modern mind it marks a shift beyond a conceptual world of binary opposites (either/or), to a conception which is literally impossible because it takes place in the excluded middle of both/and. Gregory Nazianzen (c. 330–90) declares (Oration 45, For Easter 9): "What a strange conjunction! What a paradoxical union! . . . [H]e occupies the middle ground between the subtlety of God and the density of the flesh" (Clément 1997: 88). In this paradoxical union, *either* virgin *or* mother becomes *both* virgin *and* mother, and in this reconciling movement the world is transformed from within by the divine presence through the refiguration of language around the poetry of faith. Between the virgin and the mother we encounter the Other, who comes to us as one of us if we ourselves remain within that space of wonder which we call faith.

The title New Eve has multiple associations which are also complex and diffuse, and which introduce a third term – that of woman – into early representations of Mary's virginal motherhood. New Eve refers both to Mary and the church in early Christian thought, but my concern here is with its Marian associations.[3] In patristic typology, a connection was made between Luke's account of the annunciation, and the Genesis story of creation. From this point of view, Mary became identified with the virgin earth of Paradise from which the Second Adam was created, and as the first woman of the new creation she also became known as the New Eve in relation to Christ, the New Adam. In Irenaeus's theory of recapitulation, Mary's identification with Eve signifies that all of creation from the beginning has been redeemed in Christ, in such a way that there is an "intercircling which traces back from Mary to Eve" (Irenaeus, *Against Heresies*, 3.22.4).

Such typology gave rise to a series of associations between Mary and Eve which have, in later interpretations, been understood in starkly contrasting terms. The Vatican II document on the church, *Lumen Gentium* (1964), repeats the patristic aphorism "death through Eve, life through Mary," in a series of oppositions in which Eve remains unambiguously identified with fallenness, death and sin (Flannery 1992: 416). However, once again this represents a distortion rather than a development of patristic theology. At least until the early Middle Ages, the relationship between Mary and Eve was expressed in prismatic images in such a way that Mary represented the redemption, not the condemnation, of Eve. As the New Eve in the story of salvation, Mary is the generic woman who guarantees the redemption of all women. Patristic writings on the Magnificat sometimes interpret it as Eve's song of salvation, so that Eve is the humble handmaid who is exalted in Mary. In a homily which sings the praises of Mary in the context of women's redemption, Proclus of Constantinople (d. 446) preaches (Homily 5.3) that on "account of Mary all women are blessed. No longer does the female stand accused, for it has produced an offspring which surpasses even the angels in glory. Eve is fully healed" (Proclus in Constas 2003: 261).

In art and devotion as well as in doctrine, this reconciling image of the redemption of woman has yielded to dualistic imagery in which Mary and Eve represent opposing and irreconcilable images of womanhood as either the carnal, unredeemed female flesh, or the impossible ideal of the virgin mother who is, in the title of Marina Warner's book, "alone of all her sex" (Warner 1985).[4] There are abundant images in patristic theology which lend support to such dualisms, but only if one loses sight of the fact that these functioned to develop an understanding of what it would mean to be unredeemed – a question which is only ever asked from the perspective of redemption. Mary is, in the words of Cardinal Newman, "a daughter of Eve unfallen" (Newman 1891: 47; in Graef 1985: 112), and Eve is what Mary would have been, had God not redeemed the world in Christ. This is not a dialectical struggle since the two are not in conflict. Eve is always already redeemed in Mary, and therefore Eve's suffering must be understood as the other face of redemption, not as the face of damnation. Eve represents the creative suffering of the woman who from the beginning lives in the promise of redemption, since the *protoevangelium*, the first good news of Christ, was given before she was cast out of Eden. God says to the serpent, "I will make you enemies of each other: you and the woman, your offspring and her offspring. It will crush your head and you will strike its heel" (Genesis 3.15).[5]

It is not difficult to see how these three core theological symbols – Virgin, Mother, and New Eve – gradually led the devotional imagination into complex labyrinths of kinship and nuptial relationships as Christians reflected on Mary's relationship to Christ. Ephrem was the first to call Mary the Bride of her Son (Graef 1985: 58), but such imagery does not become common in the Western church until the Middle Ages (see Balthasar 1988–98: III, 300–18), when Mary's identity increasingly becomes merged with that of the church as Bride of Christ. Although certain verses of the Song of Songs had always been applied to Mary, Rupert of Deutz, writing in the early twelfth century, was the first to give an exclusively Marian interpretation to the whole Canticle. This marked the beginning of a trend in which nuptial Marian imagery became increasingly lavish and widespread, borrowing as it did from the language of courtly love (Graef 1985: 226–9, 245–59). Philip of Harvengt (d. 1183) writes, "[n]ot only does the Mother most tenderly embrace the Son, but also the Spouse the Bridegroom; and he enjoys their mutual embraces as much as she, when he, kissing her, reposes most sweetly between her breasts" (Philip quoted in Graef 1985: 255).

Perhaps unsurprisingly in the face of such devotions, the church has been cautious about using nuptial language in Marian doctrine, and Vatican II documents do not use the word spouse in relation to Mary (see O'Carroll 1990: 333–4). However, the trajectory of Marian devotion from Ephrem to Balthasar shows that such imagery exerts a powerful hold over the Christian imagination. In Balthasar's theology, the relationship between Mary and Christ represents "the creation of an absolute relationship between man and woman that is free of all entanglement in sin: here the woman is both Mother and Bride with regard to the same man, in a real but suprasexual way" (Balthasar 1988–98: III, 327).

I turn now to consider the theological significance of the foregoing, not from the perspective of doctrine but from the perspective of the psychology of prayer and worship. These are, however, not separate concerns, for central to my argument is the belief that the separation between doctrine and spirituality does violence to the holistic and reconciling vision of the early church. The language of theology and the language of devotion should be an integrated whole which finds expression and practice in the liturgical life of the church, which in turn shapes the Christian life both communally and individually around the story of Christ. So with the insights of psychoanalytic theory, how might a theologian interpret these developments in Marian devotion? Are they evidence of repressions and neuroses which have accumulated around the symbols of the Christian faith, which should be replaced by more ethical or "healthy" concepts of relationality? Or are they potentially points of creative instability in the Christian narrative, which can push the imagination beyond the constraints of law and reason, to inhabit a once and future world where everything is possible with God? Space precludes a detailed exploration of these complex questions, so I am going to focus on the psycholinguistic theory of Julia Kristeva (for a psychological analysis of Marian devotion see Carroll 1986). My concern here is more with the analysis of culture than the individual psyche, although as cultural theorists such as Kristeva, Lacan, and Irigaray argue, culture forms the psyche in its image so that the hierarchies and values of the social order are sustained through the psychological structuring of the individual socialized subject (see Grosz 1989 and 1995). To recognize this, and to acknowledge the validity of psychoanalysis, is not to render the theological narrative redundant. On the contrary, it can demonstrate why theology goes beyond the secular discourses of modernity, without ever being free of their influence and interrogation.

The Alienated Self

Unlike Irigaray, Kristeva does not challenge the necessity of the Oedipus complex for the development of socialized subjectivity, which means that she also accepts the necessary masculinity of the subject of the symbolic order (see Grosz 1989: 63–9).[6] Through the intervention of the father in the early mother–child relationship, the child achieves the separation required to become an individuated subject, modeled on the paternal example. But for Kristeva, the masculine subject is a less stable and coherent entity than the social order acknowledges, and the cost of sustaining the illusion of a unified, unambiguously masculine self is too high. While Irigaray argues that the move towards a transformed social and sexual ethic will come about through the sexual differentiation of culture and discourse, Kristeva argues instead for the internalization of difference through an acceptance of the idea of the divided and self-alienated subject. She finds in Freudian psychoanalysis a rich resource for rethinking the ethical and religious paradigms of Western culture, in a way that takes into account the interrelatedness of language and the body in the drives of the unconscious, and also the suffering associated with the insatiable yearning for love and the unavoidable awareness of death identified with the maternal relationship. This subliminal experience of love and abjection, desire and mourning, which haunts the speaking subject of the symbolic order, finds expression in the language of the *chora*, based on Plato's concept in the *Timeaus* of "an ancient, mobile, unstable receptacle, prior to the One, to the father, and even to the syllable, metaphorically suggesting something nourishing and maternal" (Kristeva 1987a: 5). While religion sublimates this maternal language and allows it partial expression in the language of devotion, the secular symbolic order represses it altogether.[7] Although Kristeva does not rule out the efficacy of religion as a means to psychological health, she sees Christianity as an anachronism in Western culture, a dying discourse which has been replaced by the discourses of psychoanalysis (see Kristeva 1987a). While I would take issue with Kristeva on this point, I do not think her premature dismissal of the relevance of Christianity invalidates the value of her insights for Christian thinkers.

Kristeva argues that Freud exposes the extent to which the Enlightenment project, with its idea of the autonomous, coherent, and unified subject, is achieved through a process of repression and alienation which makes us "strangers to ourselves" (Kristeva 1991), because the rationalized subject is unable to accommodate the "uncanny strangeness" (Kristeva 1991: 183) associated with maternal femininity, death, and the biological drives.[8] This strangeness is projected onto others who become "foreigners" when viewed from the perspective of the various forms of nationalism and patriotism which have gripped Europe since the seventeenth century. If we seek to build a culture of peace, suggests Kristeva, we must learn from Freud in order to recognize the foreignness, the uncanny, within ourselves. "The foreigner is within me, hence we are all foreigners. If I am a foreigner, there are no foreigners" (Kristeva 1991: 192).

For Kristeva, the present crisis in Western identity and ethics will only be resolved through the displacement of the subject and a recognition of the self as psychologically divided between identity and otherness, love and abjection, desire and loss. It is in the tension between the *chora* or the semiotic, and the socio-symbolic, that we experience the truly human as "the subject in process" (Lechte 1991: 27). However, this means that we need collective access to a way of expressing the maternal semiotic, which necessitates the creation of a cultural symbolics of motherhood beyond religion, possibly based on the language and experience of mothers themselves, since in modern Western society we are confronted with "a motherhood that today remains, after the Virgin, without a discourse" (Kristeva 1987b: 262). The rediscovery of a secularized form of maternal discourse might in turn allow for "an heretical ethics separated from morality, an *herethics*, [which] is perhaps no more than that which in life makes bonds, thoughts, and therefore the thought of death, bearable: herethics is undeath [*a-mort*], love . . . *Eia mater, fons amoris . . .*" (Kristeva 1987b: 263).

But is Kristeva right in declaring the end of maternal religion and its replacement by psychoanalysis? I think she radically underestimates the ongoing potency of the Madonna as both a religious and semi-secularized symbol in Western culture. One study offers a conservative estimate of 60 to 70 million religiously motivated visits to Western European shrines every year (Nolan and Nolan 1989: 1). If one bears in mind that many of these are Marian shrines such as Lourdes, Medjugore, and Fatima, this suggests that Marian devotion is a powerful semiotic force in the modern world – semiotic because it is both dynamic and hidden, influential and largely unacknowledged by society. Even in secularized Europe, while religious devotion has declined, the Marian presence is written across the face of culture in architecture, art, music, literature, and film. The Madonna stands watch over a postmodern world in many guises, from the outrageous parodies of her pop singer namesake, to the whimsical sentimentality of the Princess Diana cult, as a reminder of a maternal tradition that has been disempowered but not destroyed, evacuated of religious meaning but not thereby rendered meaningless. The Mother of God still forms the matrix in which the Western imaginary finds collective expression in whispered, forbidden longings for God. Rather than psychoanalysis seeking to displace religion, it is surely possible for the two to encounter one another in a mutual spirit of exploration and discovery about what it means to be truly human.[9]

The Child of God

Psychoanalysis exposes a psychological world of alienation and grief focused on the trauma of childhood. Christianity offers a vision of a God who meets us with a sign of hope in the place of our sorrow, perhaps in the place where we are called to be "like a little child" (Mark 10.15) in order to enter the Kingdom of Heaven. Noel O'Donoghue, writing about Thérèse of Lisieux, says that she "saw that the figure of the child was central to the message of Jesus (how consistently dogmatic theologies overlook this)!" (O'Donoghue 1996: 73) The language of Marian devotion, configured around forbidden worlds of yearning, love, and loss, allows the Christian person as a child of God to inhabit an imaginary world wherein his or her deepest and most ancient longings can find veiled expression and partial relief. From a theological perspective, this is problematic only if our image of God is that of the stern and forbidding patriarchal Father who withholds consolation and disapproves of joy. But if, in Christ, we come to know God as a maternal father, a father identified with idealized maternal qualities of nurture and compassion, then God can be experienced as a source of *jouissance* in our ecstasy and anguish.[10] As Michael Palmer argues, "[t]he fact that Freud has defined religion as wishful-thinking does not mean that God is only a wish and not a reality because, after all, a real God might exist who corresponds to that wish" (Palmer 1997: 81).

We yearn for a God who is mother and father, lover, husband, bride, sister, brother – in other words, a God who is an epiphanic presence in our most intimate human relationships. Often, this is a God whose back seems turned to us even and perhaps especially in those relationships. Alienation can seem more real than reconciliation, the exile and estrangement of the Fall is a more credible human condition than the promise of the wedding feast, and sexual and familial relationships are the contexts wherein people are prey to the worst forms of physical and emotional abuse. But it is in the anticipatory space of such relationships perfected and liberated in love that we are invited to explore the relationship between the human and God, and through that to find a language of reconciliation which is manifest in our capacity for forgiveness and loving celebration together here in this life, as limited and vulnerable beings in communion with one another and with God.

Kristeva describes psychoanalysis as "a journey into the strangeness of the other and of oneself, toward an ethic of respect for the irreconcilable" (Kristeva 1991: 182). The paradox of the incarnation entails a life of faith situated in the impossible space of reconciliation between irreconcilable opposites. This surely could be described as "an ethic of respect for the irreconcilable," inviting us to a recognition of God as the absolute Other, the ultimate Foreigner, and yet the one who is also so close that, like Mary, I recognize this God as the stranger within myself. Maria Rainer Rilke writes:

> Strangely I heard a stranger say:
> I am with you.
> (Rilke quoted in Hillesum 1996: 23)

Mary, the stranger, the queer one, calls us to an encounter with an other self, the radically redeemed self who is an other because it is the not-yet self that is coming to birth within us, through prayer and worship, through service and love, but also through pain and separation, through failure and alienation, through the strange experience of being divine and yet human, mortal and yet eternal. The Christian life is a space of transgressive play between worlds, the playfulness of Wisdom herself, who is "ever at play" in the presence of God (Proverbs 8.30–1). It is a vocation to self-awareness, to a recognition of the limitations and possibilities of human becoming, through which we discover the freedom to "play for real, for keeps, at forming bonds: creating communities, helping others, loving, losing. Gravity becomes frivolity that retains its memory of suffering and continues its search for truth in the joy of perpetually making a new beginning" (Kristeva 1987b: 52).

As the first persons of the new beginning, the New Adam and the New Eve come into the fullness of being, not through separation and repression but in loving relationship which, in the faith of the church, comes to be described in all the language of human desire. In this encounter of woman and man made new, God's fatherly presence serves not to divide but to unite mother and child in a perfect loving union which displaces the oedipal father gods with their prohibitions and laws, and inaugurates a world in which there is only love without end.[11]

Christian personhood is situated in the space of encounter between the infinity of love and the finitude of the law, a space which might be described in terms of what Gillian Rose calls the "broken middle" (Rose 1992a; see also Rose 1992b). The middle ground I am exploring in this chapter is not yet the reconciled space of the eschaton. It is a space of ambiguity, tension, and disruption. Our experience resonates with that of our primal parents, who find themselves exiled and alienated from God and from one another in a wilderness of pain and death. But through the transgressive potency of prayer, we find ourselves at play with God and with one another, as sisters, brothers, lovers, husbands, wives, daughters, sons, and friends of God. And in this space where hope and desolation together form the shadow dance of the Christian soul, the wounded orphan (Kristeva 1987a: 55) of the Freudian psyche calls out to the Mother of God in prayer and not in despair, in a language of *jouissance* laden with insatiable longings for wholeness and peace.

> Hail, our queen, mother of mercy, our life, our sweetness and our hope.
> We cry to you, exiles as we are,
> children of Eve;
> we sigh to you, groaning and weeping
> in this valley of tears.
> Ah then, our intercessor, turn your eyes – your merciful eyes – upon us.
> And after this exile is over
> show to us Jesus, blessed fruit of your womb.
> O merciful, O holy, O sweet virgin Mary.

Notes

1   For a discussion of the difference between the virginal conception of Christ and the mythical births of the gods see Campenhausen (1964: 27, 32–3). See also Daniélou (1949: 162–4).

2   Compare Balthasar's claim that "[h]owever the One who comes forth from the Father is designated, as a human being he must be a man if his mission is to represent the Origin, the Father, in the world" (Balthasar 1988–98: III, 284).

3   For a more developed discussion of the distinction between the Church as New Eve and Mary as New Eve in patristic theology see Beattie (2000).

4   For the origins of this title in the writings of Caelius Sedulius, see Warner (1985: 368 n. 1).

5   The Vulgate translates this verse as "she (*ipsa*) shall crush thy head, and thou shalt lie in wait for her heel." It is now generally agreed that this is a mistranslation, and that the word should be *ipse* (which is masculine or neuter). See Graef (1985: 1–3).

6   See also Kristeva (1995) in which she explores the risks for women in transgressing the boundaries of the masculine symbolic order.

7   In secular society, Kristeva identifies certain forms of literature, particularly the *avant garde* of the nineteenth and early twentieth centuries, with the transgressive potency of the semiotic, i.e. the fluctuating language of desire associated with the mother. See Grosz (1989: 55–60) and Lechte (1991).

8   It should be noted that Kristeva is more Freudian than Lacanian in her interpretation of the drives, insofar as she endows them with biological significance whereas Lacan would construct them entirely in linguistic terms.

9   There is of course a vast body of literature which explores the creative interface between psychoanalysis and religion. Jungians in particular tend to take a more benign view of religion than Freudians, but in the work of post-Freudian theorists such as Irigaray, Kristeva, and Lacan there is a less negative attitude towards the ongoing relevance of religious belief than is found in Freud.

10 *Jouissance* is difficult to translate, but it is a word which suggests the eroticized language of desire associated with the Freudian unconscious and with mysticism (see Irigaray 1985a: 191–202; see also Lacan 1982).

11 See Paul Ricoeur's argument that Jewish and Christian concepts of God constitute a rejection of the oedipal father gods of the pagan cults (1974). Space precludes a discussion of the fatherhood of God in this chapter, although in a more detailed discussion it would be important to ask how the language of Marian devotion might refigure the theology of fatherhood. Kristeva writes extensively on God as the symbolic ideal of the father (see Kristeva 1987a: 139–50 and Kristeva 1987b; see also the argument in D'Costa 2000: 77–97).

Chapter 21

Desirous Saints

David Matzko McCarthy

The world is full of stories. We live by them and in them. They tell us who we are. *Elizabeth*, Shekhar Kapur's 1998 film about the Virgin Queen, is a wonderful example. The film has been criticized for its historical inaccuracies, but it is a great story with much to say about us and our history. Reviewers cannot help but disparage its outlandish historical liberties, but they love the film (Ebert 1998). Janet Maslin of the *New York Times* quips that "Elizabeth is presented as a glamorously stressed-out modern woman who must cope with a super-intense case of having it all" (Maslin 1998). She notes that Kapur's ignorance about Queen Elizabeth I "only helps to make his Elizabeth that much sassier a sovereign, slouching on her throne." Kapur is obviously more concerned to entertain and enliven than to give "just" the facts. Maslin offers an accurate list of his priorities. "His film concerns itself with elaborate appearances, anachronistically modern flourishes, Roman Catholic–Protestant intrigue, the difficulty of resolving career with personal life and the small matter of Elizabethan history, pretty much in that order" (Maslin 1998). Kapur's efforts to lift Elizabeth I out of the "formaldehyde of historical accuracy" are welcomed by a critic from *Time* magazine (Fitzgerald 1998: 44). *Elizabeth* is hagiography at its best; it is a story about an exemplary figure told through a history not entirely her own.

Kapur's Elizabeth offers an apt starting point for a consideration of saints and desire. The setting for her story is not so much sixteenth-century England or the monarchy, but her body. As the plot unfolds, she is told that her body is no longer her own, and in the end, she will give herself over to others, married to England as the Virgin Queen. I will use Kapur's *Elizabeth* as an exemplary story of the modern sexual self and as a site for inquiry about the relation between hagiography and the saints. Elizabeth will be juxtaposed with the story of St Rose of Lima. St Rose (1586–1617) presents a difficult case. Like Elizabeth, her body tells a story, but unlike Kapur's modern image of the Queen, Rose's flight from sexual desire will strike most readers as appalling. Her desire for God appears to set her against her own body. Rose seems to convey a story of oppression and violence, which are so thoroughly internalized in her as victim that she is the most formidable instrument of her own suffering. Without backing away from her suffering, I will suggest that Rose's story is redemptive only if it is distressing. If her story is wild with anguish, hers is passion of God.

A Sexual Martyr

Kapur's rejuvenation of Elizabeth is a narrative of sexual desire. He tells his story of the Virgin Queen with heavy emphasis on the queen's "virginity," which she accepts as a grim political necessity, given that she is not, nor is inclined to be, a virgin. Sex is not a subplot of the film; it is a primary conveyance of the plot and, more importantly, of character. Mary, for instance, is the queen whose husband, Philip II, is repulsed by her bed. She is a "type," like Cinderella's evil step-mother, whose wickedness only serves to ennoble the fair Princess Elizabeth. Elizabeth is a carefree, dancing lover who, at first, is under the spell of Robert Dudley's love. Her rise as mature Queen and her increasing sense of power and self-possession are mirrored in the fate of Dudley. It is he, not she, who is destroyed by their love. Dudley's degeneration is sealed through a loveless and, as it turns out, a deadly tryst with one of Queen Elizabeth's ladies-in-waiting. Unknown to Dudley, the young woman wears a dress recently given to Elizabeth, not yet worn and laced with poison. As he tears at her dress, her panting turns to frantic screams. Sex turns fatal. Dudley can do nothing but run from Elizabeth's dying surrogate. Could this have been the Queen in Dudley's arms?

Kapur's film might appear to be a simple costume drama, but *Elizabeth* carries hints of complexity, not merely in its staging and props, but also in its use of sex to deliver the meaning of events. In early scenes with Dudley, for instance, sex conveys innocence and purity. Elizabeth and Dudley are the only characters in the film that make love in the light of day. Elizabeth conceals nothing, no ulterior motives and no misgivings or shame about sex. In good modern fashion, sex is a sign of the true, unadulterated self. Later in the plot, sexual deviance becomes a convenient sign for the young Queen in a moment of decision. She has been pressured to marry, for her own safety and the good of England. She does not know how to resist. Her resolve comes to her when she witnesses her French suitor, Duc d'Anjou, in his cross-dressing exploits. After discovering him in drag, she gives a hardy laugh and announces that there will be no more talk about marriage. Duc d'Anjou's deviance puts marriage before her eyes as the true danger. If sex is innocence, it is pretense and corruption as well.

Sex is also a sign of treachery and sedition. The treachery of Elizabeth's nemesis, the Duke of Norfolk, is signaled during his first appearance on screen, by means of a lover's bite from his mistress and mole, a handmaid to the Queen. In contrast to Elizabeth and Dudley in the open air, Norfolk's mistress bites his thumb in the shadows, with subtlety and with hints of violence. Likewise, their final acts of lusty love-making are dark. At the close of the film, their erotic movements are simultaneous with the bloody undoing of Norfolk's plot against Elizabeth. Sex is intertwined with Norfolk's own brutality and with the violence that he will suffer. Sex is given the troublesome resonance of sacrifice. Ultimately, Norfolk will lose his head, and Elizabeth will bear the pallid mask of the Virgin Queen. Both are conceived as martyrdoms.

Elizabeth's martyrdom is revealed through the very structure of the narrative. It is a sexual sacrifice. Norfolk's sacrifice, in contrast, hinges upon his questionable claim to have a cause for which to die. Upon his arrest, he describes his own impending death as martyrdom, but his self-importance is quickly put to rest by Elizabeth's adviser, Walsingham, whose own cynicism allows him to see through to Norfolk's self-serving motives. Elizabeth's martyrdom is undeniable. The film opens as three Protestants, under Mary's reign, wail and shriek as their heads are shaved, and scalps cut open, in preparation for the stake. The scene is appalling to say the least. The display of sheer cruelty is witness to a true martyrdom and true sacrifice. Just before the closing scene, the meaning of these events is transferred to Elizabeth. Her ladies-in-waiting wail as her long hair is brusquely "hacked off so that she may don the garish red wig of the Virgin Queen" (Alleva 1998: 14). Although bloodlessly, she too is being prepared for martyrdom, the sacrifice of a sexless existence.

Kapur's narrative works, in large part, because Elizabeth's fate represents a type or category of modern martyrdom. Queen Elizabeth I, as a historical individual, fades because her body and her story are transferred to another time. At the beginning of the film she is natural and free. She is "in touch" with what is real and true. She is a young person with long, loose hair who dresses unconventionally and seems to disavow the conventions of her social station. In short, the narrative casts her as the sixteenth-century version of a free-loving-dancing-in-the-fields hippie. The telling of her story faces the challenge of explaining how this noble young woman of conscience becomes a colorless queen, while, at the same time, maintaining her (sexual) integrity. How is it that we are domesticated so readily when love and sex are meant to be free?

As implausible as denying the sexual self might be in our world, Elizabeth's story makes sense of it. Elizabeth, as the Virgin Queen, is clearly distinguished from Mary who plays the anti-type, the frigid hag of a half-sister. Mary is rigid and dogmatic. She has no spirit of life in her; therefore, sexual vitality is missing from her constitution. But how is it that Elizabeth allows her sexual self to be bound and repressed? How is it that she allows her body to be constrained by the needs of others? Unlike pitiful Mary, Elizabeth is a tragic figure. Her sexual goodness and the original purity of her sexual self are sustained only as they are ruined by the necessities of her duties and integrity as Queen.

Typically, the modern sexual comedy moves from inhibition and social constraints to sexual discovery. In the process, the protagonists of this tale find themselves. They awaken from a long sleep as they are enlivened by sexual desire, as desire frees the true self. Elizabeth's story retains the same construction of the sexual self, but reverses the plot. Her story begins with the true sexual self, and ends with the martyred Virgin Queen. The narrative first establishes her as a free and true sexual self, and then makes sense of her sexless future and her self-denial.

Hagiography

Kapur's Elizabeth is criticized, in historical terms, for reasons that represent modern difficulties with traditional hagiography. Writing at the beginning of the twentieth century, Hippolyte Delehaye, famous for his "scientific hagiography," is critical of popular legends in ways still prominent today. "An idealized figure," he observes, "takes the place of history's sharply defined and living portrait" (Delehaye 1962: 19). Delehaye attributes hagiographic abstraction to the subjective element of human understanding. On the one hand, we tend to see what we want to see, and on the other, even our fair understanding of events requires intuitive links that cloud the complexity of historical experience (Delehaye 1962: 12–14). Delehaye outlines a critical method for reducing the damage that hagiography brings upon its biographies, but he admits that the very nature of hagiography makes extensive historical "correction" unlikely. Like Kapur's Elizabeth, the saints are "types" rather than individuals, and their stories present explanatory schemes and markers for histories and identities not their own.

Pre-modern, pre-critical hagiographers (including those that are still with us today) expect the saints to provide imitable and theologically expressive ways of life, either as exemplary in virtue or as descriptive of God's ways, grace, and power in the world. Saints are expected to transform us. They are expected to disturb the world with God. Delehaye explains that hagiographers write according to age-old historical conventions. They hope to entertain and to enlighten, "not only to interest people, but above all to edify them, to do them good" (Delehaye 1962: 54). The life of the saint is presented for the transformation of those who receive it. The hearer is the one whose life is re-positioned and re-interpreted, like the changes put upon Ignatius of Loyola while he plays out the lives of the saints in his sickbed. Ironically, the reverse is the case as well. "Historical persons are deprived of their individuality, removed from their proper surroundings, and in a way isolated in time and space" (Delehaye 1962: 19). With the impulse to transform, the stories of saints become otherworldly.

Characteristically modern theories of sainthood attempt to break with traditional conventions by following contemporary standards of historical detachment. We like to leave things in the world as we expect they already are, and we want to keep the saints in the world as it is. For the most part, this modern project has been a failure. Historical objectivity turns out to be only as coherent or fragmented as common life, and in a "pluralistic" world, historians reproduce themselves by criticizing and consciously changing biases and perspectives. The practices of writing history belie canons of modernist historiography. Likewise, modern theories of sainthood are quite different than present-day practices of devotion and veneration. The practices look to what can be gained from or pushed upon a saint. The theories, on the other hand, promise to find something in the life of the saint that accords with some freestanding possession or quality of the saint, such as virtue, altruism, or God-consciousness.

These theories intend to reform popular practices, ancient and contemporary, by excluding many who are thought to be saints, such as Saint Jude (Orsi 1996). By bringing veneration under control, modern theories domesticate the saints as well. What is the point, for instance, of claiming that St Francis is exemplary for his "religious consciousness" when in our world, as in his, his way of life is more likely to be considered uncivilized or crazy? (Cunningham 1980) The point, it seems, is to present (i.e., divide) Francis in our modern image, to retain an internal kernel of religious subjectivity while avoiding implications of the practical husk. The idea of Francis's "religious consciousness" is useful because it makes his life meaningful for good modern capitalists who love birds and are open to loving squirrels and rabbits as well. Even though modernist hagiography may claim to depart from ancient ways of taming history, it serves to bring saints under our control.

Pre-modern elements of hagiography tend to make the lives of saints more credible to their audiences (through the testimony of miracles for instance), but at the same time, they open us to an untamed world. Historical perspectives are always anachronistic, at least to some degree, inasmuch as conceptual categories of one time are used to display the meaning of events in another. Hagiography intensifies this narrative projection insofar as the saint's life is told in order to enlighten and to underline a larger truth. Pushing beyond their own lives, saints will break with the ordinary. While a saint's story is written to the time of its readers, its goal is to change them and their world (Wyschogrod 1990).[1] In these terms, *Elizabeth* does not complete the hagiographic picture of a saint. It is true that we know her as more than a historical reconstruction. We understand her. Historians might scoff at the story's modern flourishes, but they too will recognize the personal trials and motives of this Elizabeth. We know the trials and yearnings of her body, but her transformation into the Virgin Queen is clearly not a conversion of our own.

The Saints and Sexual Desire

As different as virgin saints may be from Kapur's Elizabeth, they share a noble sexual self and a sacrifice of their desires. A clear difference is that women in the church have become saints from the low side of a social and theological hierarchy. For comparative purposes, I will consider St Rose of Lima (1586–1617), a contemporary in time but worlds away from Elizabeth I. The story of St Rose is positioned, from the start, in terms of a lack of status and power, particularly in relation to men and the church but also in a socioeconomic context. Although she is from a Spanish family in Peru, her story is shaped, in large part, by her family's financial misfortunes. Rose's purported beauty holds promise of economic advantage, as she is likely to catch the eye of a distinguished suitor. Rose resists, and like most virgin saints of the period, her resolve to stand against marriage comes at an early age (5 years old for Rose) (Bynum 1987: 24–5). Sexual nobility for Rose comes through her unwavering purity. Elizabeth's noble character is entirely different in this regard, insofar as her sexual freedom signals an equality of self amid the contradictory trappings of sixteenth-century conventions. But for both Rose and Elizabeth, virginity is a route to power, and love is the burden.

The story of St Rose presents a host of unseemly burdens. An account of her life written in 1968, by Sister Mary Alphonsus OSSP, avoids most of the gruesome details, but it retains basic themes of earlier biographies (Alphonsus 1982).[2] Rose's path to mystical union with God is agonizing. It is marked by physical and emotional pain mixed with, and usually indistinguishable from, the anguish of her intense passion for God. Rose's earthly trials seem to speak, paradoxically, of heavenly love. Her torments come, in part, through terrible visions. On one occasion, she descends to hell amid condemned souls, demons, "loathsome snakes," and "slimy lizards with distorted human faces." She is cursed and condemned by God, and plagued with confusion, "She had once loved God; she knew that. Why could she not love him now" (Alphonsus 1982: 214)?

St Rose is put to terrible tests of God's inexhaustible love, as the promises of God's ultimate embrace bring the ultimate dread. Her torture by demons is relieved, only momentarily, in visions and declarations of love by the infant Jesus. He wants to take Rose for his spouse. These visions of love are fleeting through to the end of her life when she dies with the heaving and thirsting of Christ on the cross. Like Christ, she is abandoned. Her moments of earthy joy are always ephemeral, and they serve to bring not only hope, but also more frustration and despair. Her apparent abandonment by God is a consistent theme of her life. Bereft of love, she desires it all the more. Rose plays the part of the jilted lover.

The relationship between Rose's sufferings and God's love are explained, by Mary Alphonsus, as a necessary purification. To raise her to the highest possible union of spiritual marriage, God must purify her (Alphonsus 1982: 213). For the same reason, Rose sets about to purify herself. Mary Alphonsus briefly lists examples of her penitential practices, such as frugality at table, austerity in relation to sleep, heavy chains around her waist and pins in her hair shirt. Far more self-mortification is catalogued in older accounts of Rose's life. Mary Alphonsus's restraint shows a bit of apprehension. She admits that Rose is immature, overzealous, and imprudent, and then she asks, "Why this desire? Does it not smack of sadism?" (Alphonsus 1982: 210). After an emphatic "No," Mary Alphonsus offers further explanation. First, Rose suffers "so that she might keep Christ company. Then, it was because souls in need were always storming her heart. Finally, it would seem that it was in order to arm herself against the assaults of the flesh" (Alphonsus 1982: 210).[3]

This last concern, "the flesh," takes the lead in Mary Alphonsus's narrative. Rose struggles against pride and vanity as well, but these spiritual weaknesses are part of a greater struggle that takes place through, with, and upon her body. Rose's passion for union with Christ, witnessed by nuptial moments with the infant Jesus, is "extremely unerotic."[4] Her yearning for God must be purified of sexual desire. Rose seems to be at war with herself. Every reader ought to wonder, what kind of God is this? What kind of dysfunctional love dominates Rose? What kind of sexual sickness? Ought not every attempt to justify her suffering fail?

Mary Alphonsus focuses on Rose's desire as both gift and torment, both problem and solution. She dwells upon Rose's beauty as a sign of her spiritual destiny and a basic source of her trials. The eyes of the world are set upon Rose, and she shrinks from the attention. She is an unwilling lightning rod of human desire. She is not only attractive but also irresistible in appearance and in manner. She will make a glorious spouse, of man or God. Man or God? The question goes to the heart of Rose's battles of the flesh. She is self-giving, humble, and tireless in her work to support her own family. She loves deeply. She nurses the sick and keeps company with the poor.

Rose's mother loves to highlight her daughter's beauty, dress her up and show her off. Rose desires to resist. Handsome suitors and admirers are around every corner, and even as Rose undertakes her physical austerities, men and women are drawn to her all the more. Her struggles of virginity come from without and within, from expectations of marriage to temptations of the flesh. When an esteemed lady, quite taken with Rose, compliments her fair and delicate hands, Rose runs to ruin them with lime. Mortification is a transformation of the flesh in the battle with appearances and with the ordinary appearance of things.

It might appear, at first glance, that Rose's struggles of the body present an all too common dualism of body and spirit. The body, it seems, must be disciplined so that the spirit might be set free, elevated, and redeemed. Such is not the case in the story of Rose. In Mary Alphonsus's narrative, as in earlier hagiography, Rose's body is redemptive insofar as her flesh is identified with the redemption of the suffering Christ. Rose's way toward death, as noted above, is described through a motif of unquenchable thirst brought on, simultaneously, by a deadly fever and a desire for union with God. The agony of her flesh is conceived, not as a rejection of the body, but as its purification and movement toward union with the representative body of Christ. The agony of Rose's desire accords with her desire to give her body over to God's love for the world. Lesser desires of her flesh are abandoned for greater ones. "Rose was made for God and lived for him. She loved him intensely. When she turned that love toward people, the flame flared whitehot" (Alphonsus 1982: viii).

Christ's fully human flesh appears to Rose in his helpless afflictions on the cross, suffering embodiment in the host, and as an infant under the care of his mother (Alphonsus 1982: 276, 290). Jesus asks for Rose's hand in marriage from his mother's arms. These visions are not incidental; they are key to the meaning of Rose's trials of the flesh. Rose does not endure the wrath of a divine judge, and she is not called to hate the body in order to unite with a spirit-savior. Rose's torment is not punishment or a turning away from human embodiment. She is called by a savior who needs maternal love and her protection. Rose scorns sexual desire and surface appearances of beauty inasmuch as they cloud and inhibit a broader and more profound embrace of the flesh. She plays the agonizing, jilted lover of God in order to participate in the divine agony of suffering rejection by the world (Alphonsus 1982: 280–1). "May all men adore thee, O thou the supreme Good! May all their love focus on thee, who dost love them so tenderly" (Alphonsus 1982: 280)! Unrequited love is at the heart of Rose's torment. Her physical and spiritual anguish is not suffered at the hand of God, but with God. She desires to share the agony of God's love, suffering with Christ at the hands of the world. She acts out the burning of God's own anguished passion.

As the Story Is Told

Why is this story of St Rose told in 1968 and reprinted in 1982? Mary Alphonsus suggests throughout the story that Rose's austerities and self-mortification are not a way to recommend for imitation. She recognizes them as practices of another time. Rose's self-discipline is partly explained, for instance, by her identification with Catherine of Siena and the penitential orientation of monastic practices. More importantly, Mary Alphonsus indicates that Rose is uniquely impelled by love. Rose's self-imposed trials are not practices that are recommended to Rose and certainly would not be recommended to anyone else. Rose's mortifications come from within, and influences from without, such as her mother, family, and church, serve in the biography to provide necessary limits upon her zealous behavior. Rose cannot help herself, and the story would fall apart if she were not held within the care of others. Rose cannot bear her own desires alone. Mary Alphonsus's narrative would be undermined if her agonizing love could be repeated. Rose's love stands out and disrupts the world. This is why the story is told.

Mary Alphonsus, in her preface, gives a sanguine beginning to what seems to be a morbid tale. She calls Rose's life "a spotless mirror in which we see ourselves" and "our boast, our crown, our defense, and a challenge to love completely" (Alphonsus 1982: ix). It is entirely consistent with this description and with the narrative, it seems to me, to censure its sexism and its cruelty (consider Maitland 1987). The story's violence ought not be accepted. We ought to be appalled. Rose's agony must hang before us as absurd; there is no neat means to categorize and contain it. Her pain and love are inexplicable and intractable inasmuch as they are God's own. She "keeps company with Christ." Mary Alphonsus entertains the question of sadism, but she resists putting the brutality off on Rose or God. For the narrative to work as a "spotless mirror," its violence cannot be blamed on the wrath of God or a theory of Rose's masochistic desires. Mary Alphonsus even avoids making Rose a victim, either to medieval piety or an oppressive culture. Rose willingly takes on suffering, but she takes no pleasure in it. She simply suffers in love, and in her suffering we see a mirror image of ourselves. In her passion, we see our apathy. We see the pain of the world that we would prefer to repress and evade. We see a dangerous, undomesticated love of God.

Rose's body, full of pain and passion, becomes representative of God's love for the world. The contrast between Rose and Kapur's Elizabeth is notable. Just before the film's final scenes, Walsingham advises Elizabeth to take on celestial virginity as a necessity of her rule. Princess Elizabeth indulges in the innocence of natural pleasures, but the body of the Virgin Queen must carry power through its distance and indifference to mere human desires. As she transcends to be the Virgin Queen, she elevates herself beyond mere woman or mere person. She is the divine Queen, and her power is secured by leaving behind the burdens of love. She must appear impassible. In contrast, the burdens of love destroy the pitiful Dudley who cannot carry on without Elizabeth. His weakness is mirrored in the Queen's strength. Desire in *Elizabeth* is both innocence and destruction, and the Queen moves beyond.

Rose's virginity is all too human. Her struggles with sexual desire bind her more deeply to the burdens of love. Mary Alphonsus calls St Rose our "crown" and "boast" because she shares the divine embodiment. This disturbing story of God's passion is our challenge to love.

Notes

1 Wyschogrod explains that "whether unconsciously or artfully inserted into the text, the political, economic, and social conditions of the time of writing are exhibited in hagiography. . . . Contemporary social existence therefore serves both as a system of placeholders and reference points against which changes in saintly consciousness and behavior are marked off, and as a catalyst of these transformations. 'In-text-ured,' as it were, in social catenae, the saint's life becomes transparent as a *life* when memory and expectation, desire and hope interact in wider contexts" (1990: 28).
2 Most accounts of Rose's life derive from Leonhard Hansen, OP, *Vita mirabilis, mors pretiosa, Venerabilis Sororis Rosae de S. Maria Limensis, ex Tertio ordine S. P. Dominici* (1664). For an extended rendering in English see Alban Butler (1903).
3 Bynum (1987) argues that medieval mystics like Catherine of Siena identify Christ's flesh with their female body and undergo their sufferings as the redemptive sufferings of Christ.
4 The phrase is used by Bynum in reference to Catherine of Siena (Bynum 1987: 178).

Bibliography

Abelove, Henry (2003) *Deep Gossip* (Minneapolis, MN: University of Minnesota Press).

Adams, Marilyn McCord (2002) "Trinitarian Friendship: Same-Gender Models of Godly Love in Richard of St Victor and Aelred of Rievaulx," in *Theology and Sexuality: Classic and Contemporary Readings*, edited by Eugene F. Rogers Jr (Oxford: Blackwell), 322–40.

Aelred of Rievaulx (1971) *Treatises and the Pastoral Prayer*, translated by Theodore Berkeley, Mary Paul Macpherson and R. Penelope Lawson (Kalamazoo, MI: Cistercian Publications).

Agamben, Giorgio (1993) *The Coming Community*, translated by M. Hardt (Minneapolis: University of Minnesota Press).

Agamben, Giorgio (2000) "The Face," in *Means without End: Notes on Politics*, translated by V. Binetti and C. Casarino (Minneapolis: University of Minnesota Press).

Alexander, Marilyn Bennett and James Preston (1996) *We Were Baptised Too: Claiming God's Grace for Lesbians and Gays* (Louisville: Westminster John Knox Press).

Alison, James (2003) "Honesty as Challenge, Honesty as Gift: What Way Forward for Gay and Lesbian Catholics?" (www.jamesalison.co.uk/eng10.html).

Allen, Prudence (1985) *The Concept of Woman: The Aristotelian Revolution 750 BC–AD 1250* (Quebec: Eden Press).

Alleva, Richard (1998) "The Godmother," *Commonweal* 125(22) (December 18) 14.

Alphonsus OSSR, Sister Mary (1982) *St Rose of Lima* (Rockford, IL: Tan Books).

Althaus-Reid, Marcella (2001) *Indecent Theology: Theological Perversions on Sex, Gender and Politics* (London: Routledge).

Althaus-Reid, Marcella (2003) *The Queer God* (London: Routledge).

Angela of Foligno (1993) *The Complete Works*, translated by Paul Lachance (New York: Paulist Press).

Anonymous (no date) *True Union in the Body? A Contribution to the Discussion within the Anglican Communion Concerning the Public Blessing of Same-Sex Unions. A Paper Commissioned by the Most Revd Drexel Wellington Gomez, Archbishop of the West Indies* (Oxford: Truth-Life-Way).

Anselm (1973) *The Prayers and Meditations of Saint Anselm with the Proslogion*, translated by Sister Benedicta Ward SLG, with a foreword by R.W. Southern (Harmondsworth: Penguin Books).

Apter, Emily and William Pietz, eds (1993) "Introduction," in *Fetishism as Cultural Discourse* (Ithaca NY: Cornell University Press).

Areford, David S. (1998) "The Passion Measured: A Late Medieval Diagram of the Body of Christ," in *The Body Broken: Passion Devotion in Late-Medieval Culture*, edited by A.A. MacDonald, H.N.B. Ridderbos and R.M. Schlusemann (Groningen: Egbert Forsten), 211–38.

Astell, Mary (1694) *A Serious Proposal to the Ladies, for the Advancement of their True and Greatest Interest by a Lover of her Sex* (London).

Athanasius (1974) *Against the Gentiles*, in *The Divine Office I: The Liturgy of the Hours According to the Roman Rite* (London: Collins).

Athanasius (1998) *Select Works and Letters*, edited by Philip Schaff and Henry Wace, Nicene and Post-Nicene Fathers (Edinburgh: T. & T. Clark [1893]), vol. 4.

Atkinson, Clarissa (1983) "Precious Balsam in a Fragile Glass: The Ideology of Virginity in the Late Middle Ages," *Journal of Family History* 8(2).

Aubineau, Michel (1966) *Grégoire de Nysse: Traité de la virginité*, Introduction, texte critique, traduction, commentaire et index, Source Chrétiennes (Paris: Les Éditions du Cerf).

Auerbach, Eric (1953) *Mimesis: The Representation of Reality in Western Literature*, translated by Willard R. Trask (Princeton, NJ: Princeton University Press).

Augustine (1955) *The Good of Marriage (De Bono Coniugali)*, translated by Charles T. Wilcox, The Fathers of the Church (New York: Fathers of the Church Inc.), vol. 27.

Augustine (1991a) *Confessions*, translated by Henry Chadwick (Oxford: Oxford University Press).

Augustine (1991b) *The Trinity*, translated by Edmund Hill OP, *The Works of St Augustine* (New York: New City Press).

Augustine (1991c) *Sermons 51–94 on the New Testament*, translated by Edmund Hill OP (New York: New City Press).

Augustine (1998) *The City of God against the Pagans*, edited and translated by R.W. Dyson (Cambridge: Cambridge University Press).

Augustine (2002) *On Genesis* (On Genesis: A Refutation of the Manichees; Unfinished Literal Commentary on Genesis; The Literal Meaning of Genesis), translated by Edmund Hill OP and Matthew O'Connell, *The Works of St Augustine* (New York: New City Press).

Badiou, Alain (1997) *Saint Paul: La fondation de l'universalisme* (Paris: PUF).

Badiou, Alain (2001) *Ethics: An Essay on the Understanding of Evil*, translated by Peter Hallward (London: Verso).

Bagemihl, Bruce (1999) *Biological Exuberance: Animal Homosexuality and Natural Diversity* (New York: St Martin's Press).

Balthasar, Hans Urs von (1961) *Prayer*, translated by A.V. Littledale (London: Geoffrey Chapman).

Balthasar, Hans Urs von (1968) *Man in History: A Theological Study* (London: SCM Press).

Balthasar, Hans Urs von (1979) *Heart of the World*, translated by Erasmo S. Leiva (San Francisco: Ignatius Press [1954]).

Balthasar, Hans Urs von (1982–91) *The Glory of the Lord: A Theological Aesthetics*, translated by Oliver Davies, Erasmo Leiva-Merikakis, Andrew Louth, Francis McDonagh, Brian McNeil CRV, John Riches, John Saward, Martin Simon and Rowan Williams, edited by Joseph Fessio SJ, Brian McNeil CRV and John Riches, 7 vols (Edinburgh: T. & T. Clark).

Balthasar, Hans Urs von (1986a) *New Elucidations*, translated by Mary Theresilde Skerry (San Francisco: Ignatius Press).

Balthasar, Hans Urs von (1986b) *The Office of St Peter and the Structure of the Church*, translated by Andrée Emery (San Francisco: Ignatius Press).

Balthasar, Hans Urs von (1988–98) *Theo-Drama: A Theological Dramatics*, translated by Graham Harrison, 5 vols (San Francisco: Ignatius Press).

Balthasar, Hans Urs von (1990a) *Mysterium Paschale*, translated by Aidan Nichols OP (Edinburgh: T. & T. Clark).

Balthasar, Hans Urs von (1990b) *Credo: Meditations on the Apostles' Creed*, introduced by Medard Kehl SJ and translated by David Kipp (Edinburgh: T. & T. Clark).

Balthasar, Hans Urs von (1991) *Explorations in Theology II: Spouse of the Word* (San Francisco: Ignatius Press [1961]).

Balthasar, Hans Urs von (1992) *Two Sisters in the Spirit: Thérèse of Lisieux and Elizabeth of the Trinity*, translated by Donald Nichols (San Francisco: Ignatius Press).

Balthasar, Hans Urs von (1995a) "Women Priests? A Marian Church in a Fatherless and Motherless Culture," *Communio* 22: 164–70.

Balthasar, Hans Urs von (1995b) *Presence and Thought: An Essay on the Religious Philosophy of Gregory of Nyssa*, translated by Mark Sebanc (San Francisco: Ignatius Press [1988]).

Balthasar, Hans Urs von (1998) *Elucidations*, translated by John Riches (San Francisco: Ignatius Press [1975]).

Baring, Anne and Jules Cashford (1993) *The Myth of the Goddess: Evolution of an Image* (London: Arkana Penguin [1991]).

Barnes, Kim (1996) *In the Wilderness: Coming of Age in Unknown Country* (New York: Anchor).

Barnes, Michel R. (1996) " 'The Burden of Marriage' and Other Notes on Gregory of Nyssa's *On Virginity*" (paper presented to the North American Patristics Society).

Barth, Karl (1936–75) *Church Dogmatics*, edited by G.W. Bromiley and T.F. Torrance, 4 vols (Edinburgh: T. & T. Clark).

Barthes, Roland (1972) *Mythologies* (New York: Hill and Wang).

Bataille, Georges (1962) *Eroticism*, translated by Mary Dalwood (London: Marion Boyars).

Bataille, Georges (1985) "The Notion of Expenditure," in *Visions of Excess: Selected Writing, 1927–1939*, edited by A. Stoekl (Minneapolis: University of Minnesota Press), 116–29.

Bataille, Georges (1989) *Theory of Religion*, translated by Robert Hurley (New York: Zone Books).

Bates, Stephen (2004) *A Church at War: Anglicans and Homosexuality* (London: I.B. Tauris).

Beatham, Mary (2003) " 'Woman, Who are You?': A Study of the Feminine Identity and Role of Women in the Catholic Church" (Lancaster University MA dissertation).

Beattie, Tina (1998) "One Man and Three Women: Hans, Adrienne, Mary and Luce," *New Blackfriars* 79(294): 95–103.

Beattie, Tina (1999) *God's Mother, Eve's Advocate: A Gynocentric Configuration of Marian Symbolism in Engagement with Luce Irigaray*, CCSRG Monograph Series 3 (Bristol: Bristol University).

Beattie, Tina (2000) "Mary, Eve and the Church," *Maria* 2: 5–20.

Beattie, Tina (2002) *God's Mother, Eve's Advocate: A Marian Narrative of Woman's Salvation* (London: Continuum).

Beattie, Tina (2006) *New Catholic Feminism: Theology and Theory* (London: Routledge).

Behar, Ruth (1996) *The Vulnerable Observer: Anthropology that Breaks Your Heart* (Boston: Beacon Press).

Benedict XVI (2006) *Deus Caritas Est* (London: Catholic Truth Society).

Benjamin, Walter (1999) *The Arcades Project* (Cambridge, MA: Belknap Press).

Bennett Judith and Amy Froide, eds (1999) *Single Women in the European Past, 1250–1800* (Philadelphia: University of Pennsylvania Press).

Bennett, Judith (2000) " 'Lesbian-Like' and the Social History of Lesbianisms," *Journal of the History of Sexuality* 9.

Berl, Emmanuel (1929) "Premier Pamphlet," *Europe*, 75.

Bernard of Clairvaux (1971) *Sermons on the Song of Songs I*, translated by Kilian Walsh OCSO, The Works of Bernard of Clairvaux (Kalamazoo, MI: Cistercian Publications).

Bernard of Clairvaux (1980) *Sermons on the Song of Songs IV*, translated by Irene Edmonds, The Works of Bernard of Clairvaux (Kalamazoo, MI: Cistercian Publications).

Bernauer, Michael and Michael Mahon (1994) "The Ethics of Michel Foucault," in *The Cambridge Companion to Foucault*, edited by Gary Gutting (Cambridge: Cambridge University Press, 1994), 141–58.

Bersani, Leo (1986) *The Freudian Body: Psychoanalysis and Art* (New York: Columbia University Press)

Bersani, Leo (1988) "Is the Rectum a Grave?" in *AIDS: Cultural Analysis, Cultural Activism*, edited by Douglas Crimp (Cambridge, MA: MIT Press).

Bestul, Thomas (1996) *Texts of the Passion: Latin Devotional Literature and Medieval Society* (Philadelphia: University of Pennsylvania Press).

Blackman, E.C. (1948) *Marcion and His Influence* (London: SPCK).

Blake, William (1969) *Complete Writings*, edited by Geoffrey Keynes (Oxford: Oxford University Press).

Blumenberg, Hans (1983) *The Legitimacy of the Modern Age*, translated by R.M. Wallace (Cambridge, MA: MIT Press [1966]).

Böhm, Thomas (1996) *Theoria, Unendlichkeit, Aufstieg: philosophische Implikationen zu De Vita Moysis von Gregor von Nyssa*, Supplements to *Vigiliae Christianae* (Leiden: E.J. Brill).

Bonaventure (1993) *Itinerarium* in *The Journey of the Mind to God*, translated by Philotheus Boehner, edited by Stephen F. Brown (Indianapolis: Hackett).

Boros, Ladislaus (1962) *The Moment of Truth: Mysterium Mortis* (London: Burns and Oates).

Børresen, Kari (1981) *Subordination and Equivalence: The Nature and Role of Women in Augustine and Aquinas* (Lanham, MD: University Press of America).

Boss, Sarah Jane (2000) *Empress and Handmaid: On Nature and Gender in the Cult of the Virgin Mary* (London: Cassell).

Boswell, John (1980) *Christianity, Social Tolerance, and Homosexuality: Gay People in Western Europe from the Beginning of the Christian Era to the Fourteenth Century* (Chicago: University of Chicago Press).

Bourdieu, Pierre (1977) *Outline of a Theory of Practice* (New York: Cambridge University Press, 1977).

Bowlin, John (1999) *Contingency and Fortune in Aquinas's Ethics* (Cambridge: Cambridge University Press).

Boyarin, Daniel (1993) *Carnal Israel: Reading Sex in Talmudic Culture* (Berkeley, CA: University of California Press).

Boyarin, Daniel (1995a) "Are There any Jews in the 'History of Sexuality'?" *Journal of the History of Sexuality* 5(3): 333–55.

Boyarin, Daniel (1995b) "Brides of Christ: Paul and the Origins of Christian Sexual Renunciation," in *Asceticism*, edited by Vincent L. Wimbush and Richard Valantasis (New York: Oxford University Press).

Boykin, Keith (1996) *One More River to Cross: Black and Gay in America* (New York: Anchor).

Bradshaw, Timothy (1999) "Baptism and Inclusivity in the Church," in *Baptism, the New Testament and the Church: Historical and Contemporary Studies in Honour of R.E.O. White*, edited by Stanley E. Porter and Anthony R. Cross (Sheffield: Sheffield Academic Press).

Brierley, Peter (2000) *The Tide Is Running Out* (London: Christian Research Association).

Brierley, Peter, ed. (2003) *UK Christian Handbook: Religious Trends 4, 2003/2004* (London: Christian Research Association).

Brooten, Bernadette J. (1996) *Love between Women: Early Christian Responses to Female Homoeroticism* (Chicago: University of Chicago Press).

Brown, Callum (2001) *The Death of Christian Britain: Understanding Secularization 1800–2000* (London and New York: Routledge).

Brown, Dan (2003) *The Da Vinci Code* (New York: Doubleday).

Brown, Judith C. (1986) *Immodest Acts: The Life of a Lesbian Nun in Renaissance Italy* (New York: Oxford University Press).

Brown, Peter (1988) *The Body and Society: Men, Women and Sexual Renunciation in Early Christianity* (London: Faber & Faber).

Bruce, Steve (2002) *God Is Dead: Secularization in the West* (Oxford: Blackwell).

Bruce, Steve and Tony Glendenning (2001) "Religion in Scotland 2001" (unpublished paper).

Buby, Bertrand (1996) *Mary of Galilee*, Vol. 3, *The Marian Heritage of the Early Church* (New York: Alba House).

Bullimore, Matthew (1999) "The Eschatology of Desire and Its Implications – With Reference to the Theology of Hans Urs von Balthasar" (BA dissertation, Faculty of Divinity, Cambridge).

Bultmann, Rudolf (1971) *The Gospel of John: A Commentary*, translated by G.R. Beasley-Murray (Oxford: Blackwell [1964]).

Burns, Gene (1999) "Abandoning Suspicion: The Catholic Left and Sexuality," in *What's Left? Liberal Catholics*, edited by Mary Jo Weaver (Bloomington and Indianapolis: Indiana University Press), 67–87.

Burrus, Virginia (2000) *"Begotten, Not Made": Conceiving Manhood in Late Antiquity* (Stanford, CA: Stanford University Press).

Butler, Alban (1903) *The Lives of the Fathers, Martyrs, and other Principle Saints* (New York: P.J. Kenedy).

Butler, Judith (1987) *Subjects of Desire: Hegelian Reflections in Twentieth-Century France* (New York: Columbia University Press).

Butler, Judith (1990) *Gender Trouble: Feminism and the Subversion of Identity* (New York: Routledge).

Butler, Judith (1993) *Bodies that Matter* (London: Routledge).

Butler, Judith (1997a) *Excitable Speech: A Politics of the Performative* (New York and London: Routledge).

Butler, Judith (1997b) *The Psychic Life of Power* (Stanford: Stanford University Press).

Butler, Judith (1999) *Gender Trouble*, second edition (London: Routledge [1990]).

Butler, Judith (2003) "On Emergence" (unpublished paper for the Stanford Colloquium on Emergence).

Butterman, Steven (2005) *Perversions on Parade: Brazilian Literature of Transgression and Postmodern Anti-Aesthetics in Glauco Mattoso* (San Diego: San Diego State University Press).

Bynum, Caroline Walker (1982) *Jesus as Mother: Studies in the Spirituality of the High Middle Ages* (Berkeley, CA: University of California Press).

Bynum, Caroline Walker (1987) *Holy Feast and Holy Fast: The Religious Significance of Food to Medieval Women* (Berkeley, CA: University of California Press).

Bynum, Caroline Walker (1991) *Fragmentation and Redemption: Essays on Gender and the Human Body in Medieval Religion* (New York: Zone Books).

Bynum, Caroline Walker (2001) *Metamorphosis and Identity* (New York: Zone Books).

Cameron, Averil (1991) *Christianity and the Rhetoric of Empire: The Development of Christian Discourse* (Berkeley, CA: University of California Press).

Camille, Michael (1994) "The Image and the Self: Unwriting Late Medieval Bodies," in *Framing Medieval Bodies*, edited by Sarah Kay and Miri Rubin (Manchester: Manchester University Press).

Campbell, Mary Anne (1992) "Redefining Holy Maidenhead: Virginity and Lesbianism in Late Medieval England," *Medieval Feminist Newsletter* 13: 14–15.

Campenhausen, Hans von (1964) *The Virgin Birth in the Theology of the Ancient Church*, translated by Frank Clarke (London: SCM Press [1962]).

Cannon, Katie (1988) *Black Womanist Ethics* (Atlanta: Scholars Press).

Cantarella, Eva (1992) *Bisexuality in the Ancient World*, translated by Cormac O'Culleanáin (New Haven: Yale University Press).

Caputo, Jack (2001) *On Religion* (London: Routledge).

Carlson, Eric (1994) *Marriage and the English Reformation* (Oxford: Blackwell).

Carrette, Jeremy R. (2000) *Foucault and Religion: Spiritual Corporeality and Political Spirituality* (London: Routledge).

Carrette, Jeremy R., ed. (1999) *Religion and Culture by Michel Foucault* (Manchester: Manchester University Press).

Carroll, Michael P. (1986) *The Cult of the Virgin Mary: Psychological Origins* (Princeton, NJ: Princeton University Press).

Castle, Terry (1986) *Masquerade and Civilization: The Carnivalesque in Eighteenth-century English Culture and Fiction* (Stanford: Stanford University Press).

Catholic Church (1991) *Order of Christian Funerals* (London: Geoffrey Chapman).

Catholic Church (1994) *Catechism of the Catholic Church* (London: Geoffrey Chapman).

Celsus (1987) *On the True Doctrine: A Discourse against the Christians*, translated by R.J. Hoffmann (Oxford: Oxford University Press).

Chakrabarty, Dipesh (1997) "The Time of History and the Times of the Gods," in *The Politics of Culture in the Shadow of Capital*, edited by Lisa Lowe and David Lloyd (Durham, NC: Duke Press).

Charke, Charlotte (1755) *A Narrative of the Life of Mrs Charlotte Charke, Daughter of Colley Cibber* (London).

Chenu, Marie-Dominique (1957) *La Théologie comme science au XIIIe siècle,* 3rd revised edition (Paris: J. Vrin).

Cherniss, Harold Fredrik (1971) *The Platonism of Gregory of Nyssa* (New York: Burt Franklin [1930]).

Chrétien, Jean-Louis (2002) *The Unforgettable and the Unhoped For*, translated by Jeffrey Bloechl (New York: Fordham University Press).

Church of England (1991) *Issues in Human Sexuality: A Statement by the House of Bishops of the General Synod of the Church of England* (London: Church House Publishing).

Cixous, Helene (1981) "The Laugh of Medusa," in *New French Feminisms: An Anthology*, edited by E. Marks and I. de Courtivron (Brighton: Harvester).

Clark, Elizabeth A. (1999) *Reading Renunciation: Asceticism and Scripture in Early Christianity* (Princeton, NJ: Princeton University Press).

Classen, C., D. Howes and A. Synnott, eds (1994) *Aroma: The Cultural History of Smell* (London: Routledge).

Clément, Olivier (1997) *The Roots of Christian Mysticism*, translated by Theodore Berkeley OCSO (London: New City [1982]).

Cloke, Gillian (1995) *This Female Man of God: Women and Spiritual Power in the Patristic Age, AD 350–450* (London: Routledge).

Coakley, Sarah (2000) "The Eschatological Body: Gender, Transformation, and God," *Modern Theology* 16(1): 61–73.

Coakley, Sarah (2002) *Powers and Submissions: Spirituality, Philosophy and Gender* (Oxford: Blackwell).

Cohen, David (1991) "Sexuality, Violence, and the Athenian Law of *Hubris*," *Greece & Rome* 38(2): 171–88.

Cohen, Jeffrey Jerome (2003) *Medieval Identity Machines* (Minneapolis: University of Minnesota Press).

Condorcet, Marie-Jean-Antoine-Nicholas Caritat de (1966) *Esquisse d'un tableau historique des progrès de l'esprit humain* (Paris: Editions sociales [1795]).

Constas, Nicholas (2003) *Proclus of Constantinople and the Cult of the Virgin in Late Antiquity: Homilies 1–5, Texts and Translations*, Supplements to *Vigiliae Christianae*, formerly *Philosophia Patrum*: Texts and Studies on Early Christian Life and Language, vol. LXVI (Leiden: Brill).

Crammer, Corrine (2004) "One Sex or Two? Balthasar's Theology of the Sexes," in *The Cambridge Companion to Hans Urs von Balthasar*, edited by Edward T. Oakes SJ and David Moss (Cambridge: Cambridge University Press), 93–112.

Crossan, John Dominic (1995) *Jesus: A Revolutionary Biography* (San Francisco: Harper San Francisco).

Cunningham, Lawrence (1980) *The Meaning of Saints* (San Francisco: Harper & Row).

Dale, A. Johnson (1983) *Women in English Religion 1700–1925* (New York: Edwin Mellen Press).

Daly, Mary (1973) *Beyond God the Father* (Boston: Beacon Press).

Dalzell SM, Thomas G. (1999) "Lack of Social Drama in von Balthasar's Theological Dramatics," *Theological Studies* 60(3): 457–75.

Daniélou SJ, Jean (1949) "Le Culte Marial et le Paganisme," in *Maria: Études sur la Sainte Vierge*, edited by Hubert du Manoir SJ, 8 vols (Paris: Beauchesne et se fils), I, 159–81.

Daniélou SJ, Jean (1954) *Platonisme et théologie mystique: essai sur la doctrine spirituelle de Saint Grégoire de Nysse* (Paris: Aubier).

Darwin, Charles (2004) *The Descent of Man*, edited by James Moore and Adrian Desmond (London: Penguin Books [1879]).

Davidoff, Leonore and Catherine Hall (1987) *Family Fortunes: Men and Women of the English Middle Class 1780–1850* (London: Hutchinson).

Davidson, Arnold I. (2002) *The Emergence of Sexuality: Historical Epistemology and the Formation of Concepts* (Cambridge, MA: Harvard University Press).

Dawkins, Richard (1976) *The Selfish Gene* (Oxford: Oxford University Press).

D'Costa, Gavin (2000) *Sexing the Trinity: Gender, Culture and the Divine* (London: SCM Press).

D'Emilio, John (1983) *Sexual Politics, Sexual Communities: The Making of a Homosexual Minority in the United States, 1940–1970* (Chicago: University of Chicago Press).

D'Evelyn, Stephen (2003) "A Commentary with Translations and Emended Text of Hildegard of Bingen's 'Symphonia armonie celestium revelationum' 1–50" (PhD thesis, Cambridge University, May).

De Lubac, Henri (1948) *Corpus Mysticum: l'eucharistie et l'église au Moyen Âge* (Paris: Aubier).

Delehaye, Hippolyte (1962) *The Legends of the Saints*, translated by Donald Attwater (New York: Fordham University Press).

Deleuze, Gilles (1989) *Masochism: Coldness and Cruelty* (New York: Zone Books).

Delumeau, Jean (1983) *Le péché et la peur: La culpabilisation en Occident XIII–XVIII siècles* (Paris: Fayard).

Denzinger, Heinrich and Adolfus Schönmetzer (1965) *Enchiridion Symbolorum Definitionum et Declarationum de Rebus Fidei et Morum* (Freiburg: Herder).

Derrida, Jacques (1974) *Glas* (Nebraska: University of Nebraska Press).

Derrida, Jacques (1993) *Memoirs of the Blind: The Self-Portrait and Other Ruins* (Chicago: University of Chicago Press).

Derrida, Jacques (2002) *Acts of Religion*, edited by Gil Anidjar (London: Routledge).

Descombes, Vincent (1980) *Modern French Philosophy*, translated by L. Scott-Fox & J.M. Harding (Cambridge: Cambridge University Press).

Desmond, William (1995) *Being and the Between* (Albany, NY: State University of New York Press).

Detienne, Marcel (1963) *La Notion de Daïmôn dans le Pythagorisme Ancien* (Paris: Liège).

Diamond, Sara (1989) *Spiritual Warfare: The Politics of the Christian Right* (Boston: Southend Press).

Diken, Bülent and Carsten Bagge Laustsen (2002) "Enjoy Your Fight! *Fight Club* as a Symptom of the Network Society," *Cultural Values: The Journal for Cultural Research* 6(4): 349–67.

Dinshaw, Carolyn (1999) *Getting Medieval: Sexualities and Communities, Pre- and Postmodern* (Durham: Duke University Press, 1999).

Dombrowski, Daniel (1992) *St John of the Cross: An Appreciation* (New York: State University of New York Press).

Donoghue, Emma (1993) *Passions between Women: British Lesbian Culture 1668–1801* (London: Scarlet Press).

Douglas, Ann (1977) *The Feminization of American Culture* (New York: Knopf).

Douglas, Mary (2002) *Purity and Danger: An Analysis of Concepts of Pollution and Taboo* (London: Routledge & Kegan Paul [1966]).

Dover, K.J. (1989) *Greek Homosexuality*, updated and with a new postscript (Cambridge, MA: Harvard University Press [1978]).

Dünzl, Franz (1993) *Braut und Bräutigam: die Auslegung des Canticum durch Gregor von Nyssa*, Beiträge Zur Geschicte der Biblischen Exegese (Tübingen: J.C.B. Mohr).

Durkin, Mary Greeley (1983) *Feast of Love: Pope Paul II on Human Intimacy* (Chicago: Loyola University Press).

Ebert, Roger (1998) "Elizabeth," *Chicago Sun Times*, November: http://www.suntimes.com/ebert

Edwards, Malcolm Stuart (1998) *Christianity and the Subversion of Identity: Theology, Ethics and Gay Liberation* (Cambridge University PhD dissertation).

Eilberg-Schwartz, Howard (1994) *God's Phallus: And Other Problems for Men and Monotheism* (Boston: Beacon Press).

Eilberg-Schwartz, Howard (1997) "The Problem of the Body for the People of the Book," in *Reading Bibles, Writing Bodies*, edited by Timothy K. Beal and David M. Gunn (London: Routledge), 34–55.

Ephrem the Syrian (1989) *Hymns*, translated by Kathleen E. McVey, Classics of Western Spirituality (New York: Paulist Press).

Epp, Garrett P.J. (2001) "Ecce Homo," in *Queering the Middle Ages*, edited by Glenn Burger and Steven F. Kruger (Minneapolis: University of Minnesota Press), 236–51.

Eribon, Didier (2004) *Insult and the Making of the Gay Self*, translated by Michael Lucey (Durham, NC: Duke University Press).

Escohotado, Javier Perez (1992) *Sexo e Inquisición en España* (Madrid: Temas de Hoy).

Ferguson, Everett (1976) "Progress in Perfection: Gregory of Nyssa's *Vita Moysis*," *Studia Patristica* 14(3).

Fiddes, Paul (1990) "The Status of Woman in the Thought of Karl Barth," in *After Eve: Women, Theology and the Christian Tradition*, edited by Janet Martin Soskice (London: Marshall Pickering).

Fiorenza, Elisabeth Schüssler (1995) *Jesus: Miriam's Child, Sophia's Prophet* (London: SCM Press).

Fitzgerald, Michael (1998) "Twentieth-Century Tudor," *Time* (November 2), 44.

Flannery, Austin, ed. (1992) *Vatican Collection: Vatican Council II*, Vol. 1 *The Conciliar and Postconciliar Documents* (Dublin: Dominican Publications [1974]).

Flaubert, Gustave (1975) *Madame Bovary*, translated by A. Russell (Harmondsworth: Penguin [1856–7]).

Fletcher, Anthony (1994) "The Protestant Idea of Marriage in Early Modern England," in *Religion, Culture and Society in Early Modern Britain: Essays in Honour of Patrick Collinson*, edited by Anthony Fletcher and Peer Roberts (Cambridge: Cambridge University Press).

Fletcher, Anthony (1998) "Women's Spiritual Experience," in *Studies in Church History Vol. 34, Gender and Religion*, edited by R.N. Swanson (Suffolk: The Boydell Press), 187–203.

Fletcher, Paul (2003) "Fantasy, Imagination and the Possibility of Experience," in *Difference in Philosophy of Religion*, edited by Philip Goodchild (Aldershot: Ashgate), 157–69.

Florence, Maurice (1994) "Foucault, Michel," in *The Cambridge Companion to Foucault*, edited by Gary Gutting (Cambridge: Cambridge University Press).

Ford, David (1999) *Self and Salvation: Being Transformed* (Cambridge: Cambridge University Press).

Foucault, Michel (1972) *The Archaeology of Knowledge*, translated by A.M. Sheridan Smith (London: Routledge [1969]).

Foucault, Michel (1984) "Truth and Power," in *The Foucault Reader: An Introduction to Foucault's Thought*, edited by Paul Rabinow (London: Penguin Books).

Foucault, Michel (1986) *Death and the Labyrinth: The World of Raymond Roussel*, translated by Charles Ruas (London: Athlone [1963]).

Foucault, Michel (1990–2) *The History of Sexuality*, translated by Robert Hurley, 3 vols (London: Penguin [1976–84]).

Foucault, Michel (2000) "Friendship as a Way of Life" (1981) in *Ethics: Subjectivity and Truth*, Essential Works of Foucault 1954–1984 Vol. 3, edited by Paul Rabinow (Harmondsworth: Penguin Books).

Foucault, Michel (2003) *"Society Must Be Defended": Lectures at the Collège de France 1975–1976*, translated by D. Macey (New York: Picador).

Freeman, Elizabeth (2002) *The Wedding Complex: Forms of Belonging in Modern American Culture* (Durham, NC: Duke University Press).

Gambero, Luigi (1999) *Mary and the Fathers of the Church: The Blessed Virgin Mary in Patristic Thought*, translated by Thomas Buffer (San Francisco: Ignatius Press [1991]).

Garber, Marjorie (1992) *Vested Interests: Cross-Dressing and Cultural Anxiety* (New York: Routledge).

Gardner, Lucy and David Moss (1999) "Something Like Time, Something Like the Sexes: An Essay in Reception," in Lucy Gardner, David Moss, Ben Quash, and Graham Ward, *Balthasar at the End of Modernity* (Edinburgh: T. & T. Clark), 69–137.

Gawronski, Raymond (1995) *Word and Silence* (Edinburgh: T. & T. Clark).

Gill, Sean (1998a) "How Muscular was Victorian Christianity? Thomas Hughes and the Cult of Christian Manliness Reconsidered," in *Studies in Church History Vol. 34: Gender and Religion*, edited by R.N. Swanson (Suffolk: The Boydell Press), 421–30.

Gill, Sean, ed. (1998b) *The Lesbian and Gay Christian Movement: Campaigning for Justice, Truth and Love* (London: Cassell).

Ginzberg, Lori D. (1990) *Women and the Work of Benevolence* (New Haven, CT: Yale University Press).

Girard, René (1987) *Things Hidden since the Foundation of the World*, translated by Stephen Bann and Michael Metteer (London: The Athlone Press [1978]).

Goddard, Andrew (2005) "Traditionalist and Revisionist Positions in the Church of England," in *Human Sexuality and the Churches*, edited by Tim Macquiban and Danny Rhodes (Salisbury: Sarum College Press).

Gordon, Avery (1997) *Ghostly Matters: Haunting and the Sociological Imagination* (Minneapolis: University of Minnesota Press).

Gordon, Linda (1994) *Pitied but Not Entitled: Single Mothers and the History of Welfare, 1890–1935* (Cambridge, MA: Harvard University Press).

Gornick, Vivian (1996) "The Memoir Boom," *The Women's Review of Books* 12(10–11) (July) 3.

Goss, Robert E. (1992) *Jesus Acted Up: A Gay and Lesbian Manifesto* (San Francisco: Harper San Francisco).

Goss, Robert E. (2002) *Queering Christ: Beyond Jesus Acted Up* (Cleveland: Pilgrim Press).

Gosse, Edmund (1949) *Father and Son: A Study of Two Temperaments* (Harmondsworth: Penguin Books [1907]).

Gosse, Philip (2003) *The Evolution Debate 1813–1870*. Vol. 4 *Omphalos: An Attempt to Untie the Geological Knot*, edited by David Knight (London: Routledge [1857]).

Gouldner, Alvin W. (1973) *For Sociology: Renewal and Critique in Sociology Today* (New York: Basic Books).

Graef, Hilda (1985) *Mary: A History of Doctrine and Devotion* (London: Sheed & Ward [1963]).

Gray, Chris Hables (2001) *Cyborg Citizen: Politics in the Posthuman Age* (London: Routledge).

Gray, Douglas (1963) "The Five Wounds of Our Lord," *Notes and Queries* 10: 50–1, 82–9, 127–34, 163–8.

Greeley, Andrew M. and Mary Greeley Durkin (1984) *How to Save the Catholic Church* (New York: Viking).

Greenberg, David F. (1988) *The Construction of Homosexuality* (Chicago: University of Chicago Press).

Greenberg, Steven (2003) *Wrestling with God and Man: Homosexuality in Jewish Thought* (Madison: University of Wisconsin Press).

Greenhill, Eleanor S. (1971) "The Group of Christ and St John as Author Portrait: Literary Sources, Pictorial Parallels," in *Festschrift Bernard Bischoff zu Seinem 65 Geburtstag*, edited by Johanne Autenrieth and Franz Brunhölzl (Stuttgart: Anton Hiersemann), 406–16.

Gregory of Nazianzus (1961) *Lettres théologiques*, edited by P. Gallay (Paris: Les Belles Lettres).

Gregory of Nyssa (1952) *Opera ascetica*, edited by Werner Jaeger, Johannes P. Cavarnos and Virginia Woods Callahan, Gregorii Nysseni Opera (Leiden: E.J. Brill).

Gregory of Nyssa (1955) *La vie de Moïse*, edited by Jean Daniélou SJ, Sources Chrétiennes (Paris: Éditions du Cerf).

Gregory of Nyssa (1961) *From Glory to Glory: Texts from Gregory of Nyssa's Mystical Writings*, edited and translated by Herbert Musurillo, selected and introduced by Jean Daniélou (New York: Charles Scribner's Sons).

Gregory of Nyssa (1964) *De vita Moysis*, edited by Herbert Musurillo, Gregorii Nysseni Opera (Leiden: E.J. Brill).

Gregory of Nyssa (1978) *The Life of Moses*, translated by Abraham J. Malherbe Everett Ferguson, The Classics of Western Spirituality (New York: Paulist Press).

Gregory of Nyssa (1994) *Select Writings and Letters*, translated by William Moore and Henry Austin Wilson, Nicene and Post-Nicene Fathers, Second Series (Edinburgh: T. & T. Clark [1893]) vol. 5.

Gribomont, Jean (1967) "Le Panégyrique de la virginité, oeuvre de jeunesse de Grégoire de Nysse," *Revue D'ascetique et de Mystique* 43.

Griffiths, Diana (1998) *Madness in its Place: Narratives of Severall Hospital, 1913–1997* (London: Routledge).

Grosz, Elizabeth (1989) *Sexual Subversions: Three French Feminists* (St Leonards, NSW: Allen & Unwin).

Grosz, Elizabeth (1995) *Jacques Lacan: A Feminist Introduction* (London: Routledge [1990]).

Guest, Mathew (2002) *Authority and Community in an Evangelical Church* (Lancaster University PhD dissertation).

Hadewijch of Anvers (1980) *The Complete Works*, translated by Columba Hart (London: SPCK).

Haffner, Paul (1999) *The Sacramental Mystery* (Leominster: Gracewing).

Hall, Pamela M. (1994) *Narrative and Natural Law* (Notre Dame: Notre Dame University Press).

Hallett, Judith (1989) "Female Homoeroticism and the Denial of Roman Reality in Latin Literature," *Yale Journal of Criticism* 3(1): 209–28.

Halperin, David M. (1990) *One Hundred Years of Homosexuality and Other Essays on Greek Love* (New York: Routledge).

Halperin, David M. (1995) *Saint Foucault: Towards a Gay Hagiography* (New York: Oxford University Press).

Halperin, David M. (2002) *How to Do the History of Homosexuality* (Chicago: University of Chicago Press).

Halperin, David M., John J. Winkler, and Froma I. Zeitlin, eds (1990) *Before Sexuality: The Construction of Erotic Experience in the Ancient Greek World* (Princeton, NJ: Princeton University Press).

Hamacher, W. (1998) "The End of Art with the Mask," in *Hegel after Derrida*, edited by S. Barnett (London: Routledge).

Hamburger, Jeffrey F. (1997) *Nuns as Artists: The Visual Culture of a Medieval Convent* (Berkeley, CA: University of California Press).

Hamburger, Jeffrey F. (1998) *The Visual and the Visionary: Art and Female Spirituality in Late Medieval Germany* (New York: Zone Books).

Hamburger, Jeffrey F. (2001) "Brother, Bride and *alter Christus*: The Virginal Body of John the Evangelist in Medieval Art, Theology and Literature," in *Text und Kultur: Mittelalferliche Literatur 1150–1450*, edited by Ursula Peters (Stuttgart: Verlag J.B. Metzer), 296–327.

Hamburger, Jeffrey F. (2002) *St John the Divine: The Deified Evangelist in Medieval Art and Theology* (Berkeley, CA: University of California Press).

Hamington, Maurice (1995) *Hail Mary? The Struggle for Ultimate Womanhood in Catholicism* (New York: Routledge).

Hanigan, James P. (1988) *Homosexuality: The Test Case for Christian Ethics* (New York: Paulist Press).

Harbert, Bruce (2002) "Paradise and the Liturgy," *New Blackfriars* 83(971): 30–41.

Harpham, Geoffrey Galt (1995) "Asceticism and Compensations of Art," in *Asceticism*, edited by Vincent L. Wimbush and Richard Valantasis (New York: Oxford University Press).

Harrison, Verna E.F. (1990) "Male and Female in Cappadocian Theology," *Journal of Theological Studies* 41: 465–71.

Harrison, Verna E.F. (1992) *Grace and Human Freedom According to St Gregory of Nyssa*, Studies in the Bible and Early Christianity (Lampeter: Edwin Mellen Press).

Harrison, Verna E.F. (1995) "The Allegorization of Gender: Plato and Philo on Spiritual Childbearing," in *Asceticism*, edited by Vincent L. Wimbush and Richard Valentasis (New York: Oxford University Press).

Harrison, Verna E.F. (1996) "Gender, Generation, and Virginity in Cappadocian Theology," *Journal of Theological Studies* 47: 36–68.

Harrison, Victoria S. (1999a) "*Homo orans*: Von Balthasar's Christocentric Philosophical Anthropology," *Heythrop Journal* 40(3): 280–300.

Harrison, Victoria S. (1999b) "Personal Identity and Integration: Von Balthasar's Phenomenology of Human Holiness," *Heythrop Journal* 40(4): 424–37.

Hart, Columba (1980) "Introduction," to Hadewijch of Anvers, *The Complete Works*, translated by Columba Hart (London: SPCK), i–xviii.

Hart, Lynda (1998) *Between the Body and the Flesh: Performing Sadomasochism* (New York: Columbia University Press).

Hart, Mark D. (1990) "Reconciliation of Body and Soul: Gregory of Nyssa's Deeper Theology of Marriage," *Theological Studies* 51: 468–76.

Hart, Mark D. (1992) "Gregory of Nyssa's Ironic Praise of the Celibate Life," *Heythrop Journal* 33: 1–19.

Harvey, Susan Ashbrook (1993) "Feminine Imagery for the Divine: The Holy Spirit, the Odes of Solomon, and Early Syriac Tradition," *St. Vladimir's Theological Quarterly* 37(2&3): 111–39.

Heelas, Paul and Linda Woodhead (2005) *The Spiritual Revolution: Why Religion is Giving Way to Spirituality* (Oxford: Blackwell).

Hegel, G.W.F. (1977) *Phenomenology of Spirit*, translated by A.V. Miller, with analysis and foreword by J.N. Findlay (Oxford: Oxford University Press [1807]).

Heine, Ronald E. (1975) *Perfection in the Virtuous Life: A Study in the Relationship between Edification and Polemical Theology in Gregory of Nyssa's De Vita Moysis*, Patristica Monograph Series (Cambridge, MA: The Philadelphia Patristic Foundation).

Hekman, S., ed. (1996) *Feminist Interpretations of Michel Foucault* (Philadelphia: Pennsylvania State University Press).

Hennecke, E. (1963) *New Testament Apocrypha*, edited by W. Schneemelcher (London: Lutterworth Press).

Henrici, Peter (1991) "Hans Urs von Balthasar: A Sketch of His Life," in *Hans Urs Von Balthasar: His Life and Work*, edited by David L. Schindler (San Francisco: Ignatius Press), 7–44.

Henry, Michel (2000) *Incarnation: Philosophie de la chair* (Paris: Seuil).

Heyward, Carter (1999) *Saving Jesus from Those Who Are Right: Rethinking What it Means to Be Christian* (Minneapolis: Fortress Press).

Hildebrand, Dietrich von (1984) *Marriage: The Mystery of Love* (Manchester, NH: Sophia Institute Press).

Hildegard of Bingen (2003) "O virga ac diadema," translated by Stephen D'Evelyn (unpublished).

Hillesum, Etty (1996) *An Interrupted Life and Letters from Westerbork* (New York: Henry Holt and Company).

Hinkle, Christopher (2001) "A Delicate Knowledge: Epistemology, Homosexuality, and St John of the Cross," *Modern Theology* 17(4): 427–40.

Hochschild, Arlie (1989) *The Second Shift: Working Parents and the Revolution at Home* (New York: Viking).

Hollywood, Amy (1995) *The Soul as Virgin Wife: Mechthild of Magdeburg, Marguerite Porete, and Meister Eckhart* (Notre Dame: Notre Dame University Press).

Hollywood, Amy (2001) "The Normal, the Queer, and the Middle Ages: Remarks on Carolyn Dinshaw's *Getting Medieval: Sexualities and Communities, Pre- and Postmodern*," *Journal for the Study of Sexuality* 10: 173–9.

Hollywood, Amy (2002) *Sensible Ecstasy: Mysticism, Sexual Difference, and the Demands of History* (Chicago: University of Chicago Press).

Hollywood, Amy (2004a) " 'That Glorious Slit': Irigaray and the Medieval Devotion to Christ's Side Wound," in *Luce Irigaray and Premodern Culture: Thresholds of History*, edited by Theresa Krier and Elizabeth D. Harvey (New York: Routledge), 105–25.

Hollywood, Amy (2004b) "Circa 1265: A Vision of Flowing Light," in *A New History of German Literature*, edited by David E. Wellbery and Judith Ryan (Cambridge, MA: Harvard University Press), 126–30.

Holsinger, Bruce (1993) "The Flesh of the Voice: Embodiment and the Homoerotics of Devotion in the Music of Hildegard of Bingen (1098–1179)," *Signs* 19: 92–125.

Hull, Akasha (Gloria) (1998) "Challenging the Ancestral Muse: Lucille Clifton and Dolores Kendrick," in *Female Subjects in Black and White: Race, Psychoanalysis, Feminism*, edited by Elizabeth Abel, Barbara Christian, and Helene Moglan (Berkeley, CA: University of California Press).

Hutcheon, Linda (1985) *A Theory of Parody: The Teaching of Twentieth-Century Art Forms* (New York: Methuen).

Ignatius of Loyola (1963) *Obras completas*, edited by Ignacio Iparraguirre (Madrid: Biblioteca de Autores Cristianos).

Illouz, Eva (1997) *Consuming the Romantic Utopia: Love and the Cultural Contradictions of Capitalism* (Berkeley, CA: University of California Press).

Irenaeus of Lyons (1996) "Against Heresies," in *The Apostolic Fathers, Justin Martyr, Irenaeus*, edited by Alexander Roberts, James Donaldson and A. Cleveland Coxe, Ante-Nicene Fathers, vol. 1 (Edinburgh: T. & T. Clark).

Irigaray, Luce (1985a) *Speculum of the Other Woman*, translated by Gillian C. Gill (Ithaca: Cornell University Press [1974]).

Irigaray, Luce (1985b) *This Sex Which Is Not One*, translated by Catherine Porter with Carolyn Burke (Ithaca, NY: Cornell University Press [1977]).

Irigaray, Luce (1993) *An Ethics of Sexual Difference*, translated by Carolyn Burke and Gillian C. Gill (London: The Athlone Press [1984]).

Irwin, Terence (1988) *Aristotle's First Principles* (Oxford: Clarendon Press).

Isenberg, Nancy (1998) *Sex and Citizenship in Antebellum America* (Chapel Hill: University of North Carolina Press).

Jacobus de Voragine (1993) *The Golden Legend*, translated by William Granger Ryan, 2 vols (Princeton, NJ: Princeton University Press).

James, M.R. (1924) *The Apocryphal New Testament* (Oxford: Clarendon Press).

Jansen, Katherine Ludwig (2000) *The Making of the Magdalen: Preaching and Popular Devotion in the Later Middle Ages* (Princeton, NJ: Princeton University Press).

Jantzen, Grace (1984) *God's World, God's Body* (London: Darton, Longman & Todd).

Jantzen, Grace (1987) *Julian of Norwich* (London: SPCK).

Jantzen, Grace (1995) *Power, Gender and Christian Mysticism* (Cambridge: Cambridge University Press).

Jantzen, Grace (1998) *Becoming Divine: Towards a Feminist Philosophy of Religion* (Manchester: Manchester University Press).

Jantzen, Grace (2001) "Contours of a Queer Theology," *Literature & Theology*, 15(3): 276–85.

Jantzen, Grace (2004) *Foundations of Violence* (London: Routledge).

John of the Cross (1991) *The Collected Works of St. John of the Cross*, translated by Kieran Kavanaugh and Otilio Rodriguez (Washington DC: ICS Publications).

John Paul II (1981) *The Original Unity of Man and Woman: Catechesis on the Book of Genesis* (Boston: St Paul Editions).

John Paul II (1988) *Mulieris Dignitatem: On the Dignity and Vocation of Women* (London: Catholic Truth Society).

John Paul II (1993) *Veritatis Splendor* (London: Catholic Truth Society).

Jordan, Mark D. (1997) *The Invention of Sodomy in Christian Theology* (Chicago: University of Chicago Press).

Jordan, Mark D. (2000) *The Silence of Sodom: Homosexuality in Modern Catholicism* (Chicago: University of Chicago Press).

Jordan, Mark D. (2002) *The Ethics of Sex* (Oxford: Blackwell).

Jordan, Mark D. (2005) *Blessing Same-Sex Unions: The Perils of Queer Romance and the Confusions of Christian Marriage* (Chicago: University of Chicago Press).

Jordan, Mark D. with Meghan T. Sweeney and David M. Mellott, eds (2006) *Authorizing Marriage? Canon, Tradition and Critique in the Blessing of Same-Sex Unions* (Princeton, NJ: Princeton University Press).

Julian of Norwich (1978) *Showings*, translated by Edmund Colledge and James Walsh (Mahwah, NJ: Paulist Press).

Jung, C.G. (1938) *Psychological Types or the Psychology of Individuation* (London: Kegan Paul, Trench, Trubner; New York: Harcourt, Brace & Company).

Justin Martyr (1996) *The First and Second Apologies*, edited by Alexander Roberts, James Donaldson and A. Cleveland Coxe, Ante-Nicene Fathers (Edinburgh: T. & T. Clark), vol. 1.

Kant, Immanuel (1996a) *Religion Within the Boundaries of Mere Reason* in *Religion and Rational Theology*, edited by A.W. Wood and G. Di Giovanni (Cambridge: Cambridge University Press).

Kant, Immanuel (1996b) *The Metaphysics of Morals*, translated and edited by Mary Gregor (Cambridge: Cambridge University Press).

Karant-Nunn, Susan C. and Merry E. Wesiner-Hanks, eds (2003) *Luther on Women: A Sourcebook* (Cambridge: Cambridge University Press).

Karr, Mary (1995) *The Liar's Club* (New York: Viking).

Kelley, Dean (1977) *Why Conservative Churches Are Growing*, second edition; (San Francisco: Harper and Row).

Kelly, J.N.D. (1975) *Jerome: His Life, Writings, and Controversies* (London: Duckworth).

Kempe, Margery (1994) *The Book of Margery Kempe*, translated by B.A. Windeatt, revised edition (Harmondsworth: Penguin Books [1985]).

Kerr, Fergus (2002) *After Aquinas: Versions of Thomism* (Oxford: Blackwell).

Kierkegaard, Søren (1985) *Philosophical Fragments*, translated by H.V. Hong and E. Hong (Princeton, NJ: Princeton University Press).

Kluxen, Wolfgang (1964) *Philosophische Ethik bei Thomas von Aquin* (Mainz: Matthias-Grünewald-Verlag).

Knohl, Israel (1994) *The Sanctuary of Silence: A Study of the Priestly Strata in the Pentateuch* (Minneapolis: Fortress Press [1992]).

Koester, Helmut (1968) "ΝΟΜΟΣ ΦΨΣΩΣ: The Concept of Natural Law in Greek Thought," in *Religions in Antiquity: Essays in Memory of Erwin Ramsdell Goodenough*, edited by Jacob Neusner (Leiden: E.J. Brill), 521–41.

Kojève, A. (1947) *Introduction à la Lecture de Hegel*, edited by R. Queneau (Paris: Gallimard).

Kojève, A. (1980) *Introduction to the Reading of Hegel*, edited by Allan Bloom, translated by J.H. Nichols (Ithaca: Cornell University Press).

Kojève, A. (1988) "Hegelian Concepts," in *The College of Sociology: 1937–39*, edited by D. Hollier (Minneapolis: University of Minnesota Press).

Krahmer, Shawn M. (2000) "The Virile Bride of Bernard of Clairvaux," *Church History* 69: 304–27.

Kripal, Jeffrey J. (2001) *Roads of Excess, Palaces of Wisdom: Eroticism and Reflexivity in the Study of Mysticism* (Chicago: University of Chicago Press).

Kristeva, Julia (1987a) *In the Beginning Was Love: Psychoanalysis and Faith* translated by Arthur Goldhammer (New York: Columbia University Press [1985]).

Kristeva, Julia (1987b) *Tales of Love*, translated by Leon S. Roudiez (New York: Columbia University Press [1983]).

Kristeva, Julia (1991) *Strangers to Ourselves*, translated by Leon S. Roudiez (Hemel Hempstead: Harvester).

Kristeva, Julia (1995) "Women's Time" (1986) in *The Kristeva Reader*, edited by Toril Moi (Oxford: Blackwell), 187–213.

Kristof, Jane (2001) "The Feminization of Piety in Nineteenth-Century Art," in *Reinventing Christianity: Nineteenth-Century Contexts*, edited by Linda Woodhead (Aldershot: Ashgate), 165–89.

Lacan, Jacques (1982) "God and the *Jouissance* of the Woman," in *Feminine Sexuality: Jacques Lacan and the École Freudienne*, edited by Juliet Mitchell and Jacqueline Rose (London: Macmillan), 137–48.

Lamy, Marielle (2000) "Marie en relation avec les personnes de la Trinité dans la pensée médiévale: figures de la parenté et de l'alliance" (Unpublished paper given to the XX Marian International Congress, Rome).

Laqueur, Thomas (1987) "Orgasm, Generation and the Politics of Reproductive Biology," in *The Making of the Modern Body: Sexuality and Society in the Nineteenth Century*, edited by Catherine Gallagher and Thomas W. Laqueur (Berkeley, CA: University of California Press).

Laqueur, Thomas (1990) *Making Sex: Body and Gender from the Greeks to Freud* (Cambridge, MA: Harvard University Press).

Laqueur, Thomas (2003) *Solitary Sex: A Cultural History of Masturbation* (New York: Zone Books).

Lasch, Christopher (1977) *Haven in a Heartless World: The Family Besieged* (New York: Basic Books).

Lauretis, Teresa de (1991) "Queer Theory: Lesbian and Gay Sexualities," *differences*, 3(2): iii–xviii.

Lavezzo, Kathy (1996) "Sobs and Sighs between Women: The Homoerotics of Compassion in *The Book of Margery Kempe*," in *Premodern Sexualities*, edited by Louise O. Fradenburg and Carla Freccero (New York: Routledge), 175–98.

Leahy, Brendán (1996) *The Marian Principle in the Church According to Hans Urs von Balthasar* (Frankfurt: Lang).

Lear, Jonathan (1988) *Aristotle: The Desire to Understand* (Cambridge: Cambridge University Press).

Lear, Jonathan (1990) *Love and Its Place in Nature: A Philosophical Interpretation of Freudian Psychoanalysis* (New York: Farrar, Strauss & Giroux).

Lechte, John (1991) "Art, Love and Melancholy in the Work of Julia Kristeva," in *Abjection, Melancholia and Love: The Work of Julia Kristeva*, edited by John Fletcher and Andrew Benjamin (London: Routledge).

Lehr, Valerie (1999) *Queer Family Values: Debunking the Myth of the Nuclear Family* (Philadelphia: Temple University Press).

Levine, Baruch (1989) *Leviticus*, JPS Torah Commentary (Philadelphia: The Jewish Publication Society).

Lewis, Flora (1996) "The Wound in Christ's Side and the Instruments of the Passion: Gendered Experience and Response," in *Women and the Book: Assessing the Physical Evidence*, edited by Lesley Smith and Jane H.M. Taylor (Toronto: University of Toronto Press), 204–29.

Lewis, Suzanne (1995) *Reading Images: Narrative Discourse and Reception in the Thirteenth-Century Illuminated Apocalypse* (Cambridge: Cambridge University Press).

Liddington, J. (1993) "Anne Lister of Sibden Hall, Halifax (1791–1840): Her Diaries and the Historians," *History Workshop Journal 35*.

Lincoln, C. Eric (1973) Foreword to William Jones, *Is God a White Racist?* (Garden City, NY: Anchor).

Livius, Thomas (1893) *The Blessed Virgin in the Fathers of the First Six Centuries* (London: Burns & Oates).

Lochrie, Karma (1997) "Mystical Acts, Queer Tendencies," in *Constructing Medieval Sexuality*, edited by Karma Lochrie, Peggy McCracken, and James A. Schultz (Minneapolis: University of Minnesota Press), 180–200.

Loughlin, Gerard (1998a) "Baptismal Fluid," *Scottish Journal of Theology* 51: 261–70.

Loughlin, Gerard (1998b) "Sexing the Trinity," *New Blackfriars* 79: 18–25.

Loughlin, Gerard (1999a) *Telling God's Story: Bible, Church and Narrative Theology* (Cambridge: Cambridge University Press [1996]).

Loughlin, Gerard (1999b) "Erotics: God's Sex," in *Radical Orthodoxy: A New Theology*, edited by John Milbank, Catherine Pickstock, and Graham Ward (London: Routledge), 143–62.

Loughlin, Gerard (2004a) *Alien Sex: The Body and Desire in Cinema and Theology* (Oxford: Blackwell).

Loughlin, Gerard (2004b) "Pauline Conversations: Rereading Romans 1 in Christ," *Theology and Sexuality* 11(1): 72–102.

Loughlin, Gerard (2007) "Idol Bodies," in *Idolatry*, edited by Stephen Barton (London: Continuum).

Löwith, Karl (1949) *Meaning in History: The Theological Implications of the Philosophy of History* (Chicago: University of Chicago Press).

Lüdemann, Gerd (1998) *Virgin Birth? The Real Story of Mary and Her Son Jesus*, translated John Bowden (London: SCM Press).

Luhman, Niklas (1986) *Love as Passion: The Codification of Intimacy*, translated by Jeremy Gaines and Doris L. Jones (Stanford: Stanford University Press).

Luther, Martin (1973) *Commentary on I Corinthians 7*, translated by Edward Sittler in *Luther's Works*, vol. 28, edited by Hilton C. Oswald (Saint Louis, MS: Concordia Publishing House [1523]).

Luther, Martin (2003) *The Estate of Marriage*, excerpted in *Luther on Women: A Sourcebook*, edited by Susan C. Karant-Nunn and Merry E. Wesiner-Hanks (Cambridge: Cambridge University Press [1522]).

MacCulloch, Diarmaid (2003) *Reformation: Europe's House Divided 1490–1700* (London: Allen Lane).

Maitland, Sara (1987) "Passionate Prayer," in *Sex and God*, edited by Linda Hurcombe (New York: Routledge & Kegan Paul), 125–40.

Mann, Michael (1986) *The Sources of Social Power, Vol. I: A History of Power from the Beginning to A.D. 1760* (Cambridge: Cambridge University Press).

Martin, Dale B. (1997) "Paul without Passion: On Paul's Rejection of Desire in Sex and Marriage," in *Constructing Early Christian Families: Family as Social Reality and Metaphor*, edited by H. Moxnes (London: Routledge).

Maslin, Janet (1998) "*Elizabeth*: Amour High Dudgeon in a Castle of One's Own," *New York Times*, November 6.

Matter, E. Ann (1989) "My Sister, My Spouse: Woman Identified Women in Medieval Christianity," in *Weaving the Visions: New Patterns in Feminist Spirituality*, edited by Judith Plaskow and Carol P. Christ (San Francisco: Harper).

May, Gerhard (1971) "Die Chronologie des Lebens und der Werke des Gregory von Nyssa," in *Écriture et culture philosophique dans la pensée de Grégoire de Nysse: Actes du colloque de Chevetogne (22–26 Septembre 1969)*, edited by Marguerite Harl (Leiden: E.J. Brill).

May, Elaine Tyler (1990) *Homeward Bound: American Families in the Cold War Era*, revised edition (New York: Basic Books [1988]).

McCarthy, David Matzko (1997) "Homosexuality and the Practices of Marriage," *Modern Theology* 13(3): 371–97.

McCarthy, David Matzko (1998) "The Relationship of Bodies: A Nuptial Hermeneutics of Same-Sex Unions," *Theology and Sexuality* 8: 96–112.

McClintock, Anne (1995) *Imperial Leather: Race, Gender and Sexuality in the Colonial Context* (New York: Routledge).

McCourt, Frank (1996) *Angela's Ashes: A Memoir of Childhood* (London: Collins).

McDannell, Colleen (1995) *Material Christianity: Religion and Popular Culture in America* (New Haven: Yale University Press).

McGinn, Bernard (1992) *The Foundations of Mysticism: Origins to the Fifth Century* (New York: Crossroads).

McGinn, Bernard (1994) *The Growth of Mysticism: Gregory the Great through the 12th Century* (New York: Crossroads).

McGinn, Bernard (1998) *The Flowering of Mysticism: Men and Women in the New Mysticism – 1200–1350* (New York: Crossroads).

McGrory, Mary (2000) "Routine, But Hardly Normal," *Washington Post*, 21 May: B01.

McLaren, Angus (1999) *Twentieth-Century Sexuality: A History* (Oxford: Blackwell).

McLarin, Kim (1998) *Taming it Down* (New York: William Morrow).

McNay, Lois (1992) *Foucault and Feminism: Power, Gender and the Self* (Oxford: Polity Press).

McNeill, John (1995) *Freedom, Glorious Freedom* (Boston: Beacon Press).

McPartlan, Paul (1997) "The Marian Church and Women's Ordination," in *Mary Is for Everyone*, edited by William McLoughlin (Leominster: Gracewing), 41–56.

Mechthild of Magdeburg (1998) *The Flowing Light of the Godhead*, translated by Frank Tobin (New York: Paulist Press).

Merleau-Ponty, Maurice (1962) *Phenomenology of Perception* (London: Routledge).

Miguens OFM, Manuel (1975) *The Virgin Birth: An Evaluation of Scriptural Evidence* (Westminster MD: Christian Classics, Inc.).

Milbank, John (1995) "Can a Gift be Given? Prolegomena to a Future Trinitarian Metaphysic," *Modern Theology* 11(1): 119–61.

Milbank, John (1997) *The Word Made Strange: Theology, Language, Culture* (Oxford: Blackwell).

Milbank, John (1998) "Gregory of Nyssa: The Force of Identity," in *Christian Origins: Theology, Rhetoric and Community*, edited by Lewis Ayres and Gareth Jones (London: Routledge), 94–116.

Milbank, John, Catherine Pickstock and Graham Ward, eds (1999) *Radical Orthodoxy: A New Theology* (London: Routledge).

Miles, Margaret R. (1992) *Carnal Knowing: Female Nakedness and Religious Meaning in the Christian West* (Tunbridge Wells: Burns & Oates).

Milgrom, Jacob (1992) *Leviticus 1–16,* Anchor Bible (Garden City, NY: Doubleday).

Miller, James (1994) *The Passion of Michel Foucault* (London: HarperCollins).

Mintz, Steven and Susan Kellogg (1988) *Domestic Revolutions: A Social History of American Family Life* (New York: Free Press).

Mollenkott, Virginia Ramey (2001) *Omnigender: A Trans-Religious Approach* (Cleveland: Pilgrim Press).

Moon, Michael (1998) *A Small Boy and Others: Imitation and Initiation in American Culture from Henry James to Andy Warhol* (Durham, NC: Duke University Press).

Moore OP, Gareth (1988) *Believing in God: A Philosophical Essay* (Edinburgh: T. & T. Clark).

Moore OP, Gareth (1992) *The Body in Context: Sex and Catholicism* (London: SCM Press).

Moore OP, Gareth (2003) *A Question of Truth: Christianity and Homosexuality* (London: Continuum).

Moore, Stephen D. (2000) "The Song of Songs in the History of Sexuality," *Church History* 69: 328–49.

Moore, Stephen D. (2001) *God's Beauty Parlor and Other Queer Spaces in and around the Bible* (Stanford: Stanford University Press).

Morgan, David (1998) *Visual Piety: A History and Theory of Popular Religious Images* (Berkeley, CA: University of California Press).

Moss, David and Lucy Gardner (1998) "Difference: The Immaculate Concept? The Laws of Sexual Difference in the Theology of Hans Urs von Balthasar," *Modern Theology* 14: 377–410.

Mosse, George L. (1985) *Nationalism and Sexuality: Middle-Class Morality and Sexual Norms in Modern Europe* (Madison: University of Wisconsin Press).

Muers, Rachel (1999) "A Question of Two Answers: Difference and Determination in Barth and von Balthasar," *Heythrop Journal* 40: 265–79.

Muers, Rachel (2004) *Keeping God's Silence: Towards a Theological Ethics of Communication* (Oxford: Blackwell).

Mufson, Steven (2000) "A Labor Voice Urges China Trade," *Washington Post*, 8 March: A29.

Mühlenberg, Ekkehard (1966) *Die Unendlichkeit Gottes bei Gregor von Nyssa: Gregors Kritik am Gottesbegriff der klassischen Metaphysik*, Forschung Zur Kirchen- und Dogmengeschichte (Göttingen: Vandenhoeck & Ruprecht).

Murk-Jansen, Saskia (1992) "The Mystic Theology of the Thirteenth-Century Mystic, Hadewijch, and Its Literary Expression," *The Medieval Mystical Tradition in England* 5: 117–28.

Murk-Jansen, Saskia M. (1996) "The Use of Gender and Gender-Related Imagery in Hadewijch," in *Gender and Text in the Later Middle Ages*, edited by Jane Chance (Gainesville: University Press of Florida).

Nelson, Daniel (1992) *The Priority of Prudence: Virtue and Natural Law in Aquinas* (University Park, PA: Pennsylvania State University Press).

Neville, Robert (2001) *Symbols of Jesus: A Christology of Symbolic Engagement* (Cambridge: Cambridge University Press).

Newman, John Henry (1891) "A Letter Addressed to the Revd E. B. Pusey on Occasion of his *Eirenicon*," in *Certain Difficulties Felt by Anglicans* (London: Longmans).

Niederwimmer, Kurt (1975) *Askese und Mysterium: Über Ehe, Ehescheidung und Eheverzicht in den Anfängen des christlichen Glaubens* (Göttingen: Vandenhoeck & Ruprech).

Nietzsche, Friedrich (1973) *Beyond Good and Evil*, translated by R.J. Hollingdale (New York: Viking Penguin).

Nissinen, Martti (1998) *Homoeroticism in the Biblical World: A Historical Perspective*, translated by Kirsi Stjerna (Minneapolis: Fortress Press).

Nolan, Mary Lee and Sidney Nolan (1989) *Christian Pilgrimage in Modern Western Europe* (Chapel Hill & London: The University of North Carolina Press).

Novak, David (1998) *Natural Law in Judaism* (Cambridge: Cambridge University Press).

Novosad, Nancy (1999) *Promise Keepers: Playing God* (New York: Prometheus Books).

Nussbaum, Martha C. (1999) "The Professor of Parody," *The New Republic* 22: 37–45.

Nygren, Anders (1957) *Agape and Eros*, translated by Philip S. Watson (London: SPCK).

O'Carroll, Michael (1990) *Theotokos: A Theological Encyclopedia of the Blessed Virgin Mary* (Collegeville, Minnesota: The Liturgical Press).

O'Donoghue, Noel (1996) *Heaven in Ordinarie: Prayer as Transcendence* (Edinburgh: T. & T. Clark [1979]).

O'Hanlon SJ, Gerald (1990) *The Immutability of God in the Theology of Hans Urs von Balthasar* (Cambridge: Cambridge University Press).

Olyan, Saul (1994) "Lying with a Male the Lying Down of a Woman: The Meaning and Significance of Leviticus 18:22 and 20:13," *Journal of the History of Sexuality* 5(2).

Olyan, Saul M. (2006) "'Surpassing the Love of Women': Another Look at 2 Samuel 1.26 and the Relationship of David and Jonathan," in *Authorizing Marriage? Canon, Tradition, and Critique in the Blessing of Same-Sex Unions*, edited by Mark D. Jordan with Meghan T. Sweeney and David M. Mellott (Princeton, NJ: Princeton University Press), 7–16.

Ophir, Adi (1991) *Plato's Invisible Cities: Discourse and Power in the Republic* (London: Routledge).

Origen (2001) *Commentary on the Epistle to the Romans, Books 1–5*, translated by T.P. Scheck, The Fathers of the Church 103 (Washington, DC: The Catholic University of America Press).

Orsi, Robert A. (1996) *Thank You, St. Jude: Women's Devotion to the Patron Saint of Hopeless Cause* (New Haven: Yale University Press).

Pächt, Otto (1956) "The Illustrations of St Anselm's Prayers and Meditations," *Journal of the Warburg and Courtauld Institutes* 19: 68–83.

Palahniuk, Chuck (1992) *Fight Club* (London: Vintage).

Palmer, Michael (1997) *Freud and Jung on Religion* (London: Routledge).

Parish, Helen L. (2000) *Clerical Marriage and the English Reformation: Precedent, Policy and Practice* (Aldershot: Ashgate).

Paul VI (1970) *Humanae Vitae: On Human Life*, revised edition, translated by Alan C. Clark and Geoffrey Crawfurd (London: Catholic Truth Society).

Perry, Ruth (1986) *The Celebrated Mary Astell: An Early English Feminist* (Chicago: University of Chicago Press).

Pesarchick, Robert A. (2000) *The Trinitarian Foundation of Human Sexuality as Revealed by Christ According to Hans Urs von Balthasar, The Revelatory Significance of the Male Christ and the Male Ministerial Priesthood* (Rome: Editrice Pontifica Universitit Gregoriana).

Pesch, Otto Hermann (1988) *Thomas von Aquin: Grenze und Grösse mittelalterlicher Theologie* (Mainz: Matthias-Grünewald-Verlag).

Pickstock, Catherine (1998) *After Writing: On the Liturgical Consummation of Philosophy* (Oxford: Blackwell).

Pietz, William (1993) "Fetishism and Materialism," in *Fetishism as Cultural Discourse*, edited by Emily Apter and William Pietz (Ithaca, NY: Cornell University Press).

Plato (1924) *Laches, Protagoras, Meno, Euthydemus*, translated by W.R.M. Lamb, Loeb Classical Library (Cambridge, MA: Harvard University Press).

Plato (1925a) *Lysis, Symposium, Gorgias* translated by W.R.M. Lamb, Loeb Classical Library (Cambridge, MA: Harvard University Press).

Plato (1925b) *Statesman, Philebus, Ion*, translated by H. N. Fowler and W.R.M. Lamb, Loeb Classical Library (Cambridge, MA: Harvard University Press).

Plato (1936) *The Republic I–V*, translated by Paul Shorey, Loeb Classical Library (Cambridge, MA: Harvard University Press).

Ploeger, A. (2002) *Dare We Observe? The Importance of Art Works for Consciousness of Diakonia in (Post-) Modern Church* (Leuven: Peeters).

Porete, Marguerite (1993) *The Mirror of Simple Souls*, translated by Ellen Babinsky (New York: Paulist Press).

Preller, Victor (1967) *Divine Science and the Science of God: A Reformulation of Thomas Aquinas* (Princeton NJ: Princeton University Press).

Price, A.W. (1989) *Love and Friendship in Plato and Aristotle* (Oxford: Clarendon Press).

Probyn, Elspeth (1996) *Outside Belongings* (London: Routledge).

Quash, Ben (1999) *A Critique of Hans Urs von Balthasar's Theological Dramatic Theory with Special Reference to the Thought of Hegel* (Cambridge University PhD dissertation).

Rahner, Karl (1965) "The Interpretation of the Dogma of the Assumption," in *Theological Investigations*, vol. 1: *God, Christ, Mary and Grace*, translated by Cornelius Ernst OP (London: Darton, Longman & Todd [1954]), 215–27.

Raine, Kathleen (1968) *Blake and Tradition*, 2 vols (Princeton, NJ: Princeton University Press).

Rambuss, Richard (1998) *Closet Devotions* (Durham, NC: Duke University Press).

Ratzinger, Joseph (1973) *Die sackramentale Begründung christlicher Existenz* (Feising: Kyrios).

Ratzinger, Joseph (1986) *Letter to the Bishops of the Catholic Church on the Pastoral Care [sic] of Homosexual Persons* (London: Catholic Truth Society); in *Theology and Sexuality: Classic and Contemporary Readings*, edited by Eugene F. Rogers Jr (Oxford: Blackwell), 249–58.

Ratzinger, Joseph (2000) *The Spirit of the Liturgy* (San Francisco: Ignatius Press).

Ravenhill, Mark (1996) *Shopping and Fucking* (London: Methuen).

Riches, John and Ben Quash (1997) "Hans Urs von Balthasar," in *The Modern Theologians*, edited by David Ford, second edition (Blackwell: Oxford), 124–51.

Richlin, Amy (1991) "Zeus and Metis: Foucault, Feminism, Classics," *Helios* 18: 160–80.

Richlin, Amy (1992) *The Garden of Priapus: Sexuality and Aggression in Roman Humor*, second edition (New York: Oxford University Press).

Richlin, Amy (1993) "Not before Homosexuality: The Materiality of the *Cinaedus* and the Roman Law against Love between Men," *Journal of the History of Sexuality* 3(4): 523–73.

Ricoeur, Paul (1974) "Fatherhood: From Phantasm to Symbol" (1969), translated by Robert Sweeney in *The Conflict of Interpretations: Essays in Hermeneutics*, edited by Don Ihde (Evanston, IL: Northwestern University Press), 468–97.

Riehle, Wolfgang (1981) *The Middle English Mystics*, translated by Bernard Sandring (London: Routledge & Kegan Paul).

Rifkin, Jeremy (2000) *The Age of Access: The New Culture of Hypercapitalism, Where All of Life Is a Paid-for Experience* (New York: Putnam).

Riley, Denise (1988) *Am I that Name? Feminism and the Category of "Women" in History* (London: Macmillan).

Roediger, David (1994) *Towards the Abolition of Whiteness: Essays on Race, Politics, and Working Class History* (London: Verso).

Rogers Jr, Eugene F. (1996) "The Virtues of the Interpreter Presuppose and Perfect Hermeneutics: The Case of Thomas Aquinas," *The Journal of Religion* 76: 64–81.

Rogers Jr, Eugene F. (1998) "The Narrative of Natural Law in Thomas's Commentary on Romans 1," *Theological Studies* 59: 254–76.

Rogers Jr, Eugene F. (1999a) *Sexuality and the Christian Body: Their Way into the Triune God* (Oxford: Blackwell).

Rogers Jr, Eugene F. (1999b) "Aquinas on Natural Law and the Virtues in Biblical Context: Homosexuality as a Test Case," *The Journal of Religious Ethics* 27: 29–56.

Rogers Jr, Eugene F., ed. (2002) *Theology and Sexuality: Classic and Contemporary Readings* (Oxford: Blackwell).

Rolle, Richard (1972) *The Fire of Love*, translated by Clifton Wolters (Harmondsworth: Penguin Books).

Roper, Lyndal (1989) *The Holy Household: Women and Morals in Reformation Augsburg* (Oxford: Clarendon Press).

Rose, Gillian (1992a) *The Broken Middle: Out of our Ancient Society* (Oxford: Blackwell).

Rose, Gillian (1992b) "Diremption of Spirit," in *Shadow of Spirit: Postmodernism and Religion*, edited by Philippa Berry and Andrew Wernick (London: Routledge), 45–56.

Roten SM, Johann (1991) "The Two Halves of the Moon," in *Hans Urs von Balthasar: His Life and Work*, edited by David L. Schindler (San Francisco: Ignatius Press), 65–86.

Rougemont, Denis de (1983) *Love in the Western World* (Princeton, NJ: Princeton University Press).

Roughgarden, Joan (2004) *Evolution's Rainbow: Diversity, Gender, and Sexuality in Nature and People* (Berkeley, CA: University of California Press).

Rudy, Kathy (1997) *Sex and the Church: Gender, Homosexuality, and the Transformation of Christian Ethics* (Boston: Beacon Press).

Ruether, Rosemary Radford (2001) *Christianity and the Making of the Modern Family* (London: SCM Press).

Satlow, Michael L. (1994) "'They Abused Him Like a Woman': Homoeroticism, Gender Blurring, and the Rabbis in Late Antiquity," *Journal of the History of Sexuality* 5(1): 1–25.

Sautman, Francesca Canadé and Pamela Sheingorn, eds (2001) *Same Sex Love and Desire among Women in the Middle Ages* (New York: Palgrave).

Saward, John (1990) *The Mysteries of March: Hans Urs von Balthasar on the Incarnation and Easter* (London: Collins).

Schecter, Solomon, ed. (1967) *Aboth de Rabbi Nathan* (New York: Philipp Feldheim [1887]).

Scheeben, M.J. (1961) *The Mysteries of Christianity* (St Louis: B. Herder).

Schiebinger, Londa (1987) "Skeletons in the Closet: The First Illustrations of the Female Skeleton in Eighteenth-Century Anatomy," in *The Making of the Modern Body*, edited by Catherine Gallagher and Thomas W. Laqueur (Berkeley and Los Angeles: University of California Press), 42–82.

Schindler, David L. (1993) "Catholic Theology, Gender and the Future of Western Civilisation," *Communio* 20: 200–39.

Schindler, David L. (1996) *Heart of the World, Centre of the Church: Communion Ecclesiology, Liberalism and Liberation* (Edinburgh: T. & T. Clark).

Schindler, David L., ed. (1991) *Hans Urs von Balthasar: His Life and Work* (San Francisco: Ignatius Press).

Scola, Angelo (2005) *The Nuptial Mystery*, translated by Michelle K. Borras (Grand Rapids, Michigan: Eerdmans).

Scroggs, Robin (1983) *The New Testament and Homosexuality: Contextual Background for a Contemporary Debate* (Philadelphia: Fortress Press, 1983).

Sedgwick, Eve Kosofsky (1990) *Epistemology of the Closet* (Berkeley, CA: University of California Press).

Seel, Martin (2003) "On Emergence" (Unpublished paper for the Stanford Colloquium on Emergence).

Seidman, Steven, ed. (1996) "Introduction" to *Queer Theory/Sociology* (Oxford: Blackwell).

Sells, Michael (1994) *Mystical Languages of Unsaying* (Chicago: University of Chicago Press).

Sexton, Adam, ed. (1993) *Desperately Seeking Madonna: In Search of the Meaning of the World's Most Famous Woman* (New York: Delta Books).

Shange, Ntozake (1982) *Sassafras, Cypress, and Indigo* (New York: Picador).

Shea STD, George W. (1954) "Outline History of Mariology in the Middle Ages and Modern Times," in *Mariology*, edited by Juniper B. Carol OFM (Milwaukee: Bruce Publishing Company), I: 281–327.

Shechter, Solomon, ed. (1967) *Aboth de Rabbi Nathan* (New York: Philipp Feldheim [1887]).

Sheck, T.P. (2001) *The Fathers of the Church* (Washington DC: Catholic University of America Press).

Sheils, W.J., ed. (1989) *The English Reformation: 1530–1570* (London: Longman).

Shorter, Edward (1975) *The Making of the Modern Family* (New York: Basic Books).

Sinfield, Alan (1994) *Cultural Politics, Queer Reading* (London: Routledge).

Skeggs, Beverley (1997) *Formations of Class and Gender: Becoming Respectable* (London: Sage).

Stead, Christopher (1976) "Ontology and Terminology in Gregory of Nyssa," in *Gregor von Nyssa und die Philosophie: Zweites Internationales Kolloquium über Gregor von Nyssa*, edited by Heinrich Dörrie and Margarete Altenburger (Leiden: E.J. Brill).

Steinberg, Leo (1996) *The Sexuality of Christ in Renaissance Art and in Modern Oblivion*, second edition (Chicago, University of Chicago Press).

Stevenson, Kenneth (1998) *The Mystery of Baptism in the Anglican Tradition* (Norwich: Canterbury Press).

Stout, Jeffrey (1992) "Truth, Natural Law, and Ethical Theory," in *Natural Law Theory*, edited by Robert P. George (Oxford: Clarendon).

Strukelj, Anton (1993) "Man and Woman under God: The Dignity of the Human Being According to Hans Urs von Balthasar," *Communio* 20(2): 377–88.

Stuart, Elizabeth (1995) *Just Good Friends: Towards a Lesbian and Gay Theology of Relationships* (London: Mowbray).

Stuart, Elizabeth (2003) *Gay and Lesbian Theologies: Repetitions with Critical Difference* (Aldershot: Ashgate).

Szasz, Thomas (1975) *The Age of Madness: The History of Involuntary Mental Hospitalization, Presented in Selected Texts* (London: Routledge & Kegan Paul).

Taussig, Michael (1993) "Maleficium: State Fetishism," in *Fetishism as Cultural Discourse*, edited by E. Apter and W. Pietz (New York: Cornell University Press).

Taylor, Charles (1991) *The Ethics of Authenticity* (Cambridge, MA: Harvard University Press).

Teresa of Avila (1946) "Interior Castle," in *The Complete Works of Saint Teresa of Jesus*, translated by E. Allison Peers (London: Sheed and Ward), vol. 2.

Tertullian (1870) "On the Flesh of Christ," in *The Writings of Tertullian*, vol. 2, translated by Peter Holmes, in *Ante-Nicene Christian Library* 15 (Edinburgh: T. & T. Clark).

Tertullian (1994) *On the Apparel of Women*, translated by S. Thelwall, in *The Ante-Nicene Fathers*, edited by A. Roberts, J. Donaldson and A.C. Coxe (Edinburgh: T. & T. Clark), IV: 14–25.

Thomas Aquinas (1953) *Super Epistolas Sancti Pauli Lectura*, edited by P. Raphaelis Cai, 8th revised edition (Rome and Turin: Marietti).

Thomas Aquinas (1964) *Summa Theologiae*, vol. 2 (1a.2–11), translated and edited by Timothy McDermott OP (London: Eyre & Spottiswoode).

Thornton, Bruce (1991) "Constructionism and Ancient Sex," *Helios* 18: 181–93.

Thurston, Thomas M. (1990) "Leviticus 18:22 and the Prohibition of Homosexual Acts," in *Homophobia and the Judaeo-Christian Tradition*, edited by M.L. Stemmeler and J.M. Clark (Dallas: Monument Press).

Torrell, Jean Pierre (1985a) "Les *Collationes in decem praeceptis* de saint Thomas d'Aquin: Edition critique avec introduction et notes," *Revue des sciences philosophiques et théologiques* 69: 5–40, 227–63.

Torrell, Jean Pierre (1985b) *Catechetical Instructions*, translated by J.B. Collins (New York: Wagner).

Traub, Valerie (2002) *The Renaissance of Lesbianism in Early Modern England* (Cambridge: Cambridge University Press).

Trexler, Richard C. (1993) "Gendering Jesus Crucified," in *Iconography at the Crossroads*, edited by Brendan Cassidy (Princeton, NJ: Index of Christian Art, Department of Art and Archaeology, Princeton University), 107–19.

Trible, Phyllis (1984) *Texts of Terror: Literary-Feminist Readings of Biblical Narratives* (Philadelphia: Fortress Press).

Troeltsch, Ernst (1931) *The Social Teaching of the Christian Churches*, 2 vols (London: Allen and Unwin; New York: Macmillan).

Turner, Denys (1995a) *The Darkness of God: Negativity in Christian Mysticism* (Cambridge: Cambridge University Press).

Turner, Denys (1995b) *Eros and Allegory: Medieval Exegesis of the Song of Songs* (Kalamazoo, MI: Cistercian Publications).

Vance, Norman (1985) *Sinews of the Spirit: The Ideal of Christian Manliness in Victorian Literature and Religious Thought* (Cambridge: Cambridge University Press).

Vermes, Geza (2000) *The Changing Faces of Jesus* (New York: Penguin Compass).

Vernon, Mark (2005) *The Philosophy of Friendship* (Basingstoke: Palgrave).

Vernon, Mark (2006) "Review of Stephen Bates, *A Church at War*," *Theology & Sexuality* 12(2): 220–2.

Vita, Matthew and Juliet Eilperin (2000) "On the Fence and in Demand: Pressure Mounts for House Democrats Still Torn on Trade Measure," *Washington Post*, May 19: A01.

Walter, Tony and Grace Davie (1998) "The Religiosity of Women in the Modern West," *British Journal of Sociology* 49(4): 640–69.

Walzer, Michael (1983) *Spheres of Justice: A Defense of Pluralism and Equality* (New York: Basic Books).

Ward, Graham (1999) "Bodies: The Displaced Body of Jesus Christ," in *Radical Orthodoxy: A New Theology*, edited by John Milbank, Catherine Pickstock and Graham Ward (London: Routledge), 163–81.

Ward, Graham (2000) *Cities of God* (London: Routledge).

Warner, Marina (1985) *Alone of All Her Sex: The Myth and the Cult of the Virgin Mary* (London: Picador).

Warner, Marina (1990) *Alone of All Her Sex: The Myth and the Cult of the Virgin Mary*, second edition (London: Picador).

Warner, Michael (1996) "Tongues Untied: Memoirs of a Pentecostal Boyhood," in *The Material Queer: A Lesbian Cultural Studies Reader*, edited by Donald Morton (Boulder, CO: Westview Press).

Waterworth, J., ed. (1848) *The Canons and Decrees of the Sacred and Oecumenical Council of Trent* (London: Dolman).

Watson, Nicholas (1996) " 'If wommen be double naturally': Remaking 'Woman' in Julian of Norwich's Revelation of Love," *Exemplaria* 8.

Webster, Alison (1998) "Queer to be Religious: Lesbian Adventures beyond the Christian/Post-Christian Dichotomy," *Theology & Sexuality* 8: 27–39.

Weeks, Jeffrey (2000) *Making Sexual History* (Cambridge: Polity Press).

Weisner-Hanks, Merry E. (2000) *Christianity and Sexuality in the Early Modern World: Regulating Desire, Reforming Practice* (London: Routledge).

Wesiner, Mary (1988) "Women's Responses to the Reformation," in *The German People and the Reformation*, edited by R. Po-chia Hsia (Ithaca, NY: Cornell University Press).

Westberg, Daniel (1994) *Right Practical Reason* (Oxford: Clarendon Press).

Whitbread, H., ed. (1988) *I Know My Own Heart: The Diaries of Anne Lister, 1791–1840* (London: Virago).

Whitford, Margaret, ed. (1991) *The Irigaray Reader* (Oxford: Blackwell).

Wiethaus, Ulrike (2003) "Female Homoerotic Discourse and Religion in Medieval Germanic Culture," in *Gender and Difference in the Middle Ages*, edited by Sharon Farmer and Carol Braun Pasternack (Minneapolis: University of Minnesota Press), 288–321.

Wijngaards, John (2001) *The Ordination of Women to the Catholic Church: Unmasking a Cuckoo's Egg Tradition* (Darton, Longman & Todd).

Williams, Raymond (1977) *Marxism and Literature* (Oxford: Oxford University Press).

Williams, Rowan (1986) "Rahner and Balthasar," in *The Analogy of Beauty*, edited by John Riches (Edinburgh: T. & T. Clark), 11–34.

Williams, Rowan (1999) "Afterword: Making Differences," in Lucy Gardner, David Moss, Ben Quash, Graham Ward, *Balthasar and the End of Modernity* (Edinburgh: T. & T. Clark), 173–9.

Williams, Rowan (2000) *On Christian Theology* (Oxford: Blackwell).

Williams, Rowan (2002) "The Body's Grace" (1996) in *Theology and Sexuality: Classic and Contemporary Readings*, edited by Eugene F. Rogers Jr (Oxford: Blackwell), 309–21.

Wilson, Barbara (1996) *If You Had a Family* (Seattle: Seal Press).

Wilson, Barbara (1997) *Blue Windows: A Christian Science Childhood* (New York: Picador).

Winkler, John (1989) *The Constraints of Desire: The Anthropology of Sex and Gender in Ancient Greece* (London: Routledge).

Witte Jr, John (2004) "Male Headship: Reform of the Protestant Tradition," in *Does Christianity Teach Male Headship? The Equal-Regard Marriage and its Critics*, edited by David Blankenhorn, Don Browning and Mary Stewart Van Leeuwen (Grand Rapids, MI: Eerdmans), 29–36.

Wittig, Monique (1992) *The Straight Mind and Other Essays*, foreword by Louise Turcotte (London: Harvester Wheatsheaf).

Wood, Charles (1981) "The Doctor's Dilemma: Sin, Salvation, and the Menstrual Cycle in Medieval Thought," *Speculum* 56: 710–27.

Woodhead, Linda (2004) *An Introduction to Christianity* (Cambridge: Cambridge University Press).

Woodhead, Linda (2005) "Gendering Secularization Theory," *Kvinder, Køn og Forskning* (*Women, Gender and Research*) 1: 24–35.

Woodhead, Linda, ed. (2001) *Religions in the Modern World* (London: Routledge).

Wyschogrod, Edith (1990) *Saints and Postmodernism* (Chicago: University of Chicago Press).

Zizek, Slavoj (1994) *Plague of Fantasies* (London: Verso).

Index of Biblical References

Note: "n" indicates a note.

General Index

Note: "n" indicates a note.